PRASNA

PART

PRASNA MARGA

English Translation with Original Text in Devanagari and Notes by

BANGALORE VENKATA RAMAN

Editor: The Astrological Magazine

PART I

[Chapters I to XVI]

MOTILAL BANARSIDASS PUBLISHERS PVT. LTD.
DELHI

TABLE OF CONTENTS

CHAPTER I

			Page
1.	Prayer	...	1
2.	What Astrology Comprehends	...	3
3.	Who can study Astrology ?	...	7
4.	Qualifications of an Astrologer	...	11
5.	Different Kinds of Ganitha	...	14
6.	The Five Siddhanthas	...	16
7.	Beginning the Study of Astrology	...	17
8.	Importance of Varaha Mihira	...	19
9.	Role of Horoscopy and Horary	...	23
10.	Importance of Muhurtha	...	25
11.	Similarity between Prasna and Jataka	...	28

CHAPTER II

12.	Procedure for the Astrologer	...	30
13.	Procedure for the Querist	...	32
14.	Procedure for Arudha	...	34
15.	Things to be noted at Query Time	...	36
16.	Method of Reading the Results	...	37
17.	Indications for Success	...	39
18.	The Time Factor	...	45
19.	The Place Factor	...	48
20.	Examination of Breath	...	50
21.	The Touch Analysed	...	67
22.	Sign occupied by the Querist	...	73
23.	Direction occupied by the Querist	...	83

			Page
24.	Pranakshara	...	84
25.	The Querist's Bearing	...	91
26.	The Querist's Behaviour Pattern	...	93
27.	The Querist's Mood	...	96
28.	Dress and Garments	...	97
29.	Some Peculiar Lakshanas	...	98
30.	Omens or Tatkala Lakshanas	...	98

CHAPTER III

31.	The Astrologer's Departure	...	108
32.	Omens on the Way	...	109
33.	Indicative Signs while entering the House		121

CHAPTER IV

34.	Conducting the Prasna	...	125
36.	Preparation	...	125
37.	The Lamp and the Flame	...	127
38.	Drawing the Circle or Chart	...	132
39.	Nature of the Chart	...	134
40.	How the Priest Draws the Chakra	...	134
41.	Behaviour of the Agent	...	137
42.	Invocation to the Lord	...	141
43.	Worshipping the Planets	...	142
44.	Placing the Gold Piece	...	142
45.	Sankalpa	...	144
46.	Ashtamangalam	...	145
47.	Determining the Arudha Rasi	...	146
48.	Thing to be Noted	...	148
49.	Conclusion	...	149

Page

CHAPTER V

50. Time of Query ... 150
51. Calculation of Lagna ... 150
52. Correction by Kunda ... 153
53 The Moon's Longitude ... 154
54. Position of Gulika ... 159
55. Thrisphu'a ... 162
56. Prana and Deha ... 163
57. The Death Circle ... 170
58. Planetary Longitudes ... 175
59. Arudha Position ... 176

CHAPTER VI

60. The Five Sutras ... 177
61 Diagnosing Illness ... 181
62. Results of Sutras ... 182
63. Sutras and the Bhutas ... 183
64. The Time Factor ... 184
65. The Three Sutras ... 185
66. Significance of Thrisphutas ... 188
67. Thrisphuta Indicative of Death ... 189
68. Beginning of Diseases ... 193
69. Thrisphuta Nakshatra ... 195
70. Thrisphuta Dasa ... 206

CHAPTER VII

71. Ashtamangalam ... 209
72. Results of the Sun and other Planets ... 211
73. Effects of 'Dhwajas', etc. ... 213

			Page
74.	Animal Symbols	...	215
75.	Panchabhuta Effects	...	217
76.	Reckoning of Lunar Day, etc.	...	218
77.	Results of Thithi, etc.	...	219
78.	Niryana Saturn	...	220

CHAPTER VIII

79.	Effects of Arudha	...	230
80.	Avasthas	...	233
81.	Diseases and Arudha	...	235
82.	Arudha Navamsa	...	238
83.	Planets and Vegetables	...	240
84.	Urdhwamukha and other Signs	...	241
85.	Significance of Gold Piece	...	245
86.	Effects of Lagna	...	250
87.	Effects of Prana and Deha	...	252
88.	Rahu Chakra	...	256
89.	Amazing Predictions	...	256
90.	Significance of Chandra Navamsa	...	257

CHAPTER IX

91.	Recapitulation	...	261
92.	Examination of Age	...	262
93.	Mrityu Lakshana	...	266
94.	Determining the Length of Life	...	268
95.	Lagna and Arudha	...	272
96.	Chatra Rasi	...	275
97.	Signs of Long Life	...	277
98	Longevity from Birth Chart	...	279

			Page
99.	Yogas and Longevity	...	281
100.	Long Life Again	...	286
101.	Short Life	...	288

CHAPTER X

102.	Timing Death	...	292
103.	Evil Periods	...	296
104.	Kala-Chakra Dasas	...	297
105.	Niryana Saturn	...	299
106.	Niryana Jupiter	...	302
107.	Niryana Sun	...	304
108.	Niryana Moon	...	305
109.	Pramana Gulika	....	306
110.	Death as read by the Planets	...	309
111.	Death Dealing Ascendant	...	316
112.	Time of Death as from Prasna	...	318
113.	Planetary Positions at Death	...	329

CHAPTER XI

114.	Causes of Death	...	332
115.	Nature of Death	...	341
116	Cause of Death According to Prasna	...	345
117.	Place of Death	...	355

CHAPTER XII

118.	Diseases and Their Cause	...	356
119	Types of Diseases	...	365
120.	Symptoms of Madness	...	371
121.	Symptoms for Epilepsy	...	378
122.	Treatment for Epilepsy	...	381

			Page
123.	Aberration of Mind	...	384
124.	Combinations for Diabetes	...	384
125.	Diseases indicated by Planets	...	385
126.	Combinations for Diseases	...	391

CHAPTER XIII

127.	Beginning and Ending of Diseases	...	397
128.	Direction of Beginuing of Disease	...	399
129.	Recovery	...	407
130.	Causes of Diseases	...	414
131.	Remedial Measures	...	416
132	Mrityunjaya Homa	....	417

CHAPTER XIV

133.	Fixing the Person's Age	...	420
134.	Significations of Bhavas	...	422
135.	Bhava Significations in Prasna Chart	....	426
136.	External and Internal Bhavas	...	429
137.	How Bhavas are Ruined	...	433
138.	Karakas or Significators	...	438
139	Fructification of Bhavas	...	441
140.	Favourable and Unfavourable Houses	...	441
141.	When Bhavas are Ruined	...	448
142.	Effects of Planets in Houses	...	449
143.	Effects of Gulika	...	457
144.	Effects of Tertiary Planets	...	459
145.	Time when Bhavas Fructify	...	464
146.	Favourable and Unfavourable Positions of Planets	...	472
147.	Categories of Karma	...	480

			Page
148.	Imprisonment or Captivity	...	486
149.	Quarrels and Misunderstandings	...	492
150.	Visible and Invisible Hemispheres	...	493

CHAPTER XV

151.	Favourable and Unfavourable Karma	...	496
152.	Afflictions due to Deity	...	499
153.	Palliatives for Afflictions	...	502
154.	Misappropriation of Deity's Property	...	507
155.	Nature of Misappropriated Property	....	507
156.	Intensity of Deity's Wrath	...	511
157.	Anger of Serpent God	...	513
158.	Parental Curses	...	517
159.	Curse of Elders	...	519
160.	Trouble from Ghosts	...	519
161.	Remedial Measures	...	524
162.	Evil Eye	...	525
163.	Cause of Evil Eye	...	527
164.	Places of Attack	...	528
165.	Names of Spirits Causing Evil Eye	...	529
166.	Categories of Spirits	...	530
167.	How to Distinguish Spirits	...	531
168.	Planets Favouring Spirits	...	543
169.	Houses of Harm	...	545
170.	Ascertaining the " Drishti Badha	...	546
171	Place of Attack	...	550
172.	Evil Arising from Words	...	552
173.	Bala-Graha Affliction	...	553
174.	Food Poisoning	...	553

			Page
175.	Troubles from Enemies	...	554
176.	Nature of Trouble	...	556
177.	Who is the Enemy ?	...	557
178.	Enemy's Motive	...	562
179.	Identifying the Enemy	...	565
180.	Means Adopted by Enemies	...	567
181.	Where the Kshudra is Kept	...	568
182.	Containers Used	...	569
183	Another View	...	571
184.	Removing the Mahabhichara	...	575
185.	Different Kinds of Devatas	...	578
186.	Who should Perform Remedies	...	589

CHAPTER XVI

187.	Whereabouts of the Querist	...	593
188.	Success Over Enemies	...	595
189.	Bright and Dark Future	...	596
190	Means to Adopt	...	598
191.	Locating a Treasure Trove	...	599
192.	Nature of Persons met with on the Way	...	601
193.	Characteristics of Bride and Bridegroom		602
194.	Rulers of Different Parts of Day	...	605
195.	Characteristics due to Five Elements	...	608
196.	Lakshanas Given in other Works	...	612
197.	Danger to the House	...	613
198.	Loss of Metals	...	614
199.	Interpreting First Letter of Query	...	616
200.	Predicting by Betel Leaves	...	618
201.	Acquisition of Elephants	...	622

			Page
202.	Indications for Sickness	...	623
203.	Performing Obsequies	...	637
204.	Happiness and Sorrow to Parents	...	632
205.	Afflictions to Residence	...	634
206.	Avakahada System	...	634
207.	Becoming the Head	...	639
208.	Kalachakra or Time Cycle	...	642
209.	Star Positions in Kalachakra	...	643
210.	Position of Yogini	...	646
211.	Calculating the Yogini	...	647
212.	Features of Yogini	...	654
213.	Movements of Yogini on Weekdays	...	655
214.	Longitudes of Yogini and Mrityu	...	658
215.	Movement of Mrityu	...	661
216.	Yogini Movement *Vis a-Vis* Lunar Days	...	665
217.	Hell and Heaven	...	668
218.	Signs of Krita Yuga Etc.	...	670
219.	Conclusion	...	672
220.	Appendices	...	673
221.	Index of Technical Terms	...	681
222.	Samscrit Errata	...	708

—o—

PREFACE TO SECOND EDITION

The first edition published in 1980 has been out of print for the past six years. Due to my other literary commitments, publishing the second edition had to be delayed, though there was great demand for the book.

It is my hope that this new edition will aid both the students and savants of astrology in their studies and researches and contribute to a better understanding and appreciation of the novel methods of horoscopic interpretation presented in these pages.

Thanks are due to the well-known publishers Motilal Banarsidass for having brought out this edition attractively.

Bangalore
29-4-1991

B.V. RAMAN

First Edition: Bangalore, 1980
Second Edition: Delhi, 1991

ISBN: 81-208-0914-9
ISBN: 81-208-0918-1

Also available at:
MOTILAL BANARSIDASS
41 U.A., Bungalow Road, Jawahar Nagar, Delhi 110 007
120 Royapettah High Road, Mylapore, Madras 600 004
16 St. Mark's Road, Bangalore 560 001
Ashok Rajpath, Patna 800 004
Chowk, Varanasi 221 001

PRINTED IN INDIA
BY JAINENDRA PRAKASH JAIN AT SHRI JAINENDRA PRESS, A-45 NARAINA INDUSTRIAL AREA, PHASE I, NEW DELHI 110 028 AND PUBLISHED BY NARENDRA PRAKASH JAIN FOR MOTILAL BANARSIDASS PUBLISHERS PVT. LTD., BUNGALOW ROAD, JAWAHAR NAGAR, DELHI 110 007

PREFACE

It is with justifiable feelings of pride and humility that I present herewith an English translation of *Prasna Marga* (Part I) a celebrated work on astrology largely in use in Kerala.

The idea to bring out an English edition of *Prasna Marga* first occurred to me in 1940. This was largely due to the persuasion of one Mr. P. G. Subrahmanya Iyer, then working as an assistant in my office. Mr. Iyer was well versed in astrology besides being a scholar in Sanskrit and Malayalam. With his help and co-operation a rough or tentative translation was made and the matter left there. For health reasons, Mr Iyer had to relinquish the job in my office and return to his native land. I feel indebted to Mr. Iyer for the initial help given to me.

I should say that the period between 1942 and 1962 was perhaps the most creative part of my life as it was during these years that the greater part of my intellectual productions in the shape of books were made available to the public. It was again during these years that I was busy building up THE ASTROLOGICAL MAGAZINE, organising research work etc.

Hence it was only in 1964-65 that the translation of *Prasna Marga* could be completely revised and re-written with copious notes and illustrations. But for various reasons the manuscript had to be again kept in cold storage.

In 1977, thanks to the persuasion of my son B. A. Kumar Babu and daughter Gayatri Devi Vasudev, I took up the final revision of Part I and completed the notes and the manuscript was made ready for the press.

I do not claim infallibility. Some of the stanzas may not have been correctly translated or a meaning given which may not have been intended by the original author. I am therefore open to correction.

It is hoped that the book will be received with the same warmth by my indulgent readers as all my other publications have been received by them.

Each part of this great work is self-contained and can be used without reference to the other. Hence one need not have the apprehension that in the absence of Part II, Part I may not be useful.

Though the title *Prasna Marga* suggests that the book deals with Prasna or horary astrology, I have to make it clear that the text gives equally valuable information bearing on natal astrology which can be used with advantage.

The translation of Part II (Adhyayas 17 to 32) is also ready and I hope to bring it out in 1981.

In bringing the book to its final shape, considerable assistance has been given to me by my daughter Gayatri Devi Vasudev and I must record my appreciation of this help.

My special thanks are due to my esteemed friend and colleague Dr. P. S. Sastri who has kindly prepared 'An Index of Technical Terms'.

I have also to thank Prof. M. R. Bhat and late Mr. L. Narain Rao for their helpful hints and my sons B. Niranjan Babu and B. Sachidananda Babu who have been of much help to me in proof-corrections etc.

I must put on record the helpful attitude that is being displayed by my esteemed friends P. N. Kamat and B. K. Anantharam of IBH Prakashana in coming forward to publish this book.

Bangalore.
11-8-1980.

B. V. RAMAN.

INTRODUCTION

To the ancient astrological literature of the Hindus traced to Sage Parasara there belong a certain number of complementary works without whose assistance, the student of astrology may not be able to understand the deeper implications of the subject. *Prasna Marga* may be considered as one such work. It is an exhaustive treatise on the various aspects of Prasna or Horary astrology.

This work can be considered as of exceptional interest and value.

The authorship of the work is attributed to a Namboodiri Brahmin of Kerala, written in Kollam 825 (1649 AD)in a place called Edakad near Talasseri. It appears that at that time our author had an opponent by name Easwara Deekshita living in Chola country. Another great disciple of the author was Mochhattiloyit, a well-known personality in Kerala in those days. Kerala Varma was also a great astrologer. Kerala Varma's disciple Punnasseri Nambi Neelakanta Sarma wrote a commentary in Sanskrit. And in rendering the work into English reliance has been placed on this commentary. Unfortunately the Sanskrit commentary is available only for the first part consisting of sixteen chapters.

As regards the nature and value of the work, the author appears to have been a renowned scholar and has culled information from a number of ancient sources though his favourite works appear to be *Brihat Jataka* and *Krishneeya*.

The topic of the work, though called *Prasna Marga*, covers almost the entire range of the subject: *Jataka* or predictive astrology, *muhurtha* or electional astrology, *parihara* or remedial astrology and *nimittas* or the science of omens.

Here we have essentially a work that touches on some of the most important aspects of life—longevity, death, disease etc. The value of the work is unmistakable. It not only endorses the ancient principles of astrology but also extends beyond by giving methods which are not to be found even in such celebrated books as *Brihat Jataka*.

The English translation presented herewith, as in the case of my other translations, is not word for word. It is more or less a summary of the stanzas as I have been able to understand, sometimes with the assistance of Pandits who are well acquainted with this work. It is possible my explantation may not render the intended meaning of the author. I can only crave the indulgence of my readers for any such short comings.

Though Punnasseri Neelakanta Sharma's Sanskrit text has been generally followed a manuscript traced at the Oriental Library, Madras, has also been made use of. Some verses in the former have been omitted and some in the latter included

As earlier indicated the author of *Prasna Marga* appears to have been a scholar of exceptional merits not only in different aspects of astrology proper but also in such collateral subjects as omens and *mantra sastra.* Diagnosing from the horoscope the nature of disease and the "spirits" responsible, and prescription of remedies are an important aspect of *Prasna Marga.* Today some "men of science" may smile at the author's tracing different types of insanity to "possession" by evil spirits. To rid the world of mental illness is surely the most ancient aspiration. In this our author is not alone. Some of the western thinkers have started believing in ghosts, possession etc., as causing abnormal behaviour as the various therapies employed by neuro surgeons cannot be the answer to a fight against insanity. It is on record that many persons suffering from such mental troubles (some of them seemingly incurable) have been helped by *mantra sastra.*

According to ancient thought, whatever be the modern jargon—schizophrenia, catatonia, dissociation, paranoia, reactive and endogenous depression, melancholia, maniac depressive psychosis—insanity is caused not only by organic factors but also by 'spirits' or disincarnate beings. All the modern medical magic has not been found enough to cure insanity. Hence the ancient teachings cannot be ignored as out of date.

The first part has 16 chapters and the total number of *slokas* is 1283. I shall deal briefly with the contents.

Chapter One begins with an introduction to Astrology, its branches, and who may study the science with success. The author tells us what type of *karma* is indicated by the birth-chart and *Prasna* chart under different circumstances.

How an astrologer should begin his day by prayer and what all he should note in any person who approaches him with a problem forms the crux of Chapter Two. The directions indicated by different signs and use of Arudha Lagna are explained. Answers are to be given according to *Sutra, Thrisphuta, Ashtamangala* and *Suvarnavastha.* Muhurtas, favourable and unfavourable for queries, are also mentioned. It also shows how omens, breath-variations and *avastha* or the mental state of the astrologer are used in answering queries. *Sparsa* or the part of the body touched by a querent comes in for discussion. The persons or objects encountered on the way to an astrologer, through direction, the first syllable uttered, the way he stands, or the object with him are all dealt with in this chapter. Facial expressions and the sight of certain creatures in interpreting *prasna* form the rest of the chapter.

Kala Hora and the significance of the different quarters (east, south-east, south, south-west, west, north-west, north and north-east) occupied by the Sun during his passage across the sky; the indications of omens appearing in these quarters; are all discussed in Chapter Three.

Details for conducting *Prasnakriya* are explained in the next chapter. A lighted Lamp a Rasi Chakra, flowers, gold pieces, betel leaves and nuts, fruits and other similar articles are necessary for divining the future. The lamp plays a very significant role. The shape, the size and depth of the flame, the oil and its quality, the wick and its quality as well as the container are all taken into account before coming to any conclusion. Next comes the Rasi Chakra. The thickness or otherwise of the lines constituting the chakra and any articles found in it are also indicative of results. Again there is some elaboration on 'sparsa' or the thing touched by the querent and different gestures as denoting different results. The manner in which the astrologer must next pray and invoke God, Guru and the planets is outlined. After that, predictions are to be made on the basis of rules enumerated in the previous chapters.

Chapter Five deals with determining various factors which are necessary in making predictions. Without the correct rising sign, no prediction can be made. It shows how the Lagna Sphuta using the shadow-method, and the Chandra Sphuta are to be found out. These methods bearing on astronomical calculations are not in vogue any more and they may be ignored. Determination of *Trisphuta, Chatusphuta, Pranasphuta* and other sphutas such as *Mrityu* and *Kalasphutas, Mrityu Rasi* and *Mrityu Chakras* form the rest of the chapter. It also shows how the *Arudhasphuta* is to be calculated.

How the different *Sutras* become *Jeeva, Roga* or *Mrityu* depending upon the disposition of the Arudha Lagna is explained in Chapter Six. *Jeeva, Roga* and *Mrityu* are capable of giving different results. *Nakshatra* and *Adhipathi Sutras* refer to the present. *Samanya Sutra* refers to the past. *Amsaka* and *Maha Sutras* refer to the future. The whole chart of a querent with reference to *Trisphuta, Dasas, Antardasas* and *Duta Lakshana* must all be carefully assessed. Different results are attributed to *Trisputas* falling in different signs and Navamsas. The results vary with reference to Nakshatras also. There are enumerated certain Nakshatras which when they coincide with *Trisphuta* indicate death. Chapter six limits the period of prognostication to one year which contains all the Dasas in proportion to their Vimshottari duration

How the science of *a Sankhya* or numbers can be applied to Horary Astrology, is beautifully detailed in Chapter Seven. The 3 digits of a root number starting with the unit number pertain in a reverse order respectively to the future, the present and the past. The eight planets, the *yonis* of 8 creatures, the *Panchabhutas*, etc., are assigned numerical values. Depending upon the nature of each of these, results can be good, bad or indifferent. The root number or the Ashtamangala divided by 30, 27, 7, 12, 9 and 5 respectively gives as the remainder the lunar day, the constellation, the week-day, the zodiacal sign, the planet and the element in respective order. These reckoned from the Janma Rasi and Nakshatra are used in indicating the immediate future confined to a day or a year.

Chapter Eight is comprehensive dealing with the effects of *Arudha Lagna, Navamsa Lagna, Chatra, Sprishtanga* and *Janma* results depending upon benefic or malefic associations to which they are subject. The different *avasthas* or planetary states are capable of indicating different types of reactions and states of mind of the questioner. Prepounderance of Gulika indicates death. The 8 cardinal points beginning from East are signified by Arudha and the twelve Rasis. Different planets rule different types of vegetation which can be made use of in locating lost articles and missing persons. The lay of the gold piece is again discussed in drawing conclusions. The Navamsas of Mandi, the Moon and Lagna are indicative of illness, death or incurable disease depending upon the sign in which they fall. Lagna in the Vargas of different planets gives different results. Association of Chandra Navamsa Rasi with planets gives results varying with the nature of the planets. Chandra Kriya (see Appendix) is also given a passing reference.

The longevity of a person is determined by a consideration of the Arudha Lagna, the Moon's position, Gulika and other factors together with any omens that may be observed at the time of a question. The 1st and 8th houses and their lords are also important. The author says that longevity must be judged on horoscopy as given in Varahamihira's *Brihat Jataka*. Certain *Drekkanas* such as *Sarpa, Kala* and *Gridhra* (see Appendix) associated with malefics in the Ascendant cause death. The twelve houses should be reckoned from Arudha or Lagna, whichever is stronger. If Prasna results are similar to results based on horoscopy, then the astrologer can assertively predict events. In Chapter Nine a reference is made to one's past Karma, a human life being a means to exhaust it. The horoscope reveals such Karma but it can also be overcome through *atma-jnana* or self-realisation. The author enumerates two kinds of longevity, namely, *Yogayus* and *Dasayus* which are common to most classical works. Several combinations and permutations of planetary lords for *Alpayus* (short life), *Madhyayus* (medium life) and *Purnayus* (long life) are explained in some detail.

Chapter Ten treats of determining death on the basis of the birth and horary charts. Firstly, the *Dasayus* system is explained by which the Dasa and Antardasa in which death may be anticipated are picked out from numerous candidates. An exhaustive list of maraka planets is provided. The Kalachakra Dasa system is also dealt with. Transits, particularly those of Saturn, Jupiter, the Sun and the Moon can also be effectively applied in this regard, to narrow down the range of time when death is likely. Ashtakavarga signs, the role of Gulika, when *Niryana* planets become deadly, the time of death, etc., receive due attention. On the basis of the last letter (syllable) of a query, the time of death can also be calculated aided by omens. Various factors have to be carefully reconciled before pronouncing the final word on death.

The nature and cause of death receive special attention in Chapter Eleven. The Sun, the Moon, Mars, Mercury, Jupiter, Venus and Saturn respectively in the 8th house cause death by fire, drowning, weapons, high fever, disease, thirst and hunger. Depending upon the planet influencing the 8th house and the organ ruled by that sign, death will be due to the disturbance of the humour or *dhatu* signified by it. The lord of the 22nd drekkana plays a significant role in causing death. Whether the end will be peaceful or unhappy, is to be gleaned from the nature of the planet in the 7th from the Navamsa occupied by Mandi. Certain omens coinciding with the lord of *Mrityusphuta* being a particular planet are also taken into account. An assessment of the probable time, place and nature of death can be made with accuracy.

Diagnosing and prescription for sickness are dealt with in Chapter Twelve. Malefics in houses other than 3 and 11, and benefics in 3, 6, 12 and 8 indicate bad health. Planets in 6, 8 and 12 give a clue to the disease. The region of the affection is determined according to the nature of the Lagna. The *thridoshas* and the seasons ruled by the afflicting planet, etc., also give a clue to the period of disease. Diseases are classified into two types—*Nija* or natural and *Aguntaka* or acquired. Nija ailments are divided into *sarirotha* or those relating to the body and *chittotha* or mental afflictions. Sarirotha afflictions arise out of imbalance in *vatha* (wind), *kapha* (phlegm), *pitta* (bile) or a mixture of the three. They are treated besides well-known methods of Ayurveda by supplementing the prescribed flavour or taste in food, *viz.*, sweet, sour, bitter, hot, salt and *kashaya* in different combinations. *Aguntaka* diseases are sub-divided into *Drishtanimitiya* or of known origin and *Adrishtanimitiya* or arising out of unknown causes. Ailments caused by curses, incantations and falls from elevation come under the first. To the second group belong problems of a psychic nature including lunacy caused by evil spirits. The causes of madness are enumerated and appropriate remedies (including *mantras*) suggested.

Chapter Thirteen shows how to determine the day on which sickness commenced. The computations are mostly on the basis of the constellation occupied by the Moon, or the Rasi corresponding to the first letter of the word uttered by the messenger or querent. Recovery is judged by the Moon's transit of certain Rasis. The time and possibility of recovery is also found out by noting of certain constellations coinciding with the commencement of illness.

The wrath of certain Deities is also held as the cause of even physical ailments. But the primary cause of all affliction is one's past sins denoted by planets in *Anishta* places. Atonement through repentence, gifts, feeding, prayer and *homas* as prescribed by Sayanacharya in his *Karma Vipaka* are said to alleviate or cure these afflictions.

Interpreting results and timing events cover Chapter Fourteen. It begins with how to fix the age of a querent on the basis of the lord of Lagna. Bhavas are considered as having two significations—external and internal, or the gross and the subtle. There are 21 conditions listed in which a Bhava becomes weak. The *karakatwa* of planets is also used in delineating results pertaining to the concerned Bhavas. Planets in different vargas—own, friendly, vargottama or inimical--also influence results. The effects of Gulika and the 5 Upagrahas (tertiary planets) in various Bhavas get prominence. The author also shows how the time of fructification of results can be ascertained by combining the period allotted to a planet and the Navamsa gained by it. The effects of Dasas are attributed to the Karma which is of two kinds—*Dridha* and *Adridha*. Dridha Karma is due to conscious activity—mental, verbal or physical. Adridha Karma is caused by unintentional activity. A particular thought, word or deed resulting in Karma is determined from whether a malefic is in the 5th, 2nd or 10th respectively. Then the topic of imprisonment is abruptly taken up. The Sun's position determines the place of incarceration. Planetary results are described in some detail before the chapter comes to a close.

What are the reasons for the miseries of mankind? Chapter Fifteen deals with this subject in detail. They are eleven in number. The astrologer must first determine the nature of Karma, favourable or unfavourable, that is to unfurl itself in the querent's life. Jupiter's benefic disposition indicates the Karma as being favourable while his malefic disposition implies disfavour. Different planets in different signs and Drekkanas indicate different Deities as responsible. Acts of omission or commission that transgress moral codes lead to different types of bad Karma that accumulates to show up as misery only at a later stage of time, whether in this life or some future life. Each type of Karma comes under the governance of a particular Deity. By propitiating this Deity, some sort of compromise can be obtained and the misery alleviated to a certain degree. The Satwic, Rajasic or Tamasik nature of the Deity involved is ascertained. This enables us to know the nature of the act that is responsible for bringing about the current misery suffered by the querent. The lord of the house of harm or the planet that is responsible for the suffering is called 'angry planet'. Most of the offences are related to temple idols, temple property and the conduct of temple affairs. Combinations for the displeasure of parents, preceptors, other elders and Brahmins, as the cause of suffering, are given. Ghosts cause trouble if Gulika is involved with the house of trouble. Evil eye or *drishti badha* attaches itself to people who are in extreme states, whether of passion, health, fatigue, finance, filth, hysterics of joy or sorrow, beauty or mental weakness. Women in particular states are also vulnerable to the evil eye. *Drishti badha* is said to arise by seeing mischievous *grahas* or spirits. A list of places frequented by these grahas is given. They are of 27 types, 18 being very powerful and 9, secondary and not so strong. These spirits, said to have originated from the anger of Rudra, go under the names of *Bali Kama*, *Rati Kama* and *Hanthu Kama*. Then we are enabled to differentiate the 27 spirits. The position of Arudha also helps in determining the house of harm. This chapter next deals with *Balagrahas* which trouble only children, who may suffer through poison administered through food. The particular food causing the *dosha* can be made out from Gulika or Rahu and Arudha Lagna. Poison may be administered either to harm the victim or to gain control over him. Two types of disorders are discussed, one caused by a disorder of the thridoshas and the other, through mantric spells cast by enemies. Finally, the Parihara or the method of destroying the *Kshudrabhichara* is detailed out. Different *Homas* and *Balis* are prescribed.

The last or Chapter Sixteen begins with how to find out where the questioner (in cases where someone else comes to ask a question on another's behalf due to the latter being away somewhere) is at the time of question. The nature (movable, fixed or common) of the Arudha Lagna indicates the distance at which the questioner is and the Amsa-sign shows the nature of life he is leading. Whether the period earlier to the date of question was fortunate or unfortunate is determined by whether benefics or malefics occupy the 6 houses from the latter part of the 4th house. This is for persons born in Libra to Pisces. For those born in Aries to Virgo, the past is indicated by houses 4 to 10 and the future by houses 10 to 4. There are 4 means of attaining one's objective, *viz.*, *sama* (gentle), *dana* (through bribery), *bheda* (through intimidation) and *danda* (through force). How to find out the means to be employed in gaining one's objective is explained. The next topic dealt with is how to locate treasures, if any, in a house. The importance of Arudha Lagna in regard to married partner has been stressed. The chapter also deals with certain simple methods, popular in rural parts, to answer queries. In the case of sickness, the Deity responsible for it can be determined by an arithmetical calculation of the number governing the first letter of the question. Different propitiatory remedies are also mentioned. The manner, number and state of betel leaves presented to an astrologer help us to know which *Bhavas* or significations in a chart prosper and which, suffer. On the basis of betel-leaves *Thamboola Lagna* can be determined and deductions made. There is then a mention of the principles by which queries made by rulers (applicable to ancient times) on capture of elephants etc., could be answered. The anxiety of children as to whether they will be able to perform the death-ceremonies of their parents etc., are also dealt with. The Sun and 9th lord well placed indicate a positive answer. Afflictions to them indicate obstacles, interruptions in the middle and help from third parties to complete them successfully. Combinations for getting grateful children, and the nature of relations between son and father are enumerated.

Acquisition of political power on the basis of the asterisms occupied by the Sun, the Moon, Mars, Lagna lord and 10th lord at question time is explained. Then we have the *Kalachakra*, a diagram drawn according to specification marking 28 nakashatras in it including Abhijit. Methods of locating the positions of Yogini and Mrityu in terms of zodiacal signs and constellations are given. Yogini is symbolically described as a fierce murderous female entity. Although there is no difference of opinion as to the rising of Yogini in different week-days, there is some difference, amongst astrological authors, as to its path. Questions on ascension to heaven, fall to hell or acquisition of wealth can be anwsered by making use of 3 factors, *viz.*, *Kantakastuna*, *Raktastuna* and *Stuna*. If these *stunas* afflict Lagna or Arudha Lagna, hell after death or life equivalent to death will be the querent's lot. The last chapter, also the longest, ends with the span of life of man. Longevity in different Yugas (time-cycles) is given. The signs are also divided as coming under different Yugas. Planets occupying signs and Navamsas governed by different Yugas give a proportionate part of longevity to the native. Persons born in signs or Navamsas ruled by Krita, Treta, Dwapara and Kali are classified. Thus ends Chapter Sixteen.

In conclusion we have to observe that *Prasna Marga* is a unique work on Natal and Horary Astrology, omens and remedial measures and a careful study of the work is recommended to all students and savants of astrology.

Bangalore. B. V. RAMAN.
11-8-1980.

|| श्री गणेशायनमः ||

प्रथमाध्यायः

PRAYER

मध्याटव्यधिपं दुग्धसिन्धुकन्याधवं धिया ।
ध्यायामि साध्वहं बुद्धेः शुध्यै वृध्यै च सिद्धये ॥१॥

Stanza 1.—I offer my sincere prayers to God Vishnu so that my mind may become enlightened, extensive and perfect.

NOTES

No Sanscrit writer ever commences his work without first invoking Divine Grace. In this stanza, the author Harihara makes obeisance to Vishnu who is referred to as *Dugdha Sindhu Kanyadhavam,* meaning lord of one (Lakshmi) who was evolved out of the milky ocean. The other reference is to *Madhyatavyadhipa* meaning lord of Madhyataveedhi or 'Edakad' the native place of the author. The author prays for the purification or enlightenment (Buddhi), improvement (Vriddhi) and perfection (Siddhi) of his mind.

गुरुभ्यश्च ग्रहेभ्यश्च मया बद्धोयमञ्जलिः ।
प्रसन्नमनसस्ते मे सत्यां कुर्वन्तु भारतीम् ॥२॥

Stanza 2.—I salute my preceptors and the planets, so that they may bless my speech with purity and truth.

NOTES

There is a widespread belief in India that mere learning alone cannot make an astrologer a successful predictor. One should acquire what is called *Vaksiddhi* or the gift of correct prediction and this power, it is held, could be acquired by sincere prayers to God and preceptor. Hence the invocation that the author's speech be blessed with truth.

नमः श्रीमङ्गलश्रेणीनिवासाय महात्मने ।
सर्वं जानन्ति दैवज्ञा यद्दत् श्रुति चक्षुषः ॥३॥

Stanza 3.—I bow to my Guru Mangalasseri. His pupils being doctors of science are great seers of the future

चेल्लूरीश्वरमानम्य शैलजावल्लभं मया ।
शिष्याय देशिकावाप्तं प्रश्नवर्त्मोपदिश्यते ॥४॥

Stanza 4.—I salute my village God Siva and expound *Prasna Marga* for the benefit of my pupils.

NOTES

In stanza 2, the invocation is addressed to preceptors in general while in stanza 3, the author salutes his own Guru by name Mangalasseri whose pupils, he declares, are all highly learned astrologers.

In stanza 4, salutation is made to his village God Siva (Chellureeswara or Perinchellurappa) after which the author begins his famous work on astrology which he himself learnt after due initiation and which he now intends for the benefit of his pupils.

What Astrology Comprehends

स्कन्धत्रयात्मकं ज्योतिश्शास्त्रमेतत् षडङ्गवत् ।

गणितं संहिता होरा चेति स्कन्धत्रयं मतम् ॥५॥

Stanza 5.—Ancient astrological science is divided into three *skandhas* or six *angas*. The three skandhas are Ganita, Samhita and Hora.

जातकगोळनिमित्तप्रश्नमुहूर्ताख्यगणितनामानि ।

अभिदधतीह षडङ्गान्याचार्या ज्यौतिषे महाशास्त्रे ॥६॥

Stanza 6.—Sages have classified the great science of astrology into six *angas*, *viz.*, Jataka, Gola, Nimitta, Prasna, Muhurtha and Ganita.

गोळो गणितं चेति द्वितयं खलु गणितसंहिते स्कन्धे ।

होरासंहितयोरपि निमित्तमन्यत्रयं च होराख्ये ॥७॥

Stanza 7—Ganita Skandha deals with Gola and Ganita. Hora Skandha deals with horoscopy, Prasna, Muhurtha and a part of Nimitta. Samhita Skandha deals elaborately with Nimitta.

जनपुष्टिक्षयवृष्टिद्विरदतुरङ्गादिसकलवस्तूनाम् ।
केतूल्कादीनां वा लक्षणमुदितं हि संहितस्कन्धे ॥८॥

Stanza 8.—Samhita also deals with the varying fortunes of the people, changes in weather and progress of the animal kingdom. It sketches also the nature and shape of meteors, shooting stars and all the wonderful natural phenomena.

NOTES

That astrology is divided into three principal sections or parts, *viz.*, astronomy, horoscopy and *samhita* is accepted by almost all great sages. Varaha Mihira endorses this classification when he observes thus in his *Brihat Samhita* :

ज्योतिश्शास्त्रमनेकभेदविषयं स्कंधत्रयाधिष्ठितम् ।

meaning that astrology has several divisions but can be conveniently brought under three specific sections of Ganita (astronomy), Hora (horoscopy) and Sakha (astrological mathematics).

The six angas referred to in stanza 6 may be defined thus :

(i) *Jataka*: Deals with predictions to be made on the basis of the rising sign at birth.

(ii) *Gola :* Deals with planetary systems, their nature and peculiarities and in short with spherical astronomy.

(iii) *Nimitta:* Takes into consideration *tatkalika lakshanas* or what are popularly known as omens obtaining at a particular time and makes predictions on certain gestures.

(iv) *Prasna:* This refers to forecasts being based upon the time of question.

(v) *Muhurtha:* This has reference to fixing up of auspicious times for success in religious, secular and spiritual undertakings.

(vi) *Ganita:* Broadly speaking, Ganita refers to mathematical astronomy and mathematical astrology.

As regards the three main sections or *skandhas* referred to in stanza 5, explanations as to what each of these deals with are to be found in stanzas 7 and 8.

The following extract from my English Translation of *Brihat Samhita* (in preparation) will give the reader an idea of what Samhita treats of :

*" Samhita deals with the movements of the Sun and the planets ; their nature, dimension, colour, rays, brilliancy and shape ; their risings and settings ; their regular courses and deviations therefrom ; their retrograde and somewhat retrograde motions, their conjunctions with nakshatras, and their own positions among the other planets and constellations.

---

* दिनकरादीनां ग्रहाणां चारास्तेषु च तेषां प्रकृति विकृति प्रमाण। वर्णकिरणद्युतिसंस्थानास्तमनोदयमार्गमार्गान्तरवक्रानुवक्रर्क्षग्रह समागम चारादिभिः फलानि। नक्षत्रकूर्मं विभागेन देशेष्वगस्त्यचारः। सप्तर्षिचारः। ग्रहभक्तयो नक्षत्रव्यूह ग्रहशृङ्गाटकग्रहयुद्ध ग्रहसमागम ग्रहवर्षफलगर्भलक्षणरोहिणीस्वात्याषाढीयोगाः-सद्योवर्षकुसुमलत परिधिपरिवेषपरिघ पवनोल्कादिग्दाहक्षिति-चलनसन्ध्यारागगन्धर्वनगररजोनिर्घातार्घकाण्डसस्यजन्मेन्द्रध्वजेन्द्र चापवास्तुविद्याङ्गविद्यावायसविद्यान्तरचक्रमृगचक्रश्वचक्रवात

"Samhita deals with the influences of the movements of Agastya and Saptarishi on different countries corresponding to different constellations and planets; with stellar divisions and substances; with the interpretation of appearances presented by planetary meetings; with Graha Yuddha and Samagama; with planetary years; with the nature of the pregnant clouds; with Rohini, Swati and Ashadha Yogas; with the forecasting of immediate rain; with the nature of the future crops by a consideration of the (growth of) flowers and plants; with the phenomenon of halos (*Paridhi* and *Parivesha*); with *Parigha*, winds, fall of meteors, false fires; earth tremors; the crimson sky during twilight; with cloud-castles, dust storms, thunderbolts; with trade forecasts and gardening.

"It treats of *Indradhwaja*, rainbow, house-building or architecture, *anga vidya*; of predicting from the cawing of crows, from zodiacal diagrams; of future prediction from certain phenomena connected with the deer, horse, and wind; of the construction of temples and palaces; carving of images and their installation; of abori–horticulture and under–currents; of predicting events from the flight of

---

चक्रप्रासादलक्षणप्रतिमालक्षणप्रतिष्ठापनवृक्षायुर्वेदोदगार्गल नीराजनखञ्जनकोत्पातशान्तिमयूरचित्रकघृतकम्बलखड्गपट्टकृक–वाकुकूर्मगोजश्वेथपुरुस्त्रीलक्षणान्यन्तःपुरचिन्ताापिटकलक्षणोपान च्छेदवस्त्रच्छेदचामरदण्डशयनाऽनलक्षण रत्नपरीक्षा दीपलक्षणं दन्तकष्ठाद्याश्रितानि शुभाऽशुभानि निमित्तानि सामान्यनिच जगतः प्रतिपुरुषं पार्थिवे च प्रतिक्षणमनन्यकर्माभियुक्तेन दैवज्ञेन चिन्तयितव्यानि

Kanjana and from appearance of abnormal phenomena; of shantis or propitiatory ceremonies; of various planetary phenomena, *ghrita-kambala, khadga and patti;* of the features of *kukkuta*, crab, cow, goat, horse, elephant, man and woman. It also deals with matters connected with harems; with moles, injuries to footwear and clothes, chamara (hairy fans), danda (sticks), bedding, seats; testing of precious stones, lamps, tooth-brush and the like."

WHO CAN STUDY ASTROLOGY?

प्रमाणफलभेदेन द्विविधं च भवेदिदम् ।
प्रमाणं गणितस्कन्धः स्कन्धावन्यौ फलात्मकौ ॥९॥

Stanza 9.—Astrology can also be divided into two, *viz.*, Pramana and Phala. Ganita Skandha comes under Pramana while the other two skandhas go under Phala.

NOTES

Ganita or astronomy comes under *pramana* according to which the test of truth is actually demonstrative, *i.e.*, truth is perceived by measurements and calculations. Phala on the other hand is not capable of immediate demonstration. Phala is based upon cause-effect phenomena. The horoscope merely indicates the results of one's previous Karma. Hence the future of man is only the fruit (phala) of his past actions.

ज्योतिः कल्पो निरुक्तं च शिक्षा व्याकरणं तथा ।
छन्दो विचितिरेतानि षडङ्गानि विदुः श्रुतेः ॥१०॥

Stanza 10.—The Vedas have six limbs, *viz.*, Jyotisha, Kalpa, Nirukta, Siksha, Vyakarana and Chhandas.

छन्दः पादौ शब्दशास्त्रं च वक्त्रं
कल्पः पाणी ज्यौतिषं चक्षुषी च ।
शिक्षा घ्राणं श्रोत्रमुक्तं निरुक्तं
वेदस्याङ्गान्येवमाहुर्मुनीन्द्राः ॥११॥

Stanza 11.—For the Vedas, the six important limbs, *viz.*, the feet, the face, the hands, the eyes, the nose and the ears are represented by Chhandas, Vyakarana, Kalpa Jyotisha, Siksha, and Nirukta respectively.

वेदस्य चक्षुः किल शास्त्रमेतत्
प्रधानताङ्गेषु ततोस्य युक्ता ।
अङ्गैर्यतोन्यैरपि पूर्णमूर्ति
श्चक्षुर्विना कः पुरुषत्वमेति ॥१२॥

Stanza 12.—As astrology is the eye of the Vedas, it is given the pride of place. No person possessing all the organs intact but without eyesight can have an individuality.

NOTES

Stanzas 10 to 12 stress the importance of astrology. The Vedas have six angas or auxliaries and astrology is the first and foremost as representing the eyes. The other five are Chandas, Vyakarana, Kalpa, Siksha and Nirukta representing respectively legs or feet, face, hands, nose and ears respectively. *Chandas* sastra treats about Rishis and Chanda Devatas mentioned in the Vedas and they form the basis (legs). *Vyakarana* or *Sabda* treats about the grammatical peculiarities found in the Vedas. It is as it were the face of the Vedas. *Kalpa* treats about the procedure to be followed in sacrifices and the *Dharmas* of the sacrificial priests. It represents the hands. *Siksha* is concerned with the 'sounds', the 'phonetics' of the Vedas. *Nirukta* deals with the special meaning of the Vedic words and sounds. Chandas, Kalpa and Vyakarana are in the shape of *sutras*. Nirukta is in prose and *Siksha* and *Jyotisha* are in the form of verses. *Jyotisha* or Astrology is, of course, the most important limb of the Veda Purusha (Vedas Personified). The allusion by way of a simile to want of individuality (purushatwa) in the absence of eye-sight, made in stanza 12, is merely to emphasize the importance given to sight or vision (astrology) as against all the other limbs (angas) of the body (Vedas).

अध्येतव्यं ब्राह्मणैरेव तस्मात्
ज्योतिश्शास्त्रं पुण्यमेतद्रहस्यम् ।
एतद्बुध्वा सम्यगाप्नोति यस्मा-
दर्थम् मं धंमोक्षमग्रयं यशश्च ॥१३॥

Stanza 13.—The exalted and recondite science of astrology is to be studied only by

Brahmins. A proper study of the subject leads one to the acquisition of wealth, merit, salvation, respect and fame.

म्लेच्छा हि यवनास्तेषु सम्यक्छास्त्रमिदं स्थितम् ।
ऋषिवत्तेपि पूज्यन्ते किं पुनर्दैवविद्द्विजः ॥१४॥ इति ।

Stanza 14.—When even Mlechchas and Yavanas well versed in astrology are held in the same esteem as Rishis, who would deny respect to an astrologer who happens to be a Brahmin?

NOTES

Though stanza 13 implies that the study of astrology should be restricted to Brahmins alone yet from the reference made to Yavanas and Mlechchas well versed in astrology being held in same respect as Rishis, it is clear that all intelligent persons, irrespective of their caste, creed or religion, can take to the study of the subject through proper initiation. The Brahmin, unlike as commonly understood, can be anyone who leads a simple and pious life. Sage Vyasa in the *Mahabharata* says that everyone is born a *sudra* and becomes a Brahmin through his deeds as per the statement:

जन्मनो जायते शूद्रः कर्मणो भवति ब्राह्मणः ।

The same meaning is implied in the *Srimad Bhagavad Gita* wherein Lord Krishna says the four-fold division was on the basis of one's nature and one's work. Brahmins, according to the Lord, are those who lead lives of piety, are forbearing, calm, self-controlled and seekers of knowledge.

Stanza 14 is merely a reproduction of stanza 15 of Chapter II of *Brihat Samhita*.

It is difficult to define the term Mlechcha. But by a careful perusal of the literature connected with ancient scientific thought, I would venture to say that the inhabitants of Afghanistan, Arabia and Persia were probably intended by the term Mlechcha. It is not correct to suggest that *mlechcha* means *neecha*. On the contrary the term *mlechcha* meant a person inhabiting a certain tract of land which I would identify as the strip beginning from Afghanistan and extending upto and including modern Iran. The Yavanas are, of course, the Greeks.

This stanza furnishes us with the clue that the ancient Hindus had cultural relations with Middle East and Southern European countries. In fact the astrological writings of Yavanacharyas seem to have been held in such high esteem by a celebrated scientist like Varaha Mihira that he does not hesitate to give them the respect due to a Maharshi. There seems to have been considerable intermingling of Indian, Greek and Arabian cultures during the time of Mihira, though it cannot be denied that all those countries were highly indebted to India, the mother of all arts and sciences.

QUALIFICATIONS OF AN ASTROLOGER

ज्योतिश्शास्त्रविदग्धो गणितपटुर्वृत्तवांश्च सत्यवचाः ।

विनयी वेदाध्यायी ग्रहयजनपटुश्च भवतु दैवज्ञः । ॥१५॥

Stanza 15.—That person, who has mastery of this science, who has a good knowledge of mathematics who leads a religious life, who is truthful, who is free from conceit and who is well versed in the *Vedas*, *mantras* and *tantras*, he alone can be called a Daivajnya or seer.

दैवविदेवंभूतो यद्वदति फलं शुभाशुभं प्रष्टुः ।

तत्सर्वं न च मिथ्या भवति प्राज्ञैस्तया चोक्तम् ॥१६॥

Stanza 16.—All the predictions made by such a person will come true and will never be false. The learned support this statement.

दशभेदं ग्रहगणितं जातकमवलोक्य निरवशेषं यः ।

कथयति शुभमवशुभं वा तस्य न मिथ्या भवेद्वाणी ॥१७॥

Stanza 17.—The predictions of one who has studied the ten kinds of planetary motions and who has understood the inner principles of astrology will never be falsified.

अनेकहोरातत्वज्ञ पञ्चसिद्धांतकोविदः ।
ऊहापोहपटुः सिद्धमन्त्रो जानाति जातकम् ॥१८॥ इति ।

Stanza 18.—He who has acquired a thorough knowledge of the different Horas, who is an adept in the five siddhantas, who has inferential ability and who is initiated into a secret mantra by a preceptor, can alone know horoscopy.

NOTES

Qualifications of an astrologer have been laid down in stanzas 15 to 18. In this connection, reference may also be made to similar qualifications laid down by Varaha-Mihira in his *Brihat Samhita*. One, who wishes to be a correct predictor, should not only be an adept in Astrology, Astronomy, Vedas and Mantra Sastras, but also must be a man of character, religious, righteous and must have obtained *siddhi* of certain secret mantras which would confer on the astrologer the uncanny power of correct predictions.

Varahamihira goes to the extent of suggesting that the astrologer should be of noble birth, and agreeable appearance. Humility must characterise his behaviour. His personal habits must be disciplined and above opprobium. He should be well versed in ritual and expiatory ceremonies. He should be gifted to resolve independently any tough problems. Disciplined life, faith in God, a helpful nature and scrupulous adherence to certain types of austerity would enable him to develop his power of intuition considerably and this would be a great asset to anyone who aspired to be a successful astrologer.

The ten kinds of astrological mathematics referred to in stanza 17 are explained in the following two stanzas. Stanza 18 is also to be found in a slightly varied form in *Satya Samhita*.

DIFFERENT KINDS IN GANITA

द्युगणानयतं खेटमध्यमस्फुटयोरपि ।
ग्रहणद्वितयं खेटकलहस्तत्समागम ॥१९॥
अस्तोदयौ च खेटानां नक्षत्राणां च सङ्गमः ।
इति भेदास्तु विज्ञेयाः ग्रहाणां गणिते दश ॥२०॥ इति ।

Stanzas 19 and 20.—Kali day, mean positions of planets, true positions of planets, solar eclipses, lunar eclipses, planetary fights, lunar conjunctions combustion, heliacal risings and settings and planetary conjunctions with constellations are the ten kinds of calculations.

NOTES

As I do not propose to explain the astronomical aspect of astrology, I would refer the readers to such works as *Surya Siddhanta* and *Siddhanta Siromani* for the elucidation of the astronomical references. The astrologer is expected to be thoroughly conversant with the method of calculating eclipses, planetary longitudes, heliacal risings and settings and other astronomical phenomena. Kali day is the number of days passed from the beginning of Kali Yuga to the epoch in question. The mean position of a planet is the position which it would have attained at a uniform rate of motion and the corrections to be applied in respect of the eccentricity of the orbit are not considered. The mean longitude is reckoned on the assumption that the orbits of planets are concentric circles. Because the orbits are elliptical and not circular, equations are later on applied to the mean positions to get the true longitudes. Two planets are said to be in fight (*graha yuddha*) when they are in conjunction and the distance between them is less than one degree. All the planets excepting the Sun and the Moon can enter into 'war'. The conquering planet is the one whose longitude is less. The heliacal setting and rising of planets (*asthodaya*) occur when they are at certain distances from the Sun. For instance, Jupiter can become *asta* when he is at a distance of 11° from the Sun. *Surya-siddhanta* gives the following limits for the *asta* or combustion of the planets :—

Mars	17°
Mercury	12° (retrograde) 14° (acceleration)
Jupiter	11°
Venus	8°
Saturn	15°

For a fuller appreciation of the astrological importance of combustion reference may be made to a special number (September 1978) of THE ASTROLOGICAL MAGAZINE devoted mainly to this subject.

Chandra Samagama, eclipses, etc., etc., involve elaborate calculations. I do not propose to discuss them in these notes.

Modern Nautical almanacs give all astronomical details required for astrological purposes.

THE FIVE SIDDHANTAS

ब्राह्मः सौरश्च वासिष्ठो रौमशः पौलिशस्तथा ।
सिद्धान्ता इति पञ्च स्यु कथ्यन्ते खलु तद्विदाः ॥२१॥

Stanza 21.—The five siddhantas are Brahma, Surya, Vasishta, Romasa and Poulasa.

स्पष्टा ब्राह्मस्तु सिद्धान्तस्तस्यासन्नस्तु रोमशः ।
सौरः स्पष्टतरोऽस्पष्टौ वासिष्ठ पौलिशश्च तौ ॥२२॥
कदाचिद् ब्रह्मसिद्धान्तः सावित्रस्तु कदाचन ।
कदाचिद्रोमशः स्पष्टो न कदाचित्तथेतरौ ॥२३॥

Stanzas 22 and 23.—Brahma Siddhanta is accurate. Romasa is more accurate and Surya is the most accurate. Vasishta and Poulasa are not accurate. The first three can be relied upon. And the last two are archaic in character.

NOTES

Hindu astronomy makes reference to 18 siddhantas, *viz.*, Surya, Paitamaha, Vyasa, Vasishta, Atri, Parasara, Kasyapa, Narada, Garga, Marichi, Manu, Angirasa, Lomasa, Paulasa, Yavana, Chyavana, Manu and Saunaka. Of these, only five seem to have merited the admiration of Varahamihira, who, as will be seen subsequently is generally the source of inspiration for our author. According to this author, Paitamaha or Brahma, Romasa and Surya Siddhantas can be relied on, while Vasishta and Paulasa, are not accurate. But Varahamihira in his **Pancha-siddhantika* (which is a summary of the five siddhantas above referred to) clearly says* that the siddhanta made by Paulasa is accurate ; near to it stands the siddhanta of Romaka and more accurate is the Saura. And the remaining two, *viz.*, Paitamaha and Vasishta are far from truth. Romaka and Surya are accepted as accurate by Varahamihira even though pride of place is invariably given to Surya.

BEGINNING THE STUDY OF ASTROLOGY

मन्त्रं यथाविधि गुरोः सुदिने ग्रहीत्वा
तद्देवतां जपहुतिप्रमुखैः प्रतोष्य ।
ज्ञानाय जातकफलस्य तु सिद्धमन्त्रः
स्यादेव दैवविदिहाप्तव वात्तथा हि ॥२४॥

Stanza 24.—One should get initiation into the appropriate *mantra* from a qualified Guru, at an auspicious moment, and propitiate the *mantra devata* suitably. This will enable him to master all astrological knowledge.

---

*पौलिशतिथिस्फुटोसौ तस्यासन्नस्तु रोमकः प्रोक्तः ।
पसष्ठतरः पवित्रः परिशेषौ दुरविभ्रष्ठौ ॥

दातव्यमपापेभ्यो निपुणमतिभ्यः प्रशान्तशीलेभ्यः ।
शुभदिवसे गुरुलग्ने चन्द्रे मृदुशीघ्रवर्गस्थे ॥२५॥

Stanza 25.—An intelligent, calm and pious person should begin study of astrology on an auspicious day when Jupiter is in Lagna and the Moon occupies *mridu* (benefic) and *seeghra* (fast) vargas.

NOTES

Mridu (soft) and seeghra (fast) vargas are interpreted by some as the vargas of Mercury. According to another reading, *mridu* vargas are Mrigasira, Anuradha and Revati and *seeghra* vargas are Aswini, Hasta and Pushyami.

बलिहोमगन्धपुष्पैरादित्यादीन् ग्रहान् समभ्यर्च्य ।
प्रारभ्यमिदं शास्त्रं विधिवत्कृत्वा गुरोः पूजाम् ॥२६॥

Stanza 26.—The study of this science should begin only after worshipping the nine planets (*navagrahas*) and the preceptor in the prescribed form.

NOTES

Apart from the planets being huge masses of matter they are also supposed to have their subtle or spiritual aspects. The *navagraha pujas* are intended to establish some sort of resonance between thought-vibrations of the individual and those released from the planetary bodies.

विधिवन्मन्त्राः पठिताभवन्ति सर्वार्थसाधका लोके ।
एवं सफलं शास्त्रं भवति हि विधिपूर्वकं पठितम् ॥२७॥
इति ।

Stanza 27.—Mantras when properly practised and recited give the desired results. So does this science when properly cultivated.

IMPORTANCE OF VARAHAMIHIRA

तस्याः पुनः पटुधियामपि दुर्गमोऽर्थः ।
भट्टोत्पलादिरचिता विवृतीर्विलोक्य स्पष्टं करोतु हृदि दैवविदर्थमस्याः ॥२८॥

Stanza 28.—*Brihat Jataka* by Varahamihira, though short, is a very suggestive treatise pregnant with ideas Though difficult to be comprehended by even intelligent persons, yet with the aid of the commentaries of Bhattotpala and others, it is possible to understand the book.

NOTES

Compare Varahamihira's own admission,

स्वल्पम् वृत्तविचित्रमर्थबहुळ

meaning that his work is " concise, of a variety of meter and full of meaning ".

होरां वराहमिहिरास्यविनिर्गतां ये
मालामिवादधति दैवविदः स्वकण्ठे ।
कृष्णीयशास्त्रमपि भर्तृमतीव सूत्रं
तेषां सभासु महती भवतीह शोभा ॥२९॥

Stanza 29.—One wearing the garland of Varahamihira in his neck along with the necklace of *Krishneeya* can win laurels in any astrological assembly.

NOTES

Brihat Jataka deals with horoscopy and *Krishneeya* with Prasna. One well acquainted with these two books can, according to the author, safely claim good scholarship.

होरायास्तु दशाध्याय्यां व्याख्यायां क्रियतां श्रमः ।
दैवज्ञेन विशेषेण फलमादेष्टुमिच्छता ॥३०॥

Stanza 30.—An astrologer who wants to make predictions should specially study *Dasadhyayi* carefully.

दशाध्याय्यां विशेषेण श्रमौ नैव कृतो यदि ।
दुष्करः फलनिर्देशस्तद्विदां च तथा वचः ॥३१॥

Stanza 31.—Without a thorough study of the *Dasadhyayi*, it would be difficult to make correct predictions. So say the learned.

अदृष्ट्वा यो दशाध्यायीं फलमादेष्टुमिच्छति ।
इच्छत्येव समुद्रस्य तरणं स प्लवं विना ॥३२॥

Stanza 32.—One, who attempts to predict without studying the *Dasadhyayi*, would be like a man trying to cross an ocean without a boat.

NOTES

Several commentaries have been written on *Brihat Jataka*, Bhattotpala's being the most popular and *Dasadhyayi* being the the most recondite. The author or *Prasna Marga* seems to have had such great regard for *Dasadhyayi*, that he regards this commentary as a suitable boat for crossing the grand ocean of astrological knowledge. As the name implies, *Dasadhyayi* is a commentary on only the first ten chapters of *Brihat Jataka*. The name of the commentator is still obscure, though some hold that one Govinda Somayaji wrote these commentaries. As to why he chose to comment on only ten chapters, remains inexplicable. He must have had his own reasons. A careful study of *Dasadhyayi* reveals that the commentator has very intelligently tried to read some secret or hidden meanings into Varahamihira's writings other than they would ordinarily imply. To gratify the curiosity of readers as to the uniqueness of *Dasadhyayi*, I shall just refer to the first sloka of Chapter I of *Brihat Jataka*. The first line of the sloka runs thus :

मूर्तित्वे परिकल्पितः शशभृतो वर्त्माऽपुनर्जन्मना—

This sloka, according to Bhattotpala, is merely an invocation addressed to the great and glorious Sun. But *Dasadhyayi* sees in it a variety of meanings, consistent with

Varahamihira's own claim to this effect in stanza 2 of Chapter I of *Brihat Jataka.* It is said that the method of casting unknown horoscopes (*Nashta Jataka*) is contained in this sloka, apart from other equally important or significant meanings. Each word of the sloka, apart from what it ordinarily connotes, is supposed to stand for some other meaning. Thus while by the word *moorthithve* is meant one of the *astamurthis* of Siva (*vide* English Translation of *Brihat Jataka* by B. Suryanarain Rao) it is also said to imply *moorthibhava* or Lagna. Similarly each word of the sloka is held to be capable of a variety of meanings and interpretations. Again taking the words *Moorthithve-parikalpitassasabritha:* To start with 'moorthithve' is converted into numbers. From this the number 'parika' should be subtracted. Again from the remainder, got by subtracting 'parika' from 'moorthithve' the number of 'pitha' after being inverted should be subtracted, as the commentary says that the number 'pitha' should be subtracted only after it is inverted (*sodhayed vilomena*). Then to this remainder the number 'sasa' should be added. This gives the number of slokas contained in *Brihat Jataka.* When this is calculated, we will get the number as shown hereunder :—

(1) The number of 'moorthithve' is 465 (as 'thve' is 4, 'rthi' is 6 and 'mu' is 5).

(2) The number for 'parika' is 121.

(3) When (2) is subtracted from (1) we get 465 — 121 =344.

(4) From this the number for 'pitha' =61 should be subtracted after it is reversed. Then we get 344 — 16=328.

(5) To this 328 the number for 'sasa' should be added. Then we get (328 plus 55) 383. This is the total number of slokas contained in the work *Brihat Jataka*.

The above observations, it is hoped, will give the reader an idea of how the author of *Dasadhyayi* has tried to interpret *Brihat Jataka*.

ROLE OF HOROSCOPY AND HORARY

स्वर्गाद्यनुभवक्षीणशिष्टप्राचीनकर्मणाम् ।
भोगाय जननं नृणां मोहभाजां मुहुर्मुहुः ॥३३॥

Stanza 33.—A man is born in this world to enjoy or suffer the consequence of his deeds from his past birth. A portion of this he reaps in heaven or hell but for the remnant he has to take a new birth.

अत्र तु द्विविधं कर्म प्राक्कर्म निजयत्नतः ।
अन्ल्यस्यानुभवोमुत्र भुक्त्वेहाद्यस्य संक्षयः ॥३४॥

Stanza 34.—There are two kinds of Karma, *viz.*, *sanchita* and *prarabdha*. The effects of *sanchita* will be exhausted in heaven or hell. The result of the *prarabdha karma* will be lessened only by experiencing them.

NOTES

In stanzas 33 and 34, the theory of Karma is cryptically expounded. The subject of Karma is so vast that it would be impossible to make justice to it by way of a short note.

Karma has its philosophical as well as astrological aspects. The author of this work has tried to explain that *sanchita karma* can be exhausted by our sojourn in heaven or hell, whereas *prarabdha karma* must be experienced in this life. *Prarabdha karma*, at the end of this life, will result in our re-birth, this cycle of births and deaths going on till the attainment of gnana or true knowledge.

I have dealt with the theory of Karma exhaustively in my book *Astrology and Modern Thought* and I would refer my esteemed readers to this book for more details.

स्वकर्म भोक्तुं जायन्ते प्रायेणैव हि जन्तवः ।
क्षीणे कर्मणि चान्यत्र पुनर्गच्छन्ति देहिनः । ॥३५॥

Stanza 35.—Souls take fresh births for reaping the fruits of previous lives. This cycle of births goes on until the attainment of *moksha*.

यदुपचितमन्यजन्मनि शुभाशुभं तस्य कर्मणः पक्तिम ।
व्यञ्जयति शास्त्रमेतत्तमसि द्रव्याणि दीप इव ॥३६॥

पूर्वजन्मार्जितं कर्म शुभं वा यदि वाशुभम् ।
तस्य पक्तिं ग्रहाः सर्वे सूचयन्तीह जन्मनि ॥३७॥

Stanzas 36 and 37.—Just as a lamp illumines objects in darkness, astrology reveals to us the effects of our previous Karma, good or bad. All the planets indicate clearly whether we are enjoying or suffering now as a result of our actions in our previous birth.

IMPORTANCE OF MUHURTHA

सुखदुःखकरं कर्म शुभाशुभ मुहूर्तजम् ।
जन्मान्तरेपि तत् कुर्यात् फलं तस्यान्वयेपि वा ॥३८॥

Stanza 38.—What is done at an auspicious moment results in happiness. What is done at an inauspicious time, begets evil. However remote our deeds, the results are bound to be experienced in the family.

NOTES

According to stanza 36 astrology merely indicates the results of past Karma. Planets are only an index of things to happen and they do not cause the events. The same idea is expressed by almost all classical writers. This definition must enable us to appreciate the real significance and scope of astrology and its relation to the theory of Karma. Stanzas 37 and 38 repeat the same idea. It is also suggested in stanza 38 that accumulated Karma during the past birth may be experienced not only by the person concerned but also by his descendants.

प्राग्जन्मार्जितपुण्याधप्राबल्योद्रेकहेतुतः ।
प्रारब्धसंज्ञि मानुष्यजातौ जातकचिन्तनम् ॥३९॥

Stanza 39.—The balance of good or bad Karma brought forward from the previous birth is *prarabdha*, and it is the reading of this that goes under the name of Jataka or Astrology.

आ मरणादिह जन्तुः प्राक्कृतनिजकर्मपाकमनुभवति ।
तद्वक्तुमलं जातकमथ किं प्रश्नेन कथ्यते सत्यम् ॥४०॥

Stanza 40.—One undergoes the consequences of one's previous Karma from birth to death and this can be known from his horoscope. Then what is the use of Prasna?

NOTES

As the name of the book implies, *Prasna Marga* has primarily to do with Prasna or horary astrology, though, almost all the principles may be used with advantage in interpreting radical horoscopes. In stanza 40, the author queries as to what use a Prasna chart could be put to when horoscopy can deal with all important events. He answers the question in the following stanzas :—

कस्य पक्तिरिति ज्ञातुमिदानीं पूर्वकर्मणाम् ।
इहार्जितं च विज्ञातुं कर्म प्रश्नो विधीयते ॥४१॥

Stanza 41.—Prasna reveals to us whether a man reaps the fruits of his deeds in his previous birth or the fruits of his actions in this birth. Here a question arises.

प्राग्जन्मानि कृतानां च कृतानां चेह कर्मणाम् ।
विभागोपि कथं ज्ञेय इति चेत्सोपि कथ्यते ॥४२॥

Stanza 42.—How can we distinguish whether it is the result of our previous Karma or present Karma that is yielding its result now?

यदा जातकतः प्रश्नो गुणदोषैर्विभिद्यते ।
तदा शुभाशुभं विद्यात् कर्मभेदैरिहार्जितैः ॥४३॥

Stanza 43.--If the horoscope has beneficial planetary patterns and the Prasna chart malefic ones, then it is to be understood that the native is experiencing the fruits of evil Karma done in this birth. If *vice versa*, then also the native is experiencing the effects of good Karma done in this birth.

यदानुसरति प्रश्नो जातकं ग्रहभादिभिः ।
तदा प्राक्कर्मपाकः स्यादित्यारूह्यं हि धीमता इति । ॥४४॥

Stanza 44.–If the planetary patterns in the horoscope as well as in the Prasna chart are similar, then a clever astrologer should divine that the native is experiencing the fruits of his past Karma only.

NOTES

In stanzas 41 to 44, the author explains the relative utilities of the Prasna and the birth charts. There is repeated emphasis on the influences of Karma and the importance of Prasna in finding out the nature of Karma to be enjoyed in this birth. The horoscope by itself reveals the nature of past Karma and the Prasna chart acts as some sort of a supplement to the birth chart. Suppose we see in a man's horoscope a good period and in a query of his (Prasna chart) a very bad time, then we have to assume that the person is reaping the bad effects of his Karma done in this life. Suppose we see in his horoscope a bad period and in his Prasna chart a good period, it is to be inferred that the person is reaping the favourable effects of good deeds done in this birth only. If the horoscope and Prasna are similar in positions and combinations, then the person is reaping the result of Karma done in his previous birth. Since some sort of a balancing of the birth and Prasna charts is involved, it is clear that the current indications in the birth chart, *i.e.*, the indications obtaining at the time of a query—the benefic and malefic dispositions of current Dasa lords, Yogakarakas, etc., have to be studied along with the Prasna chart to know the nature of Karma now being experienced.

SIMILARITY BETWEEN PRASNA AND JATAKA

बुध्वा शास्त्रं यथान्यायं बलाबलविधानतः ।
सयोक्तं जातके सर्वं तद्वत् प्रश्नेपि चिन्तयेत् ॥४५॥ इति ।

Stanza 45.—The Prasna chart should be read just as the horoscope is examined with reference to its relative merits and demerits.

संप्रेर्यमाणस्त्ववशः शरीरी प्रसह्य दैवेन शुभाशुभेन ।
ज्योतिर्विदः सन्निधिमेति यस्मात् प्रश्नोऽप्यतो
जन्मसमः फलेषु ॥४६॥

Stanza 46.—A person goes to an astrologer prompted by Providence to know his future.

Therefore there is a close similarity between Prasna and Jataka.

जन्मलग्नतया प्रश्नलग्नं संकल्प्य पण्डितः ।
जातके यद्यदुद्दिष्टं तत्तत् प्रश्नेपि चिन्तयेत् ॥४७॥ इति ।

Stanza 47.—As Prasna Lagna is similar to Janma Lagna, all events should be read from Prasna as you would do in a horoscope.

NOTES

The sum and substance of these three stanzas is that the time of question (Prasna) should be given the same importance as the time of birth. Human births are regulated according to the law of Karma and hence the time of birth is significant. Similarly a person proceeds to an astrologer to ascertain his future prompted by a Divine force and hence the time of question is equally important. There are no doubt certain points of difference in reading Prasna charts and horoscopes. They are discussed by the author in their proper places. But unless otherwise implied, all events revealed in a horoscope can also be read from a Prasna chart. The principles given in this book may be used with advantage in studying horoscopes.

There are some points of difference in reading which the author details in Chapter XIV and XVII.

॥ इति प्रश्नमार्गे प्रथमोऽध्यायः ॥

द्वितीयाध्यायः

PROCEDURE FOR THE ASTROLOGER

उत्थायोषसि देवतां हृदि निजां ध्यात्वा वपुश्शोधनं
कृत्वा स्नानपुरःसरं सलिलविक्षेपादि कर्माकिलं ।
कृत्वा मन्त्रजपादिकं च विधिवत् पञ्चाङ्गवीक्षां तथा
खेटानां गणनं च दैवविदथ स्वास्थान्तरात्मा भवेत् ॥१॥

Stanza 1.—An astrologer should get up early in the morning, pray to the family Deity, cleanse the various parts of the body, bathe, do his Nitya Karmas and perform *mantra japa* (by invoking the presiding Deity according to shastraic injunction), study the planets with the help of an almanac and remain calm without being ruffled by any anxieties, ever expecting the visit of someone anxious to have his difficulties solved with the help of astrology.

NOTES

In this sloka, the author explains what everyone expects of an astrologer to do. Obviously this chapter also gives us an insight into the social life of the people of

Kerala (in particular and India in general) at the time of this author. We are informed that even now in Kerala where this science had developed much, there are many families which have own astrologers to consult with as we find elsewhere family physicians attending to the health of a family. The astrologer is called in and asked to read the past, present and the future of the family by *astha mangala prasna*. The first part of this treatise deals with this art and the author has detailed every aspect of it for the benefit of Daivajnas (astrologers). An astrologer is expected to be very learned and to lead a godly life. The astrologer believes that what he foretells, will never be satisfactory, unless his preceptor and his initiated mantra lead him on to find out the real truth in spite of the diversity of views revealed therein (Ashta Mangala Prasna).

आलोके खलु यस्य कस्यचिदसावायाति यत्किंचन
प्रष्टुं मां प्रति नूनमित्यवहितस्तन्न्यस्तदृष्टिर्दृढम् ।
तच्चेष्टादिकमाकलय्य सकलं तत्कालजातं
पुनर्ज्ञानीयात्सदसन्निमित्तमपि च श्वासस्थितिं
चात्मनः ॥२॥

Stanza 2.—The astrologer should always be on the lookout if any person is approaching him for a prediction. He should carefully examine the appearance, dress, movements, actions, etc., of the querist. He should also note down any ominous sound or indicative sign. Lastly, he should very carefully diagnose the nature of his own breath.

PROCEDURE FOR THE QUERIST

तियौ शुभायां शुभादेऽनुकूले तारे दिने भानुशुभग्रहाणाम् ।
प्रष्टेप्सितं प्राभृतदानतुष्टं ज्योतिर्विदं प्रातरुपेत्य
पृच्छेत् ॥३॥

Stanza 3.—The querist should select an auspicious lunar day, a favourable constellation and auspicious week-days. Early in the morning, the querist should meet the astrologer with some humble presents and ask his question in a reverential attitude.

NOTES

In this stanza, the author explains what a person who is anxious to know his future should do. The person consulting is not, of course, expected to know this treatise but the details furnished are for the information of the astrologer. Favourable constellations are the 2nd, 4th, 6th and 8th from birth star. Saturday and Tuesday are not auspicious.

नापृष्टः कस्यचिद्ब्रूयान्नान्यायेन च पृच्छतः ।
परमार्थफलज्ञानं यतो नैवेह सिध्यति ॥४॥ इति॥

अपृच्छतः पृच्छतो वा जिज्ञासोर्थस्यकस्यचित् ।
होराकेन्द्रत्रिकोणेभ्यः शुभाशुभफलं वदेत् ॥५॥

वसिष्ठवचनादस्माज्जिज्ञसोरप्यपृच्छतः ।
दर्शने दैवविद्ब्रूयादारूढेन शुभाशुभम् ॥६॥

Stanzas 4, 5 and 6.—Only humble requests deserve an answer. No prediction should be offered to any person unasked for, nor to one who wishes to test an astrologer. If the astrologer attempts to answer him, he will not be able to get at the truth. Whether requested or not, if there is the desire to know the future, the astrologer should give predictions on the basis of Lagna, Kendras and Kona Bhavas. As Vasishta says "those who have a desire to know the future, whether they ask or not, deserve to be given predictions on the basis of Arudha" at the time of Prasna.

NOTES

Some sort of a professional code is laid down in stanzas 4 to 6. Unasked for, no prediction should be given. If a person comes to test an astrologer, no predictions should be given. But when the motive is pure and the person is anxious to consult the astrologer, it is immaterial whether or not one expresses a desire to consult. Such a person must receive the attention of the astrologer.

PROCEDURE FOR ARUDHA

ऐन्द्र्यां मेषवृषावग्निकोणे मिथुनभं स्थितम् ।
याम्यां कर्कटसिंहौ स्तो नैऋत्यां दिशि कन्यका ॥७॥
वारुण्यां तु तुलाकीटौ वायुकोणे धनुःस्थितिः ।
सौम्यां मृगघटौ स्यातामैशान्यां दिशि मीनभम् ॥८॥
भूमिचक्रमिति प्रोक्तं विष्वग्दैवविदःस्थितम् ।
तत्र यत्र स्थितः प्रष्टा पृच्छत्यारूढभं हि तत् ॥९॥

Stanzas 7. 8 and 9.—In the terrestrial sphere or circle, Mesha and Vrishabha represent east; Mithuna south-east; Karkataka and Simha south; Kanya south-west; Thula and Vrischika west; Dhanus north-west; Makara and Kumbha north; and Meena north-east. The *Arudha* Rasi is the sign corresponding to the direction occupied by the questioner at the time of putting the query.

आरूढत्वात्पृच्छकेन राशिरारूढ उच्यते ।
तस्मिन् सम्यक्परिज्ञाते सर्वं तेनैव चिन्त्यताम् ॥१०॥

Stanza 10.—As the sign comes to be mounted upon by the questioner, it is termed *arudha*. A careful consideration of *arudha* leads to a proper assessment of the chart concerned.

तस्मिन्ननिश्चिते चक्रं विलिख्यास्मिन् सुपूजिते ।
प्रष्टा स्वर्णेन यं राशिं स्पृशेदारूढ एव सः ॥११॥

इति ।

Stanza 11.—In uncertain cases, *arudha* is to be found thus: A circle is drawn marking the directions and zodiacal signs, and after due invocation, the questioner is asked to place a piece of gold on any point and *arudha* is accordingly ascertained.

NOTES

Arudha is a very important factor in Prasna or Horary astrology. In stanzas 7 to 11, the method of finding *arudha* is indicated. The twelve signs are assigned to the eight directions and according to the direction held by the person consulting the astrologer at the time of a query, the *arudha* is found. In doubtful cases, or when a questioner being agitated, walking up and down puts a question, a diagrammatic representation is made and the person asked to place a bit of gold or merely touch any point. This sign is taken as *arudha*.

It will be seen that if the circle is divided by 8, each cardinal point gets 45°. According to the assignment of Rasis, the common signs (Gemini, Virgo, Sagittarius and Pisces) get each 45°, while the other signs get only 22½°. If for instance the questioner stands, say at a distance of 30° towards S.E. direction, the sign will undoubtedly be Taurus and this will be the *arudha*. It is better the astrologer always keeps ready a circle (see appendix) drawn according to the instructions in the above stanzas, and when a questioner comes, ask him to touch a place in the circle and then note down the *arudha* Rasi. Otherwise the direction where a person stands can be easily noted and *arudha* Lagna determined.

THINGS TO BE NOTED AT QUERY TIME

दैवज्ञेन समाहितेन समयो देशः स्ववायुर्दशा
प्रष्टुः स्पर्शनामाश्रितर्क्षहरितौ प्रश्नाक्षराणि स्थितिः ।
चेष्टाभावविलोकने च वसनाद्यन्यच्च तत्कालजं
पृच्छायाः समये तदेतदखिलं ज्ञेयं हि वक्तुं फलम्
॥१२॥

Stanza 12.—When a query is put, the astrologer should take stock of the exact time (*samaya*), the nature of the spot occupied by the questioner (*desa*), the nature of his own breath (*swarayu*), his own condition or state (*avastha*), what the querist touches (*sparsa*), *arudha* Rasi, the direction, the letters of the words uttered (*prasnakshara*), deportment of the querist (*sthiti*), movements (*cheshta*), mental attitude (*bhava*), his looking at particular direction or thing (*vilokanam*), his dress (*vasanam*), and ominous sounds or indicative signs at the time (*nimittas*).

NOTES

Fourteen items have been listed in this stanza which the author wants an astrologer to consider carefully when answering a query. It is interesting to note that according to this stanza every gesture, emotion and suggestion, both of the astrologer and the querist have their own role to play in indicating the outcome of a query. The author poses a very intriguing problem to modern thinkers, when he brings together a variety of apparently unconnected matters as having a bearing on our future thinking and actions. Modern psychologists and para-psychologists will do well to find why or how the state of mind of a person, or the dress he wears or the direction he faces, give a clue to the pattern of what is likely to happen to him in the future. Prasna takes into account not only the external influences, the planets, but also the internal ones, the psychic impulses which mould life. It enjoins a thorough examination of the minds of the astrologer and the querist.

Method of Reading the Results

पृच्छानिर्गममार्गमन्दिरगतिप्रश्नक्रियासंभवम्
सूत्रात्रिस्पुटजाष्टमङ्गलफलारूढोदयेन्दूद्भवम् ।
आयुः खेटवशाच्च जातकवशात्संचिन्त्य भावान् परान् ।
देवानामनुकूलतादि च वदेद्बाधाभिचाराद्यपि ॥
इति ॥१३॥

Stanza 13.—The astrologer should reveal to the querist God's grace towards him, the troubles from enemies, diseases and appropriate remedial measures by observing and taking into account everything around him in the shape of omens or signs at the time of the query, when he starts from the house of the native, when he is on his way to the house, when he enters his house and when the Chakra or casting is being prepared and on the basis of *sutra*, *thrisphuta*, *ashtamangala*, *arudha*, laying of the gold piece (*suvarnavastha*) amongst the flowers in the Chakra, the rising sign, the position of the Moon, planetary states at the time and the Bhavas in the horoscope of the questioner.

NOTES

This sloka is not easily amenable to translation. The author wants the astrologer to follow a particular order in answering queries. First he should predict the leanings of God towards the native and then give indications of any impending troubles from enemies, diseases, etc., and suggest suitable remedial measures to counteract the evil effects. These predictions should be based on three factors, *viz.*, (*a*) the Prasna chart, (*b*) the birth chart and (*c*) Nimittas—an all-embracing subject, not capable of concise definition. If the astrologer is invited to the house of the questioner, then he should all the while closely and carefully watch all omens or other signs that he may come across from the time he starts from his residence to the time of his giving the predictions. Nature is a source of eternal inspiration for man. Prof. Rao used to tell me that by a certain code of interpretation of the sounds, gestures and movements of certain species of animals, the future could be ascertained with considerable accuracy. I am not attempting an explanation of the other technical terms used in this stanza, such as *thrisphuta*, etc., as the meanings become clear to the reader as he goes through further chapters.

दैवज्ञसावधानत्वे प्रष्टुश्च प्रश्नसौष्ठवे ।
सति प्रश्नेषु सर्वेषु शुभाप्तिर्वचनं तथा ॥१४॥
दैवज्ञसावधानत्वं प्रष्टुश्च प्रश्नसौष्ठवम् ।
इष्टद्रव्यभृतीक्षे च सम्यगिष्टोपलब्धये ॥ इति ॥१५॥

Stanzas 14 and 15.—If the mind of the astrologer is steady and the person to whom the future is read is humble and devout in temperament, then the reading will be correct and the answer to all the queries will be invariably good. If the astrologer is calm, if the querent frames his question in the proper form and if anybody talks about it or if he sees anything connected with the topic, then the questioner will attain his desired object. So says a great authority.

THE TIME FACTOR

बालान्नवर्ज्यतारासु गण्डान्तोष्णविषेषु च ।
अष्टमीविष्टिरिक्तासु स्थिरेषु करणेषु च ॥१६॥

तिथिनक्षत्रराश्यंशसन्धौ च गुलिकोदये ।
चक्रार्द्धे ग्रहणे सार्पशिरस्येकार्गले तथा ॥१७॥

मृत्युदग्धादियोगेषु पापदृश्युदयेषु च ।
त्रयोदश्यां प्रदोषे च निशीथे रविदर्शने ॥१८॥

संक्रान्तौ च तथा प्रष्टुर्विपत्प्रत्यरयोर्वधे ।
अष्टमे च तथा राशौ जन्माष्टमगते विधौ ॥१९॥

इत्यादि दुष्टकालेषु प्रश्नस्त्यादशुभप्रदः ॥२०॥

Stanzas 16 to 20.—The unfavourable times for putting questions are: the eleven constellations not considered auspicious for the first feeding of the child; *gandantha, ushna* and *visha* nakshatras, the four evil lunar days, *vishti* and *sthira* karanas; junctions of *tithi, nakshatra*, *rasi* and *amsa; gulikodayakala*, *vyatheepatha*, *sarpa siras,* eclipses and *ekargala; mrityu* and *dagdha yogas*; when malefics rise in or aspect evil signs, thirteenth lunar day; at dusk; at midnight; when the Lagna is aspected by the Sun; at a solar ingress; on a day ruled by the 3rd, 5th or 7th star from the birth star of the querent; when the Lagna of query is the 8th from the querent's birth Lagna; and when the query Moon is in the 8th from the natal Moon. Queries put under such evil times are indicative of inauspicious results.

NOTES

According to stanzas 16 to 20, an astrologer has to consider innumerable astronomical factors before pronouncing judgement. There are nearly 22 doshas or afflictions or inauspicious periods. When a question is put under these doshas, the indication should be deemed to prove harmful or inauspicious. For the information of the readers, I propose to list these doshas *seriatim*. There is a slight difference between the definition of the following doshas as given here and as found in some works on *Muhurtha*.

I. *Constellations considered inauspicious for first feeding :* They are Bharani, Krittika, Aridra, Aslesha, Makha, Pubba, Visakha, Jyeshta, Moola and Poorvashadha.

II. *Gandantha :* The first pada or quarter of Aswini, Makha and Moola and the last pada of Aslesha, Jyeshta and Revati.

III. *Ushna :* From 7½ to 15 ghatikas of Aswini, Rohini, Punarvasu, Makha and Hasta ; 55 to 60 ghatikas of Bharani, Mrigasira, Pushyami, Pubba and Chitta ; 21 to 30 ghatikas of Krittika, Aridra, Aslesha, Uttara, Swati ; 1 to 8 ghatikas of the 1st quarter of Visakha, Moola, Sravana and Poorvabhadra ; 52 to 60 ghatikas of Anuradha, Poorvashadha, Dhanishta, Uttarabhadra ; 20 to 30 ghatikas of Jyeshta, Uttarashadha, Satabhisha and Revati.

IV. *Visha:* 50, 24, 30, 4, 14, 11, 30, 20, 32, 30, 20, 18, 22, 20, 14, 14, 10, 14, 20, 24, 20, 10, 10, 18, 16, 24, 30; 4 ghatis from these limits in each of the 27 constellations respectively. For example, in Krittika that part of the constellation coming between 30 and 34 ghatis becomes Visha.

V. *Riktha Thithis:* The 4th, 8th, 9th and 14th lunar days.

VI. *Bad Karanas:* Vishti and Sthira. Vishti is the 7th Karana. The first seven come by rotation eight times in a lunar month commencing with the second half of the first lunar day. There are 11 Karanas, the four, *viz., sakuna, chatushpada, naya* and *kimstughna* being sthira or permanent Karanas which occur in order from the second half of the 29th lunar day.

VII. *Sandhis or junctional points:*

(*a*) The first and the last ghati (24 minutes) of a lunar day and nakshatra.

(*b*) The first and the last five vighatis (2 minutes) of a sign.

(*c*) The first and the last vighatika (24 seconds) of each Navamsa.

VIII. *Gulikodaya Kala:* This is the time at which the tertiary planet Gulika rises. Each day at a particular interval of time from sunrise as given below Gulika is said to rise.

	Day	Night
Sunday	26	10
Monday	22	6
Tuesday	18	2
Wednesday	14	26
Thursday	10	22
Friday	6	18
Saturday	2	14

It is this moment that is meant.

IX. *Vyathipatha :* This is an evil Yoga prohibited for all auspicious works.

The method of calculation of *Vyathipatha* has been detailed in all Hindu astronomical treatises. Roughly *Vyathipatha* falls in the following asterisms in the corresponding solar months :

Aries and Libra	Makha and Satabhisha
Taurus and Scorpio	Sravana and Pushyami
Gemini and Sagittarius	Poorvashadha and Aridra
Cancer and Capricorn	Rohini and Jyeshta
Leo and Aquarius	Bharani and Swati
Virgo and Pisces	Revati and Hasta

X. *Eclipses :* For three days from the time of the commencement of solar or lunar eclipse, the time is said to be inauspicious.

XI. *Sarpasiras :* The latter half of Vyathipatha.

XII. *Ekargala :* This yoga is powerful during the daytime.

The following is a rough method for calculating Ekargala :

Subtract the Sun's longitude from 360°. Divide the balance by 13° 20′. Reject the remainder and the quotient plus 1 is the Ekargala nakshatra. The 2nd, 7th, 10th, 11th, 14th, 16th, 18th and 20th from this asterism are also Ekargala stars.

Example : The Sun's longitude is 116°.

$$360-116: \frac{244°}{13° 20'} = 18\ 3/10$$

The 19th from Aswini, *viz.*, Moola is Ekargala star. Other Ekargala stars are Poorvashadha, Poorvabhadra, Aswini, Bharani, Mrigasira, Punarvasu, Aslesha and Pubba.

XIII. *Mrityu and Dagdha Yogas:* Sunday to Saturday coinciding with Makha, Visakha, Aridra, Moola, Satabhisha, Rohini, Poorvashadha respectively causes Mrityu Yoga in the first eighth part of the day concerned. Dagdha Yoga arises when Sunday to Saturday respectively coincide with the 12th, 11th, 5th, 2nd, 6th, 8th and 9th lunar days.

XIV. *Rise and Aspect of Evil Planets:* The Sun, Mars, Saturn and Rahu are malefics. Their aspect of or association with the rising sign is considered inauspicious.

XV. The 13th lunar day.

XVI. *Pradosha:* At dusk, *i.e.*, just before and immediately after sunset.

XVII. *Nishi:* At the time of midnight.

XVIII. *Ravi Darshana:* When the Lagna at the time of the query is aspected by the Sun. According to some the 7th sign from that occupied by the Sun.

XIX. *Sankranti:* At the time of the solar ingress into a zodiacal sign. The 16 ghatikas (6h. 24m.) both before and after the Sun's entry can be considered as inauspicious.

XX. When the ruling constellation is the 3rd, 5th or 7th from that of the birth, it goes under the name of Vipat, Pratyak and Naidhana respectively and hence inauspicious.

XXI. The Lagna at the time of query should not be the 8th from the Lagna at the time of birth.

XXII. The Moon at the time of query should not be in the 8th from the radical Moon.

Thus it will be seen that in these stanzas, some sort of a brief summary of Muhurtha or electional astrology has been given. Then there are other equally inauspicious phenomena like fall of meteors and appearance of comets, etc., which should also be considered.

THE SPACE FACTOR

इत्यादिदोषरहिते कालेमृतघटीषु च ।
शुभानामुदये दृष्टौ मुहूर्तेषु शुभेषु च ।
सिद्धामृतादियोगेषु पृच्छाभीष्टफलप्रदा ॥२१॥

Stanza 21.—If the query is made at a time which is free from the above doshas, in the Amrita ghatis, when benefics rise in the Lagna or aspect it, in auspicious Muhurthas and in Siddha, Amrita and other good yogas, it will lead to success.

NOTES

Amritaghatikas are auspicious moments and they vary with regard to each constellation. In the table given below, the moments of the commencement of the Amritaghatikas are given, along with the moments of the commencement of Vishaghatikas and Ushnasikha and also the Mrityubhagas or fatal degrees, for ready reference.

Durmuhurtha.—Muhurtha technically means 48 minutes or 2 ghatis in terms of time. A sidereal day consists of 30 muhurthas. The 1st fifteen diurnal muhurthas named are : (1) Rudra, (2) Ahi, (3) Mitra, (4) Pitru. (5) Vasu, (6) Vara, (7) Vishwedeva, (8) Vidhi, (9) Satamukhi, (10) Puruhuta, (11) Vahni, (12) Naktanchara, (13) Varuna, (14) Arama, and (15) Bhaga. The nocturnal muhurthas are : (1) Girisa, (2) Ajipada, (3) Ahirbudhya, (4) Pusha, (5) Aswi, (6) Yama, (7) Agni, (8) Vidhatru, (9) Chanda, (10) Aditi, (11) Jeeva, (12) Vishnu, (13) Yumigadyuti, (14) Thyasthur, and (15) Samdram.

In regard to the diurnal muhurthas the 1st, 2nd, 4th, 10th, 11th, 12th and 15th are inauspicious while in nocturnal muhurthas the 1st, 2nd, 6th and 7th are inauspicious.

In calculating the Muhurtha or the Visha or Amrita-ghatikas, the exact length of day and night or the exact duration of the nakshatra concerned should be ascertained. Each Muhurtha is said to last for 48 minutes on the assumption that the duration of day and night is of equal proportion *viz.*, 30 ghatis. Similarly the periods of commencement and termination of the amrita or visha-ghatikas are given on the assumption that the duration of a nakshatra is 60 ghatis.

No.	*Asterism*	*Visha-ghatika*		*Ushna-sikha*		*Amrita-ghatika*		*Mrityu-bhaga*
		B.	*E.*	*B.*	*E.*	*B.*	*E.*	
1	Aswini	50	54	7½	15	42	46	8
2	Bharani	24	28	55	60	48	52	4
3	Krittika	30	34	21	30	54	58	12
4	Rohini	40	44	7½	15	52	56	2
5	Mrigasira	14	18	55	60	38	42	6
6	Aridra	11	15	21	30	35	39	14
7	Punarvasu	30	34	7½	15	54	58	10
8	Pushyami	20	24	55	60	44	48	16
9	Aslesha	32	26	21	30	56	60	24
10	Makha	30	34	7½	15	54	58	20
11	Pubba	20	24	55	60	44	48	22
12	Uttara	18	22	21	30	42	46	2
13	Hasta	22	26	7½	15	45	49	26
14	Chitta	20	24	55	60	44	48	30
15	Swati	14	18	21	30	38	42	38
16	Visakha	14	18	1	8	38	42	38

No.	Asterism	*Visha-ghattka* B.	*Visha-ghattka* E.	*Ushna-sikha* B.	*Ushna-sikha* E.	*Amrita-ghatika* B.	*Amrita-ghatika* E.	*Mrityu bhaga*
17	Anuradha	10	14	52	60	28	34	36
18	Jyeshta	14	18	20	30	38	42	34
19	Moola	20	24	1	8	44	48	32
20	Poorvashadha	24	28	52	60	48	52	42
21	Uttarashadha	20	24	20	30	44	48	44
22	Sravana	10	14	1	8	34	38	46
23	Dhanishta	10	14	52	60	34	38	48
24	Satabhisha	18	22	20	30	42	46	50
25	Poorvabhadra	16	20	1	8	40	44	52
26	Uttarabhadra	24	28	52	60	48	52	52
27	Revati	30	34	20	30	54	58	54

[B stands for Beginning and E, for End]

For example: in Aslesha Vishaghatikas commence at 32 ghatis and end at 26 ghatis. The Ushnasikha in Aslesha begins at 21 ghatis and goes on upto 30 ghatis. The Amritaghatikas in Aslesha are between 56 and 60 ghatis. The Mrityubhaga or fatal degrees of Aslesha are those in the 24th ghati.

THE PLACE FACTOR

फलप्रसूनसंपूर्णमहीरुहसमाकुले ।
स्निग्धभूमितले रत्नकाञ्चनादिसमन्विते ।।२२।।

पञ्चेन्द्रियमनःप्रीतिकरे गोमयवारिणा ।
तत्क्षणप्रोक्षितक्षोणितले समवसुन्धरे ॥२३॥
मङ्गल्यकर्मसंयुक्ते मङ्गलस्त्रीसमाकुले ।
मन्दिरे पुत्रभार्यादिहृष्टपुष्टजनाश्रिते ॥२४॥
यः पृच्छतीदृशे देशे साप्नोत्यभिमतं ध्रुवम् ॥२५॥

Stanzas 22 to 25.—When the spot where the question is put is the following, the querist's object will be realised : sites filled with trees or plants blooming with fruits and flowers and free from all dirt and dust and abounding in gold, gems and the like; a place agreeable to the mind and senses, or a spot washed with diluted cowdung, pleasant spots filled with beautiful women; a happy corner resounding with the echoes of auspicious ceremonies such as marriage, etc., and a healthy home with smiling families.

महावने श्मशानान्ते निम्नोच्चे शून्यमन्दिरे ।
गृहे चार्तजने प्रेतक्रियाद्यशुभकर्मणि ॥२६॥
जलाग्निशुष्कवृक्षान्ते तथैवेन्द्रियचेतसाम्
अनिष्टदे प्रदेशे च प्रष्टा नाप्नोत्यभीप्सितम् ॥२७॥

Stanzas 26 and 27.—A dreadful forest, a burning ghat, a bleak and rugged place; a deserted house, or a home where poverty and disease abound; a place where obsequies are being performed; neighbourhood of water, fire or lifeless trees; and in brief, all spots which sicken our mind and body are bad and the questioner's object will not be realised.

EXAMINATION OF BREATH

कार्यं श्वासपरीक्षणं प्रतिदिनं बुध्वा प्रभातागमे
तस्येडादिगतिर्द्धराप्रभृतिसञ्चारश्च विज्ञायताम् ।
तेनात्मीयशुभाशुभं हि सकलं ज्ञेयं पुनः पृच्छतां
तत्कालात्मसमीरणेन च तथा नष्टादिकं चोच्यताम्
॥२८॥

Stauza 28.—Everyday the astrologer should examine his breath early in the morning. He should diagnose through which 'Nadi' it passes, and to which Bhuta it can be assigned. From this he can know beforehand what is likely to happen to him that day. In the same manner, the future of the questioner can be read in the case of Nashta Prasna (query regarding lost wealth) and the like, through the nature of the astrologer's breath at the time of query.

वारेष्विन्दुबुधाङ्गिरोभृगुसुतां वामे चरन् मारुतो
भौमार्कार्किदिनेषु दक्षिणगतो नृणाममीष्ट स्मृतः ।
सौम्यानां दिवसेषु दक्षिणगतोऽनिष्टो सतां वामगो
वक्ष्यन्ते मरुतोः शुभाशुभदयोर्भेदाः फलानामथ ॥२९॥

Stanza 29.—If the breath is seen to pass through the left nostril on Monday, Wednesday, Thursday and Friday, it is favourable. If it is through the right nostril on Sunday, Tuesday and Saturday, it is also equally favourable. But if it passes through the right nostril on the days of good planets and through the left nostril on the days of evil planets, the effects will be adverse. Significant happenings can be anticipated by a study of the passing of the breath through the nostrils.

सर्वेषामपि वासरेषु पवनेभीष्टे वपु स्वस्थता
लाभोर्थस्य च मृष्टभोजनमितीष्टानां भावोन्यथा ।
श्वासश्चेदहितो न मृष्टमशनं नार्थागमो विग्रहः
सर्वैर्ना शयनं सुखेन च सुखंविण्मोक्षणादिष्वपि ॥३०॥

Stanza 30.—If the 'breath' is found favourable on any day, then be rest assured that his health will be good, he will gain money and he will get sumptuous meals and such other favourable things that day. If unfavourable, the effects also will be reverse, *i.e.,* he will not get good food, he will have quarrels with everybody, he will not have sound sleep, nor will he have ease and comfort even in respect of answering calls of nature.

श्वासस्य प्रतिकूलता यदि दिने भानोर्वपुर्वेदना
शीतांशोः कलहः कुजस्य मरणं दूरप्रयाणं विदः ।
राज्यापद्धिषणस्य शुक्रदिवसे कार्यस्य कस्यापि नो
सिद्धिर्मन्ददिने स्ववीर्यकृषिनाशोर्थिवादळादयः ॥३१॥

Stanza 31.—If the breath is unfavourable on Sundays, he will have pain all over his body ; on Mondays, quarrel ; on Tuesdays, death for himself or his relatives ; on Wednesdays, distant trips ; on Thursdays, some calamities to his country ; on Fridays, failure in all his undertakings ; and on Saturdays, monetary loss, loss of valour, failure of crops and litigation regarding land.

NOTES

The great author has explained in the above stanzas the method of prediction by examining the nature of one's breath or *swasa*. This may seem strange to some but a careful scrutiny will bear out its usefulness not only to the astrologer but to the layman at large. Readers are referred to books on Swara Sastra for greater details.

वायुर्भानुदिनाष्टके यदि चरेद्वामे गुरोः पञ्चता
व्याधिर्वा सुमहांस्तथैव हिमगोर्वाराष्टके दक्षिणे ।
पुत्रापत् क्षितिजस्य बन्धनमरेर्वामे विदो दक्षिणे
मृत्युः स्वस्य निरंन्तरं सुरगुरोर्मृत्युर्गुरोः संभवेत् ॥३२॥

शुक्रस्यावनिहेतुर्धनक्षयो दक्षिणे शनेर्वामे ।
यदि चरति मातरिश्वा भार्यानाशो निवासनाशो वा ॥३३॥

Stanzas 32 and 33.—If you find on 8 consecutive Sundays, that your breathing is through your left nostril, then predict death of or calamity equivalent to death to your Guru (preceptor) or senior relative; on 8 consecutive Mondays if the breath passes through your right nostril, some ill-luck to your children or junior relations; on 8 Tuesdays, breath through the left nostril involves imprisonment at the hands of your enemies; on 8 Wednesdays, breath through the right nostril brings in severe illness or even death; on 8 Thursdays, breathing through the right nostril causes danger to your Guru; on 8 Fridays, breath through the right nostril causes loss of money in respect of lands ; and on 8 Saturdays, breathing through the left nostril brings about the ruin of your house or death of your wife.

NOTES

Some interpret these two stanzas to mean 8 consecutive days from Sunday, Monday, etc. and not 8 consecutive Sundays or 8 consecutive Mondays etc.

मेदिन्याः खलु षोडशांगुलमपां दैर्घ्यं दिनेशांगुलं
वह्नेर्दन्तिमितांगुलं मरुत एतद्द्व्यूनमग्न्यंगुलम् ।
आकाशस्य च वेद्यमेतदुदितं भूम्यादिभूतात्मक-
स्वीयश्वासगतिप्रमाणमुभयोरेतत्समं घ्राणयोः ॥३४॥

Stanza 34.—The dimensions of the five Maha Bhutas (great primordial compounds) are as follows :—Prithvi or earth—16 inches ; apa or water—12 inches ; teja or fire—8 inches ; vayu or air—6 inches ; and akasa or ether—3 inches. This is true of both nostrils. Here 8 inches make one foot.

NOTES

Here the author tells us under what Bhuta the breath can be brought. If the breath thrown out through a particular nostril, measures, say, 16 inches, then it falls under Prithvi Bhuta ; if 12, under Tejo Bhuta and so on. These measurements can be correctly ascertained only by trained Yogis and not by ordinary human beings. The science of breath 'Swara Sastra' is a complete discipline in itself and requires many years of diligent study and practice before it can be mastered.

पक्षेच्छे खलु पक्षतौ क्षितिरिडायातोऽन्नमन्मन्दिर
प्राकारादिगृहप्रवेशनकरी पट्टाभिषेकप्रदा ।
कुर्यादन्यदभीष्टकर्म सलिलं वामस्थमेवं शुभं
कूपादे रचनं करग्रहणमंबूत्थं च कुर्यादभयम् ॥३५॥

वह्निर्वारिभयायुधक्षतिशरीरारुग्गृहप्लोषणं
पातं वा शिशुकादिकस्य दहने कुर्याद्भजेतेश्वरम् ।
वायुश्चोरभयं पलायनमपि स्थानं विमृज्यात्मनो
दन्त्यश्वाद्यधिरोहणं च वितरेद्व्योमोदयश्चेत् पुनः ॥३६॥

मन्त्रादेरुपदेशलब्धिरसकृद्देवप्रतिष्ठापनं
दीक्षा व्याधिसमुद्भवश्च नितरां पीडा तनोः सन्ततम् ।
विज्ञेयं खलु भूतपञ्चकफलं नाड्योः समं चोभयोः
श्वासः संहतदीर्घ इष्ट उदितः शीर्यच्छिखो नेष्टदः ॥३७॥

Stanzas 35, 36 & 37.—Suppose on a first lunar day after the New Moon, you discover in your breath passing through your left nostril, the earthly element, then predict good effects such as getting good and lofty houses and coronation. If you find the watery element, then say he will have wells and tanks dug up for the use of the people and will celebrate marriages. If it is the fiery element, he will be troubled by enemies, will have wounds from weapons and ulcers, his house will be burnt down, he will fall down from a height and his children will be injured by fire. To avert this, Lord Iswara should be propitiated. If it is airy, there will be fear from thieves, flight from one's native place and there, he will ride horses and elephants. If it is ethereal, he will be initiated into the old mantric lore, will be spending money for building temples and take Diksha though his health may cause him some anxiety. These are the effects of the five elements in both the Nadis. If the breath is long and continuous, it is auspicious. If its tip is broken, it is bad.

भूमौ निखातमवनेरुद्ये जलेपां
वातस्य धूमवति खस्य तथोर्ध्वदेशे ।
भुपृष्ठगं हुतभुंजः खलु वास्तु नष्टं
ब्रूयात् कृतेह यदि नष्टपदार्थपृच्छा ॥३८॥

Stanza 38.—In a query involving loss or theft, one can make use of this (different elements in breath) and predict the result boldly. If you find the breath to be earthy (prithvi), then say the lost article is hidden under the earth; if it is watery, it will be under water; if it happens to be airy, say it is in a smoky corner; if it happens to be 'ethereal', then say that it is somewhere up; and if it is fiery, say it is kept on the ground.

भागे यत्र मरुत्स्थितिः पुनरिह क्षोण्या जले वा यदा
भागे तत्र तदेक्ष्यते यदि पुमान् ज्योतिर्विदा कश्चन ।
दीर्घायुर्गुणवत्कलत्रतनयः पुष्यद्धनश्चाधिकं
विज्ञेयः स तथा स्त्रियोपि विपरीततः फलं चान्यथा ॥३९॥

Stanza 39.—If the astrologer meets the querist on the same side as his breath of the earthy or watery type, he will be blessed with long life, good wife and children and plenty of wealth. If she is a woman she will have a worthy husband, etc. If, on the other hand, the querist stands on the opposite side or if the breath is of other types, the effect will be quite the reverse.

इडा वामा भवेन्नाडी सोमस्याऽर्कस्य दक्षिणा ।
पिङ्गलाख्या सुषुम्नाख्या मध्यमाग्नेरुदीरिता ॥४०॥

Stanza 40.—In the left nostril, there is a nerve known as Ida; in the right, Pingala. Through the centre which is covered, there is Sushumna. These are governed by the Moon (Chandra), the Sun (Surya) and fire (Agni) respectively.

निर्गमे तु शुभदा भवेदिडा पिङ्गला तु शुभदा प्रवेशने ।
योगसाधनविधौ तु मध्यमा शस्यते न तु परेषु कर्मसु ॥४१॥

Stanza 41.—Ida is good at the starting time and Pingala is favourable for entering a place. Sushumna is good only for Yogic practices.

देवे दक्षिणभागगेथ पुरुषो रोगातुरो दक्षिणे
स्थित्वा पृच्छति पृच्छकेथ पुरुषो जीवत्यरोगश्चिरम् ।
वामायां तु रुजाकुलीकृततनौ वामाश्रिते चेधरे
वामे पृच्छति चेद्दृढं गतगदा वामा चिरं जीवति ॥४२॥

Stanza 42.—In a query relating to sickness, if the question comes from the right when the breath passes through the same side, then predict that sickness will be cured. If the question comes from the left when the breath passes through the same sign, predict aggravation of the illness. If the sick person happens to be a woman, it should be from the left side for relief and from the right side for aggravation of the illness.

देवे गते पृच्छति वामभागे
स्थितो नरो दक्षिणतो यदि स्यात् ।
व्यत्यासतोऽस्मादपि कृच्छ्रसाध्यं
वदन्ति सन्तः खलु रोगजातम् ॥४३॥

Stanza 43.—When the question is put from the left and the breath flows through the right or *vice versa*, then the sick man will get relief only with great difficulty.

अन्तर्गते पृच्छति पृच्छकश्चेद् वै नरो जीवतिवीतरोगः ।
तेनैव मार्गेण बहिर्गतश्चेत् परेतराजस्य पुरीं प्रयाति ॥४४॥

Stanza 44.—If the query is made when the astrologer inhales, then there will be relief; if when he exhales, the sick man will die.

वामे वा दक्षिणे भागे प्रश्नश्चेद्वायुसंयुते ।
जीवेन्नरश्च नारी च तथानुष्ठानपद्धतिः ॥४५॥

Stanza 45.—In *Anushthana Paddhathi*, it is stated that a sick man will get relief if the astrologer's breath and the side from which the question comes, are in agreement. Here, left side alone is good for women and right side for men.

लयलिङ्गश्रवणेक्षास्मरणाभावे तु दूतमारुतयोः ।
एकदिशावस्थाने जीवति रोगी विपर्यये म्रियते ॥४६॥

Stanza 46.—At the time of the query if there is no indication of death, inauspicious sight, talk or thought and if the messenger and the breath are on the same side, the sick person will live; otherwise not.

NOTES

In Kerala, there appears to have been a custom of sending a messenger to take the astrologer home and do Prasna business in the house of the sick man. Hence frequent reference to *duta* or messenger.

अग्रे वामेपि च यदुपरि स्थायिना पृच्छयमानं
शुक्ले पक्षे तदिह सकलं लभ्यते चन्द्रचारात् ।
पृष्ठेधस्तान्नियतमसिते दक्षिणे सूर्यचारा-
दात्मावस्थासदृशमखिलं पृच्छकस्यापि वाच्यम् ॥४७॥

Stanza 47.—If the query is made when the Moon is waxing (*sukla paksha*), the messenger or querist standing in front or in a raised place or on the left side and the astrologer's breath is governed by the Moon (left), then the questioner will have all his desires satisfied. If when the Moon is waning (*krishna paksha*), the messenger stands below or behind or on the right side and the breath is governed by the Sun (right), then also predict good results.

NOTES

In all these cases—questions being put from certain sides when the astrologer's breath passes through certain sides etc.—it will be seen that the effects on the querist will be similar to the experiences or mental conditions of the astrologer at the time.

स्नानभोजननिद्रादिनिजकर्मसु यादृशः ।
आत्मनोनुभवस्तेषु तादृशः प्रष्टुरुच्यताम् । ॥४८॥

Stanza 48.—At the time of query, as the astrologer happens to feel comfortable or otherwise, when doing his daily work such as sleep, bath and taking meal, so will be the effects on the questioner.

NOTES

Here the author deviates a little from his main topic (breath) and dwells a little on *avastha* or mental state.

यत्रकुत्र स्थितः पृष्ट्वा पुनर्दूतः समारुते ।
स्थिरस्तिष्ठति चेद्रोगी जीवत्येव न संशय ॥४९॥

Stanza 49.—Irrespective of where the questioner stands or where the breath flows, if after putting the query the person stands still and unwavering, predict that the sick-man will not die.

ऐन्द्याद्यास्तु दिशो ज्ञेयाः पृथिव्याद्युदयैः क्रमात् ।
आकाशोदयतो मध्यं नष्टं तत्रैव वा स्थितम् ॥५०॥

Stanza 50.—In a query regarding 'lost wealth', say that the article will be found in the east, south, west or north from the querist's place, according as the nature of the astrologer's breath is earthy, watery, fiery or airy. If the breath is ethereal, then the article will be found somewhere in the middle or in the same place where it was before.

शुभवारे शुक्लपक्षे सिद्धिदा वामनाडिका ।
पापवारे कृष्णपक्षे नाड्यन्या सिद्धिदाधिकम् ॥५१॥

Stanza 51.—In benefic weekdays when the Moon is waxing, if the breath is in the left, it is good. In malefic weekdays when the Moon is waning, if the breath is in the right, it is also good.

NOTES

Benefic weekdays are Monday, Wednesday, Thursday and Friday. Tuesday, Saturday and Sunday are malefic.

गृहाच्चन्द्रेण निर्यातः प्रविष्टो भानुना रणे ।
शून्याङ्गे वैरिणं कृत्वा कातरोपि जयी भवेत् ॥५२॥
निष्क्रान्तो भानुना गेहात् प्रविष्टः शशिना रणे ।
जीवांशे यस्य वा शत्रुः स शूरोपि विनश्यति ॥५३॥

Stanzas 52 & 53.—In Yuddha Prasna, if a soldier starts with his breath in his left and reaches the battleground when his breath is on the right, and if his enemy stands on that side where he has no breath, then he will surely defeat his opponent. The reverse will be the effect in reverse position.

NOTES

A soldier starting when breathing through his left nostril and reaching the battlefield when he is breathing through the right nostril will be victorious ; while, if he starts with his breath in his right nostril and reaches the battlefield when his breath is in the left nostril, he is likely to be vanquished, however powerful. In either case, the enemy should be standing on the side where the soldier has no breath.

दस्यवः शत्रवो भूपाः कितवा व्यवहारिणः ।
एते शून्यगताः सौम्याः पूर्णस्था भयदाः स्मृताः ॥५४॥

Stanza 54.—Whenever thieves, enemies, kings or those in authority, saints, his brother-gamblers with whom he plays and his rivals in litigation, are put on that side of his nostril through which breath does not pass, they will be utterly powerless to do him any harm. But on the other side, they will inflict defeat on him.

विवादे द्यूतयुद्धे च स्नानभोजनमैथुने ।
व्यवहारे भये भङ्गे भानुनाडी प्रशस्यते ॥५५॥

Stanza 55.—Right breath is favourable at the time of bathing, eating, cohabitation, transacting business, debating, gambling and fighting. It is also good when you are in fear or disappointment in anything.

यात्रादानविवाहेषु वस्त्रालङ्कारभूषणे ।
शुभे सन्धौ प्रवेशे च वामनाडी प्रशस्यते ॥५६॥

Stanza 56.—Left side breath is good for travel, putting on new dress or ornaments, marriage, bringing about reconciliation, making a gift and entering the presence of another.

गर्भिणीदर्शने वायुर्दक्षिणे चेत् पुमान् वधूः ।
गर्भस्था वामभागे चेद्द्वयोर्नो चेदसत्प्रजा ॥५७॥

Stanza 57.—When you see a pregnant woman at the time when you breathe through the right, then predict that the child is male; if through left say it is female. If it is in *sushumna*, predict that she will give birth to a lifeless child.

गर्भे मे किमिति प्रश्ने सवायौ गर्भिणी यदि ।
पुमान् स्त्री वीरणे भागे युग्मं वायुर्द्वयोर्यदि ॥५८॥

Stanza 58.—Suppose a pregnant woman asks an astrologer 'what is the sex of the child that I will give birth to', then tell her it is to be male if she asks from the side you have breath. If not, say it will be a female. If breath passes through both sides, then she will give birth to twins.

निर्गत्य शशिना गेहात् प्राप्यं प्रासस्य भानुना ।
कार्यस्य दुर्लभस्यापि लाभः स्यादप्रयत्नतः ॥५९॥

Stanza 59.—If one wants to succeed easily in any undertaking in life, one should start when the

5

breath is in the left and reach his destination when the breath is in the right.

रिपोरागमनप्रश्ने वामगे मातरिश्वनि ।
नागमोनुक्तसिद्धैव तदागतिरतोन्यथा ॥६०॥

Stanza 60.—In a query regarding an invasion, if the breath passes through the left, predict there will be no invasion ; if through the right, there will be an attack.

अङ्कयुद्धे ममैतस्मिन् जयो वा किं पराजयः ।
प्रश्नोयं पूर्णभागे चेज्जयोन्यत्र पराजयः ॥६१॥

Stanza 61.—To a query whether one will be successful in a friendly dual, if the question is made from the side where there is breath, then say he will succeed.

सन्नहनं निर्गमनं खल्लूरिकारोहणं च शुभमिडया ।
पिङ्गलया पुनरितरं प्रहरति यदि वामगं जयो नियतम्
॥६२॥

Stanza 62.—When the breath passes through the left, a wrestler can prepare, start and enter the arena. If he strikes the opponent in the left, when the breath is in the right, success is assured for him.

इडयाप्याऽरूढवतः खल्वरिकामेनयैव पुनरपि चेत् ।
चरति मरुन्नैव जयः प्राग्वोदक्स्थीयतां तदा तस्याम्
॥६३॥

Stanza 63.—Even if the contestant enters the ring with the breath in the left nostril, he will be defeated when he moves on with the breath in the same nostril. In such a contingency he should resort to the East or North of the ring in order to avoid defeat.

वायोराकाशसञ्चारो गर्भस्थमृतिसूचकः ।
पृष्ट्वा सवायावन्यत्र स्थितौ चासत्प्रजां वदेत् ॥६४॥

Stanza 64.—In a question pertaining to birth of issue, when the astrologer's breath is ethereal, say the child in the womb will die. If the person asks the question from the side where there is breath and passes to the side where there is no breath, then predict that a lifeless child would be delivered.

THE 'TOUCH' ANALYSED

प्रष्टा वाक्षोदेशे स्पृशेद्यदि क्षिप्रमीप्सितं लभते ।
मङ्गलवस्तुनि च तथा विपरीतं फलममङ्गलस्पर्शे ॥६५॥

Stanza 65.—If at the time of query the questioner is feeling with his hand his chest or breast or any auspicious object, then predict good. If not, evil results will happen.

NOTES

In this stanza, the method is switched on to *sparsa* or touch.

संस्पृशन्नाभिनासास्यकेशरोमनखद्विजान् ।
गुह्यपृष्ठस्तनग्रीवाजठरानामिकांगुलीः ॥६६॥
रन्ध्राणामपि नवकं करपद्योस्तलं च सर्वपर्वाणि ।
प्रष्टा लभतेऽनिष्टं निम्नस्पर्शे तथैव विज्ञेयम् ॥६७॥

Stanzas 66 and 67.—If he touches his own navel, nose, mouth, locks of hair on his head or hair anywhere in his body, nails, teeth, private parts, anus (पृष्ठ), breasts, neck, stomach, ring finger, the nine openings in his body, the palm of his hand, the soles of his feet and joints in his body, or any depression, then predict evil.

प्रागादिदिक्षु मूर्द्धादिष्वङ्गेष्वष्टसु च स्थिताः ।
ध्वजाद्यास्तत्स्थितिस्पर्शफलमप्यथ कथ्यते ॥६८॥

Stanza 68.—The eight cardinal points and the eight bodily limbs have their counterparts symbolised in the eight Yonis like Dhwaja, Dhuma, etc. Results good or bad happen when these points are touched by the questioner.

ध्वजो धूमश्च सिंहश्च सारमेयो वृषः खरः ।
दन्ती काकः क्रमादेते दिशास्वैन्द्र्यादिषु स्थिता ॥६९॥

Stanza 69.—Dhwaja (flag), Dhuma (smoke), lion, dog, bull, an ass and cow, an elephant correspond respectively to east, south-east, south, south-west, west, north-west, north and east.

मूर्ध्नि ध्वजो घ्राणपुटे तु धूम
श्चास्ये हरिः श्रोत्रदृशोः श्वसंज्ञः ।
कण्ठे वृषः पाणियुगे खरश्च
गजश्च हृद्यंघ्रियुगेथ काकः ॥७०॥

Stanza 70.—The head, nose, mouth or face, eyes or ears, neck, arms or hands, chest and legs symbolically correspond respectively to Dhwaja, Dhuma, etc., mentioned in stanza 69.

NOTES

In these three stanzas, there is some sort of an allocation of the eight main limbs to the eight cardinal points and the sex organs of eight animals. The touching of any of these parts by the questioner seems to imply the success or otherwise of the object in view. The following is a tabular representation of the allocations suggested in the above stanzas :—

Direction	*Yoni*	*Limb*
East	Dhwaja	Head
South-east	Dhuma	Nose
South	Lion	Mouth or face
South-west	Dog	Eyes or ears
West	Bull	Neck
North-west	Ass	Arms, hands
North	Elephant	Chest, breast
North-east	Crow	Legs

केतुस्थो ध्वजसिंहगो वृषगजस्थानानि देहे स्पृशन्
संप्राप्तोति नरः क्रमेण धनगोयानानि भूषामपि ।
सिंहस्थोपि च सिंहगो वृशकरिश्रेष्ठध्वजान् संस्पृश-
न्नायाति प्रतिपक्षनाशकमलसत्पुत्रबन्ध्वागमान् ॥७१॥

Stanza 71.—If the questioner stands in the east and touches his own head, then predict monetary gains; his mouth, gain of cows; his neck, gift of vehicles; chest, gift of ornaments. If the questioner stands in south and touches his face or mouth, destruction of enemies; neck, monetary gains; chest, begetting good children; head, arrival of relatives.

गच्छेद्गोवृषसिन्धुरध्वजहरिस्पर्शेन तिष्ठन् वृषे
सद्योऽसौ वृषयानधातृदयितामित्रास्तिपमव्याहताम् ।
दन्तिस्थो गजकेतुसिंहवृषभस्थानं स्पृशन् पाणिना
यायाद्दन्तिविभूषणोत्तमसुहृत्सत्पुत्रलाभान् क्रमात् ॥७२॥

Stanza 72.—If the questioner stands in the west and touches his head, gain of knowledge; mouth, acquisition of friends; neck, gift of cows; chest, gain of vehicles. If the questioner stands in the north and touches his head, ornaments; mouth, good friends; neck, good children; chest, acquisition of elephants or elephant-ride.

धूमस्थोऽपि च धूमकुक्कुरखरध्वाङ्क्षप्रदेशान् स्पृशन्
मृत्युक्लेशभयव्रतक्षयकुटुम्बध्वंसमप्याप्नुयात् ।
श्वारूढः श्वखराभिधानवलिभुग्धूमस्थलानि स्पृशन्
व्याधिं पुत्रविनाशमेति विपदं वित्तक्षयं मानवः ॥७३॥

Stanza 73.—If the questioner stands in south-east and touches his nose, danger to life; eyes and ears, fear of troubles; arms, breaking of vows; and legs, ruin of one's family. If the questioner stands in south-west and touches his nose, loss of money; eyes and ears, sickness; arms, loss of children; and legs, danger.

स्प्रष्टा गर्दभकाकधूमशुनकान् मर्त्यः स्थितो गर्दभे
सद्यो याति विवादगोहतिमहाशस्त्रार्तिभार्यारुजः ।
काकस्थोपि च काकधूमभषकस्थानं स्पृशन् गर्दभं
भनृध्वार्तिं द्विजभङ्गमेति च मृतिं नीचात्तनूजापदम् ॥७४॥

Stanza 74.—If the questioner stands in north-west and touches his nose, fear from fearful weapons; eyes and ears, wife's sickness; arms, litigation or dispute; and legs, killing cow. If the questioner stands in the north-east and touches his nose breaking of teeth; eyes and ears, death from evil-minded people; arms, danger to children; and legs, sickness to relation.

ध्वजहरिवृषदन्तिस्थो धूमश्वखराख्यवायसस्पर्शी ।
विपरीतो वा याति च विपदं वा सम्पदं च नात्यन्तम्
॥७५॥

Stanza 75.—If the questioner, standing in east south, west or north, touches nose, eyes, arms or legs respectively or standing in south-east, south-west, north-west or north-east, touches neck, chest, head or mouth respectively, the effects will neither be very bad nor very good.

शास्त्रान्तरमपीहास्ति दूतदैवविदोर्दशा ।
यादृशी तादृशी वाच्या दशा व्याधिमतामपि ॥७६॥

Stanza 76.—In any query regarding longevity, the cure of a sick man will depend on the Avastha, state of the messenger or astrologer at the time of query.

SIGN OCCUPIED BY QUERIST

पृच्छकाधिष्ठितं राशिं विज्ञायानेन पृच्छताम् ।
अनुभूतं हि वक्तव्यं किमपि प्रत्ययाप्तये ॥७७॥

Stanza 77.—In order to create conviction in the questioner, the astrologer should study the Arudha Lagna and read therefrom what experience the questioner had on the way.

राहुर्वार्किः पृच्छकाधिष्ठितर्क्षे यदा तस्मात् पञ्चमे वाष्टमे वा ।
चण्डालानां पंक्तिरग्रे प्रदृष्टा शूद्रा दृष्टास्तत्र चेद्भूमिजज्ञौ ॥७८॥

Stanza 78.—If Rahu or Saturn is in Arudha or fifth or eighth house from it, then the messenger might have seen very low people on his way. If Mars or Mercury stands at the above positions, he might have met people belonging to Sudra caste·

लग्नसुताष्टसंस्थौ गुरुशुक्रौ चेद्द्विजादिभिर्योगः ।
पापयुतौ दृष्टौ चेद्ब्राह्मणतन्तुधारिभिर्योगः ॥७९॥

Stanza 79.—If Jupiter or Venus is in Arudha or 5th or 8th from it, then Brahmins must have been seen. If these are associated with or aspected by evil planets, then thread-wearing Hindus.

अर्के यद्येषु नृपैश्चन्द्रसितौ चेत्स्त्रिया योगः ।
चन्द्रार्कजौ स्थितौ चेद्दुष्टस्त्रीभिः सितः कुलस्त्रीभिः ॥८०॥

Stanza 80.—If the Sun, then distinguished personages or officials; if the Moon or Venus, then a woman. If the Moon and Saturn are together there, he might have seen bad women; if Venus (without any evil planets), chaste women.

अशुभशुभदृष्टियोगात्तज्जातीयैश्च योगमपि विद्यात् ।
दूतस्य चेष्टयातः परं वदेल्लक्षणं दिशागतया । इति॥८१॥

Stanza 81.—The nature of the people he has met on the way depends on the association or aspects of evil or good planets. Further, predictions will have to be made from the direction of querent and his gesticulations.

अर्केऽष्टमे बहुजनैर्नृपसेनया वा
याते रवेरहनि नूनमुपद्रवोऽभूत् ।
जीवांशके नृपतिनेति वदेद्दिनांशा-
द्धात्वादिवस्तुविहतिश्च विचिन्त्य वाच्या ॥८२॥

Stanza 82.—If the Sun occupies the eighth house from the Arudha, then predict royal displeasure or trouble from the army and this must have happened on the previous Sunday. If he occupies Jiva Navamsa, then say it was the ruler himself. Predict also some loss befitting the Navamsa the Sun occupies—Dhatu, Jeeva or Moola (mineral, vegetable or animal).

NOTES

In odd signs (Aries, Gemini, Leo, etc.) the 1st, 4th and 7th Navamsas refer to Dhatu (mineral), the 2nd, 5th and 8th refer to Moola (animal) and the 3rd, 6th and 9th refer to Jeeva (vegetable). In even signs (Taurus, Cancer, Virgo, etc.) the 1st, 4th and 7th refer to Jeeva (vegetable), the 2nd, 5th and 8th to Moola (animal) and the 3rd, 6th and 9th to Dhatu (mineral).

In 80 नृपे has been translated as distinguished personality or officer.

अष्टमस्थे निशानाथे प्रष्टुर्वाच्यमभोजनम् ।
यवागूपानमात्रं वा गते चन्द्रस्य वासरे ॥८३॥

Stanza 83.—If the Moon occupies the eighth house, then say that the querist had to starve on the previous Monday or he had to live on mere rice-water.

NOTES

According to the commentator, if the Moon was strong then the querist would have lived on rice-water.

आरेष्टमे पदभ्रंशो मान्दियुक्तस्स चेत् क्षतिः ।
धात्वांशेसृजि शस्त्रेण मूलांशे कण्टकादिना ॥८४॥

वाच्या जीवांशके दन्तनखाद्यैरंशकोदितैः ।
सरीसृपांशे तद्दंशो वारस्य गतवासरे ॥८५॥

Stanzas 84 and 85.—If Mars is in the 8th, then the questioner had a fall. Mars with Gulika reveals that the person was wounded severely. According as Mars occupying a dhatu, moola or jeeva or sarisripa Navamsa, the querist was hurt by some weapon, lacerated by thorns, scratched or wounded by nail or teeth or was bitten by a snake or scorpion, on the previous Tuesday.

NOTES

Sarisripa Navamsas are Cancer, Scorpio and Pisces.

अष्टमस्थे विधोः पुत्रे भङ्ग इष्टस्य कर्मणिः ।
मूलांशे पूगतांबूलनाशोऽभावोथवानयोः ॥८६॥

धात्वंशे वपुषः सादो वाच्यो जीवांशके पुनः ।
पारुष्यं वचसश्चूर्णाभावो वा गतविद्दिने ॥८७॥

Stanzas 86 and 87.—If Mercury occupies the 8th from Arudha Lagna, the questioner was obstructed in his work the previous Wednesday. According as Mercury is in Moola, Dhatu or Jeeva Navamsa, the questioner had to lose or be without betel leaves and nuts, or was sick, or had to exchange harsh words or be without chunam (lime).

रन्ध्रस्थितेऽमराचार्ये नित्यकर्मविलम्बनम् ।
द्विजानां द्रव्यनाशो वा वाच्यं गुरुदिने गते ॥८८॥

भृगुपुत्रेष्टमं प्राप्ते वियोगः प्रिययोषिता ।
वक्तव्यो वस्त्रनाशश्च तत्र धात्वंशगे भृगौ ॥८९॥

वसने पङ्कसम्पर्को जीवांशेऽस्य नखक्षतिः ।
पिपीलिकाखुवाभ्राद्यैः क्षतिरंशे सरीसृपे ॥९०॥

कण्टकाद्यैस्तु मूलांशे यद्वा जीवांशगे पुनः ।
अन्यस्मै वस्त्रदानं वा गतासन्ने भृगोर्दिने ॥९१॥
अष्टमस्थे रवेः पुत्रे वाच्यं भुक्तिविलम्बनम् ।
अत्यापत्तिश्च मन्दस्य समीपस्थे गतेऽहनि ॥९२॥

Stanzas 88 to 92.—If Jupiter stands on the eighth, say on the last Thursday his performance of daily religious duties was delayed (in the case of twice-born) or there was loss of articles. If Venus is in the 8th house, he had separation from his beloved or loss of clothes or his clothes were soiled by dirt. If he is in Moola Navamsa, his clothes were torn by thorns. If he occupies Jeeva Navamsa, they were torn by his finger nails or he gave them away as gifts. If he occupies Sarisripa Navamsa, his clothes were bitten by mice or eaten away by white ants on the previous Friday. If Saturn stands on the eighth from Arudha, say that he had to take food very late or had to face a great danger on Saturday last.

रन्ध्रगे सिंहिकासूनौ वाच्या पादव्यथा पथि ।
मूलांशे कण्टकेनं पाधात्वंशेश्माभिघाततः ॥९३॥
जीवांशे सध्वसं सपात् गते मन्दस्य वासरे ।
केतौ रन्ध्रस्थिते वाच्यं पादे पाषाणघट्टनम् ॥९४॥

मान्दियुक्तोत्र केतुश्चेत्पादो नूनमभिद्यत ।
भौम्यसाम्यात्फले केतोर्गते भौमस्य वासरे ॥९५॥

Stanzas 93, 94 and 95.—If Rahu stands on the eighth, say that his legs were affected by some pain on the way. If he stands on *dhatu* Navamsa, say it was caused by stones. If he stands in *moola* Navamsa, some thorns pierced into his feet. If he is in *Jeeva* navamsa, the querist was bitten by a serpent on the previous Saturday. If Kethu stands on the eighth house, say that his legs dashed against rocks last Tuesday. If he is with Gulika, then predict that his legs were very much wounded.

पापस्तृतीयसंस्थश्चेद्वक्तव्यं स्यादुपोषणम् ।
गते तु तत्तद्दिवसे सुविचार्यैवमादिशेत् ॥९६॥

Stanza 96.—If evil planets occupy the third house from Arudha, then the questioner had to fast on the days governed by such planets.

व्ययः षष्ठस्तृतीयं च भावा नेष्टा यथाष्टमः ।
दिनेष्वनिष्टसंस्थानां यातेष्वशुभदं वदेत् ॥९७॥

Stanza 97.—The third, sixth and twelfth houses are also evil as eighth house. Hence predict evil to have happened last week allotting suitable days to those planets that occupy the above houses.

NOTES

These stanzas are clear enough and they do not need any explanations. The situation of the different planets in the 3rd, 6th, 8th and 12th houses from Arudha Lagna and in certain Navamsas indicate the happenings—some trivial—on certain week-days, pertaining to the planets concerned. Readers may test these principles and find out for themselves, the usefulness of these combinations in the modern age.

We can illustrate with a chart here.

Suppose at the time of query Aquarius is the Arudha Lagna.

Sun 4 Merc. 19 Venus 16 Kethu 14–32			Jup. 5 Moon 6
Arudha Lagna	17–3–1978		Mars 1
			Saturn 2–52
			Rahu 14–32

	Saturn	Rahu	
	NAVAMSA		Mars
			Sun
Mercury	Moon Jupiter Kethu Venus		

Rahu is in the 8th in Rasi and in Taurus Navamsa which is the 5th Navamsa. Virgo being an even sign, the 5th Navamsa would belong to Moola or vegetable.

So, the querent can be expected to have trodden over thorns which must have pierced through his soles while on his way to the astrologer.

इष्टस्थितानां वारेषु शुभप्राप्तिं च निर्दिशेत् ।
उदयेनैष्यवारेषु फलमप्येवमादिशेत् ॥ इति । ॥९८॥

Stanza 98.—Suppose planets occupy favourable houses, then predict good as having happened on the days governed by the occupants. These predictions can also be made from Udayalagna, in which case, predict good or bad on the ensuing weekdays.

द्यूनस्थेष्वशुभेषु दुष्टशकुनं सौम्येषु तच्छोभनं
दूतारूढवशादमुष्य कथयेत् प्रश्नाधिरूढेन वा ।
कर्मारूढसुखस्थितैर्बलयुतैरप्येवमादिश्यतां
यातुर्वा शकुनं शुभाशुभमिति प्रस्थानलग्नाद्वदेत् ॥९९॥

Stanza 99.—In *Prasna Bhasha* it is stated thus: If there are strong malefics in the 7th from the Arudha of the messenger or query, he must have had bad omens; if benefics, good ones. The same results can be read from planets in the 4th and 10th from Arudha. The omens at a journey can be read from the Ascendant at the time of starting and the 4th and the 10th therefrom. The same results can be read from planets in the 4th and 10th from Arudha.

तत्रस्थे चतुरंघ्रिसंज्ञविहगे मातङ्गपश्व.दयोभ्यायाताः
पथि पक्षिसंज्ञखचरे दृष्टाश्चकोरादयः ।
सूर्यारौ तु चतुष्पदौ निगदितौ मन्देन्दुजौ पक्षिणौ
शीतांशुस्तु सरीसृपोष्टचरणः शास्त्रे प्रदिष्टः फणी
॥१००॥

Stanza 100.—If the Sun and Mars occupy 1, 4, 7 and 10, then say he has met some quadrupeds like elephants or cows as indicative signs on his way. Mercury and Saturn are bird-planets and indicate birds like *chakoras*. The Moon indicates serpents or scorpions and Rahu, spiders.

NOTES

It must be noted that if Jupiter or Venus occupies such a position, the questioner must have come across some human being.

चण्डालाभ्यागमो यद्यहिशिखिगुलिकब्रध्नजस्तत्र संस्थः
शुक्रेन्दु चेद्वधूनां यदि शशितनयस्तत्र विद्वज्जनानाम् ।
विप्राणां वाक्पतिश्चेद्यदि धरणिसुतः शस्त्रिणां कीर्तनीयो
वर्त्मन्यभ्यागमः प्रास्यदि पुनररुणः श्रैष्ठ्यभाजां जनानाम्
इति ॥१०१॥

Stanza 101.—If Saturn, Rahu, Ketu or Gulika occupies 1, 4, 7, 10, say he met low-caste people on his way. If the Moon and Venus occupy the above houses, say that he has met women on the way. If it is Mercury, say he met learned men. If it is Jupiter, he met pious Brahmins. Mars indicates soldiers. The Sun represents men of distinction.

DIRECTION OCCUPIED BY QUERIST

पृच्छकस्य दिशि स्थानं विशेषाच्छुभदं नृणाम् ।

पृच्छकस्य स्थितिः कोणे प्रश्ने स्त्रीविषये शुभा ॥१०२॥

Stanza 102.—If the messenger puts in his question from east, south, west or north, it is good. If he occupies south-east, south-west, north-west or north-east, it is bad. This applies to men only. The reverse holds good for women.

दक्षिणाशाभिमुख्यं च प्रष्टुर्यमदिशि स्थितिः ।

अशुभया भवेन्नूनमायुः प्रश्ने विशेषतः ॥१०३॥

Stanza 103.—If the questioner faces or stands in the south, it indicates evil especially regarding the question of longevity.

PRANAKSHARA

आकाशावायुवह्न्यर्णपूर्वं तद्गणपूर्वकम् ।
भूतार्थवाचकश्चापि वचनं न शुभप्रदम् । ॥१०४॥

Stanza 104.—If the first syllable or Gana of the words uttered by the querent happens to be one owned by any of the Bhutas—Akasa, Vayu, Agni, Apa and Prithvi, the effect of the query will not be happy.

NOTES

Gana is a term used in prosody, where there are 8 syllable groups, *viz*., (1) Ma, (2) Ya, (3) Ra, (4) Sa, (5) Ta, (6) Ja, (7) Bha and (8) Na.

आद्यैस्स्वरैस्तु काद्यैश्च वर्गैर्भिन्ना लिपिर्द्विधा ।
स्वरा जीवस्तनुर्वर्गा इति ज्ञेया च मातृका ॥१०५॥

Stanza 105.—The alphabet is divided under two heads, *viz*., the vowels headed by Aa (अ) and the consonants headed by the gutterals (कवर्ग) including the liquids, semi-vowels and sibilants. The vowels constitute the 'Life' and consonants the 'Body'.

प्रश्नवाक्यं स्वराद्यं चेज्ज्ञेयं जीवगतं शुभम् ।
दोषश्च देहविषयो हलाद्यं चेदतोन्यथा ॥१०६॥

Stanza 106.—If the sentence of a query begins with a vowel, the query may be about the person's longevity and the effect will be beneficial. The trouble, if any, is only physical. Similarly if the sentence begins with a consonant, the trouble is not so much with the body as with his longevity.

वर्गेश्वक्षरपञ्चकं पवनवन्हीन्द्रांबुनापुंसकं ।
वाक्यादौ तु नपुंसकाक्षरमतीवानिष्टदं पृच्छताम् ॥
दुष्टौ मारुतपावकौ वलरिपुर्मध्यः प्रशस्तं जलं
दीर्घह्रस्वविभागतः स्वरगणाश्चाम्भोमहेन्द्रात्मकाः ॥इति
॥१०७॥

Stanza 107.—The five vargas or groups of consonants have five syllables each presided over by Vayu, Agni, Indra, Jala and Napumsaka. If the first letter of the question happens to fall under Napumsaka, the result will be extremely bad; if under Vayu and Agni, evil results befall; if under Indra, neutral effect; if under water, favourable results. In vowels too, the short and long belong respectively to Indra and Jala.

NOTES

The five vargas or groups of consonants are :—

Kavarga :	(Gutterals)	Ka, Kha, Ga, Gha, Gna
Chavarga :	(Labials)	Cha, Chcha, Ja, Jha, Jna

Pavarga :	(Palatals)	Pa, Pha, Ba, Bha, Ma
Tavarga :	(Dentals)	Ta, Tta, Da, Dda, Na
Thavarga :	(Linguals)	Ta, Tha, Da, Dha, Na

In each varga, the first to last syllable is presided over respectively by Vayu (air), Agni (fire), Indra, Jala (water) and Napumsaka (eunuch). If for instance, you take Kavarga, the letters Ka, Kha, Ga, Gha and Jna are ruled by Air, Fire, Indra, Water and Napumsaka respectively. Suppose the first letter of a certain query commences with the letter *ma*, the result will be harmful as the syllable is presided over by Napumsaka or eunuch. In this way, other syllables should be interpreted. The syllables ya, ra, la, va, sa, sha, sa, ha, la and ksha have similar lords as mentioned above.

Assign short vowels अ इ उ ऋ ए to Indra Bhuta and आ ई ऊ ॠ ऐ to Jala Bhuta.

मध्यान्ताद्यखिलेषु गाजसभमाः सूर्यानिलेन्दुक्षमा
देवा स्फीतरुगन्यदेशगमनप्रख्यातकीर्तिश्रियः ।
तद्वत्स्युर्लघवो गुणा रतयना वह्न्यम्बरांभोदिवो
मर्त्याःस्युर्मृतिशून्यतोत्तमसमृध्द्यायूंषि ते तन्वते ॥ इति
॥१०८॥

Stanza 108.—

Ganas	*Presiding Deities*	*Effects*
Jhagana (u — u)	The Sun (Surya)	Increase of illness

Ganas	*Presiding Deities*	*Effects*
Sagana (u u —)	Air (Vayu)	Going to another country
Bhagana (— u u)	The Moon (Chandra)	World-wide renown
Magana (— — —)	Earth (Bhoomi)	Prosperity
Ragana (— u —)	Fire (Agni)	Death
Thagana (— — u)	Ether (Akasa)	Emptiness or poverty
Yagana (u — —)	Watar (Jala)	Exceptional prosperity
Nagana (u u u)	Heaven (Swarga)	Long Life

NOTES

This sloka is from the *Anushtanapaddhati*.

Letters are divided into hard (*guru*) and soft (*laghu*) ones. Long ones are said to be hard and short ones soft. In the word uttered by the questioner, the first three letters make up a *gana*. Ganas are divided into eight on the basis of soft and hard ones. For instance in stanza 108, 1st line of the three letters constituting Jhagana, the first (u) is *laghu* or soft, the second is *guru* or hard and the third is *laghu* the whole Jhagana being ruled by the Deity Sun. Likewise in the *Sagana* the first letters (u u) are soft and the third (—) hard. In Magana all the three letters (— — —) are hard (*guru*). In the words uttered by the questioner, take the first three letters and fit them to the above classification of *ganas* and then give appropriate prediction.

With due deference to the author and his eminent desciples I must confess that the method given in stanza 108 is not easily applicable in actual practice.

श्रोत्रप्रियं वदति वा वचनं शुभं वा
यद्वार्थपुष्टगिरमस्खलितां तदनीम् ।
प्रष्टाभियात्यभिमतं त्वितरोनभीष्टमन्ते
विसर्गसहितं वचनं च वक्ता ॥१०९॥

Stanza 109.—If the questioner utters words that are very pleasing to the ears. auspicious, coherent and expressive, predict success of his undertaking; therwise not. If his sentence closes with a Visarga, then too the effect will be unfavourable.

प्रष्टुर्वाक्यादिवर्णेन लग्नं संगृह्य चामुना ।
वाच्यं शुभाशुभं सर्वं तत्प्रकाऽथ कथ्यते ॥११०॥

Stanza 110.—Moreover find out the Lagna from the first letter of the querent's statement and then predict the results, good or bad as the case may be.

अकचटतपया वर्गा रविकुजासितसौम्यजीवसौराणाम् ।
चन्द्रस्य च निर्दिष्टं प्रश्ने प्रथमोद्भवं वर्णम् ॥१११॥

Stanza 111.—There are seven Vargas, *viz.*, Aa (अ), ka (क), cha (च), ta (त), tha (ट), pa (प) and ya (य) belonging to the Sun, Mars, Venus, Mercury, Jupiter, Saturn and the Moon respectively.

ज्ञात्वा तस्माल्लग्नं संगृह्य शुभाशुभं वदेत्प्रष्टुः ।
वर्गादि मध्यचरमैर्वर्णैः प्रथमोद्भवैर्विषमम् ॥११२॥

Stanza 112.—By a consideration of this varga division, ascertain the Lagna on the basis of the first, second and third letters and answer the questioner.

राशिं लग्नं प्रवदेच्छिष्टैर्युग्मं कुजज्ञजीवानाम् ।
सितरविजयोश्च नैवं रविशशिनोरेकराशित्वात् ॥११३॥

Stanza 113.—In the case of Mars, Mercury, Jupiter, Venus and Saturn, each having two signs, take their odd or even signs according as the syllable is odd or even in the Vargas. In the case of the luminaries, there is no such difference, as they own only one house each.

तस्माल्लग्नात्प्रवदेत् पृच्छासमये शुभाशुभं सर्वम् ।
कालस्याविज्ञानादेतच्चिन्त्यं बहु प्रश्ने ॥११४॥

Stanza 114.—This plan is made use of when neither the Arudha nor the Udaya Lagna is known. So too when there are many questions put practically at the same time.

NOTES

Some sort of a connection is established between sound vibrations and the zodiacal signs. There are seven vargas or groups of letters.

Planet	*Varga letters commencing from*								
Sun	अ	आ	इ	ई	उ	ऊ	ऋ	ॠ	
	a	aa	i	ee	u	oo	ri	rii	
	लु	लू	ए	ऐ	ओ	औ			
	lu	loo	e	ai	o	ow			
Mars	क	ख	ग	घ	ङ				
	k	kha	ga	gha	gna				
Venus	च	छ	ज	झ	ञ				
	cha	chha	ja	jha	nya				
Mercury	ट	ठ	ड	ढ	ण				
	ta	tah	da	dah	na				
Jupiter	त	थ	द	ध	न				
	tha	thha	da	dha	na				
Saturn	प	फ	ब	भ	म				
	pa	pha	ba	bha	ma				
Moon	य	र	ल	व	श	ष	स	ह	ळ
	ya	ra	la	va	sa	sha	sa	ha	la

According to stanza 111, the above vargas are ruled by the Sun, Mars, Venus, Mercury, Jupiter, Saturn and the Moon respectively. Stanza 112 is interpreted by different scholars in different ways. Mr. P. G. S. Iyer who assisted me in translating this work and who was well versed in Malayalam and Sanscrit, thinks that by taking the first word in the query and tracing it to the varga concerned and thence to the planet, the Lagna should be found out. Suppose the first word of a query commences with Aa (अ): the presiding planet being the Sun, the Lagna would be Leo. In regard to two signs owned by a planet, the odd or even position of the first letter in the appropriate varga should be taken. Suppose a query commences with ba (ब); it is the third letter in Pavarga: presided over by Saturn. Since 3 is an odd number, you must take Aquarius, the odd sign, as Lagna. If instead, the query commences with bha (भ): This is the 4th letter and 4 being an even number, the Lagna will be Capricorn, the even sign owned by Saturn.

This method of ascertaining Lagna should be resorted to in the absence of Arudha or Udaya Lagnas or when a number of queries are put simultaneously.

Stanzas 112 to 114 are taken from *Prasna Gnana* of Bhattotpala.

THE QUERIST'S STHITI OR BEARING

वामांघ्रिरग्रे निहितः शुभः स्याद्‌दूतस्य दोपाय च
दक्षिणांघ्रिः ।

दोषाय चांघ्रेश्चलनं हि तस्य स्थितिः स्थिरा तस्य
शुभप्रदा स्यात् ॥११५॥

Stanza 115.—Watch the questioner as to how he stands. If he puts his left foot in front, then predict it to be good ; if he places his right foot in front, it is bad. If he shakes his leg, it is productive of evil only. If he stands firmly, it is wholesome.

सुखोपविष्ट ऋज्वङ्गस्तुङ्गदेशे शुभासने ।
दैवज्ञाभिमुखश्चैव शुभं यात्यन्यथाऽशुभम् ॥११६॥

Stanza 116.—If he sits at ease, straight, facing the astrologer in an elevated place and on a good seat, it is good. If he sits in a low place on a bad seat, then it is bad.

उत्तिष्ठति यदि प्रश्नं कुर्वन्नासीत आसनात् ।
स्थितश्चोपविशेत् कुर्वन् भद्रमेवोभयं मतम् ॥११७॥

Stanza 117.—If the querist puts a question seated, then stands up or makes the query standing and then sits down, the results will be good.

प्रष्टा दृष्टिपथं प्राप्य स्थित्वा स्थित्वागमद्यदि ।
अतीत्य स्थितिसंख्याहान्यस्य कार्यस्य साधनम् ॥११८॥

Stanza 118.—Suppose the questioner having come within the orbit of the astrologer's vision halts here and there, then predict 'delay' by the number of days corresponding to the number of his halts.

अन्तरा दूतमात्मानं यदि कश्चन गच्छति ।
अनागमं सहायस्य कल्पितस्यास्य निर्दिशेत् ॥११९॥

Stanza 119.—Suppose a stranger crosses between the astrologer and the questioner, then failure of the expected help should be predicted.

THE QUERIST'S BEHAVIOUR PATTERN

हस्तौ धून्वन् विमृदंश्च तिरश्चीनमुखः स्थितः ।
विस्मृतस्वार्थ इत्येतैर्यत्पृष्टं तद्विनश्यति ॥१२०॥

Stanza 120.—Suppose the questioner shakes or wrings his hands or rubs them, or looks sideways, or he forgets the object of his visit, then puts in the query after much hesitation, then predict failure.

स्वाङ्गेष्वन्यत्र वा द्रव्ये गाढसंताडनं क्षणात् ।
मृत्युदं लयलिङ्गानां चिन्तेक्षाश्रवणादिकम् ॥१२१॥

Stanza 121.—Suppose suddenly he strikes hard his own body or anything near him, then predict death. The effect is the same when there is a thought, sight or news of indications of death.

सुप्ते मुक्तकचेऽशुचौ रुदति वा भग्नागमे मुण्डिते
नग्ने छिन्दति निन्दति द्रवति वा वह्नौ हविर्जुह्वति ।
दूते हस्तपदां च बन्धनपरे दोष्णाक्षि संमर्दने
दीने काष्ठतृणादिमर्दनपरे न स्याद्विचारः शुभः ॥१२२॥

Stanza 122.—Suppose he feels sleepy or is unclean, or is weeping, or has his hair dishevelled or has his face cut or has head shaved clean or stands naked or bemoans his fate or is engaged in cutting or flees in fear or performs his Homa to Agni or ties up something round his legs or hands, or frequently rubs his eyes with his hands or feels despondent or is seen trampling on a piece of wood or a bunch of grass, then know that the effects will be evil.

पाशोद्वर्तनके नखैर्लिखति वाप्युत्सारिते वारिते
साभ्यङ्गे भासिताग्थिसीसशकृतां भर्तर्यपि व्याधिते ।

वस्त्रप्रावृतकन्धरे च मलिने रूक्षाशुभालापिनि
प्रश्नो नैव शुभाय निर्वपति वा पिण्डान् परेतान् प्रति
॥१२३॥

Stanza 123.—If the questioner is found engaged in twisting a rope, marking the ground with his nails, is forced to change his place or is obstructed, has his body smeared with oil, engaged in carrying ashes or bones, lead or dung, or discovered to be sickly ; has a cloth wound up round his neck ; has his body painted with mud ; is found uttering unpleasant and harsh sounds or words ; is found performing Sraddha ; then you can very well count that you have nothing good to predict.

व.सीरखड्गपलालजालकतुपापादत्रपिच्छत्वचां
शृङ्गस्यापि च वाहके च विकले संमार्जनीधारिणि ।
प्रेतालंकृतिशूर्पपाशमुसला.न् भर्तर्थुपेते क्षुधा
दैवज्ञेपि च पृच्छके न च शुभो ज्ञेयो विचारः क्वचित्
॥१२४॥

Stanza 124.—Suppose he has with him a knife or a sword, a bundle of hay, net, chaff, shoes, peacock feathers, leather, decorations of dead body, horn, broom, winnowing basket, ropes, pestles, or he is found to be starving or is crippled, then also predict evil.

QUERIST'S MOOD OR BHAVA

दौर्मुख्यं वदनारूढशोकक्रोधश्रमादिभिः ।
वैमनस्यं च दूतस्य येनकेनापि दोषकृत् ॥१२५॥

Stanza 125.—If he has his face distorted either by anger or sorrow or exertion, or if his mind is much worried, then also effects will be bad.

सुन्दरश्च कुलीनश्च विनयी च निरामयः ।
सुप्रसन्नश्चदूतश्चेत्प्रष्टा सुखामवाप्नुयात् ॥१२६॥

Stanza 126.—If the messenger or questioner is handsome, healthy and modest, has the mark of nob'e birth and breed and possesses a happy face, then take these as good and predict accordingly.

उन्मिषदम्बकयुगलो मङ्गलपदार्थ दृढथरनिहितेक्षः ।
अध ऊर्ध्वेक्षणरीहतो लभतेभीष्टं प्रतीपदृग्दुःखम् ॥१२७॥

Stanza 127.—If his eyes are opening wide or he is looking at auspicious objects, and is free from downward or upward looks, then predict good effects. If his eyes are half-closed, if he looks at dirty or inauspicious things, or looks upwards or downwards, the results will be very bad.

DRESS AND GARMENTS

तोयार्द्रभिन्नमलिनारुणनीलवासा
रक्तप्रसूनभृदपि व्यसनं प्रयाति ।
वासः सितं सुरभिगौरसुमानुलेपभूषा
दधच्च खलु मङ्गलमेति नूनम् ॥१२८॥

Stanza 128.—If the questioner puts on wet, torn, dirty clothes, in red or blue colour, or decorates himself with red flowers, the Prasna effects will be sorrowful. If he has white neat clothes, fine ornaments, fragrant white flowers and rich perfumes on his person, then the effects will be good.

बिभ्राणो मङ्गलद्रव्यं पृच्छको याति मङ्गलम् ।
रिक्तपाणिरमङ्गल्यद्रव्यभृच्चाशुभं व्रजेत् ॥१२९॥

Stanza 129.—If the questioner comes with any auspicious things in his hand, then predict good. If he comes with nothing or with any inauspicious things as broom, etc., then predict evil effects.

SOME PECULIAR LAKSHANAS

प्रश्नकाले शुभे प्रष्टुः स्थितिस्पर्शेक्षणादिके ।
दैवज्ञचित्ते तुष्टे च स्यादिष्टार्थसमागमः ॥१३०॥

Stanza 130.—If at the time of query, the astrologer is free from all anxieties, and if the questioner's posture, movements and looks are favourable, then predict good.

मनोगतफलप्राप्तिरशुभेष्वेषु नो भवेत् ।
मिश्रेषु येषामाधिक्यं फलं तेषां विनिर्दिशेत् ॥१३१॥

Stanza 131.—If these are bad, then the achievement of his desired objects will not take place. If these are of mixed nature, then the effects will be mixed according to the strength of good and bad indications.

OMENS OR TATKALA LAKSHANAS

प्रश्ने यदुच्यते यच्च श्रूयते यच्च दृश्यते ।
तत्सादृश्येन सकलं प्रष्टुर्वाच्यं शुभाशुभम् ॥१३२॥

Stanza 132.—All the effects of a query can be fully understood by a careful study of what you see before you or what you hear or what others speak at the time of the query, in the shape of ominous sounds or expressive signs.

यस्यकस्यापि कार्यस्य पृच्छायां प्रस्थितावपि ।
तत्कार्यसाधनं वस्तु दृष्टं चेत्तत्तु सिध्यति ॥१३३॥

Stanza 133.—The sight of certain objects brings in comfort and welfare. Note these suggestive signs when you begin to make predictions. This will be useful also when you go or start for another place.

नववस्तुद्वयादीनां दर्शनं करसङ्ग्रहे ।
सद्वये तदसिध्यै स्याद्वियोगास्तु कयोरपि ॥१३४॥

Stanza 134.—While discussing marriage affairs or when starting for a marriage ceremony, the sight of 'fresh dress' and the like indicate a happy marriage. Then if you happen to see two persons bidding farewell to each other and parting away, then the marriage tie will be broken or dissolved.

रन्ध्रेङ्गुलिप्रवेशे तु कन्यया दूषणं वदेत् ।
यस्या यः कश्चिदागच्छेद्विवाहोस्यां दिशीर्यताम् ॥१३५॥

Stanza 135.—If you see any person thrusting his finger into any hole, then say that the bride in question is immoral. If however you notice any person coming towards you from any side, you may predict that a gentleman from that direction will marry her.

घुटिकापुस्तकाद्यं यद्विद्याभ्यासनसाधनम् ।
किङ्किणीकटकादीनि भूषणानि शिशोरपि ॥१३६॥
मेखलाजिंनदण्डाश्च गर्भिणी बालकस्तथा ।
एतेषां दर्शनादीनि भवेयुः पुत्रसिद्धये ॥१३७॥

Stanzas 136 and 137.—In a query regarding 'birth of children' a casual sight of the following at the time brings in luck and attainment of object: a book, pen and the like, a small jingling bell, bangle, a necklace and other ornaments of children, a small piece of deer-skin, a stick, a belt of *darbha* grass, a pregnant woman, smiling children : these indicate clearly that the questioner will get children.

दर्शनं ज्वलितस्याग्नेर्मलादित्यजनं तनोः ।
यानं कस्यापि तद्देशाद्गर्भच्छिद्रस्य सूचकम् ॥१३८॥

Stanza 138.—If you happen to see near, anybody cleaning his body or going away from your midst or anything burning brilliantly, say that the pregnant woman in question will have abortion.

दक्षिणांघ्रिंस्थिरीकृत्य स्थितिरायुधचालनम् ।
मर्दनं दक्षहस्तस्य ज्वलिताग्निप्रदर्शनम् ॥१३९॥

पुरुषस्य प्रसिद्धस्य प्रसन्नस्य च दर्शनम् ।
एतत्षट्कं विशेषेण युद्धप्रश्ने जयावहम् ॥१४०॥

Stanzas 139 and 140.—In a Yuddha Prasna, the following are considered as favourable signs: a person standing on his right leg or shaking his weapons pressing his right hand ; a burning fire or a distinguished, august or calm personage.

वामपादं स्थिरीकृत्य स्थितिर्विक्लबता गिरः ।
सश्रुता मलिनेक्षा च नियम्यायुधधारणम् ॥१४१॥
पराजवकराः पञ्च युद्धप्रश्ने विशेषतः ॥१४२॥

Stanzas 141 and 142.—A person standing firmly on his left leg, a person shedding tears or speaking in a faltering voice, a dirty person and one sheathing his sword : these sights indicate defeat in a fight.

यत्किञ्चित् कार्यमुद्दिश्य प्रस्थाने यदि तिपश्य ।
सुवर्णं वा फलं वा स्याद्द्रव्यलाभो न संशयः ॥१४३॥

Stanza 143.—In a query pertaining to an enterprise, the sight of a piece of gold or some fruits suggests financial gain.

आरुह्य वा समाश्रित्य जीववद्वस्तु पृच्छति ।

प्रश्ने चागच्छति प्राणी तं देशं प्रति कश्चन ॥१४४॥

जीवत्येव ध्रुवं रोगी म्रियते वैपरीत्यतः ॥१४५॥

Stanzas 144 and 145.—In a query bearing on disease, the sight of a living being or person on horseback or on an elephant portends immediate cure of the disease. But standing on a lifeless object will bring about the death of the questioner.

पितृपुष्पं तिलं वह्निर्नूतनं वसनं तथा ।

दर्भदध्यादि निखिलं संभृतं पितृकर्मणे ॥१४६॥

मरणानन्तरापेक्षं द्रव्यं यत्सकलं तु तत् ।

एतेषां दर्शनं नृनामायुः प्रश्नेमृतिप्रदम् ॥१४७॥

Stanzas 146 and 147.—Flowers for funeral rites, sesamum seeds, burning cinder, unwashed clothes, darbha grass (kusa grass), curd, all things used in obsequies—burial or cremation—these when seen indicate the death of the sick man.

शयनं चोपवेशश्च पृष्ट्वा यात्रा विघातकृत् ।
पादव्यत्याससङ्कोची विलम्बनकरौ ध्रुवम् ॥१४८॥

पृष्टोत्थानञ्च यानं च यात्रालाभाय सत्वरम् ॥१४९॥

Stanzas 148 and 149.—In a question pertaining to travel, if the messenger sits down or lies down after the question is put, then you can say that some obstructions will impede his trip. If he gets up on one leg and keeps standing on the other and contracts them, some delay will be caused in his trips. If he gets up or walks up as soon as the query is made, predict that the intended trip will take place soon.

पाणिग्रहणमन्योन्यं द्वयोः कस्यापि चागमः ।
सन्धये छेदभेदादि सर्वं संधिविरोधकृत् ॥१५०॥

Stanza 150.—If you chance to meet two persons with their hands clasped or if you find a stranger walking towards you, then a dispute will end in compromise. Separations, breaks, etc., lead to the obstruction of peace.

हाहाखेदरवं क्षुतं च पतनं चैत्यध्वजादेस्तथा
वस्त्रच्छत्रपदत्रविक्षतिमपि ध्वंसार्थनानागिरः ।
क्रूराणां मृगपक्षिणां प्रतिदिशं वाचश्च दीपक्षयः
पातं पूर्णघटादिकस्य च बुधाः कष्टं निमित्तं विदुः
॥१५१॥

Stanza 151.—The following are considered as evil omens indicating failure :—Intermittent cries of Oh! Oh!—sniffing sounds, the falling of the flag-post or the family tree of worship, clothes, umbrella, or shoes getting spoiled or words connoting ruin or loss heard from all directions, or bad birds or cruel animals making unpleasant cries, light being extinguished unexpectedly—any vessel full of water or so firmly fixed that it tumbles down.

मार्जारडुण्डुभोलूकगोधाद्यशुभदर्शनम् ।
गौळ्या रुतं च नाशाय वामे दक्षे तथा क्षुतम् ॥१५२॥

Stanza 152.—At the time of prasna, if you see on your left, cats, owls, a kind of snake, or Godha it is considered bad ; if you hear the cry of a lizard on the left side, the effect is the same.

Sneezing of persons to the right side also is harmful.

प्रशस्ताः कीर्तने कोलगोधाहिशशजाहकाः ।
न दर्शने न विरुते वानरर्क्षावतोन्यथा ॥१५३॥
मातङ्गाश्ववृषादीनां पृच्छाकाले रुतं यदि ।
तेषां वा दर्शनं तर्हि प्रष्टाभीष्टमवाप्नुयात् ॥१५४॥

Stanzas 153 and 154.—If you hear anybody uttering the names of hogs, serpents, hare, Godha, etc., it is good. But to see these or hear their cries is bad. To see or to hear the cries of the monkey and the bear is good. But to hear their names uttered is bad. To see or to hear the cries of an elephant, a horse, or an ox is also good.

वीणावेणुमृदङ्गशंखपठहध्वानं च भेरीरवं
गीतं मङ्गलमङ्गनां च गणिकां दध्यक्षातेक्ष्वादिकम् ।
दूर्वाचन्दनपूर्णकुम्भकुसुमं मालां फलं कन्यकां
घण्टां दीपसरोरुहे च शुभदं विद्यान्निमित्तं बुधः ॥१५५॥

Stanza 155.—A veena, flute, drum, conch, —the sounds of these instruments are auspicious. General music, pleasant objects and beautiful women, dancing girls, pot of curd, coloured rice, sugarcane, Durva grass, sandal paste, pot filled with water, flowers and garlands, fruits and virgins, bells, lights and lotus flowers—all these are auspicious both for hearing and seeing.

छत्रं तोरणहृद्ययानशकटं स्तोत्रं च वेदध्वनिं
बद्धं चैकपशुं वृषं च मुकुरं स्वर्णं सवत्सां च गाम् ।
भक्ष्यं चोद्धृतमृत्तिकां बुधवरं यच्चान्यदिष्टं श्रुतं
दृष्टं श्रोत्रदृशोश्शुभं तदखिलं प्रश्ने निमित्तं विदुः ॥१५६॥

Stanza 156.—Umbrella, arches, agreeable palanquins or carriages, hymns of prayer, or utterances of the Vedas, a cow tied with a rope, a bull, a mounted mirror, gold, a cow and its calf, eatables, fresh mud, or a learned pandit, are good. In brief, all those things which are agreeable to our ears and which are pleasant to our eyes can be considered as good omens at a query.

लोकाच्छास्त्रमुखात्तथा गुरुमुखादन्यन्निमित्तान्तरं
विज्ञातव्यमतः शुभाशुभफलं प्राज्ञैः प्रयत्नादिह ।
यद्यत्पृच्छति पृच्छकोन्तिकगतं तन्नाशचिह्नं भवे-
न्नाशः स्यादिह तस्य तस्य न चिरात्तद्व्यत्यये व्यत्ययः
॥१५७॥

ज्ञात्वैतत्सकलं सम्यक्समयादि शुभाशुभम् ।
एतैरेवाखिलं वस्तुं शक्यं प्रष्टुः शुभाशुभम् ॥१५८॥

Stanzas 157 and 158.—Other signs and omens should be learnt from other treatises on the subject or under the guidance of a Guru or according to the code of conduct sketched by learned men. For general guidance, it may be taken as granted that whatever things or signs that help us to attain our objects, are good and all those things that are inauspicious indicate the contrary results. Knowing benefic or malefic nature of the omens, it is possible to make appropriate predictions.

Thus concludes the 2nd chapter of *Prasna Marga*.

॥ इति प्रश्नमार्गे द्वितीयाध्यायः ॥

तृतियाध्यायः

THE ASTROLOGER'S DEPARTURE

प्रश्नकालोद्भवं बुध्वा सदसत्समयादिकम् ।
निर्गच्छेत्समये जीवकालहोरादिके शुभे ॥१॥

Stanza 1.—When the astrologer sets out to the house of a person whose future he has to read, he must recall all those ominous indications which he noted when the querent approached him. He must apply now the same rules and start at an auspicious time to the house of the querent. The Kalahora of benefics is particularly good.

शुभाशुभनिमित्तं यत्प्रश्नकालसमुद्भवम् ।
उक्तं निखिलमप्येतच्चिन्तनीयं हि निर्गमे ॥२॥

Stanza 2.—All those good and bad omens suggested for the time of putting a query in the last chapter may be applied now when the astrologer sets out to the house of the querist.

निर्गच्छतोम्बरं सङ्गमेति भूमौ ततेच्च वा ।
छत्राद्यं य त्करस्थं वा भवेदेवाशुभाय तत् ॥३॥

आगच्छ तिष्ठ मा गच्छ प्रविश क्व नु गच्छसि ।
इत्यादिवाचः प्रस्थाने भवन्त्यशुभदा दृढम् ॥४॥

पाषाणादिषु पादस्खलनं स्तम्भादिके तथा शिरसः ।
नेष्टं निर्गमनेन्यान्यपि चिन्त्यानि लोकसिद्धानि ॥५॥

Stanzas 3. 4 and 5.—The astrologer's dress gets entangled on anything; his walking stick or umbrella tumbles down, somebody calls him from behind and says "come here, stop, do not go, enter in, where do you go?", etc; his head dashes against a post or pillar; his legs strike against a stone or piece of wood. These are bad omens indicating inauspicious results. He should also refer to his experience for other omens.

Omens on the Way

अन्यजन्मान्तरकृतं शुभं वा यदि वाशुभम् ।
यत्तस्य शकुनः पाकं निवेदयति गच्छताम् ॥६॥

Stanza 6.—These omens simply indicate what is going to happen as a result of your good or bad karma in your last birth.

NOTES

This sloka is from *Brihat Samhita.*

सदसच्छकुनोद्भूतौ कर्तृभिदास्त्येव तत्फलानुभवे ।
मार्गादिभेदवशतस्तदपि च शास्त्रान्तरे कथितम् ॥७॥

पथ्यात्मानं नृपं सैन्ये पुरे चोद्दिश्य देवताम् ।
सार्थे प्रधानं साम्ये तु जातिविद्यावयोधिकम् ॥८॥

Stanzas 7 and 8.—Whom an ominous sign affects has to be understood by the then situation. If a person going alone notes a sakuna or omen, he is himself affected ; in an army, the king is affected ; in the capital of a country, it is a warning from the goddess of the place ; a company of people, the effects will be felt by the important man in the group according to seniority in age, wisdom or birth.

शकुनफलानामपि भूतानागतवर्तमानत्वम् ।
तत्सम्भवदिग्वशतो ज्ञेयं शास्त्रान्तरोक्तमेतदपि ॥९॥

Stanza 9.—The effects of any sakuna—whether it has been experienced in the past, or whether it is being felt at present, or whether it will be experienced in the future, have been explained in some other works according to the direction of its occurrence.

आरभ्य स्वोदयादर्कः पूर्वाद्यष्टासु दिक्ष्वपि ।
सञ्चरत्यर्द्धसंयुक्ताः सप्तनाडीर्दिवानिशम् ॥१०॥

मुक्तप्राप्तैष्यसूर्यासु फलं दिक्षु तथाविधम् ।
अङ्गारदीप्तधूमिन्यस्ताश्च शान्तास्ततोपराः ॥११॥

Stanzas 10 and 11.—Beginning from sunrise, the Sun travels through the eight directions commencing from the east, at the rate of seven and a half ghatis in each direction. The directions under traverse, the preceding and the succeeding ones go under the name of *deeptha*, *angara* and *dhumni* respectively. The remaining five are *santha*.

NOTES

The day is to be reckoned from sunrise to sunrise. The Sun is supposed to symbolically go round the different directions in the order of east, south-east, south, south-west, west, north-west, north and north-east respectively, staying in each direction for $7\frac{1}{2}$ ghatis or three hours. From sunrise to say about 9 a.m. the Sun will be in the east. During these three hours, the east goes under the name of *deeptha* or ablaze. The quarter left, *viz.*, south-east is *angara* or burning and the quarter to succeed, *i.e.*, south-east is *dhumni* or smoky. The rest, *viz.*, south, south-west, west. north-west and north are *santha* or tranquil. Three hours after sunrise, the Sun stays in S.E. Then this quarter or direction becomes deeptha. The preceding one (east) and the succeeding one (south) become angara and dhumni respectively ; and the other directions—south-west to north-east reckoned in clockwise order become santha.

Six hours after sunrise the position is shifted to the south, which becomes deeptha, south-east and south-west going under the name of angara and dhumni respectively. In this way note the position of the Sun and determine the nature of the directions. *Angara* refers to the past, *deeptha* refers to the present and *dhuma* refers to the future. The following diagram will also be useful in understanding the above two stanzas :—

North-east 3 a.m. to 6 a.m.	East 6 a.m. to 9. a.m.	South-east 9 a.m. to 12 noon
North 12 midnight to 3 a.m.	Sunrise 6 a.m.	South 12 noon to 3 p.m.
North-west 9 p.m. to 12 midnight	**West** 6 p.m. to 9 p.m.	South-west 3 p.m. to 6 p.m.

Suppose at 10–20 p.m. the nature of the diks or directions is to be ascertained. The Sun's position will be at north-west—deeptha; west will be angara; the north will be dhuma and north-east, east, south-east, south, south-west and west will be santha. In actual practice, the actual time of sunrise should be taken and each direction allotted three hours. Depending upon the direction of the past, present and future of the querist is to be noted.

तत्प्रश्नदिशां तुल्यं फलं त्रैकाल्यमादिशेत्
परिशेषदिशोर्वाच्यं यथासत्वं शुभाशुभम् । इति ॥१२॥

Stanza 12.—To the five directions (going under the name of santha) should be suitably assigned the sequence of the "time–effect". The remaining two directions will be similar to those of their adjacent ones.

NOTES

I have given a very liberal translation of this stanza. In the preceding stanza, reference is made to the dik or directions falling under the name of santha. What does this refer to? Is it present or past or future? This is answered in this ṣloka. The fifth dik from each is also

	N. E.	E.	S. E.	
	3 a.m. to 6 a.m. *Angora* **Past**	6 a.m. to 9. a.m. SUN *Deeptha* **Present**	9 a.m. to 12 noon *Dhumni* **Future**	
N	1–30 a.m. to 3 a.m. ↑ ↓ 12 midnight to 1–30 a.m.	Sunrise 6 a.m.	12 noon to 1–30 p.m. ↑ ↓ 1–30 p.m. to 3 p.m.	S
	9 p.m. to 12 midnight Omen	6 p.m. to 9 p.m.	3 p.m. to 6 p.m.	
	N. W.	W.	S. W.	

the same in time-effect. It has already been suggested that the direction, the Sun is in, is *deeptha* (present) and the preceding and the succeeding ones are respectively *angara* (past) and *dhumni* (future). Suppose the Sun is in east direction (6 a.m. to 9 a.m.) and an omen is sighted in north-west, its effect will be felt only in the future, because it is the fifth from south-east which is dhumni (future). Regarding the effects of the south and north, the first half will correspond to the previous direction and the second half to the next quarter. Thus the first half of south indicates future and the second part, the present. The first half of north refers to future and the next half to past.

राजा कुमारो नेता च दूतः श्रेष्ठी चरो द्विजः ।
गजाध्यक्षश्च पूर्वाद्याः क्षत्रियाद्याश्चतुर्दिशः ॥१३॥

Stanza 13.—The eight quarters, beginning from east to west in the clockwise order, signify respectively a king, an heir apparent, a commander-in-chief, a messenger, a learned man, a spy, a priest, and a controller of elephants. Again, the east, south, west and north respectively signify a Kshatriya, a Vaisya, a Sudra and a Brahmin.

गच्छतस्तिष्ठतो वापि दिशि यस्यां प्रतिष्ठितः ।
विरौति शकुनो वाच्यस्तद्दिक्स्थेन समागमः ॥१४॥

Stanza 14.—Omens seen in the various directions by the astrologer standing or walking indicate contact with the class of people mentioned in stanza 13.

प्राच्यां खलु शकुनखो यदि खलु भविता समागमो
राज्ञा ।
राजकुमारेणाग्नौ याम्यादिष्वेवमेव नेतृमुखैः ॥इति ॥१५॥

Stanza 15.—Suppose an omen is notified in the east, then assume that you will meet with a royal personage; in south-east, a prince and so on.

पाषण्डाश्रमवर्णानां सवर्णाः कार्यसिद्धये ।
त एव विपरीताः स्युर्दूताः कार्यविपत्तये ॥१६॥

Stanza 16.—If the messenger be of the same caste, etc., the object of the query will be realised. If not, the effects will be adverse.

NOTES

The above stanzas are quite clear and they do not require an explanation. The eight cardinal points beginning from the east are held to signify a king, an heir apparent, etc., and an omen seen in a particular direction signifies meeting with the class of people according to the above allocation.

कार्पासौषधकृष्णधान्यलवणं जालादि हिंसार्थकं
भस्माङ्गारमयश्च तक्रमुरगं पूतिं च विट्छर्दिते ।
भ्रान्तापन्नजलान्धमूकबधिरक्लीबांश्च संन्यासिनो
यद्यद्दृङ्मनसोरनिष्टमखिलं कष्टं निमित्तं विदुः ॥१७॥

Stanza 17.—Cotton, medicines, black-gram, salt, net, trap, and other destructive appliances, ashes, burning cinder, iron, buttermilk, serpents, foul-smelling things as human refuse, or vomitted dirt, mad man, a sick man, an idiot, a blind man, a mute, a deaf man, a eunuch, an ascetic—in brief all those things which are repugnant to the eye or mind, are all evil omens.

NOTES

Meeting any of these on his way is considered bad.

पथश्छेदोऽहि मार्जारगोधानकुलवानरैः ।
सर्षपेन्धनपाषाणतृणानीतिश्च दोषकृत् ॥१८॥

Stanza 18.—If a serpent, a cat, a godha (a kind of alligator), a mongoose or a monkey crosses your path, something bad is sure to happen The sight of mustard seed, fuel, stone, grass, is also bad.

आमं मांसमथासवं मधुघृते धौतांशुकालेपनं
रत्नेभद्विजवाजिनश्च नृपतिं संवर्द्धमानं नरम् ।

देवं पाण्डरचामरं सुमधुरस्निग्धान्नपाने शवं
विप्रौ च ज्वलदग्निमत्र शुभदं विद्यान्निमित्तं बुधः
॥१९॥

Stanza 19.—Raw flesh, liquor, honey, ghee, white clothes, white ointment, jewels, elephant, birds, horse, king, a prosperous family-man, deities in procession, white chowries, delicious food or drinks, dead body, Brahmins coming in twos, and burning fire, are good omens.

प्रदक्षिणं खगमृगा यान्तो नैवं श्वजम्बुकौ ।
अयुग्माश्च मृगाश्शस्ताः शस्ता नित्यं च दर्शने ॥२०॥

Stanza 20.— Birds and animals going clockwise, jackal and dog moving anti-clockwise, and good animals found in odd numbers, indicate good.

चाषभासभरद्वाजनकुलछागबर्हिणः ।
मत्स्यौ घटीति पद्योक्तं निमित्तं च शुभप्रदम् ॥२१॥

Stanza 21.—The sight of wild crow, Bhasa and Bhardwaja birds, mongoose, goats, peacock, is good besides what is expressed in the sloka, "matsyau ghati", etc.

NOTES

The sloka referred to here is from Varahamihira's *Brihat Jataka*.

Two fishes, a man bearing a pot, a man and woman bearing a mace and veena, a person carrying bows and arrows, crocodile, a person carrying a balance, an unmarried girl sailing with corn in one hand and fire in the other, are indicative of auspiciousness.

श‍ृगालनकुलव्याघ्रचकोरोरगपोत्रिणः ।
गच्छन्तो दक्षिणे वामे श्वकाकाजमृगाद्विपाः ॥२२॥
दृष्टाः प्रशस्ता एते तु न शुभाः स्युर्विपर्ययात् ॥२३॥

Stanzas 22 and 23.—Jackal, mongoose, tiger, chakora bird, serpent or a pig crossing you on the right side is indicative of good. If they cross your left, it foretells evil. A dog, a crow, a goat, an elephant or a stag, passing on your left, indicates good, if not it forebodes evil.

NOTES

These birds and beasts if seen in the suggested directions produce good. Otherwise evil results are said to flow.

शान्तादीप्तत्वमाशानां शुकुनानां च तद्वशात् ।
शुभाशुभत्वमस्त्येतदपि शास्त्रान्तरोदितम् ॥२४॥

रविमुक्तादयस्तिस्रो दीप्ता नेष्टास्ततोपराः ।
शान्ताः शुभाः स्वदिक्तुल्यफलं हि शकुनं मतम् ॥ इति
॥२५॥

Stanzas 24 and 25.—The omens too become 'tranquil' and 'blazing' according to the directions in which they are situated. They yield their results too accordingly. The three quarters—left behind, occupied at present and to be occupied next—by the Sun, are called Deeptha or 'blazing'. These three quarters are unfavourable and the remaining ones termed 'Santha' or tranquil are favourable. The omens seen in these quarters also yield similar effects.

NOTES

Suppose the Sun is in the eastern quarter (6 a.m. to 9 a.m.). Then the north-east, east and south-east directions go under the name of deeptha. The other five directions are santha. An omen seen in a deeptha quarter indicates evil results and that sighted in a santha quarter denotes favourable happenings.

यामार्द्धमुदयात्पूर्वमारभ्याष्टासु दिक्ष्वपि ।
परिभ्रमति तिग्मांशुर्यामेष्वष्टासु सर्वदा ॥२६॥

रवौ ज्वाला ततो धूमच्छायामृद्वारिभूमयः ।
भसिताङ्गारकाश्चेति प्रदक्षिण्येन संस्थितम् ॥२७॥

अङ्गारादित्रयं दीप्तं शान्तं मृत्स्नादिकत्रयम् ।
छाया पूर्वं शुभं भस्म पश्चाच्चैवं शुभं भवेत् ॥२८॥

Stanzas 26 to 28.—Commencing from an hour and a half before sunrise the Sun travels through the 8 directions during the 8 *yamas* of the day. The names of the 8 quarters are :—*jwala* (flame), *dhuma* (smoke), *chaya* (shadow), *mrittika* (mud), *jala* (water), *bhumi* (earth), *bhasma* (ashes) and *angara* (charcoal). The three quarters from angara are termed deeptha or blazing and the three from mrittika, santha or tranquil. The first half of chaya and the last half of bhasma are good. The other halves are bad.

NOTES

Here the allocation of the Sun's symbolic motion clockwise in the eight cardinal points is of a different type. The following table is self-explanatory. The table holds good if sunrise is at 6 a.m.

Time	*Direction*	*Nature of motion*
4–30 a.m. to 7–30 a.m.	East	Jwala or flame
7–30 a.m. to 10–30 a.m.	South-east	Dhuma or smoke
10–30 a.m. to 1–30 p.m.	South	Chaya or shadow
1–30 p.m. to 4–30 p.m.	South-west	Mrittika or mud
4–30 p.m. to 7–30 p.m.	West	Jala or water
7–30 p.m. to 10–30 p.m.	North-west	Bhumi or earth
10–30 p.m. to 1–30 a.m.	North	Bhasma or ashes
1–30 a.m. to 4–30 a.m.	North-west	Angara (charcoal)

The three directions beginning from *angara*, *i.e.* north-west, east and south-east fall under *deeptha* and produce the same results as suggested in stanza 25. The three directions commencing from *mrittika*, *viz.*, south-west, west and north-west are santha and denote favourable results. The first half of *chaya* (south) and the last half of *bhasma* (north) are good. In this connection 'notes' given under stanzas 10 and 11 may be re-read with advantage.

एकादशादिमेनिष्टे द्वितीये शकुने पुनः ।
प्राणायामाः षोडश स्युस्तृतीये तु न च व्रजेत् ॥ इति ॥२९॥

Stanza 29.—A person meeting with a bad omen on the way must go back home, wash his feet and do *pranayama* (breath-regulation) 11 times and start again. If he meets again with a bad omen, he should return home and do *pranayama* 16 times. After that if he again sees a bad omen for the third time, he should not proceed at all.

INDICATIVE SIGNS WHILE ENTERING THE HOUSE

प्रश्ने तत्कालजं यद्यन्निर्गमे यद्यद्ध्वनि ।
प्रोक्तं प्रष्टृगृहप्राप्तौ तत्तत्प्रायेण चिन्त्यताम् ॥३०॥

Stanza 30.—When the astrologer enters the house, he should take stock of all the effects of the indicative signs and omens occurring at the time of starting, going along the way and entering the house, and apply their effects.

आर्तालयं विशति दैवविदीत एतद्द्वारा निरेति यदि
कोपि सरुङ्म्रियेत ।
द्वरा तथैव विशतीह यदीतरश्चेज्जीवेत्स नूनमिति मे
गुरुणोपदिष्टम् ॥३१॥

Stanza 31.—As the astrologer enters the place, if some other person issues out through the same gate, then the patient will die. On the contrary, if another person enters the place (with the astrologer) the sick man will soon improve. So am I taught by my Guru.

गृहान्तिकं प्रष्टुरिहाभियाते ततो वधूः
प्रश्नविचारिणीत्थम् ।
विनिर्गता मूलफलोपपन्ना रजस्वलोन्मूलविनाशिनी
स्यात् ॥३२॥

Stanza 32.—If a woman in menses, carrying fruits and roots issues out of the house which the astrologer enters, it may safely be predicted that the querist's life and career are doomed.

NOTES

According to some this verse is an interpolation.

वेदाध्ययनघोषश्च तथा पुण्याहनिस्स्वनः ।
गन्धश्च सुरभिर्वायुः सुखस्पर्शः प्रदक्षिणः ॥३३॥

वृषस्य चानुलौमस्य स्वनस्तद्वद्गवामपि ।
प्रवेशसमये प्रष्टुरारोग्यादिफलाप्तये ॥३४॥

Stanzas 33 and 34.—While entering, if one hears Vedas being chanted, mantras recited, a bull facing the house, bellows or cows mooing sweetly, or finds a gentle and fragrant breeze blowing, then predict good health and prosperity.

शयनासनयानानामुत्तानानां च दर्शनम् ।
न्युब्जानामितरेषां च पात्रादीनामशोभनम् ॥३५॥

Stanza 35.—Cots, chairs, vehicles, etc., if found upturned or vessels down-faced, consider they are evil indicators.

आतुरस्य गृहे यस्य भिद्यन्ते वा पतन्ति वा ।
अतिमात्रममत्राणि दुर्लभं तस्य जीवितम् ॥३६॥

Stanza 36.—If you hear anything falling or breaking to pieces, then also the sick man is not likely to survive.

निवाते दीपनाशः स्यान्मन्दिरे यस्य रोगिणः ।

स न जीवति चुल्यादो चाग्निनाशः सतीन्धने ॥३७॥

Stanza 37.—If the light is put out though there is no violent wind and the fire is soon extinguished though there is sufficient fuel, consider that the sick man will die.

॥ इति प्रश्नमार्गे तृतीयोऽध्यायः ॥

—o—

चतुर्थोऽध्यायः

CONDUCTING THE PRASNA

प्रश्नानुष्ठानमेतेन लक्षणान्यपि कानिचित् ।
शास्त्रान्तरेषु दृष्टानि कथ्यन्ते खल्वनन्तरम् ॥१॥

Stanza 1.—In this chapter is explained how *prasna kriya* is to be conducted and how the future can be divined on the basis of certain indications given in sastras.

NOTES

In Kerala, it seems people generally ask astrologers to do *ashtamangala prasna* and have their varying fortunes unfolded to them. It is said that most family people took part in it and in fact, the daily routine of some families was regulated by these Prasnikas. Remedial measures were taken to alleviate the sufferings caused by their previous evil actions. Hence the author has taken great pains to detail how this Prasna must be conducted. The first three chapters cover the first stage in dealing with Prasna. In this chapter, the author explains further how the future can be divined by Time with the help of God, omens, signs and significations.

PREPARATION

स्नात्वा धृतसितवासा भृतभस्मा प्राङ्मुखः सुखासीनः
आलोच्याथ निमित्तं प्रश्नविधिं प्रारभेत् गुरुभक्त्या ॥२॥

Stanza 2.—After taking a clean bath, dressing himself in tidy neat robes and wearing sacred ashes, the astrologer seated at ease must open the Kriya with great devotion to God and Guru facing east, and observing carefully all around, noting omens if any.

अनासन्ने तु समये मध्याह्नोदययो रवेः ।
प्रश्नकर्म हि कर्तव्यं सुप्रसन्ने दिवाकरे ॥३॥

Stanza 3.—The time for this must be neither too early in the morning nor too advanced in the midday. It must be done when the Sun is bright and pleasing.

प्रश्नानुष्ठानसम्भारसम्भृतौ प्रक्तु भस्मनः ।
आनीतिर्मृतिदा तस्य दीपस्य तु शुभप्रदा ॥४॥

Stanza 4.—Of the accessories used for Prasna or query, if sacred ashes are first brought inadvertently, then it forebodes evil. If a lighted lamp is taken to the Prasna-room, it denotes general welfare and God's blessing.

SIGNIFICANCE OF THE LAMP

सर्वप्रश्नेषु सर्वेषु कर्मस्वपि विशेषतः ।
प्रसादेनैव दीपस्य भविष्यच्छुभमादिशेत् ॥५॥

Stanza 5.—In all prasnas, why in all karmas, the lamp plays a prominent part, a messenger of the future. If the flame is pleasant and bright, it forebodes good

वामावर्तो मलिनकिरणः संस्फुलिङ्गोल्पमूर्तिः
क्षिप्रं नाशं व्रजति विमलस्नेहवर्त्यन्वितोपि ।
दीपः पापं कथयति फलं शब्दवान् वेपथुश्च
व्याकीर्णार्च्चिर्विमलमसकृद्यश्च नाशं प्रयाति ॥६॥

Stanza 6.—If the flame of the lamp (used in the Prasna) moves in an anti-clockwise direction, if it is not bright, if it frequently emits sparks, if it is too small in shape, if it is suddenly put out though there is good oil and sufficient wick, if it is extinguished in spite of repeated efforts to light it, if it is found broken in two halves, if it makes 'cracking sounds' and if it shakes to and fro though there is no adverse wind, then prognosticate 'evil'.

दीपः संहतमूर्तिरायततनुर्निर्वेपथुर्दीप्तिमान्
निश्शब्दो रुचिरः प्रदक्षिणगतिर्वैडूर्यहेमद्युतिः ।
लक्ष्मीं क्षिप्रमभिव्यनक्ति रुचिरां यश्चोच्छिखो दृश्यते
शेषं लक्षणमग्निलक्षणसमं योज्यं यथा युक्तितः ॥७॥

Stanza 7.—If the flame is fairly dense and long in appearance, if it moves only in a clockwise way, if it is steady and bright, if it produces no sound, if it is beautiful to look at, if it is golden or jewel-like in hue and if it burns straight without being bent, then predict prosperity and success.

स्नेहो यस्येह देहो भवति तदुदरे वर्तिनी वर्तिरात्मा
ज्वाला चायुस्तदीये विमलमलिनते सौख्यदुःखे क्रमेण ।
पात्रं गेहं समीरो मृदुपरुषगुणो बन्धुशत्रुस्वरूपः
प्रष्टुः प्रायेण वृत्तं पिशुनयति महादेवतात्मा स दीपः
॥८॥

Stanza 8.—The oil in the lamp represents the physical body; the wick, soul; the flame, longevity; its brightness and dimness, happiness and misery; the can, its size and shape, the house; and the wind, relatives and friends. The lamp symbolising divinity indicates the future.

NOTES

Light is the basis of all divinity in the Universe. It is said to foretell clearly the present and the future events of man. Oil in the lamp is equivalent to the physical body of a person. Its quality and quantity determine the physical and mental features of a man. It is said that the quantity of the oil, its purity, its clearness, its density and everything that is found in it, its temperature, colour, etc., all these can be skilfully applied to the physical and mental qualities of the questioner. If the quantity is small, divine that the questioner also is weak in blood ; if the temperature of the oil is high, say that he is suffering from fever or worried in mind. If many things are found floating in the oil, then say that he is suffering from worms. The wick that burns can be considered as the soul of the person. If the wick is dirty, then say he is not sharp in intellect. If two wicks are found to be intertwined say his Prana, Apana and other vayus are not working in order and hence ill-health and mental troubles. The flame of the lamp is ' life '. Its size determines longevity. If it is bright, he is happy, and if it is dim, he is afflicted.

The can that contains the oil is the house of the questioner. If it is fair in size or neat in shape, say he is in a spacious and neat house. If you happen to shift the lighted lamp from its original position, then predict that the questioner will change his house. If a gentle breeze blows against the light, say that he has bosom friends to help him. If an adverse wind blows, say he has innumerable enemies. In this way this idea can be expanded intelligently by astrologers.

In this connection, reference may be made to *Dasadhyayi* an annotation of Varaha Mihira's *Brihat Jataka*, Sloka 18 Chapter V. Here ' sneha ' is considered as happiness or misery of a person. The wick is considered the physical body, the flame is compared to the soul. Accordingly some change the reading and say that the wick represents longevity and the flame, soul.

The significance of a lamp in Prasna, so elaborately dealt with by the author, may have to be ignored in modern times, in view of the fact that oil lamps are today conspicuous by their absence electric lights having taken their place.

पूर्वाभिप्रेतदात्री शिखिनि शिखिभयं दक्षिणे प्राणहानि-
र्नैरुत्यां विस्मृतिः स्याद्वरुणदिशि शिखा शान्तिदा
वायुकोणे ।
शून्या मृत्युश्चयी स्याद्धनददिशि शिखा शं विधत्ते
शिवाख्ये
वह्नेरूर्ध्वा शिखैषा वितरति वपुषोभीष्टवस्तूनि सद्यः ॥९॥

Stanza 9.—If the flame burns towards the east, then it foretells prosperity; if the flame is found towards the south-east, predict 'fear from fire'; if it is towards the south, say 'death'; if it is south-west 'diseases like epilepsy or apoplexy or sudden fits'; if it is towards west, say 'improvement' or peace; if it is towards the north-west, predict 'poverty and decline'; if it is towards the north, predict 'he has just overcome a great danger or death'; if it is north-east, conclude 'general good health'. If the flame blazes vertically, state that success and gains will attend the questioner's efforts.

NOTES

In all these, the astrologer should carefully divine the situation, environment and context and apply the *lakshanas* above mentioned.

प्रश्नार्थमापादितपत्रपुर्वान् छित्वा च भित्वा
गुळिकस्थराशौ ।
प्रष्टृष्टमर्क्षे यदि निक्षिपेच्चेत्सद्यो मृतिः स्यान्न तु
जीवदृष्टे ॥१०॥

Stanza 10.—If any of the articles brought while putting a query are placed on that side or Dik occupied by Gulika or that side indicated in the Rasis as the 8th Rasi from Arudha or from the Janma Rasi of the questioner, then the questioner will meet with an early death, if it is not aspected by Jupiter.

NOTES

Usually when putting questions, the custom is to bring such articles as flowers, betel leaves, sandalwood sticks, etc. The placement of these articles in a particular direction or quarter with reference to Gulika or Arudha or Janma Rasi of the querist seems to have its own significance in determining the outcome of a query. Jupiter's aspect will avert the crisis. For purposes of this stanza, the different directions are denoted thus: Aries and Taurus—east; Gemini—south-east; Cancer and Leo—south; Virgo—

south-west ; Libra and Scorpio—west ; Sagittarius—north-west ; Capricorn and Aquarius—north ; and Pisces—north-east. Suppose, at the time of the query, Gulika is in Gemini (south-east) and the articles are placed on the south-east side. It means that questioner may die unless Jupiter aspects the sign.

Drawing the Circle or Chart

शुद्धतण्डुलसम्पूर्णप्रस्थदीपाद्यलंकृते ।
समे सुमृष्टसंसिक्ते चक्रं लिखतु भूतले ॥११॥

Stanza 11.—Draw a diagram on an even and clean spot, made pure and tidy, and covered by a layer of raw rice and adorned with a lamp and flowers and other ornaments.

NOTES

Chakra here refers to the zodiacal diagram. It should be drawn on an even and clean spot covered with rice and adorned with flowers, etc.

Meena *Pisces*	Mesha *Aries*	Vrishabha *Taurus*	Mithuna *Gemini*
Kumbha *Aquarius*	PADMA *LOTUS*		Kataka *Cancer*
Makara *Capricorn*			Simha *Leo*
Dhanus *Sagittarius*	Vrischika *Scorpio*	Thula *Libra*	Kanya *Virgo*

After drawing the diagram, Puja has to be offered to the Padma (the central portion). The gold piece has to be put in one of these parts, to be detailed later. Stanza 12 gives measurements of the Chakra.

हस्तप्रमाणे चतुरश्रखण्डे षडङ्गुलांशैर्विभजेद्दळानि ।
चतुर्दळं पद्ममिहास्तु मध्ये चतुर्भिरन्यान्यजपूर्वभानि
॥१२॥

Stanza 12.—Draw the Chakra or figure on the ground aforesaid measuring 24 angulas square. Divide it into 16 equal parts of 6 angulas each. Then you will get at the centre a 'Lotus' with four petals. The remaining 12 parts will constitute the 12 signs of the zodiac beginning with Aries.

केचिन्निन्दन्ति दैवज्ञा भस्मना चक्रलेखनम् ।
तथापि तत्र भस्मैव गृहणन्ति बहवोधुना ॥१३॥

Stanza 13.—Some astrologers condemn the use of sacred ashes (bhasma) for drawing this Chakra. Still many make use of it nowadays.

प्रदक्षिणतया कार्यं राशिचक्रविलेखनम् ।
अनुलोमविलोमेन लेखने विघ्नसम्भवः ॥१४॥

Stanza 14.—This Chakra should be drawn clockwise. Many obstacles are indicated, if it is drawn first in the anti-clockwise manner and then in the opposite direction.

NATURE OF THE CHART

स्थूलरेखा सुखकरी सूक्ष्मा दुःखप्रदायिनी ।
रेखाच्छेदो भवेत् प्रष्टुः सुखकार्यविघातकः ॥१५॥

Stanza 15.—Bold lines indicate prosperity. Indistinct lines indicate misery and affliction. Broken lines show that obstacles are ahead both for happiness and work

HOW THE PRIEST DRAWS THE CHAKRA

लिखिता सौम्यरेखा प्राग्यदि नूनं धनागमः ।
वारुणी यदि रोगाप्तिरैन्द्रो चेत्सन्ततिर्भवेत् ॥१६॥
याम्यरेखा यदि भवेन्मरणायैव पृच्छताम् ॥१७॥

Stanzas 16 and 17.—If it so happens that the northern line is drawn first, then the questioner may be told that he will have monetary gains. If the western line is drawn, then diseases will increase. If the eastern line is drawn, 'birth of children' can be told. If the southern line is drawn first, death can be foretold.

NOTES

Generally the Chakra is drawn by the temple-priest and not the astrologer. Therefore, the mode of drawing of the diagram is to be interpreted by the astrologer.

चक्रस्य यत्र निम्नत्वमौन्नत्यं वापि दृश्यते ।
प्रष्टुर्निवासभूमिश्च तत्र तत्र नतोन्नता ॥१८॥

Stanza 18.—If any portion of the Chakra is found to be a little raised, then the astrologer should predict that in the house and compound of the questioner there is a spot, which is elevated; if there is any depression anywhere in the Chakra, there is a deep pit in his compound or house.

NOTES

The astrologer must intepret the Rasi Chakra as the house and compound of the questioner.

चक्रे यत्र तृणानि तत्र तरवस्तत्रांबुसिक्ते जलं
ग्रावा यत्र शिलेह यत्र सिकतास्तत्र स्थलं चोन्नतम् ।
केरा वा खलु नालिकेरसदृशाकाराः परे भूरुहो
वल्मीकोत्र पिपीलिकाहृतमृदो यत्र क्षितौ पृच्छताम्
॥१९॥

Stanza 19.—If anywhere in the Chakra, pieces of grass are found scattered, then deduce there are trees on that side in the compound of the querist. If the Chakra is found wet anywhere, say there are ponds and wells. If you discover a piece of stone, then say there are rocky spots. If you note small particles of sand, then conclude that certain portions of the compound are elevated or cocoanut or some other trees of the kind are there. If you find wet mud anywhere sprinkled by ants in the Chakra, state that there will be ant-hill in the compound of the questioner.

NOTES

In these 9 slokas, the author deals with 'Lekhaka Sparsa Lakshanam', *i.e.*, effects of the touch and posture of the man who draws the Chakra.

संस्पर्शनाद्यैरपि चक्रकर्तुः प्रष्टुः क्षितेर्लक्ष्म विचारणीयम् ।
विलिख्य चक्रं प्रददाति किञ्चिद्द्रव्यं परस्मै यदि
भूमिरेषा ॥२०॥
परस्वतामेष्यति यत्परस्मादादानमन्यक्षितिलाभशंसि ।
यद्युद्धरेत्स्वाभिमुखं प्रसार्य हस्तं नगाः स्युर्यदि सांगुलीयः
॥२१॥
करः स वल्लीपरिवेष्टिताङ्गा ग्रीवा विभूषालभनेपि तद्वत् ।
शाखाविहीनास्तरवोङ्गुलीनामाकुञ्चने स्थाणव एव
मुष्टौ ॥२२॥

Stanzas 20 to 22.—After finishing the Chakra, if he gives away anything to anyone, then conclude that the property of the questioner will be soon sold away. If he takes anything from anybody, then he will gain fresh landed property. If he raises his hand up, then think that there are trees in the lands of the questioner. If he wears rings in his raised fingers or touches his necklace, then say there are creepers in the trees; if he raises his palms with the fingers folded, then say that the trees are without branches; if he clenches his fist, then say there are more stumps of trees. If he feels the hair in his face, then say there are trees with thorns. If he feels his nostrils or earholes, then say there are rat-holes and snake-holes in his gardens.

BEHAVIOUR OF THE AGENT

मुखरोमार्द्धच्छिन्नं स्पृशेद्यदि वदेत्सकण्टकान् वृक्षान् ।
नासाश्रवसो रन्ध्रस्पर्शे तु विलं भुजङ्गमाखूनाम् ॥२३॥

केशान् विश्लथितांश्च रोन सुखजं यद्वा स्पृशेन्निर्दिशे-
न्मुञ्जोशीरकुशादिकानपि नसो वल्मीकमामर्शने ।
मेढ्रक्रोडदशां कुचास्यविलयोश्चामर्शनेन्तर्जलं
प्रष्टुर्वास्त्वनिशोद्यदम्बु कथयेत् स्विन्नाङ्गसंस्पर्शने ॥२४॥

Stanzas 23 and 24.—If he touches his dishevelled locks or hair on the head or moustache, then state there are *kusa* and other kinds of grass. If he touches his nose, you will find ant-holes. If he however feels his stomach, privities, eyes, mouth and breast, then say there is plenty of water in his gardens. If he happens to touch any of the perspiring parts of his body, you will find his lands to be very fertile with water flowing through always.

कक्षापानस्पर्शने वारि दुष्टं बाहून्नत्यां भूरुहोतीव दीर्घाः ।
हस्तानत्यां तत्र वृक्षोतिखर्वो लोहानि स्युः स्पर्शने
दन्तनखानाम् ॥२५॥

Stanza 25.—If he places his hands in his armpit or anus, then the water in his gardens will be very bad. If he raises his arms too high, there are very tall trees; if he lowers his hands very low, the trees are stunted ones. If he feels his teeth or nails, then metal ores (mineral wealth) can be discovered in his gardens.

जान्वादिकेऽङ्गेऽस्थियुते स्पृशेच्चेत् पाषाणजालैर्निचिता-
स्थिमिश्र ।
नाभ्यादिनिम्नावयवाभिमर्शे श्वभ्रान्विता पृच्छकभूः
सकुल्या ॥२६॥

स्वपृष्ठभागस्थनतप्रदेशस्पर्शेन कुल्यां प्रवदेन्नदीं वा ।
रहस्यलक्ष्मेत्यथ तत्प्रसङ्गाद्दूताश्रयं किञ्चन लक्ष्म
वक्ष्ये ॥२७॥

Stanzas 26 and 27.—If he touches his knee-cap and other bony spots in his body, then many stones and bones can be found in his compound. If he touches his navel or any other depressed limb, then many pits and ponds can be seen in his gardens. There will be rivers or small streamlets in his gardens if he touches the ridge of his back. We shall now deal with other secrets pertaining to the messenger.

दृश्यन्ते दिशि यत्र यत्र मनुजा दूतस्य विष्वक्स्थिता
दिक्ष्वास्वासु गृहाणि सन्ति सदृशां जात्या च तैः
संख्यया ।
आयानेन धनुष्मतोत्र हरिति स्थानं च शास्तुर्वदे-
द्व्यास्तद्दिशि योषितः कुपृथुकायाने पिशाचस्थितिः
॥२८॥

Stanza 28.—The astrologer must carefully mark the other persons, if any, accompanying the messenger, at the time of invitation. He should ascertain the nature of the people and state that the questioner has houses all around his home inhabited by people similar in occupation and caste to the persons already noted. If at the time of first invitation a bowman turns up, say that there is a temple in that direction of the questioner's house where God Sasta is worshipped. If a woman turns up, predict that there is a temple dedicated to Goddess Lakshmi or Durga in that direction of house. If dirty boys turn up, then predict that evil spirits live near.

विप्रायाने ब्रह्मरक्षोनिवासश्चोरोत्थापद्दुर्मतेरागमेन ।
दूतस्यैतत्सम्भवेद्यद्दिशायां प्रष्टुर्द्धाम्नस्तत्फलं तद्दिशि
स्यात् ॥ इति ॥२९॥

Stanza 29.—If a Brahmin turns up, say that a Brahma Rakshasa resides in that direction of his house. If a wicked man happens to come, then say that the questioner is molested by thieves and robbers.

NOTES

All these lakshanas can be applied to Prasna time and first invitation time.

चक्रं विलिख्य चरणौ प्रक्षाल्य तनुशोधनम् ।
आत्मपूजां गणेशार्चामपि कृत्वा महेश्वरम् ॥३०॥

चक्रमध्यस्थिते पद्मे पीठपूजापुरस्सरम् ।
परिवारनिवेद्याढ्यंपञ्चाक्षर्याभमर्चयेत् ॥३१॥

Stanzas 30 and 31.—After the Chakra is drawn, the astrologer should wash his feet, sanctify his body with Vedic mantras, worship the Atman and Lord Ganesa. Thereafter he should worship Lord Maheswara with Panchakshari Mantra in the lotus at the centre of the Chakra after the preliminary worship, and keep ready the offerings to be made to the subsidiary Deities.

INVOCATION TO THE LORD

कैलासाध्रीशकोणे सुरविटपितटे स्फाटिके मण्डपे स-
न्मातङ्गारातिपीठोपरि परिलसितं सेव्यमानं सुरौघैः ।
जानुस्थं वामबाहुं मृगमपि परशुं ज्ञानमुद्रां वहन्तं
नागोद्यद्योगवेष्टं ददतमृषिगणे ज्ञानमीशानमीडे ॥३२॥

Stanza 32.—The Lord's meditation is as follows:—"I invoke the Lord who is gracefully seated on the grand throne placed on a crystal platform at the foot of a celestial tree in a quiet place on the Great Mount Kailasa, who is attended upon by the entire host of Gods, whose left hand is placed on his knee, who holds a deer, axe and the symbol of knowledge, whose body is gist up with the yogic bands in the form of snakes and who teaches the Supreme Knowledge to the group of Sages."

WOSHIPPING THE PLANETS

मेषाद्या राशयः स्वस्वस्थाने स्वाश्रितभे ग्रहाः ।
परिवारतया पूज्या गुळिकश्च स्वनामभिः ॥३३॥
ब्रह्मार्पणान्ते वाग्देवीं गुरुंश्चाप्यष्टमङ्गले ।
पुष्पैराराध्य वन्देत् प्रदीपे च तथा श्रियम् ॥३४॥

Stanzas 33 and 34.—Aries and other signs, the planets posited in different signs and Gulika should be worshipped with thier names as sobordinate Deities. At the end of the worship he should adore Saraswati and Guru in the auspicious objects kept by the side of the Chakra and worship Lakshmi in the lamp.

NOTES

Stanza 32 is to be recited as Dhyana Mantra for worshipping Lord Maheswara.

PLACING THE GOLD PIECE

अथ प्रक्षाळ्य तोयेन स्वर्णं चन्दनभूषितम् ।
पत्रे विन्यस्य कुसुमैरक्षतैरपि योजयेत् ॥३५॥

Stanza 35.—After this puja, take a piece of of gold, wash and place it in a basin or in a plantain leaf. Apply sandal paste and cover it with some flowers, coloured rice, etc

वामहस्ते निधायाथ पिधायान्येन पाणिना ।
पञ्चाक्षरीं साष्टशतं मनूनन्यांश्च भक्तितः ॥३६॥

Stanza 36.—Keep it in the left hand and covering it with the right hand, repeat with devotion the Panchakshari Mantra 108 times.

जप्त्वाथैकत्र विन्यस्य प्रारभेताष्टमङ्गलम् ।
संक्षेपेणाथ तत्कर्म कथ्यते गुरुणोदितम् ॥३७॥

Stanza 37.—Then the Ashtamangala Kriya is solemnly begun. The details are given below as advised to me by my Guru.

कृत्वा दक्षिणतो राशिचक्रं प्राङ्मुख आसने ।
आसीनः फलकेभिन्ने वराटीस्साष्टकं शतम् ॥३८॥

Stanza 38.—Sit on the left side of the Chakra facing east. Sit on a neat place. Place before you a plank of wood to the north of the Chakra. Take 108 cowries and place them on the plank.

विधाय मन्त्रवत्प्रोक्ष्य गन्धपुष्पाक्षतैश्च ताः ।
अलंकृत्यार्चयेत्तासु शिवमावाह्य चक्रवत् ॥३९॥

Stanza 39.—Sprinkle them with holy waters and cover them with sandal paste, flowers, etc Then worship Siva in them as before.

प्रागाद्याशासु सूर्यारार्येज्ञाच्छार्किविधूरगान् ।
अपि संपूज्य ताः स्पृष्ट्वा स्पृष्ट्वा साष्टशतं जपेत् ॥४०॥
पञ्चाक्षरीं मनूनन्यानपि गुर्वाननाच्छ्रुतान् ।
ततः संप्रार्थयेदेवं गुरूनपि निजान् ग्रहान् ॥४१॥

Stanzas 40 and 41.—You should then do the navagraha puja invoking the Sun in the east, Mars in the south-east, Jupiter in the south, Mercury in the south-west, Venus in the west, Saturn in the north-west, Moon in the north and Rahu in the north-east, and repeat the Mantra 108 times.

NOTES

Repeat Panchakshari and other mantras derived from Guru and invoke the Guru and the nine planets.

SANKALPA

एतन्नक्षत्रसंजातस्यैतन्नाम्नोस्य पृच्छतः ।
भूते च वर्तमाने च समये च भविष्यति ॥४२॥

शुभाशुभानि चेदानीं चिन्तितस्य विशेषतः ।
सम्भवासम्भवाद्यन्यान्यर्थपुत्रगृहादिषु ॥४३॥
शुभाशुभानि यान्येतान्यखिलान्यपि तत्वतः ।
युष्मत्प्रसादतः स्पष्टं मम चित्ते स्फुरन्त्विवति ॥४४॥

Stanza 42, 43 and 44.—May it occur to me through your grace to find out the real truth, good and bad, regarding the person born in such and such a nakshatra and bearing such and such a name, and happenings about him in the past, present and the future in respect of money, children and house affairs.

ASHTAMANGALAM

ततः कन्याकुमारो वा स्नात्वा वस्त्राद्यलंकृतः ।
राशिग्रहस्थितिज्ञानशून्यो वा कश्चनापरः ॥४५॥
उपेत्याराधयेत् पुष्पैर्दीपविघ्नखगेश्वरान् ।
ततोस्य दक्षिणे हस्ते स्वर्णं साक्षतपुष्पकम् ॥४६॥
दद्यादेतद्वहन् सोपि कृत्वा चक्रप्रदक्षिणम् ।
पश्चात्समीपतस्तिष्ठेच्चक्रस्य प्राङ्मुखः सुधीः ॥४७॥
ततः प्रष्टा निजाभीष्टं ध्यायंस्तिष्ठतु साञ्जलिः ।
दैवज्ञोथ स्मरन् प्रष्टुरभीष्टं ता वराटिकाः ॥४८॥

संस्पृशन् संस्पृशन् मन्त्रं मूर्तित्वेपूर्वकं जपेत् ।
त्रिवारं तज्जपस्यान्ते दूतं ब्रूयान्न्यसेरिति ॥४९॥

तदैव विन्यसेद्दूतः स्वर्णं निजकरस्थितम् ।
चक्रस्थभेषु चैकत्र दैवज्ञस्ता वराटिकाः ॥५०॥

Stanzas 45 to 50.—Then call the girl or boy not conversant with astrology who has just bathed and is well-dressed. He or she should worship the lamp, Ganesa and the planets with flowers. The astrologer should then place the gold piece along with flowers, etc., in the right hand. He or she should then go round the Chakra and then stand near it facing the east. in the meanwhile the questioner should be meditating on God. Then the astrologer reflecting on the problem of the querist should touch the cowries repeating the mantras thrice and at the end ask the boy or girl to place the gold piece in any one of the signs.

Determining the Arudha Rasi

विभजेत्तिरुदक्पूर्वं निमित्तानि च चिन्तयेत् ।
प्राक्पृच्छासमये यद्यच्छुभाशुभमुदीरितम् ॥५१॥

तत्तत्सकलमत्रापि चिन्त्यं स्पर्शशरादिकम् ।
अथ दूतः पदच्छायामानं कुर्यात्समक्षितौ ॥५२॥
यस्मिन् राशौ स्थितं स्वर्णं स स्यादारूढसंज्ञकः ।
ज्ञात्वा दैवविदारूढं स्वर्णस्योत्तानतादि च ॥५३॥

Stanzas 51 to 53.—Then the astrologer should divide the cowries which he has before him into three groups, placing one on the left hand side, another in front of him and the last one on his right hand side. The omens also should be taken into consideration. Note this time also. The nature of the breath too is to be noted. Then one may be asked to go out and measure the Sun's shadow. That Rasi where the gold piece is deposited by the boy or girl is known as the Arudha Rasi. The astrologer should carefully observe the lay of the gold piece amidst the flowers in the Chakra and point out some effects from its position.

पृच्छकाय फलं किञ्चित्प्रोच्य पूजां समाप्य च ।
वराटीरष्टशस्त्यक्त्वा स्थानत्रितयतः पृथक् ॥५४॥
शिष्टसंख्यामपि ज्ञात्वा रक्षणीया वराटिकाः ॥५५॥

Stanzas 54 and 55.—After finishing the worship the astrologer should give the predictions.

He should solemnly take the cowries kept in three places one after another. Count each separately and expunge all multiples of 8 and keep the remainder. This forms the third digit, second digit and the unit (respectively) of a number he is making.

NOTES

The remainder in the left hand is 'hundred', in front ten and on the right hand side one unit. Thus a number containing three digits is obtained. This number is technically termed the Ashtamangala Number. Some more details on the results that can be gleaned from the lay of the gold coin are dealt with in stanzas 32 to 36 of Chapter VIII.

THINGS TO BE NOTED

आरूढं स्वर्णसंस्थानं छायामप्यष्टमङ्गलम् ।
विलिखेन्मासयाताहःप्रष्टृतारापुरस्सरम् ॥५६॥

यदत्र कथितं कर्म चक्रलेखनपूर्वकम् ।
संक्षेपेण तदेवाथ पुनरप्युच्यते क्रमात् ॥५७॥

Stanzas 56 and 57.—Note carefully the Arudha, the lay of the gold piece, the shadow of the Sun measured in feet,[ashtamangala number, deepa lakshana and other lakshanas perceived at the time. The nature and number of the betel leaves, year, month, date, week-day, the name of the questioner, his house name, his nakshatra and sankalpa (object of the Prasna) must also be noted.

CONCLUSION

विलिख्य चक्रं प्रविकीर्य चाक्षतं
संपूज्य भक्त्याथ कृतेष्टमङ्गले ।
आराध्य राशिं कनकेन संस्पृशेत्
प्रष्टा वराटिर्विभजेच्च दैववित् ॥५८॥
रक्तानि कुसुमान्यत्र गृह्यन्ते कैश्चनापरैः ।
शुक्लानि दृश्यते प्रायेणाद्य तुम्बाभीधार्तवम् ॥५९॥

Stanzas 58 and 59.--Draw a chakra and scatter coloured rice over it. Perform the puja with devotion. Worship the cowries for ashtamangala. See that a piece of gold is asked to be deposited in one of the squares of the chakra and find out the ashtamangala number. For puja purposes, white flowers (especially tumbe) alone should be used.

NOTES

In these stanzas, the author recapitulates what he has already treated of in this chapter.

॥ इति प्रश्नमार्गे चतुर्थोऽध्यायः ॥

पञ्चमोऽध्यायः

TIME OF QUERY

प्रश्नकालविलग्नस्य स्फुटावगमने सति ।

फलादेशस्य साफल्यं तथा शास्त्रान्तरोदितम् ॥१॥

Stanza 1.—Without knowing correctly the exact rising sign at the time of a question, no prediction is possible. This point has been repeatedly explained in treatises on this subject.

तन्त्रे सुपरिज्ञाते लग्ने छायांबुयन्त्रसंविदिते ।

होरार्थे च सुरूढे नादेष्टुर्भारती वन्ध्या ॥इति॥२॥

Stanza 2.—The astrologer's statement can never be fruitless if he has studied well the astronomical and astrological treatises and if he has correctly calculated the Lagna through the shadow, water appliances, etc.

CALCULATION OF LAGNA

छायां तत्कालजां न्यस्य त्यक्त्वा वाक्यं तदूर्ध्वगम् ।

तच्छेषमङ्गुलीकृत्य षष्ठ्या हत्वा विभाजयेत् ॥३॥

तत्कालांघ्रिप्रभापा श्र्ववाक्ययुग्मान्तरांगुलैः ।
लब्धा विनाडिकास्त्यक्तवाक्यनाड्याः परित्यजेत् ॥४॥

लभ्यन्तेह्नस्तदा याता नाडिकाश्च विनाडिकाः ।
ततस्तत्कालसूर्यस्य गम्यलिप्तांशकान् हरेत् ॥५॥

अर्कयुक्तर्क्षहारेण लभ्यतेर्कोदयात् परम् ।
नाड्यादिकं हि तद्राशेरेतद्दिनगतात्त्यजेत् ॥६॥

ऊर्ध्वराशिप्रमाणानि त्याज्यान्यपि ततस्त्यजेत् ।
शेषं तद्राशिहारघ्नं लग्नं स्याद्गतराशियुक् ॥७॥

Stanzas 3 to 7.—The length of the shadow at the time of query should be noted down and from that the *vakya* for the next stage should be deducted. The balance should be converted into inches (angulas) and multiplied by 60. The product should be divided by the difference in inches between that vakya and the following vakya taken in inches. The quotient will be the *ghatikas* and *vighatikas* past in the day. Then from the position of the Sun at that instant, find out the balance in degrees of the sign ; multiply this by the multiplier (Rasi gunaka) of the sign occupied by the Sun, when the balance of the sign remaining after sunrise will be got. Deduct this from the number of ghatikas-vigatikas past in the day and also the durations of the following signs till a balance is left over. Multiply the balance by 30 degrees and divide by the duration of the sign which is not covered. This will give the degrees past in the particular sign, to which prefix the number denoting the past signs. This will be the Lagna

NOTES

The author shows how the Ascendant may be determined by noting the length of the shadow at the time of the question. This was the standard method until almost a few decades back for determining the Ascendant.

Briefly, a circle is described on a level floor. The gnomon (a rod of 12 digits meant specifically for this purpose) is placed vertical at the centre of the circle. The length of the shadow of the gnomon at the time of question is noted and from this the Lagna for the instant in question calculated.

Vakyas are astronomical formulas given in terse Sanskrit sutras. Thier use and application require diligent study under a competent teacher.

For example, there are 248 vakyas for the Moon giving its anomalies which enable one to find the geocentric longitude of the Moon at sunrise on any day. These are called lunar vakyas. These vakyas or formulae are very much in use even today in certain parts of Kerala for the determination of the position of the Moon, nakshatra and tithi on any particular day, The difference (as alluded to in stanzas 3 to 7) between 2 consecutive vakyas gives the orbital velocity of that particular planet at sunset. The difference of two alternate vakyas divided by two gives the orbital velocity at sunrise.

The method prescribed by the author is both impractical as well as impossible in present times. There are standard ephemerides available with which the Ascendant for the time of query can be determined with greater ease and better accuracy.

CORRECTION BY KUNDA

कुन्दनिघ्ने पृथग्लग्ने प्रष्टृतारा न चेद्भवेत् ।

क्षिप्त्वा काश्चित्कलास्त्यक्त्वा वानेयं प्रष्टृजन्मभम् ॥७॥

Stanza 8.—Having arrived at correct Lagna Sphuta, multiply this by 81 (Kunda). Expunge all multiples of 12. From the remainder, find out the Nakshatra. If this Nakshatra happens to be the constellation of the questioner, or its trines, then be sure that this Lagna is accurate. If it is not Janma or Anujanma Nakshatra, add or subtract some minutes and shift the Lagna in such a manner as to have the asterism (Janma or Anujanma) of the questioner.

ऊर्ध्वासन्ने क्षिपेत्त्याज्या अधश्चेत्पृच्छकोड्डनि ।

स्वर्णं दशदशैकैकनक्षत्रस्येह लिप्तिकाः ॥९॥

Stanza 9.—Add to the Lagna or subtract from it 10 minutes of arc for each asterism. If the asterism of the questioner is Aswini and Kundagata Sphuta as got from verse 8 is Krittika, subtract 20 minutes from the Lagna Sphuta. If the Kundagata Sphuta is Satabhisha, add 40 minutes. Adjust this change in the *dinagata* also similarly.

NOTES

Suppose the ascendant is 11° 34′ and the birth asterism is Mrigasira. Applying stanzas 8 and 9 we get Lagnasphuta (11° 34′ = 694′) × Kunda (81) = 56214. Dividing this by 12, *i.e.*, by expunging multiples of 12, the remainder is 6, which counted from Aswini gives Aridra. As the Kundagata star is Aridra and birth star given is Mrigasira, subtract 10 minutes from the Lagnasphuta. That is, the Lagna will be 11° 24′. Adjust the given time of birth accordingly.

THE MOON'S LONGITUDE

चन्द्रे परहितानीते वीरलिप्तासमन्विते ।
"कालभीमतिशोभाङ्गाये"ति कन्याझषार्कतः ॥१०॥
प्रारभ्यर्णं धनं वीणाचापार्कादृद्दग्विधुर्भवेत् ।
कोलम्बे मुरहासंख्ये चन्द्रे वीरयुतिर्मता ॥११॥
सुंभाब्देष्वथ यातेषु संयोज्यैकैकलिप्तिका ॥१२॥

Stanzas 10, 11 and 12.—To the Moon got from the Parahita system of calculation, 24 minutes should be added. To this the following figures—1, 3, 4, 5, 6, 5, 4, 3 and 1—should be applied for every 10 days, negative from 10th day of Virgo to 10th day of Sagittarius and from 10th day of Pisces to the 10th day of Gemini; so also positive from 10th day of Sagittarius to 10th day of Pisces and from 10th day of Gemini to 10th day of Virgo. This will be the Drik Ganita Moon. In the Kollam Era 825, it was the view that 24 minutes should be added to the Moon. Following has been stated in the work called *Kanthabharana* regarding bringing out the correct Drik Moon.

कोळम्बोसुकलान्तरैरयनयुक्तकालसूर्योद्भवैः
सौम्यघ्नाप्रियभाजितै रहितयुग्भास्वद्भुजाकोटितः ।
संयुक्तः शिवकेन वाक्यभिदया निघ्नो धनेशोर्हृतो
लिप्तायां खलु योजितः परहितग्लावः सदृक्चन्द्रमाः ॥
इति ॥१३॥

Stanza 13.—Find out the *asus* with the help of the function got by adding the precession relative to the Kollam year to the Sun's position for the instant. Multiply this by 17 and divide the product by 12. This will be negative or positive according to the Bhuja or Koti position of the Sayana Sun. Then 145 divided by 509 converted into minutes added to the Parahita Moon will make it equal to the Drik Chandra.

NOTES

In stanzas 10 to 13, the author gives the methods for calculating Chandra Sphuta on the basis of Parahita, a system of calculation that was in vogue in Kerala.

Though it is not necessary for the reader to bother himself with this method, I have given some clarifications based on the commentary of Sri Punasseri Nambi Neelakantha Sarma.

The word *asu* has not been specific. Perhaps it is *charasu*. While finding out the Lagna, the word ' nadika ' includes ' vinadika' also. To find out the time from the sunrise to the required instant, a method is indicated which makes use of the knowledge of the length of the shadow.

From *chaya* to *angula* it is the rule of three ; measure is by difference in inches. 60 vinadikas is the effect. The adjoining vakya is subtracted from the observed shadow and this gives the starting point. As for the vakya, it begins with *simha jagate dinape* and is given in *Jyotishastra Subodhini*. When the Sun is at the end of a sign, the process becomes intricate and for places where it is difficult to calculate, these have already been laid down. Therefore, these *vakyas* have to be framed according to the times and places. Even the method of proportion is only approximate for the shadow decreases rapidly. When greater accuracy is required recourse has to be had to " computation of shadows ". At other than junction points, the time arrived at from these can also be used. In any case, either according to the method indicated or by " shadow computation ", the time past in the day has to be arrived at. For determining the portion yet to elapse in the sign occupied by the rising Sun, recourse has to be had only to the rule of three.

After subtracting the balance (of duration) of the sign at sunrise and the following signs (their duration) from the time of question, the portion elapsed in the rising sign is got. From the rule of three, the Lagnasphuta is got. Rasi durations and divisors vary with time and place, a fact which should always be kept in view.

The word 'Vira' represents 24. *Kala seemathi sobhangaya* by figure notation represents 1, 3, 4, etc., to apply to months from 10th day of Virgo and Pisces 10th day for every 10 days. For months from Virgo 10 to Sagittarius 10 and from Pisces 10 to Gemini 10 these figures should be deducted from the Parahita Moon. For the rest of the months, they should be added. According to *Parahita Ganita* while working out the duration of the day only the *charaphala* from the Sun's Bhuja is taken into account and not *pranakalantara*. But in Drik system, Pranakalantara also is taken into account. Therefore this new correction is intended to regularise this. In this context, it may be said that this work was written at a time when the precession of equinoxes was about 20°. That is why the 10th day of Virgo and Pisces were taken. The work 'Arka' in notation refers to 10 and that was why the 10th day was taken. At present the precession is about 22° and as such **the 8th day should be taken.**

As explained above, the application of the constants, *viz.*, 1, 3, 4, 5, etc. (*vide* stanzas 10 to 13) to Parahita Moon to convert it into Drigganita Moon is related to the position of the Sun. Thus when the Sun occupies the following positions, the correction to be applied will be as follows :—

Virgo 10° to Sagittarius 10°

Virgo	10 to 20	... 1	Negative
	21 to 30	... 3	
Libra	1 to 10	... 4	
,,	11 to 20	... 5	
,,	21 to 30	... 6	
Scorpio	1 to 10	... 5	
,,	11 to 20	... 4	
,,	21 to 30	... 3	
Sagittarius	1 to 10	... 1	Positive
,,	11 to 20	... 1	
,,	21 to 30	... 3	
Capricorn	1 to 10	... 4	
,,	11 to 20	... 5	
,,	21 to 30	... 6	
Aquarius	1 to 10	... 5	
,,	11 to 20	... 4	
,,	21 to 30	... 3	
Pisces	1 to 10	... 1	
,,	11 to 20	... 3	Negative
,,	21 to 30	... 4	
Aries	0 to 10	... 5	
,,	10 to 20	... 6	
,,	21 to 30	... 5	
Taurus	0 to 10	... 4	
,,	10 to 20	... 3	
,,	21 to 30	... 1	
Gemini	0 to 10	... 1	

Gemini	11 to 20	...	3	
,,	21 to 30	....	4	
Cancer	1 to 10	...	5	
,,	11 to 20	...	6	
,,	21 to 30	...	5	Positive
Leo	1 to 10	...	4	
,,	11 to 20	...	3	
,,	21 to 30	...	1	
Virgo	0 to 10	...	3	

Suppose the Moon's position on a particular day during this year is 24° 30′ as per Parahita and the Sun is in 25° Leo which means the 25th day of the solar month Leo.

Adding 24 minutes to 24° 30′ we get 24° 54′. The Sun is in 25° of Leo. The solar date is 25th of Leo. From the table given above, when the Sun is in 20° 30′ Leo, the value to be added is 1. Therefore 24° 54′ + 1′ gives the Drigganita Moon as 24° 55′.

The word *stungo* represents 74 and by about 74 years the precession amounts to 1°. Even this is approximate. This difference will be clear from the disparity in the mean longitude of the Moon in the Drik and Parahita systems which can be detected as real or otherwise only by astronomers and astrologers.

Since accurate planetary positions based on correct observations (Drik) are now available, it is not necessary for a student of astrology to bother himself with the methods here. These methods are now obsolete.

POSITION OF GULIKA

मान्दिकालायनाढ्यार्कचरज्यां विभजेत्त्रिभिः ।
लब्धा विनाडिकास्ताभिर्हत्वा मान्दिघटीः पृथक् ॥१४॥

हरेर्नीलैर्विघटिका लब्धा स्वर्णं यथाक्रमम् ।
मान्दिनाड्यां सायनार्के मेषजूकादिसंस्थिते ॥१५॥
मान्दिनाड्यस्तदा स्पष्टास्ताभिस्तु गुळिकस्फुटम् ।
अनेतव्यं यथा लग्नं नाड्या दिवसयानया ॥१६॥

Stanzas 14, 15 and 16.—These three stanzas give the method of calculating the longitude of Gulika.

NOTES

The above three stanzas give a cumbersome method of finding out the position of Gulika on the basis of the "Charajya" of the Sun. Readers need not bother themselves with this cumbersome method.

There appears to be some confusion as to whether Gulika and Mandi are the same or they are different "planets". I shall briefly deal with the method of finding the position of Mandi.

MANDI

From Sunday onwards during daytime the position of Mandi will correspond to the rising degree at the end of 26, 22, 18, 14, 10, 6 and 2 ghatikas after sunrise ; provided the sunrise is at 6 a.m. If the length of the day is more or less than 30, these figures have to be appropriately changed. Thus for example if the length of the day is 32 ghatis on a Sunday, the sunrise being at 5–40 a.m. then Mandi's position will correspond to the rising degree at the end of 27.73 ghatis after sunrise.

During night times, the position of Mandi will correspond to the rising degree at the end of 10, 6, 2, 26, 22, 18 and 14 ghatis respectively from sunset from Sunday onwards. These figures hold good provided the duration of night is 30 ghatis. Appropriate alterations should be made if the nocturnal duration is more or less than 30 ghatis. If for instance on a Saturday, the duration of night is 34 ghatis then the position of Mandi corresponds to the rising degree at 15.86 ghatis after sunset.

GULIKA

In daytimes the lords of the first 7 parts are the seven planets reckoned from the lord of the week-day chosen in the order, the Sun, the Moon, Mars, Mercury, Jupiter, Venus and Saturn. The 8th or last portion has no lord. Therefore Gulika's position corresponds to the ascendant rising at the end of Saturn's part.

In the night the lords of the first seven portions or Muhurthas are the seven planets counted from the lord of the 5th week-day from the day chosen. Here again Saturn's Muhurtha is Gulika.

Both Mandi and Gulika are said to be Saturn's sons.

Let us find out the position of Mandi and Gulika on a Friday; during daytime, when the duration of the day is 30 ghatis and the Sun rises at 6 a.m.

Mandi : On Friday, Mandi's position corresponds to the rising degree at 6 ghatis after sunrise.

Gulika : As the duration of the day is 30 ghatis, each part is equal to $3\frac{3}{4}$ ghatis. The ruler of the first part is

Venus (lord of the week-day) and that of the second part (upto 7½ ghatis) is Saturn. Therefore Gulika's longitude corresponds to the rising degree at 7½ ghatis after sunrise.

But so far as our author is concerned, he seems to have accepted both Gulika and Mandi as the same 'planets' and consequently Gulika's position so far as this book is concerned should be obtained according to the method given for Mandi.

एवं लग्नं विधुं मान्दिमानीय विलिखेत्पृथक् ।
तेषां त्रयाणां संयोगस्त्रिस्फुटं विलिखेच्च तत् ॥१७॥

Stanza 17.—Keep the Sphutas or longitudes of the three, *viz.*, the ascendant, the Moon and Gulika separately. Then add up the three. This is called Thrisphuta.

लग्नेन्दुमान्दिसंयोगस्त्रिस्फुटं तच्च भानुयुक् ।
चतुस्फुटं राहुयुक्तमेतत्पञ्चस्फुटं भवेत् ॥१८॥

Stanza 18.—Add the Sun's Sphuta to Thrisphuta, you get Chathusphuta. By adding the Rahusphuta to Chathusphuta, you get Panchasphuta.

NOTES

The stanzas are simple and need no elucidiation. Take an example in which the longitudes or Sphutas of the Sun, the Moon, Lagna, Gulika and Rahu are : the Sun 301° 12′; the Moon 18° 29′; Lagna 43° 9′; Gulika 64° 26′; and Rahu 6° 9′.

Lagna	+	Moon	+	Gulika	=	Thrisphuta
43° 9′	+	18° 29′	+	64° 26′	=	126° 4′
Thrisphuta	+	Sun			=	Chatusphuta
126° 4′	+	301° 12′			=	67° 16′
Chatusphuta	+	Rahu			=	Panchasphuta
67° 16′	+	6° 9′			=	73° 25′

In all these cases expunge multiples of 360 degrees.

PRANA AND DEHA

लग्नेन्दूमानदानाभ्यां हत्वा मान्दिं क्षिपेद्द्वयोः ।
प्राणदेहौ क्रमात्स्यातां पुनर्मान्दिस्सुताडितः ॥१९॥

Stanza 19.—Multiply Lagnasphuta by five. Add Gulikasphuta to it, we get Pranasphuta. Multiply Chandrasphuta by 8. Add Gulika to it, we get Dehasphuta Multiply Gulikasphuta by 7. Add the Sun's Sphuta to it, we get Mrityusphuta.

NOTES

Lagnasphuta	×	5	+	Gulika	=	Pranasphuta
43° 9′	×	5	+	64° 26′	=	280° 11′
The Moon	×	8	+	Gulika	=	Dehasphuta
18° 29′	×	8	+	64° 26′	=	212° 18′
Gulika	×	7	+	The Sun	=	Mrityusphuta
64° 26′	×	7	+	301° 12′	=	32° 14′

भानुयुक्तो भवेन्मृत्युर्विलिखेत्त्रीनिमानपि ।
प्रश्नकालगता नाडिर्निरयघ्ना विभाजयेत् ।
दिवसस्य प्रमाणेन लब्धं राश्यादिकं फलम् ॥२०॥
तत्कालार्के क्षिपेदर्कः स्थिरराशिगतो यदि ।
भचतुष्कं त्यजेच्चास्माद्द्वन्द्वगो यदि योजयेत् ॥२१॥
त्यागयोगौ चरे न स्तः प्राणाप्त्यै विलिखेच्च तत् ॥२२॥

Stanzas 20 to 22.—Multiply Prasna ghatis by 120 and divide the product by the duration of the day. Add to the quotient the Sun's longitude. Call this X.

If the Sun is in a fixed sign subtract 4 signs from X. If the Sun is in a common sign, add 4 signs to X.

If the Sun is in a movable sign, no addition or deduction is needed. This is Pranasphuta.

NOTES

In stanzas 20, 21 and 22, another method for calculating Pranasphuta as given in other works is explained.

The time of question in ghatis is to be multiplied by 120 and divided by the duration of the day (in ghatis) of Prasna. To this is added the Sphuta or longitude of the Sun. From the total, four signs (120°) are subtracted if the Sun is in a fixed sign ; four signs are added if the Sun is in a common sign. No addition or subtraction is needed if the Sun is in a movable sign. The result is Pranasphuta.

Determination of Pronasphuta :

Step (*a*) Prasna ghatis × 120 = product

(*b*) $\frac{\text{Product}}{\text{duration of day}}$ = quotient

(*c*) quotient + Sun's longitude = X.

(*d*) If Sun is in fixed signs, X 4 signs = Pranasphuta

If Sun is in common signs, X + 4 signs = Pranasphuta

If Sun is in movable signs, X = Pranasphuta.

Illustration :

Suppose, Sun = 24° Gemini = 84°
Prasna *time* = 25–42 ghatis after sunrise
Duration of day = 31 ghatis.

For determining Pranasphuta :

(*a*) 25–42 × 120 = 25.7 × 120 = 3084

(*b*) $\frac{3084}{31}$ = 99.48

= 99s 14° 24′

Expunging multiples of 12, we get the quotient as 3s 14° 24′ = 104° 24′

(*c*) X = 104° 24′ 84° = 188° 24′
X = 6s 8° 24′.

Since the Sun is in a common sign,

Pranasphuta = X + 4 signs, *i.e.*, 6s 8° 24′ + 4s
= 10s 8° 24′

Pranasphuta = Aquarius 8° 24′.

In calculating the Pranasphuta etc., due to difference of opinion amongst the ancient scholars different methods are given by different authors. Therefore, we can calculate Pranasphutas as per the method given by the author himself in stanza 19 and the method given in stanzas 20 to 22 may be used for research purposes.

याता नाडीस्तिलघ्ना विभजतु दिनमानेन राश्यादि लब्धं
सूर्यार्याच्छेन्दुवारेष्वजमुखचरभान्त्येष्वसृक्ज्ञार्किवारे ।
वीणादिद्वन्द्वमध्येष्वपि धनमुदितं मृत्युलब्ध्यै विजह्यात्
स्थानेभ्यश्चोदितेभ्यस्तदिदमपि भवेत् काल एतौ लिखेच्च
॥२३॥

Stanza 23.—Mrityu and Kalasphutas are obtained thus:

Multiply Prasna ghatis by 35 and divide the product by the duration of the day. You get Y. Depending upon the week-day of the Prasna being Sunday, Monday, etc., Mrityusphuta is obtained by adding 1 sign, 10 signs, 2 signs and 15 degrees, 5 signs and 5 degrees, 4 signs, 7 signs and 8 signs and 15 degrees respectively to Y. By subtracting these figures from Y, Kalasphuta is obtained.

NOTES

The rationale of the mathematics employed is not very clear. But it is given for what it is worth. Any research-minded student can study the implications of Mrityusphuta or Kalasphuta in birth horoscopes also and come to his own conclusions.

Determination of Mrityusphuta and Kalasphuta :

Step.—(*a*) Prasna ghatis × 35 = product

(*b*) $\frac{\text{Product}}{\text{duration of day}} = Y$

(*c*) *For Mrityusphuta :*

If day of prasna is Sunday. Mrityasphuta = Y + 1 sign

If day of prasna is Monday, Mrityusphuta = Y + 10 signs

If day of prasna is Tuesday, Mrityusphuta = Y + 2 signs 15°

If day of prasna is Wednesday Mrityusphuta = Y + 5 signs 5°

If day of prasna is Thursday. Mrityusputa = Y + 4 signs

If day of prasna is Friday, Mrityusphuta = Y + 7 signs

If day of prasna is Saturday, Mrityusphuta = Y + 8 signs 15°

(*d*) *For Kalasphuta,*

If Sunday, Kalasphuta = Y – 1 sign

If Monday, Kalasphuta = Y – 10 signs

If Tuesday. Kalasphuta = Y – 2 signs 15°

If Wednesday, Kalasphuta = Y – 5 signs 5°

If Thursday, Kalasphuta = Y − 4 signs
If Friday, Kalasphuta = Y − 7 signs
If Saturday, Kalasphuta = Y − 8 signs

Illustration :

Taking the previous illustration, prasna ghatis = 25–42

Duration of day = 31 ghatis

(*a*) 25–42 gh. × 35 = 25.7 × 35 = 899.5

(*b*) $\frac{899.5}{31} = 29.01$

Expunging multiples of 12, Y = 5s 0° 18′
Suppose the week day is a Thursday, then

(*c*) Mrityusphuta = 5s 0° 18′ + 4s = 9s 0° 18′
i.e., Mrityusphuta = Capricorn 0° 18′

(*d*) Kalasphuta = 5s 0° 18′ − 4s = 1s 0° 18′
i.e., Kalasphuta = Taurus 0° 18′.

Therefore Mrityu and Kalasphutas are Capricorn 0° 18′ and Taurus 0° 18′ respectively.

सार्द्धेन नाडीद्वितयेन गच्छत्यारभ्य सूर्योदयतो दिनेशः ।
चापद्विलोमादनुलोपयामी भानोरमुष्यास्तगतः शशाङ्कः
॥२४॥

राहुर्मृगमृगारातिकर्किमेषालिजूकभे ।
कर्किकुम्भैणमेषाक्षजूकेषु प्रतिलोमतः ॥२५॥

चरत्यर्कोदयात्सार्द्धनाडीद्वितयतोन्वहम् ।
लिखेदेतानपीनेन्दुराहुचक्रमिदं स्मृतम् ॥२६॥

Stanzas 24 to 26.—It is assumed that the Sun passes through the 12 Rasis from sunrise staying 2 ghatikas and 30 vighatikas in each in a retrograde motion beginning from Sagittarius, and passing through Scorpio, Libra, etc., in that order. The Moon is always assumed to be in the 7th house from the Sun. Rahu passes through Capricorn, Leo, Cancer, Aries, Scorpio, Libra, again Cancer, Aquarius, Capricorn, Libra, Taurus and Aries staying $2\frac{1}{2}$ ghatikas in each from sunrise. This is to be known as Sun–Moon–Rahu Chakra.

NOTES

Pisces	Aries	Taurus	Gemini Moon at sunrise
Aquarius	Passage of Sun starting from Sagittarius		Cancer
Capricorn			Leo
Sagittarius Sun at sunrise	Scorpio	Libra	Virgo

Pisces	Aries 4, 12	Taurus 11	Gemini
Aquarius 8	Passage of Rahu starting from 1		Cancer 3, 7
Rahu Capricorn 1, 9			Leo 2
Sagittarius	Scorpio 5	Libra 6, 10	Virgo

Pisces	Aries	Taurus	Gemini Moon
Aquarius	Sun-Moon-Rahu Chakram at Sunrise		Cancer
Capricorn Rahu			Leo
Sagittarius Sun	Scorpio	Libra	Virgo

The use of this chakra is detailed in Chapter VIII.

THE DEATH CIRCLE

गुळिकेन्दुणीक्ष्णमहसांक्रमान्निजोदयनवांशराशिगतैः ।
प्रतिगृहचारो ज्ञेयो नवतिप्राणैस्तु वामतो गुळिकः ॥२७॥

सोर्कयुतो मृत्युकरो भयदः सेन्दुश्च मृत्युचक्रमिदम्
॥२८॥

Stanzas 27 to 28.—It is assumed that the Sun, the Moon and Gulika transit through various Rasis from their Navamsa Rasi staying 15 vighatikas in each. The Sun and the Moon travel in the usual order, while Gulika moves in retrograde motion. In this Mrityu Chakra, Gulika conjoining the Sun or the Moon causes sure death or great fear respectively.

NOTES

These two stanzas enable us to cast the Mrityu Chakra or chart of death and place the Sun, the Moon and Gulika in this chart.

This involves the determination of the "death sign" (Mrityurasi) and the longitude of the *Navamsa Rasi* of the planet concerned. The position of the planet in the chart of death is obtained by adding the Navamsa-rasi longitude to the longitude of the death Rasi.

(*a*) Convert the number of Ghatis (of birth or question) from sunrise into vighatis and divide this by 15. The quotient represents the number of degrees (from the first point of Aries) of the death Rasi. The remainder may be converted into minutes, etc.

(*b*) Multiply the longitude of the planet (devoid of the sign) by 9 and divide the product by 30. The quotient plus 1 represents the Navamsa which the planet occupies and the remainder, the longitude of the planet within this Navamsa-rasi.

(*c*) Add the longitude of the death sign to the Navamsa-rasi longitude of the Sun and the Moon and deduct the longitude of the death-sign from the Navamsa-rasi longitude of Gulika to obtain their respective positions in the Mrityu Chakra.

In the chart of death if Mrityu Gulika and the Mrityu Sun are in the same Rasi, death of the questioner is likely. If Mrityu Gulika conjoins Mrityu Chandra, the querist will be in great fear and danger. If Mrityu Gulika stands alone in a Rasi, general improvement in all matters can be predicted.

Determination of Mrityu Rasi and Mrityu Chakra

(*a*) $\dfrac{\text{Prasna ghatis from sunrise converted into vighatis}}{15} = \text{Mrityu Rasi}$

(*b*) $\dfrac{\text{Longitude of Sun (or Moon or Gulika) in sign of occupation} \times 9}{30} = \text{Quotient}$

Quotient + 1 = Navamsa occupied by Sun (or Moon or Gulika)

Remainder = longitude of Sun (or Moon or Gulika) in above Navamsa.

(*c*) Mrityu Rasi + longitude of Sun (or Moon) in Navamsa = position of Sun (or Moon) in Mrityu Chakra.

Longitude of Gulika in Navamsa − Mrityu Rasi = position of Gulika in Mrityu Chakra.

Illustration :

Suppose Prasna or birth-time = 33–53 ghatis
Sun = Cancer 24° 25′
Moon = Taurus 25° 11′
Gulika = Gemini 12° 44′

(*a*) Gh. 33–53 $= \dfrac{\text{Vigh. } 2033}{15} = 135° \, 32'$

∴ Mrityu Rasi (death sign) is Leo 15° 32′

(*b*) The Sun : (Cancer) $\dfrac{24° \, 25' \times 9}{30} = \dfrac{219° \, 45'}{30} = 7\dfrac{9° \, 45'}{30}$

Quotient + 1 (*i.e.*, 7 + 1 = 8) represents the Navamsa-rasi of the Sun—the 8th from Cancer, *viz.*, Aquarius and the Navamsa-rasi longitude is 9° 45′.

(3) The Moon : (Taurus) $\dfrac{25° \, 11' \times 9}{30} = \dfrac{226° \, 39'}{30}$

$= 7\dfrac{16° \, 39'}{30}$

The quotient 7 plus 1, *viz.*, 8, represents the Navamsa rasi and the 8th Navamsa in Taurus is Leo and the longitude of the Navamsa rasi is Leo 16° 39′.

(4) Gulika (Gemini) $\dfrac{12° \, 40' \times 9}{30} = \dfrac{114° \, 36'}{30} = 3\dfrac{24° \, 36'}{30}$

The Navamsa is the 4th (3 + 1) in Gemini, *viz.*, Capricorn and the longitude of Navamsa rasi is 24° 36′.
Therefore :

(1) Mrityu Rasi is Leo 15° 32′
(2) Navamsa-rasi of the Sun—Aquarius 9° 45′
(3) Navamsa-rasi of the Moon—Leo 16° 39′
(4) Navamsa-rasi of Gulika—Capricorn 24° 36′.

Add Mrityu Rasi to the Navamsa-Rasis of the Sun and the Moon and we get respectively the Mrityu sphutas of the Sun and the Moon. Subtract Mrityu Rasi from the Navamsa-rasi of Gulika and the Mrityu Rasi of Gulika is obtained.

(*c*) Mrityu Rasi		4s 15° 32′
Navamsa-rasi of Sun		10 9 85
Mrityu Rasi of Sun	=	2s 25° 17′
	=	Gemini 25° 17′

Likewise the Mrityu Rasis of the Moon and Gulika are :

The Moon : Capricorn 2° 11′
Gulika : Virgo 9° 4′

			Sun 25° 17′
	Mrityu Chakra		
Moon 2° 11′			
			Gulika 9° 4′

In the Mrityu Chakra, Gulika is not in conjunction with either the Moon or the Sun, and it stands alone. Therefore general improvement can be expected.

अर्केन्द्वारूढोदयभांशेशाः स्पष्टगणितशास्त्रेण ।
दृक्तुल्येनानेया ग्रहाश्च सर्वे तथैवान्ये ॥२९॥

Stanza 29.—The positions of the Sun, the Moon, Arudha Lagna, etc., should be correctly calculated through Drigganita.

PLANETARY LONGITUDES

योगे ग्रहाणां ग्रहणेर्कसोमयोर्मौढ्ये तथा वक्रगतौ च पञ्चसु ।
दृष्टानुरूपं करणं यदन्वहं तेन ग्रहेन्द्रान् गणयेत्त्रिवारम् ॥३०॥

यदा यश्चैव सिद्धान्तो गणिते दृक्समो भवेत् ।
तदा तेनैव संसाध्यं जातकं गणयेद्बुधः ॥ इति ॥३१॥

Stanzas 30 and 31.—Planetary movements and conjunctions, the solar and lunar eclipses, the setting and rising of planets, retrogression, etc., should be ascertained according to Drigganita or observational methods and worked out thrice to ensure accuracy. Thus even Siddhanta calculations will be as accurate as Drik calculations.

NOTES

In these three stanzas emphasis is laid on the need for accuracy in the calculation of the planetary movements and the other attendant phenomena.

Today accurate ephemerides giving the correct positions of planets are available and therefore there is no need for students af astrology to bother themselves with the ancient astronomical methods.

The author seems to favour Drik in prefereace to Parahita.

ARUDHA POSITION

लग्नस्फुटस्य भं त्यक्त्वा कलाभागांश्च योजयेत् ।
आरूढभे स्फुटावाप्त्या अमुष्य विलिखेच्च तत् ॥३२॥

Stanza 32.—The longitude of the ascendant (devoid of the sign) added to the Rasi or sign of the Arudha gives the Arudha Sphuta or the longitude of Arudha.

NOTES

Suppose the Lagna is Aquarius 12° 25′ and the Arudha Rasi is Virgo. Then adding the degrees in the Lagna (devoid of the sign), *viz.*, 12° 25′ to the Arudha Rasi, *viz.*, Virgo we get *Arudha Sphuta* or the exact longitude of Arudha as Virgo 12° 25′.

॥ इति प्रश्नमार्गे पञ्चमाध्यायः ॥

षष्ठाध्यायः

THE FIVE SUTRAS

आरूढोदयलग्नाभ्यां सूत्रं सामान्यसंज्ञितम् ।
तदीशाभ्यां तु यच्चिन्त्यं तत्स्यादधिपसंज्ञकम् ॥ १ ॥
लग्नांशारूढराशिभ्यां सूत्रमंशकसंज्ञितम् ।
लग्नोडुपृच्छकोडुभ्यां चिन्त्यं नक्षत्रसंज्ञितम् ॥ २ ॥
आरूढतद्दशमतो महासूत्रं विचिन्तयेत् ।
पृथ्वी सामान्यसूत्रं स्यादापस्त्वधिपसंज्ञितम् ॥ ३ ॥
तेजस्त्वंशकसूत्रं स्यादुडुसूत्रं तु मारुतः ।
आकाशस्तु महासूत्रमित्येतत्सूत्रपञ्चकम् ॥ ४ ॥

Stanzas 1 to 4.—Samanya Sutra is determined by Arudha and rising Lagna ; Adhipati Sutra is to be noted by the lords of these two signs. Amsaka Sutra is arrived at by the Lagna Navamsa and Arudha. Nakshatra Sutra is calculated by noting the Janma Nakshatra of the questioner and the asterism of the sign rising at the time of the query. Mahasutra is worked out by Arudha and the 10th from it Samanya, Adhipati, Amsaka, Nakshatra and Maha Sutras respectively are earthy, watery, fiery, and ethereal

प्राधान्येन विचिन्त्यं स्यात्पञ्चभूतात्मकत्वतः ।
आरूढोदययोर्द्वन्द्वं चरराशिगतं यदि ॥ ५ ॥
द्वन्द्व एकं स्थिरेन्यद्वा जीवसूत्रमिति द्विधा ।
आरूढोदययोरेकं चरे स्यादुदये परम् ॥ ६ ॥
द्वितयं वा स्थिरे तद्वन्मृतिसूत्रमपि द्विधा ।
चरसंस्थं तयोरेकमपरं स्थिरसंज्ञितम् ॥ ७ ॥
द्वयं वोभयराशिस्थं रोगसूत्रमपि द्विधा ।
चिन्तनेंशकसूत्रस्याप्ययं न्यायो विचिन्त्यताम् ॥ ८ ॥

Stanzas 5 to 8.—If Arudha and rising sign are both movable or if one is common and the other is fixed, it is Samanya Sutra termed Jeeva. If both of these are fixed Rasis or if one is movable and the other common, it is Mrityu Sutra. If both are common or if one is movable and the other fixed, it is Roga Sutra. The same applies to Amsaka Sutra also.

NOTES

Five kinds ot sutras have been enumerated in stanzas 1 to 4. They are Samanya, Adhipati, Amsaka, Nakshatra and Maha Sutras. The method of their determination is also given. Samanya Sutra and Amsaka Sutra come to be called Jeeva (life), Mrityu (death) and Roga (disease) by the following dispositions of Arudha and Lagna:

Jeeva	*Mrityu*	*Roga*
(1) Both movable	(1) both fixed	(1) both common
(2) One common and other fixed	(2) one movable and other common	(2) one movable and other fixed.

चरे चरस्थिर द्वंद्वास्थिरे द्वंद्वचरस्थिराः ।
द्वंद्वे स्थिरोभयचरा जीवो रोगो मृतिः क्रमात् ॥ ९ ॥

Stanza 9.—If Arudha and rising sign are both movable or one is fixed and the other common, it becomes Jeeva. If both are common or if one is movable and the other fixed, it is Roga. If both are fixed or one is common and the other movable, it is Mrityu.

NOTES

This stanza is merely a repetition of the previous one, applicable to Samanya and Amsaka Sutras.

आरूढस्य च लग्नस्य पत्योरैक्ये च सौहृदे ।
जीवसूत्रं विजानीयात्समत्वे रोगदं भवेत् ॥१०॥

तयोश्शात्रवभावे तु सूत्रं तु मरणप्रदम् ।
गणयेल्लग्ननक्षत्रादारभ्य प्रष्टृजन्मभम् ॥११॥

त्रिभिस्तां गणयेत्संख्यामेकशेषे तु जीवकृत् ।
द्विशेषे रोगदं सूत्रं निश्शेषे मरणप्रदम् ॥१२॥

Stanzas 10, 11 and 12.—If the lords of Arudha and Lagna are the same or if they be mutual friends, it is Jeeva Sutra. If they are neutral, then it is Roga Sutra. If they happen to be enemies, then it is Mrityu Sutra. Count from Udaya Lagna Nakshatra to the Janma Nakshatra of the questioner and divide it by 3. If the remainder is one, it is Jeeva Sutra; if the remainder is 2, it is Roga Sutra; if the remainder is zero, it is Mrityu Sutra.

NOTES

Here a question arises that in the Adhipati Sutra if the lords happen to be neither neutral nor friendly nor inimical, as one planet may be friendly towards another while the other planet may be only neutral, how we should proceed? The answer would be as follows :—

Friend + Friend is Jeeva
Friend + Neutral is Jeeva
Friend + Enemy is Roga
Neutral + Friend is Jeeva
Neutral + Neutral is Roga
Neutral + Enemy is Mrityu
Enemy + Friend is Roga
Enemy + Neutral is Mrityu
Enemy + Enemy is Mrityu

आरूढतद्दशमयोर्द्वितयं चन्द्रराशिगम् ।
यदि जीवनदं सूत्रं द्वयं चेत्सूर्यराशिगम् ॥१३॥

मृत्युसूत्रं तदा ज्ञेयं यदा तु पुनरेनयोः ।
एकं चान्द्रं परं सौरं रोगसूत्रं तदाभवेत् ॥१४॥

Stanzas 13 and 14.—If both Arudha Rasi and 10th from it are lunar signs, then it is Jeeva. If both are solar signs. then it is Mrityu. If one is lunar and the other solar, then it is Roga.

NOTES

Mesha, Vrishabha, Mithuna, Karkataka, Dhanus, Makara and Meena are lunar or Chandra Rasis or Nocturnal signs,

Simha, Kanya, Thula, Vrischika and the latter half of Kumbha are solar or Surya Rasis or Diurnal signs.

DIOGNOSING ILLNESS

जीवसूत्रफलं दीर्घमायू रुक्शमनादि च ।
रोगोत्पत्तिश्च रुग्दैर्घ्यं रोगसूत्रफलं मतम् ॥१५॥

मृतिसूत्रफलं मृत्युः प्रष्टुस्सम्बन्धिनामपि ।
प्रेप्सिताप्तिरपि प्रष्टुः सूत्रे जीवनदायिनि ॥१६॥
रोगदे कार्यनाशादिर्दुःखं भीरपि मृत्युदे ।
अत्र ग्रन्थान्तरं चास्ति तदैवानु विलिख्यते ॥१७॥

Stanzas 15, 16 and 17.—The effect of Jeeva Sutra is long life and recovery from sickness. Roga Sutra indicates prolongation of illness and attack from fresh diseases. The effect of Mrityu Sutra is death of the questioner's relative. In a Karya Prasna, Jeeva, Roga and Mrityu Sutras denote respectively success in undertakings, sorrow and failure in undertakings and fear.

NOTES

After ascertaining the various major sutras such as Samanya, Adhipatya, etc., and their location in the three important sub-sutras, *viz.*, Jeeva, Mrityu and Roga, results of a question have to be guaged as per stanzas 15, 16 and 17. The effects are continued further in the next sutra.

RESULTS OF SUTRAS

आयुर्वीर्यं धनमपि तथा वर्द्धते जीवसूत्रे
रुक्सूत्रं चेद्धनहतिमनोभङ्गदेहप्रपीडाः ।
भीरुग्वृद्धिर्दिनमनुमनःकर्मभङ्गोऽन्त्यसूत्रे
प्रष्टुर्वाच्यं फलमिति दृढं सर्वपृच्छासु सूत्रैः ॥१८॥

Stanza 18.—In regard to all questions Jeeva Sutra confers longevity, vitality and wealth. Roga Sutra gives loss of money, mental worry and ill-health. And Mrityu Sutra denotes increase of illness, fear, failure in undartakings and mental derangement.

सूत्रं यद्भूतसम्बन्धि मृत्युकृद्वाथ रोगकृत् ।
तद्भूतांशभवान् देहे रोगान् प्रष्टुर्विनिर्दिशेत् ॥१९॥

Stanza 19.—The nature of the diseases is to be ascertained from the Bhuta governing the Sutra. The questioner will have the disease appropriate to the Bhuta.

NOTES

If Roga Sutra is seen in Samanya, you have to say that it is caused by earth. The seat of the disease can be stated according to the lord of that Bhuta or element. Every Bhuta governs a particular part of the body.

SUTRAS AND THE BHUTAS

मांसास्थित्वक्सिरारोम पृथ्वी देहभृतां तनौ ।
स्वेदासृङ्मूत्रशुक्लास्यतोयं तोयमुदाहृतम् ॥२०॥

क्षुत्तृडालस्यनिद्राभास्तेजोङ्गचलनं मरुत् ।
द्वेषरागौ च मोहश्च साध्वसं च जरा नभः ॥२१॥

एवं हि सर्वजन्तूनां पञ्चभूतमयी तनुः ।
पञ्चोक्तान्यत्र सूत्राणि त्रीण्येवान्ये प्रचक्षते ॥२२॥

Stanzas 20, 21 and 22.—In the human body flesh, bones, skin (veins), hair are earthy. Blood, urine, sweat, saliva and seminal fluid are watery. Hunger, thirst, sleep, bodily splendour, dullness of the mind are 'fiery'. Movement or throbbing of limbs, and shaking of the body are airy. Affection, hatred, infatuation, fear, old age, these are mental qualities and are ethereal. We have described so far five sutras, but some writers deal with three sutras only.

NOTES

The earthy (bhumi), watery (jala), fiery (agni), airy (vayu) and ethereal (akasa) bhutas (primordial elements) have as their lords Mercury, Venus, Mars, Saturn and Jupiter respectively.

THE TIME FACTOR

नक्षत्राधिपसूत्रे द्वे वर्तमानफलप्रदे ।
सामान्यं भूतकालेन्ये भविष्यत्फलसूचके ॥२३॥

Stanza 23.—Nakshatra and Adhipati Sutras refer to the present. Samanya Sutra refers to the past. Amsaka and Maha Sutras refer to the future.

NOTES

This is a very important stanza enabling us to find out whether a question refers to the past, present or future.

Determination of the major sutras and their reference to the Jeeva, Mrityu or Roga Sutras clearly reveal the outcome of a query.

लग्नादापञ्चमगैरानवमस्थैश्च पञ्चमान्नवमात् ।
आलग्नगैरपि भवद्भावि च भूतं शुभाशुभं ज्ञेयम् ॥२४॥

Stanza 24.—Planets occupying the first four Bhavas indicate the present, the next four indicate the future and the remaining four indicate the past.

NOTES

Lord of Samanya Sutra is Mercury. Lord of Adhipati Sutra is Venus. Lord of Amsaka Sutra is Mars. Lord of Nakshatra Sutra is Saturn. Lord of Maha Sutra is Jupiter.

If these lords occupy the first four houses (1–4), then say that it is present. If these lords occupy the next four houses (5–8), then say it is future. If they occupy the next four (9–12), then say it is past.

THE THREE SUTRAS

सूत्राणां त्रितयस्य कीर्तितमिह प्राधान्यमन्यैः परं
तत्कण्ठाभरणे समीरितामिहाप्येतत्फलं चोच्यते ।
आरूढोदययोर्द्वयोरपि तयोः सम्बन्धि चाङ्काशयो-
रादित्यांशकयोश्च यच्च तदिहारूढस्फुटं गृह्यताम् ॥२५॥

Stanza 25.—Kanthabharana deals with three sutras only. They are Arudha Rasi and Udaya Lagna Rasi constituting Samanya Sutra ; Arudha Dwadasamsa and Udaya Lagna Dwadasamsa making up the second Sutra ; and Arudha Navamsa and Udaya Lagna Navamsa causing the third Sutra.

NOTES

We have already seen above how Arudha Sphuta has to be calculated. The degree and minutes of the Lagna Sphuta have to be added to the Arudha Rasi, to get Arudha Sphuta.

आरूढोदययोस्तयोश्च नवभागार्कांशसम्बन्धि यत्
सूत्राणां त्रितयं मृतिप्रदमिदं यद्येनयोर्नाथयोः ।
स्वस्वाङ्कांशदिवाकरांशकपती स्यातां च चेद्वैरिणौ
दोषे त्रिस्फुटदूतलक्षणदशादीनां म्रियेताप्यरुक् ॥२६॥

Stanza 26.—If these *sutras* happen to be Mrityu Sutras, if the lords of Arudha Navamsa and Arudha Dwadasamsa happen to be the enemy of the lord of Arudha ; if Thrisphuta, Duta Lakshana, Dasas and Antardasas, according to the native's horoscope happen to be bad, you have to predict that the questioner will die though healthy at present.

सूत्राणां त्रितयेत्र जीवनकरे चांशेशयोः सौहृदे
शस्ते त्रिस्फुटदूतलक्षणदशाछिद्रादिके चाखिले ।
अत्यासन्नमृतेरपीह न मृतिर्मिश्रेथ सूत्रादिके
जीवेत्कर्मभिरेव नैव सुकरं दोषेधिके जीवनम् ॥ इति ॥
॥२७॥

Stanza 27.—If these three *sutras* happen to be Jeeva, if the lords of Arudha Navamsa and Arudha Dwadasamsa happen to be friendly towards the lord of Arudha, and if the lords of Lagna Navamsa and Lagna Dwadasamsa happen to be friendly to the lord of Udaya Lagna; if Thrisphuta, Duta Lakshana (omens) and if Dasas and Antardasas of the native, according to his horoscope, happen to be good, then predict that the questioner will never die though very sick and bed-ridden. If there is a combination of Jeeva and other sutras, then there will be recovery by recourse to remedial measures.

NOTES

If some of these sutras happen to be Jeeva and some otherwise and if the lords of Arudha Navamsa and Dwadasamsa and the lord of Arudha happen to be neutral or some inimical: or Thrisphuta, Duta Lakshana and Dasas and Antardasas happen to be mixed in effects (good and bad), then predict that the sick man will recover by remedial measures.

SIGNIFICANCE OF THRISPHUTA

कुळीरभृङ्गमत्स्येषु दोषजं स्याद्यथोत्तरम् ।
तत्राप्यहीन्द्रपौष्णेषु तथैव त्रिस्फुटं भवेत् ॥२८॥

Stanza 28.—If Thrisphuta falls in Karkataka, Vrischika or Meena, it is productive of intense trouble which is greatest for Meena and least for Karkataka.

NOTES

Even in Karkataka Rasi, it is least intensive in asterism Punarvasu and most intensive in Aslesha. In Vrischika, it is least effective in Visakha and most effective in Jyeshta. In Meena, it is least intensive in Poorvabhadra and most intensive in Revati.

कर्किवृश्चिकमीनानां त्रिस्फुटं चरमांशगम् ।
मृत्युप्रदं भवेत्प्रष्टुरब्दमासदिनैः क्रमात् ॥२९॥

Stanza 29.—If the Thrisphuta falls in ths last Navamsa of Karkataka, the questioner will die in a year. If it falls in the last Navamsa of Vrischika, he will die in a month. If it falls in the last Navamsa of Meena, he will die in a day.

मेषात् केसरिणस्तथैव धनुषो भानां चतुष्कं क्रमा-
त्सृष्टिस्थानविनाशसंज्ञमजतो दस्रात्तथा भानि च ।

त्रीणि त्रीणि नवांशका भवनवन्नाशर्क्षसन्ध्याह्वये-
ष्वष्टाशीतितमांशकादिषु तथा नो शोभनं त्रिस्फुटम्
॥३०॥

Stanza 30.—The four signs beginning from Mesha, Simha and Dhanus respectively constitute the creative, protective and destructive areas. Movable, fixed and common signs and Navamsas are respectively creative, protective and destructive. If Thrisphuta falls in a destructive area, Rasi or Navamsa or Nakshatra, predict that evil alone will happen.

NOTES

Aswini is Srishti Nakshatra. Bharani ls Sthiti Nakshatra. Krittika is Samhara Nakshatra. Rohini again Srishti and so on in a cyclic order with regard to the other Nakshatras. If Thrisphuta falls in Samhara Rasi, Navamsa or Nakshatra in Riksha Sandhis (junctions of two signs) or in the 88th pada or quarter calculated from the pada of questioner's asterism at birth, or if it happens to be the 3rd or 5th or 7th asterism from this Janma Nakshatra, evil is bound to happen.

Thrisphuta Indicative of Death

कर्कटान्त्यनवभागसंश्रितं त्रिस्फुटं मरणदायि वत्सरात् ।
मासतो मधुकरान्त्यभागगं रेवतीचरमभागगं दिनात्
॥३१॥

Stanza 31.—If the Thrisphuta falls in the last Navamsa of Karkataka, the questioner will die in a year. If it falls in the last Navamsa of Vrischika he will die in a month. If it falls in the last Navamsa of Meena, he will die in a day.

NOTES

This verse conveys the same idea as stanza 29. It is repeated because of its importance. In this chapter, you will find that the author has repeated the same ideas in different verses. Most of these ideas are borrowed from other writers and repeated in order that the readers may know that they are important and dependable.

त्रिस्फुटं नवहतं निहन्त्विनैर्भं विना यदि तदृक्षसन्धिगम् ।
जन्मगं यदि च तत्त्रिकोणगं मृत्युदं भवति पृच्छतां
ध्रुवम् ॥३२॥

Stanza 32.—Multiply the Thrisphutas by 9 and drop off the Rasis. Multiply the degrees and minutes that remain by 12 and expunge all 'twelves' from the Rasi. If the result falls in Riksha Sandhis, Navamsas, or in the asterism of the questioner, he will certainly die.

त्रिस्फुटस्य भनवांशयोर्बलं यस्य तेन जनिचन्द्रसङ्गमः ।
मृत्यवेजहरिकार्मुकांशगं त्रिस्फुटं यदि महत्तरायुषे
॥३३॥

Stanza 33.—If the Thrisphuta Rasi or Navamsa Rasi, whichever is stronger, happens to be the Janma Rasi of the questioner, then also he will meet with death. If it falls in the Amsa of Mesha, Simha or Dhanus, he will live long.

संयुक्तं गुळिकेन वा यदि खरैर्नो शोभनं त्रिस्फुटं
तत्र स्यात्तदुडुद्भवो यदि निजे गेहस्य कल्प्यो गदः ।
दोषाणां नवकेन चान्वितमिदं प्रष्टुर्विपत्त्यै भवे-
त्सृष्ट्यृक्षादिगतं च सद्ग्रहयुतं दीर्घायुरारोग्यदम् ॥३४॥

Stanza 34.—If Gulika or evil planets occupy Thrisphuta Rasi, it forebodes evil. If anybody in the questioner's house is born in the Thrisphuta Nakshatra, he will fall sick. If this Thrisphuta is afflicted by Nava Doshas, then the questioner will meet with calamities. If Thrisphuta occupies creative elements or if it conjoins with good planets, then predict longevity and good health.

आद्यक्षोणिसुरागमो विधनविप्रायानमग्नेर्भयं
वासोहानिरथ क्रमात्कलहभग्नायानमह्यागमः ।
भूदेवत्रितयागमोऽथ चतुरंध्रचापच्च बन्ध्वागमो
मृत्योर्लक्षणमश्विभादिनवकत्रय्याश्रिते त्रिस्फुटे ॥३५॥

Stanza 35.—If Thrisphuta falls in Aswini and its trines, Bharani and its trines, etc , and an event of the following kind takes place on each of these days, then predict that the questioner will die. A rich and learned Brahmin visits the house; a penniless Brahmin visits the house; a conflagration takes place; loss of clothes; a man comes after being vanquished in a quarrel; a serpent is seen in the house; three Brahmins turn up at the house: destruction of cattle; and arrival of a relative.

NOTES

The death of the questioner can be predicted when Thrisphuta falls in Aswini, Makha or Moola, and on this day a rich and learned Brahmin visits the house; when the Thrisphuta falls in Bharani, Pubba or Poorvashadha, a penniless Brahmin visits the place; when the Thrisphuta falls in Krittika, Uttara and Uttarashadha and a conflagration takes place and so on in regard to other constellational groups in the order of events cited above.

यस्मिन् राशौ नवांशे वा त्रिस्फुटं तद्गते विधौ ।
त्रिकोणस्थेथवार्के वा प्रोक्तलक्षणसम्भवः ॥३६॥

Stanza 36.—These events must take place when the Sun or the Moon occupies Thrisphuta Rasi, or its Navamsa Rasi or their trines. Then only death can happen.

मूर्द्धोष्णज्वरतापकृदविरतीसारं शशिमं कुजः
स्तम्भं वाङ्मनसोः करोत्यपि बुधो दृक्पारवश्यं गुरुः ।
बुद्धिभ्रंशशरीरतोदकृतः शोफं भृगुः पादयो-
स्सङ्गोचं कुरुतेर्कजोथ पतनं राहुः शिखी भौमवत् ॥३७॥

Stanza 37.—The Sun causes fever, internal heat, and severe pains in the head due to heat. The Moon causes dysentery. Mars brings in all sorts of sores and wounds. Mercury causes inability to talk and think, *i.e.*. disorder in the vocal organ and the head. Jupiter causes weakness of the eyes; Venus causes mental ill-health, excruciating pains in the body and swelling; and Saturn produces disorders to one's hands and legs; Rahu is the cause of sudden fall from an elevated place; and Ketu causes ills like Mars.

NOTES

In this stanza, the author details the nature of the diseases governed by the planets.

BEGINNING OF DISEASE

सूर्याद्यंशकसंस्थिते रविमुखैरप्यन्विते त्रिस्फुटे
तेषामीरित आमयो यदि भवेत्प्रष्टुर्मृतिः स्याद्ध्रुवम् ।

यत्र त्रिस्फुटमङ्कनिघ्नमुडुनि स्यात्तत्रभे स्याद्रुजः
प्रारम्भोथ ततः परोडुनि भवेन्मोहस्तृतीये मृतिः ॥३८॥

Stanza 38.—Planets occupying Thrisphuta Rasis or lords governing Thrisphuta Navamsas bring about the above diseases and disorders. By multiplying Thrisphuta by 9 we get Thrisphuta Navamsa. Sickness begins on that Nakshatra day indicated by Thrisphuta Navamsa. On the next Nakshatra day, the sick man becomes unconscious, and on the following day he dies.

त्रिस्फुटस्थैष्यनाडीभिरानीय भदशां तथा ।
अपहारं छिद्रमतो वत्सरान्तः फलं वदेत् ॥३९॥

Stanza 39.—Find out the Dasas, Antardasas and Chidras from the unexpired portion of the Nakshatra held by Thrisphuta. The Dasa period is to be 1 year or 12 months only from the Prasna day and not 120 years as in Vimshottari.

आरूढाष्टमरिःफषष्ठपतयस्तत्स्थाश्च नीचस्थिता
मूढाः केन्द्रधनत्रिकोणगखरा मान्द्यशराशीश्वरौ ।
ये च त्रिस्फुटतारसङ्गमभपास्ते दोषदाः पृच्छतां
केन्द्रादिस्थशुभादयोत्र शुभदा एतद्रहस्यं परम् ॥४०॥

Stanza 40.—The lords of the 8th, 12th and 6th from Arudha, planets that occupy these houses, planets in debilitation, in combustion, evil planets that occupy the 2nd, kendra and trikona houses, the lords of the house and Navamsa occupied by Gulika, and the lords of the 3rd, 5th and 7th asterisms from Thrisphuta Nakshatra bring in evil. Good planets occupying the 2nd, kendras and trikonas, and the lords of the 9th and 11th bring about invariably good results. These principles are a special secret.

THRISPHUTA NAKSHATRA

योंशस्त्रिस्फुटगोस्य यातघटिका घीघ्ना विभज्य स्थिरैः
शिष्टं त्रिस्पुटतारकादि गणयेदत्रागतं मृत्युभम् ।
तारं चाथ चतुस्पुटस्थमिह तु व्याधेः शमः स्याद्यदि
प्रष्टुस्तर्हि चतुस्फुटोडुजनुषं बन्धुं विशेदामयः ॥४१॥

Stanza 41.—Note down the Thrisphuta Navamsa. Find out the expired portion in ghatis. Multiply this by 9, and divide the product by 27. Count the remainder from the Thrisphuta Nakshatra. The result is Mrityu Nakshatra. On that day the questioner will die. Chathusphuta Nakshatra also may be taken as Mrityu Nakshatra

—not for the questioner but for any one in the family born on the Chathusphuta Nakshatra day. On that day, the relative concerned will fall ill.

त्रिस्फुटस्थगृहगो यदा भवेद्भानुरिन्दुरथवात्र वा मृतिः ।
निर्णयस्त्विह गुरूपदेशतो जायते बहुपरीक्षणैरपि ॥४२॥

Stanza 42.—When the Sun or the Moon transits the Thrisphuta Rasi, death will take place. The conclusion must be based upon experience and the guidance of the preceptor.

लग्नाहिमान्दीन्दुरविस्फुटानां योगे भवेयुर्यदि जन्मभानि ।
वधर्क्षत्रैनाशिकपौष्णभानि मृत्युर्विपत्प्रत्यरयोश्च सद्यः ॥४३॥

Stanza 43.—If Panchasphuta happens to be the Janma Nakshatra of the questioner, or its trines or the 3rd, 5th or 7th Nakshatras, or the 88th quarter from the quarter of his asterism, or Revati, then predict that the questioner will die soon.

लग्नस्यांशमसुं वपुश्शशभृतो मान्देश्च मृत्युं विदु-
स्तद्योगेक्षणवर्जितो वपुरसू युक्तक्षितौ चेन्मिथः ।

दीर्घायुर्दृढमादिशेद्यदि तनोर्मृत्योर्युतीक्षादिकं
पीडा स्याद्वपुषो रुजाथ तदसोर्मोहप्रदं पृच्छताम् ॥४४॥

Stanza 44.--By multiplying Lagnasphuta by 9, we get Pranasphuta. By multiplying the Moon by 9, we get Dehasphuta. By multiplying Gulika by 9, we get Mrityusphuta. If Pranasphuta and Dehasphuta mutually aspect or combine, and they are free from the aspect or association of Mrityusphuta, then predict 'long life'. If Dehasphuta is afflicted by Mrityusphuta, predict long sickness. If Pranasphuta is in any way conjoined with Mrityusphuta, say there will be fits and unconsciousness.

द्वन्द्वांशे यदि लग्नचन्द्रगुळिका मृत्युप्रदा रोगदाः
प्रष्टुस्ते स्थिरभागगा यदि चरांशेष्वायुरारोग्यदाः ।
अन्योन्यं यदि ते त्रिकोणभगताभागा महारोगदा
दृष्टा मोहकरा युता मरणदाः कर्किंत्रिकोणे दृढम् ॥४५॥

Stanza 45. If Lagna Navamsa, Chandra Navamsa and Gulika Navamsa happen to be common signs, predict death. If they are fixed signs, predict sickness and in movable signs, predict sound health and long life. If these

Amsas happen to be in mutual trines, severe illness will result; if they aspect mutually, they cause stupor; and if they are conjoined in a house trine to Cancer, death is certain.

प्राग्लग्नं पञ्चनिघ्नं गुलिकयुतमसुं प्राहुरिन्दुं वसुघ्नं
मान्द्याढ्यं चापि देहं मुनिहतगुलिकं भानुयुक्तं च
मृत्युम् ।
प्राणाधिक्ये तु रोगः शमनमथ रुजां देहवृद्धौ प्रवृद्धे
मृत्यौ स्यात्तेषु मृत्युर्जनिभमुपगते सार्पपौष्णेन्द्रभे वा
॥४६॥

Stanza 46.—Multiply Lagnasphuta by 5 and add Gulikasphuta to it; then we get Pranasphuta. Multiply Chandrasphuta by 8 and add Gulika, we get Dehasphuta. Multiply Gulikasphuta by 7 and add Suryasphuta, we get Mrityusphuta. If Pranasphuta is greater, predict 'recovery from sickness'; If Dehasphuta is greater, predict 'improvement in health'; If Mrityusphuta is greater or if Mrityusphuta falls in Aslesha, Jyeshta or Revati, predict death.

NOTES

In this stanza, the author speaks of a Sukshma Thrisphuta (a more accurate one). The methods of calculation are simple and do not need any explanation or illustration.

युक्ते तत्त्रितयं भवेद्यदिह भं तत्स्थेषु सूर्यादिषु
ब्रूयात्तातसुखापदं मृतिमिह प्रष्टुस्समान्दावहौ ।
मान्दौ दैवविदो शुभानि शिखिनि प्रश्नस्य कर्तुस्तथा
दूतस्यास्य विनाशमर्कतनये प्रष्टेह यः प्रेषितः ॥४७॥

Stanza 47.—Add up all these and you get Sukshma Thrisphuta. You have to predict danger to the persons signified by the planets occupying this Sukshma Thrisphuta. If the Sun occupies this, predict danger to father; if the Moon, say that calamities will visit mother; if Mercury, calamities to uncle; if Mars, brothers; if Jupiter, son; if Venus, wife; and if Saturn, servants. In a prasna regarding a woman, Venus governs husband. If Rahu and Gulika occupy this Rasi, the questioner will die. If Gulika alone stands, the astrologer will himself have some troubles. If Kethu occupies this Rasi, trouble will come to the man who placed the gold piece in the prasna. If Saturn occupies this, the messenger sent will be involved in trouble.

गतासुतः प्रोक्षणभक्तभादिना
विहीनमान्दिर्जनिगो मृतिप्रदः ।

न चेन्निजाधिष्ठिततारजन्मनो
मृतिप्रदो बन्धुजनस्य पृच्छताम् ॥ इति ॥४८॥

Stanza 48.—Take the time of prasna in ghatikas and vighatikas; convert it into vighatikas; multiply it by 6. Then divide the number by 562. Then we get the Rasi and from the remiander, calculate dagrees and minutes. The Sphuta so got must be then subtracted from Gulikasphuta. If this happens to fall in the asterism of the native, predict death; or if any of his relatives happen to be born in this Sphuta Nakshatra, then predict that relative will die.

संहारगमसद्यक्तं प्रष्टुर्देहांशकादिगम् ।
जन्मतारात्रयस्थं च नियमेन मृतिप्रदम् ॥४९॥

Stanza 49.—If Thrisphuta occupies Samhara (destructive) Khanda, Rasi or Nakshatra, or if it is in conjunction with evil planets, or if it happens to be the 28th quarter from his 'Nakshatra Pada' or if it happens to be the 3rd or 5th or 7th Nakshatra from his Janma Nakshatra, or if it happens to be his Anujanma Nakshatra, then predict 'death'.

NOTES

Anujanma is the 10th star from Janma Nakshatra, *e.g*, Pubba is the Anujanma Nakshatra of Bharani.

सृष्टिखण्डगृहोडुस्थमथवा शुभसंयुतम् ।
यद्वाजहरिचापांशगतं त्रिस्फुटमायुषे ॥५०॥

Stanza 50.—If Thrisphuta happens to fall in Srishti Khanda (zone), Srishti Rasi, Srishti Nakshatra, or if it conjoins with good planets or if it occupies Aries, Leo or Sagittarius Navamsas, predict longevity to the questioner.

त्रिस्फुटस्य दृगाणादि वर्गेशाश्रितराशिपैः ।
तातमातृभ्रातृबन्धुपुत्र भार्याशुभाशुभम् ॥५१॥

Stanza 51.—Find out the Shadvargas of the Thrisphuta and note down the respective lords. From them, read good and bad for father, mother, brothers, relatives, children and wife respectively.

NOTES

For example, see in what Rasi in Drekkana the Thrisphuta has fallen. Note the lord of this Rasi. From the nature of this lord, read the fortunes of the father. In this way, the indications of other relatives should be given in the order of relatives in the stanza, the vargas being taken into consideration in the order of Drekkana, Hora, Navamsa, Thrimsamsa, Dwadasamsa and Rasi.

सुगुणैस्तैश्शुभं वाच्यं सदोषैश्च तथाशुभम् ।
दोषा दुर्बलतानिष्टस्थितिपापान्वयादिकाः ॥५२॥

Stanza 52.—If the lord is well disposed, then good will befall the concerned relative. If the lord is afflicted, then predict evil. By affliction is meant debility, evil disposition and aspect of evil planets.

इष्टभावस्थितिर्वीर्यं सद्योगेक्षे च तद्गुणाः ।
द्रेक्काणाद्यधिपैरेव कैश्चिदेवं निरूप्यते ॥५३॥
त्रिस्फुटेर्कादिभिर्युक्ते पित्रादीनामशोभनम् ।
चतुष्पदांशके भे वा त्रिस्फुटं पापयुग्यदि ॥५४॥
वाच्यश्चतुष्पदां नाश एवं युक्त्या विचिन्त्यताम् ॥५५॥

Stanzas 53, 54 and 55.—By 'strength' of planets is meant their residence in appropriate bhavas, good strength and association or aspect of benefics. If the Sun, etc., conjoins Thrisphuta, father, etc., will be in peril. If Thrisphuta occupies Chathushpada Rasi or Navamsa and conjoins with evil planets, destruction of quadrupeds such as cattle or horses may be predicted.

NOTES

If the Sun, the Moon, Mars, Mercury, Jupiter, Venus and Saturn conjoin the Thrisphuta, affliction will befall father, mother, brothers, relatives, children, wife or husband and servants or dependents respectively.

दिवसत्रितयादर्वाक्कलहो हेतुना विना ।
धनहीनस्य वृद्धस्य भूसुरस्य समागमः ॥५६॥

अग्निभीतिस्ततो नाशः पात्रस्य वसनस्य वा ।
ततः क्षतशरीरस्य रोगिणो वा समागमः ॥५७॥

ततः सर्पागमः शुद्धविप्रस्यागमनं ततः ।
नाशश्चतुष्पदां यद्वा दासस्य पतनं ततः ॥५८॥

समीपे कस्यचिन्मृत्युर्व्याधिताष्टमगे विधौ ।
भृङ्गाद्यैर्दीपहानिर्वा लक्षणानि मृतेर्नव ॥५९॥

दस्रादिनवताराणां त्रिस्फुटे तु त्रिकोणगे ।
त्रिस्फुटांशस्य राशेर्वा त्रिकोणेन्द्रौ तदुद्भवः ॥६०॥

Stanzas 56 to 60.—When Thrisphuta falls in a particular Nakshatra and the following events—a quarrel within three days, a poor old Brahmin turning up in three days, fear from fire or a huge conflagration, loss or destruction of vessels or clothes, sickness or wounds to any one in the family, a serpent seen anywhere in the house, a pious and noble Brahamin's visit, death of a quadruped or fall from a tree of a servant and putting out of the light by a destructive fly or death news—are noticed, the order coinciding with the order of Aswini, Bharani, etc. (and their trines), then predict death.

NOTES

If in the Prasna chart, the Thrisphuta falls in Aswini, Makha or Moola and within three days, a quarrel takes place without cause, then death may be predicted. Likewise, when the Thrisphuta falls in the following constellations, and an appropriate event takes place as follows :–

1.	Aswini, Makha, Moola	A quarrel within three days.
2.	Bharani, Pubba Poorvashadha	A poor old Brahmin turning up in three days.
3.	Krittika, Uttara, Uttarshadha	Fire or conflagration.
4.	Rohini, Hasta, Sravana	Loss or destruction of vessel or cloth.
5.	Mrigasira, Chitta, Dhanishta	Sickness or wound.
6.	Aridra, Swati, Satabhisha	Appearance of a serpent.
7.	Punarvasu, Visakha, Poorvabhadra	Visit of a religious and noble Brahmin.
8.	Pushyami, Anuradha, Uttarabhadra	Death of a quadruped or fall of a servant.
9.	Aslesha, Jyeshta, Revati	Putting out of the light.

In all the said cases, any happening similar to the specific events mentioned should also be taken as an indicative sign and death predicted.

ज्वरस्तापस्तनौ मूर्ध्नि विशेषेणोष्णतेजसः ।
अतिसारः सुधा भानोर्भूमिपुत्रस्य तु व्रणः ॥६१॥

Stanza 61.—The Sun governs fever, rise of temperature all over the body and brain fag. The Moon rules dysentery. Mars indicates wounds and sores.

ज्ञस्य वाङ्गनसोः स्तम्भः पारवश्यं च नेत्रयोः ।
वेदना सकलाङ्गेषु धीभ्रमश्च गुरोः स्मृतः ॥६२॥

Stanza 62.—Mercury denotes diseases that make one unable to think or speak or see. Jupiter causes pain all over the body and mental upsets.

शोफः शुक्रस्य मन्दस्य सङ्कोचः करपादयोः ।
राहोस्तु पतनं केतोर्व्याधिर्व्रण उदाहृतः ॥६३॥

Stanza 63.—Venus causes swelling. Saturn governs disability to stretch or to fold one's hands and legs. Rahu governs fall from an elevated place. Kethu indicates wounds.

त्रिस्फुटेन समेतस्य त्रिस्फुटांशकपस्य वा ।
रोगिणो यदि रोगः स्यान्मरणं तस्य निश्चितम् ॥६४॥

Stanza 64.—If the sick man has the diseases signified by the lord of Thrisphuta Navamsa or by the lord associated with Thrisphuta, then predict death.

THRISPHUTA DASA

दशामपहृतिं छिद्रमानीय त्रिफुटोडुनः ।
एष्याभिर्घटिकाभिस्तैर्वत्सरान्तः फलं वदेत् ॥६५॥

Stanza 65.—Calculate Dasas and Antardasas from the unexpired portion of Thrisphuta Nakshatra (for one year) and predict the results.

NOTES

Here the Dasa period for the Sun is 18 days, the Moon 30 days, Mars 21 days, Rahu 54 days, Jupiter 48 days, Saturn 57 days, Mercury 51 days, Ketu 21 days and Venus 60 days. Vimshottari Dasa period multiplied by 3 gives the Prasna Dasa period in days. The order of succession is also according to Vimshottari. Here the duration of the year is taken as 360 days.

त्रिफुटोडुसमूलेशा आरूढानिष्टभावगाः ।
तदंशा नीचगा मूढा मान्दीशाश्चाशुभप्रदाः ॥६६॥

Stanza 66.—If the lord of the Thrisphuta constellation is in the Vipat, Pratyak or Naidhana stars; or occupies Arudha Rasi or evil houses; and if lords of these Rasis are in debilitated, combust or in association with the lord of the sign occupied by Mandi, the Dasa results will be unfavourable.

NOTES

Suppose the Thrisphuta longitude is Leo 21° 3′. This means the constellation involved is Poorvaphalguni. If the lord of this constellation, *viz.*, Venus is in the Vipat (Hasta, Sravana and Rohini), Pratyak (Swati, Satabhisha and Aridra) or Naidhana (Anuradha, Uttarabhadra and Pushyami) the effects will be bad. Likewise if Venus occupies Arudha Rasi or evil houses (6th, 8th or 12th) or if the lord of the Rasi occupied by Venus is in debilitation, combust or in association with the lord of the Mandi-sign, the results can only be unfavourable.

प्रश्नोडुत्रिस्पुटाभ्यां विधिवदुडुदशां मान्दिनापि प्रतीपं
याताभिर्नाडिकाभिर्नयतु तिसृषु वै गृह्यतां तासु चैका ।
प्रश्ने यात्रानुरूपा शुभतदितरदे चाब्दिके मासिके वा
खेटाब्दा वासराः स्युत्रिगुणितविहृता वैव नेया दशेन्दोः
॥६७॥

Stanza 67.—Calculate the Dasas from the Moon, Thrisphuta and also Gulika. Consider which would be appropriate in regard to the question concerned. Prasna results are to be told either for 1 year or for 1 month on the basis of the yearly or monthly Dasa. Some are of the opinion that the Dasa worked on the Moon's position alone is sufficient.

NOTES

In stanza 67. we are asked to determine the Dasas with reference to the constellations occupied by the Moon, Gulika and also Thrisphuta and consider that which appears appropriate according as the overall effects of Prasna chart are either generally good or generally evil.

Here much responsibility rests on the shoulders of the astrologer. He should carefully assess the chart as a whole and then decide the appropriate Dasa. If the Prasna chart shows benefic results, then the least powerful Dasa of the three Dasas calculated should be considered. One is of course to be guided by one's Guru in these matters.

Prasna effects are told either for one year or for one month. If it is for one year, we have seen how to work out the Dasa period before. If it is only for one month, then divide the Dasa periods by 4 and we get the periods in days. The Sun $1\frac{1}{2}$ days, the Moon $2\frac{1}{2}$ days, Mars $1\frac{3}{4}$, Rahu $4\frac{1}{2}$, Jupiter 4, Saturn $4\frac{3}{4}$, Mercury $4\frac{1}{4}$, Ketu $1\frac{3}{4}$, and Venus 5 days.

॥ इति प्रश्नमार्गे षष्ठोऽध्यायः ॥

सप्तमाध्यायः

ASHTAMANGALAM

वामस्थेन फलं भूतं वर्तमानं तु मध्यतः ।
दक्षिणस्थेन भावीनि फलानि च विनिर्दिशेत् ॥ १ ॥

Stanza 1.—In the (Ashtamangala) number (consisting of three digits), the digit on the left-hand side (100th) denotes the past, the middle one (10th) the present, and the one on the right-hand side (unit), the future.

अधोमध्योर्ध्वभागेषु वपुषो दक्षिणादयः ।
युग्मसंख्यावपुर्भागे ग्रहोक्तव्याधिमादिशेत् ॥ २ ॥

Stanza 2.—The lower, middle and upper parts of the body are signified respectively by the unit, tenth and hundredth digits. In the part of the body denoted by the even number, there is some disorder appropriate to the planet.

NOTES

The stanza is suggestive. The Ashtamangala number consisting of three digits denotes the entire physical body. The left-hand number signifies the condition and nature of the body above the neck; the central digit refers to the part of the body below the neck and above the waist and the right-hand digit governs the part of the body below the waist. Suppose the Ashtamangala number is 247. The centre digit 4 is an even number. This means that there is some disorder or defect in the middle part of the body—below neck and above waist. This number is governed by some planet (noted below) and the nature of the defect or disease would be appropriate to the nature of the planet concerned. This particular chapter deals in a way with Hindu Numerology.

स्थानेषु त्रिषु चैकादिशेषे स्युर्भास्करादयः ।
ध्वजाद्या गरुडाद्याश्च पञ्चजूतानि च क्रमात् ॥ ३ ॥

अर्कारजीवविच्छुक्रमन्दचन्द्राहयः क्रमात् ।
ध्वजधूमहरिश्वोक्षखरमातङ्गवायसाः ॥ ४ ॥

तार्क्ष्यमार्जारसिंहश्वाह्याखुद्विपशशास्तथा ।
ध्वजसिंहौ मही दन्तिवृषौ जलमयौ मतौ ॥ ५ ॥

धूमो वह्नि खरो वायुः श्वकाकौ वियदात्मकौ ॥ ६ ॥

Stanzas 3 to 6.—The eight planets, yonis, animals and Bhutas (elements) beginning from the Sun, Dhwaja, Garuda and Prithvi respectively correspond to numbers one to eight in the order Sun, Mars, Jupiter, Mercury, Venus, Saturn, Moon and Rahu; to the respective yonis of

Dhwaja, Dhuma, Simha, Dog, Ox, Donkey Elephant and Crow ; and to the creatures Garuda, Cat, Simha, Dog, Serpent, Mouse, Elephant and Hare respectively. Dhwaja and Simha yonis come under Prithvibhuta ; Gaja and Vrishabha under Jala ; Dhuma under Agni ; Khara (donkey) under Vayu ; and Dog and Crow under Akasa.

NOTES

This stanzas are simple enough and do not call for detailed explanations. 8 numbers are taken into consideration. Each number denotes a particular planet, a particular yoni, a particular animal and a particular Bhuta. The number is always to be taken in three digits, the 100th digit referring to the past, the 10th to the present and the unit to the future. In the subsequent stanzas, the results due to the ruling planet yoni, etc., are explained.

RESULTS OF THE SUN AND OTHER PLANETS

अभीष्टार्थागमं कीर्तिं जयं भूपतिमाननम् ।
सभाजनपदग्रामसत्कृतिं कुरुते रविः ॥ ७ ॥

चोरभूपायुधाग्निभ्यो भयं स्कन्दाच्च भैरवात् ।
कलहज्वरपित्तासृक्शिरानेत्रगदान् कुजः ॥ ८ ॥

गुरुदैवतविप्राणां प्रसादजशुभागमम् ।
दुकूलहेमदन्त्यश्वसुताप्तिं कुरुते गुरुः ॥ ९ ॥

श्वगोमृगादितो भीतिं विष्णुकोपं विचर्चिकाम् ।
त्वग्रोगान् सन्निपातं च कुरुते शीतरश्मिजः ॥१०॥

भूषणांबरशय्याप्तिं स्त्रीसुखं मृष्टभोजनम् ।
कृषिगोमहिषीलाभं कुरुते भृगुनन्दनः ॥११॥

वातशूलामयं चोरदुर्जनेभ्यो भयं शनिः ।
कुरुते मरणाद्भीतिं दुर्ग्रहाणां च पीडनम् ॥१२॥

वेश्मसौख्यं मनःप्रीतिं सुहृत्स्वजनसङ्गमम् ।
जलोत्थसस्यपानान्ननार्याप्तिं पूर्णचन्द्रमाः ॥१३॥

कुष्ठपामादिकान् रोगान्नेत्रपादभवानपि ।
विषभीतिं च नीचानां विरोधं कुरुते फणी ॥१४॥

Stanzas 7 to 14.—If the planet happens to be the Sun, there will be success in undertakings, fame, victory, honour from rulers, and honour in councils, villages, etc.; Mars—troubles from thieves, princes and weapons, fear from fire, wrath of God Subramanya, trouble from Bhairava quarrels, fever, diseases of the head, and the eyes and blood affections; Jupiter—grace of gods and Brahmins, help of Gurus, and gains of clothes, gold, elephants and horses; Mercury—fear from animals, anger of God Vishnu, skin diseases and typhoid fever; Venus—ornaments, fine clothes, cots and beds, happiness from wife, good food, better yield in lands and acquisition of cows and buffaloes; Saturn—rheumatism, stomach pains, trouble from thieves, fear from wicked people, fear of death and affliction from wicked spirits; full Moon—family happiness, mental peace, association with relatives and friends, acquisition of aquatic products, good food and drinks and company of women; and Rahu—virulent skin troubles, diseases in the eyes and legs, fear from poison and quarrel with bad people.

NOTES

Here we see that odd numbers are good and even numbers are bad.

EFFECTS OF "DHWAJA"

आरोग्यमर्थलाभं च लभते शत्रुनाशनम् ।
पुत्रलाभं च नियमाद्‌ध्वजसन्दर्शनान्नरः । ।।१५।।

चित्तदुःखं महाव्याधिं शत्रुपीडां निरर्थताम् ।
स्थानभ्रंशं विवादं च लभते धूमदर्शनात् ।।१६।।

नीरोगत्वं सुतप्राप्तिं मनःप्रीतिं धनागम्मम् ।
द्विजभूपालसम्मानं लभते सिंहदर्शनात् ।।१७।।

विप्रवासं भयं चैव द्रव्यनाशं रुजं तथा ।
अपमृत्युं विवादं च निर्दिशेच्छ्वप्रदर्शनात् ॥१८॥

स्त्रीलाभं पुत्रलाभं च धनलाभं गृहं सुखम् ।
लभते चायुरारोग्यं वृषसन्दर्शनान्नरः ॥१९॥

द्विषदागमनं रोगं स्थाननाशं धनक्षयम् ।
कार्यहानिं मनःक्लेशं लभते खरदर्शनात् ॥२०॥

स्त्रीभोगं धनधान्याप्तिं सुहृदां सङ्गमं सुखम् ।
भूपालरत्नलाभं च कथयेद्गजदर्शनात् ॥२१॥

स्थानभ्रंशं सुहृन्नाशं स्थाननाशं महाभयम् ।
जीवनाशमरेमृत्युं लभते काकदर्शनात् ॥२२॥

Stanzas 15 to 22.—If Dhwaja happens to be the 'Yoni', there will be health, monetary gains, destruction of enemies and birth of children; Dhuma—mental worry, serious diseases, troubles from enemies, poverty, degtfdation in one's position and disputes; Simha—health, birth of a son, mental peace, gain of money, rewards from rulers and Brahmins; Dog—exile from one's place, fear, loss of money, illness, dispute and fear from accidental death; Vrishabha—marriage, birth of son, gain of money, family happiness, long life and good health ; Khara—troubles from enemies, deprivation of house, loss of money, failure in undertakings and sorrows ; Gaja—intercourse with women, acquisition of money and brains, association with friends and relations and awards and presents from rulers ; and Crow—loss of profession or degradation, quarrels with relatives, loss of house, great mental affliction, fear of suicide or death.

ANIMAL SYMBOLS

सर्पादयः क्रमान्मध्ये चत्वारो दक्षिणे पुनः ।
तार्क्ष्याद्यश्च चत्वारो यदि ते मरणप्रदाः ॥२३॥

Stanza 23.—If the middle and unit digits are represented by serpent and Garuda, or mouse and cat, elephant and lion or hare and dog respectively, the questioner will die.

NOTES

You will see in this that serpent and Garuda are enemies, mouse and cat are enemies and so on with the rest. Death is likely when the central and unit digits are disposed as follows :—

Central digit		*Unit digit*
Serpent	...	Garuda
Mouse	...	Cat
Elephant	...	Lion
Hare	...	Dog

एवं क्रमात्स्थितेष्वेषु मार्जारस्याखुभक्षणम् ।
चकोरश्येनपूर्वाणामुरगग्रहणं तथा ॥२४॥

शशस्य ग्रहणं मांसखण्डं वादाय चागमः ।
कुक्कुरस्य गृहे प्रष्टुरेतन्मरणलक्षणम् ॥२५॥

Stanzas 24 and 25.—If the animals are found in the above order, the cat being discovered eating a mouse or a Garuda catching a serpent or a dog in pursuit of a hare, it is a sign of death.

ओतौ मध्यस्थिते वाच्यं प्रष्टुस्तल्लङ्घनादिकम् ।
सारमेये ततो भीतिर्व्याघ्रादिभ्योथवा भयम् ॥२६॥

मूषिके मूषिकैर्वस्त्रशयनादिनिकृन्तनम् ।
वायसे वायसस्पर्शः शकृत्पातोस्य वा तनौ ॥२७॥

खरे चतुष्पादाद्क्रीदिर्द्धूमे तु भयमग्निजम् ।
एतत्तु सकलं प्रष्टु रोगाद्यशुभसूचकम् ॥२८॥

Stanzas 26, 27 and 28.—If the middle digit happens to belong to cat (or if the questioner jumps over a cat), the querist will be attacked by diseases; dog—he will be bitten by a dog; mouse—clothes, beds, etc., will be torn by rats; crow—a crow will excrete or scratch the body; Khara—danger from quadrupeds or wild animals;

Dhuma—calamities from fire. Any of these in the middle digit indicates that the questioner will be affected by bad diseases and other misfortunes, but not death.

एकस्य यदि वैर्यन्यो मध्यदक्षिणसंस्थयोः ।
खेटयोरुभयत्रापि पापौ चेच्चाशुभं वदेत् ।
सुहृदावुभयत्रापि पापावपि शुभप्रदौ ॥२९॥

Stanza 29.—If the 'lords' of the centre and right-hand digits are inimical to each other or if both are malefic planets, then evil should be predicted. If these lords, though malefic, are friendly, then evil will not happen.

PANCHA BHUTA EFFECTS

भूतेषु शुभदा पृथ्वी तथैवापः प्रकीर्तिताः ।
वह्निर्वायुस्तथाकाशस्त्रयोमी चाशुभप्रदाः ॥३०॥

Stanza 30.—Of the 'Bhutas', Prithvi and Jala are auspicious. Agni, Vayu and Akasa are evil.

एकत्र स्यादग्निः परत्र तोयं च मध्यदक्षिणयोः ।
यदि तर्हि विनिर्देश्यं प्रष्टू रोगोथवा मरणम् ॥३१॥

Stanza 31.—Of the central and the right-hand digits, if one is Agni and the other Jala, then there will be diseases or death also may happen.

RECKONING OF LUNAR DAY ETC.

एकस्थानदशस्थानशतस्थानतया पुनः ।
स्थानत्रयं प्रकल्प्यातो नीलभक्तावशेषतः ॥३२॥

शुक्लप्रतिपदाद्याः स्युस्तिथयः सारशेषतः ।
तारावाराः सप्तशेषात् प्रियशेषात्तु राशयः ॥३३॥

नवभक्तावशेषात्तु विज्ञेयाः स्युर्नवग्रहाः ।
तथैव पञ्चभूतानि पञ्चभक्तावशेषतः ॥३४॥

Stanzas 32 to 34.—The (Ashtamangala) number divided severally by 30, 27, 7, 12, 9 and 5 and the remainder counted from the first lunar day of the bright half, Aswini, Sunday, Aries, the Sun and Prithvi respectively gives the lunar day, constellation, week-day, Rasi, Planet and Bhuta.

NOTES

Suppose the number is 183. Divide this by 30. The remainder is 3. Counted from first lunar day, we get the third tithi. Similarly dividing the number by 27, 7, 12, 9 and 5 we get remainders 21, 1, 3, 3 which means the (Ashtamangala) nakshatra is Uttarashadha (21st), the week-day is Sunday (1st), the Rasi Gemini (3rd) and the Bhuta is Fire (3rd).

RESULTS OF TITHI ETC.

प्रष्टृष्टमो भवेद्राशिः प्रष्टृनिष्टाश्च तारकाः ।

यदि चेदिह वक्तव्यं पृच्छकस्याशुभं ध्रुवम् ॥३५॥

Stanza 35.—If the (Ashtamangala) Rasi obtained as above happens to be the 8th Rasi from the Janma Rasi of the questioner, or if the (Ashtamangala) Nakshatra be 3rd, 5th or 7th from the birth nakshatra of the questioner, then something evil is certain to happen.

एभिस्तिथ्यादिभिर्योगा मृत्युदग्धादयो यदि ।

प्रष्टुर्विपत्तिरादेश्या सुधायोगादयः शुभाः ॥३६॥

Stanza 36.—According as the Ashtamangala factors (Tithi, Nakshatra, Vara, etc.) are afflicted by such evil doshas as Mrityu or Dagdha or fortified by good yogas such as Suddha, etc., the querist will meet with some imminent danger or good.

स्थानत्रयेपि युग्माः स्युर्यदि संख्या मृतिर्भवेत् ।

वाममध्यमयोर्युग्मा यदि स्यान्महती रुजा ॥३७॥

Stanza 37.—If all the three digits are even numbers, then death will happen. If the left and the centre figures are even, there will be dangerous diseases.

NOTES

Here, we have to note that even numbers cannot occupy all the three places. Hence to predict according to this is not possible. Writers explain this sloka in many ways attempting to overcome this difficulty but none of these explanations satisfy the real intention of the author. Hence the explanation is left to the intelligence of the readers.

संख्यां मध्यगतां हत्वा शुभेन विभजेद्दिनैः ।
निश्शेषे मरणं प्रष्टुर्द्विशेषे सुतपश्चता ॥३८॥
स्वजनापच्चतुः शेषे षट्च्छेषे पृच्छकामयः ।
ओजसंख्यासु शिष्टासु सुखारोग्यादिसम्भवः ॥३९॥

Stanzas 38 and 39.—Multiply the number by 45 and divide the product by 8. According as the remainder is 0, 2 or 4, there will be death, loss of children or danger to relatives. If the remainder is an odd number, there will be good health, recovery from illness, etc.

NIRAYANA SATURN

न्यस्य स्थानत्रयं द्वाभ्यां वामस्थं मध्यगं त्रिभिः ।
चतुर्भिर्दक्षिणं स्थानं हत्वा पक्षः सितो यदि ॥४०॥

चलाङ्कं दैवतं कृष्णे पक्षे क्षिप्त्वा हरेद्भुजैः ।

फलराशिगते जीवे शिष्टं प्रियनगैर्नतैः ॥४१॥

हत्वा वेदाक्षराश्यादि गते च रविजे मृतिः ४२॥

Stanzas 40, 41 and 42.—Keep the Ashtamangala number. Multiply the left-hand digit by 2, the central digit by 3, the right-hand digit by 4. If the Prasna happens to be in Sukla Paksha, (Bright half) add to this 336. If it is in Krishna Paksha (dark half) add 648. Divide this total by 84. Divide the remainder by 12; we get the number of Rasis. Multiply the balance by 30 and divide it by 12; we get 'Degrees'. Multiply the remainder by 60 and divide it by 12 when we get minutes (respectively). When Jupiter transits through this Rasi, predict that the questioner will die. When Saturn transits this sphuta, consider that the death of the man will take place.

NOTES

Here we have worked the Ashtamangala Nirayana Jupiter and Saturn. As the prasna is intended to cover one year and sometimes one month, you have to state that if these transits take place within one year or one month, the questioner will die in one day. In this way, make the calculations.

अष्टमङ्गलमित्युक्तं संक्षेपेण गुरूदितम् ।
गुरुभक्त्येश्वरं ध्यायन् वदेत्सत्यं भवेद्ध्रुवम् ॥४३॥

Stanza 43.—Here has been described Ashtamangala as I studied from my Guru. If predictions are made with devotion to the preceptor and God, then they will come correct.

NOTES

The principles adumbrated in this chapter may be used for answering questions based on numerology. We are summarising again the whole chapter for the benefit of readers.

The science of numbers has always been a fascinating study with the Hindus. Everything in the universe is vibration. The mystery of sound vibration had been well understood by the Maharishis and the whole science of Mantra Sastra is based on the importance of sound vibrations. Unfortunately, as has been the case with other sciences, educated Hindus neglected the knowledge bequeathed to us by the ancient sages and began to study and appreciate books on the so-called numerology written by the Western savants. There is a lot of difference between the Sankhya Sastra as propounded by the Hindus and numerology as understood and expounded by the Westerners. The former is based on a correct appreciation of the working of the law of periodicity and the great significance of vibratory laws while the latter arbitrarily allots certain numbers for certain letters of the English alphabet. English is not Sanskrit and 'Sanskrit' means Samyuk kirt or that which is perfect. The vibrations released by the Sanskrit alphabets have their own peculiar importance. The numerology of the Hindus has an important bearing on Prasna or Horary astrology since the latter comes to our rescue in moments of the most profound anxiety.

The questioner should be asked to mention a number of three digits. We shall call this as the root number. The one on the left-hand side (100th) denotes the past, the central one (10th) denotes the present and the digit on the right-hand side (unit) suggests the future. More importance is attached to the 10th and unit digits as they deal with the present and future.

The different planets are assigned the following numbers: The Sun—1, the Moon—7, Mars—2, Mercury —4, Jupiter—3, Venus—5, Saturn—6 and Rahu—8.

In order to appreciate the general trend of affairs the root number is subjected to certain manipulations. Divide the root number by 30, 27, 7, 12 and 9 respectively. The remainder left in each case represents the Tithi (lunar day counted from 1st of the bright half), constellation, week-day, sign of the zodiac and the Bhuta respectively that will have a predominating influence. You can predict that some evil will befall the questioner if the root number Rasi happens to be the 8th from his Janma Rasi or the root number constellation happens to be the 1st, 3rd, 5th or 7th from his birth constellation. Imminent danger may also be anticipated if the root number constellation, Rasi and planet are afflicted by evil or malefic conjunctions, aspects and associations at the period in question. If all the three digits (of the root number) are even numbers, something serious can be expected to happen. If the 100th and the 10th units have even numbers, the questioner will suffer from serious diseases.

Multiply the root number by 45 and divide it by 8. Ascribe the following results for the remainders thus: If the remainder is 0, predict death (or a crisis for life); 2—loss of children or illness to them; 4—danger to some relatives. If the remainders are odd numbers such as 1, 3, 5, 7, etc., predict good health, recovery from illness, etc.

I have given above a list of planetary numerals. Now different numbers which indicate the different yonis, animals and the primordial elements etc., will be enumerated. Numbers 1 to 8 respectively represent the yonis (sex instincts) of Dhwaja, Dhuma, Hari (lion), Swana (dog), Vrishabha (ox). Khara (donkey), Matanga (elephant) and Vayasa (crow). Numbers 1 to 8 represent respectively Garuda, Cat, Lion, Dog, Serpent. Mouse, Elephant and Hare. The panchabhutas (five primordial elements) are represented as follows :—

Prithvi (earth)—1 and 3 : Jala (water)—5 and 7 ; Agni (fire)—2 ; Vayu (air)—6 ; and Akasa (ether)—4 and 8.

These details are given below in a tabular form for easy comprehension.

Number	*Planet*	*Yoni or Sex*	*Animal*	*Bhuta or primordial element*
1	Sun	Dhwaja	Garuda	Earth
2	Mars	Dhuma	Cat	Fire
3	Jupiter	Lion	Lion	Earth

Number	*Planet*	*Yoni or Sex*	*Animal*	*Bhuta or primordial element*
4	Mercury	Dog	Dog	Ether
5	Venus	Ox	Serpent	Water
6	Saturn	Donkey	Mouse	Air
7	Moon	Elephant	Elephant	Water
8	Rahu	Crow	Hare	Ether

Reduce the root number to a single digit and find out the planet presiding over it and predict the following results. If the Sun presides over the number—the object in view will be gained. If the question refers to politics, success will attend and honour will flow. The Moon—mental peace, domestic happiness, plenty of food, and acquisition of desired object.

The Moon at the time of question should be powerful to give all these results in full measure.

Mars—accidents, injuries from fire and weapons, quarrels, head diseases and troubles from thieves.

Prasna always refers to immediate future—1 day to 1 year—and these results are to happen within this period.

Mercury—itches, skin eruptions and sores in the body, lingering or intermittent fever, troubles from domestic animals such as dogs, cats, etc., and losses in trade and business. Jupiter - access to gold, realisation of objects, blessings from preceptors and holy people and smooth sailing in all affairs. Venus—good sexual enjoyments, happiness with wife, good income and acquisition of monies and ornaments. Saturn—colic pains, sorrow, misunderstandings, fear from spirits and hobgoblins, rheumatism and bad results in general. Rahu—skin diseases of a virulent type, eye troubles, misunderstandings, fear from poison, snakes and reptiles.

There is difference of opinion as to whether the unit digit of the root number is to be taken or the root number should be reduced to a single digit for purposes of predictions. The unit represents the future and it seems reasonable to take the unit digit for ascertaining anything pertaining to the future.

For purposes of answering questions pertaining to Medical astrology the root number as a whole represents the physical body. The left-hand digit describes the condition and nature of the body above the neck, the central digit suggests the condition of the body between the neck and the waist while the unit figure reveals the defects in the body below the waist. Even numbers indicate some disorder and the nature of the affliction is denoted by the planet representing the number and the diseases ruled by it. Suppose the root number is 563. The centre figure is an even number. The part of the body is between neck and waist. 6 is ruled by Saturn. Therefore the questioner suffers from a disease indicated by Saturn in the portion of the body between the neck and the waist.

If the central and unit digits are represented by the following pairs of animals, much evil will befall the questioner :

Central digit	*Right hand digit*
Serpent	Garuda
Mouse	Cat
Elephant	Lion
Hare	Dog

The above disposition is even indicative of early death and the questioner or his relatives should be duly warned of the impending disaster. If the middle digit is the one representing cat's yoni, you have to predict that the questioner simply suffers from diseases; if dog's yoni say he will be bitten by a dog and that he should be careful. If the crow's yoni comes in the middle number, then you will have a scratch made on your body by a crow. Danger from quadrupeds or wild animals should be suggested if the middle number is that of a donkey's yoni. Calamities from fire are likely if the dhuma yoni comes in the middle. In all the above circumstances, misfortunes and diseases should be predicted and not death.

Likewise if the planets ruling the middle and last numbers are inimical to each other or both are natural malefics, then predict evil. If the evil planets are friendly, then no evil can happen. In a like manner, if the middle and the last digits represent prithvi (earth) and jala (water), it indicates good. Agni, Vayu and Akasa portend evil. Thus Agni and Vayu are good and Agni and Jala are evil.

An Example

Let Janma Rasi be Taurus and the root number 563. Let Janma constellation be Mrigasira.

	Past	*Present*	*Future*
Root Number :	*5*	*6*	*3*
	Venus	Saturn	Jupiter
	Ox-yoni	Donkey-yoni	Lion-yoni
	Serpent	Mouse	Lion
	Water	**Air**	**Earth**

Dividing the root number by 30, 27, 7, 12, 9 and 5 respectively we get:

Root number lunar day—8th of dark half.

Root number constellation--Dhanishta--5th from Moola.

Root number	week-day	Tuesday
Root number	sign	Aquarius
Root number	planet	Venus

The root number Rasi is 10th from Janma Rasi. The root number constellation is the 1st from birth star. The root number planets own the Janma Rasi. Thus the root number dispositions are fairly powerful and favourable. Multiplying root number by 45 and dividing the product by 8, $\frac{(563 \times 45)}{8}$, we get 7 as remainder, indicating good health, and recovery from illness.

The hundredth digit is presided over by Venus a benefic indicating a good past, 6 being ruled by Saturn, the present is evil and the questioner suffers from a disease indicated by Saturn between the neck and waist. The number in the unit place is that of Jupiter suggesting realisation of the object. The middle number is presided over by donkey-yoni foreboding troubles from quadrupeds.

Summing up: The disposition of root number, lunar tithi, etc., towards your birth elements being favourable, good time is indicated in the immediate future. Saturn rules the middle number and this suggests that you are having either colic or some rheumatic troubles in the region between the neck and the waist. This is likely to disappear shortly. Good health is indicated. The immediate past was good while the present indicates anxious moments. You need not have to worry about the future as Jupiter ruling the unit digit will confer happiness and enable you to realise the objects in your mind. As the middle number is ruled by a donkey-yoni, be careful as trouble from quadrupeds is indicated.

We see how the science of numbers is of immense use to us in its application to Prasna or Horary astrology. One should be very careful in the discrimination of the astrological evidences as otherwise the conclusions are bound to go wrong.

॥ इति प्रश्नमार्गे सप्तमाऽध्यायः ॥

अष्टमाऽध्यायः

EFFECTS OF ARUDHA

आरूढोदयलग्नांशछत्रस्पृष्टाङ्गराशयः ।
चन्द्राधिष्ठितराशिश्च चिन्त्याः षट्प्रश्नकर्मणि ॥ १ ॥

Stanza 1.—In Prasna Kriya, six Rasis, *viz.*, Arudha, Lagna, Navamsa Lagna, Chatra, Sprishtanga and Janma should be examined.

NOTES

In this chapter. the author goes on to deal with the effects of Arudha. Sprishtanga Rasi is the sign corresponding to the organ touched by the querist. The allocation of organs to the twelve signs should be considered as given by Varahamihira, *viz.*, the head, face, chest, heart, belly, waist, abdomen. sex organs, thighs, knees, buttocks and feet are governed in regular order by Aries and the succeeding signs.

Chatra Rasi is determined by noting what is called the *Veethi Rasi*. If the Sun occupies Vrishabha, Mithuna, Kataka and Simha, the Veethi Rasi is Mesha. If the Sun occupies Vrischika, Dhanus, Makara and Kumbha, Veethi Rasi is Mithuna. If the Sun occupies Kanya, Thula, Meena and Mesha, Veethi Rasi is Vrishabha. Count the number of Rasis from Arudha to Lagna and mark the same number of Rasis from Veethi Rasi, then we get the Chatra Rasi.

Illustration: Supposing Arudha is Vrishabha and Lagna is Simha. Let the Sun be in Mesha. The number from Arudha to Lagna would be 4. The same number counted from Veethi, *viz.* Vrishabha, would be Simha or Chatra Rasi.

एषां सदसद्योगादारोग्यसरोगतादि शुभमशुभम् ।
अशुभशुभावस्थाया बलवत्वात्प्रष्टुरुक्तमिति शास्त्रे ॥ २ ॥

Stanza 2.—If the Rasis suggested in stanza 1 are beneficially disposed, then there will be health and other favourable results. The benefic, malefic and weak dispositions should be carefully considered and then the answer given to the querist. This is the injunction of the Sastras.

NOTES

The six signs should be strong by association or aspect of good planets. If they are weak by the presence or aspect of evil and afflicted planets, the questioner will be miserable in general conditions of life. The astrologer's power of judgement should be fully exploited.

यदङ्गराशिः संस्पृष्ट आरूढ उदितोऽथवा ।
तस्मिन् पापयुतेब्रूयात्तदङ्गे रुग्व्रणादिकम् ॥ ३ ॥

Stanza 3.—If Arudha or Lagna is occupied by evil planets, then the questioner will suffer from diseases or wounds in the organ governed by these Rasis.

NOTES

If Arudha is Mesha and Lagna is Cancer and both are afflicted, then both the head and the heart will be seats of disease.

आरूढोदयपेन्द्वर्का अपि तद्युक्तराशिपाः ।
तुङ्गांशे बलवन्तश्चेत्पूर्णावस्थां तु पृच्छताम् ॥ ४ ॥

Stanza 4.—If the lords of Arudha and Lagna and the Moon and the Sun and lords of houses occupied by these four lords, are exalted in Navamsa and otherwise strong, then the questioner will be fortunate and happy.

NOTES

According to some Thungamsa means the degrees of exaltation and not the exaltation in the navamsa.

एते बलविहीनाश्चेद्रिक्तां च कथयेद्दशाम् ।
नीचार्यंशगतास्ते चेदनिष्टफलदा दशा ॥ ५ ॥

Stanza 5.—If the above-mentioned ones are weak, the condition of the questioner will not be good. If they occupy neecha or inimical Navamsa, then the condition of the querist will be really unfortunate.

NOTES

Here a distinction is made between the Rasi lords being weak and their occupying inimical or debilitated Navamsas—the latter being definitely more harmful.

आरूढेशे बलविरहिते रन्ध्रपे वीर्ययुक्ते
तस्मिन् काले विपदतितरां जायते पृच्छकस्य ।
अरूढेशः शुभपतिरपि प्राप्तवीर्यौ विवीर्या
यत्रायायुर्व्ययभपतयः सर्वभाग्यागमोत्र ॥ ६ ॥

Stanza 6.—If the lord of Arudha is devoid of strength and the lord of the 8th is strong, then the questioner will be beset on all sides by danger. If the lords of Arudha and 9th are strong and the lords of the 6th, 8th and 12th are weak, then there will be influx of all kinds of fortune.

AVASTHAS

अवस्थासप्तकद्वन्द्वं ग्रहाणामस्ति तत्समा ।
भवेच्च पृच्छकावस्था प्रोक्तं शास्त्रान्तरे तथा ॥७॥

Stanza 7.—There are two categories of 'Planetary Avasthas', each being divided into seven kinds. The state or condition of the questioner will be similar to the planetary avastha concerned.

समबन्धुनिजर्क्षस्वत्रिकोणोच्चारिनीचभे ।
सप्तावस्था ग्रहाणां स्युरतिबाल्यादयः क्रमात् ॥ ८ ॥
अतिबालश्च बालश्च कुमारो युवभूमिपौ ।
वृद्धो मृत इति स्थानभेदतः क्रमशो दशाः ॥ ९ ॥

सूर्यादुदितमात्रो यः सोतिबालो भवेद्ग्रहः ।
दिनानि सप्त बालः स्यात्कुमारः स्यादतः परम् ॥१०॥

युवा वक्रसमारम्भे वक्रगत्यां महीपतिः ।
आसन्नास्तमयो वृद्धः सूर्यलुप्तकरो मृतः ॥११॥

एवं द्विधा ग्रहावस्था प्रोक्ता वाच्या तु पृच्छताम् ।
आरूढलग्नच्छत्राणामीशेषु बलिनो दशा ॥१२॥

Stanzas 8 to 12.—Neutral, friendly, own, Moolathrikona, exaltation, inimical and debilitation are the seven planetary avasthas corresponding regularly to the seven avasthas, *viz.*, infant (atibalya), child (balya), adolescent (kaumara), youth (yauvana), royal (bhupa), servile (vriddha) and death (mrita). A planet will be infant for a day after combustion; a child 7 days after combustion; kaumara till the planet becomes stationary; yauvana till the commencement of retrogression; king for the period of retrogression; of vriddha, a few days before combustion and mrita, when in combustion. Thus there are two kinds of planethary avastas. The strength of the lords, Arudha, Lagna and Chatra should be considered under these various avasthas.

NOTES

Stanzas 8 to 12 are very important. Two types of planetary avasthas or states are recognised. They are *sthanavastha* or positional state and *kālavastha* or temporal state. Sthanavasta of a planet can be known thus by its occupation of different signs—friends, neutral, inimical. The kalavastha can be ascertained by the distance of the planet from the Sun. It will be seen that retrogression (vakra), combustion (moudhya), etc., are due to a planet's movement with reference to the Sun, The following table will enable the reader to guess the *sthana* and *kalavasthas.*

Avastha	*Nature of Rasi*	*Nature of Kala*
Atibalya	Neutral or sama	for 1 day after combustion
Balya	Friendly	7 days after above
Kaumara	Own house	till stationary
Yauvana	Moolathrikona	till beginning of retrogression
Raja	Exaltation	as long as retrogression lasts.
Vriddha	Enemy's sign	7 days before combustion
Mrita	Debilitation	when in combustion

You have to take the lords of Arudha Rasi, Lagna and Chatra Rasis, see who is the most powerful and then find out the *avastha* of that planet.

DISEASES AND ARUDHA

अतिबालादिकानां ये स्वभावाः प्रथिता इह ।

यूनः स्त्रीसक्ततेत्याद्यास्त एवेह दशा मताः ॥ इति ॥१३॥

Stanza 13.—If a planet's avastha is atibalya etc., the results will be appropriate to the avastha. The 'yauvana' and other stages indicate sexual instincts and appropriate results.

NOTES

The author suggests that when a planet acquires a certain state or avastha, the results he indicates would be in accordance with the nature of the avastha. Here, we are required to guess the results ourselves thus :

Atibalya (infant stage) indicates inability to speak, tendency to sleep, extreme selfishness and a tendency to cry and smile by turns. The Balya stage (child) is marked by a tendency to play, to do things topsy-turvy, inquisitive to know everything. The Kaumara (youthful) stage is distinguished by learing to study and think, to work and do something always. The Yauvana (adolescent) stage is noted for sexual instincts. Then manhood stage (Raja) is characterised by a domineering nature always commanding and ruling. This is followed by the Vriddha stage when inattention, inertia, pessimism, and sleep come in turns. The last stage is the Mrita (practically dead) and this is marked by absence of any activity, living in a perpetual state of fits and unconsciousness. All these characteristics can be attributed to the questioner according to the strength of the planets.

उच्चे राशावंशके वा स्थितो यो वारेमुष्यारूढराशिस्तदुच्चः ।
यद्यारोग्यं दीर्घमायुश्च वाच्यं प्रष्टुर्मृत्युर्वैपरीत्ये त्वमुष्मात्
॥१४॥

Stanza 14.—If Arudha Rasi coincides with the exaltation Rasi or Navamsa of the lord of the week-day of the question, then the querist will live long enjoying sound health. If on the contrary, the Arudha Rasi falls in the debilitated Rasi or Navamsa of the lord of the week-day concerned, etc., death will occur.

सिंहे कुक्ष्यक्षिजो व्याधिरात्मपीडोष्णरुक्तथा ।

वक्षोजिह्वास्यरोगोरुच्यम्बुरोगास्तु कर्कटे ॥१५॥

Stanza 15.—If Arudha is Leo, he will have stomach and eye troubles, spiritual affliction, diseases caused from extreme heat. If Cancer is Arudha, he will suffer from diseases in his breasts, tongue and face; want of taste for anything and swelling and watery complaints.

शिरोनेत्रभवव्याधिज्वरव्रणविचर्चिकाः ।

भौमभे बुधभे वायुरोधनासात्वगामयाः ॥१६॥

Stanza 16.—If Arudha Rasi is Aries or Scorpio, he will suffer from diseases in the head and eyes, high fever, itches and wounds. If Gemini or Virgo, he will have nose, skin and breathing troubles.

अरूढे जीवभे बुद्धिभ्रमकर्णामयादयः ।
शुक्रभे व्यञ्जनोत्था रुगरुचिश्वांबुजो गदः ॥१७॥

Stanza 17.—If Arudha Rasi is that of Jupiter, the questioner will suffer from mental troubles and ear complaints. If the Rasi is that of Venus, diseases in the testicles, aversion to eat and drink, swelling and other watery diseases.

बुद्धिभ्रमोऽङ्गसादश्च मलया न हतिः शनेः ।
विचर्चिकां च कण्डूतिंब्रूयात्सर्पान्वितेक्षिते ॥१८॥

आरूढे पापसंयुक्ते नियमेन वदेदिदम् ॥१९॥

Stanzas 18 and 19.—If a saturnine sign is the Arudha, it indicates mental troubles, extreme debility, dyspepsia and inability to walk. If Rahu is in Arudha Rasi, then he will suffer from itches and wounds. These diseases can be predicted only when the Arudha is found to be afflicted by evil planets.

Arudha Navamsa

आरूढलग्नभांशानां मान्दिराशिनवांशयोः ।
योगो रोगप्रदस्तत्र बहुयोगो मृतिप्रदः ॥२०॥

Stanza 20.—If Arudha, Lagna or thier Navamsas happen to be the Rasi or Navamsa holding Gulika, then the questioner will have bad diseases. If the majority are connected with Gulika, the questioner will die.

NOTES

Four factors have to be taken. They are Arudha Rasi, Arudha Navamsa, Lagna and Navamsa Lagna. If one of these is afflicted by Gulika, disease must be predicted. If three are afflicted by Gulika, then death of the questioner should be anticipated. Here affliction means that the Rasi or Navamsa position of Mandi should coincide with the Rasi positions or Amsa positions of Arudha and Lagna. In all these cases, especially when predicting death, one should give more weight to the birth horoscope.

आरूढे वा विलग्ने वा गण्डान्तांशः सपापदृक् ।
उदेति चेद्भवेन्मृत्युरारूढाष्टमभे तथा ॥२१॥

Stanza 21.—If *Gandanthamsa* happens to be in Arudha or Lagna and aspected by malefics, then death will happen. The same result will take place with regard to the 8th from Arudha.

NOTES

Gandanthamsa is the last Navamsa of Cancer, Scorpio and Pisces, and the first Navamsa of Aries, Leo and Sagittarius. If Gandanthamsa also falls in the 8th from Arudha, death can be predicted. Suppose Lagna or 8th from Arudha is 2° of Simha. Then this has reference to Gandanthamsa.

आरूढे मीनभे प्रष्टा पङ्गुः स्यात्पापवीक्षिते ।
कूपादौ पतनं वाच्यमारूढेऽलिनि वेन्दुभे ॥२२॥

Stanza 22.—If Pisces being Arudha is aspected by evil planets, the questioner will lose his legs and become lame. If Scorpio or Cancer is Arudha (aspected by evil planets), then he may fall into a well or a tank.

PLANETS AND VEGETABLES

प्राच्यदीत्युक्तवद्राशीनारूढादीन् न्यसेत् क्षितौ ।
वृक्षादीन्निर्दिशेत्स्वोक्तान् केन्द्रगैश्च बलान्वितैः ॥२३॥

Stanza 23.—The eight cardinal points beginning from East are signified by Arudha and other Rasis. Strong planets in kendras suggest the presence of trees governed by such planets in the directions appropriate to the trees.

NOTES

Arudha and 2nd from it represent East, 3rd denotes S.E. 4th and 5th South, 6th S.W., 7th and 8th West, 9th N.W., 10th and 11th North and 12th N.E.

गिरितरुकदळीकण्टकिवेणूनां क्रमुकनाळिकेराणाम् ।
तालानां च वनानि क्रमशोऽर्कात्स्वामिवत्तु राशीनाम्॥२४॥

Stanza 24.—Trees found in the hills, plantains (banana), thorny trees, shrubs, bamboos, arecanut trees and cocoanut trees are indicated by the Sun, Moon, Mars, Mercury, Jupiter, Venus and Saturn respectively. The signs ruled by these planets also indicate the appropriate trees.

NOTES

Trees are allotted to different planets and signs. For instance, the Moon rules plantain trees. Cancer also rules the same trees. Similarly the trees ruled by Mars come also under Aries and Taurus. Suppose as per stanza 24, a strong planet is in Sagittarius—a kendra from Arudha Rasi. This happens to be the 7th and the direction is west. Since Sagittarius is a Jupiterian sign, and since Jupiter rules bamboo, it may be inferred that bamboo trees are to be found in the western direction. In my humble opinion, these principles can be used for finding out the direction of lost articles in a question involving theft or finding the direction in which a missing person may have gone.

URDHVA MUKHA AND OTHER SIGNS

आरूढस्योर्ध्ववक्त्रत्वं प्रष्टुरभ्युदयवृद्धिकृत् ।
आधोमुख्यं क्षयाय स्यात्तत्कृष्णीयादिषूदितम् ॥२५॥

Stanza 25.—If Arudha is Urdhwa Mukha Rasi, the questioner will have increase of prosperity. If Arudha is Adhomukha Rasi, then he will have a downfall. This is the view of *Krishneeya.*

ऊर्ध्वमुखो यदि राशिर्होरा प्रश्ने नरस्यसिद्धिकरी ।
अन्ये विफले ज्ञेये शुभयुतदृष्टे शुभाख्ये च ॥२६॥

Stanza 26.—If in a Prasna, Arudha happens to be Urdwa Mukha, then he will succeed in his undertakings. If otherwise, he will meet with failure. But if good planets occupy or aspect these Rasis, the evil effects will be considerably minimised.

NOTES

The Rasi occupied by the Sun is Adhomukha Rasi. That Rasi which he has just left is Urdhwa Mukha Rasi and the one to which he will be going is Thiryang Mukha Rasi. Kendra Rasis from these are also of the same nature. In stanza 27, by "if otherwise" is meant Adhomukha and Thiryang Mukha Rasis. Even if Arudha falls in these Rasis, the effects will be good provided the Rasi is occupied or aspected by benefic planets.

ऊर्ध्वास्ये तनुगे प्रसूतगतकार्यारंभिणां पृच्छता-
मौन्नत्यं महदर्थपौरुषयशः स्थानादिकानां भवेत् ।
यद्यारूढमधोमुखं भमखिलैर्हीयेत वित्तादिभि-
स्तयज्येतापि सुहृज्जनैरपि पतेद्ग्राहादितः पृच्छकः ॥२७॥

Stanza 27.—If Lagna, at the time of birth, or at the time of a journey, or at the commencement of a work, etc., happens to be Urdhwa Mukha then success will attend all of them and status, fame, wealth and position will increase. On the contrary, if Arudha Rasi is Adhomukha, there will be decline of wealth, power, fame and position, desertion of his friends and fall from position.

NOTES

The astrological principle given in stanza 28 can be applied to Prasna (horary), Jataka (horoscopy) or Yatra (travel). In the 2nd part of the sloka, 'Arudha Rasi' is specifically used implying its application to prasna only. But there is no harm in extending the scope of its application as in the first part of the sloka.

आरूढाधिपतिः शुभग्रहगृहे प्रश्ने यदि स्यात् स्थितः
क्षोणीशामरमन्दिरादिषु मनोज्ञेषु स्थितिः पृच्छताम् ।
पापक्षेत्रगतः स चेदिह भवेन्म्लेच्छप्रदेशे स्थितिः
सोम्यासौम्यदृगन्वयात्सदसतां योगश्च तत्रोह्यताम्
॥२८॥

Stanza 28.—If the lord of Arudha occupies the Rasi of a benefic planet, it is to be inferred that the questioner lives in a beautiful house, palace or temple. If the lord occupies the Rasi of a malefic planet, then the house will be situated in the locality of mlechhas or the house will be unclean. According as the lord is associated with benefics or malefics, the person will have company of good or bad men.

NOTES

If Arudha lord occupies a house owned by good planets but is in conjunction with bad planets, then the person lives in a good mansion but in very bad company.

शुभवर्गे लग्नगते लग्ने वा सौम्ययोगमायाते ।
ब्रयादभिमतसिद्धिं प्रष्टु स्थानान्तरप्राप्तिम् ॥२९॥

Stanza 29.—If the Lagna has a number of benefic vargas or if the Lagna is occupied by good planets, then before long, the querist's position will be improved and his ambitions satisfied.

NOTES

The commentator suggests that by 'Lagna is implied Arudha. The position of Lagna in the Saptavargas (Rasi, Hora, Drekkana, Saptamsa, Navamsa, Dwadasamsa and Thrimsamsa) should be considered in order to know whether the Lagna has more benefic vargas or malefic ones.

द्विपदे चतुष्पदे वा भवने लग्नोपगो ग्रहः पापः ।
तिष्ठति तन्नाशकरो ज्ञेयः सौम्योपि वृद्धिकरः ॥३०॥

Stanza 30.—If the Lagna being a biped or a quadruped sign is occupied by malefics, the questioner's dependents and relatives or live-stock will be destroyed. If benefics occupy the Lagna, they will prosper.

NOTES

If the Lagna is a biped sign and malefics are in Lagna, the person's dependents and relatives will be afflicted or destroyed. If the occupants are benefics, good will happen to dependents and relatives. If the Lagna is a quadruped sign, effects will pertain to live-stock belonging to the querist.

SIGNIFICANCE OF GOLD PIECE

स्वर्णेनारूढविन्यस्तेनापि प्रष्टुः शुभाशुभम् ।
ज्ञेयं शास्त्रान्तरेषूक्तं तदप्यथ निगद्यते ॥३१॥

Stanza 31.—The gold piece is Arudha and in fact it is more important than Arudha because it is the gold piece that determines the Arudha.

NOTES

The 'lay' of the gold piece has been discussed in stanzas 51 to 53 of Chapter IV to which the readers may refer once again.

जलगन्धार्तवव्रीहितण्डुला भूतपञ्चकम् ।
तन्मयं हि पुनर्ज्ञेयं जीव एव हि काञ्चनम् ॥३२॥

Stanza 32.—The five Bhutas (used in a Prasna) are water, sandal paste, paddy, rice and flowers. Their importance should be understood once again. The gold piece represents Jeeva the life element.

NOTES

It will be seen that before laying the gold piece, worship is offered to the Chakra or the zodiacal diagram and the materials used are water, sandal paste, paddy, rice and flowers. These materials are symbolic of the human body which is composed of the Panchamahabhutas (five primordial elements). It is said that from the gold piece and the pooja materials, many things can be gleaned regarding the future of the questioner or the outcome of the question. If the five materials are found in contact with the gold piece, the questioner would live long. If they are found away, the person's life will be short. The conjunction of Jeeva (gold piece) and Deha (the five materials) is life. Their separation is death. If the materials used are in small quantities, then the constitution of the man is weak. If they are dirty, he is suffering from diseases. In this way by a careful examination of the gold piece and the materials, Kerala astrologers, who practise Ashtamangala Prasna, glean a lot about the future of the querist.

पुष्पाक्षतोपरि स्वर्णमुत्तानं पृच्छकायुषे ।
तिर्यङ्मृत्युकरं भूस्थं न्यक्तु बाधागदावहम् ॥३३॥

Stanza 33.—If the gold piece is found on the top of the materials, facing up, the man will live long. If it lies inclined not facing the ground, it indicates danger to life. If it is facing the ground, he will have sickness and troubles from evil spirits.

ऊर्ध्वं पुष्पाक्षतानां निहितमिह भवेत्स्वर्णमूर्ध्वाननं चे-
त्तत्काले वर्द्धनं स्याद्धनसुखयशसां पृच्छकस्योर्ध्वमूर्ध्वम् ।
तत्त्राधोमुखं चेत्क्षय उपचयतः किञ्चिदारब्ध एवा-
थोर्ध्वास्यं चेदधस्तात्क्षयत उपचयारम्भणं तत्र वाच्यम्
॥३४॥

Stanza 34.—If the gold piece is at the top lying in its normal position, the period before him is bright and his wealth, happiness and fame will all increase. If it has fallen with the face down, then his times so far were good but the future will be bad. If the gold piece is found under the flowers and other materials with the face upwards in a normal way, his period till now was bad, but hereafter better days will soon dawn.

NOTES

If the gold piece is found mixed with other materials his period was good so far; if aloof from materials, his period so far was bad; if found with the face up normally, the future will be good; if discovered in an abnormal posture, the future will be bad.

सर्वाधोधोमुखं चेत्क्षय इह तु पुनश्चापि सर्वक्षयः स्या-
न्मध्यस्थे हेम्नि चोह्यां फलमपि सकलं प्रोक्तयैवात्र
रीत्या ।
दीर्घायुर्मृत्युनैस्त्रै उपचितधनता प्राग्दिगादिप्लवत्वे
स्वर्णस्याग्न्यादिकोणप्लवन इह पुनर्मृत्युरोगाद्यनर्थाः ।
इति ॥३५॥

Stanza 35.—If the lay of the gold piece is towards the ground, it is bad; if it is towards or amidst the flowers, it is good; if inclined towards the East, South, West and South, there will be long life, death, poverty, and increase of wealth. If inclined towards the corners, there will be poverty, sickness, danger to life and everything.

मान्दीन्दूदयलग्नांशा मृत्युदेहासवश्वरे ।
आयुरारोग्यदास्त्वेते रोगदैर्घ्यप्रदा स्थिरे ॥३६॥
द्वन्द्वगास्संयुताश्चैते त्रयः प्रष्ठमृतिप्रदाः ।
मोहदाः स्युर्मिथो दृष्टास्त्रिकोणस्था महारुजे ॥३७॥

Stanzas 36 and 37—If the Navamsas of Mandi, Moon and Lagna (going under the names of Mrityu, Deha and Prana respectively) fall in Chara Rasis, then there will be long life and good health. If they fall in fixed signs, the sickness will drag on for a long time. If they fall in common signs or if they are found in one and the same Rasi, then he will die. If these aspect one another, there will be sudden fits and unconsciousness. If they are in trines, he will suffer from incurable disease.

NOTES

Multiply Gulika Sphuta (*i.e.*, Gulikas longitude by 9) and divide the product by 30. We get its Navamsa Sphuta which is known as Mrityu Sphuta. If Chandra Sphuta is multiplied by 9, and divided by 30, we get a Sphuta known as Deha Sphuta. Multiply Udaya Lagna Sphuta by 9 and divide the product by 30 to get Prana Sphuta.

Determination of Mrityu, Deha and Prana Sphutas

$$\frac{\text{Gulika Sphuta} \times 9}{30} = \text{Mrityu Sphuta}$$

$$\frac{\text{Chandra Sphuta} \times 9}{30} = \text{Deha Sphuta}$$

$$\frac{\text{Udaya Lagna Sphuta} \times 9}{30} = \text{Prana Sphuta}$$

योगदृष्ट्यादिसम्बन्धस्त्वायुषे प्राणदेहयोः ।

देहमृत्योस्तु रोगाय प्राणमृत्योस्तु मोहकृत् ॥६८॥

Stanza 38.—If Prana and Deha or Deha and Mrityu or Prana and Mrityu Sphutas are found in the same sign or aspect each other, then there will be long life, increase of sickness, and fits and unconsciousness respectively.

NOTES

Prana and Deha must be together or in opposite signs to cause long life. Deha and Mrityu should be similarly disposed to give rise to disease. Fits and unconsciousness can result if Prana and Mrityu are situated in the same manner.

EFFECTS OF LAGNA

क्षीणेन्द्वर्कसुतारतीक्ष्णमहसां वर्गा विलग्नस्थिता
मृत्युव्याधिधनक्षयाद्यशुभदाः प्रष्टुर्यदीमे विदुः ।
धीसामर्थ्यकृतोथ पूर्णशशिनः शुक्रस्य वा वाक्पते-
रेते कुर्युररोगतार्थतनयप्राप्त्याद्यभीष्टागमान् ॥३९॥

Stanza 39.—If Lagna is in the Vargas of waning Moon, Saturn, Mars and the Sun, there will be death, disease, loss of money and other unfavourable results; in those of Mercury, increase of intelligence; if in the vargas of waxing Moon, Jupiter and Venus, good health, influx of money, birth of children and realisation of ambitions.

लग्ने तदीश्वरे वोष्णयुक्ते जूर्त्यादिपित्तरुक् ।
दाहश्च भवनस्याथ सविषत्र्यंशनाडिके ॥४०॥

Stanza 40.—If Lagna or the lord is conjoined with ushna the person is suffering from fever and other phlegmatic diseases. If with Visha Drekkana, or Visha Nadi or Ekargala, his house will be set fire to.

NOTES

These doshas have been referred to in Chapter II, stanzas 17-21. Refer also to Appendix.

Visha Drekkanas are: the first Drekkana of Mesha, Kataka, Simha, Kanya, Dhanus and Makara; the 2nd Drekkana of Vrishabha, Mithuna, Thula, Kumbha and Meena; and the last Drekkana of Vrischika.

यद्राशिसंज्ञो लग्नांशः स राशिश्चेच्छुभान्वितः ।
गतकालः शुभः प्रष्टुरशुभो यदि पापयुक् ॥४१॥

Stanza 41.—If the Rasi denoting Navamsa Lagna has the association of good planets, then the past of the man can he said to be good. If it has bad associations, his past was bad.

लग्नांशराशिगे चन्द्रे लोहपात्रक्षतिर्मृतेः ।
लक्ष्मंमान्द्यंशराशिस्थे तथा मृद्भाण्डभञ्जनम् ॥

मृत्युप्राणशरीरराशिसहितैस्तद्वीक्षकैर्वा ग्रहै-
स्तत्तत्प्रोक्तपदार्थलाभविहति वाच्ये शुभायापदे ॥४२॥

Stanza 42.—Chandra occupying Lagna Navamsa Rasi, and any metal vessel getting broken ; or Chandra occupying Gulika Navamsa Rasi and any earthen vessel getting broken are the indications for death.

NOTES

Some writers read that if Guliku Navamsa Rasi turns out to be Lagna Navamsa Rasi, and an earthen vessel breaks, then also death can be predicted.

Effects of Power and Deha

संज्ञाध्यायदशाधनाप्तिकथनास्त्वन्यत्र वोक्ता हि ते ।
ताम्राद्या नखपूर्वकास्तृणमुखाः पत्यास्य वा ते न चेत्
॥४३॥

Stanza 43.—If, during the period of Prasna, articles signified by planets aspecting or occupying Prana, Mrityu and Deha Rasis (as per sloka 36) are obtained or lost (by the questioner) auspicious or inauspicious results respectively should be predicted. The assignment of articles should be taken according to *Samgnadhyaya* and principles of Dasa Phala. If there are no planets occupying or aspecting, the materials signified by the Rasis themselves should be taken.

NOTES

In all standard books on astrology and in the earlier chapters of this work different articles have been allotted to different planets and signs. In predicting profession or in predicting Dasa results, different articles are referred to different planets. It is these 'articles' that should be considered.

लग्नेन्दूमानदानाभ्यामित्युक्तानामथो फलम् ।
प्राणमृत्युशरीराणामधुना समुदीर्यते ॥४४॥

Stanza 44.—Now the effects of Prana, Deha, Mrityu, as calculated in Chapter V, Sloka 10, are enumerated.

प्राणमृत्युशरीरेषु देहाधिक्ये रुजां शमः ।
प्राणेधिके महान् रोगो मृत्युश्चेदधिको मृतिः ॥४५॥

Stanza 45.—Of Prana, Mrityu and Deha, if Deha is greater, the sickness of the man will abate. If Prana is greater, sickness will increase. If Mrityu is greater, he will die.

NOTES

Suppose Prana is in Gemini 25° and Deha is in Cancer 26°. Then 'Deha' is greater. The sickness of the querent will abate. If both are in the same Rasi, the difference in degrees should be taken. If the degrees are also the same, then the minutes must be taken

मृत्यौ ज्येष्ठाहिपौष्णस्थे जन्मभस्थे च पञ्चता ।
मृत्युः प्राणश्च देहश्च क्रमवृद्धाः शुभप्रदाः ॥४६॥

Stanza 46.—If Mrityu occupies Jyeshta, Aslesha, Revati or the Janma Nakshatra or Anujanma Nakshatra of the questioner, he will die. If Mrityu, Prana and Deha are found in an ascending order, one greater than the other, it will be very good for the questioner.

लग्नेन्दुगुलिकांशैरप्याधिक्याद्विविचिन्तनम् ।
एतत्तु क्रियते कैश्चिदप्यथ विलिख्यते ॥४७॥

Stanza 47.—The above-mentioned effects can also be gleaned by a consideration of the greater longitude of the Navamsas of the Lagna, the Moon and Gulika.

NOTES

In the earlier pages, we have learnt the method of calculating the longitudes of the Navamsa Rasis of the ascendant, the Moon and Gulika. In this sloka the reference is to these Navamsas. According to some authorities, these Navamsas should be considered in judging whether the questioner will die or if his fortune will improve.

लग्नांशकेधिके वृद्धी रुजां चन्द्रांशके शमः ।
मान्द्यंशे मृतिराधिक्यं गताभिर्घटिकादिभिः ॥ इति ॥४८॥

Stanza 48.—If the Lagna longitude is greater than Chandra's longitude, the result is, increase of sickness. If *vice versa*, there will be abatement of the disease. If Mandyamsa which is Mrityu is greater, then the result could be fatal.

मृत्युकालसतां प्राणे मध्यगे तद्युतेक्षिते ।
प्रष्टुर्मरणमादेश्यं शुभदोस्येन्दुसङ्गमः ॥४९॥

Stanza 49.—If Prana Sphuta comes between Mrityu Sphuta and Kala Sphuta or between the sphutas of two evil planets, or is aspected by these, or is associated with these, then death will result. The Moon's association causes benefic results.

आरूढेन तदीशेन लग्नांशकाधिपैः ।
इन्द्वंशेनेन्दुना युक्तौ मृत्युकालौ मृतिप्रदौ ॥५०॥

Stanza 50.—If Mrityu or Kala happen to conjoin Arudha, Lagna, Lagna Navamsa, Chandra, Chandra Navamsa or their lords, death will result.

RAHU CHAKRA

लग्ने राहुयुते चोरारिपुपीडा रवौ मृतिः ।

चन्द्रे देहव्यथा कैन्दु राहुचक्रफलं त्विदम् ॥५१॥

Stanza 51.—If Rahu conjoins Lagna, there will be troubles from enemies and thieves; with Sun, death; and with Moon diseases and pains all over the body.

NOTES

Here the reference is to Rahu Indu Chakra explained in Chapter V, stanzas 24 to 26.

AMAZING PREDICTIONS

कालहोराफलं वाच्यं प्रष्टुर्विस्मापनं परम् ।

विश्वासार्थं स्वभारत्या तदप्यथ विलिख्यते ॥५२॥

Stanza 52.—The astrologer must deduce effects from Kala Hora to amaze the questioner, so that convinced at the accuracy of predictions, he may be led to place faith in the astrologer's words.

सूर्यस्त कालहोरायां प्रश्नश्चेद्भूमिपागमः ।

नार्यागमः शशाङ्कस्य भूमिपुत्रस्य शस्त्रिणाम् ॥५३॥

बौध्यां पारशवायानमथवा विद्वदागमः ।
गुरोर्विप्रवरायानं भृगोर्वेश्याङ्गनागमः ॥५४॥
मन्दस्य वणिगायानं भृत्यबौद्धागमोथवा ।
केन्द्रगाश्चेदमी खेटा नियमेन वदेदिदम् ॥५५॥

Stanzas 53 to 55.—If Prasna time is in the Kala Hora of the Sun, then a king or a distinguished personage will turn up. If the Moon, some woman; if Mars, some armed man; if Mercury, a flower-maker or a learned man; if Jupiter, a true Brahmin; if Venus, a dancing girl; and if Saturn, a merchant, a servant or a Buddhist monk. If lord of Kala Hora is in a kendra from Lagna, the results will be further confirmed.

NOTES

The persons suggested in this stanza are supposed to arrive at the time of Prasna, either at the place of Prasna or at the residence of the querist.

So much regarding Udaya Lagna.

SIGNIFICANCE OF CHANDRA NAVAMSA SIGN

यद्राशिसंज्ञश्चन्द्रांशः स राशिश्चेच्छुभान्वितः ।
भावी कालः शुभो वाच्यः पापयुक्चेदशोभनः ॥५६॥

Stanza 56.—If Chandra Navamsa Rasi is associated with good planets, a good period ahead is indicated. If this Rasi is afflicted, then a bad future is going to set in.

जीवस्सुतप्रदो विप्रवरकृत्रीचभांशगः ।
शुक्रो वस्त्राङ्गनादायी विवादे जयकृद्बुधः ॥५७॥
पूर्णचन्द्रो मनोहारिद्रव्यलाभं प्रयच्छति ।
देवभूमिपयोः कोपं कुर्यादर्कोथ भूमिजः ॥५८॥
वृथैव विग्रहं भूमिविवादं च समावहेत् ।
सूर्यपुत्रः कृषिप्रेष्यपश्वादीनां विनाशकृत् ॥५९॥
चण्डालापच्छिरोरोगविषसर्पभयं फणी ।
प्रेतबाधां शिखी कुर्यान्मान्दिश्चूर्णाद्युपद्रवम् ॥६०॥
बुधः पापयुतश्चेत्स विवादे परिभूतिकृत् ।
क्षिणचन्द्रो मनःपीडां करोति परिपृच्छताम् ॥६१॥

Stanzas 57 to 61.—Jupiter in the Chandra Navamsa Rasi gives rise to the birth of a son. Jupiter debilitated, denotes quarrels with Brahmins. Venus in Chandra Navamsa Rasi gives fresh clothes and happiness from women; Mercury—success in litigation. A full Moon denotes beautiful things. The Sun causes anger of rulers and gods. Mars causes strife without reason, and litigation connected with lands; Saturn brings about loss of produce in lands, diseases to cattle, and sufferings to servants. Rahu causes fear from poison, serpents, and troubles to his inferior servants. Ketu causes troubles from ghosts. Gulika causes trouble in the shape of Abhichara. Afflicted Mercury will give rise to failure in litigation and weak Moon causes mental worry.

कालः प्रोक्तांशमासोत्र लग्नांशेपि विधिस्त्वयम् ॥६२॥

Stanza 62.—These results will be experienced within the number of months denoted by the number of Navamsas traversed by the Moon; or the number of Navamsas counted from Aries. The period can be fixed by taking into consideration the number of Navamsas the Lagna has gained

प्रश्नकालसुधाभानुक्रियणां सदृशं फलम् ।

प्रष्टुर्वक्तव्यमित्युक्तं जीवेनैतद्विलिख्यते ॥६३॥

Stanza 63.—The great author Jeeva wants the astrologers to calculate Chandra Kriya at the time of Prasna and explain the effects.

क्रमाच्चन्द्रक्रियाः पञ्च पञ्च मेषादिराशिषु ।
प्रकल्प्य तत्समंत्रयात्सर्वकार्येषु तत्फलम् ॥६४॥

Stanza 64.—Allot 5 Chandra Kriyas for each Rasi from Aries. From this find out the Chandra Kriya of the Moon.

प्रश्नकाले गुणश्चेन्द्वोः शुभो यदि शुभप्रदः ।
तथा चाशुभकर्मस्थे चन्द्रो प्रश्नोशुभप्रदः ॥६५॥

Stanza 65.—If the Chandra Kriya is good at at the time of Prasna, there will be good ; if Chandra Kriya is bad, evil results will happen. The nature of Chandra Kriyas has to be learnt from Horoscopy.

NOTES

Astrological writers talk of Chandra Kriyas (60), Chandravastas (12) and Chandravelas (36). Convert the are traversed in a constellation by the Moon into minutes. Multiply this by 60 and divide the product by 800. The quotient plus represents the number of Chandra Kriya.

Determination of Chandra Kriya :

$$\frac{\text{Are traversed by Moon in a constellation in minutes} \times 60}{803} = X$$

$X+1$ = Chandra Kriya,

॥ इति प्रश्नमार्गे अष्टमोध्यायः ॥

नवमाध्यायः

RECAPITULATION

आयुर्विवाहसन्तानप्रभृतिप्रश्नकर्मसु ।

साधारणफलाः प्राय: समयाद्या इतीरिताः ॥ १ ॥

Stanza 1.—What has been explained so far can be applied to all questions pertaining to longevity, marriage and birth of children.

तत्कालजैर्निमित्तैः प्रष्ट्रारूढोदयेन्दुगुलिकाद्यैः ।

आयुः प्रथमं चिन्त्यं स्वस्थातुरविषयभेदमवगम्य ॥ इति ॥ २ ॥

Stanza 2.—First the longevity of the person should be ascertained by a consideration of Arudha Lagna, Moon's position, Gulika, etc., and by observing the *nimiththas* at the time of the query and then the results the querist wishes to know.

NOTES

Stanzas 1 to 3 are from *Anusthana Paddhati*, a work presumably earlier to *Prasna Marga*. It is not known who its author is. Very little is known of the work itself.

EXAMINATION OF AGE

आयुः पूर्वं परीक्षेत पश्चाल्लक्षणमादिशेत् ।
अनायुषां तु मर्त्यानां लक्षणैः किं प्रयोजनम् ।। इति ।।३।।

Stanza 3.—Longevity must be examined first and then the other aspects. What use would be the other indications in the absence of longevity?

इत्यादिभिस्तु वचनैः पूर्वमायुनिरूपणम् ।
कर्तव्यमिति लग्नाष्टमेशप्रभृतिभिर्ग्रहैः ।। ४ ।।

Stanza 4.—According to these sayings, the longevity of the person must be first found out by looking at Lagna and the 8th and their lords.

आयुरेव विशेषेण प्रथमं चिन्त्यतेधुना ।
स्वस्थमुद्दिश्य वा प्रश्न एष वातुरमित्ययम् ।। ५ ।।
विवेको विहगैः कार्य इति शास्त्रान्तरोदितम् ।। ६ ।।

Stanzas 5 and 6.—The age of the questioner must first be examined. It should be ascertained from other works whether a Prasna relates to health or disease.

लग्नेशो यदि केन्द्रगः खलु बली राशौ चरे चांशके
प्रश्नःस्वस्थगतोथ रिःफरिपुगो लग्नाधिपश्चेत्स्थिरे ।

निर्वीर्यश्च महागदार्तविषया पृच्छाथ मिश्रः स चे-
त्तोयर्द्धिक्षयवन्मुहुः प्रशमनं वृद्धिश्चवाच्ये रुजाम् ॥७॥

Stanza 7.—If the lord of Lagna is in a movable Rasi or Navamsa or in kendras or in a strong position, then it is Swastha Prasna. If the lord of Lagna occupies fixed signs or fixed Navamsas or is in the 6th or the 12th houses or found weak in all respects, then it is to be inferred that the querist is suffering from severe illness and the question relates to disease. If the lord of Lagna is subject to mixed influences, the man's illness increases sometimes and decreases sometimes like the ebb and flow of water.

NOTES

Swastha means doing well. Swastha Prasna means a question that does not pertain to illness or disease. Disposition of the Lagna lord in a kendra, his strength, his placement in a movable sign and a movable Navamsa are the four factors favouring good health. His situation in the 6th or 12th, his weakness, and his placement in a fixed sign and fixed Navamsa favour the opposite results.

तुङ्गस्थिते तनुपतौ सधनः सवीर्यो
जेता द्विषां खलु भवेत्प्रथमानतेजाः ।
प्रष्टाभिमानसहितोथ निजत्रिकोणे
वासो विभूषणलसत्तनुरात्तसौख्यः ॥८॥

बन्धोर्गृहे निजगृहे च विनष्टवैरी
भार्यातनूजधनबन्धुभिरिद्धमोदः ।
वैर्यृक्षगे रुगनिशं सुतमित्रभार्या-
नाशश्च भूमिपतिपावकचोरपीडा ॥ ९ ॥

नीचस्थिते रिपुनिपीडनतोन्यदेश-
यानं पदाच्च चलनं धनहानिदैन्ये ।
मूढे सपापगुळिके च नृपारिहेतो-
र्वैकल्यवानितरदेशगतो मृतो वा ॥१०॥

Stanzas 8 to 10.—If the lord of Lagna is exalted, the person will be wealthy and strong, will have fame and good name and will overcome his enemies; if in Moolatrikona, he will have plenty of clothes and ornaments and happiness; if own or friendly house, he will live happily with money, wife and children and relations overcoming his enemies and difficulties; if in inimical place, there will be sickness, trouble from kings and thieves, fear from fire and calamities to wife children and friends. If in debilitation, the person lives in a foreign place being driven out by poverty, loss of position, etc. If in combustion or in association with Gulika or malefic planets, the person lives maimed in a foreign place, through the machinations of enemies or the orders of the rulers, or he will be dead.

लग्नेशोऽष्टमपश्च नीचगृहगौ यद्वास्तगौ चेदुभौ
भ्रष्टा भग्नमनाः सुखेन रहितः पीडार्तदेहः सदा ।
स्वल्पायुष्टश्चलितः पदादपि निजादूर्ध्वाङ्गरोगार्दितो
योगेष्वप्यशुभेषु सत्सु कथयेत्केमद्रुमाद्येष्विदम् ॥११॥

Stanza 11.—If lords of Lagna and the 8th are debilitated or combust, the person will have a frustrated mind being devoid of happiness, and suffering afflictions If there are Kemadruma, etc., the person will be short-lived, suffering from sickness in the upper parts of the body.

लग्नाधिपश्च मृतिपश्च मिथः समेतौ
यद्वा स्वतुङ्गनिजगेहसुहृद्गृहस्थौ ।
लग्नेशशुक्रधिशणाश्च धनत्रिकोण-
केन्द्रस्थिता विदधते खलु दीर्घमायुः ॥ इति॥१२॥

Stanza 12.—If the lords of Lagna and the 8th conjoin, or are exalted or occupy own or friendly houses; or if the lord of Lagna, Jupiter and Venus occupy trines or quadrants or the 2nd house, the person will have a long life.

MRITYU LAKSHANA

प्रष्टुस्तारात्रिकोणे स्थितवति गुळिके जन्मचन्द्राष्टमे वा
नक्षत्रेशे च मान्द्याश्रितभवनपतौ सत्यपि प्रष्टरि स्वे ।
स्थातर्यप्यष्टमर्क्षे निहित इह पणे चात्र या जन्मतारा
प्रश्नोडुमान्दिगोडुत्रितयपतिषु वा षट्स्वपि स्वस्थमृत्युः
॥१३॥

Stanza 13.—The following eight combinations indicate death :—Gulika occupying the person's Janma Nakshatra or its trines ; Gulika joining the 8th from the Janma Rasi ; lord of the sign held by Gulika happening to be lord of Janma Nakshatra ; the messenger or questioner standing in the 8th from the Janma Rasi ; depositing of the gold piece in the 8th from Janma Rasi ; and the lord of Janma Nakshatra, or the lord of Prasna—Nakshatra, or the lord of the Nakshatra occupied by Gulika (at the time of Prasna) standing in the 8th Rasi from the Janma Rasi.

NOTES

The eight conditions listed above are simple. If any of the above conditions prevail at the time of query, the person will die even though at the time of query he may be hale and healthy.

होराया इह जीवः स्यात्प्रष्टुरायुर्निरूपणम् ।
देहः फलान्तरज्ञानमिति शास्त्रान्तरोदितम् ॥१४॥

Stanza 14.--According to other authorities, there are two aspects to be considered, *viz.*, Jeeva (life), and Deha (body), the former dealing with the determination of longevity and the latter with the delineation of the other aspects of the horoscope.

आयुश्च लोकयात्रा च शास्त्रेस्मिन् द्वे प्रयोजने ।
निश्चेतुं कोनु शक्नोति वसिष्ठो वा बृहस्पतिः ॥१५॥
किं पुनर्मनुजास्तत्र विशेषात्तु कलौ युगे ।
लोकायात्रापरिज्ञानं शरीरं कथ्यते बुधैः ॥१६॥
आयुषस्तु परिज्ञानं होराया जीव उच्यते ॥ इति ॥१७॥

Stanzas 15 to 17.—The two uses of astrology are the derermination of longevity and the discernment of life's journey. When even sages like Vasishta and Brihaspathi find it difficult to scan the future, how can men understand it clearly especially in Kaliyuga? Learned men say that by Deha or 'body' is meant the knowing of life events while 'jeeva' implies the determination of longevity.

Determining the Length of Life

लग्नं विलग्नपतिमृत्युतदीशचन्द्राः
प्रष्ट्रायुषोवगमने खलु साधनानि ।
तेषां शुभाशुभदृगन्वयवीर्यवत्ता
निर्वीर्यतादिगुणदोषवशाद्विचिन्त्यम् ॥१८॥

Stanza 18.—The factors to be considered in determining the length of life are Lagna, the 8th house, their lords and the Moon. The longevity should be ascertained by considering whether these factors are associated with or aspected by benefics or malefics and whether they are powerful or weak.

पापान्तरस्थितिशुभेतरदृष्टियोगा
दोषा गुणास्त्रयं इमे वपुषः शुभानाम् ।
स्वेशस्य सङ्गमदृशौ च गुणौ भवेतां
दोषा गुणाश्च खलु लग्नवदष्टमस्य ॥१९॥

Stanza 19.—Lagna becomes afflicted if it is hemmed in between malefics or if it is in association with or aspected by evil planets. Lagna is said to be strong if it is conjoined with or aspected by benefics or the lord of Lagna or if it stands between two benefic planets. The strength and weakness of the lord of the 8th are similarly constituted. Instead of Lagna, consider the 8th.

पापान्वयेक्षणशुभेतरमध्यवास-

मौढ्यारिनीचभगमास्तनुपस्य दोषाः ।

तुङ्गात्मबन्धुभवनस्थितिसौम्ययोग-

वीक्षान्तरस्थितिविलोमगमा गुणाः स्युः ॥२०॥

Stanza 20.—The lord of Lagna becomes afflicted if he is associated with (or hemmed in between) or aspected by evil planets, is combust, or debilitated or occupies the house of an enemy. The lord can be said to be strong if he is associated with or aspected by or hemmed inbetween benefic planets, is exalted or occupies his own house or the house of a friend or is retrograde.

लग्नपस्य गुणा दोषास्तुल्याः स्युर्मृतिपस्य च ।

केन्द्रस्थितिर्मृतीशस्य दोषो लग्नपतेर्गुणः ॥२१॥

Stanza 21.—What is said above regarding the strength or affliction of lord of Lagna is also applicable to the lord of the 8th. While lord of Lagna in a kendra becomes strong, the lord of the 8th becomes a malefic in a similar situation.

NOTES

Thus we see in these two stanzas 8 gunas for lord of Lagna and 7 gunas for the lord of the 8th.

चन्द्रस्यारिमृतिव्ययस्थितिरसन्मध्यस्थितीक्षन्वयाः
क्षीणत्वं तनुगत्वमत्र निजनीचाप्तिश्च दोषा इमे ।
पूर्णत्वं शुभमध्यवासयुतिदृद्वेड्यकेन्द्रस्थिता
स्थानं तुङ्गगृहे युतिश्च गुरुणा साङ्के विशेषाद्गुणाः
॥२२॥

Stanza 22.—The Moon becomes evil if he occupies the 6th, 8th or 12th house or is situated between the evil planets or is associated with or aspected by malefics or he is weak (waning) or occupies Lagna or is debilitated. The Moon can be considered good and strong if he is in Taurus or full, or is between two benefics or is associated with or aspected by benefic planets, or is exalted or is in conjunction with or in a kendra from Jupiter.

त्र्यायारिष्वसदा वासो दीर्घायुष्यकृदीरितः ।
वराहमिहिरेणैव पद्येन गुरुशादिना ॥२३॥

Stanza 23.—If malefics occupy 3, 6 and 11, they give rise to long life. So says Varahamihira.

लग्नं मूर्द्धोदयं चेच्छुभपतिनिहितं त्रीक्षितञ्चाखिलानां
दीर्घायुष्यप्रदं स्यान्निधनमपि तथैवान्यभावा विचिन्त्यः ।

रन्ध्रेशो लग्नपो वा यदि बलसहितौ चानयोर्वाऽधिमैत्री
चारूढश्चोर्ध्ववक्त्रः समयजलसमृद्धः स मूर्द्धोदयाख्यः
॥२४॥

Stanza 24.—If Lagna and the 8th happen to be Urdhodaya Rasis or if they are associated with or aspected by benefic or by their own lords; or if the lords of Lagna and the 8th are strong or are intimate; or if Arudha happens to be Urdhwa Mukha, Urdhodaya or Samaya Jala Samriddha Rasis, long life can be predicted.

NOTES

Urdhodaya Rasis are also called Sirshodaya Rasis.

Samaya Jala Samriddha Rasis are :—(1) Three Rasis from the Moon can be considered as rise or ebb. (2) The next three as fall or flow; the next three are the same as (1) and the next three same as (2). Meena is Ubhayodaya Rasi and Mesha, Vrishabha, Kataka. Dhanus and Makara are Prishtodaya Rasis. The remaining ones are Sirshodaya Rasis.

द्रेक्काणाः फणिभूषणा मृतिकराः कोलाभ गृध्रननाः ।
सक्रूरा यदि शीतगौ निधनगे हीनस्य च व्याधिना ।
रन्ध्रे शीतकरो भवेन्मृतिकरः पृष्ठोदयो लग्नगः
पापाः केन्द्रमृतिस्थिताश्च मृतिदा रोगार्दितानां नृणाम् ॥
इति ॥२५॥

Stanza 25.—Death will happen even in the absence of any diseases if Lagna rises in Sarpa, Kola and Gridhra Mukha Drekkanas; or if evil planets conjoin the same; or if the Moon occupies the 8th house. If the Moon is not in the 8th, then the querist will die only if he is already sick. If Lagna is Prishtodaya Rasi and the Moon is in the 8th house, death will happen. If evil planets occupy kendras and the 8th house, the man will die in case he is sick.

NOTES

Sarpa Drekkanas.—The first Drekkana of Vrischika, the last Drekkana of Kataka and Meena.

Kola Mukha Drekkana.—The first Drekkana of Kataka and Makara and the last one of Vrischika.

Gridhra Mukha Drekkana.—The last ones of Simha and Kumbha and 2nd Drekkana of Thula.

LAGNA AND ARUDHA

तत्कालोघद्राशिः प्रष्ट्रारूढश्च लग्नशब्दोक्तौ ।
कृष्णीयादिषु कथितं ताभ्यां द्वाभ्यां फलं हि वाच्यमिति ॥२६॥

भूमिष्ठंस्थिरचक्रं चरति तथाकाश एव चरचक्रम् ।
चक्रद्वितयेन फलं प्रश्नादौ पृच्छतां वाच्यम् ॥२७॥

Stanzas 26 and 27.—By Lagna or Arudha is meant the rising sign at the moment. *Krishneeya* and other works say that results must be read either from the one or from both. A Rasi Chakra is of two kinds, *i.e.*, Sthira and Chara. The fixed circle (sthira chakra) is posited on the earth (all around the astrologer). The movable circle (chara chakra) on the other hand moves in the sky. It is by a consideration of both the chakras that predictions should be made.

NOTES

The sthira chakra is indicated by Mesha, Vrishabha (East), Mithuna (South-East), etc. It is on this that Arudha has been based. Avaha Vayu drives this chakra. Its speed is unequal and not the same at all times. The chara chakra is driven by Pravaha with uniform speed: Lagna is based on this.

उदयारूढर्क्षाभ्यां शुभाशुभं प्रष्टुरादिशेद्यद्वत् ।
दैवविदो व्ययभाभ्यां तदायभाभ्यां तथैव दूतस्य ॥२८॥

Stanza 28.—Just as you read the good and bad for a querist from Lagna and Arudha, the future of the astrologer can also be read from the 12th (from Lagna or Arudha) and that of the messenger from the 11th.

अथोदयारूढभयोर्ध्वयोस्तदा बलान्वितादद्वादशभावजं फलम् ।
तथात्मपित्रादिपदार्थकारकैरपि ग्रहैरर्कमुखैर्विमृश्यते ॥ इति ॥२९॥

Stanza 29.—The results of the twelve houses should be read from Lagna or Arudha—whichever is stronger. In the same way, read from the Sun all about the father and one's own soul and other events from the appropriate Karakas.

Questions are of two types being based on the ascendant and on the Arudha.

प्रश्नः खलूदयारूढप्रधानान्येन द्विधा मतः ।
भास्करोदयवेलायां सञ्चरत्यपि पृच्छके ॥३०॥
पृच्छके विद्याया युक्ते यात्रादिचरकर्मसु ।
उदयेन फलं ब्रूयादेवमादिषु दैववित् ॥३१॥

Stanzas 30 and 31.—If the questioner is a learned man or if the query is made early in the morning walking up and down, if he asks any question regarding journeys, then follow Udaya Lagna.

NOTES

When the querist is moving about or when a question is put from a position from which Arudha cannot be easily fixed, then one has to have recourse to the rising sign (Udaya Lagna).

कर्मान्ते च दिनान्ते च शयिते पृच्छके निशि ।
प्रदेशे जन सम्पूर्णो मुष्टौ चान्तर्गृहस्थ च ॥३२॥
विषये स्थावराणामित्यादिष्वारूढराशिना ।
चिन्त्यमत्रोभयत्रापि स्वं स्वं छत्रं तदुच्यते ॥३३॥

Stanzas 32 and 33.—If any question is put after the questioner has finished his work, or in the evening twilight, or lying down, or from a place crowded with people, or just to test the astrologer, or from inside a house; or if he questions anything about lands and trees, then follow Arudha Rasi. Whether you follow Arudha or Udaya Lagna, note the Chathra Rasi from these Rasis.

CHATRA RASI

मार्ताण्डे वृषतोलितश्च चतुरो राशीनतोन्यांस्तथा
प्राप्तेऽजो मिथुनं क्रमेण च वृषो वीथ्योयु यावान् भवेत् ।
आरूढादुदयोथ वीथिभवना—त्तावद्भवेच्छत्रभं
ग्राह्यंस्यात्स्थिरचक्र एतदद्दढे लग्नांशकश्छादकः ॥ इति
॥३४॥

Stanza 34.—According as the Sun occupies Taurus to Leo, Scorpio to Aquarius and the remaining four signs, Veethi Rasi will respectively be Aries, Gemini and Taurus. Chatra Rasi is the sign arrived at by counting from the corresponding Veetha Rasi as many signs as Lagna is removed from Arudha. This Chathra Rasi is applicable to Arudha. Chatra Rasi of Udaya Lagna is its own Navamsa.

NOTES

This is important in horoscopy and all Prasnas where Udaya Lagna is followed. For further clarification of Chatra Rasi, see Notes given for stanzas 1 and 2 in Chapter VIII.

निरन्तरोद्यतां भानां कस्याप्यस्त्युदयः सदा ।

तथाप्यारूढवाञ्छा यत्ततोऽस्यैव प्रधानता ॥३५॥

Stanza 35.—Arudha is more important than Udaya Lagna for Prasna purposes. Hence wherever Lagna is stated before, take it as Arudha unless otherwise specified as Udaya Lagna.

NOTES

It is the author's own view that Arudha is more important than the rising sign.

SIGNS OF LONG LIFE

एतेषु दोषरहितेषु गुणान्वितेषु
निरोगताद्यखिलसौख्यमनल्पमायुः ।
दोषान्वितेषु विणेषु मृतिश्च रोग—
दैर्घ्यादिकंतु गुणदोगुपविमिश्रितेषु ॥३६॥

Stanza 36.—In the various conditions prescribed already to determine longevity, if all are devoid of afflictions and are favourable, the person will live long. If the combinations are all evil, he will die soon. If the influences are mixed, then the querist will neither die nor recover from his diseases.

NOTES

Happiness and misfortunes will alternately trouble him.

लग्नं दोहोष्टमो जीवस्तयोरधिपयोर्बलम् ।
अन्योन्यदृष्टियोगौ च दीर्घाय प्रष्टुरायुषे ॥३७॥

Stanza 37.—Lagna indicates Deha. The 8th is Jeeva. If their lords are strong, or are in conjunction or in mutual aspect, the querist will have long life.

लग्नादिपश्च जीवश्च शुक्रश्चारूढकेन्द्रगः ।
एकैकोप्यायुषे प्रष्टुः किमु द्वौ किं पुनस्त्रयः ॥३८॥

अन्योन्यकेन्द्रखेष्वेषु दीर्घमायुरितीतरे ॥३९॥

Stanzas 38 and 39.—If the lord of Lagna or Jupiter or Venus is placed in a kendra from Arudha or if these lords, Jupiter, Venus and lord of Lagna are in mutual kendras, there will be long life.

सौम्यस्त्रिकोणधनकेन्द्रभवाष्टमस्था
दीर्घायुषे सहजषड्भवगाश्च पापाः ।
अन्यत्रगा मरणरोरकराश्च तेस्यु—
र्मान्दिर्मृतौ मृतिकरोपि गुणेषु सत्सु ॥४०॥

Stanza 40.—If benefics are in kendras, trikonas, the 2nd and 8th or 11th and malefics are in the 3rd, 6th and 11th, there will be long life. If malefics occupy houses other than 3, 6 and 11 and benefics are in 3, 6 and 12, death and mortal illness will be the result If Gulika occupies the 8th, then the questioner's death cannot be doubted.

सर्वेषामपि पापानां मान्दिर्दोषप्रदाधिकम् ।
सोतिदोषकरो योगदृग्वर्गवशतः शनैः ॥४१॥

Stanza 41.—Of all the malefic planets, Gulika contributes the worst evil. If Gulika has the association, aspect or vargas of Saturn, his evil becomes more intensified.

LONGEVITY FROM BIRTH CHART

वराहमिहिरो होराषष्ठाध्यायेऽभ्यधत्त याम् ।
योगान् मृतिकरान् सद्यस्तत्संवादो विचिन्त्यताम् ॥४२॥

Stanza 42.—Varahamihira has detailed the Yogas for determining longevity in the sixth chapter of his *Brihat Jataka*. Carefully make a study of it and apply the same here.

NOTES

Till now the author has given methods for finding longevity on the basis of Horary. In the following stanzas he deals with combinations applicable to horoscopy.

ग्रहचारदशाप्रश्नफलसंवादसम्भवे ।
सत्येव फलामादेश्यं शुभाशुभसंशयम् ॥४३॥
इत्येतया तु शास्त्रोक्त्या प्रश्नजातकयोरिह ।
संवादश्चिन्त्य इत्यायुश्चिन्त्यते जातकेन च ॥४४॥

Stanzas 43 and 44.—If the results, good and evil, deduced from Prasna are confirmed by the results based on horoscopy such as Dasa periods or planetary transits (Gocharas), one can boldly assert these results. Here comes the necessity for comparing the Prasna results with Jataka.

पूर्वकर्मफलं भोक्तुं जन्तोर्यदिह जीवनम् ।
आयुस्तत्कर्मशक्त्याऽस्य धीर्घमध्यात्मतादिकम् ॥४५॥

Stanza 45.—All beings take fresh births to experience the results of their actions done in their previous birth. Depending upon the past Karma the longevity will be long, medium and short.

NOTES

People are born in this world just to finish off or exhaust their Karma Phala. This existence is known as 'Life'. According to some only Prarabdha Karma is meant here and not Sanchitha Karma.

For details about the various categories of Karma and main alibis to ward off evils read my book *Astrology and Modern Thought*.

अवश्यमनुभोक्तव्यं यत्किंचित फलपस्ति चेत् ।
येनकेनापि योगेन नभुक्त्वायं म्रियेत् तत् ॥४६॥

Stanza 46.—Even if there is a little Karma left over, it has to be experienced. Effects of Karma can however be overcome by Atma Jnana (self-realisation).

शास्त्रान्तरोदितं योगशब्दनिर्वचनं तथा ।
योगस्वरूपसंख्याश्च तत्प्रकारोथ लिख्यते ॥४७॥

Stanza 47.—Yogas reveal to us the results of Karma. The nature and meaning of these yogas and their number have been well explained in other works.

ग्रहाणां स्थितिभेदेन पुरुषान् योजयन्ति हि ।
फलैः कर्मकमुद्भूतैरिति योगाः प्रकीर्तिताः ॥४८॥

Stanza 48.—Yoga means that which joins or connects. Purusha is that which has body. Yogas connect Purusha with Karma Phalas. Planets indicate how these yogas connect the Purusha with Karma Phala from their position.

YOGAS AND LONGEVITY

स्थानतो भावतः खेटैः स्थानभावनभश्वरै ।
स्थानभावसभायोगाद्भावखेचरयोगतः ॥४९॥

योगाः स्युः षड्विधाः स्थानखेचराभ्यां तु सप्तमः ।
उच्चमूलत्रिकोणादिग्रहाणां स्थानमुच्यते ॥५०॥

भावा लग्नादयः प्रोक्ताः खेचरा भास्करादयः ।
भावस्थानग्रहैः प्रोक्ते योगे ये योगहेतवः ॥५१॥

तेषां बली यः कर्ता स्यात्स एवास्य फलप्रदा ॥५२॥

Stanzas 49 to 52.—There are seven varieties of yogas. (*a*) Those formed by position, (*b*) those formed by Bhavas, (*c*) those formed by planets, (*d*) those formed by position, Bhavas and planets, (*e*) those formed by *sthana* and Bhava, (*f*) those formed by Bhavas and planets and (*g*) those formed by position and planets. By *sthana* is meant the residence of planets in uchcha, moolathrikona, etc. By Bhava is meant Lagna, etc. The planets are the Sun, etc. Bhava Sthana and Graha are the cause of Yoga. The strongest in bringing about a yoga is the yoga-karta (composer of yoga) and it is he who gives the results of the yoga.

योगायुश्च दशायुश्चेत्यायुर्वै द्विविधं नृणाम् ।
योगोक्तमायुर्योगायुश्चदशाः कृतम् ॥५३॥

Stanza 53.—There are two types of longevity, *viz.*, Yogayus—that which is contributed by yogas; and Dasayus, that which is contributed by Dasas.

योगायुः षड्विधं योगैः षड्विधैस्तान् वदाम्यथ ।
सद्योरिष्टा अरिष्टाख्या योगारिष्टाह्वयास्तथा ॥५४॥

मध्यदीर्घामितितादा इति योगास्तु षड्विधाः ।
सद्योरिष्टाह्वया योगा वत्सरान्तर्मृतिप्रदाः ॥५५॥

रव्यब्दान्तररिष्टाख्या नापेक्षन्ते दशामिमे ।
योगारिष्टाह्वयाव्द्याष्ठिवत्सरान्तर्मृतिप्रदाः ॥५६॥

अब्दानां सप्ततेरन्तर्योगा ये मध्यमायुषः ।
दीर्घायुषश्शतस्यान्तर्दशापेक्षान्वितास्त्रयः ॥५७॥
शताधिकसमा जीवेद्योगे जातोमितायुषि ।
आयुर्दायविधिं योगा नापेक्षन्तेमितायुषः ॥५८॥

Stanzas 54 to 58.—There are six kinds of Yogayus, *viz.*, Sadhyorishta, Arishta, Yogarishta, Madhya, Deergha and Amita. The terms of life of these six kinds of Yogayus are respectively within a year, twelve years, thirty-two years, seventy years, hundred years and above hundred years. Amitayuyoga, Sadhyorishta and Arishta Yogas are independent of Dasas.

NOTES

The author, quite in line with earlier classical writers, considers two types of longevity, *viz.*, Yogayus and Dasayus. There are six types of Yogayus indicating death within one year (Sadhyorishta), death within 12 years (Arishta or Balarishta), death within 32 years

(Alpayu or Rishta), death within 70 years (Madhyayu), death within hundred years (Deerghayu) and death after 100 years (Amithayu).

Sadhyorishta, Arishta and Amithayu are independent of Dasas. As students of astrology know, there are marakas or death-inflicting planets with reference to each Lagna. The period of death (maraka Dasa) should be fixed consistent with the term of longevity indicated in the horoscope. By noting whether one's term of life refers to Alpayu (32 years), Madhyayu (70 years) or Deerghayu (100 years), the appropriate Dasa and Bhukti for death should be fixed, taking into consideration the death-inflicting planets and their Dasas. If there are Sadhyorishta, Arishta or Amithayur yogas, then they function without reference to the Dasas and Bhuktis. This is the view of the author.

In actual practice however, leaving aside Amithayur Yogas, it is found in our humble experience that Sadhyorishta and Arishta Yogas also can be brought within the purview of Dasas. If Arishta Yogas are present, then death is likely before 12 years. The planets who cause the yoga can bring about death in the course of their Dasas and Bhuktis.

एते योगास्तु विज्ञेयाः सारावल्यादिशास्त्रतः ।

त्रिविधं च पुनस्त्वायुर्दीर्घमध्याल्पतावशात् ॥५९॥

Stanza 59.—These yogas can be studied in astrological treatises such as *Saravali.* Thus the longevity of a man can be divided into Alpayu, Madhyayu and Deerghayu

लग्नजन्मपयोः शत्रू निजाष्टमपती यदि ।
समौ वा यदि वा बन्धू स्वल्पमध्यचिरायुषः ॥६०॥

Stanza 60.—According as lords of Lagna and the 8th therefrom and lords of Chandra Lagna and the 8th therefrom are mutually inimical, neutral or friendly, the length of life would be Alpa (short), Madhya (medium) or Poorna (full)

चन्द्रांशेशस्य तद्भूषा नवांशेशोथवा रवेः ।
लग्नेशो वापि यद्येवं स्वल्पमध्यचिरायुषः ॥६१॥

Stanza 61.—If the lord of Chandra Navamsa is inimical, neutral or friendly to the lord of the 64th Navamsa therefrom, the longevity of the person will be short, medium or full. The Sun and lord of Lagna should be similarly reckoned.

NOTES

In these two stanzas, combinations for different terms of longevity are given. They can be tabulated thus :—

Alpayu or Short life

1. Lords of Lagna and the 8th should be inimical.
2. Lords of Chandra Lagna and the 8th from it should be enemies.

3. Lord of the Navamsa occupied by Chandra and the lord of the 64th from Chandra Navamsa should be enemies.

4. Lord of Lagna and the Sun should be enemies.

Madhyayu or medium life

The four pairs listed above should be neutrals.

Purnayu or full life

The four pairs should be friends.

Suppose the Moon, in Navamsa, is in Leo. The lord is Sun. The 64th Navamsa from the Moon's Navamsa would be Scorpio and the lord is Mars. The Sun and Mars are friends. Relationships should be considered in this way.

Long Life Again

अथ केचन लिख्यन्तेत्रायुर्दैर्ध्यकरा गुणाः ।
बलवत्त्वं विलग्नेद्वोः शुभयोगः शुभेक्षणम् ॥६२॥
केन्द्रत्रिकोणरन्ध्रार्थेष्वनयोः शुभसंस्थितिः ।
त्रिषडायेष्वसद्वासो विशेषेण गुरूदयः ॥६३॥
गुरुचन्द्रमसोर्योगः केन्द्रलग्पतेः स्थितिः ।
जन्मेशसंस्थितिश्चात्र बलवत्त्वं तयोर्द्वयोः ॥६४॥
अनयोरायसंस्थानमायुर्दैर्ध्यकरा गुणाः ॥६५॥

Stanzas 62 to 65.—The Lagna and Chandra Lagna are strong; are occupied or aspected by benefics ; benefics are in quadrants, trines, 2nd and 8th ; malefics are disposed in the 3rd, 6th and 11th ; Jupiter rises in Lagna ; Jupiter and the Moon are in association ; and the lord of Lagna is in a kendra ; the lord of Chandra Lagna is strong. Lagna lord occupies the 11th from Lagna. The above combinations confer long life.

NOTES

Wherever Lagna is mentioned in the above stanzas, Chandra Lagna should also be considered. Combinations for long life given in stanzas 62 to 65 may be listed thus :—

(1) Lagna is strong. (2) Chandra is strong. (3) Lagna is aspected by good planets. (4) Chandra is aspected by good planets. (5) Lagna is occupied by good planets. (6) Chandra is conjoined with good planets. (7) Good planets should occupy quadrants, trines, the 2nd and 8th houses. (8) Good planets should occupy quadrants, trines, 2nd and 8th houses from Chandra. (9) Evil planets should occupy 3rd, 6th and 11th from Lagna. (10) Evil planets should occupy 3rd, 6th and 11th from Chandra. (11) Jupiter in Lagna. (12) Jupiter and the Moon are in one Rasi. (13) The lord of Lagna is in a kendra from Lagna. (14) The lord of Chandra Lagna is in a kendra from Chandra Lagna. (15) The lord of Lagna is strong. (16) Lord of Chandra Lagna is strong. (17) The lord of Lagna occupies the 11th house from Lagna. (18) The lord of Chandra Lagna occupies the 11th house from Chandra Lagna. **These are the 18 yogas indicating long life.**

SHORT LIFE

आयुशोल्पत्वदा दोष विलिख्यन्तेथ केचन ।
बलहानिर्विलग्नेन्द्वोः पापदृष्टिसमन्वयौ ॥६६॥

लग्नजन्मेशयोर्मौढ्यं स्थितिश्चारिव्ययाष्टमे ।
अनयोरपि दौर्बल्यं परिवेषोपरागयोः ॥६७॥

सन्ध्यायां दिक्प्रदाहादि दुर्निमित्तेषु वा जनिः ।
राशीनां मृत्युभागेषु सन्दिष्वपि तथा जनिः ॥६८॥

पीनं धनं खरः क्रूरो मन्त्ररत्नं वनं गिरौ ।
दिव्यनारी वरा नित्यं मृत्युभागा अजादिषु ॥६९॥

मृत्युभागस्थचन्द्रस्य स्थितिः केन्द्रेषु वाष्टमे ।
केन्द्रायुमृत्यु भागस्थविधोश्चासत्समन्वयः ॥७०॥

चन्द्रो रम्यो लयो मित्रे भूरिकार्यं चिरं भयम् ।
गोपमात्रे मनोरम्यं मृत्युभागा विधोरजात् ॥७१॥

ग्रहदृष्टस्य चन्द्रस्य स्थितिरष्टमषष्ठयोः ।
शुभानां वक्रिभिः पापैर्दृष्टानां चात्र संस्थितिः ॥७२॥

केन्द्रत्रिकोणरन्ध्रेषु तथैवाशुभसंस्थितिः ।
आयुरल्पत्वदा दोषा इति केचित्प्रकीर्तिताः ॥७३॥

Stanzas 66 to 73.—The Lagna and the Moon are weak; they have evil aspects or associations; lords of Lagna and Chandra Lagna are combust; they are in the 6th, 8th or 12th; birth takes place when the Sun or the Moon is surrounded by a halo or when there is an eclipse, or at twilight, or at the time of earthquakes or other evil omens or in the Mrityubhagas of Rasis or Rasi Sandhis; Chandra occupies Mrityubhagas in kendra Rasis or the 8th from Lagna; Chandra is in the 6th or 8th aspected by planets; benefics occupy the 6th or 8th aspected by retrograde malefics; evil planets are in kendras, trikonas or in the 8th. The above combinations indicate short life.

NOTES

Combinations for short life are listed in these stanzas, Chandra Lagna has been given equal prominence with Lagna. The Mrityubhagas or fatal degrees are the 1st, 9th, 22nd, 23rd, 25th, 2nd, 4th, 23rd, 18th, 20th, 24th and 10th in Aries onwards in regular order. Chandra Mrityubhagas, *i.e.*, the degrees considered fatal for the Moon are 26th, 12th, 13th, 25th, 24th, 11th, 26th, 14th, 13th, 25th, 5th and 12th in Aries, etc. According to stanzas 66 to 73, short life is indicated :—(1) If Lagna is weak. (2) If Chandra is weak. (3) If Lagna is associated with bad planets. (4) If Lagna is aspected by bad planets. (5) If Chandra is conjoined by bad planets. (6) If Chandra is aspected by bad planets. (7) If the lord of Lagna is in combustion. (8) If the Lord of Chandra Lagna is in combustion. (9) If Lagnadhipa occupies 6th, 8th and 12th houses from Lagna. (10) If Chandra Lagnadhipa occupies 6, 8, 12 from Chandra Lagna. (11) If Chandra Lagnadhipa is weak. (12) When the Sun or the Moon is surrounded by a halo (Parivesha) and is eclispsed. (13) If birth takes place in Sandhyas. (14) Dikdaha or earthquakes or Ulkapatha take place at the time of birth. (15) If birth takes place in the Mrityubhagas of Rasis. (16) If born in Rasi Sandhyas. (17) If the Moon occupies the Mrityubhaga of kendras and the 8th house from Lagna. (18) If Chandra occupies kendras or 8th house or Mrityubhagas in conjunction with evil planets. (19) If Chandra occupies the 6th or 8th house aspected by any planet. (20) If good planets occupy 6th or 8th house aspected by evil planets with retrograde movement. (21) If evil planets occupy the kendras and trines and the 8th house. Thus there are 21 yogas.

दीर्घायुषो गुणेषु स्युः सत्सु दोषेष्वनायुषः ।

काल्प्यमायुर्विमिश्रेषु तेषामल्पाधिकत्वतः ॥७४॥

Stanza 74.—If there are more yogas for long life, long life is to be predicted. If there are more yogas fōr short life, short life is to be expected. If the yogas are found mixed, the intensity and strength of these yogas should be examined and then the prediction given.

एवं प्रश्नवशाच्च जातकवशात् कृत्वायुषो निर्णयं
निर्णीते मरणेस्य रोगसमयौ वाच्यावथो रोगिणाम् ।
निर्णीतं यदि जीवितं तु शमनारम्भादिकं वा रुजां
सन्दिग्धं यदि तद्द्वयं तदुचितं ब्रूयात्सुधीर्लक्षणम् ॥७५॥

Stanza 75.—If after examining Prasna and Jataka, it is found that the questioner will die, by what diseases and when he will die, should be predicted. If he has a long life, when his recovery will begin should be ascertained. If there are any doubts, the Thrisphutas also should be examined and the indications for death and recovery determined. These should be well balanced.

Here ends the examination of life with the help of a horoscope.

॥ इति प्रश्नमार्गे नवमाध्यायः ॥

दशमाध्यायः

TIMING DEATH

प्रश्नेनापि च जातकेन च मृतेश्चिन्त्यं हि कालादिकं
तत्र प्राक्समयो गदश्च जनुषा देशश्च सञ्चिन्त्यते ।
कार्यं कालविचिन्तनं खलु मृतेर्योगैर्दशान्तर्दशा
मन्दाचार्यदिनेशशीतकिरणस्थानैर्विलग्नेन च ॥ १ ॥

Stanza 1.—The question of death should be examined from the birth and horary charts. In order to ascertain the nature of death, its cause and the time of its occurrence, the yogas, the nature of Dasas and the nature and positions of Saturn, Jupiter, the Sun and the Moon should all be first studied.

योगेषु तत्सु योगोक्तवत्सरान्ते मृतिर्भवेत् ।
दशापेक्षान्विते योगे तत्संवादोपि चिन्त्यताम् ॥ २ ॥

Stanza 2.—Death takes place at the end of the period indicated by Yogayus. Sometimes the age as contributed by Dasas goes counter to the age given by yogas. This should be carefully understood.

दशापहारचारेषु ग्रहाणां दोषदायिषु ।
मरणं निर्दिशेन्नणां योगाभावेत्वयं विधिः ॥ ३ ॥

Stanza 3.—In the absence of any yogas in the horoscope indicating age, we have to be guided by the Dasas and determine the period of death.

NOTES

From this we see that 'Dasayus' is very important. But 'Yogayus' is no less valuable. Certain yogas as Sadhyorishta, Arishta, etc., are not said to be controlled by Dasas. Certain yogas as Rishta Yogas, Madhyayus or Deerghayur yogas are to be checked by the age contributed by Dasas and Bhuktis. If *Yogayus* indicates, say 75 years, and according to Dasas also the same age is obtained, then one can boldly declare the length of life.

लग्नाद्वा यदि जन्मतो मृतिपती मृत्युस्थतद्वीक्षकौ
मन्दः क्रूरदृगाणपो गुळिकपस्तैर्युक्तराश्यंशपः ।
राहुश्चैषु सुदुर्बलो जनुषि यो भावेनभीष्टे स्थितः
पापालोकितसंयुतोस्य हि दशावान्तर्दशा मृत्युदा ॥ ४ ॥

Stanza 4.—Death can happen in the Dasa or Antardasa of the weakest—that which occupies the 6th, 8th, 12th or that which is associated with or aspected by malefics of the following: Lords of 8th from Lagna and the Moon; planets occupying or aspecting the 8th from Lagna and the Moon; Saturn; lords of the 22nd Drekkana from Lagna and the Moon; lord of the house occupied by Gulika; lords of the houses and Navamsas occupied by these factors; and Rahu.

NOTES

An exhaustive list of marakas is furnished in this stanza. Wherever Lagna is mentioned, Chandra Lagna is automatically meant. A discriminating astrologer should very carefully pick out the appropriate maraka. Of all these lords, the weakest—by occupying 6th or 8th house or subject to affliction—should be selected. The marakas can be listed thus:

1. The lord of the 8th house from Lagna.
2. The lord of the 8th house from Chandra.
3. The planets that occupy the 8th house from Lagna.
4. The planets that occupy the 8th house from Chandra.
5. The planets that aspect the 8th house from Lagna.
6. The planets that aspect the 8th house from Chandra.
7. Saturn.
8. The lord of 22nd Drekkana from Lagna.
9. The lord of 22nd Drekkana from Chandra.
10. The lord of the house occupied by Gulika.
11. The lords of the houses occupied by the ten lords noted above.
12. Navamsa lords of the above-mentioned planets.
13. Rahu.

With due deference to the great author's accomplishments, it seems to us that to select a maraka out of this formidable number--almost all planets seem to get involved somehow—is a herculean task. A much simpler method would be to consider all the lords except those mentioned in 11 and 12 and then decide the weakest. Generally the 7th and 2nd are considered houses of death.

पापानां चेद्दशायामपहृतिरसतां चिन्तनीयोत्र मृत्यु-
र्गोमासर्क्षेश्वराणामपि निजजनिभाद्दोषदः पाककालः ।
द्वित्रादीनां दशानां युगपदवसितिर्यत्र कालः स कष्टः
सर्वासां वा दशानामवसितिरशुभा दोषदानां विशेषात्
॥ ५ ॥

Stanza 5.—Death can take place in the sub-periods of malefics and the major periods of malefics. The Dasas and Bhuktis of the 3rd, 5th and 7th Nakshatras from Janma Nakshatra can also cause death. If 2 or more Dasas terminate at the same time, then that period also may be taken as time of death. Again, the end of all Dasas is not good. Especially the last period of all Dasas indicating evil has to be considered as bad.

दोषो रन्ध्राधिपत्यादिजातः सर्वदशासमः ।
दशासूद्भवास्वेव गोमासर्क्षाधिपत्यजः ॥ ६ ॥

Stanza 6.—The lordship of the 8th house, etc., is bad for all Dasas. The Dasas of lords of the 3rd, 5th and 7th Nakshatras from Janma Nakshatra are bad in Vimshottari Dasa.

NOTES

The lord of a Dasa owning the 8th is bad whatever be the type of Dasa applied—Vimshottari, Ashtottari, Kalachakra, etc. But the Dasas of the lords of the 3rd, 5th and 7th Nakshatras are bad only with reference to Vimshottari.

EVIL PERIODS

दशा नीचस्थमूढानां नियमेन मृतिप्रदा ।
कालचक्रदशायास्तु विशेषोथ निगद्यते ॥ ७॥

Stanza 7.—Dasas of the planets that are in debilitation or combustion cause death. In Kala chakra Dasa, however, there are special considerations which have to be noted for determining maraka periods.

NOTES

This stanza is highly suggestive. A Dasa lord in combustion or in debility can cause death. But it occurs to us that in actual practice the word 'death' should not be treated very literally. In this context, "maraka" may also imply great misfortune, suffering and troubles consistent with the other qualities of the planets concerned. A planet, in order to kill, should acquire combined afflictions. Suppose a planet is the lord of the 8th and he is in the 12th aspected by malefics and otherwise afflicted as well. In such a case, provided the Dasa of the planet concerned is appropriate to the term of longevity fixed according to Yogayus, death can be predicted. Otherwise if there are only minor afflictions such as the 8th lord being combust, etc., then death may not be caused. The Dasa or Bhukti of such a planet is only capable of conferring great misfortunes.

KALACHAKRA DASA

मीनाद्वृश्चिकभं वृजेद्यदि तदा षष्ठादथो कर्कटं
सिंहाद्वा मिथुनं ततोपि हरिभं चापाच्च मेषं तथा ।
कष्टाः स्यादिह तत्प्रवेशसमयः कष्टा दशा चोत्तरा
चारो राश्यनतिक्रमेण शुभदो राश्यन्तरस्थोशुभः ॥ ८ ॥

Stanza 8—The beginning of the Dasa 'movement', from Meena to Vrischika, Kanya to Karkataka, Simha to Mithuna, Mithuna to Simha and Dhanus to Mesha, will be a difficult period as also the subsequent Dasa. Whether the order is regular or otherwise, the Dasa 'movement' will be good if there is no deviation but evil if the 'movement' is at the junction of two Rasis.

देहो दक्षिणतारासु वाक्योक्तेष्वादिमं गृहम् ।
जीवः स्यादन्तिमो राशिर्विपरीतं हि वामभे ॥९॥

देह जीवेशयोरेकस्यासद्योगो गदप्रदः ।
द्वयोस्सह स चेन्मृत्युर्दशा चेदशुभा दृढम् ॥१०॥

Stanzas 9 and 10.—In regard to the Dakshina (clockwise) group of stars, the first and last 'signs' indicated by the formula are Deha and Jeeva respectively, while the reverse will be the case in regard to Vama (anti-clockwise) group of stars. If malefics afflict Deha or Jeeva, there will be sickness. If both are afflicted and the Dasa is also evil, then there will be death.

NOTES

In the above three stanzas, the referece is to Kalachakra Dasa. Here, I propose to make only a few observations on this system. For more details reference may be made to standard treatises or to my own forthcoming book *Kalachakra Dasa.*

The 27 constellations have been divided into two groups—the Dakshina or the Savya group where the reckoning is clockwise and the Vama or the Apasavya group where the reckoning is anti clockwise; the former group consisting of five triads of stars and the latter four triads. For those born, say in the first pada of Aswini, Punarvasu or Hasta, the Dasas run in the order of Mesha–Kuja, Vrishabha–Sukra, etc., upto Dhanur–Guru. For those born in the

2nd pada of the same stars, the succession of Dasas would be in the order of Makara–Sani, Kumbha–Sani, *Meena–Guru*, Vrischika–Kuja, Thula–Sukra, *Kanya–Budha*, Kataka–Chandra, *Simha–Ravi* and *Mithuna–Budha*. Here it will be seen that the movement or 'jump' of the Dasa is from Meena to Vrischika, Kanya to Kataka and also Simha to Mithuna, and hence, deviating. The junctions of the Dasas mentioned above would be harmful. The three important movements indicative of extremely bad results are *simhavalokana* (leap from Meena to Vrischika) or *mandukagamana* (leap from Kanya to Kataka) and *prishtathogamana* (Simha to Mithuna). These stanzas will prove useful to those who are familiar with the Kalachakra system of directing.

NIRYANA SATURN

परागपर्ययेष्वार्केरल्पमध्यच्चिरायुषाम् ।
मरणं निर्दिशेन्नृणां चतुर्थेऽपि च्चिरायुषाम् ॥११॥

Stanza 11.—In regard to the different terms of longevity—short, medium, full and unlimited—death takes place respectively during the 1st, 2nd, 3rd or 4th round of Saturn's revolution.

NOTES

After deciding the term of longevity and the likely Dasa and Bhukti of death, the author enables us in this and subsequent stanzas, to locate the time of death—year, month and even the day—by considering the transit movements of Saturn, Jupiter, the Sun and the Moon. The transit of Saturn helps to locate the event within $2\frac{1}{2}$ years; that of Jupiter within one year, and that of the Sun within a month. The Moon's transit helps to find out even the day of death.

The principles given here should not be applied *verbatim*. The astrologer's judgment power should help him to adapt these various rules to suit individual horoscopes. These transiting planets go by the special names of Niryana Sani, Niryana Guru, Niryana Ravi and Niryana Chandra.

There is always a certain correlation between the time of death as indicated either by Yoga or by Dasa and the transit movements of planets--principally Saturn. The period of Saturn's revolution is 30 years. If Alpayu or short life is indicated, then death generally takes place during the first round of Saturn's transit, *i.e.*, before Saturn completes one cycle with reference to his own radical position or the radical position of the Moon or Mandi, etc. If the term of life indicated in the horoscope is medium, then death can happen during the second term of Saturn's cycle. When the native has Purnayu or long life, death can happen during the third revolution. When one has 'unlimited' longevity—over 100 years—death generally takes place during the fourth revolution of Saturn. These are only general principles and they have to be suitably adapted to individual cases in the light of a number of other astrological factors.

मान्दित्रिकोणगे मन्दे मरणं रात्रिजन्मनाम् ।
दिनभेहर्भुवामस्तत्रिकोणस्थेस्य भांशयोः ॥१२॥

Stanza 12.—According as birth is during the day or night, death takes place when Saturn transits the sign held by Mandi or the trinal places from it, or the 7th from Mandi or its trinal places.

NOTES

If the birth is during the day, then death will happen when Saturn passes through the sign occupied by Mandi or the 5th or 9th from it. When birth is during the night, then Saturn's passing through the 7th, 11th or 3rd from Mandi should be taken, It will be seen that the 11th and 3rd from Mandi happen to be trinal signs from the 7th. Transit Saturn with reference to death is known by the technical term *Niryana Sani*, and the Rasi transited as Niryana Rasi.

मन्दरन्ध्रेशयोरंशराश्योर्वार्कौ त्रिकोणगे ।
अर्कारूढगृहस्यार्थरिःफयोर्वा त्रिकोणगे ॥१३॥
द्वाविंशत्र्यंशपो यस्मिन् भवने जन्मनि स्थितः ।
तत्त्रिकोणगते वार्कौ निर्दिष्टं मरणं नृणाम् ॥१४॥

Stanzas 13 and 14.—The Rasis and Navamsa Rasis occupied by Saturn and the lord of the 8th and the Sun at birth; the trines from there; the 2nd and 12th from the Sun and their trines; the sign occupied by the lord of the 22nd Drekkana and its trines are all Niryana Rasis for Saturn.

NOTES

In stanzas 13 and 14 are given the signs or Rasis transiting which, Saturn can cause death, either in the 1st, 2nd, 3rd or 4th round according to the term of longevity vouched for the horoscope. Whenever a Rasi is mentioned, the Navamsa Rasi is automatically implied. Thus we can catalogue the Niryana Rasis thus: (1) Mandi's sign and its trines, (2) Mandi's Navamsa and its trines, (3) the 7th from Mandi and its trikonas, (4) the 7th from Mandi (in Navamsa) and its trines, (5) Saturn's Rasi and its trines, (6) Saturn's Navamsa and its trines, (7) sign occupied by the 8th lord and its trines, (8) the Navamsa held by the 8th lord and its trines, (9) the 2nd from the Sun and its trines, (10) the 12th from the Sun and its trines. (11) the sign occupied by the lord of the 22nd Drekkana and its trines. In this way, we have 33 Rasis.

NIRYANA JUPITER

लग्नत्र्यंशेश्वराक्रान्तराशेर्जीवे त्रिकोणगे ।
कालहोरेश्वराक्रान्तराशेर्वा मरणं नृणाम् ॥१५॥

Stanza 15.—Death can happen when Jupiter transits the Rasis occupied by the lords of the 22nd Drekkana and Kala hora or their trines.

यो राशिः सूर्यजाक्रान्तस्तद्धनस्य व्ययस्य वा ।
बृहस्पतिस्त्रिकोणस्थो मरणाय भवेन्नृणाम् ॥१६॥

Stanza 16.—Jupiter's transit in the 2nd and 12th from the Rasi, occupied by Saturn or its trines, can bring about death.

देहजीवेशयोर्योगराशिगोपि बृहस्पतिः ।
पापग्रहाश्च तत्रस्था नृणां मरणदायिनः ॥१७॥

Stanza 17.—Death can also happen when Jupiter transits the Rasi arrived at by the addition of the longitudes of the lords of Lagna and the 8th, provided other malefics also pass through the same sign simultaneously.

राशेर्मन्दाधिरूढस्य तृतीयायात्मजारिपु ।
यत्र स्वदर्शनं न्यूनं तत्रस्थो मृतिदो गुरुः ॥१८॥

Stanza 18.—Note in the birth chart which out of the 3rd, 5th, 6th and 11th from Saturn receives the least aspect of Jupiter. When this sign is transited by Jupiter death may occur.

NOTES

Stanzas 15 to 18 deal with Jupiter's Niryana Rasis, *i.e.* the signs, when transiting which Jupiter becomes capable of causing death. According to stanza 17, Jupiter's transit of the Rasi resulting from adding the sphutas of the lords of the Lagna and 8th can cause death only when other malefics afflict the sign.

According to another view this stanza can be translated thus: Increase Saturn's longitude by adding 2, 4, 5 and 10 signs. Of the resulting Rasis, that which receives the minimum of Jupiter's aspect becomes Niryana Rasi for Jupiter.

Niryana Sun

अष्टमेशाश्रितं राशिमावहत्यहिमत्विषि ।
जन्मतारं विलग्नस्थतारकां वा मृतिर्भवेत् ॥१९॥

Stanza 19.—When the Sun transits the sign occupied by the lord of the 8th or Janma Nakshatra or the Nakshatra of Janma Lagna, death can take place.

आत्मार्कांशकभत्रिकोणसहिते सूर्ये चरस्थः स चे-
द्यर्कः स्थिरभेष्टमेशनवभागेशर्क्षकोणस्थिते ।
लग्नेशस्थनवांशराशिसहिते तस्यं त्रिकोणेथवा
सूर्ये मृत्युमुशन्ति यद्युभयगः सोयं भवेज्जन्मनि ॥ इति ॥
॥२०॥

Stanza 20.—Death can occur when the Sun transits his own Dwadasamsa Rasi and its trines; the Rasi occupied by the lord of the Navamsa the 8th lord is in, and its trines; or the Navamsa Rasi of lord of Lagna and its trines according as the Sun is in a movable, fixed or common sign respectively in the birth horoscope.

NOTES

When the Sun transits (1) the sign occupied by the lord of 8th; (2) the birth asterism; (3) the asterism of Lagna; (4) his own Dwadasamsa Rasi and its trikonas if he is in a movable sign in the birth chart ; (5) the Rasi occupied by the lord of the Navamsa held by the lord of the 8th, if the Sun is in a fixed sign at birth; (6) the Navamsa Rasi occupied by lord of Lagna, if the Sun is in a common sign; and (7) the trines from all the other six places, he becomes Niryana Ravi capable of causing death.

NIRYANA MOON

सूर्याश्रितर्क्षगे चन्द्रे रन्ध्रेशाश्रितवेश्मनः ।

त्रिकोणोपगते वेन्दौ राहारूढोडुनस्तथा ॥२१॥

रन्ध्रेशाधिष्ठितोडौ वा निर्दिष्टं मरणं नृणाम् ॥२२॥

धनेशाश्रितराशेर्वा तस्य सप्तमभस्य वा ।

त्रिकोणस्थे धनेशांशराशिगे वा विधौ मृतिः ॥२३॥

Stanzas 21 to 23.—Death happens when the Moon transits the signs occupied by the Sun and lords of the 2nd and 8th; 7th from the sign oecupied by, or the Navamsa Rasi of the 2nd lord; the Nakshatras occupied by the lord of the 8th or Rahu; and the trines from all these places.

NOTES

The Moon becomes Niryana Chandra in (1) the sign occupied by the Sun, (2) in the sign occupied by the lord of 8, (3) the constellation held by Rahu, (4) the constellation occupied by the lord of 8, (5) the sign occupied by lord of the 2nd, (6) the seventh from the sign occupied by the lord of the 2nd, (7) the Navamsa Rasi of the 2nd lord and (8) the trines from all these places.

निजजन्मनि यस्मिन् भे गुळिकस्तत्रगे विधौ ।
रोगारम्भस्तदस्तस्थे मरणं दृढमादिशेत् ॥२४॥

Stanza 24.—When the Moon transits the Rasi occupied by Gulika sickness begins. The person's death may take place when the Moon passes through the 7th therefrom.

NOTES

Here too the trines may be included. When the Moon transits the sign occupied by Gulika or the trines from it, sickness sets in and when the Moon transits the 7th from Gulika or trines from it. death may ensue.

PRAMANA GULIKA

प्रमाणगुळिकानीतिस्तद्दशान्मन्दजीवयोः ।
सूर्येन्द्वोश्च स्थितिमृत्यौ शास्त्रोक्ताथ निगद्यते ॥२५॥

Stanza 25.—We shall now consider the Pramana Gulika and from it fix the places of Saturn, Jupiter, the Sun and the Moon at the time of death.

जातस्याह्नि स षड्गृहो गतनिशा मान्दिः प्रमाणाह्वयो
रात्रौ प्राग्दिनमान्दिरेव न परं तद्राशिनाथालये ।
मान्दोमुष्य नवांशपाश्रितगृहे मृत्युप्रदायी गुरु-
र्भानुर्द्वादशभागपाश्रितगृहे त्रिंशांशपर्क्षे शशी ॥२६॥

Stanza 26.—If birth is during daytime, then the position of Gulika the previous night increased by 180° gives Pramana Gulika. If birth is in the night, the position of Gulika during the daytime is itself Pramana Gulika. When Saturn passes through the Rasi occupied by Pramana Gulika, when Jupiter passes through the Rasi occupied by Pramana Gulika Navamsadhipa, when the Sun passes through the Rasi occupied by Pramana Gulika Dwadasamsadhipa and when the Moon passes through the Rasi occupied dy Pramana Gulika Thrimsamsadhipa, death takes place.

NOTES

For a day birth, add 180° to the position of Gulika the previous night, Pramana Gulika is obtained. For a night birth, the position of Gulika during the day is itself Pramana Gulika. Death happens when Saturn transits this Rasi, when Jupiter passes through the Rasi occupied **by the lord of the Navamsa held by the lord of Pramana**

Gulika Rasi (Pramana Gulika Navamsadhipa), when the Sun transits the Rasi occupied by the lord of the Dwadasamsa in which the lord of Pramana Gulika is placed (Pramana Gulika Dwadasamsadhipa) and when the Moon moves through the Rasi occupied by the lord of Thrimsamsa held by the lord of Pramana Gulika Rasi (Pramana Gulika Thrimsamsadhipa).

Illustration :—Let us take the following example :

Lagna Kethu		Pramana Gulika 24°	Jupiter
	RASI		Mars
Sun, Mercury, Venus			Saturn
Moon			Rahu

Mercury		Moon; Saturn Rahu	
	AMSA		Sun
			Lagna, Mars Venus, Pramana Gulika
	Jupiter Kethu		

Pramana Gulika occupies 24° of Taurus. Applying the above rules :

(*a*) Death can happen when Saturn passes through Taurus.

(*b*) Lord of Pramana Gulika Rasi is Venus. He occupies Leo Navamsa. Lord of Leo *viz.*, the Sun is in Capricorn. Therefore death can happen when Jupiter transits Capricorn.

(*c*) Lord of Pramana Gulika, *viz.*, Venus occupies Libra Dwadasamsa. The lord of this. *viz.*, Venus is in Capricorn. Therefore death happens when the Sun transits Capricorn.

(*d*) Lord of Pramana Gulika Rasi, *viz.*, Venus occupies the Navamsa of Saturn. And Saturn is in Leo. Death can happen when the Moon transits Leo.

Summing up, death is possible (during the maraka period) when Saturn transits Taurus, Jupiter transits Capricorn, the Sun transits Capricorn and the Moon transits Leo.

DEATH AS READ BY THE PLANETS

मन्दजीवार्कचन्द्राणां प्रोक्तेष्वेतेषु राशिषु ।
मृतिदा स्वाष्टवर्गेषु हीनाक्षभवनस्थितिः ॥२७॥

Stanza 27.—Of the several Niryana Rasis mentioned above for Saturn, Jupiter, the Sun and the Moon, that alone can be considered as the

Niryana Rasi, which has the least number of points in the concerned Ashtakavarga.

NOTES

Work out the Ashtakavarga of Saturn, Jupiter, the Moon and the Sun separately. Mark that sign amongst the various Niryana Rasis which has the least number of points. When the planet concerned transits through this Rasi having the least number of bindus, death takes place. It will be seen that for Saturn nearly 37 Rasis have been assigned, for Jupiter 17, for the Sun 12 and for the Moon 21. The author suggests here a method for deciding the correct Rasis for Niryana Saturn, Niryana Jupiter, Niryana Sun and Niryana Moon by a process of elimination. I am not at all able to conceive why so many Rasis have been allotted to Saturn, Jupiter, etc., to cause death by their transits. In actual practice it may be difficult to consider all these factors.

मन्देनास्य दृगाणरन्ध्रतपनांशेशैर्युतेर्के पृथग्राशि-
योंस्य तदस्तभस्थं यदि वा प्राप्ते त्रिकोणं क्रमात् ।
चन्द्रे तीक्ष्णकरे गुरौ रविसुते योगांशभस्थेषु वा
मृत्युस्तेष्वथ तैर्निजांशगुणितैः संवाद ईक्ष्यस्त्विह ॥२८॥

Stanza 28.—The Niryana Rasis for the Moon, the Sun, Jupiter and Saturn are respectively the Yogasphuta Rasis of the Sun and Saturn, of the Sun and the lord of the Drekkana occupied by Saturn, of the Sun and the lord of the Navamsa occupied by Saturn, and the Sun and the lord of the Dwadasamsa occupied by Saturn. Their respective Navamsas and the 7th from the respective Yogasphutas and Rasis and the trines of all these places.

NOTES

In this stanza another method for the determination of the Niryana Rasis of Chandra (the Moon), Ravi (the Sun), Guru (Jupiter) and Sani (Saturn) are given. The elements required for calculating these Niryana Rasis are the longitudes (sphutas) of the Sun, Saturn and lords of the Drekkana, Navamsa and Dwadasamsa occupied by Saturn. By Yogasphuta Rasi is meant the sign arrived at by adding the longitudes of two or more planets, bhavas or planets and bhavas.

Illustration:—I. The Sun's longitude is Kumbha 1° 12′, *i.e.*, 311° 12′,. Saturn's longitude is Mithuna 3° 20′, *i.e.*, 63° 20′.

	Moon 18.29 Rahu 6.9	Lagna 13.9	Saturn 3.20
Sun 1.12 Mercury 8.27 Jupiter 21.38			
Venus 20.33		Mars 1 Kethu	

Therefore, Yogasphuta Rasi of Sun and Saturn
=301° 12′ + 63° 20′
=4° 32′ Mesha (expunging 360°)

II. The lord of Drekkana occupied by Saturn is Mercury. His longitude is 308° 27′.

∴ Yogasphuta Rasi of the Sun and lord of Drekkana held by Saturn is 301° 12′ + 308° 27′ = 609° – 39′. Expunging 360°, we get 249° 39′ or Dhanus 9° 39′.

III. The lord of Navamsa occupied by Saturn is Venus and his longitude is Dhanus 20° 33′ or 260° 33′.

∴ Yogasphuta Rasi of the Sun and lord of Navamsa occupied by Saturn is 301° 12′ + 260° 33′ = 201° 45′ (expunging 360°) or Thula 21° 45′.

IV. The lord of the Dwadasamsa held by Saturn is Moon and his longitude is Mesha 18° 29′ or 18° 29′.

∴ Yogasphuta Rasi of the Sun and the lord of the Dwadasamsa held by Saturn is 301° 12′ + 18° 29′ = 319° 41′ or Kumbha 19° 41′.

I. *Chandra Niryana Rasis in this horoscope are :—*

(*a*) Yogasphuta Rasi of Sun and Saturn—
Mesha 4° 32′.

(*b*) The Navamsa Rasi of (*a*)—Simha,

(*c*) The 7th from (*a*)—Thula and

(*d*) The trines from above–Simha, Dhanus, Dhanus, Mesha Kumbha and Mithuna.

II. Ravi Niryana Rasis are :—

(*a*) Yogasphuta Rasi of San and the lord of the Drekkana occupied by Saturn—Dhanus 9° 39′.

(*b*) The Navamsa Rasi of (*a*) —Mithuna.

(*c*) The 7th from (*a*)—Mithuna.

(*d*) Trines from above—Mesha, Simha, Thula, Kumbha, Thula, Kumbha.

III. Guru Niryana Rasis are :—

(*a*) Yogasphuta Rasi of Sun and the lord of the Navamsa occupied by Saturn—Thula 21° 45′.

(*b*) The Navamsa of (*a*)—Mesha.

(*c*) The 7th from (*a*)—Thula.

(*d*) Trines from above—Mithuna, Kumbha, Simha, Dhanus, Mithuna, Kumbha.

IV. Sani Niryana Rasis are :—

(*a*) Yogasphutn Rasi of the Sun and the lord of the Dwadasamsa held by Sani—Kumbha 19° 41′.

(*b*) The Navamsa of (*a*)—Meena.

(*c*) The 7th from (*a*)—Simha.

(*d*) Trines from above—Thula, Mithuna, Kataka, Vrischika. Mesha, Dhanus.

With due deference to the author I feel that it is enough to consider Yogasphuta Rasis and Navamsas of the Sun, Moon, Jupiter and Saturn and ignore items given *c* and *d* above.

द्वेधा न्यस्य विहङ्गमस्फुटमजाद्यातांशसंख्याहते
तत्रैकत्र कलीकृतादितरतस्तत्रांशकस्योद्यतः ।

निघ्नाद्यातकलाभिरानखहृता लिप्ताः समायोजये-
त्तत्रायतगृहे भवेत्स मरणे शुद्धेऽथवा चक्रतः ॥२९॥

Stanza 29.—Multiply the sphuta or longitude of a planet (devoid of the degrees passed in the current Navamsa) by the number of expired Navamsas reckoned from Aries: Call this x: convert the degrees passed in the current Navamsa into minutes and multiply it by the Navamsas from Aries. Divide the product by 200. Add the quotient (which will be in minutes) to x and the result is the Niryana Rasi of the planet.

NOTES

The stanza is a bit confusing.

Each planet is said to have its own *Niryana Rasi* or death-dealing sign. When the said planet transits its own Niryana Rasi, death may happen. Here one is enabled to find out the death-dealing Rasi of all the planets.

Illustration :—Suppose, for instance, Saturn's longitude is Cancer 25° 32′, *i.e.*, 3s 25° 32′. This means that Saturn has covered 34 Navamsas (*i.e.*, 3s 23° 20′) from Aries and has passed 2° 12′ in the 35th Navamsa (8th in Cancer).

1st step :—Multiplying the longitude of Saturn (less the degrees in its current Navamsa), *viz.*, 3s 23° 20′ by 34, we get 128s 13° 20″. Expunging multiples of 12, the result is 8s 13° 20′.

2nd step :—Converting the degrees passed in the current Navamsa, *viz.*, 2° 12′ into minutes we get 132′, Multiplyiug this by 34 and dividing the product by 200, the results is

$$\frac{132 \times 34}{200} = \frac{4488'}{200} = 22'\ 26''\ \text{(seconds ignored)}$$

3rd step :—Adding this to *x* we get :

x	=	8s 13° 20′
		22′
		8s 13° 42′

Niryana Sani's place is 13° 42′ in Sagittarius. Saturn's transit of this position may cause death, provided of course other appropriate factors are also present.

According to another view simply multiply the sphuta or longitude of a planet by the number of expired Navamsas. The resulting figure becomes the planet's Niryana Rasi.

According to this view

3s 25° 32′

= 115° 32′ × 34 = 318° 8′ = Saturn's Niryana Rasi

= 318° 8′ = Aquarius 18° 8′.

In our humble opinion, the latter view appears to be more acceptable.

आत्मारूढादर्थरिप्फत्रिकोणेष्वत्यल्पाक्षे मन्दिरे स्वाष्टवर्गे ।
न्यूनालोके चाखिलानां ग्रहाणां सञ्चारः
स्यान्मृत्युदोनर्थदो वा ॥३०॥

Stanza 30.—Considering the 2nd, 5th, 9th and 12th Rasis (from a planet's position in the horoscope), find out the Rasi having the least number of 'bindus' in the Ashtakavarga of the planet concerned and the Rasi least aspected by the respective lord. When planets pass through such Rasis, either there will be death or at least some calamities.

NOTES

Suppose in a horoscope, the Sun is in Cancer. Then consider Leo (2nd), Scorpio (5th), Pisces (9th) and Gemini (12th). Find out in the Sun's Ashtakavarga, the Rasi, out of these four, which has the least number of bindus and also the Rasi out of these four, that receive the least aspect from the Sun. Planets when transiting such Rasis cause death or calamity. Other planets should also be similarly considered.

Death–Dealing Ascendant

विलग्नादष्टमो राशिरष्टमेशाश्रितश्च यः ।
लग्नेशांशकराश्योर्यो रन्ध्रराशी इतीह ये ॥३१॥

चत्वारस्तत्त्रिकोणेषु लग्नगेन्यतमे मृतिः ।
यद्वा लग्नांशकर्क्षस्य लग्नेशभवतस्य वा ॥३२॥
मरणं निर्दिशेन्नृणां चतुर्थभवनोदये ॥ इति ॥३३॥

द्वित्रिसंवादतः स्पष्टमादेश्यमिति यत्र भे ।
लक्षणानि बहून्यत्र वाच्या मान्दादयः स्फुटम् ॥३४॥

परस्परं च संवादं मन्दादीनां निरीक्ष्य च ।
पञ्चतासमये तेषां सम्यङ्निश्चिनुयात्स्थितिम् ॥३५॥

Stanzas 31 to 35.—The 8th from Lagna, the sign occupied by the lord of the 8th, the 8th from the sign occupied by the lord of Lagna, the 8th from the Navamsa Rasi of lord of Lagna, the trines from all these four, the 4th from Navamsa Rasi of Lagna and the 4th from the sign occupied by the lord of Lagna are all death-dealing signs. Whether a sign has two, three or more indications for causing death and whether it has the aspect of transit Saturn, etc., should all be considered. Only after careful reconciliation and adjustment the correct death-dealing sign should be found out.

NOTES

Hitherto, the author has enabled us to calculate the year, month and day of death. In these stanzas, he deals with the method of finding out *Marana Lagna*, or the ascendant in which one would die. After finding the day of death, the time should be found out according to the principles dealt with in stanzas 31 to 35. The exact sign that would be rising at the time of death should be decided by a process of elimination, taking into account that Rasi, which gets a larger percentage of ' indications ' and which also receives the aspect of Saturn and of course, the other planets too. Taking again the example horoscope given above, we find the Niryana Rasi or Marana Rasi as follows :—

(*a*) 8th from Lagna—Dhanus,

(*b*) the sign in which the lord of the 8th is placed—Kumbha,

(*c*) the 8th from the sign occupied by lord of Lagna—Cancer,

(*d*) the 8th from Navamsa Rasi of lord of Lagna—Vrishabha,

(*e*) the trines from the above : Mesha, Simha. Thula—Mithuna, Vrischika. Meena, Kanya, Makara,

(*f*) the 4th from the Navamsa Rasi of Lagna—Cancer,

(*g*) the 4th from the sign occupied by lord of Lagna—Meena.

On 12th March 1937 of the sign given above Mithuna, Thula and Makara were receiving the aspect of Saturn. Mithuna in the birth horoscope is also occupied by Saturn. The native died in Mithuna Lagna.

TIME OF DEATH AS PER PRASNA

प्रश्नेनापि च वक्तव्यो मृतिकालस्ततो मृतौ ।
मन्दार्यार्कविधुस्थानलग्नादिकमथोच्यते ॥३६॥

Stanza 36.—The time of death should be ascertained on the basis of Prasna. Hence the positions of Saturn, Jupiter, the Sun, the Moon and Lagna as indicated by Prasna will be explained.

NOTES

Hitherto the principles dealt with the method of finding the time of death with reference to the birth chart and on the basis of the Niryana Sani, etc., as applied to birth chart. Now, the method of ascertaining the period of death with reference to the time of query will be given.

मान्द्यंशराशिगो मन्दो गुरुर्लग्नांशराशिगः ।
आरूढराशिगो भानुर्मान्दिराशिगतः शशी ॥३७॥
एते मृतिप्रदाः प्रष्टुः संवादश्चेत्परस्परम् ॥३८॥

Stanzas 37 and 38.—Saturn in Gulika Navamsa Rasi, Jupiter in Lagna Navamsa Rasi, the Sun in Arudha Rasi and the Moon in Gulika Rasi indicate the death of the querist. Adjust and reconcile the positions of these Rasis.

दूतवाक्यान्त्यवर्णोक्तराशिगेत्यन्तदोषदे ।
मन्दगुर्वर्कचन्द्रेषु मृतिस्तद्भवनोदये ॥३९॥

Stanza 39.—That planet which is most unfavourable amongst Saturn, Jupiter, the Sun and the Moon in the Rasi indicated by the last letter of the query of the messenger (Prasna Akshara) or in Prasna Lagna indicates death.

NOTES

The unfavourable nature of these planets should be judged by their situation in Arishta-bhavas or by their association with or aspect of malefics, or by their debilitation, etc.

द्रामिळा द्वादशाचः स्युर्वर्गाद्यन्ता यरान्विताः ।
येषादिषु क्रमाद्योज्याः शेषा मेषादिषट्स्वपि ॥४०॥

Stanza 40.—The letters a (अ), aa (आ), e (इ), ee (ई), u (उ), oo (ऊ), ru (ऋ), roo (ॠ), ae (ए), aai (ऐ). o (ओ), ou (औ) represents respectively the 12 signs from Aries Similarly the letters ka (क), gna (ङ), cha (च), jna (ञ), ta (ट), nna (ण), tha (त), na (न), pa (प), ma (म), ya (य), and ra (र) signify the 12 signs of the zodiac. The remaining la (ल), va (व), lla (ळ), lla (ळ), ra (र), na (न) cannote the six signs from Aries.

NOTES

The author gives a method for determining the Lagna on the basis of the name. In Tamil and in the old Dravidian language of Malabar, it appears there were only thirty letters. Hence only these are given. It occurs to me that the method given in *Prasna Tantra* (see my English translation) could be used.

लग्नांशराशिगे चन्द्रे प्रष्टु रुग्वर्द्धनं यदि ।
स्वांशराशिगते मोहो मृतिन्मांद्यंशराशिगे ॥४१॥

Stanza 41.—If the sickness shows signs of increase when the Moon is in the Navamsa Rasi of Lagna, then the period of uncosciousness and death of the querist will correspond to the transit of the Moon through his own Navamsa Rasi and Gulika Navamsa Rasi respectively.

NOTES

Supposing at the time of a query relating to a person whose illness is growing worse, the Navamsa Lagna is Leo, the Moon occupies Leo in Rasi and Libra in Navamsa and Gulika is in Meena in Navamsa, then he will become unconscious when the Moon by transit passes through Libra (Navamsa-Rasi of the Moon) and he may die when the Moon transits Meena (Navamsa Rasi of Gulika). What is given in stanza 41 can be applied only when the sick man shows signs of increase of sickness.

चन्द्रमान्धंशकौ युक्तौ यदि तद्राशिगे विधौ ।
मोहः सत्यर्कमांधंशयोगे तत्र गते मृतिः ॥४२॥

Stanza 42.—If the Moon and Mandi are in the same Navamsa, then the querist becomes unconscious when the Moon transits the sign corresponding to this Navamsa. If the Sun and Mandi occupy the same Navamsa, he will die when the Moon transits the Rasi corresponding to the said Navamsa.

NOTES

Supposing the Moon and Mandi are in association in Leo Navamsa and the Moon occupies Mesha Rasi, then the querist becomes unconscious when the Moon transits Leo (the Rasi corresponding to the Navamsa occupied by the Moon and Mandi). Suppose again at the time of query the Sun and Mandi are in Virgo Navamsa and the Moon in Mesha Rasi. Then the querist's death can be anticipated when the Moon transits Virgo (the Rasi corresponding to the Navamsa occupied by the Sun and Mandi).

लग्नेन्दू मानदानाभ्यामित्यानीतस्फुटत्रये ।
यमकण्टकमायोज्य योडुस्तस्यां च पञ्चता ॥४३॥

Stanza 43.—When the Moon transits through the asterism represented by the sum of the sphutas of Prana, Deha, Mrityu and Yamakantaka, death takes place.

NOTES

Suppose the total of Prana, Deha and Mrityu sphutas is 215° and the longitude of Yamakantaka is 106°. The sum of these would be 321°. The asterism corresponding to this longitude is the 25th, *i.e.*, Poorvabhadra. The Moon's transit of this is dangerous.

गुळिकोडुत्रिकोणस्थस्तथा रन्ध्रेशराशिगः ।
मृत्युदोर्कस्तथा मान्दिनक्षत्रं च मृतिप्रदम् ॥४४॥

Stanza 44.—When the Sun is in the Nakshatra occupied by Gulika, or its trines or in the Rasi occupied by the lord of the 8th from Arudha, when the Moon occupies the Nakshatra of Mandi, death takes place.

NOTES

Here three combinations are given.

(1) The Sun should be in the constellation occupied by Gulika, or the trinal constellation therefrom.

(2) The Sun should be in the sign occupied by the lord of the 8th from Arudha.

(3) The Moon should be disposed in the Nakshatra of Gulika.

त्रिस्फुटस्थोडुतो यावत्त्रिकोणमुरगोडुनः ।
तावद्वत्सरमासाहर्नाडिकांते भवेन्मृतिः ॥४५॥
लग्नेशस्य तदंशेशे बन्धुमित्राहिताभ्यरौ ।
स्वभप्रतीपतो मान्दिर्दिनरात्रौ मृतिप्रदः ॥४६॥

Stanzas 45 and 46.—Count from Thrisphuta Nakshatra to the nearest of either Aslesha, Jyeshta or Revati. The number so got indicates the number of years, months or days, the questioner will live from the time of Prasna according as the lords of Lagna and Navamsa Lagna are intimate friends or mere friends, or neutral, or enemies.

Death occurs in the night or during the day according as Mandi occupies a diurnal or nocturnal sign.

NOTES

If the lords are bitter enemies, then say so many ghatikas should pass. If the lords happen to be same, then the querist will not die but recover. This view is not accepted by all.

एष्यनाडीसमाहर्मासाब्दांन्ते लग्नचन्द्रयोः ।
बलीयसो नवांशस्य दोषाधिक्याल्पतावशात् ॥४७॥

Stanza 47.—Note the number of unexpired ghatikas in the Navamsa of the stronger between Lagna and the Moon. Depending upon the intensity or otherwise of the affliction, the number of days, months, years, etc., corresponding to the number of the unexpired ghatis, should be predicted.

NOTES

If the Prasna is very unfavourable, say he may die in the number of days so calculated. If it is neither favourable nor unfavourable, put the number as so many months. If the Prasna is favourable, take the number as years.

लग्नांशैष्यविनाडीभिः ममाहर्मासवत्सरैः ।
मृतिर्लग्नपतेः शत्रौ समे बन्धौ तदंशपे ॥४८॥

Stanza 48.—Find the number of vighatikas unexpired in Lagna Navamsa. According as lords of Lagna and Navamsa Lagna are friends, neutrals or enemies, death takes place in so many years, months or days.

मृत्युप्रदनवांशैष्यविनाड्यश्च मृतिप्रदाः ।

प्रोक्तवल्लग्नपारातिसमबन्धौ तदंशपे ॥४९॥

Stanza 49.—Similar results can be predicted by considering the unexpired portion of the Navamsas of the death-inflicting planets.

NOTES

Count the unexpired portion of the Navamsa of the Mrityupada or death-inflicting planet in vighatikas (treating the said planet as Lagna itself) and consider that number in years, months or days, according as lord of Lagna is friendly, neutral or inimical to lord of Navamsa Lagna. Death-inflicting planets are those that own or occupy the 8th house or that which is the most unfavourable amongst Gulika, Mrityu Kala or Thrisphuta.

क्रूराहिमृत्युगुळिकादिषु यावति स्या-

ल्लग्नांशकात्प्रभृति कष्टतमो नवांशे ।

तत्कष्टभाववशतः खलु तावतीषु

वाच्यो गतासु दिनमाससमासु मृत्युः ॥५०॥

Stanza 50.—The number of Navamsas from Lagna Navamsa to the Navamsa occupied by the most evil planet amongst Mandi, etc., represents the number of days, months or years, according to the intensity of affliction, within which the querist's death may take place.

NOTES

Count the number of Navamsas from Lagna Navamsa to the Navamsa of the most unfavourable (by position or otherwise) amongst the Sun, Mars, Saturn, Rahu, Gulika, Thrisphuta and Mrityu. Note this number. If that planet is very unfavourable, treat it as the number of days ; if he is less unfavourable, treat this as number of months ; if he is least unfavourable, treat it as number of years. Then predict that the questioner will live for such length of time as is in accordance with the evil nature of the planet mentioned.

कष्टोऽहिमृत्युगुळिकादिषु यत्र राशौ
तत्कालजं निधनदं यदि वा निमित्तम् ।
तस्य त्रिकोणजुषि कष्टतमे तदानीं
चन्द्रार्कजीवरविजेषु मृतिर्विचिन्त्या ॥५१॥

Stanza 51.—Note the Rasi occupied by the most unfavourable amongst Rahu, Mrityu, Gulika, Thrisphuta, etc., and the one wherefrom any indication suggesting death is observed at the time of Prasna. When the most evil amongst the planets Saturn, Jupiter, the Sun or the Moon transits these two Rasis or their trines, death may take place.

NOTES

Two Rasis—one occupied by the worst malefic from among Rahu, Saturn, Mandi, Thrisphuta, etc., and the other indicated by the direction in which an omen suggesting death is observed at the time of the query are considered. The transit of the most afflicted amongst Saturn, Jupiter, Sun or the Moon over these signs causes death of the querist. The directions ruled by different signs have already been discussed previously.

लग्नारूढपयोर्द्वयोर्बलवतः प्रारभ्य यस्मिन् गृहे ।
नक्षत्रेथ दृगाणके नु भवति प्रश्ने नवांशेपि वा ।
वृक्षादेः पतनाद्यनिष्टमसुभत्प्राणप्रणाशोपि वा
स्थानं वा गुळिकादिकस्य भविता तावद्दिनादौ मृतिः ॥

इति ॥५२॥

Stanza 52.—The number of Rasis or Nakshatras or Drekkanas or Navamsas counted from the Rasi, Nakshatra, etc., occupied by the lord of Lagna or the lord of Arudha—whichever is stronger—to the Rasi, Nakshatra, etc., in which any unfortunate accident such as death or fall of a tree is observed; or to the Rasi, Nakshatra, etc., occupied by the most unfavourable amongst Gulika, Mrityu, Thrisphuta. etc., represents the number of days, months or etc., in which death takes place.

NOTES

The number so counted may be taken as days or months or years according to the intensity of the evil represented by the above planets. This stanza is taken from *Anushtana Paddhati* and requires very careful consideration. Whether days, months or years have to be considered, whether Rasis, Nakshatras, Drekkanas or Navamsas have to be looked into should be very carefully examined by the astrologer by weighing the intensity of the evil indicated.

If we take Rasis, the number cannot be more than 12; if 'Nakshatras', not more than 27; if Drekkanas 36; if Navamsas 108. The Rasi indicated by the 'Dik' where the incident takes place should be taken into consideration. Some are of the opinion that, instead of the stronger of the two, Lagnadhipa or Arudhadhipa, one of these can be taken. 'Lagnarudha Ubhayadho' is another reading.

Stanzas 49 to 52 are from *Anustana Paddathi*.

आरूढोदययोरष्टमेष्टमेशाश्रितालये ।
पिण्डाष्टवर्गे हीनाक्षे राशौ वा लग्नगे मृतिः ॥५३॥

Stanza 53.—The eighth from Lagna or Arudha, the signs occupied by the lords of the 8th from Lagna and Arudha and the sign containing the least number of bindus in Sarvashtakavarga, can also be death-inflicting signs.

श्लोकस्यास्योत्तरार्द्धं यत्तज्जन्मविषयं तथा ।
स्वभप्रतीपतो मान्दिरित्यर्द्धं च पुरोदितम् ॥५४॥

Stanza 54.—The latter half of the above stanza and stanza 46 can be applied to horoscopy also.

NOTES

That part of the stanza dealing with the Rasi counting the least number of bindus in Sarvashatakavarga, can also be applied to birth horoscope for determining marakas, What is stated in stanza 46 is also applicable to birth horoscopes and not merely to horary charts.

द्वादशजन्माष्टमगाः पुंसां दिननाथभौमशनिजीवाः ।
वित्तक्षयं प्रवासं रोगान् जनयन्ति भीतिं वा ॥५५॥

Stanza 55.--When the Sun, Mars, Jupiter and Saturn transit the Janma Rasi, its 8th or 12th house, there will be loss of money, wanderings, sickness and fear.

PLANETARY POSITIONS AT DEATH

चन्द्रस्तु निधनं प्राप्तः सप्तमं बुधलोहितौ ।
द्वादशं भास्करः षष्ठं भृगुपुत्रः समाश्रितः ॥५६॥
तृतीयं देवमन्त्री च राहुकेतुशनैश्चराः ।
जन्मस्थाः प्राणसन्देहं कुर्वन्त्येते न संशयः ॥५७॥

Stanzas 56 and 57.—The period, when transit Moon is in the 8th, Mercury and Mars in the 7th, the Sun in the 12th, Venus in the 6th, Jupiter in the 3rd and Saturn, Rahu and Ketu in the Janma Rasi itself should be considered as most fatal.

प्रथमे च चतुर्थे च सप्तमेचाष्टमे ऽव्यये ।

क्रूरग्रहाः प्रदीप्यन्ते दीप्तपावकसन्निभाः ॥५८॥

Stanza 58.—Malefic planets transiting the 1st, 4th, 7th, 8th and 12th are always indicative of fatal happenings.

NOTES

In stanzas 55 to 58, the author deals with Gochara or transits. The movements of the planets with reference to radical Moon (the sign occupied by the Moon at the time of birth) should be considered. In these stanzas, the significance of transits with reference to the occurrence of *maraka* or death should be noted.

चतुर्थे निधने चान्त्ये चन्द्रो नित्यमरिष्टकृत् ।

शुभः शशी च जन्मस्थो न स्याज्जन्मदिनं तथा ॥ इति ॥५९॥

Stanza 59.—The periods when the Moon transits the 4th, 8th and 12th from it, have to be considered as bad. Though the Moon's transit in Janma Rasi is good, his passing through the Janma Nakshatra is not good.

इत्थं विचिन्त्य निश्चित्य ससंवादं परस्परम् ।

खेचराणामवस्थानं समयः कथ्यतां मृतेः ॥६०॥

Stanza 60.—In this way, predict 'death' after carefully weighing the 'pros' and 'cons' of the positions of planets.

॥ इति प्रश्नमार्गे दशमाध्यायः ॥

एकादशाध्यायः

CAUSE OF DEATH

क्रमेण मरणं वह्निसलिलायुधजूर्तिभिः ।
अज्ञातरोगतृट्क्षुद्भिरर्काद्यैरष्टमस्थितैः ॥ १ ॥

Stanza 1.—Death will be due to fire or burns, drowning, weapons, high fever, an inexplicable disease, thirst or hunger according as the eighth house is occupied by the Sun, Moon, etc.

NOTES

In this chapter causes that bring about death are enumerated. If the Sun is in the 8th, death will be due to fire or burns; if the Moon—drowning; if Mars—weapons; if Mercury—high fever; if Jupiter—due to a disease that cannot be diagnosed; if Venus—thirst or *pranita* and if Saturn—death will be due to starvation or inability to eat or drink. The scope of this stanza can be widened to include innumerable other causes. The Sun in the 8th may cause death by electric shock, suffocation, train and aeroplane accidents, outbreak of fire, etc. Accidental drowning or suicide, falling in a well, tank, river or sea may occur if the Moon is in the 8th. Mars, of course, can cause death by accidents, explosions, fire arms and similar happenings. 'High fever' is assigned to Mercury. Several variations of this may be thought of. All sorts of complications may set in rendering the nature of illness difficult to diagnose if Jupiter is the planet occupying the 8th. Similarly with regard to the other two planets, all appropriate causes must be considered.

दृष्टेष्टमे तु सूर्याद्यैस्तत्प्रोक्तास्थ्यादिजामयैः ।
मृत्युर्यद्वाथ तत्प्रोक्तपित्तवह्न्यादिसम्भवः ॥ २ ॥

Stanza 2.—Death will be due to the disease, affecting the appropriate organ by the excitement of one of the doshas, as indicated by the planet aspecting the 8th.

NOTES

If a planet aspects the 8th house, study it and see what disease it indicates and where (in which part of the body) it is found, what Dhatu it governs, and what dosha or humour it rules and then ascertain the cause of death.

अस्थि रक्तं च मज्जा त्वग्वसा शुक्रं च वस्नसा ।
एवं हि धातवः सप्त सूर्यादीनां प्रकीर्तिताः ॥ ३ ॥

Stanza 3.—The seven Dhatus, *viz.*, asthi (bone), raktha (blood), majja (muscle), twak (skin), vasa (flesh), sukla (seminal fluid) and vasmasa (nervous material) are governed respectively by the Sun, the Moon, etc.

NOTES

According to this stanza, planetary allocations of the *Sapta Dhatus* are distributed as follows :

Planet	*Dhatu*
The Sun	Asthi or bone
The Moon	Raktha or blood
Mars	Majja or muscle
Mercury	Twak or skin
Jupiter	Vasa or fat
Venus	Sukla (sperm and ovum)
Saturn	Vasmasa (nervous material)

पित्तं वातकफौ पित्तं वातपित्तकफाः कफः ।
कफवातौ च वातश्च सूर्यादीनां प्रकीर्तिताः ॥ ४ ॥

Stanza 4.—The tridoshas are ruled by the seven planets thus: The Sun—pitta; the Moon--vata and kapha; Mars—pitta; Mercury—vata, pitta and kapha; Jupiter—kapha; Venus—kapha and vata; and Saturn—vata.

कालाङ्गेष्वष्टमो राशिर्ग्रहो वाष्टमवीक्षकः ।
जन्मकाले स्थितो यत्र तत्राङ्गे तद्गदोद्भवः ॥ ५ ॥

Stanza 5.—The 8th Rasi and the Rasi occupied by the lord aspecting the 8th determine the diseases and the part of the body affected.

NOTES

In *Brihat Jataka*, we have the stanza 'Kalangani'—allotting different parts of the body to different Rasis. The allocation of organs should be considered on this basis.

ग्रहयोगेक्षणाभावे निधने निधनाधिपः ।
द्वाविंशत्र्यंशपो वापि स्वगुणैर्मरणप्रदः ॥ ६ ॥
धातवश्च त्रिदोषाश्च प्रोक्ता वह्न्यादयोगुणाः ॥ ७ ॥

Stanzas 6 and 7.—If the 8th house is not occupied or aspected by any planet, then death will be due to the *dathu*, *tridosha*, etc., indicated by the lord of the 8th or the lord of the 22nd drekkana.

NOTES

The stanza is clear. If there is no planet in the 8th or no planet aspects the 8th, consider the lord of the 8th or the lord of the 22nd drekkana. Death will come by the diseases caused by the humour or dhatu ruled by such a lord.

मन्दे सूर्यादिसंयुक्ते तेषां योस्थयादिरीरितः ।
रोगेण तत्र जातेन पुरुषस्य भवेन्मृतिः ॥ ८ ॥

Stanza 8.—If Saturn is associated with the Sun and other planets, they determine the nature of disease causing death.

भानुना वासृजा दृष्टे दक्षांगेरुरसृग्भवः ।
अतिसारो निशाभर्त्रा वेपथुश्चन्द्रसूनुना ॥ ९ ॥
गुरुणाश्वयथुः पादे दक्षिणाङ्गे च वेदना ।
क्षयः शोफश्च शुक्रेण कासश्वासादि नेक्षिते ॥१०॥

राहुणा सन्धिसादादि मान्दिनोन्मादसंभवः ।
मूर्च्छा द्राघीयसी मन्दे यमकण्टकवीक्षिते ॥११॥

अरुरर्द्धप्रहारेण समासन्ने सुनिर्गमे ।
कालदृष्टे रवेः पुत्रे नृणां सञ्चरतां मृतिः ॥१२॥

Stanzas 9 to 12.—Death will be owing to boils or eruptions due to blood impurities on the right side of the body, diarrhoea, shivering, swellings in the legs, and pain in the right side of the body, consumption and cough, difficulties in breathing, pains in the joints, unmada or madness, swooning, sores, no disease respectively according as Saturn is aspected by the Sun, Mars, Moon, Mercury, Jupiter, Venus, no planet, Rahu, Mandi, Yamakantaka and Ardhaprahara respectively. If Saturn is aspected by Kala, death occurs while travelling.

NOTES

In these stanzas, the nature of disease causing death is discussed. Since Saturn is the Ayushkaraka, the disease will be according to the planet aspecting Saturn. If the Sun or Mars is the aspecting planet, the cause of death will be due to *aru* (nlcers, boils, etc. skin eruptions due to blood impurities, etc.). We may also include blood-poisoning. The range of diseases should be widened keeping in view the primary indications. It is the left side of the body that will be affected by these troubles. If the Moon aspects Saturn, *athisara* (diarrhoea) will be cause. Dysentery and similar types of bowel disorders can also be taken into account. When Mercury aspects Saturn, the cause of death will be *Vapatha* or shivering. If Jupiter is the planet there will be swelling in the feet (ayath) and pain (vedana) in the right side of the body. Venus denotes kshaya (consumption) and kapha (cough). Cough and breathing troubles should be predicted if Saturn has no aspect. Weakness and aches in the joints are likely if Rahu is the planet aspecting Saturn. Rheumatic troubles come under this category. Unmada or madness or mental aberration is said to arise if Mandi is the aspecting planet. Yamakantaka brings about *moorcha* or swooning, while Ardhaprahara denotes death by sores. If Saturn is aspected by Kala, there will be no ostensible cause and death can occur while travelling.

The diseases allotted to different planets should be ascertained very carefully. It is suggested that if Saturn is aspected by no planet, there will be cough and brealhing diffculties. There are several instances of death having occured due to breathing difficulties, even in cases where Saturn is not free from any aspects. Here comes the importance of 'discrimination' and inferential ability on the part of the astrologer. He should remember that these rules are intended only for our guidance and that they should not be considered as axiomatic truths applicable to all cases.

मान्द्यारूढनवांशकामगृहगाः सौम्याः सुमृत्युप्रदाः
पापस्तत्रगतास्तु दुर्मृतिकरास्तेष्वर्क उर्वीपतेः ।
क्षीणेन्दुः सलिले युधि क्षितिसुतः सूर्यात्मजो वञ्चना-
द्राहुः पन्नगदंशनान्मरणदो यद्वा विषस्पर्शनात् ॥१३॥

Stanza 13.—The person will have peaceful or painful death according as the 7th from the *mandyarudha Navamsa* is occupied by benefic or malefic planets. The Sun in the 7th denotes death due to royal displeasure; weak Moon—by drowning; Mars—in a battle-field; Saturn by deceit; and Rahu—by snake-bite or poisoning.

NOTES

These slokas are highly suggestive and are not amenable to easy translation. Malefics and benefics should occupy the 7th from the Navamsa Rasi held by Mandi at the time of birth. According to some, these rules are also applicable to Prasna charts. Regarding the violent nature of death, what is stated in this stanza can be extended to include a number of other similar causes. Thus death by royal displeasure may mean, hanging, execution for treason, or liquidation as in communist countries. Death in secrecy may mean being murdered. In all these cases, Satyacharya's dictum that an astrologer should use *uhapoha* (proper guessing) should be carefully remembered.

जूत्यां तोयविकारतश्च पिटकाद्युष्णा मयैर्वायुना
गुल्माङ्गोत्थितवेदनाभिरधिकं शोफप्रमेहक्षयैः ।
कासश्वाससमीरतो मृतिरिनादीनां शनौ त्र्यंशगे
त्र्यंशेशा यदि तेऽहिवीक्षितयुता मृत्युर्विषोत्थामयैः ॥१४॥

Stanza 14.—If the lord of the Drekkana occupied by Saturn is the Sun, death will be due to fever ; the Moon swelling, tumor and *mahodara*; Mars—boils, pox, etc ; Mercury—disorder in breathing ; Jupiter—*gulma* (a disease inside the stomach) and intense pains in the body ; Venus—swelling and consumption ; Saturn—cough troubles and rheumatism. If the Drekkana lord is in association with or aspected by Rahu, poison will be the cause of death.

NOTES

This sloka is simple. Saturn occupies some drekkana. The lord of this Drekkana indicates the cause of death. If the lord is the Sun, fever will be the cause ; if Moon—there will be swelling, etc. If the lord of the drekkana is combined with or aspected by Rahu, then death will be due to poisoning.

सौम्यानामंशराशीन् गतवति रविजे स्वर्क्षतुङ्गादिगे वा
जीवर्क्षस्थे विशेषान्म्रियत इह गृहे पुत्रमित्राद्युपेतः ।
नीचारात्यालयस्थे रविभुवि रहितो बन्धुभिर्दुखितः सन्
सर्पत्र्यंशेत्र तिष्ठत्यहिगुळिकसमेतेक्षिते सर्पदष्टः ॥२५॥

Stanza 15.—The person will die peacefully in the middle of friends and relatives if Saturn occupies benefic Navamsas or his own house or Moolatrikona or exaltation, or if he is in jovian signs. If Saturn is in inimical houses or in debilitation, the person will die unfriended and unhelped. If Saturn happens to be in *Sarpa drekkana* or if he is associated with or aspected by Rahu or Mandi, the native will die of snake-bite.

NOTES

Here again the nature of death is dealt with by taking into consideration the situation of Saturn. If Saturn is in benefic Navamsas, own, friendly, or exaltation or moolathrikona sign. one's end will be peaceful. Otherwise it will be unhappy. Saturn's situation in a Sarpa drekkana (the 1st of Scorpio, the last of Cancer and the last of Pisces) or his association with Rahu is not desirable as it denotes death by snake-bite poisoning, etc.

मन्दे भौमयुतोथवा रवियुते क्षेत्रस्थिते चानयो—
र्भूते वह्निमये स्थितेगुगुळिकोपेतेक्षितेग्नौ मृतिः ।
एवंभूतशनौ जलग्रहयुते तप्तांबुपातादिभि-
र्दोषेऽसत्युदितेम्बुभूतखचरक्षेत्रान्विते वारिणि ॥१६॥

Stanza 16.—If Saturn is in association with Mars or the Sun in Aries, Scorpio or Leo, occupies *agnibhuta* in association with or aspected by Rahu or Gulika, the person will be burnt to death. If Saturn is associated with watery planets, death will be due to falling in boiling waters. If Saturn occupies *jalabhuta* or watery signs, he will die by drowning.

NOTES

The first part of the sloka is clear. Saturn must occupy a sign of Mars with Mars or the sign of Sun and should have the aspect or association of Mandi or Rahu besides being posited in Agnibhuta, to be burnt to death. So far as the second part of the sloka is concerned, death by falling in boiling water being poured on takes place if Saturn is associated with *jalagrahas* (Moon and Venus). If Saturn is in *jalabhuta* or occupies the signs of jalagrahas (Cancer, Taurus and Libra), death takes place by drowning or slipping into rivers, tanks etc. Here also, the affliction due to Rahu's and Mandi's association or aspect should be considered. Where there is an intermingling of influences of both Jala Rasis and Agni Rasis, predictions must be accordingly varied.

In applying this stanza, a distinction should be noted between Agnitatwa Rasis and Agnibhuta, Jalatatva Rasis and Jalabhuta, Vayutatwa Rasis and Vayubhuta and Prithvitatwa Rasis and Prithivibhuta.

Agnitatwa (fiery), *Bhutatwa* (earthy), *Vayutatwa* (airy) and *Jalatatwa* (watery) signs are respectively Aries, Taurus, Gemini and Cancer and their triangular ones.

Agnibhuta, Jalabhuta etc , are to be understood as follows :

According to the commentator, a Drekkana has 3 Navamsas and a Navamsa has 4 *yamas* equal to 15 ghatis, so that each yama becomes equal to $3\frac{3}{4}$ ghatis. Putting this differently, we can say that if 4 yamas equals 1 Navamsa or 200′ of arc 1 yama will be equal to 50 minutes of arc. In a Navamsa, the four yamas are distributed thus :

1st yama 0′ to 50′ of arc
2nd yama 51′ to 100′ of arc
3rd yama 101′ to 150′ of arc
4th yama 151′ to 200′ of arc

The Bhuta a planet falls in, can be found out by noting the longitudes of the planet concerned.

Illustration :

Suppose Saturn's longitude is 25° 32′ of Cancer. This means, Saturn has covered 2° 12′ or 132′ of arc in the 8th Navamsa. Since each yama is equivalent to 50′ of arc, Saturn is in the 3rd yama having covered 32′ in it.

The order of Bhutas in the 1st and 3rd yamas are :

Prithvi or Bhumi (Fire)	16′ 40″
Apa or Jala (water)	13′ 20″
Teja or Agni (fire)	10′ 00″
Vayu or Air (wind)	6′ 40″
Akasha (Ether)	3′ 20″
Total	50′ 00″

The order is reversed in the 2nd and 4th yamas.

In the above example, Saturn is in the 3rd yama having covered 32′ in it ; which means he is in Agni or Fire Bhuta.

Yama—3rd

Bhumi	16′ 40″
Jala	13′ 20″
Totol	30′ 00″

Agnibhuta lasts from 30′ to 40′ and hence Saturn is in Agnibhuta.

Illustration 2 : Mars is in 203° 15′ or Libra 23° 15′ This means that in Aries Navamsa, Mars has gained 3° 15′ or 195′ of arc. Since each yama is equal to 50′, Mars is in the 4th yama (151′ to 200′) in which he has covered 45′: In the 4th yama the order of succession of Bhutas is

Akasa	3′ 20″
Vayu	6′ 40″
Agni	10′ 00″
Apa	13′ 20″
Total	33′ 20″

Since Mars is in 45′ in 4th yama the Bhuta is Bhumi or Prithvi.

त्र्यंशे कोलमुखे स्थिते मृगगणैर्गृध्रानने पक्षिभि-

स्तत्राप्यस्तु बलोनता गुळिकयोगेक्षादिकं भास्करेः ।

नेष्टस्थानगताश्च मान्दिगृहपाः सुर्यादयौ दुर्बला-
स्तातान्मातृसहोत्थबन्धुतनयस्त्रीभ्यः स्वतो मृत्युदाः
॥१७॥

Stanza 17.—According as weak Saturn aspected by or associated with Gulika or Rahu joins *Kolemukha Drekkana* or *Pakshimukha Drekkana*, death will be due to beasts or birds. If the Sun, Moon etc., being weak happen to own the sign occupied by Gulika, the person's death will be brought about respectively by father, mother, brothers, relatives, son wife and his ownself.

NOTES

One will be done to death by beasts if Saturn who must be weak and who must be aspected by or associated with Rahu occupies a Kolemukha drekkana. Saturn similarly placed in Pakshi drekkana indicates death by birds. Similarly if the Sun is weak and owns the sign occupied by Gulika, and occupies an evil place, the native's death will be brought about by his father. The Moon similarly placed, causes death at the instigation of the mother, Mars at the instigation of brother, Mercury at the instigation of relatives, Jupiter at the hands of the son, Venus at the hands of women or wife ; and Saturn so placed, will make the native commit suicide.

The first Drekkanas of Scorpio, Capricorn and Cancer are Kolemukha Drekkanas. The second Drekkana of Libra, and the first of Leo and Aquarius are Pakshi Drekkanas.

दौर्बल्यदियुतु शनौ क्षितिभुवा युक्तेक्षिते पञ्चता
चामुण्ड्यादिनिपीडयारगुळिकोपेतेरिवाणादिभिः ।
मन्दे मान्दिविवस्वदीक्षितयुते कोपेन शम्भोस्तदी-
यावासाहितवासभूतकृतया जूत्यां मृतिं निर्दिशेत् ॥१८॥

Stanza 18.—If a weak and badly situated Saturn occupies a sign of Mars or has the association or aspect of Mars, death results from the troubles of evil spirits as Chamundi, etc; of Mars and Gulika, he will be affected by an enemy's *aabichara;* the Sun and Gulika, death will be due to the wrath of God Siva.

NOTES

Saturn must be weak, badly situated and occupy a sign of Mars. In this state if he has the association or aspect of Mars and Gulika death will ensue due to enemy's black magic; if such a Saturn has the association or aspect of the Sun and Gulika death will be due to the wrath of God Shiva.

CAUSE OF DEATH ACCORDING TO PRASNA

मृत्युरोगनिमित्तानि कथितानीति जातकात् ।
अथ मृत्युप्रदा रोगाः कथ्यन्ते प्रश्नलग्नतः ॥१९॥

Stanza 19.—After having detailed the cause of death through horoscopy, we shall pass on to discussing the nature of disease leading to death on the basis of Prasna.

वीक्षिते योष्टमं खेटस्तस्य रोगस्तु मृत्यवे ।
तदभावेष्टमस्तस्य द्वयाभावे तदीशितुः ॥२०॥

Stanza 20.– Death will be due to the disease indicated by the planet aspecting the 8th or in its absence the planet occupying the 8th or in its absence by the lord of the 8th.

NOTES

The aspecting planet is the most important. Next comes the occupant and then the lord. It will be seen that according to standard works, the least powerful in causing death is the lord.

अत्यग्निं वेदनामन्तर्ज्वरं चार्कोथ चन्द्रमाः ।
छर्दिमूर्ध्वानने तिर्यग्वक्त्रे मूत्रादिबन्धनम् ॥२१॥
अतिसारं तृषं चाधोवक्त्रे शोफं तु सर्वगः ।
उष्णप्रसरणं दाहं रक्तक्षोभभवं व्रणम् ॥२२॥
भूमिजोथ बुधः कुर्याच्छीतज्वरमतिभ्रमौ ।
सन्निपातरुजं चाथ गुरुर्बुद्धेरनार्जवम् ॥२३॥
अजीर्तिं श्वयथुं चाथ दाहं मोहं च भार्गवः ।
तृष्णारुचिसमस्ताङ्गतोदांस्तरणिनन्दनः ॥२४॥

वायुक्षोभमहिमांन्दिर्हिक्कामपि सिरोद्गमम् ।
सूर्यादिगुळिकान्तानामिमे रोगाः प्रकीर्तिताः ॥२५॥

Stanzas 21 to 25.—Excessive heat and internal fever are the diseases of the Sun. In Urdhwa Mukha Rasis, the Moon gives rise to 'vomitting'; in Thiryugamukha Rasis, urinary diseases; diarrohea and thirst in Adhomukha Rasis and a *sophan* (swelling ?) generally in all Rasis. Mars causes diseases due to heat in the body, thirst, impure blood and ulcers. Shivering fever, mental disorders and typhoid are caused by Mercury. Jupiter denotes dullness af mind. Indigestion, dropsy (swayuthan), extreme heat in the body, sex-troubles and swoons are all diseases of Venus. Saturns governs thirst, want of appetite, and pains all over the body. Windy complaints and breathing difficulties are indicated by Rahu. Mandi denotes contraction of the nerves of cerebral complaints (siro सिरो).

सूर्याद्यैर्भास्करादीनामंशैर्वा त्रिस्फुटे युते ।
ये रोगा मृत्युदाः प्रोक्ताश्चिन्तयेदिह तानपि ॥२६॥

Stanza 26.—The diseases of appropriate planets can be predicted if the Sun to Saturn occupy the Navamsa of Thrisphuta. This can be used in all places where diseases have to be diagnosed.

चन्द्रे लग्नांशराशिस्थे वृद्धिमेति मनागपि ।
आमयो यो भवेदेष मरणायैव पृच्छताम् ॥२७॥

Stanza 27.—If the disease shows any signs of increase when the Moon transits the Navamsa Rasi or Lagna, then the person will die of the disease indicated in the previous slokas.

NOTES

The Lakshanas discussed in Chapter IV (slokas 55-60) may be advantageously used here for prediction.

लग्नमांद्यंशकाभ्यां यदुदितं पात्रभञ्जनम् ।
त्रिस्फुटस्थोडुना यच्च लक्ष्म तच्चेह चिन्त्यताम् ॥२८॥

Stanza 28.—The Navamsas of Lagna and Mandi, the nimityas (omens) such as breaking of vessels etc., the constellation of the Thrisphuta etc., should all be considered.

मृत्युपतिर्यदि भानुः प्रबलजनस्यांगमो विगृह्य भवेत् ।
आसन्ने सति मरणे प्रष्टुः स्यात् कोपि कलहो वा ॥२९॥

चन्द्रश्चेद्वनितागमो यदि कुजः कांक्षा गुळक्षीरयो-
र्वक्तव्यामयिनोथवा खलु वदेदानीतिमात्रानयोः ।

आयानं विदुषो बुधो यदि गुरुर्विप्रस्य शुक्रो यदि
व्यापद्विप्रचष्पादां यदि शनिः स्याछुष्टनीचागमः ॥३०॥
मृत्युश्चेप्फणियुक्स वा शिखियुतो भिक्षाशिसर्पागम-
स्तस्मिन् केतुयुते भवेच्च पतनं तलारचन्द्रान्विते
भयाद्भाजनभञ्जनं मरणलक्ष्माथायुरारोग्यदे
प्रश्ने रुक्च्छमलक्ष्म चैतदुदितं देहासुनाथादिभिः ॥३१॥

Stanzas 29 to 31.—If the lord of Mrityu-sphuta (at the time of query) happens to be the Sun, some persons of distinction arrive quarrelling among themselves or some unexpected quarrel takes place in the house. If the Moon is the lord a strange woman turns up; Mars—some persons take milk and sugar to the house or the questioner takes up a sudden fancy to drink sugared milk. Mercury—a learned man visits the house; Jupiter—a Brahmin makes his appearance; Venus—nearby the death of a Brahmin or a quadruped takes place; Saturn—some low born and evil-minded men turn up; Rahu—a beggar or a serpent is found near; Ketu—somebody falls down from an elevated place; and Mars and the Moon—some vessels get broken. These indications show that *death is near*.

If instead of Mrityu Sphuta the planets are disposed as above in regard to Prana or Deha

Sphuta and the above omens are observed, then the sick man will recover.

NOTES

Certain omens should happen coincident with the lord of Mrityu Sphuta being a certain planet at the time of Prasna. In regard to questions pertaining to disease, early death must be predicted. Recovery is possible if the omens suggested in stanzas 29 to 31 coincide with the Sun, Moon etc., being lords of Prana Sphuta or Deha Sphuta. For example, if a strange woman tu'ns up when Mrityu Sphuta happens to be owned by the Moon, early death of the person may be predicted. If on the other hand, the same omen takes place but the Moon insted of being in Mtityu Sphuta, occupies Prana or Deha Sphuta, then the patient will recover.

छर्दिः शोफोतिसारो मरणकरगदास्त्रिस्फुटांशेब्जभृग्वो-
र्धाम्न्यूर्ध्वास्याद्यभेदाद्दिनकरकुजयोरुष्णसञ्चारदाहौ ।
चेतोवाक्स्थम्भनं वा विद इह तु गुरोर्द्धाभ्रमोपेतवाणी-
रोधः श्वासस्य वायोः स्खलनमपि शनेर्दष्टयुक्तैश्च तैस्तैः
इति ॥३२॥

Stanza 32.—According as the Thrisphuta Navamsa owned by Venus (or the Moon) happens to be *Urdwa*, *Adho* or *Tiryag* sign the disease causing death will be pneumonia, vomitting or diarrohoea. If the lord owning the said Navamsa happens to be the Sun (or Mars) Mercury, Jupiter or Saturn, death is caused respectively by excessive heat, loss of speech, mental trouble or asthama and suffocation. The same results should be predicted if the different planets aspect or occupy the said Navamsa Rasi.

NOTES

With regard to Venus and the Moon, Urdhwa Mukha, Adhomukha and Thiryagmukha Rasis are noticed. The Thrisphuta Navamsa, *i.e.*, the Rasi having reference to this should be the sign of a particular planet or be associated with or aspected by the said planet to give the result attributed. Thus if Aries, Scorpio or Leo is the Thrisphuta Navamsa or Mars or the Sun is in the said Rasi or aspects it, then suffering from heat should be predicted. If the Thrisphuta Navamsa happens to be the house of Mercury or Mercury associates with that Navamsa, then one will suffer from inability to talk or think. If the said Navamsa happens to be the house of Jupiter or if he is connected with it, say the person dies because of unsound mind. If Navamsa happens to be the sign of Saturn, or if Saturn is connected with it, then the person is suffering from asthama, suffocation etc., and death will be due to these troubles.

प्राणो लग्ननवांशश्चन्द्रनवांशः समीरितो देहः ।
गुळिकनवांशो मृत्युः कालः स्यात्त्रिस्फुटस्यांश ॥
इति च ॥३३॥

Stanza 33.—The longitudes of Lagna, the Moon, Mandi and Thrisphuta multiplied by nine gives Prana, Deha, Mrityu and Kala sphutas respectively.

NOTES

So far, the author death with death-causing disease on the basis of Prasna chart. Now he proceeds to locate the place of dea'h based on birth chart

मृत्युः स्याच्चरभे विदेश उभये मार्गे स्वदेशे स्थिरे
ग्राम्यारण्यजलात्मके तु निधने ग्रामे जलेम्ब्वन्तिके ।
स्वच्छम्लेच्छनतोन्नतेषु सदसत्क्षेत्राध ऊर्ध्वानने
दीपादीनपि निर्दिशेज्जननवद्रन्ध्राष्टमेनामुना ॥३४॥

Stanza 34.—According as the 8th Rasi is movable, common or fixed; grama (village), aranya (forest) or jala (watery) owned by benefics or malefies; Adhomukha or Urdhwamukha death happens in a foreign place, on the way, or own place; in a village, or a forest or a watery place; in a clean or dirty spot; in plains or table lands respectively. The nature of the lamp etc., can be known considering the 8th instead of Lagna, as is done at the time of birth.

NOTES

Find the place of death from the nature of the 8th house If it is movable, say he will die in a foreign place.

If it is fixed, he will die in his own native place If it is common, he will die on the way. If the 8th is a village Rasi, he will die in a village. If it is a forest Rasi, he will die in a forest. If it is a Rasi owned by good planets, he will die in a clean spot. If it is owned by evil planets, he will die in a place occupied by low people. If it is Adho-mukha Rasi, he will die in plains or places below the sea-level. If it is Urdhwa Mukha Rasi, he will die in high table-lands or elevated places. Whether there is light or a lamp burning at the time of death can also be stated. Varahamihira has described the nature of deepa or lamp at the time of birth by asking us to study Lagna. Here instead of Lagna,read the 8th house and we can predict the nature of deepa at the time of death.

स्वजन्मानि विलग्नांशपत्योः प्राण्याश्रितेन च ।
राशिना स्वपराध्वादिप्रदेशेषु वदेन्मृतिम् ॥३५॥

Stanza 35.—The nature of the place of death can also be known by applying the principles given in sloka 34 to the Rasi held by the stronger of the lords of Lagna and Navamsa Lagna.

NOTES

Marana lakshana cau be aseertained by examining the strongest of the two lords at the time of birth, *viz.*, the lord of Lagna and the lord of Lagna Navamsa. If that Rasi is *Chara* (moveable), he dies in a foreign place. If it is fixed, he dies in his own house ; if it is common, he dies on the way. If it is Gramya or Aranya, say he will die respectively in a village or forest. If it is watery, he will die in a watery house. If that Rasi is *Subha* he will die in a clean place and if it is a *Papa*, he will die in a bad place. For the rest, refer to the previous sloka and repeat the results.

स प्राणी चेदन्यखेटैः समेतः संदृष्टो वा तेषु
वीर्यान्वितस्य ।
लग्नांशाधीशस्य वा देहभाजां देवांब्वादिस्थानभेदेषु
मृत्युः ॥३६॥

लग्नलग्नेशयुग्द्रष्टा वास्तिचेत्कश्चनामुना ।
जीर्णसंस्कृतगेहादौ मरणं कैश्चनेरितम् ॥३७॥

Stanzas 36 and 37.—We can also examine the strogest of the planets who associate or aspect lord of Lagna or lord of Navamsa Lagna(whichever is stronger) and from that we can determine the place where the questioner will die. We can also consider the strongest amongst (*a*) the planet who occupies Lagna; (*b*) the planet who associates with the lord of Lagna ; (*c*) the planet who aspets Lagna ; and (*d*) the planet who aspects the lord of Lagna.

ज्ञात्वा कालादि सर्वं तदशुभशुभते चापि बुध्वाथ तेषां
सर्वेषां चेच्छुभत्वं गदशमनमरं दीर्घमायुश्च वाच्यम् ।
सर्वेषां चाशुभत्वं यदि मृतिरचिरान्मिश्रतायां तु तेषां
मन्दं शान्ती रुजां वा मृतिरधिकतया स्यात् सतां
चासतां च ॥३८॥

Stanza 38.—The time, the place, the air the querist breathes,etc., the omens in the road when departing, should all be carefully examined. If they are favourable,the person will have long life. If they are adverse, the sick man will not recover.

एवं निरूप्य निर्णिते मरणे सति पृच्छताम् ।
तस्य कालं च रोगांश्च देशांश्चेति विनिर्दिशेत् ॥३९॥

Stanza 39.—After considering carefully, if you come to the conclusion that the sick man will die, then decide the nature of his sickness and the probable period and place at which his death may take place.

॥ इति प्रश्नमार्गे एकादशाध्यायः ॥

द्वादशाध्यायः

DISEASES AND THEIR CURE

निर्णीते सति जीवने खलु रुजां शान्त्यै चिकित्सां वदे-
दज्ञातेषु गदेषु·दुष्करतरा सा चापि यस्मात्ततः ।
कर्तव्यो गदतत्वबोध इह तद्बोधाय भेदा रुजां
कथ्यन्ते खलु तत्र रोगशमने कार्याः क्रियाश्चोचिताः
॥ १ ॥

Stanza 1.—After ascertaining whether the sick man will recover or die, the nature of treatment to be given should be considered. In order to give the best medical treatment, a careful diagnosis of the nature of disease, its cause, etc., is essential.

NOTES

In this chapter the author describes in his own inimitable way the various diseases, how they are caused, and how they are to be diagnased. He shows how astrology can be made use of in medical treatment.

तत्तदुक्तामया वाच्या अनिष्टस्थानगैर्ग्रहैः ।
इष्टस्थितैस्तथारोग्यं तदेवाथ निगद्यते ॥ २ ॥

Stanza 2.—Planets occupying *anishta* or unfavourable houses bring about appropriate diseases. Planets occupying *ishta* or favourable houses indicate good health.

पापा लाभतृतीयगाः सहजवैर्यन्त्याष्टमेभ्योन्यगाः
सौम्या मान्दिरपि त्रिकोणमृतिकेन्द्रेभ्योपरत्र स्थितः ।
सर्वेमी कथयन्त्यनामयतनुं प्रष्टारमेवं स्थिता
रोगग्रस्तकळेबरं च कथितेभ्योन्यत्र ते संस्थिताः ॥ ३ ॥

Stanza 3.—When malefics occupy the 3rd and 11th houses ; benefics occupy houses other than 3rd, 6th, 12th and 8th ; and Gulika is in places other than the 5th, 9th, 8th or kendras ; good health is indicated. Those occupying unfavourable places indicate ill-health and disease.

NOTES

Ishta Bhavas or favourable houses for malafics are 3rd and 11th. In the rest of the houses they are unfavourable. Ishta Bhavas for benefics are 1st, 2nd, 4th, 5th, 7th, 9th and 10th. Gulika produces good results when occupying 2nd, 3rd, 6th, 11th and 12th.

When malefics, benefics and Gu!ika occupy houses other than those given in the above paragraph, they denote ill-health and diseases. When favourably disposed, the querist will be healthy.

आरोग्यदा ग्रहा यत्र सुस्थसंज्ञास्तु तत्रगाः ।
रोगदा यत्र ते दुस्थास्तदुक्तं सारसंग्रहे ॥ ४ ॥

Stanza 4.—According to *Sarasangraha* planets become *susthas* in favourable houses giving rise to health and *dusthas* in unfavourable houses causing diseases.

षष्ठान्त्याष्टमदांबुलग्ननमापत्येषु ये दुर्बलाः
पापाः षष्ठमृतिव्ययेष्वपि शुभा दुस्था भवन्ति ग्रहाः ।
लग्नेशाध्यरयोतिरोगमृतिदा दुस्थेषु सुस्थाश्च ते-
नुक्तस्थानगताः शशाङ्कसहिताः स्वं स्वं फलं कुर्वते ॥ ५ ॥

Stanza 5.—Weak malefics occupying 1st, 4th, 5th, 6th, 7th, 8th, 9th and 12th and benefics occupying 6th, 8th and 12th become *dusthas*, Amongst dusthas, the bitter enemy of lord of Lagna is most violent in giving diseases and causing death. Planets that are found in conjunction with the Moon also give rise to results consistent with their own nature.

द्विण्मृत्युव्ययसंस्थितैस्तदुदितान् व्याधीन् वदेल्लग्नव-
द्रष्ट्रा तत्सहितेन वा तनुगतैस्तद्रष्ट्रभिर्वा ग्रहैः ।

ऊर्ध्वास्ये चरभे गळोपरि गलात्तिर्युङ्मुखे च स्थिरे
द्वन्द्वेधोमुखगेप्यधः कटितटात् लग्नस्थिते व्याधयः ॥६॥

Stanza 6.—Diseases have to be read from the planets occupying 6th, 8th and 12th; those associating with or aspecting the lord of Lagna; those that occupy or aspect the Lagna. According as Lagna is moveble and *urdhwamukha*, or fixed and *ihirayangmukha*, and common and *adhomukha* the seat of disease will be above the neck, below the neck and above the waist, or below the waist respectively.

सूर्यादीनां कुक्षिहृन्मूर्द्धवक्षांस्यूरू वक्त्रं जानुनी
चांघ्रियुग्मम् ।
अङ्गानि स्युर्व्याधयोऽङ्ग ग्रहाणां वक्तव्या
दौर्बल्यदौस्थ्यादिभाजाम् ॥ ७ ॥

Stanza 7.—The eight planets from the Sun to Rahu signify respectively the stomach, heart, head, chest, thighs, face, knees and the feet. By considering the intensity of affliction or otherwise of these planets, the strength or weakness of the respective organs can be ascertained.

NOTES

Some say that the left foot is governed by Ketu.

वाराङ्गपूर्वावयवा निधेया लग्नादिभावेष्वधिपेषु चैषाम् ।
सक्रूरभावग्रहसंस्थमङ्गं सव्याधिकं प्रष्टृजनस्य वाच्यम्
॥ ८ ॥

Stanza 8.—The twelve houses signify the twelve organs from head to feet. Disease occurs in the part of the body indicated by the afflicted house or planet.

NOTES

Lagna and the lord of Lagna indicate the head, the 2nd Bhava and the lord of the 2nd indicate the face, the 3rd Bhava and the lord of the 3rd indicate the chest. In this way, the different parts of the body should be assigned to different houses and their lords as explained by Varahamihira in his *Brihat Jataka*.

The parts of the body signified by an afflicted house will be the seat of disease or disorder. Supposing the third house is afflicted. We can indicate that there is some disorder and trouble in the chest region. Similarly if the lord a of Bhava is afflicted, the part of the body signified by the Bhava in question will be the trouble-spot.

स्पृष्टेन राशिना प्रष्ट्रा चारूढेनोदयेन च ।
रोगस्थानं वदेदुक्तमारूढविषये हि तत् ॥ ९ ॥

Stanza 9.—The location of the disease can be known from the Rasi symbolical of the limb touched at the time of query, Arudha Lagna or Udaya Lagna. This has been explained already.

NOTES

Suppose the querist touches a certain Bhava in the Prasna chart ; then the limb signified by that Bhava will be the seat of trouble. The limbs signified by that sign of Arudha Lagna or even the ascendant can also be taken as the seat of disease.

प्रोक्तस्त्रिदोषसम्बन्धो वराहमिहिरोदितः ।
ग्रहाणां प्रागथेदानीं वच्म्युक्तं सारसङ्ग्रहे ॥१०॥

Stanza 10.—Varaha Mihira's classification of 'Thridoshas' has already explained. Below is given the view contained in *Sarasangraha.*

पित्तं वातयुतं करोति दिनकृद्वातं कफं शीतगुः
पित्तं भूमिसुतस्तथा शशिसुतो वातं च पित्तं कफम् ।
जीवो वातकफौ सितोनिलकफौ वातं च पित्तं शनिः
क्षीणेन्दुः स्थिरराशिनाथकथितं पूर्णः कथं तोयभे ॥ इति॥ ॥११॥

Stanza 11.–The Sun governs pitta(bile) combined with vata (wind) ; the Moon governs vata and kapha (phlegm); Mars rules pitta ; Budha indicates vata, pita and kapha; Jupiter rules over kapha with vata ; Venus also denotes vata and kapha; and Satura governs vata combined with pitta; waning Moon brings about the dosha of the lord of the Rasi which he occupies; full Moon brings about kapha only.

NOTES

According to this view, we see that the Sun governs mostly pitta and little of vata. Saturn governs more of vata and a little of pitta. Jupiter indicates more of kapha and a little of vata.

रोगान् कुर्युर्ग्रहाः स्वोक्तपञ्चभूतवशादपि ।
तत्कालाश्चर्तवः स्वोक्तास्तथा शास्त्रान्तरोदितम् ॥१२॥

Stanza 12.—The planets cause diseases befitting their Pancha Bhuta nature. And diseases appear at the various seasons governed by the planets.

दुस्थयोरर्कभूसून्वो रोगाः स्युः पित्तसम्भवाः ।
शुक्रेन्द्वोर्जलजा मन्दे वातजा ज्ञे त्रिदोषजाः ॥१३॥

बाधिर्याद्या नभोजाता अनिष्टस्थानगे गुरौ ।
अनिष्टगा निजान् रोगान् कुर्युर्निजनिजर्तुषु ॥ इति ॥१४॥

रोगदायिषु खेटेषु तत्तत्प्रोक्तेषु धातुषु ।
अपि रोगोद्भवो वाच्यः प्रोक्तं ग्रंथान्तरे तथा ॥१५॥

Stanzas 13 to 15.—If the Sun and Mars become dusthas, diseases due to pitha will be caused ; if the Moon and Venus, watery diseases ; if Saturn, diseases due to vata ; if Mercury, due to all the three doshas ; Jupiter in an *anishta* place brings about diseases caused by *akashabhuta.* These diseases make their appearance in the Ritus or seasons signified by the concerned planets. Planets also indicate the appropriate dhatus from which diseases arise. The occurrence of diseases has also been dealt with in other treatises.

NOTES

The places where planets become dusthas have been enumerated in the stanzas 3, 4 and 5 above. Stanzas 13 to 15 deal with diseases due to vata (wind), pitta (bile) and kapha (phlegm), etc., caused by the planets becoming dusthas. If the Sun and Mars are dusthas, diseases due to the inflammation of pitta (bile) become manifested. According to the famous Ayurvedic scientist Vagbhata, pitta has the characteristic of fire (pittamvahnihi). Therefore if the Sun or Mars becomes a dustha, one suffers from diseases due to heat such as constipation, measles, ulcers, skin eruptions, small-pox, burning sensation, etc. The Moon and Venus as dusthas produce diseases caused by water such as swellings in different parts of the body. Saturn brings about diseases due to vata (wind). Mercury brings about diseases such as brain fever, typhoid, etc., due to the inflammation of all the three doshas. Jupiter brings about deafness. If in the birth horoscope, any planet is dustha, then, during the *ritu* or season ruled by the *dustha* planet, the appropriate disease makes its appearance. The allocation of seasons to different planets should be taken according to Varahamihira. Venus rules Vasantharitu or spring (March–April); the Sun and Mars Greeshma or windy season (May–June); the Moon—Varsha or rainy season (July–August); Mercury—Sarat—Autumn (September-October); Jupiter—Hemanta or Fall (November–December) and Saturn—Sasira (January-February)

Suppose in a horoscope, the Sun is a dustha. The native is sensitive to the diseases of pitta and heat. The Sun rules the ritu or season of spring and the dhatu *raktha* or blood. Therefore during the season of spring, the native suffers from a disease due to blood impurity, caused by excessive heat and bile. In this way, the other planets should also be dealt with. The next sloka explains the method.

दुस्थितास्थ्यादिधातुस्थो रोगिणां रोग ईर्यताम् ।
रोगप्रश्नेऽथवा रोगदाश्रितांशपधातुगः ॥ इति ॥१६॥

Stanza 16.—A man will suffer from the diseases affecting the dhatu governed by dustha or the lord of the Navamsa occupied by it.

NOTES

Reference may be made to sloka 3 of Chapter XI, for details about different dhatus and the planets governing them. According to this stanza not only the dustha but its Navamsa lord should also be considered.

सन्ति प्रकारभेदाश्च रोगभेदनिरूपणे ।
ते चाप्यत्र विलिख्यन्ते यथा शास्त्रान्तरोदिताः ॥१७॥

Stanza 17.—There are other principles to ascertain the nature of the disease and they are enumerated in other works.

TYPES OF DISEASES

रोगास्तु द्विविधा ज्ञेया निजागन्तुविभेदतः ।
निजाश्चागन्तुकाश्चापि प्रत्येकं द्विविधाः पुनः ॥१८॥
निजा शरीरचित्तोत्था दृष्टादृष्टनिमित्तजाः ।
तथैवागन्तुकाश्चैवं व्याधयः स्युश्चतुर्विधाः ॥१९॥
वातपित्तकफोद्भूताः पृथक्संसर्गजास्तथा ।
सन्निपातभवाश्चैते शारीराः कीर्तिता गदाः ॥२०॥

Stanzas 18 to 20.—There are two types of diseases, *viz.*, *nija* and *aganthuka*. These two can again be sub-divided thus: *nija* into *sarirotha* and *chittotha*; and *aganthuka* into *drishta nimittaja* and *adrishta nimittaja*. Bodily diseases are of four kinds, *viz.*, those caused by vata, those caused by pitha, those caused by kapha and those caused by sannipatha.

NOTES

The classification of diseases suggested in the above slokas can be represented thus :

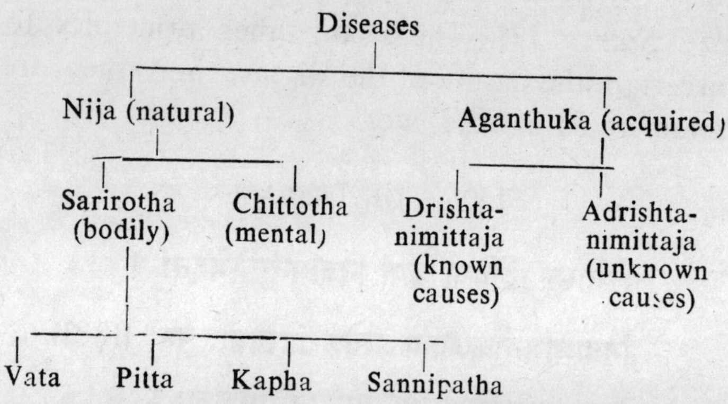

Diseases arising in the body may also be due to a combination of vata and pitta, vata and kapha and pitta and kapha. Thus there are seven variations of bodily troubles arising from (1) vata, (2) pitta, (3) kapha, and a combination of (4) vata and pitta, (5) vata and kapha, (6) pitta and kapha and (7) vata, pitta and kapha.

अष्टमेन तदीशेन तद्द्रष्ट्रा तद्गतेन वा ।
विज्ञातव्याः स्युरेतेषां वीर्यतस्तत्कृता गदाः ॥२१॥

Stanza 21.—The bodily diseases (*sarirotha*) can be determined by considering the strength of the 8th house, its lord, the planet aspecting or occupying it.

क्रोधसाध्वसशोकादिवेगजातस्तु मानसाः ।
ज्ञेया रन्ध्रमनोनाथमिथोयोगेक्षणादिभिः ॥२२॥

Stanza 22.—Anger, fear, sorrow, desires and such emotions bring about mental diseases. They have to be determined by considering the relationship between the lords of the 5th and the 8th.

NOTES

To the 5th house is allocated to Manas or mind. By relationship is meant the disposition of the lords of the 5th and 8th in mutual aspect, association, kendras, etc. Chithottas are diseases arising from emotional disturbances as different from bodily peculiarities. The ancients, it will be seen, clearly recognised the distinction between the mental or psychic disturbances and physical or bodily ailments.

शापाभिचारघातादिजाता दृष्टनिमित्तजाः ।
ज्ञेयाः षष्ठतदीशाभ्यां तद्द्रष्ट्रा तद्गतेन वा ॥२३॥
रन्ध्रेशषष्ठसम्बन्धे शापाद्याः प्रबलाश्च ते ।
अदृष्टहेतुजा ज्ञेया बाधकग्रहसम्भवाः ॥ इति ॥२४॥

Stanzas 23 and 24.—The *drishtanimittaja* diseases—curses, incantations and falls from elevation—should be ascertained from the 6th, its lord or the planet aspecting the 6th or the planet occupying the 6th. If the lords of the 6th and 8th are related, then the intensity of the diseases will be much. The *adrishitanimittaja* diseases should be known from the attack of evil spirits.

NOTES

In the stanzas 21 and 22 Nija diseases have been explained. In starzas 23 and 24 the author deals with Agunthaka diseases. There are two types, *viz.*, *drishta-nimittaja* and *adrishtanimittaja.* To the former category belong the curses of great men, elders, parents, Gurus. etc., the incantations (Kshudra Mantras) of enemies and sudden fall from elevations and accidents. Examine the 6th lo d, the planets aspecting the 6th and the planets occupying the 6th. Consider the stiongest and determine the disease. If the 6th and 8th lords are related (*i.e.*, in mutual aspect, association, etc.), then the effect of the curses, incantations, etc , will be powerful and the native will have to constantly suffer. The *adrishtanimittaja* diseases are said to be brought about by spirits, devils, hobgoblins, ghosts, etc. (Badhaka Grahas).

It is within our humble experience that when there is a conjunction of the 6th and 8th lords, the native especially during the Dasas of the 6th or 8th lord has passed through untold suffering mentally and also physically, though medically no abnormality is suspected. Another interpretation is, such diseases for which no immediate cause could be traced are karmic in origin and are caused by the Badhaka Planets.

दृष्टं वा यच्छ्रुतं द्रव्यं प्रश्नकाले यदृच्छया ।
तद्वशाच्च रुजां भेदा ज्ञेया ग्रन्थान्तरे तथा ॥२५॥

Stanza 25.—The nature of the disease can be known also by a careful observation of materials seen or the names mentioned at the time of Prasna. The things seen and the sounds heard should be purely accidental.

यस्य रोगस्य यद्द्रव्यमपथ्यं तस्य वीक्षणे ।
श्रवणे वास्य विज्ञेयः स रोगो रोगचिन्तने ॥२६॥

Stanza 26.—By seeing anything or hearing about anything which would indicate that the disease will aggravate, increase in the sickness of the man can be predicted.

रसाः स्वाद्वम्ललवणातिक्तोषणकषायकाः ।
तत्राद्या मारुतं घ्नन्ति त्रयस्तिक्तादयः कफम् ॥२७॥
कषायतिक्तमधुराः पित्तं पुष्णन्ति चेतरे ।
वातः पित्तं कफश्चेति त्रयो दोषाः समासतः ॥२८॥

Stanzas 27 and 28.—Of the six rasas or tastes—(1) madhura, (2) amla, (3) lavana,

24

(4) thiktha, (5) ushna and kashaya, the first three remove vata and aggravate kapha; the remaining three remove kapha and aggravate vata. Pitta is destroyed by the 1st, 4th and 6th and aggravated by 2nd, 3rd and 4th.

NOTES

The above two stanzas are from *Astanga Hridaya.* The *shadrasas* are said to remove or aggravate the three doshas as followas :—

Vata (wind) is removed by madhura (sweetness), amla (sourness) and lavana (salt); kapha (phlegm) is neutralised by thiktha (bitter), ushna (hot) and kashaya. Pitta is destroyed by madhura (sweet), thiktha (bitter) and kashaya. Contrarily, vata is aggravated by thiktha (bitter), ushna (hot) and kashaya. Kapha is increased by madhura (sweet), amla (sour), lavana (salt) and ushna (hot).

यस्य ग्रहस्य यो दोषः पित्तादिष्विह कीर्तितः ।
तेन रोगे तु वक्तव्ये वाच्यस्तद्दोषजो गदः ॥२९॥

Stanza 29.—The disease one will suffer from arises from the *dosha* governed by the planet causing the disease.

NOTES

Different planets govern different doshas. For example, if the Sun is the disease-causing planet, then the disease will be due to excitation of pitta. If it is the Moon then the disease will be due to vata and pitta. In this way should be ascertained the cause of diseases from the planets.

पापालोकितयोराद्यैर्योगैर्होरादिषूदितैः ।
अपि ज्ञेया रुजां भेदाः प्राग्जन्मदुरितोद्भवाः ॥३०॥

Stanza 30.—The disease caused by past Karma in a person's birth can be ascertained by studying works on Hora.

NOTES

Here the reference is to Varaha Mihira's *Brihat Jataka*. In Chapter XXI the diseases one suffers from past sins are enumerated. The nature of *unmada* (lunacy) is detailed in the following stanzas.

SYMPTOMS OF MADNESS

लग्नस्थे धिषणे दिवाकरसुतो भौमोथवा द्यूनगो
मन्दे लग्नगते मदात्मजतपः संस्थो महीनन्दनः ।
भूतौं मूढशशीन्दुजौ कुशशशी मन्दश्च रिष्फस्थितौ
पापोपेतकृशामृतांशुरुदयायस्वान्तधर्मोपगः ॥३१॥
अस्ते पापयुतो मान्दिर्त्रित्रिषष्ठाष्टमान्त्यगः ।
उन्मादददायिनो योगा एवमष्टौ समीरिताः ॥३२॥

Stanzas 31 and 32.—Jupiter in the ascendant and Saturn or Mars in the 7th; Saturn in Lagna and Mars in the 7th, 5th or 9th; the Moon and Mercury in combustion in Lagna; weak Moon and Saturn in the 12th; weak Moon associated with a malefic in Lagna, 5th, 8th or 9th; Mandi in the 7th in association with a malefic; and afflicted Mercury in the 3rd, 6th, 8th or 12th; These 8 combinations cause madness or *unmada*.

NOTES

The first combination actually suggests two combinations, *viz.*, (1) Jupiter in Lagna and Saturn in the 7th and (2) Jupiter in Lagna and Mars in the 7th and hence the total number of combinations is 8. These yogas for *unmada* or madness are quite clear and need no explanation.

कारणमुन्मादानामुन्मत्तानां तथैव चेष्टाद्यम् ।
कथ्यत इह तद्भेदास्तत् खलु शास्त्रान्तरेषु निर्दिष्टम् ॥३३॥

Stanza 33.—The causes that usher in 'lunacy' and the bodily movements of persons suffering from mental disease and the different types of mental patients are noted below. Some of them have been taken from other works.

हर्षेच्छाभयशोकादेर्विरुद्धाशुचिभोजनात् ।
गुरुदेवादिकोपाच्च पञ्चोन्मादा भवन्त्यथ ॥३४॥
त्रिदोषजाः सान्निपाता आगन्तव इति स्मृताः ।
हसनास्फोटनाक्रन्दगीतनर्तनरोदनम् ॥३५॥
अस्थानमङ्गविक्षेपस्ताम्रा मृदुकृशा तनुः ।
जीर्णे बलं च वाग्बह्वी वातोन्मादस्य लक्षणम् ॥३६॥

Stanzas 34 to 36. –The causes for madness are excessive delight, desire, fear, sorrow, eating disagreeable and dirty food and the wrath of preceptors and gods. There are five types of madness; three kinds arise from the three doshas individually, one kind from Sannipatha and the last one caused by external influences. Signs of madness due to *vata* are: laughing, clapping hands, speaking aloud, singing, dancing, crying, moving about, shaking bodily organs, the body becoming copper coloured, soft and emaciated. The disease shows signs of increase as soon as the food is digested and the person eats too much.

NOTES

The main causes of mental dislocation are due to excessive pleasure and delight, too much fear, too many desires and sorrows, eating all kinds of dirty and undesirable foods and curses of parents, teachers and deities.

Moderation in food, drink, sleep, sex life, etc., is the keynote of mental equilibrium. A man getting too elated when things go in his favour and very depressed at the slightest misfortune are all signs of imbalance.

If one wounds the feelings of one's elders, preceptors and parents, the reaction is always adverse to the person. Therefore the curses and blessings are concentrated forms of thought vibrations capable of hitting the defaulter for good or bad.

Lunacy given rise to by vata or wind goes under the name of *vatonmada*. This can be deteced by the following symptoms. A mad person laughs (*hasano*) at all wrong moments irrespective of time,circumstance or age or situation. He claps his hands often (*aspotan vada*), speaking aloud, singing songs (*geeta*) and dancing (*nartana*) round and round. He wails or cries bitterly (*rodana*), constantly moving about (*asthana*). He wrings his hands and shakes his legs (*angavikshepa*).His body becomes copper-coloured, soft and emaciated (*thamra mridu krisa tanu*). The disease shows signs of increase as soon as the intaken food is digested. He speaks too much.

संरम्भामर्षवैदग्ध्यमभिद्रवणतर्जनम् ।
छायाशीतान्नतोयेच्छा रोषः पीतोष्णदेहता ॥३७॥
नारीविविक्तप्रियता निद्रारोचौ मनाग्वचः ।
लाला छर्दिर्बलं भुक्तौ नखादिषु च शुक्लता ॥३८॥

एताः पित्तकफोन्मादचेष्टाः श्लोकोदिताः क्रमात् ।
संमिश्रलक्षणो वर्ज्य उन्मादः सान्निपातिकः ॥३९॥

Stanzas 37 to 39.—Seeking solitude and women, sleeping too much, showing aversion for everything, speaking little, drops of saliva trickling down, vomitting always, sickness increasing with intake of food, the finger nails turning pale and white, hating all, growing impatient, exhibiting a tendency to do very clever acts, flying in a fury at the face of all, showering abuses, longing to drink water and eat food, avoiding great heat or cold and ever angry and the body becoming yellow and hot : are respectively the signs of kapha and pitta unmada. In sannipatha unmada, all the above characteristics will be found mixed.

आगन्तवो ग्रहा ज्ञेयास्तेतु देवासुरादयः ।
अमर्त्या बलवाक्ज्ञानविक्रमादिसमन्विताः ॥४०॥

Stanza 40.—By the slow and invisible influence of certain Devagrahas and Asuragrahas, lunacy is caused. When one is 'possessed' by a Devagraha, he becomes strong and his words will be learned and studied.

वातोन्मादे स्नेहपानं पित्तोन्मादे विरेचनम् ।
श्लैष्मिके नस्यवमनमागन्तुष्वखिलाः क्रियाः ॥४१॥

सर्वे नश्यन्ति चोन्मादा जपहोमादिकर्मतः ॥४२॥

Stanzas 41 and 42.—Medicated oils and ghee can cure *vatonmada.* Strong purgatives will give relief in *pittonmada.* Madness caused by kapha can be got rid of by medicines for inhaling and vomitting. There is no treatment for *sannipatha unmada.* All types of madness can however be cured by *Japa*, *Homa* and similar remedial measures.

संप्रदायविशेषोस्ति पूर्वाचार्यैरुदाहृतः ।
उन्मादकारणादीनां कथने स च लिख्यते ॥४३॥
विषमाशुचिभोजनोपवासैर्भयवैराग्यशुधाक्रुधाभिचारैः ।
गुरुपावकदेवतापवादैस्त्रिविधोन्मादउदाहृतास्त्रिदोषैः ॥४४॥
दशेति हेतवो भ्रान्तौ दशहेतुभवा अपि ।
त्रिदोषजाः स्युरुन्मादाः पित्तजे बन्धनं भवेत् ॥४५॥

Stanzas 43 to 45.—In dealing with this subject, some writers have taken another point of view. Eating at irregular hours either too much or too little, unhygienic food, fasting, fear, indifference to or aversion for all sensual pleasures; anger, enemies, villifying elders, preceptors and superiors; making wrong use of fire and getting the dissatisfaction of Devas by censuring them; all these can be brought under the three types of *unmada* caused by the three doshas. A man affected by *pitta unmada* will be angry and rushing about and hence he is to be bound hand and foot or to be caged.

चन्द्रशुक्राष्टमाधीशा गोचरेतरगा यदि ।
विषमाद्द्युपवासोत्थ उन्माद इति निर्दिशेत् ॥४६॥
केतुमान्द्यहियुक्तेषु चैतेष्वशुचिभुक्तिजः ।
सपापे पञ्चमे भीतिवैराग्योत्थः स भूमिजे ॥४७॥
क्रोधजोथाभिचारोत्थः षष्ठगेष्वशुभेषु सः ।
गुर्वादिशापसम्भूतः पापे नवमसंस्थिते ॥४८॥
कल्याणपञ्चगव्याज्यसेवाद्येषु विधीयताम् ॥४९॥

Stanzas 46 to 49.—Lunacy will be due to starvation or irregular use of food ; unhygienic food ; fear or renunciation ; anger ; abhichara ; and curses of preceptors, Agni or Gods, according as the Moon, Venus and the lord of the 8th are in evil places ; these lords are in conjunction with Rahu, Ketu or Mandi ; malefics are in the 5th; Mars is in 5th; malefics are in the 6th; and malefics are in the 9th. For all these, *kalyana ghrita* and *pancha-gavya ghrita* are very efficacious medicines.

NOTES

If the Moon, Venus and the lord of the 8th occupy evi places, then it must be inferred that the lunacy is caused by starvation, fasting or irregular use of food. If these lords are in conjunction with Rahu, Ketu or Gulika, then the person's lunacy is due to unhygienic food. If evil planets other than Mars occupy the 5th house, the mental disease is caused by fear or renunciation. If Mars is in the 5th, anger is the cause of disease. If evil planets occupy the 6th house, abhichara or black magic is the reason. If evil planets occupy the 9th house the disease is the outcome of the curses of preceptors or Fire God or wrath of Deities.

SYMPTOMS FOR EPILEPSY

मन्दे रन्ध्रगतेहौ च त्रिकोणे बलिनो शुभाः ।
योगोपस्मारदो भानुर्भौमश्च गददौ यदि ॥५०॥

Stanza 50.—If Saturn is in the 8th, powerful malefics are in trines and the Sun and Mars are in the 12th, then the native suffers from *apasmara* or epilepsy.

NOTES

This sloka can be interpreted thus :

1. The Sun occupies an evil position such as the 8th house.

2. Mars also occupies a similar position.

3. Rahu and Saturn occupy the 8th house and other evil planets occupy the 5th and 9th.

भिन्नो द्वादशभिर्भेदैरपस्मारः स्वरूपतः ।
स च तस्य च भेदास्ते निगद्यन्ते स्वरूपतः ॥५१॥

Stanza 51.—Though actually *apasmara* is only one disease, it can be recognised in 12 forms.

विस्रस्ताङ्गः पतति सहसा भूतले नष्टसंज्ञः
फेनोद्गारी रसति परुषं सन्नकायश्चिराय ।
व्यावृत्ताक्षो दशति दशनं पीतवर्णः प्रमादी
तोयासक्तो विकृतवदनः स्यादपस्मारः एषः ॥५२॥

Stanza 52.—A man faints all of a sudden and falls on the ground; some dirty sphutums flow out of his mouth; he produces disagreeable sounds; he lies on the ground tired and limps; his eyes roll alround; he bites his teeth; he becomes pale; he gets excited; he feels thirsty and shows awry faces. These are the signs of epilepsy.

NOTES

After some time the person gets up as if he is not affected by anything. Some are of the opinion that this is not a disease but it is the attack of a Devata or Deity. But it has to be said that the ancients deified every disease. In Sayaniya every disease has been given 'a shape' befitting a deity. Further, even trees and mountains have been given a shape. Hence it is to be inferred that all things have two forms—one immovable or sthoola (sthavara) as we see, and one movable or sookshma (jangama) from which we do not see.

श्वासना मलिना निद्रा जृंभिकानशना तथा ।
त्रासिनी मोहिनी चाथ रोदनी क्रोधनी तथा ॥५३॥
तापनी शोषणी चैव ध्वंसिनी चेति कीर्तिताः ।
दूत्यो द्वादश विख्याता अपस्मारस्य सुप्रियाः ॥५४॥
एताः समस्ता व्यस्ता वा संश्रयन्ति नरं किल ।
स्वाख्यानार्थवतीं चेष्टां तत्राभिव्यञ्जयन्ति च ॥५५॥

Stanzas 53 to 55.—Svasani, Malina, Nidra, Jrimbhika, Anasana, Thrasini, Mohini, Rodani, Krodhini, Thapani, Soshani, and Dhwamsini are the twelve minds of apasmara. They attend the person affected by this disease in the manner of their names finding expression in the behaviour of the sick person.

NOTES

The twelve names listed are self-explanatory as

follows :—Svasana means gasping; malina—soiling of body ; nidra—sleepiness ; jrimbhika—yawning; anasana—no interest in food; thrasini—fearful; mohini—beguiling; rodani—wailing ; krodhani—angry ; thapani—excited; soshani—drying up; dhwamsini—destructive.

TREATMENT FOR EPILEPSY

शमायादावपस्मारे कूश्माण्डीबलिमाहरेत् ।

सुदर्शनेन जुहुयात्तिलैः क्रोधाग्निनाथवा ॥५६॥

प्रत्यक्षरसहस्रेण घोरापस्मारशान्तये ॥ इति ॥५७॥

Stanzas 56 and 57.—With the aid of *kushmanda* bali and *tilahoma* with *sudarsana mantra* or *krodhagni mantra*, even the most violent form of apasmara can be got rid of.

NOTES

In these two stanzas, remedial measures for the cure of epilepsy have been suggested. As the performance of these remedial measures involves Mantrasastra techniques, it is advisable to consult the specialists in Mantra Sastra before attempting anything on the point.

दृष्टा ग्रन्थान्तरे प्रश्नविषयेपस्मृतौ हिताः ।

लिखितास्त्वत्र लिख्यन्ते चिकित्सा अपि काश्चन ॥५८॥

Stanza 58.—The question of apasmara has been dealt with in other suitable works on the subject. A few methods of treatment are given herewith.

सिन्धूत्थवृश्चिकाळीकुष्ठकणाभार्ङ्गिभिः कृतं चूर्णम् ।
नसि योजयेत्तु शस्तं तीव्रापस्मारशान्तये पुंसाम् ॥५९॥

Stanza 59.—Powder of sindutha, vrischikali, kushta, vanga, bhangee should be inserted in the nose. Violent apasmara in males will be pacified.

ब्रह्मीरसे धृतवचामयशंखपुष्पधात्रीसमुद्भवरसे
मधुकान्वितं च ।
सिद्धार्थहिंगुसहिते वृषबस्तमूत्रे पानादिना हरति
सर्पिरपस्मृतिं तत् ॥६०॥

Stanza 60.—The juice of *brahmi* combined with *vacha* (baje), *amaya*, *sankhapushpa*, the juice of *dhatri* (nellikayi) and honey, *siddhartha* (white mustard), *hingu*, urine of cow taken in or inhaled pacifies apasmara.

त्रिवृद्विळङ्गत्रिफलाग्निविश्वव्याघातसिन्धूत्थकणैः-
यथावत् ।
ब्रह्मीरसे सर्पिरिदं प्रशस्तं पुंसामपस्मारविनाशनाय
॥६१॥

Stanza 61.—Thrivridu (trigathi), *vilanga* (vayuvilanga), *thriphala* (tili, alale), *agni* (bitra), *viswavyadhata* (shunti), *sindhoota*, *kana*, made into a paste with *brahmirasa* will be an appropriate remedy for apasmara.

मञ्जिष्ठाग्निविळङ्गकुष्ठरनीमुस्तात्रिवृच्छारिबा-
दार्वीतिक्तकशंखपुष्पसहितैरेलावचायष्टिभिः ।
पाठामागधिसंयुतं घृतमिदं गव्येषु सिद्धं नृणां
तीव्रापस्मृतिदोषविस्मृतिहरं कुष्ठापहं कांतिदम् ॥६२॥

Stanza 62.—Manjishata, *agni-vilanga*, *kushta*, *ranimustha*, *thrivridu*, *suriba*, *darvee* (dalchinni), thikthaka, sankhapushpa, ela (elakki), vacha (baje), yashti (madhu), patha (balegadde), *magadhi*—all made into ghee and mixed with *gavya* destroys violent apasmara, leprosy, loss of thinking (*vismruti*) and increases the shining of body.

NOTES

Stanzas 58 to 62 give details of medicines to be used for curing *apasmara*. By *gavya* is meant a mixture of cowdung, cow's urine, milk and curds. The proportion of mixing the four items is given as 1 : 2 : 16 : 5. English equivalents of several medicines suggested in the above slokas are not available. Therefore it is advisable to seek the help of a specialist in Ayurveda to understand the prescription clearly. A layman should never attempt to give this treatment.

ABERRATION OF MIND

पापग्रहेक्षितं लग्नं रन्ध्रं रविजवीक्षितम् ।
रन्ध्रेशो विबलो योग एष भक्तविरोधकृत् ॥६३॥

Stanza 63.—If malefics aspect Lagna, Saturn aspects the 8th house and the lord of the 8th house is weak, then the person suffers from the disease of inability to take the good (bhakta virodha).

NOTES

What is meant by the disease *bhakta virodha* is to be ascertained from books on Ayurveda.

COMBINATIONS FOR DIABETES

लग्ने पापेक्षिते लग्ननाथे नीचारिराशिगे ।
शुक्रयुक्तेक्षितं रन्ध्रमेषयोगः प्रमेहकृत् ॥६४॥

Stanza 64.—If malefics aspects Lagna and the lord of the Lagna is debilitated or in the sign of enemy, and Venus occupies or aspects the 8th, the person suffers from diabetes.

सिंहे कुक्ष्यक्षिजेत्याद्यैर्व्याधयो येत्र कीर्तिताः ।
आरूढविषये पूर्वं चिन्तयेदिह तानपि ॥६५॥

Stanza 65.—Diseases described earlier about stomach, eye, etc., in respect of Arudha (VIII Chapter) may be looked into now in this connection.

मूर्तिभेदा रुजां भेदाः प्रश्नानुष्ठानपद्धतौ ।
प्रोक्ता दुस्थविहङ्गानां लिख्यन्तेत्र च ते तथा ॥६६॥

Stanza 66.—Different types of constitutions and diseases due to planets becoming *dusthas* and discussed in *Anushtana Paddahati* are given herewith.

NOTES

Diseases are of two kinds. Medical treatment is essential for some and mantriac measures are unimportant for them. *They are diseases.* For some mantriac and tantric measures are very essential and medical treatment is only subsidiary. They are said to be 'troubles from devatas' (influence of spirits). Planets show these two types of diseases.

Diseases Indicated by Planets

पित्तोष्णज्वरतापदेहपतनापस्मारहृत्क्रोडज-
व्याधीन् वक्ति रविर्दृगार्त्यरिभयं त्वग्दोषमस्थिस्त्रवम् ।
कुष्ठाग्न्यस्त्रविषार्त्तिदारतनयव्यापच्चतुष्पाद्भयं
चोरक्ष्मापतिधर्मदैवफणभृत्भूतेशभूताद्भयम् ॥६७॥

Stanza 67.—Diseases pertaining to the Sun are: those arising from inflammation of bile (*pitta*), fever with pains (*ushnajwara*), sudden fall, epilepsy (*apasmara*); heart, stomach and eye trobles; fear from enemies; cutaneous diseases (*thwaka-dosha*), bone troubles (*asthisrava*), leprosy, burns, danger from weapons and poison; affliction to wife and son; fear from quadrupeds, thieves, rulers; and wrath of the family deity, serpent gods and Siva Bhutas.

निद्रालस्यकफातिसारपिटकाः शीतज्वरं चन्द्रमाः
शृङ्ग्यब्जाहतिमाग्निमान्द्यकृशतायोषिव्द्यथाकामिलाः ।
चेतश्शांतिमसृग्विकारमुदकाद्भीतिं च बालग्रहात्
दुर्गाकिन्नरधर्मदैवफणभृद्यक्षाच्च पीडां वदेत् ॥६८॥

Stanza 68.—Increase of sleep and inertia, diseases of phlegm (*kapha*), diarrhoea, shivering fever, wounds caused by the horns of animals, troubles from watery animals, dyspepsia (*agni-mandya*), anaemia, sorrow from wife, jaundice, mental and emotional affliction, blood-poisoning, fear from water, troubles from Bala Grahas; and wrath of the goddess Durga, kinnaras, family deities, serpents and *yakshis*, are the troubles arising from the Moon.

तृष्णासृक्कोपपित्तज्वरमनलविषास्त्रार्तिंकुष्ठाक्षिरोगान्
गुल्मापस्मारमज्ञाविहतिपरुषतापामिकादेहभङ्गान् ।

भूपारिस्तेनपीडासहजसुतसुहृद्वैरयुद्धं विधत्ते
रक्षोगन्धर्वघोरग्रहभयमवनीसूनुरूर्ध्वाङ्गरोगम् ॥६९॥

Stanza 69.—The diseases of Mars are: thirst, blood pressure, fever due to inflammation of the bile, diseases caused by heat; poison and weapons, leprosy, eye and spleen troubles, epilepsy, bone decay, loss of lustre in the skin, itching, troubles from rulers, enemies and thieves; quarrels with brothers, sons and relatives; fight with others, fear from demons, Gandharva and destructive spirits and diseases above the neck.

भ्रान्तिं दुर्वचनं दृगामयगळघ्राणोत्थरोगान् ज्वरं
पित्तश्लेष्मसमीरजं विषमपि त्वग्दोषपाण्ड्वामयान् ।
दुस्स्वप्नं च विचर्चिकां निपतनं पारुष्यबन्धश्रमान् ।
गन्धर्वक्षितिहर्म्यवासिमयुभिर्ज्ञो वक्ति पीडां खगैः ॥७०॥

Stanza 70.—Mercury causes mental aberration, a tendency to use abusive language, diseases of the eye, throat, nose; fever caused by the fury of all three doshas; fear from poison, skin diseases, bad dreams. itches, sudden falls, fear of imprisonment and the wrath of gandharvas and kinnaras usually found in beautiful mansions, and troubles from birds.

गुल्मान्त्रज्वरशोकमोहकफजश्रोत्रार्तिमेहामयान्
देवस्थानानिधिप्रपीडनमहीदेवेशशापोद्भवम् ।
रोगं किन्नरयक्षदेवफणभृद्विद्याधराद्युद्भवं
जीवः सूचयति स्वयं बुधगुरू कृष्णापचारोद्भवम् ॥७१॥

Stanza 71.—Spleen diseases (gulma), fever, sorrow, fainting, ear troubles due to phlegm, diabetes ; afflictions due to the removal of temple treasure and the curses of Brahmins ; troubles from kinnaras, yakshas, devas and vidyadhara ; and diseases caused by the anger of serpents and God Vishnu are the results due to Jupiter.

पाण्डुश्लेष्ममरुत्प्रकोपनयनव्यापत्तितन्द्रीश्रमान्
गुह्यास्यामयमूत्रकृच्छ्रमदनव्यापत्तिशुक्लस्रुतीः ।
वासस्त्रीकृषिदेहकान्तिविहतिं शोफामयं योगिनी-
यक्षीमातृगणाद्भयं प्रियसुहृद्भङ्गं सितः सूचयेत् ॥७२॥

Stanza 72.—Venus brings about leucoderma (pandu) disease arising from phlegm and wind, diseases in the eye, laziness, tiredness and exhaustion (diabetes is another reading); diseases in the private parts, face and urinary system; affliction due to avarice for money or girls ; loss of seminal fluid, loss of clothes, wife; cultivation, fading away of the lustre in the body, swelling, and fear from yogini, yakshis, *matrus* and the death of near relations.

वातश्लेष्मविकारपादविहतीरापत्तितन्द्रीश्रमान्
भ्रान्तिं कुक्षिरुगन्तरुष्णभृतकध्वंसं च पश्वाहतिम् ।
भार्यापुत्रविपत्तिमङ्गविहतिं हृत्तापमर्कात्मजो
वृक्षाश्मक्षतिमाह कश्मलगणैः पीडां पिशाचादिभिः
॥७३॥

Stanza 73.—Windy (*vata*) and phlegmatic (*kapha*) diseases, troubles in the legs, unforeseen dangers, laziness, weakness due to over-exertion, mental affliction, stomach troubles, loss of servants and quadrupeds, danger to wife and children, bodily accidents, heat troubles, injuries from the fall of trees or stones and troubles from evil spirits and ghosts, are all denoted by Saturn.

स्वर्भानुस्तनुतापकुष्ठविषमव्याधीन् विषं कृत्रिमं
पादार्तिं च पिशाचपन्नगभयं भार्यातनूजापदम् ।
ब्रह्मक्षत्रविरोधशत्रुजभयं केतुस्तु संसूचयेत्
प्रेतोत्थं च गदं विषं च गुळिकः सर्पार्त्तिमाशौचकम्
॥७४॥

Stanza 74.—Rahu signifies heat in the body, leprosy, *vishama vyadhi* (incurable diseases ?), risk of being poisoned, diseases in the feet, troubles from devils and serpents; danger from wife and children, quarrels with Kshatriyas and Brahmins and troubles from enemies in the shape of *abhichara.* Ketu brings about all these besides causing troubles from pretas (disembodied souls) and poison. Besides giving the troubles attributed to Rahu and Ketu, Gulika brings about troubles from snakes and pollution by the death of near relatives.

Combinations for Diseases

बाधां वक्ति पिशाचजां दशमगो मन्दोथ सर्पेक्षितो
वीक्षाघ्राणभवं विषं च गुळिको देहाष्टमस्थानगः ।
पापाः षष्ठगतास्तथोदररुजं रन्ध्रास्तगारो ज्वरं
लग्नास्तोपगतोप्यजीर्णजरुजं चन्द्रोरिपीडां रिपौ ॥७५॥

Stanza 75.—Saturn in the 10th house denotes troubles from pisachas; Gulika in Lagna or the 8th house aspected by Rahu generates poison in the system due to smelling or evil eye; malefics in the 6th cause stomach troubles; Mars in the 8th gives rise to fever, in Lagna or the 7th, indigestion. When the Moon is in the 6th troubles arise from enemies.

ग्रहाश्रितभभावान्यग्रहयोगेक्षणादिकम् ।
दौस्थ्याधिक्यं च सञ्चिन्त्य सर्वं वाच्यं यथोचितम्
॥७६॥

Stanza 76.—The intensity of evil a planet is subject to should be properly assessed by noting where he stands, who associates with him, who is aspecting him, and so forth, and then the prediction must be made suiting the circumstance.

लाभतृतीयौ हित्वा परत्र पापा स्थिता भवन्ति यदि ।
रोगवतैव प्रष्टा भाव्यं तत्प्रोक्तदोषतो नियतम् ॥७७॥

Stanza 77.—It should be examined whether any malefic planets occupy houses other than 3rd and 11th. Then it should be inferred that the person is suffering from a disease, appropriate to the malefic.

कादीति कन्दगित्याभ्यां प्रष्टुरङ्गानि चिन्तयेत् ।
पापादृष्टयुते गात्रे व्रणरोगादिकं वदेत् ॥७८॥

Stanza 78.—There will be wounds or diseases in the limbs typified by the signs aspected by or associated with malefic planets, according to the dictum *kandruk*, etc.

NOTES

Here the reference is to the sloka beginning from *kandruk strotra* in the V Chapter (24) in *Brihat Jataka*. For details refer to Prof. B. Suryanarain Rao's English translation of *Brihat Jataka*.

चरोर्ध्ववक्त्रशीर्षोदयादीनां लग्नगत्वतः ।
ककण्ठवरितपूर्वाङ्गंग्रहणं न दृगाणतः ॥७९॥

Stanza 79.—If Lagna is movable, urdhwamukha and sirshodaya, the seat of disease will be above the neck. The drekkana classification given by Varahamihira refers only to horoscopes.

NOTES

If Lagna is sthira, thiryaugmukha and ubhayodaya, the disease will be below neck and above waist. If Lagna is ubhaya, adhomukha and prishtodaya, it will be below waist.

राश्यंशयोश्चरादित्वसंवादे तु चरादिभिः ।
तदभावे न च ज्ञाते चांश ऊर्ध्वाननादिभिः ॥८०॥

Stanza 80.—If Rasi and Navamsa are similar *i.e.*, chara, etc., then consider the limbs according to Rasi classification. If they differ, consider on the basis of urdhwamukha, etc.

NOTES

If the ascendant in the Rasi and Navamsa are in movable signs, or in fixed signs or in common signs, take the Rasi classification of limbs. If on the other hand, the Rasi and Navamsa Lagnas fall in different categories—one in chara and the other in sthira, one in sthira and the other in dwiswabhava, etc., adopt the method given in stanza 6.

अत्यन्तविबलोऽर्कोऽङ्गग्रहणं कोदयादिभिः ।
नीचांशस्त्रीतुलान्त्याद्यात्र्यंशेष्वर्कोऽतिदुर्बलः ॥८१॥

Stanza 81.—The Sun becomes very weak in the last Drekkana of Virgo, in the first Drekkana of Libra and Libra Navamsa of any sign. If the Sun is weak, then see whether Lagna is sirshodaya, prishtodaya or ubhayodaya and classify the area of disease accordingly.

विलग्नादिषु काद्यङ्गन्यासोऽथ निगद्यते ।
कृष्णीये तु यथा ग्राह्यः स एव प्रश्नकर्मणि ॥८२॥

Stanza 82.—For purposes of Prasna, the allocation of organs to different houses beginning from Lagna as done in Krishneeya should be followed.

होरोत्तमाङ्गसंस्था दक्षिणवामावनागतातीतौ ।
कर्णाक्षिनासिकापुटकपोलहनवोऽथ वक्त्रान्ताः ॥८३॥

ग्रीवांसभुजौ पार्श्वे पृष्ठे हृदयोदरे कटिश्चान्त्या ।
नाभिर्वस्तिगुदाण्डा मुष्का पूर्वादयो द्वौ द्वौ ॥८४॥

Stanzas 83 and 84.—The expired and unexpired portions of Lagna represent the right and left sides of the head, the neck and navel. Two Bhavas each beginning from Lagna—1st in the invisible half and the other in the visible half indicate the right and left sides respectively of the other organs thus: the 2nd and 12th—ears, shoulders and sex organs; 3rd and 11th—eyes, sides and testicles; 4th and 10th—nostrils, back and thighs; 5th and 9th—cheeks and knees; 6th and 8th—chin, stomach and legs; and the unexpired and expired portions of the 7th—mouth, waist and feet.

NOTES

These two stanzas are very suggestive. The human body is divided into three parts, *viz.*, head, the region below the neck and above the waist, and the region below the waist. By the situation of a *dustha* in a particular place, one can locate the seat of disease in one of the three parts. After this has been done, the organs affected should be ascertained according to the allocation given in these stanzas. In the three regions, the right and left sides of the different organs are thus allocated.

Parts of the body			Right side ruled by	Left side ruled by
Above neck	*Below neck and above waist*	*Below waist*		
Head	Neck	Navel	Lagna (un-expired portion)	Lagna (expired (portion)
Ears	Shoulders	Sexual organs	II	XII
Eyes	Sides	Testicles	III	XI
Nostrils	Chest	Thighs	IV	X
Cheeks	Back	Knees	V	IX
Chin	Stomach	Legs	VI	VIII
Mouth	Waist	Feet	VII (expired portion)	VII (unexpired portion)

कंदृक्श्रोत्रेति होरायां वराहमिहिरोदितः ।
योऽङ्गेषु भावविन्यासो ग्राह्य एव स जातके ॥८५॥

Stanza 85.—The allocation of organs to different Bhavas by Varahamihira according to the sloka 'Kandruk srotra' should be considered as applying to horoscopy only.

NOTES

In Chapter V, stanza 24, the great Mihira assigns different organs of the human body to the different signs of the zodiac. Here also the body is divided into three parts—above the neck, below the neck and above the waist, and below the waist. Organs in the left and right sides in each of these parts are assigned to Bhavas in the visible and invisible halves, but Drekkanas are considered in locating the particular region or part of the body. We are informed that Varaha Mihira's allocation is applicable to horoscopy only and not to Prasna.

रोगभेदानिति ज्ञात्वा चिकित्सामुचितां वदेत् ।
तीव्रे कर्मविपाकोक्तप्रायश्चित्तं च शान्तये ॥७६॥

Stanza 86.—Having understood the nature of different types of diseases, suitable medical treatment should be recommended. If the disease is serious, remedial measures as suggested in Karma Vipaka of Sathyacharya, should be adopted.

॥ इति प्रश्नमार्गे द्वादशाध्यायः ॥

त्रयोदशाध्यायः

BEGINNING AND ENDING OF DISEASES

लग्नोदितोहुतश्चस्द्रो यावत्युडुनि संस्थितः ।
तस्मात्तावति नक्षत्रे रोगारम्भमुदीरयेत् ॥ १ ॥

Stanza 1.—The sickness will have commenced on the day ruled by the asterism arrived at by counting as many asterisms from the Moon's, as that of the Moon is removed from the asterism of Lagna.

NOTES

The explanation is simple. Suppose the positions of Lagna and the Moon at the time of query are respective by 16° Mesha and 12° Simha. This means Lagna is in the constellation of Bharani and the Moon is in the constellation of Makha. Counting from the constellation of Lagna (Bharani) to that of the Moon (Makha) we get 9. Counting this number from Makha (Moon's star) we get Jyeshta. The sickness will have commenced on the day (prior to the day of query) ruled by Jyeshta. Suppose when the query was put, say on 31st July 1978, the Lagna was in Aslesha and the Moon was in Mrigasira : Counting from Aslesha to Mrigasira we get 24. Counting 24 from Mrigasira we get Aswini. The illness commenced (before the day of query) on a day ruled by Aswini which means 27th July 1978.

यद्वा मान्दिनवांशस्थ द्वादशांशर्क्षगे विधौ ।
मान्दीन्दुयोगभे वैषु ग्राह्यं प्रष्टुरनिष्टभम् ॥ २ ॥

Stanza 2.—Either in the Nakshatras arrived by multiplying Mandi's longitude by 9 and 12 or in the Nakshatra corresponding to the sum of the longitudes of the Moon and Mandi, sickness might have commenced.

NOTES

Suppose the longitude of Mandi is Cancer 9° (99°). Multiplying this by 9 and 12 we get 171° and 188° (after expunging multiples of 360°) respectively. 171° corresponds to *Hasta* and 188° corresponds to *Swati*. Taking the second part of the stanza : suppose the Moon's longitude is 108°. The sum of the longitudes of the Moon and Mandi would be 207° corresponding to Vishakha. Therefore the sickness might have commenced (prior to the day of Prasna) when the Moon was transiting Hastha, Swati or Visakha. It is also suggested that the 3rd (Vipat), 5th (Pratyak) and the 7th (Naidhana) stars from the above three may also be considered.

दूतवाक्याद्यवर्णोक्तराशिगेत्यन्तदोषदे ।
चन्द्रार्कगुरुमन्देषु रोगारम्भमुदीरयेत् ॥ ३ ॥

Stanza 3.—Sickness might have commenced when the most unfavourable planet amongst the Moon, the Sun, Jupiter and Saturn transited the Rasi corresponding to the first letter in the communication brought by the messenger.

NOTES

The first letter of the message, in case a messanger comes to put the question or the first letter of the question in case the querist personally comes, should be taken and the Rasi corresponding to this letter noted. The prediction must then be given that sickness commenced when the most unfavourable planet amongst the Sun, the Moon, Jupiter and Saturn transited this Rasi. In actual practice, it is difficult to apply this method. Saturn takes 2½ years to transit a sign. If Saturn is the most malefic and he happened to transit the Rasi in question, then the time at which sickness commenced would spread over 2½ years—a practical impossibility.

DIRECTION OF BEGINNING OF DISEASE

यदाशाभिमुखो रोगी दृश्यते दूत एव वा ।
रोगारम्भणमेतस्यां दिशि प्रष्टुरुदीर्यताम् ॥ ४ ॥

Stanza 4.—The direction towards which the sick man or messenger was found facing by the astrologer indicates the place where the querist had his first attack of illness.

ऐन्द्रीतो दिशि यावत्यां दूतः पृच्छति संस्थितः ।
यामे तत्समसंख्ये स्यात् प्रष्टुर्व्याधिसमुद्भवः ॥ ५ ॥

Stanza 5.—The number of the direction from which the messenger or the sick man put in his first query to the astrologer, counted from the East, will give the time in terms of *yamas* when sickness began.

NOTES

Suppose the questioner or messneger put his query facing north-west or *vayavya*. Then from east to north-west counted in the order of east, south-east, south, south-west, west and north-west would be 6. This means 6 yamas beginning from sunrise which will be equivalent to 18 hours or midnight. It must be inferred that sickness actually began at midnight on the day already fixed according to previous stanzas.

यावन्तो व्याधिते सन्ति निमग्ननयना जनाः ।
व्याध्यारम्भेन्तिकस्थाः स्युस्तावन्तः सदृशाश्चतैः ॥ ६ ॥

Stanza 6.—The number of men found along with the sick man or messenger at the time of query indicates the number of persons attending the sick man during his illness. The nature of the people will also be similar.

रोगेशाश्रितराशौ तद्भुक्तभोक्तव्य भागतः ।
रोगस्य गतगन्तव्यकालाधिक्याल्पते वदेत् ॥ ७ ॥

Stanza 7.—According as the expired portion of the sign occupied by the lord of the 6th is less or more than half, the person's sickness will linger long or will be cured soon.

NOTES

This is an important stanza. The lord of the 6th occupies some Rasi. If the longitude of this planet is less than half Rasi, then the person will suffer for a long time. If the longitude traversed by the lord is more than half, the querist will have passed through the worst and the disease will be cured soon.

षष्ठाधिपे दिवावीर्ये यद्वा षष्ठगते ग्रहे ।
दिवारम्भश्च वृद्धिश्च रोगाणामन्यथा निशि ॥ ८ ॥

Stanza 8.—If the lord of the 6th or the planet occupying the 6th is a planet of diurnal strength then the sickness began during day-time. If it is a planet of nocturnal strength, then the attack was during night.

NOTES

The Moon, Mars and Saturn are nocturnal planets. The Sun, Jupiter and Venus are strong during the day. Mercury is always strong.

अरूढाद्भवने तु यावति गदस्थानाधिपः संस्थितो
मासे तावति वाह्निभास्वदुडुचारे वाथ रुग्जायते ।
यावत् प्रश्नभतोरिपाप्तमुडु तावन्तं गदारम्भणे
ब्रूयात् कालमनेन भुक्तनवभागघ्नं गदेशस्य वा ॥ ९ ॥

Stanza 9.— The sickness commenced as many months back as are signified either by the (1) number of Signs passed by the lord of the 6th from Arudha Lagna; or by (2) the number of asterisms from Prasna asterism to that held by the lord of the 6th; or by (3) the number arrived at by multiplying (2) by the number of Navamsas gained by the lord of the 6th.

NOTES

Let us take an example where Lagna is Pisces, Arudha Lagna is Capricorn, lord of the 6th (Sun) is in Libra 6° in Chitta nakshtra and the Prasna nakshatra is Makha. (1) From Arudha Lagna, the lord of the 6th is in the 10th house. (2) From Prasna nakshatra (Makha) the lord of the 6th is in the 5th asterism (Chitta). (3) The lord of the 6th, *viz.*, the Sun has gained 2 Navamsas in Libra. Multiplying 5—the number in (2)—by 2 we get 10. Thus the sickness must have commenced 10, 5 or 10 months prior to the day of Prasna. Here again it is by a consideration of the relative strengths of the planets and asterisms concerned that one of the the three alternatives is to be fixed.

The above two slokas are from *Kantabharanam*.

षष्ठेशाश्रितराशिस्थे चन्द्रे वा रोगसम्भवः ।
शमनं च रुजां वाच्यं सुखेशाश्रितराशिगे ॥१०॥

Stanza 10.—The disease will have begun when the Moon transited the sign occupied by the lord of the 6th and recovery will begin when the Moon enters the sign occupied by the lord of the 4th.

लग्नस्याधिपतेश्च तस्य शशिनो वा पापयोगेक्षणं
यत्राभूत्समये तदामयसमारम्भः समादिश्यताम् ।
सौम्यानां युतिरीक्षणं च भविता तेषां त्रयाणां यदा
रोगाणां शमनं तदाथ शमनारम्भस्तदेकान्वये ॥११॥

Stanza 11.—The disease will have commenced when Lagna, lord of Lagna, or the Moon was afflicted last by malefics. When benefics associate or aspect any one of them, recovery will begin. When all the three get the association or aspect of good planets, the person will completely recover.

NOTES

The illness will have commenced or the disease will have set in when the Moon transited the sign occupied by the lord of the 6th. When the Moon transits the Rasi occupied by the 4th lord, recovery or cure will take place.

In applying these principles, the astrologer must be very careful. First of all he must diagnose astrologically, the intensity or otherwise of the disease, whether it is curable or incurable and whether the querist has good longevity and then he must proceed on to find out when the illness commenced. In stanza 11, another method is given involving consideration of three factors. The disease will have commenced at the time of affliction of Lagna, lord of Lagna or the Moon by malefics. Here also, the astrologer must fall back on his power of judgement to infer the likely result when either two factors or all the factors had been afflicted. There may have been a slow beginning of the illness, gradually increasing, or suddenly flaring up. According to the next part of the stanza, when either Lagna, lord of Lagna or the Moon conjoined with benefics, the recovery wlll commence. When all the three factors are involved in association with or aspect of benefics, there will be full recovery or probably even sudden recovery.

लग्नोदितनवांशस्य द्वादशांशगराशिगे ।
मान्दिराशिमतिक्रान्ते चेन्दौ स्याच्छमनं रुजाम् ॥१२॥

Stanza 12.—When the Moon enters Lagna Rasi, Navamsa Rasi, or a Dwadasamsa Rasi or the Rasi occupied by Gulika, the illness will subside.

अष्टमेन्दु पुरोधाय यदि चेद्व्यधिसम्भवः ।
अतियातेष्टमं राशिं शशाङ्के शमनं रुजाग् ॥१३॥

Stanza 13.—If the sickness had begun in the asterisms preceding Ashtama Rasi from the radical Moon, then relief will be obtained after the lapse of the said Ashtama Rasi Nakshatras.

NOTES

Suppose Aries is Janma Rasi. The 8th or Ashtma Rasi is Scorpio or Vrischika. Since it is made up of one quarter of Visakha, Anuradha and Jyeshta, these are the Ashtma Rasi Nakshatras. If sickness began in an asterism previous to these three, then recovery takes place after the Moon's transit of these Nakshatras. In other words relief can be expected when the Moon enters Moola or the sign Sagittarius.

दुस्थखेटवशतो रुजागमं सुस्थखेटवशतः शमं वदेत् ।
मन्त्रनृत्तबलिपूजनौषधैर्देवताभजनधातुपोषणैः ॥१४॥

Stanza 14.—The occurrence of disease should be predicted from *dustha* planets and the recovery should be foretold from *sustha* planets. Chanting of mantras, conducting 'dances', Bali Karma, administering medicines, worship of God and *dhatuposhana* will give relief.

दुस्थानामतिदोषदाश्रितगृहं प्राप्तेषु चन्द्रादिषु
व्याध्यारम्भ इहातिदुस्थखगसम्बन्धीशकोपोद्भवः ।
सुस्थानामपि तद्वदिष्टतमखेटाधिष्ठितर्क्षाश्रिते-
ष्विन्द्वाद्येषु तदीयदेवभजनाच्छान्तिश्च वाच्या रुजाम्
॥१५॥

Stanza 15.—When the Moon, the Sun and Jupiter transited the sign occupied by the most *dustha* planet, sickness might have commenced. The disease is brought about by the dissatisfaction of the deity indicated by the dustha concerned. When however these three planets enter the Rasi occupied by the most favourable planet, the symptoms of recovery can be seen. For recovery the aid of the appropriate deities governed by favourable planets should be sought.

NOTES

According to this stanza, the cause of disease is the wrath or displeasure of the deity indicated by the worst dustha. The disease will have commenced when the Moon, the Sun or Jupiter entered the sign occupied by such a dustha. Similarly, the disease vill be cured when the three planets pass through the Rasi held by the most favourable sustha planet by invoking the deity indicated by the sustha planet concerned by appropriate worship, Bhajanas, etc. Elsewhere it has already been suggested that the Sun's deity is Sambhu, the Moon's Durga, etc.

The above two slokas are from *Anushtanapaddhati.*

RECOVERY

वैश्वे सौम्ये च मासादुपरि तु वसुमत्रश्नस्त्रयेषु पक्षाद्रोगी
चित्राप्रचेतोयमहरिषु सुखं विन्दते रुद्रसंख्यात् ।
विंशादङ्को मघायां गुरुभगसूरसूबुध्निवेधस्सु भूभृत-
संख्यान्मूलाश्वियुक्ते हुतभुजि नवमान्मित्रपूष्णोस्तु
कृच्छात् ॥१६॥

Stanza 16.—If diseases begin in the asterisms, Uttarashadha and Mrigasira, recovery will be visible after one month; if they begin in Dhanishta, Hasta and Visakha, recovery will take place after 15 days; if in Chitta, Satabhisha, Bharani and Sravana, 11 days are required for recovery; if in Makha, 20 days; if in Pushyami, Uttara, Punarvasu, Uttarabhadra and Rohini, 7 days; if in Moola, Aswini, and Krithika, 9 days; if in Anuradha and Revati a very long time and the disease is difficult to be cured.

ज्येष्ठासमीरोरगरौद्रपूर्वात्रयेषु न प्राणिति जातरोगः ।
छिद्रासमेतुतेषु सपापवारेष्वाग्नेयवस्वन्तकवारुणेषु ॥१७॥

Stanza 17.—If Jyeshta, Swati, Aslesha, Aridra, Pubba, Poorvashadha and Poorvabhadra happen to be the commencement asterisms, recovery is impossible. If Krittika, Dhanishta, Bharani and Satabhisha happen to fall on Sunday, Tuesday and Saturday and if *chidra* or *riktha tithis* also coincide, death may result.

NOTES

Chidra or Riktha tithis are 4th, 9th and 14th lunar days.

अष्टमीपर्वरिक्तासु पापवारे त्रिजन्मभे ।
गोमासाष्टमचन्द्रेषु रोगारम्भो मृतिप्रदः ॥१८॥

Stanza 18.—If the disease commences on *ashtami, parva days riktha tithi days,* malefic week-days, or trijanma nakshatra days, or vipat, pratyak and naidhana nakshatra days, chandrashtama days, the person will meet with death.

NOTES

Trijanma nakshatras are the birth constellation, the 10th and 19th from it. The *vipat, pratyak* and *naidhana* nakshatras are the 3rd, the 5th and the 7th from the birth constellation. Malefic week days are Sunday, Tuesday and Saturday. Chandrashtama days mean the period when the Moon transits the 8th from his radical position. Disease should not commence on these days and on the

4th, 9th and 14th lunar days (riktha tithis), New Moon day (parva) and on Tuesday, Saturday and Sunday. We have given here a combination of three Nakshatras, week-days and tithis. If the evil tithi, nakshatra and week-day—all the three combine, death will be certain. If tithis alone combine with the week days, the sick man will recover with great difficulty.

अर्कारूढेस्य धीमान्यपुत्रभे वा रुगागमः ।
यदि मृत्युर्भवेत्सार्कतारकोभयपार्श्वयोः ॥१९॥
त्रिषु त्रिषु च धीमान्यपुत्रपार्श्वगतोडुषु ।
रुग्वृद्धिः परिशीष्टेषु द्वादशस्वथ जीवति ॥२०॥

Stanzas 19 and 20.—If the illness starts on a day ruled by the constellation occupied by the Sun, or the 9th, 15th or 21st from it, there will be no recovery. If the stars are the three preceding and the three succeeding ones to that occupied by the Sun or the one previous to or the one next to the three already mentioned above, sickness will increase but there will be no death. In the remaining twelve constellations, there will be recovery.

NOTES

If a person falls ill on the days governed by the following constellations, he may not survive.

(i) (*a*) The constellation occupied by the Sun 1

(*b*) The 9th, 15th and the 21st therefrom 3

(ii) *Increase of sickness but no death under the following* :

The 26th, 27th, 28th, 2nd, 3rd and 4th from that held by the Sun 6.

(iii) Recovery under the following :—

The tithi owned and the one next to those mentioned in (i), that is, the 8th, 10th, 14th, 16th, 20th and 22nd from the one occupied by the Sun ... 6

Total ... 16

Here since the total number of constellations are 28, Abhijit is also considered. Suppose the Sun at the time a person puts a query is in the constellation of Makha :

Fatal constellations will be :

(i) (*a*) Makha, Jyeshta, Satabhisha and Krittika.

Constellations denoting increase of illness but no death will be:

(ii) Punarvasu, Pushyami, Aslesha, Pubba, Uttara, and Hasta.

Constellations denoting early recovery :

(iii) Anuradha, Moola, Dhanishta, Poorvabhadra, Bharani and Rohini.

The allocation of constellations with reference to the Sun's constellation goes under the name of *soola chakra.*

तारावारतिथीनां मृतिदानां शूलचक्रभानां च ।
जन्मप्रभृतीनां वा मृतिर्ध्रुवं सङ्गमे तु पञ्चनाम् ॥२१॥

Stanza 21.—We have considered so far certain asterisms, week days, lunar days, certain asterisms in soola chakra and certain nakshatras as reckoned from the birth constellation. If all these coincide, death is certain.

NOTES

In the earlier stanzas, it has been suggested that appearance of sickness on a day coincident with a certain malefic asterism, malefic tithi and malefic week day would prove fatal. In addition to these three, if the constellation on the day on which the illness started is the 3rd, 5th or 7th from Janma Nakshatra and it also happens to be one declared fatal according to *soola chakra*, death is certain.

रोगारम्भणतारकान्तगणने जन्मर्क्षतो या भवेत्
संख्या तां त्रिगुणां हरेज्जलधिभिः शेषैः फलानि क्रमात् ।
एकद्वित्रिचतुर्भिराशु मरणं मृत्युः शनैर्जीवनं
कृच्छ्राज्जीवनमप्रयत्नत इद प्राग्द्वादशाद्वाच्छिशोः ॥
॥२२॥

Stanza 22.—Count from Janma Nakshatra to the Nakshatra on the day the sickness commenced. Multiply this by 3. Divide the product by 4. According as the remainder is 1, 2, 3 or 4 respectively the sick child will die, will linger long and then die, will survive with great difficulty or recover very easily. This is applicable only to children below 12 years of age.

षष्ठेशे मन्दगतौ स्थिराश्रिते वा रुजां शनैः शमनम् ।
शीघ्रगतौ चरयाते शमनं रोगस्य न चिरेण ॥२३॥

Stanza 23.—If the lord of the 6th possesses slow motion or occupies a fixed sign, recovery will be very slow. If his speed is great or he occupies a movable sign, recovery will be rapid.

NOTES

It is implied that if the planet has medium motion or occupies a common sign, there will be neither too rapid nor too slow a recovery.

पापानामुदयश्च मध्यवसतिर्लग्नस्य लग्नेशितु-
र्दौर्बल्यं कथितं द्वयं च हिमगोस्तच्चोभयं क्षीणता ।
रिष्फारातिमृतिष्वपूर्णहिमगोस्तत्र स्थितिश्चासतां
केनाप्यामयदैर्घ्यमेषु बहुभिर्वक्तव्यमेतैः किमु ॥२४॥

Stanza 24.—If Lagna is joined by or hemmed in between malefics; or lord of Lagna is weak or associated with or situated between malefics; or the Moon is similarly disposed; or the waning Moon occupies the 6th, 8th or 12th; or evil planets occupy the abovementioned places, the sickness of the person will linger long. If all these are found, he will not live.

प्रायश्चित्तं दुश्शमरोगशनाय तत्तदुदितमपि ।
कार्यं सर्वैष्ववदत् स्वग्रन्धे सायणोस्य वचनमिदम् ॥२५॥

Stanza 25.—Cases where recovery is difficult, should be carefully looked into and the necessary remedial measures should be recommended as given by Sayanacharya in his famous work *Karma Vipaka*.

यथा कार्येषु सामग्री दृष्टादृष्टोभयात्मिका ।
तथोक्ता रोगनाशेषु प्रायश्चित्तौषधात्मिका ॥२६॥

Stanza 26.—Drishta and Adrishta are the two important causes for everything. To bring about the cure of any diseases, *prayaschitta* and medical treatment should be resorted to.

NOTES

Generally speaking, we can find two reasons for everything. One that can be perceived by our senses (drishta) and another that cannot be gauged by our our senses (adrishta). Punya (*virtue*) and Papa (*vice*) come under adrishta. For every disease, we have ***adrishta** karma* (unknown cause) and *drishta karma* (known cause). To bring about the cure of any disease, these two must be looked into. Remedial measures (prayaschitta) for the sins committed, and expert medical treatment for the disease, must be prescribed.

परिपूर्णतनुश्चन्द्रो लग्नोपगतो निरीक्षितो गुरुणा ।
गुरुशुक्रौ केन्द्रे वा पीडार्तस्तत्र सुखितः स्यात् ॥२७॥

Stanza 27.—The full Moon in Lagna aspected by Jupiter or Jupiter and Venus in Kendras, indicate disappearance of affliction, and recovery.

उपचयसंस्थश्चन्द्रः सौम्याः केन्द्रत्रिकोणधनमृतिगाः ।
लग्नं वा शुभदृष्टं सुखितस्तत्रातुरो वाच्यः ॥२८॥

Stanza 28.—There will be recovery from sick-sickness if the Moon occupies Upachayas and benefic planets are in Kendras, Trikonas, the 2nd or 7th, or Lagna is aspected by benefics.

Causes of Diseases

जन्मान्तरकृतं पापं व्यधिरूपेण जायते ।
तच्छन्तिरौषधै र्दानैर्जपहोमार्चनादिभिः ॥२९॥

Stanza 29.—Diseases are the resultant of sins done in our past births. The remedial measures are medicines, gifts, *japas*, *homas* and divine worship.

रोगार्तानमिह तु बहुधा कल्प्यते रोगहेतु-
र्भूतावेशाद्ग्रहगतिवशाद्वातपित्तादिकोपात् ।
एतत्तथ्यं त्रिविधमुधितं प्रायशः स्वीयपाप्या
रोगोत्पत्तेर्भवति हि नृणां हेतुरेकस्त्रिधा स्यात् ॥३०॥

Stanza 30.—People ascribe all sorts of causes for diseases. Evil influences of Bhutas, the effects of planetary movements and the fury of the three doshas Vata, Pitta and Kapha are perhaps these three causes. It must be noted that all these originate from one cause, *viz.*, one's own sins.

दुष्टे चारे ग्रहाणां भवति तनुभृतां पीडनं दुर्ग्रहाणां
जायन्ते तेन दोषत्रियचलनतस्तद्भवा व्याधिभेदाः ।
सर्वेषामेव तेषां खलु निजदुरितं प्राक्तनं हेतुरेकः
प्रायश्चित्तं च तत्तत्कथितमपि चिकित्सास्तु
रोगोपशान्त्यै ॥३१॥

Stanza 31.—When planets are in *anishta* place the appropriate 'spirits' stir up attacking the body. The *thridoshas*, in their turn get agitated. And this external agitation is the disease. The primary cause is however one's own sins in past births. Hence in order to get rid of diseases, *prayaschittas* (palliatives) must be recomended along with the medical treatment.

पापभेदश्च तत्प्रायश्चित्तभेदाश्च विस्तरात् ।
सायणेनोदिताः कर्मविपाके ग्रन्थ आत्मनः ॥३२॥

Stanza 32.—The different kinds of sins and the different kinds of palliatives (prayaschitta) to get rid of them have been elaborated by Sayanacharya in his famous treatise *Karma Vipaka*.

NOTES

Different diseases are due to different types of sins. The primary causes and what appropriate remedial measures have to be adopted to tide over such sins have all been detailed by Sayanacharya.

Remedial Measures

राजयक्ष्मादिरोगाणां ब्रह्महत्यादि कारणम् ।
वस्त्रदानादिकं प्रायश्चित्तं तद्द्विगितीरिता ॥३३॥

Stanza 33.—For consumption, the primary cause is the wilful murder of a Brahmin. The appropriate remedy is gift of clothes after due repentance.

कर्मविपाकं वक्ष्याम्यध्यायेस्मिन् खलु त्रयोविंशे ।
ज्ञात्वा तस्मात्तत्तत्प्रायश्चित्त विधीयतां रुक्षु ॥३४॥

Stanza 34.—In Chapter XXIII of this book, I am detailing about 'Karma Vipaka'. By going through it, appropriate remedial measures are to be prescribed.

औषधं पथ्यमाहारं तैलाभ्यंङ्गं प्रतिश्रयम् ।
रोगिभ्यः श्रद्धया दद्याद्रोगी रोगनिवृत्तये ॥३५॥

Stanza 35.—A sick man should respectfully cater to the needs of other sick men by providing them with free medical treatment, oil bath, diet, and other amenities.

NOTES

Free medical hospitals and free medical treatment should be given to sick men.

Mrityunjaya Homa

मृत्युंञ्जयहवनं खलु सर्वरुजां शान्तये विधेयं स्यात् ।
सर्वेष्वपि होमेषु ब्राह्मणभुक्तिंस्तथा तथाप्तवचः ॥३६॥

Stanza 36.—Mrityunjaya Homa is indeed the panacea for any type of disease. The feeding and worship of Brahmins as an auxiliary to all Homas is also recommended.

तीव्रज्वराभिचारादिशान्तिदं हवनं मतम् ।
मृत्युञ्जयाख्यमन्त्रेण नैव केवलमायुषं ॥३७॥

Stanza 37.—Mrityunjaya Mantra gives relief to intermittent and all baneful influences of evil spirits and it even conquers death.

तीव्रज्वरे तीव्रतराभिचारे सोन्मोदके दाहगदे च मोहे ।
तनोति शान्तिं नचिरेण होमः सञ्जीवनश्चाष्टसहस्र-
संख्यः ॥३८॥

Stanza 38.—Severe illness, dangerous abhicharas, madness, fainting and fits and other diseases can all be got rid off by performing Mrityunjaya Japa for 8000 times.

शान्तिके पौष्टिके चापि वशीकरणकर्मणि ।
हुतसंख्यासमानं स्यादुत्तमं द्विजभोजनम् ॥३९॥

Stanza 39.—Whenever this 'Homa' is performed a number of Brahmins equal to the number suggested for the Homa must be fed and worshipped.

NOTES

Stanzas 29 to 39 deal with the primary cause of diseases and the remedial measures to be adopted. Planets are in certain malefic places in an individual's horoscope. Each planet governs a certain deity or 'spirit'. This stirs up and attacks the tridoshas. Again the dosha governed by the afflicted planet is excited or gets agitated and this agitation expresses itself as a disease. Ultimately the cause of disease is traced to one's previous Karma—the sin or wrong action committed by him. We are informed that the cause of such dosha and the appropriate remedy—medical and spiritual—have been discussed in Sayana's *Karma Vipaka*. Mantra Sastra is a recondite subject. There are Kshudra Mantras as well as Maha Mantras—the former capable of invoking certain spirits and generally used for destructive purposes and the latter requiring for their *siddhi* or control a highly disciplined and moral life and always used for the good of man. Mantras are indestructible forms of subtle vibrations capable of causing the greatest good or greatest evil. It is not advisable to have recourse to the performance of remedial measures of this type merely on bookish knowledge without the sound advice and guidance of an expert.

॥ इति प्रश्नमार्गे त्रयोदशाध्यायः ॥

चतुर्दशाध्यायः

वाच्याः सुतादयो भावाः परोक्षस्यापि पृच्छतः ।
सुवाचास्ते वयो ज्ञात्वा यतस्तदपि कथ्यते ॥ १ ॥

Stanza 1.—Sometimes it so happens that the questioner is away and wants to know about the 5th and other houses. In such a case, the age of the person must be fixed first and then the horoscope studied.

Fixing the Person's Age

लग्नेशे क्षितिजे च बालहिमगौ नो पञ्चसंवत्सराः
पूर्णाः अष्टुरथेन्दुजेष्ट भृगुजे षट्संयुता वा दश ।
त्रिंशद्देवगुरौ रवौ दशगुणा शैलाश्च वृद्धोडुपे
अष्टा वृद्धतरोर्कजे फणिनि वा चैषां तथैवोदये ॥ २ ॥

Stanza 2.—The person will be under five, eight, sixteen, thirty or seventy or over 70 years of age according as the lord of Lagna happens to be the infant Moon or Mars, Mercury, Venus, Jupiter, Sun or aged Moon, and Saturn or Rahu respectively.

NOTES

The Moon is infant (Bala Chandra) till 5th lunar day of bright half. He is aged (Vriddha Chandra) from the 8th lunar day of the dark half till New Moon. Between 5th lunar day (Sukla Paksha) and the 23rd lunar day (Krishnashtami) the age can be calculated by the rule of proposition. The age of the person should be determined on the basis of the principles given in this stanza.

If Mars or the infant Moon owns Lagna (or occupies Lagna), then the age of the man will be below five years. If Mercury occupies or owns the Lagna, then the age is below 8. If Venus occupies or owns Lagna, the person is not yet 16 years old. If Jupiter is lord of Lagna or is posited in it, then he is below 30 years. If the Sun or aged Moon occupies Lagna, or if they are owned by them then the native is 70 years. If Saturn or Rahu occupy Lagna or it is owned by Saturn, then he is past 70 years in age.

Some construe the stanza thus : "If aged Moon is in Lagna or if Lagna is owned by aged Moon, predict that the man is past 70 years". According to this explanation, the correct age can be told by noting the nature of the Moon. If Cancer is Lagna, examine carefully the 'Avastha' (state) of the Moon and work out the age. Similarly, if the Moon occupies Lagna, examine his state and then predict. Readers should be able to decide for themselves the correct method of ascertaining the 'age' by experience. In our humble view, the age will be according to the years allotted to the different planets as in the stanza, when they own Lagna. So far as Rahu is concerned his occupying the Lagna is important and denotes a very aged man.

SIGNIFICATIONS OF BHAVAS

देहस्य सौष्ठवं स्वास्थ्यं स्थितिः श्रेयो यशस्सुखम् ।
जयो वपुश्च तत्सर्वं चिन्तनीयं विलग्नतः ॥ ३ ॥

Stanza 3.—From Lagna should be read everything about one's body, shape, health, strength, etc., welfare, fame, general happiness, and success in all undertakings.

भर्तव्यमखिलं वित्तं वाणी चक्षुश्च दक्षिणाम् ।
विद्याश्च विविधा ह्येतत्सर्वं चिन्त्यं द्वितीयतः ॥ ४ ॥

Stanza 4.—From the 2nd house should be ascertained one's family, wealth, speech, right eye and all kinds of knowledge.

धैर्यं वीर्यं च दुर्बुद्धिः सहोदरपराक्रमौ ।
दक्षकर्ण सहायौ च चिन्तनीयं तृतीयतः ॥ ५ ॥

Stanza 5.—The 3rd house rules courage, vitality, evil inclinations, brothers, right ear and help.

माता सुहुन्मातुल भागिनेयौ क्षेत्रं सुखं वाहनमासनं च ।
लालित्यमंभः शयनं च वृद्धिः पश्वादिकं जन्मगृहं
चतुर्थात् ॥ ६ ॥

Stanza 6.—The 4th house signifies mother, relatives, uncle, nephew, house and property, happiness, vehicles, things to set on, popularity, water, beds and cots, general affluence, cattle and the house where one is born.

प्रज्ञा प्रतिभा मेधा विवेकशक्तिः पुरातनं पुण्यम् ।
मन्त्रामात्यतनूजाः पश्चमभात्सौमनस्यमपि चिन्त्यम्
॥७॥

Stanza 7.—From the 5th house should be ascertained one's intelligence, prudence, memory, power of discrimination, merit earned in previous births, capacity to advise, ministers, children and condition of mind.

तस्कराराति विघ्नाधिव्याधयश्च तनुक्षतिः ।
मरणं वारिशस्त्रेण चिन्तनीयं हि षष्ठतः ॥८॥

Stanza 8.—The 6th house rules thieves, enemies, obstacles, mental worries, diseases, wounds and death due to enemies or weapons.

विवाहमदनालेकभार्याभर्तृसमागमाः ।
शय्यास्त्रीसद्मनष्टार्थमैथुनान्यपि सप्तमात् ॥ ९ ॥

Stanza 9.—The 7th house deals with marriage, sexual instincts, wife or husband, general relations with others, beds and cots, wife's birth place, lost or hidden things and sex relations.

सर्वप्रणाशो विपदोपवादो हेतुप्रदेशौ मरणस्य दासः ।
मठाधिकं वेश्म गदाश्च विघ्ना विचिन्तनीयाः
पुनरष्टमेन ॥१०॥

Stanza 10.—The 8th house signifies ruin of everything, dangers, evil repute, cause and place of death, servants, out houses, chronic diseases and obstructions.

भाग्यधर्मदयापुण्यतपस्तातसुतात्मजाः ।
दानोपासनसौशील्यगुरवो नवमादमी ॥११॥

Stanza 11.—The 9th house indicates luck or fortune, righteousness, kindness, merit, spirituality, father, grand children, charities, spiritual quest, good conduct or culture and preceptors.

देवालयनगरसभामार्गालयदाससर्वकर्माणि ।
आज्ञालम्बनमेतत्सर्वं चिन्त्यं हि दशमेन ॥१२॥

Stanza 12.—Places of worship, towns, council halls, wayside inns, servants, all actions, power to command and service under others come under the 10th house.

सर्वाभीष्टागमो ज्येष्ठभ्राता जाता निजात्मजाः ।
वामकर्णोर्थलाभाश्च चिन्त्या ह्येकादशेन ते ॥१३॥

Stanza 13.—The gain of everything desired, elder brother, sons already born, left ear and monetery gains should be read from the 11th house.

पापं व्ययश्च पतनं निरये वाममम्बकम् ।
स्थानभ्रंशश्च वैकल्यं द्वादशेन विचिन्तयेत् ॥१४॥

Stanza 14.—The 12th house signifies sinful actions, expenses, breaks and falls, left eye, loss of position or profession, and bodily injuries.

NOTES

These 12 stanzas (3 to 14) give the events or significations ruled by the twelve different Bhavas. There is not much difference between allocation of different events to different Bhavas given in this work and the details furnished in other classical works.

चिन्त्यं चंक्रमणं लग्नाच्छ्यनं हि चतुर्थतः ।
सप्तमेनोपवेशश्च चिन्त्या दशमत स्थितिः ॥१५॥

Stanza 15.—The Lagna, the 4th, the 7th and the 10th signify respectively various postures as 'walking', 'lying or resting', 'sitting' and 'standing'.

हिबुकेनाधः सलिलं नद्यागमनं तु सप्तमेनैव ।
दशमेन वृष्टिपतनं ब्रूयादुदयेन तत्रितयम् ॥१६॥

Stanza 16.—The four cardinal houses beginning from the 4th, in regular order, signify water inside the earth, water in rivers, fall of rain and all these three together respectively.

NOTES

These stanzas will be particularly useful in regard to predicting rainfall (Varsha Prasna) and digging of wells (Kupa Prasna). Water inside the earth indicates undercurrents, wells and springs while water in rivers means the rise or flow of water. Fall of rain includes the fall of snow, hail, etc. Lagna rules over all the indications attributed to the 4th, 7th and 10th houses.

Bhava Significations in Prasna Chart

विशेषाः सन्ति भावानां भुक्तिप्रश्ने च भूपतेः ।
ते चाप्यत्र विलिख्यन्ते लग्नाद्या द्वादश क्रमात् ॥१७॥

Stanza 17.—The twelve Bhavas beginning from Lagna have certain peculiarities in Raja

Prasnas and Bhukti Prasnas. They are noted below.

मूर्तिरमत्रं भक्ष्यं भोज्यं भोजायितृभाव उपदेशः ।
सेचनमन्नं सहभुक्पूर्तिकथा शयनमपि विलग्नात् ॥१८॥

Stanza 18.—In Bhojana Prasna, the Lagna and other Bhavas signify respectively (1) the person concerned and his constitution, (2) the eating plate or leaf, (3) dishes, (4) the menu, (5) drinks such as milk, (6) mood of the person, (7) auxiliary dishes, (8) butter-milk, etc., (9) the persons who eat along with the person, (10) the quantity eaten, (11) the nature of the conversation at the time of eating, and (12) the rest taken after meal.

मूर्तिः कोशो धात्विनो वाहनानि मन्त्रः शत्रुमार्गं
आयुर्मनश्च ।
व्यापारश्च प्राप्तिरप्राप्तिरेवं लग्नाद्भावा भूमिभर्तुर्विचिन्त्याः
॥१९॥

Stanza 19.—In a Raja Prasna, Lagna and the twelve Bhavas signify respectively, (1) the physical body of the king, (2) the treasure, (3) the army (4) vehicles, (5) diplomacy, (6) the enemy, (7) communications, (8) longevity, (9) the mind of the king, (10) trade and commerce, (11) the income and (12) expenditure.

NOTES

Stanzas 17 to 19 deal with questions relating to Bhukti (eating) and Raja (king or ruler). Whatever might have been the significance of questions pertaining to Bhukti or eating food, during the time of the author, we are of opinion that they are of no practical utility now except as a matter of curiosity.

Stanza 19 is however highly important. It can be used in national or mundane astrology. In a monarchy, the first house signifies the king or ruler. In a democracy, it may signify the person of the President. The 2nd rules the treasury and the finances. The 3rd denotes not only the army but also weapons of offence and defence. From the 4th, we may study the royal or governmental paraphernalia. The 5th indicates diplomacy and counsels. The 7th has reference to communications. The 8th rules the term of life. The 9th denotes the working of the mind of the king or the ruler. The trade and commerce of the country should be read from the 10th house. The 11th or 12th of course denotes the revenue and the expenditure. The principles given in this stanza will be useful in making political forecasts.

External and Internal Bhavas

बाह्याभ्यन्तरभावाद्द्विविधा भावाः समीरिता ह्येते ।
बाह्याः खलु तत्वाद्या ज्ञेयाः पुनरान्तरास्तु कल्याद्याः
॥२०॥

Stanza 20.—Bhavas can be considered to have two significations, *viz.*, external and internal. The external ones are as mentioned in the stanza Thanu, etc., and the internal ones are as given in the stanza Kala, etc.

NOTES

Here is a new method of classification of Bhavas into *bahya* or external and *antara* or internal ones. The author is a great admirer and follower of Varahamihira. The verse *thanukutumba sahotta*, etc., given in *Brihat Jataka* explains the external things while in the same book the verse *kalyaswa vikrama*, etc., gives the internal attributes.

Bhava	*External*	*Internal*
I	Thanu	Kala
II	Kutumba	Swa
III	Sahotta	Vikrama
IV	Baudhn	Gruha
V	Putra	Pratibha
VI	Ari	Kshata
VII	Patni	Chitotta
VIII	Marana	Randhra
IX	Subha	Guru
X	Aspada	Mana
XI	Aya	Bhava
XII	Ripha	Vyaya

The exact significance of the external and internal division of the Bhavas can be understood only after considerable experience in horoscopic interpretation. The 'internal' always refers to the abstract while the 'external' actually refers to concrete events. Thus the external significance of the 5th house is children, a physical entity while the internal significance is *pratibha* which is only an abstract quality meaning intelligence.

यद्यल्लग्नादिभिश्चिन्त्यं तत्तत्स्वामि समागमे ।
आभ्यन्तरं भवेत्सर्वं विज्ञेयं बाह्यमन्यथा ॥२१॥

Stanza 21.—If the Bhavas are in any way connected with their lords, they indicate the internal attributes. Otherwise they refer only to the external aspects.

NOTES

For example, if the 5th house is conjoined with or aspected by the 5th lord, then it denotes the internal significance of the Bhava, *viz.*, *Pratibha.* Otherwise, the external significance of the Bhava, *viz.*, children, becomes prominent. Hence we should be careful in reading the Bhavas.

मूर्द्धास्यगळस्कन्धा हृदयोदरवस्तिदेशगुह्यानि ।
ऊरु जानू जंघे पादौ भावाः क्रमाद्विलग्नाद्याः ॥२२॥

Stanza 22.—Beginning from the Lagna, the twelve houses represent (1) head, (2) face,

(3) neck, (4) shoulders, (5) heart, (6) stomach, (7) waist, (8) sexual organs, (9) thighs, (10) knees, (11) legs, and (12) feet, respectively.

NOTES

According to Varahamihira's classification, the 4th rules the heart, the 5th stomach, the 6th waist and the 7th lower stomach and the 11th buttocks.

अङ्गानां ह्रस्वादीर्घत्वं लग्नाद्याश्रितराशिभिः ।
वाच्यं तत्कथने प्राय एवेदमुपयुज्यते ॥२३॥

Stanza 23.—The different limbs of the body will be long or short according as the Rasis representing them are of long or short ascension.

NOTES

If, for example, Lagna is a sign of long ascension, the head will be long. If it is short, then the head also will be small. In this way, the nature of the other limbs of the body as indicated by the other Bhavas may be noted.

लग्नराशिः स्वयं प्रष्टा तत्सम्बन्धिधनादयः ।
द्वितीयाद्यन्यभावास्तत् पुष्टिहानी शुभाशुभैः ॥२४॥

Stanza 24.—The ascending sign is the 'querist' and the other Bhavas are the querist's wealth, brothers, etc. According as the Bhavas are connected with benefics or malefics, they will be well or ill-disposed.

NOTES

The significance of Bhavas suggested in natal astrology are here extended to Prasna or Horary astrology.

यो यो भावः स्वमिदृष्टो युतो वा सौम्यैर्वा स्यात्तस्य तस्याभिवृद्धिः ।
पापैरेवं तस्य भावस्य हानिर्विज्ञातव्या प्रश्नतो जन्मतो वा ॥२५॥

Stanza 25.—Whether in Prasna or horoscopy, such Bhavas as are associated with or aspected by their appropriate lords or benefics are said to thrive well. Those conjoined with or aspected by malefics will suffer annihilation.

NOTES

This stanza is from *Shatpanchasika* of Prithuyasas. Most principles of horoscopy so far as strength of Bhavas, etc., are concerned, are also applicable to Prasna charts. But the astrologer is expected to use much discretion in the manner of adapting rules of natal astrology to horary charts and *vice versa*.

यो यो भावाः प्रभुणा युक्तो दृष्टेथवा भवेत् प्रश्ने ।
गुरुबुधशुक्रैरेवं वक्तव्यं तस्य तस्य शुभम् ॥२६॥

यस्मिन् यस्मिन् भावे द्विद्वादशसप्तमे स्थिताः सौम्याः ।
तस्मिन् तस्मिन् वृद्धिर्दशमचतुर्थस्थितैस्तद्वत् ॥२७॥

Stanzas 26 and 27.—In Prasna, good results should be predicted in respect of Bhavas aspected by or conjoined with their respective lords or by Jupiter or Mercury or Venus. Bhavas, which have benefics in the 2nd, 7th and the 12th or 4th and 10th from them, can also be considered as favourable.

NOTES

If the lord, Jupiter, Mercury or Venus joins or aspects a Bhava, its indication will be fortified or promoted. Similarly good results will flow in respect of a Bhava which has benefics disposed in the 2nd, 7th and 12th or 4th and 11th from it. These are general principles of astrology. Bhavas generally get strengthened if subject to *subhakaratariyoga* or if Kendras are occupied by benefics.

How Bhavas are Ruined

षष्ठाष्टमरिप्फेशा भावापरिपवः शुभाश्च भावहनः ।
भावतदीश्वरकारकदुर्बलता चास्ति तद्वादाप्तवचः ॥२८॥

Stanza 28.—The benefic nature of Bhavas is destroyed by their connection with the lords of

6th, 8th and 12th or with the natural foes of their respective lords. If the Bhava, or its lord or the Karaka is weak, then also the Bhava comes to grief.

NOTES

The lords of the 6th, 8th and 12th are always said to be evil. If a Bhava is associated with or aspected by the lord of the 6th, 8th or 12th, the Bhava gets afflicted. Similarly if a Bhava is occupied by a planet who is a natural enemy to the lord, then also the Bhava becomes afflicted. If the Bhava, the lord or Karaka is weak, then also, the Bhava suffers annihilation. In what manner, a Bhava suffers damage, has to be ascertained by a careful balancing of the intensity of the affliction to which it is subject. If the 2nd Bhava is afflicted in the manner suggested in this stanza, then the native may become poor; or even though rich, he may get involved in debts.

षष्ठं द्वादशमष्टमं च मुनयो भावनानिष्टान् विदु-
स्तन्नाथान्वितवीक्षिता तदाधिपा ये वा च भावाः
स्वयम् ।
तत्रस्थाश्च यदीश्वरास्त्रय इमे नश्यन्ति भावा नृणां
जाता वा विफला विनष्टविकलास्तत्रातिकष्टोष्टमः ॥२९॥

Stanza 29.— Sages have declared that the 6th, 8th and 12th lords are malefic in nature. (1) Bhavas aspected by or associated with the lords of these; (2) Bhavas, the lords of which are associated with or aspected by the lords of these houses; and (3) Bhavas whose lords occupy 6th, 8th or 12th: these three sets of houses get destroyed. Even if they remain, they are found to be impotent or distorted in effect.

NOTES

Lords of the 6th, 8th and 12th are evil. The following Bhavas become afflicted :

(1) Those that are aspected by the lords of 6th, 8th and 12th.

(2) Those that are occupied by the lords of 6th, 8th and 12th.

(3) Those whose lords are aspected by the lords of 6th, 8th and 12th.

(4) Those whose lords are associated with the lords of 6th, 8th and 12th.

Here the intensity of the affliction of a Bhava is directly proportional to the number of evil associations or aspects.

In actual practice it is not advisable to apply these combinations literally. For purposes of illustration, the following example is given.

Mars Rahu			Moon Jupiter
Sun			Ketu
Ascendant Mars Venus	Saturn		

Lords of the 6th, 8th and 12th are Venus, the Moon and Mars. Theoretically the following houses become sterile or afflicted.

(1) Houses aspected by Venus, the Moon and Mars, *viz.*, VII, II, IV, VII and VIII.

(2) Houses occupied by Venus, the Moon and Mars, *viz.*, I, I and VIII.

(3) Houses whose lords are aspected by Venus, the Moon and Mars. Venus does not aspect any lord. Mars aspects Moon (lord of VIII)and Jupiter (lord of I and IV). The Moon aspects the Sun (lord of IX).

Therefore Bhavas that get afflicted are VIII, I, IV and IX.

(4) Houses whose lords are associated with Venus, the Moon and Mars. Venus associates with Mars (owning V and XII): Mars associates with Venus (owning VI and XI); the Moon associates with Jupiter (owning I and IV).

It must be noted that according to cannons of astrology, since some planets own two houses, the affliction due to lordship of the 8th or the lordship of the 12th or the lordship of the 6th gets neutralised under certain conditions. Hence the necessity of not applying the principles verbatim. In this connection, reference may be made to my book *How to Judge a Horoscope*.

भावाधीशे च भावे सति बलरहिते च ग्रहे कारकाख्ये
पापान्तस्थे च पापैररिभिरपि समेतेक्षिते नान्याखेटैः ।
पापैस्तद्बन्धुमृत्युव्ययभवनगतैस्तत्त्रिकोणस्थितैर्वा ।
वाच्या तद्भावहानिः स्फुटमिह भवति द्वित्रसंवादभावात्
॥३०॥

Stanza 30.—A Bhava should be considered to be weakened under the following circumstances: The said Bhava, its lord or the Karaka is weak; they are hemmed in between, or are combined with, or are aspected by malefic planets or their respective enemies; benefics do not associate with or aspect them; and the evil planets are disposed in the 4th, 8th, 12th or 5th or 9th; out of these various afflictions, even if two or three are present, the Bhava may be rendered extinct.

NOTES

The factors to be considered in judging whether a Bhava is strong or weak are the concerned Bhava, its lord and the appropriate Karaka. There ara twentyone points of affliction, which are as follows :—

The three factors being weak	3
,, subject to Papakarthari Yoga	3
,, are combined with or aspected by malefics	3
,, are conjoined with their respective enemies	3
,, are not associated with or aspected by benefics	3
,, have evil planets disposed in in the 4th, 8th and 12th.	3
,, evil planets are disposed in the 5th and 9th.	3
	21

Of these 21 items of affliction, even if there are two or more, then the Bhava becomes weak or ruptured. Here again great care must be exercised in balancing the afflictions.

KARAKAS OR SIGNIFICATORS

तातश्चात्मप्रभावो द्युमणिरथ मनोमातरौ शीतरश्मि-
र्भ्राता सत्वं च भौमः क्षितिरपि वचनं ज्ञानमिन्दो-
स्तनूजः ।
धीचित्पुत्रांगसौख्यं सुरगुरुरबलाभोगयानानि शुक्रो
मृत्युर्व्याधिश्च दुःखं शनिरिह गदितो दासभृत्यादिकोपि
॥३१॥

Stanza 31.—The Sun is karaka for father and spiritual influence ; the Moon for mother and the mind ; Mars for brothers, landed property and courage ; Mercury for speech and knowledge ; Jupiter for intelligence, children, wisdom and bodily health ; Venus for vehicles, wife and sense-pleasures ; and Saturn for death, diseases, sorrow, servants and followers.

आत्मादयो गगनगैर्बलिभिर्बलवत्तराः ।
दुर्बलैर्दुर्बला ज्ञेया विपरीतं शनेः स्मृतम् ॥३२॥

Stanza 32.—If the different karakas such as the Sun, the Moon, etc., are strong, then the events attributed to them will be predominantly seen. If weak, these will exist only in name. With regard to Saturn, however, it is just the reverse. If he is strong, miseries and diseases decrease; if weak, these will be felt in abundance.

NOTES

This is an important stanza. If the Karakas are strong, they promote their respective indications. But Saturn is an exception. If he is strong, he will lessen the indications.

अर्कांशे शौर्यं स्वं तातश्चाद्युदितसर्ववस्तूनाम् ।
कारकताकादीनां विज्ञेयापोषणे तथा हनने ॥३३॥

Stanza 33.—Besides being karakas of events explained above, the various planets govern all the other indications attributed to them in the texts.

भाग्याद्यभीष्टभावेशोप्यशुभो भावपुष्टिकृत् ।
"लग्नात्पुत्रे"ति पद्ये तद्वराहमिहिरोदितम् ॥३४॥

Stanza 34.—The lords of the 9th and other favourable houses, though they may be malefics, nourish a Bhava. This point has been well emphasized by Varaha Mihira in the verse 'Lagnath puthre'.

NOTES

The relevant stanzas referred to in stanza 33 are

Arkamsetrunakanaka urna bheshajadhai (see Chapter on Karmajeevadhay and *Sauryamswamnakhadanta*, etc., in Dasaphaladhyaya). Details of *Karakatwas* have also been given in my book *Hindu Predictive Astrology*.

शुभदानां प्राबल्ये शुभपौष्कल्यं पुनश्च दोषकृताम् ।
वैबल्ये दोषाणां पौष्कल्यं वदति तद्वदभियुक्तः ॥३५॥

Stanza 35.—Benefics if strong contribute good fully. Malefics if weak give evil in full.

पञ्चमसंस्थः पापः पुत्रविनाशं करोति बलहीनः ।
सौम्याः सुतं तिदत्ते बलसहितश्चाष्टमाधिपं हित्वा ॥३६॥

Stanza 36.—If a weak malefic occupies the 5th, there will be loss of children. If it is occupied by a strong benefic other than the lord of the 8th, there will be birth of children.

NOTES

Here by lord of the 8th is also implied the lords of the 6th and 12th.

FRUCTIFICATION OF BHAVAS

येन ग्रहेण यत्प्रोक्तमशुभं वा शुभं फलम् ।
बली चेत्स शुभं पूर्णमशुभं दुर्बलो यदि ॥३७॥

Stanza 37.—A planet, capable of giving rise to both bad and good, confers only good results if he is strong, only evil results if he is weak.

NOTES

According to stanza 35, a strong benefic can contribute good results fully, but according to this stanza, a planet capable of producing both good and bad results—where no mention is made about the planet being a benefic or a malefic—can give rise to exclusively good or exclusively evil results according as the said planet is strong or weak.

भावेष्विष्टेषु वर्गोत्तमनिजरिपुभेष्वास्थितो यो ग्रहोसौ
पूर्णं मध्यं तथाल्पं दिशति शुभफलं स्त्रोदितं
पृच्छकानाम्।

भावेष्विष्टेतरेष्वप्य शुभमपि तथा पुष्टमध्याल्परूपं
वैरिस्वीयांशवर्गोत्तमगत उदितं द्रव्यनाशामयाद्यम्
॥३८॥

Stanza 38.—A favourable planet is capable of conferring benefic results fully, moderately or feebly—according as the Navamsa it occupies is Vargottama, own or friendly, or inimical. Similarly an unfavourable planet is capable of giving rise to malefic results—fully, moderately or feebly, according as the Navamsa he holds is inimical, own or friendly or Vargottama.

NOTES

The good that a favourable planet can do, if he is in Vargottama Navamsa, is full. If he is in own Navamsa, the effects will be half. If he is in the Navamsa of his enemy, the results will be very little. The effect of a friendly Navamsa is similar to own Navamsa. An unfavourable planet, if he is in Vargottama brings in very little evil. If he is in his own or friendly Navamsa, the evil effects will be partly mixed. If he is in the Navamsa of his enemy, the evil that he does will be intense. Views differ as to whether in this stanza by the terms 'favourable' and 'unfavourable' are meant natural benefics and natural malefics or benefic lords and malefic lords. I am inclined to accept 'benefic' and 'malefic' lords. Suppose Leo is Lagna and the 5th house is occupied by Mars. Here Mars is a benefic lord. His position in the Navamsa suggests the good and bad results he can give pertaining to the Bhava he occupies. Here again when *bandhu* (friend) and *ari* (enemy) are mentioned, they refer to natural friends and natural enemies.

स्वामी कारकखेचरश्च बलिनौ यस्येष्टभावस्थितौ
सम्पूर्णानुभवक्षमश्च नियतं भावः स नृणां भवेत् ।
रिःफारातिमृतिस्थितौ च विबलौ यत्कारकाधीश्वरौ
भावोयं नहि सम्भवेदपि नृणां कस्यानुभूतौ कथा ॥३९॥

Stanza 39.—If the lord and the Karaka are strong and occupy favourable houses, then the indications of the Bhava will be fully experienced. On the contrary if they are weak and occupy the 6th, 8th or 12th, the results of the concerned Bhava will be negative, and as such, the question whether the native gets its influence need not be raised.

NOTES

Here the disposition of the lord and the Karaka in favourable and unfavourable houses should be reckoned from Lagna.

स्वोच्चाभीष्टगृहेषु कारकपती रन्ध्राद्यनिष्टस्थितौ
यद्भावस्य स सम्भवेदविमलो नास्यानुभूतिर्नृणाम् ।

नीचाद्याश्रयतो बलौ शुभतरे लाभादिभावे स्थितौ
यद्भावाधिपकारकौ स विकलोप्यस्यानुभूतिर्भवेत् ॥४०॥

Stanza 40.—If the lord and Karaka are strong but occupy an unfavourable position, then though the effects of Bhava may be seen, the native will not enjoy them. On the contrary, if the lord and Karaka are weak but occupy favourable positions, the effect will be experienced by the native however little it may be.

NOTES

Strength here implies own, exaltation and friendly places. Unfavourable position means the 6th, 8th and 12th. By weakness is meant debilitation; favourable positions are the angles, trines and the 11th. When the Bhava is strong (by virtue of strength of the lord and Karaka), it implies existence of the indications of the Bhava. Weakness of the Bhava implies its extinction. When a Bhava exists and the lord and Karaka are weak, the native will not enjoy the results. On the contrary if the Bhava (that is the lord and Karaka) is weak but occupy favourable houses, the results of the Bhava, however feeble, will be experienced.

Here we have to note that strength gives the Bhava its existence, and position gives its influence on the native.

नाथकारकयोरेको बलवानिष्टभावगः ।
अन्योन्यथेति मिश्रत्वेप्युक्तरीत्योह्यतां फलम् ॥४१॥

Stanza 41.—Of the two, the lord of a Bhava and its Karaka, if one is strong and the other is weak, then the influence should be considered to be mixed in nature.

भावात्तदीश्वरे सुस्थे भावसम्पन्न चान्यथा ।
लग्नादनुभवश्चैवं चिन्त्यतामिति केचन ॥४२॥

Stanza 42.—If the lord of a Bhava occupies a favourable house from it, then the effects of that Bhava will be full. If the lord occupies a favourable house from Lagna, the effects of the Bhava will be well experienced. This is the view of some.

NOTES

If the lord occupies an unfavourable house from it, the Bhava itself will be distorted. If the lord happens to occupy an unfavourable house from Lagna, the native will not experience the results in full. This is the opinion of some writers.

यस्य यस्य विलग्नेन सम्बन्धो लग्नपेन वा ।
दृग्योगकेन्द्रगत्याद्यैः स स भावोनुभूयते ॥४३॥

Stanza 43.—Such Bhavas as have any relationship with Lagna or its lord, such as aspect, association, Kendra disposition, etc., will be surely experienced.

सौम्यानां व्ययमृत्युशत्रुसहजा नेष्टा अभीष्टाः परे ।
पापानामभिमातिसोदरभवा इष्टा अनिष्टाः परे ।
भावेष्वेषु हि मुख्यता तु वपुषो धर्मात्मजौ तत्समौ
तेषु त्रिष्वधिकं शुभाशुभफलम् विद्यात् सतां चासताम्
॥४४॥

Stanza 44.—Benefics in the 3rd, 6th, 8th and 1?th become unfavourable. Malefics in the 3rd, 6th and 11th become favourable. The most important of all the houses is Lagna. The 5th and the 9th houses are equally important. It is in these three Bhavas that benefics show their greatest good, and malefics their worst evil.

ताम्रहेमादिवस्तूनां स्वोक्तानां लाभदा अपि ।
रुक्प्रदत्वात्तु रोगादिप्रश्नेनिष्टा रिपौ खराः ॥४५॥

Stanza 45.—Malefic planets (in the 6th) confer all the articles governed by them. But the Bhava gets spoiled. In questions pertaining to diseases, an evil planet in the 6th house is harmful.

पुष्णन्ति शुभा भावान् मृत्यादीन् घ्नन्ति संस्थिताः
पापाः ।
सौम्याः षष्ठेरिप्राः सर्वे नेष्टा व्ययाष्टमगाः ॥४६॥

Stanza 46.—Benefics vitalise the houses. Malefics destroy them. Benefics in the 6th house destroy enemies and malefics increase them. All planets are harmful in the 8th and 12th.

NOTES

The stanza is clear and needs no clarification. Benefics strengthen the house they occupy. Malefics on the other hand spoil the Bhavas. Even in the 6th benefics destroy enemies and other significations of this house, *viz.*, debts and enemies. Malefics produce harmful effects because they increase the 6th house indications. All planets—benefic or malefic—will give rise only to evil when they occupy the 8th and 12th houses.

This above sloka is from *Swalpajathakam.*

दशाफलानि यान्युक्तान्यशुभानि वा ।
प्रश्नेपि तानि वाच्यानि दुःस्थे सुःस्थे च खेचरे ॥४७॥

Stanza 47.—The good and bad significations ascribed to different planets should be used when describing the effects of Dasas. In the matter of Prasna the inappropriate ones from the planetary situations in *dustha* and *sustha* places should be weeded out.

FAVOURABLE AND UNFAVOURABLE HOUSES

इष्टानिष्टगतत्वेन शुभाशुभफलप्रदे ।
ग्रहे सत्यखिलं योज्यं संज्ञाध्यायसमीरितम् ॥४८॥

Stanzas 48.—Planets give rise to favourable or unfavourable results according as they occupy *ishta* or *anishta* Bhavas. On the basis of *samgnadhyaya*, the various effects should be inferred.

NOTES

In *samgnadhyaya* or chapter on General Principles. planetary effects have been explained. If, for instance, the Sun is in an *ishta Bhava*, he indicates benefits from rulers, grace of lord Siva and acquisition of copper vessels etc. If he is in *anishta* Bhavas, then the Sun's indications would be wrath of the rulers, wrath of God, loss of copper vessels, illness etc. The results will happen in the Sun's Dasa.

WHEN BHAVAS ARE RUINED

मूर्त्याद्या निजरन्ध्रपेण शनिना वा स्युर्यदा संयुता
स्वस्वारिव्ययरन्ध्रपापहृतयस्तत्स्थस्य वा चेत्तदा ।
तत्तद्भावविपत्तिरस्ति नियमादेवं वराङ्गादिषु
ब्रूयादंघ्रियुगान्तिमेषु च वपुर्भागेषु रोगान् सुधीः ॥४९॥

Stanza.—49.—When the lord of the 8th from a certain Bhava or Saturn transits the Bhava in question and when at the same time, the Dasa (or Bhukti) of the lord of 6, 8 or 12 operates, the Bhava concerned will come to grief. Similarly diseases in the various parts of the body as signified by the Bhava concerned can also be predicted.

NOTES

In stanza 49, the time when a Bhava fructifies is given. Let us take an example The Lagna is Aquarius and the lord of the 4th Venus is in Leo. The lord of the 8th from the 4th is Jupiter. When this planet or Saturn transits the 4th (Taurus) and simultaneously the Dasa (or Bhukti) of the lord of the 6th (the Moon), 8th (Mercury) or the lord of the 12th (Saturn) operates, indications of the 4th Bhava should suffer. Under the same directional influences, the native may suffer from diseases pertaining to or in the organ signified by the 4th house, *viz.*, chest or heart.

EFFECTS OF PLANETS IN HOUSES

लग्नाद्यैर्वाच्यमसत्सद्योगे सति फलं समुच्चित्य ।
सौकर्यार्थं प्रष्टुः फलानिर्देशस्य कथ्यते तदनु ॥५०॥

Stanza 50.—The effects of various planets occupying different Bhavas will now be given to facilitate easy prediction.

पापे लग्नगते पराजयशिरोरुग्दुःखदुष्कीर्तयः
स्थानभ्रंशधनक्षयाखिलशरीरास्वास्थ्यदुःखासिकः ।
सौम्ये लग्नगते सुखस्थितिजयारोग्यार्थसम्पत्तयः
कीर्तिस्थानविशेषलब्धिरिति विज्ञेयं फलं पृच्छतात् ॥५१॥

Stanza 51.—If an evil planet occupies Lagna, there will be failure, diseases in the head, sorrows, dishonour. displacement, loss of money, pains all over the body, and discomfort in all ways. A benefic in Lagna gives general comfort, success, good health, financial prosperity, fame and promotions to higher positions.

पापे वित्तगते स्वपूर्वनिचितद्रव्यक्षयो वक्त्र-
रुग्भर्तव्यामयदक्षिणाक्षिरुजो दुष्टोक्ति पात्रक्षती ।
सौम्ये वित्तगते पुरार्जितधनानामेव वृध्युद्भवः
पात्राप्तिर्भरणीरयञ्जनसुखं प्रष्टेति यायात्फलम् ॥५२॥

Stanza 52.—A malefic in the 2nd house indicates loss of ancestral property, diseases in the face, sickness for the family members, diseases in the right eye, scandals, and loss of vessels. A good planet brings in increase of family wealth and gains of vessels and family amity and happiness.

पापे भ्रातृगते सहायविगमः सोदर्यरोगादिकं
वक्षःकन्धरदक्षिणश्रवणरुग्धीदौष्टचधैर्यक्षयाः ।
सौम्ये भ्रातृगते सहोदरसहायारोग्यलाभाधिकं
सद्बुद्धेरुदयश्च धैर्ययुतिरित्येतत्फलं पृच्छताम् ॥५३॥

Stanza 53.—A malefic in the 3rd house brings in misunderstanding with friends and people who help. Misfortunes to brothers, diseases in the chest, neck and right ear ; mental affliction, bad conduct and cowardice. A benefic indicates good conduct, courage, happiness to brothers, increase or help from others and good health.

मातुर्मातुलभागिनेयसुहृदां गोवेश्मशय्यासन-
क्षेत्राणामपि वाहनस्य च विपध्द्दहेशरुक्चासुखम्
कूपाद्यम्बुविदूषणं सुखगते पापे शुभे वाहनं
क्षेत्रं गोशयनासनानि सुखमित्येषां हि लाभो भवेत्
॥५४॥

Stanza 54.—A malefic in the 4th house causes distress to mother and maternal relations, loss of cattle, beds, cots, landed property and vehicles, heart trouble, general misery and discomfort due to impure water. A benefic in the 5th confers vehicles, lands, cattle, beds and general prosperity and health.

पापे पञ्चमगेस्य दोषवशतो मौढ्यादिना रुङ्मृति-
र्वापत्यस्य पुराणपुण्यविलयो वेद्या मनः कुण्ठता ।

क्रोधामात्यरुगादिकं त्वथ शुभे पुत्रस्य लाभोथवा-
रोग्यं धीप्रतिभोदयश्च मनसस्तुष्टिश्च पुण्योदयः ॥५५॥

Stanza 55.—If a malefic is in the 5th, afflicted by way of combustion, etc., there will be illness, death or danger to children ; leaving of Sanchita Karma, mental uneasiness, irritable temperament, and illness to the native's advisers. If a benefic is in the 5th, there will be birth of children or good health, peace of mind, influence and increase of good deeds.

NOTES

If the malefic is afflicted considerably, then alone there will be death of children. Otherwise, they will be ill or meet with accidents; the native will lose the spirit of optimism and enthusiasm and will frequently lose his temper to the detriment of his own interests. A benefic gives quite the opposite results.

पापे षष्ठगते तु षष्ठभवनोक्ताङ्गे व्रणस्योद्भव-
श्चोरारिव्यसनं च नाभिकादिरुग्विघ्नोद्भवः कर्मसु ।
पापस्यास्य च दोषसम्भवगदः सौम्ये च शत्रुक्षयो
रोगाणामभवः सतां तु शमनं प्रष्टुः समादिश्यताम्
॥५६॥

Stanza 56.—A malefic in the 6th denotes occurrence of a wound or ulcler in the organ ruling the 6th sign, fear from thieves and enemies, trouble in the waist and navel, obstacles in undertakings and ailments signified by the occupying planet. If a benefic planet is in the 6th, enemies will be vanquished, diseases will disappear and new ones do not sprout out.

NOTES

If a benefic occupies the 6th house, remember that the nature of the house is improved though the planet is spoiled by its position.

पापे सप्तमगे कळत्रमरणं रोगो वियोगोस्य वा
भर्तुर्वा गमनान्तराय उदियात्स्युर्मूत्रकृच्छ्राण्यपि ।
सौम्ये सप्तमगे विवाहघटन नष्टार्थलाभः
सुदृग्भोगावाप्तिविदेशयानसुहृदायानादिकं स्यात् फलम्
॥५७॥

मदने पापसमेते दाहादिकमपि गृहस्य भार्यायाः ।
बलवच्छुभसंयुक्ते गृहकरणं सम्भवेच्च जायायाः ॥५८॥

Stanzas 57 and 58.—When malefics are in the 7th, there will be sickness or death to or separation from the life-partner, disturbance to journeys and urinary troubles. Fire may break out in the wife's house.

Benefics in the 7tn indicate marriage, recovery of lost wealth, enjoyment and happiness and safe return of relations gone to foreign countries. The native is likely to build a good house.

NOTES

Benefics in the 7th also indicate trips to foreign countries and safe return.

पापे रन्ध्रगते तु दासजनरुक्प्रत्युहगुह्यामया
लोकैर्विग्रहणं धनादिहरणं चोरैर्नृपैर्वारिभिः ।
रोगाश्चारुचिपूर्वकाः स्युरपि च स्याच्छङ्कनीया मृतिः
सौम्ये रन्ध्रगते तु रोगविरहो दैर्घ्यं तथा चायुषः ॥५९॥
अपवादो मठापत्तिरपि पापेऽष्टमस्थिते ।
मठाद्यालयसम्पत्तिमपि कुर्याच्छुभोऽत्रगः ॥६०॥

Stanzas 59 and 60.—Malefics in the 8th bring illness to servants, obstacles in all works, diseases in the anus, quarrels with all; loss of wealth due to thieves, rulers or enemies; loss of appetite for food, diseases and bad name. A benefic indicates freedom from disease, courage, longevity and facilities to acquire new houses, building mutts, etc.

पापे धर्मस्थिते स्याद्गुरुजनपितृपौत्रादिरुग्भाग्यहानि-
र्वैद्यं धर्मेश्वरानुग्रहसुकृत तपोहानयो निष्कृपत्वम् ।

सौम्ये धर्मस्थिते स्याद्गुरुपितृमनसश्चेश्वराणां प्रसादो
वृद्धिर्भाग्यस्य धर्मस्य च शुभतपसामार्द्रता
पौत्रसौख्यम् ॥६१॥

Stanza 61.—In the 9th malefics are capable of causing illness to elders, father and grand-children ; ill luck, divine wrath, disinclination to acts of charity, gradual decline of hard earned merits, ruin of one's power of penance and hard-heartedness. Good planets bring in blessings from elders and parents, mental happiness, God's grace, increase of fortune, inclination to do good acts, increase of Tapas, humanitarian tendencies and happiness from grand-children.

पापे कर्मगते तु कर्मविहतिर्दुष्कीर्तिराज्ञाक्षति-
र्दासालम्बनयोर्विनाशनमपि स्यज्ञानुरुक्प्रोषणम् ।
सौम्ये पद्धतिमण्डपामरगृहाद्युत्पादनं कर्मणा
माज्ञालम्बनयोश्च सिद्धिरपि दासावाप्तिकीर्त्युद्गमौ ॥६२॥

Stanza 62.—Malefics in the 10th denote failures in efforts, bad name, loss of respect, ruin to servants, breaks in profession, diseases in the ankle and exile. Benefics in the 10th, indicate construction of wayside inns, new roads, council halls and temples; success in all attempts, increase of prestige and influence, rise in profession and acquisition of servants.

पापे लाभे स्थितवति सुतज्येष्ठयोरामयाद्यं
जंघावामश्रवणरुगपूर्व्योक्तताम्रादिलाभः ।
सौम्ये दुःखप्रशमनसमस्तेप्सितार्थार्थलाभाः
संज्ञाध्यायादिषु तदुदितस्यापि लाभागमाद्यम् ॥६३॥

Stanza 63.—When malefics occupy the 11th, there will be illness to elder brothers and sons, fresh ailments in the left ear and legs, and gain of articles (such as copper mentioned in *Brihat Jataka*). Benefics indicate abatement of grief, accomplishment of desired objects, gain of fresh sources of wealth and material objects signified by the benefic planet or planets concerned.

पापे द्वादशगे तु दुर्व्ययपदभ्रंशांघ्रिवामाक्षि-
रुक्पाताः पापमतिप्रवृद्धमिति वक्तव्यं फलं पृच्छताम् ।
सौम्ये द्वादशगे व्ययो वितरणप्रायो न दुष्टव्ययः
पापानामभवः सतां तु शमनं चेत्यादिकं स्यात्फलम् ॥६४॥

Stanza 64.—Malefics occupying the 12th indicate squandering of money, fall from position, troubles in the soles of the feet and the left eye, and falls due to carelessness and sinful actions. Benefics in the 12th cause heavy expenditure for good purposes, gradual termination of sinful actions and abatement of sickness.

सदसत्सामान्यफलम् लग्नादिष्विति पुनर्विशेषफलम् ।
शूरस्तब्धाद्युदितं होरायामिह विचिन्त्य वाच्यमिह
॥६५॥

Stanza 65.—Thus far the effects of planets in the various Bhavas have been outlined in a general manner. For special effects, reference may be made to the stanza *soorasthabdhadyuditam* in Varaha Mihira's *Hora Sastra*.

THE EFFECTS OF GULIKA

होरायां नोदितं मान्देर्विलग्नादिस्थितेः फलम् ।
विलिख्यते तदप्यत्र दृष्टं ग्रन्थान्तरे क्वचित् ॥६६॥

Stanza 66.—The effects of Gulika in the various houses have not been given by Varaha Mihira They have been enumerated here as found in other treatises.

रोगी क्षताङ्गो गुळिके तनुस्थे निन्द्याभिभाषी धनगे
विवेषः ।

सोत्थं द्विषन् भ्रातृगते सशोर्थः सुखादिहीनः सुखगेरि
भीतः ॥६७॥

गुर्वादिनिन्दाकृदनात्मजः स्याच्छूली सुतस्थे रिपुगे
निजद्विड् ।

विषक्षणो वंशविदूषणश्च कळत्रहन्ता मदगेतिकामः ॥६८॥

धीमान् बहुव्याधिरनायतायुर्विषाग्निशस्त्रैर्मृतिरष्टमस्थे ।

धर्मस्थिते धर्मतपोमनूनः खस्थे सुकीर्तिः परकार्यसक्तः
॥६९॥

कुर्याच्च पौरुषयुतो धनवाहनार्थानैश्वर्यवान् भवगते
बहुभृत्ययुक्तः ।

दुस्स्वप्नवांश्च कुनखी विकलो व्ययस्थे लग्नादिभावगत-
मान्दिफलम् प्रदिष्टम् ॥७०॥

Stanzas 67 to 70.—Gulika in Lagna—sickly body, suffering from sores and ailments; in the 2nd—untidy in dress, generally uses abusive language; in the 3rd—hates brothers, but valorous; in the 4th—generally unhappy and fear from enemies; in the 5th—no respect for elders and preceptors and deprived of issues; in the 6th—tendency to find fault with relatives; in the 7th—affliction to wife, strong sex instinct; in the 8th—short life, chronic complaints, sharp intelligence, and death from poison, weapon or fire; in the 9th– irreligious and uncharitable; in the 10th—unsullied fame and inclination for social work; in the 11th—greatness, prosperity and courage, wealth, attendants and servants; and in the 12th —hideous dreams, diseases in the nails and loss of limbs.

लग्नादिगता वपुराद्युपचयहानी शुभाशुभाः कुर्युः ।
विपरीतं षष्ठमृतिद्वादशगाः कथितमिति हि सत्येन ॥७१॥

Stanza 71.—Benefics nourish Bhavas while malefic planets destroy them. But in the 6th, 8th and 12th contrary results happen. This is the view of Satyacharya.

NOTES

In the 6th, 8th and 12th benefics lessen the malefic effects while malefics aggravate the evil effects.

Effects of Tertiary Planets

धूमादिपञ्चदोषाणां विलग्नादिषु संस्थितौ ।
फलं यल्लिख्यते तच्च समं प्रश्ने च जातके ॥७२॥

Stanza 72.—The results of the occupation of the various Bhavas by the Pancha doshas Dhuma, etc., should be carefully looked into both in Prasna and horoscopy.

NOTES

The five *doshas* (or tertiary planets) are Dhuma, Vyatheepatha, Parivesha, Indrachapa and Kethu. Their situations or longitudes can be ascertained thus :

Dhuma	=	Sun's longitude + 133°
Vyatheepatha	=	360° – Dhuma
Parivesha	=	180° + Vyatheepatha
Indrachapa	=	360° – Parivesha
Kethu	=	Indrachapa + 17°
The Sun	=	Kethu + 30.

It will be noted that by adding 30° to Kethu – this Kethu is evidently different from the Moon's descending node – the longitude of the Sun is obtained.

कूपे स्यात्पतनं तनौ यदि वचस्खालित्यमर्थे स्थितः
पङ्गुर्भ्रातरि सोदरः सुरगृहं रक्षेत्सुखे मातुलः ।
क्रुद्धः पञ्चमभेऽरिभे खलु भवेद्व्याघ्रेण दष्टो मुखे
याति भ्रष्टतया मदे तु निधने धूमः क्षतः शस्त्रतः ॥७३॥
धर्मे स्वल्पतपाः खभेशनिहतिर्लाभे लभेतेतर-
द्वेश्मापि प्रवसेद्व्ययेथ तनुगः स्योऽस्त्रेव्द्यतीपातकः ।

श्वित्री वाचि सकौशलः सहजभे गानी सुखेऽब्वागमो
दुःखं पुत्रभवं सुतेऽरिभवने छिद्रावहोस्तेऽधनः ॥७४॥
वेत्ता सर्वकला मृतौ तपसि भाग्योनौ नभस्यग्निभी-
र्लाभे भूपतिसत्कृतो व्ययगृहे भ्रष्टोथ सर्पान्मृतिः ।
लग्नस्थे परिवेषनाम्नि निधिकृत्स्वेभ्रान्तिमान् सोदरे
बासो नात्मगृहे सुखे मनसि बद्धोन्तस्थचोरो रिपौ
॥७५॥
काणोस्ते क्षतिरायुधेन निधने गुर्वाघभक्तो गुरौ
ह्योदार्यं दशमे भवे तु जळवाग्दीर्घामयो द्वादशे ।
वातव्यभ्यवशीकृताखिलतनुर्वृत्रारिचापोदये
बाधिर्थं वचसि द्विजन्मवधपूर्वाकृत्यकृद्विक्रमे ॥७६॥
वेश्मस्थे गणरक्ष्यहा मनासि वाग्भीमन्त्रवादावुभौ
षष्ठे शत्रुभयं मदेङ्गविकलो भार्यानुभूतिश्च नो ।
बद्धो भूरितराशया प्रकटयन् जाळ्यं चरेदष्टमे
बन्धाद्भ्रातमजतो मृतिस्तपसि खे स्वल्पांबरः शीघ्रभुक्
॥७७॥

Stanza 73 to 77.—Dhuma in the first house indicates fall into a well; in the 2nd, indistinct speech; in the 3rd, brother becomes lame; in the

4th, maternal uncle becomes the guardian of temple property; in the 5th, irritable; in the 6th, injury from wild tigers; in the 7th, excommunication; in the 8th, injury by weapons; in the 9th, an atheist; in the 10th, death by lightning; in the 11th, acquisition of new residences; and in the 12th, going away from home.

Vyatheepatha in the 1st indicates skin diseases; in the 2nd eloquence; in the 3rd, musical talents; in the 4th owns horses; in the 5th, affliction to children; in the 6th, quarrels in the family; in the 7th, poverty; in the 8th learned in fine arts; in the 9th unlucky; in the 10th, danger from 'burns' or fire; in the 11th, favoured by rulers; and in the 12th, a bhrashta or fallen person.

If Parivesha is in 1st house, there will be death from serpents; in the 2nd, acquisition of treasures; in the 3rd unsound mind; in the 4th, will not live in his own house; in the 5th incarceration; in the 6th, becomes a thief; in the 7th, loses one eye; in the 8th, danger from weapons; in the 9th, disrespectful towards elders; in the 10th, generous; in the 11th, poor in speech; and in the 12th, affected by chronic diseases.

Indrachapa in Lagna gives rheumatism; in the 2nd, deafness; in the 3rd inclination to kill

Brahmins ; in the 4th, squandering public wealth; in the 5th, a magician and a coward ; in the 6th, fear from foes ; in the 7th, deformed limbs ; in the 8th, a wanderer in quest of impossible things; in the 9th death through son or incarceration ; in the 10th shabby dress and quick eating.

लाभे भूरिपराक्रमश्च मृगयासक्तो व्यये प्रोषणं
कोपाद्भूमिपतेरथोदयगते केतौ विकेशोग्रतः ।
दौर्बल्यं गिरिसानुनासिकवचा वाग्भीश्च सोस्थेत्द्वयं
वेश्मस्थे सुरभिः सदा हृदि नरः शूली वधूर्युग्मसूः
॥७८॥

Stanza 78 —If Indrachapa is in the 11th, the person will be valiant and a good hunter ; and in the 12th,leaving native place through Government disfavour. Kethu in Lagna makes one bald-headed ; in the 2nd, physical debility and speech through the nose ; in the 3rd, highly sensitive and speaking through the nose ; in the 4th, fond of perfumes and scents ; in the 5th, 'soola' disease (birth of twins in the case of women).

NOTES

Kethu in the 5th can give rise to " soola disease ", heart trouble, weakness of the heart, etc. In regard to a female such a position indicates birth of twins.

अन्धो रुद्धमरुन्म्रियते परगेहेरौ मदे मोषणा-
द्रन्ध्रस्थे विषभोजनात्तपसि विक्रान्तश्च दुर्मृत्युभाक् ।
वृक्षेणाभिहतो निपत्य तरुतो वा खे मृतिं प्राप्नुया-
दाये शेवधिभाग्यये शयनसौख्याभावदुःखव्ययाः ॥७९॥

Stanza 79.—In the 6th Kethu makes one sand-blind and gives death through kapha diseases in a stranger's house; in the 7th, death while thieving; in the 8th, death by posion; in the 9th, performs wonderful deeds and dies in the end; in the 10th, death by fall; in the 11th, gets treasure; and mines; in the 12th, he will be sleepless, squanders money and meets with calamities in life.

लाभनाशादिकं सर्वभावानां यदिहोदितम् ।
कदा तत्सम्भवेदित्याकांक्षयां काल उच्यते ॥८०॥

Stanza 80.—The nature and strength of the Bhavas, their completeness and incompletness and their progress and decay have been explained hitherto. The exact period, when the Bhavas fructify, will now be explained.

TIME WHEN BHAVAS FRUCTIFY

फलाप्तिः कल्प्यते येन तस्य कालोयनादिकः ।
तद्भुक्तांशकसंख्याभिस्तत्सिद्धौ समुदीर्यताम् ॥८१॥

Stanza 81.—The time of fructification is to be known by multiplying the time-periods allotted to the different planets as Ayana, Kshana, etc., by the number of Navamsas gained by the planet in the Rasi.

NOTES

The time-periods allotted to different planets as per *Brihat Jataka* are: the Sun—Ayana (6 months); the Moon—Kshana (48 minutes): Mars—Vasara (one week); Mercury—Rithu (two months); Jupiter—Masa (one month), Venus—Ardha (a fortnight) and Saturn—Sama (one year).

लग्ने यावानुदेत्यंशस्तत्संख्याघ्नोयनादिकः ।
कालो वाच्योंशकेशस्य कार्ये वैरिजयादिके ॥८२॥

Stanza 82.—The period indicated by the lord of Lagna Navamsa, multiplied by the number of Navamsas traversed by the said lord gives the time of fructification.

NOTES

Suppose the rising Navamsa is Leo. Its lord is the Sun. The period indicated by the lord is Ayana or 6 months. Suppose the Sun is in the 5th Navamsa. Then the event, say marriage, will happen within $(5 \times 6) = 30$ months.

लग्नाद्यावति भे पापस्तावत्यब्देह्नि मासि वा ।
पक्षे क्षणेयने वर्तौ लग्नेशस्योचिते व्यथा ॥८३॥

Stanza 83.—The 'time' signified by the lord of Lagna multiplied by the number of Rasis intervening between the Lagna and the Rasi holding a malefic planet indicates the period of sorrow.

NOTES

Here, there is a certain ambiguity discernible. We are asked to multiply the 'time' ruled by the lord of Lagna by the number of signs intervening between the Lagna and the sign holding a malefic. Suppose there are two or three signs holding malefics. Which is to be preferred? No light is thrown on this. Here we have to take recourse to commonsense. The sign holding the most powerful malefic, must be considered. Suppose Lagna is Virgo and Mars is in the 3rd. The lord of Lagna is Mercury. The time signified by Mercury is 'a fortnight'. Multiply this by 3 (the number of signs Mars is removed from Lagna) and the evil effect will fructify within three fortnights.

According to the same reasoning if instead of a malefic, a benefic is concerned, within the appropriate time a benefic event can take place. This is the view of some.

अन्येनापि प्रकारेण कालो ग्रन्थान्तरोदितः ।
शुभाशुभफलप्राप्तौ स च सम्प्रति लिख्यते ॥८४॥

Stanza 84.—Other methods of fixing the 'time' of happening of the good and evil results are given elsewhere. They are herewith explained.

भावाद्भावपतौ तु दृश्यदळगे तद्भावलाभोऽचिरा-
त्तत्रादृश्यगते शनैरिति भिदाभावात्पुनस्तत्पतिः ।
राशौ यावति तत्समे तु दिवसे मासेऽथवा भावना
थारूढालयगेऽथवा हिमकरे भावस्य लाभो भवेत् ॥८५॥

Stanza 85.—If the lord of a house is in the visible hemisphere, the effects of the Bhava will be experienced very shortly. If the lord is in the invisible hemisphere, the results will happen very late. The time of happening corresponds to the period in months or days signified by the number of Rasis intervening between the Bhava concerned and the Rasi occupied by the lord of the said Bhava. Or the results may happen when the Moon next transits the sign occupied by the lord of the concerned Bhava.

NOTES

In this stanza, methods are given for ascertaining the period of happening of the results pertaining to a Bhava. If the lord of a Bhava is in the visible half of the horoscope (7th to 12th houses), the Bhava results materialise very early. If the lord is in the invisible half (1st to 6th), the indications manifest rather late. The other method suggested is this. Find the number of Rasis separating the Bhava and the sign occupied by the lord. Here instructions are not clear as to when to predict 'days' and when to predict 'months'. One has to fall back on one's experience. It is to be assumed that if the concerned planet is in the visible half, the time reckoning should be in terms of days ; if in the invisible half, in terms of months.

The results of the Bhava can also happen when the Moon next transits the sign held by the lord of the Bhava concerned. Suppose in a Prasna chart, one wishes to know the time of marriage. The lord of the 7th Bhava (Sun).is in the 6th, *i.e.*, in the invisible half. This means marriage will be delayed. The lord of the 7th Sun is separated from the 7th, by 12 signs. Marriage may take place within 12 months. Or, the Moon will next transit the sign held by the lord of the 7th after about 24 days. The events may take place then. These are all clues for a clever astrologer to make predictions and he should fall back on his interpretative skill.

लग्नं वा फलदातृगेहमथवा तस्यो च्चभं वा यदा
यायादिन्दुरिनोथवाथ फलदो वाच्यं तदा तत्फलम् ।
भूते वा समये भविष्यति यदा लग्नस्य पापन्वय-
स्तत्कालेऽशुभमादिशेच्छुभसमायोगे शुभं पृच्छताम्
॥८६॥

Stanza 86.—When the Sun or the Moon or the effect-giving planet transits the Lagna, or the sign occupied by the effect-giving planet, or his exaltation sign, the indicated events happen. Whether in the past or in the future good and bad happenings coincide with the transit of Lagna by benefics and malefics respectively.

NOTES

This stanza enables us to predict when good and bad will happen. By good is implied good health etc., while by evil is meant loss of wealth, illness, etc. Three points are considered, *viz.*, (*a*) Lagna, (*b*) the sign occupied by the phaladatru or the effect-giving planet, (*c*) the exaltation sign of (*d*) The indicated event can happen when the Sun or the Moon or the phaladatru transits the above three points. Here an ambiguity arises. Would the Sun and the Moon, whenever they transit the three points, give uniform results or those indicated by the *Phaladatru*. One has only to guess. The 2nd part of the stanza is also open to two kinds of application. One is the happening of good and bad results pertaining to an indicated event—if we confine the malefics and benefics to the three lords mentioned in the first part of the stanza; or good and evil results in a general sense can happen if we interpret the term *benefics* and *malefics* rather widely. I leave it to my intelligent readers to take either interpretation in the light of their experience.

In the following chart suppose the *phaladatru* (effect giver)is Jupiter. Results in his Dasa have to be considered. Then when the Sun or the Moon or Jupiter transits Aquarius (Lagna), Scorpio (sign occupied by effect-giving planet) or Cancer (exaltation sign of phaladatru), the results indicated (by ownership, position etc.) will come to fruition. Out of these three planets here considered,

Rahu		Moon Saturn	
Ascendant			Sun
			Mars Mercury Venus
	Jupiter		Ketu

the Moon and the Sun are malefics. During the earlier transits of these planets over Aquarius, good and bad results (pertaining to Jupiter's indications) will have happened in the past and will happen in the future when they transit Lagna. Instead of assigning the terms malefics or benefics to all the malefic and benefic planets, I would favour their restriction to the three factors considered.

फलप्रदानसमयाः सर्वेषां व्योमचारिणाम् ।
विद्यन्ते केचनान्येपि लिख्यन्ते तेपि सम्प्रति ॥८७॥

Stanza 87.—There are other methods of noting the times of happening of events and they are given below.

कालः स्वर्क्षदिनर्तवो निजगृहस्थार्केन्दु जीवादयः
सर्वेषां स्वदशानिजापहृतयः स्वीयोदयादावपि ।

खेटानां रविचन्द्रयोरयनमप्यत्रोत्तरं दक्षिणं
दातुं स्याद्गुणदोषसम्भवफलं सर्वं बुधैरुह्यताम् ॥८८॥

Stanza 88.—They are (*a*) constellation days of the planets; (*b*) their week-days; (*c*) the Ritus of the planets; (*d*) the period when the Sun, the Moon, Jupiter transit the radical sign by the planet concerned; (*e*) Dasa and Bhukti periods of the planets; (*f*) when the sign of a concerned planet rises or sets. The Sun signifies Uttarayana and the Moon Dakshinayana. The benefic and malefic results to be given by the planets should be intelligently inferred.

NOTES

Suppose Venus occupying Scorpio is the planet in question. He signifies certain events in respect of certain houses, *e.g.*, marriage. Then the event can manifest (*a*) on a day ruled by Bharani, Poorvaphalguni and Poorvashadha; (*b*) on Friday; (*c*) during Vasanta Ritu or spring (March–April); (*d*) when the Sun or the Moon or Jupiter transit Scorpio; (*e*) in the Dasa (major period) and Bhukti (sub-period) of Venus and (*f*) when Scorpio rises or sets.

दशाफलादिनेष्टानिष्टादिना चोक्तमत्र यत् ।
संक्षेपेण तदेहेव विस्तरेण निगद्यते ॥८९॥

Stanza 89.—The good and bad results likely to happen during the different Dasas have already been given briefly earlier. They will be elaborated now.

NOTES

Here the reference is to stanzas 47 and 48 in this chapter.

FAVOURABLE AND UNFAVOURABLE POSITIONS OF PLANETS.

मार्तण्डेनिष्टसंस्थे नृपशिवपितृकोपादि हृत्कोडनेत्र-
व्याध्यस्थिस्रावपित्तामयशिखिपशुभीतास्रनाशात्मपीडाः ।
इष्टस्थे सात्विकत्वं शिवपितृनृपतिप्रीतयस्ताम्रलाभ-
श्चार्थाप्तिः कंबलाध्वाटनतृणकनकाद्यौषधैश्चोद्यमः स्यात्
॥९०॥

Stanza 90.—When the Sun occupies an unfavourable position, the native will suffer from the wrath of the rulers, God Siva, and his own father; diseases in the heart, stomach and the eyes; troubles in the bones; diseases caused by Pitta, fear from quadrupeds and fire, destruction of copper vessels and decline of personal influence. When the Sun is well disposed, the results will be: satwic nature, favour of Siva, father and rulers; acquisition of copper utensils;

increase of wealth through journeys and by trade in woollen goods, grass, gold, leather and medicines.

कोपो राज्ञ्या जनन्या रुगपि कफसमीरास्त्ररुग्वीर्यवत्स्वै-
वैरं कोपश्च दौर्गः कृषिधनयशसां संक्षयोनिष्टगेब्जे ।
राज्ञीदुर्गाप्रसन्नां मुदणुतिलगुलाच्छादनाज्यद्विजस्त्री-
गोनौरत्रादितोर्थः कृषिधनयशसां वृद्धिरिष्टस्थितेब्जे
॥९१॥

Stanza 91.—An unfavourable Moon will give during his Dasa: Queen's anger, dissatisfaction of the mother or her illness; diseases caused by Vatha, Pitta, and impure blood; enmity with superiors and relatives; the fury of Durga, loss of crops, danger to life and ill fame. If favourable: grace of the Queen and Durga, satisfaction of the mother, gain of money by trading in ghee, sugar, clothes, etc., income by chanting mantras, by breeding cattle, and by marine traffic and by dealing in diamonds through the help of women and by increase of crops and increase of fame and riches.

प्रद्वेषः सोदराद्यैः क्षितिकनकविनाशोग्निचोरारिभीतिः
सेनानीरक्तकोपज्वरनयनरुजापातशस्त्राङ्गभङ्गाः ।

भौमेनिष्टस्थितेस्मिन् पुनरितरगते भूमिहेमायुधाप्तिः
सेनानितुष्टतास्याद्धनमरिवधतो भ्रातृतो भूपतेश्च ॥९२॥

Stanza 92.—An unfavourable Mars brings about during his Dasa : Misunderstandings with brothers, loss of landed property and gold, fear from fire, thieves and enemies ; wrath of God Subrahmanya and trouble from military personnel, ailments arising from impure blood, fever, eye diseases, loss of vessels and cuts and wounds in the body caused by weapons. If favourable, there will be acquisition of landed property, gold, weapons, favour of the commander-in-chief, and grace of Lord Subrahmanya, profits from the loss of enemies, brothers and kings.

ज्ञेनिष्टस्थे तु कोपो हरियुवनृपयोर्दुर्वचस्तस्करार्ति-
स्तत्रेष्टस्थेऽश्वहेमक्षितिसुहृदवनीदेवगुर्वर्थलाभाः ।
अर्थो दौत्याच्च शिल्पैः स्तुतिरपि विदुषां वर्धनं बुद्धिवृत्तेः
सिद्धिर्धर्मक्रियाणां लिपिगणितधनं गोपसून्नुप्रसादः ॥९३॥

Stanza 93.—If Mercury is unfavourable, the native suffers from the ire of God Vishnu, and the anger of the heir-apparent, abusive language and troubles from thieves. If favourable, there will be acquisition of horses, gold and lands, friends increase, wealth is acquired through the help of Brahmins and good advisers, sculptural skill and arbitration work. There will be increase of fame, performance of righteous deeds, earning by writing and figures and winning of the grace of God Vishnu.

जीवेनिष्टस्थिते स्याच्छ्रवणतनयरुग्विप्रदेवप्रकोपो
वैरं वा धर्महीनैः पुनरितरगते वर्धनं धीगुणानाम् ।
नित्यं यज्ञेन वेदाध्ययनमनुजपैर्भूपतेश्चर्थलाभो
लाभो दायादहेमांबरहयकरिणां विप्रदेवप्रसादः ॥९४॥

Stanza 94.— Jupiter if unfavourable will indicate ear troubles, sickness to sons, anger of Gods and Brahmins and enmity with wicked people. If favourable : increase of clarity of mind, gain from religious practices, through persons well–versed in recitation of Vedas and through the favour of rulers. Gold, horses and elephants come in unsolicited. Brahmins and Gods bestow blessings.

शुक्रेनिष्टस्थिते स्त्रीजनगदवसनापायलक्ष्मीवियोगाः
शोकः स्नेहान्निषादक्षितिपतिसचिवद्वेषगोरुप्यनाशः ।

इष्टस्थे रूप्यवस्त्राभरणमणिनिधिस्त्रीविवाहार्थलाभः
श्रद्धा गीते क्रियादिष्वपि च महिषगोमित्रमृष्टान्नलाभाः
॥९५॥

Stanza 95.—When Venus is unfavourable, there will be sickness to wife and other female relations, destruction of clothes and decrease of general prosperity ; sorrow caused by love, hatred towards Government servants and low born people come by turns, quadrupeds die in numbers, and silverware is lost. When Venus is favourable, there will be gain of silver utensils, fine clothes, ornaments, diamonds, underground treasures, marriage, gain of money, increase in taste for music, and access to cattle and luxurious food.

मन्देनिष्टस्थिते स्यादनिलकफरुजाज्ञानचौर्यादिकोप-
व्यापत्तन्द्रीश्रमा स्त्रीभृतकतनुभुवां भर्त्सनं व्यङ्गतेष्या ।
इष्टस्थे दुःखनाशः परिणतवनिताभोगदासायसां
पूश्रेणिग्रामाधिपत्यस्य च वरकमहिष्यादिकानां
च लाभः ॥९६॥

Stanza 96.—Saturn afflicted brings in diseases caused by wind and phlegm, ignorance, tendency to steal, etc., irritability, calamities, inertia, physical and mental debility, sarcasm of women and servants and children, dislocation of the limbs and jealousy. If Saturn is favourable, it denotes abatement of sorrows, association with old women, increase of servants and iron goods, headship of a town, acquisition of buffaloes and growth of *varaka* grain.

मन्दोदितं स्वाश्रितभेश्वरोक्तं स्वोक्तं च राहोरथ
भूमिजोक्तम् ।
स्वोक्तं निजाधिष्टितराशिपोक्तं केतोश्च वाच्यं त्रितयं
फलानाम् ॥९७॥

Stanza 97.—The effects of Rahu are similar to those of the lord of the Rasi occupied by him and of Saturn. Ketu will confer results similar to those of lord of the Rasi occupied by him and of Mars.

दोषाः केवलमेव चेद्विपदतीवाराद्विनिर्दिश्यतां
प्रश्ने केवलमेव चेत्खलु गुणा वाच्यास्तथा सम्पदः ।
मिश्रत्वे गुणदोषयोरधिकतामालोच्य वाच्यँफलं
यद्वा दोषजमेव भाग्यविकलाः प्रायोत्र लोका यतः
॥९८॥

Stanza 98.—On analysis, if it is found that the malefic influences alone predominate, then evil should be predicted. If benefic influence predominates, then good must be anticipated. If the influences are mixed, then prediction must be made according to the predominating factor.

निर्याणं विषमामयो निजजनापायो गृहप्लोषणं
स्थानभ्रंशनरेन्द्रकोपजनविद्वेषार्थभूरिव्ययाः ।
चोरार्थापहृतिश्च मानविहतिर्दुष्कीर्तिरेवंविधा
वाच्याः स्युर्विपदो विलोक्य विहगान् भावांश्च
दोषप्रदान् ॥९९॥

Stanza 99.—Death, serious diseases, danger to near relatives, destruction of house, fall from position, wrath of the rulers, unpopularity and loss, waste of money and lands, theft of property, dishonour, ill fame, are the various evil effects. The exact nature of the evil should be determined by carefully studying the different Bhavas.

आरोग्यं नृपमाननं धनसमायानं सुहृत्संभवः
साफल्यं सकलक्रियासु सततं चित्तप्रसादोदयः ।
स्थानप्राप्तिजनानुरागसुयशःसन्तानलाभादयो
वाच्याः स्युः खलु सम्पदोभिमतभावोपेतखेटोचिताः
॥१००॥

Stanza 100.—Good health, royal or governmental favours, gain of money, reconciliation with friends, success in all enterprises, mental peace, elevation to high positions, popularity, fame, birth of children, are the good effects to be predicted by a consideration of the appropriate dispositions of planets.

NOTES

The stanzas giving the results of Dasas of planets, when they are favourable and unfavourable, are clear and need no explanation. But in stanzas 98 to 100 the good and bad effects have been defined with the suggestion that planetary influences should be correctly weighed. If the afflictions predominate, then evil alone should be predicted. The person may, die, become seriously ill, or his relatives, children, wife, brothers etc., may suffer. His house may be set on fire. He may incur the displeasure of the authorities; he may lose his position and influence. His lands may be auctioned. His property may be stolen. He may face dishonour and his reputation may suffer.

If the good influences predominate, disappearance of enemies, access to wealth, gain of property, increase in reputation, mental peace, etc., will be the indications.

When the good and bad aspects are mixed up, the astrologer should use his discrimination and find out whether benefic or malefic aspects are in excess or whether both are equally disposed and then arrive at a conclusion.

In predicting the good or bad nature of the results, the appropriate Bhavas and planets should be considered. Thus if the Sun is the planet afflicted and he is in the 10th, the native suffers the displeasure of the rulers. The Sun in the 4th with a fiery planet may cause destruction of the house due to fire. Similarly if the Sun is the elevated planet in the 10th, there will be rise in official life. If in Lagna with benefic, there will be good health. The task of the astrologer indeed becomes very arduous in balancing the different shades of planetary influences. It is here that he should bring to bear his keen powers of analysis and the gift of synthesis.

CATEGORIES OF KARMA

दृढादृढ क्रियाप्तत्वाच्छुभाशुभफलं द्विधा ।
मनोवाक्कर्मजं तच्च त्रिविधं तद्विदोच्यते ॥१०१॥

Stanza 101.—The good and bad effects are the resultant of two kinds of Karma—Dridha and Adridha. These can again be subdivided into three types of action, *viz.*, mental, verbal and physical.

NOTES

This stanza gives in a nutshell, the theory of Karma. Our actions are of two kinds, *viz.*, Dridha (fixed) and Adridha (not fixed). Whether Dridha or Adridha—Karma may be due to speech (verbal), thought (mental) and bodily actions (physical). The gamut of Karma is all-comprehensive and it cannot be restricted to any particular sphere of thinking or activity.

It is not my purpose to elaborate the theory of Karma in these notes as I have already dealt with it in detail in my *Astrology and Modern Thought*. Reference may also be made to *An Introduction to the Study of Astrology* by my revered grandfather Prof. B. Suryanarain Rao.

छत्रारूढेन्दुलग्नव्ययरिपुमृतिगाः सद्ग्रहाः पापखेटा-
स्तेषां केन्द्रत्रिकोणेष्वपि यदि कथयेद्दुष्कृते सम्प्रवृद्धम् ।
कोपाद्देवस्य शापात्सितिविबुध भवाद्विद्विषां चाभिचारा-
ल्लोकाक्रोशाच्च तत्स्याददृढमपि दृढं चेति वेद्यं द्विधैतत्
॥१०२॥

Stanza 102.—The cause of one's evil Karma and whether it is Dridha or Adridha, is to be ascertained from the disposition of benefics in the 6th, 8th and 12th and of malefics in quadrants and trines. According as these dispositions are from Chathra Rasi, Arudha, Chandra or Lagna, the evil Karma is due to divine wrath, a Brahmin's curse, spells of enemies or people's hatred.

NOTES

In this stanza, we are given a clue to find out the cause of one's bad Karma which has resulted in the man suffering from afflictions. If benefics occupy 6, 8 and 12 from Chathra Rasi and malefics occupy 1, 4, 5, 7, 9, 10, the sins and consequent evil effects are due to fury of Gods. If planets are found in the above places from Arudha at the time of Prasna, the sins are the outcome of Brahmin's curses. If planets occupy such places from the Moon at the time of Prasna, the sins are due to the incantation (mantraic) of enemies. If planets are found in the above mentioned places from the rising sign, the sins and the consequent evil effects are due to people's hatred.

These bad actions may be either deliberate or done out of ignorance or both combined. Here the reference is mainly on Prasna Chart. But we can apply the principles to radical horoscopes also.

चेतोवाक्कर्मजं तद्द्विविधमपि विधोस्तत्र होरादिवर्गे
तिष्ठन् खेटः प्रदद्याद्दृढफलमदृढं भास्वतो गोचरस्थे ।
खेटे पुण्यस्य पाकः पुनरितरगते कर्मणोन्यस्य वेद्य-
श्चित्ताद्ये तत्त्रिके यद्द्विबलखरयुतं तेन दोषानुभूतिः
॥१०३॥

Stanza 103.—The nature of the evil Karma will be Dridha or Adhridha according as the indicative planet is in the house of the Moon or the Sun. When planets are favourably placed, they indicate fruition of good Karma, otherwise that of evil Karma. The mental, verbal or bodily nature of the Karma is revealed by the position of a malefic planet in the 5th, 2nd or 10th house.

NOTES

Man suffers from misfortunes in the shape of loss of wealth, humaliation, loss of name, death of kith and kin. diseases,etc., as a result of evil Karma done in his previous life. This Karma is either Dridha—intentional and deliberate or Aridha accidental or unintentional. In either case the consequence is felt. Whether Dridha or Adridha, the Karma can again be divided into three categories—*kayaka*, arising from bodily actions such as causing physical injury,etc.,*manasika*—arising from mental actions—entertaining evil thought and wishing others evil, and *vachaka* or due to verbal actions—indulging in abusive and filthy language, etc.Benefics in the 6th, 8th and 12th and malefics in trines and quadrants—these planets can be called as indicators—denote that the troubles are due to evil Karma. If these dispositions are from Chakra Rasi, the Karma will be due to God's wrath. Here by God are also meant persons held in reverence such as parents, preceptors and elders. Suppose one deliberately insults or assaults one's parents or elders. Here the nature of Karma is Dhridha, Vachaka and Dridha kayaka. The same is the case when the person harbours evil thoughts. The Karma is Dridha manasika. If on the other hand, one uses impolite language towards an elder through ignorance or slip of tongue or accidentally inflicts physical injury, the nature of Karma is Adridha manasika and Adridha kayaka. The aggrieved party feels pain and this rebounds on the perpetrator of the Karma. Similarly if the benefics are in the above places from Arudha, the evil Karma will be due to a Brahmin's curse. If from Chandra Lagna, the sins are due to black-magic indulged in by enemies. If from Lagna, people's hatred will be the cause. If the indicator is in the Moon's sign or hora, it is Dridha karma—sins deliberately committed. If the indicator is in the house of the Sun, the sins are ignorantly or accidentally got. Similarly planets favourably placed, *i.e.*, benefics in quadrants and trines and malefics in the 6th, 8th and 12th, indicate merit derived from good deeds. If a weak malefic is in the 5th, the sins may be considered as the outcome of mental actions. If he is in the 2nd, they are the results of his words, cruel and unwanted. If he is in the 10th, they are the fruits of his bodily actions.

Venus	Ketu	Mercury Saturn	
Mars			
		Ascendant Rahu Moon Sun, CR.	Jupiter

In the illustration given herewith, Chakra Rasi (CR) is Libra. The three benefics Venus, Mercury and Jupiter are in the 6, 8 and 12 respectively. Malefics are in Kendras. Therefore the person's misfortunes are the result of evil Karma which in turn is due to the wrath of divinity or persons held in equal esteem. Let us assume that the majority of planets occupy Chandra Hora. The Karma is Dridha that is deliberatejy committed. Saturn aspects the 2nd and 10th. The Karma is Kayaka—born out of bodily actions, *i.e.*, the native must have deliberately attacked his parents, men equal to God, preceptors, etc. Some suggest that Chandra and Surya Vargas should be considered instead of thei houses. When malefics are in 3, 6, 8 and 12 from Lagna, from Chandra Lagna, Arudha, etc., then the intensity of the evil Karma gets proportionately increased. If some planets indicate Dridha and some Adridha, here also a certain delicate balancing is called for.

चित्ते वाचि च कर्मणि त्रिषु खरोपेतेषु तैश्च त्रिभि-
र्जायन्ते दुरितानि कर्म सशुभं सासच्च चेतो वचः ।
यद्यत्र क्रियमाणकर्मसु मनःखेदाद्दिरानिष्टया
पापश्चेतसि वाक्च खं च शुभयुक्चेत्कर्म चाश्रद्धया
॥१०४॥

तद्दोषस्तनयापदेधिकतरः पापः परं वाचि चेत्सौम्याः
कर्मणि मानसे च दुरितं वाग्दोषतो जायते ।
तद्दोषोधिकमर्थहाथ रिपुनीचर्क्षे च मौढ्ये खरा-
स्तुङ्गस्वर्क्षसुहृद्ग्रहेष्वपि शुभा दोषे गुणे चाधिकाः
॥१०५॥

Stanzas 104 and 105.—If malefics occupy the 2nd, 5th and 10th houses, evil Karma would have emanated from all the three—thought, word and deed. If malefics occupy only the 2nd and 5th while benefics occupy the 10th, we have to conclude that when we do any work we do it unwillingly, complaining bitterly. If malefics occupy the 5th house while good planets are in the 2nd and 10th, we do our duties carelessly or indifferently without proper attention. Careless actions generally bring in loss of children. If malefics occupy the 2nd, while benefics join the 5th and 10th houses, the evil has issued out of 'words'. This brings about loss of money. If these malefics are in debilitation or occupy inimical places or comust, they cause intense evil. If benefics are in exaltation, in own or friendly houses, the good they give will also be great. On the contrary, if malefics are exalted and if benefics are debilitated, their effects will be little.

IMPRISONMENT AND CAPTIVITY

सूर्यात्सप्तमधर्मधीष्वशुभभे पापौ पितुर्बन्धदौ
कार्यादावृणतश्च बन्धनमिनप्राबल्यदौर्बल्यतः ।

सूर्यस्थर्क्षवशाच्च दूरसविधाद्यूह्यं नवांशैरपि
स्याद्योगोयमिदं स्वकारकवशाद्योज्यं सुतादिष्वपि
॥१०६॥

Stanza 106—If from the Sun two malefics occupy the 7th, 9th and 5th houses which happen to be owned by evil planets, then the father of the questioner is in prison. If the Sun is strong, prison–life is due to some action not liked by the King. If he is weak, it is due to debts. The place of incarceration will be far off, near or midway according as the Sun is in a movable, fixed or common sign. The same principle can be applied to mother, son, brothers, etc., by substituting the appropriate karaka. Navamsa also can be taken into consideration.

कृत्वा लग्नं रवेः स्थाने प्रष्टुर्बन्धोत्र कथ्यताम् ।
लग्ने चरस्थिरद्वन्द्वे बन्धो दूरान्तिकाध्वसु ॥१०७॥

Stanza 107.—By substituting Lagna for the Sun, the questioner's own imprisonment will have to be predicted. If Lagna is movable, jail will be far off; if it is fixed, it will be near and if it is common, it will be midway.

वराहमिहिरेणापि स्वहोरायां समीरितम् ।
लक्षणं बन्धनस्यथ तदप्यत्र विलिख्यते ॥१०८॥

Stanza 108.—Varahamihira, in his *Brihat Jataka*, has touched upon this topic and that has also been noted here.

व्ययधनसुतधर्मगैरसौम्यैर्भवनसमाननिबन्धना विकल्प्या ।
भुजगनिगळपाशभृद्दृगाणैर्बलवदसौम्यनिरीक्षितैश्च तद्वत्
॥१०९॥

Stanza 109.—If malefics occupy the 12th, 2nd, 5th and 9th from Lagna, or if Lagna Drekkana happening to be Sarpa, Nigala or Pasa, is aspected by powerful malefics, the native suffers imprisonment. The nature of jail life corresponds to the nature of Lagna.

NOTES

Either malefics should occupy the 12th, 2nd, 5th and 9th or Lagna falling in the Drekkana of Sarpa, Nigala or Pasa, should be aspected by malefics to cause imprisonment. The nature of the place of incarceration will be in accordance with the nature of the signs where the afflicted planets are situated. In these days of democracy, even when criminals can lead comfortable lives in jails, the last part of the stanza should be applied with great care.

वेश्याहेतुऋणेन वाव्ययगते पापे धनस्थे पुनर्बन्धो
राजकृतोस्य दूषणवशात्पुत्रस्थिते कथ्यताम् ।

तद्धेतुर्नवमस्थिते पितृनिमित्तोयं यथा बध्यते
मेषादिः खलु लग्नगो भुवि तथा पाशादिभिः पृच्छकः
॥११०॥

Stanza 110.—One's incarceration will be due to chronic debts or dancing girls; treason; son or father; according as the evil planets occupy the 12th, 2nd, 5th or 9th. The person will be 'bound' by rope, chain, etc., according to the nature of the Lagna Rasi.

NOTES

If evil planets occupy all the places mentioned in this stanza, then the strongest must be taken as indicating the cause of imprisonment. Aries rules ram, Taurus oxen, etc. If Aries or Taurus is Lagna, the man will be bound by rope. If Leo, by chains, etc.

सौरद्रेकाणे वा भुजङ्गपरिवेष्टितेथवा लग्ने ।
शशिसौराभ्यां दृष्टे बन्धनमिह वाच्यमादेशे ॥१११॥

Stanza 111.—If Lagna falls either in the Drekkana of Saturn or is a Sarpa Drekkana, and is aspected by the Moon and Saturn, then the subject will be imprisoned.

NOTES

This verse is from *Krishneeya*. Saturn's Drekkanas are the last ones of Taurus and Gemini, the 2nd of Virgo and Libra, the 1st of Makara and Kumbha and Surya Drekkanas are the middle of Aries, the first of Leo and the third of Sagittarius.

पापक्षेत्रेषु यमे त्रिकोणचतुरश्रसप्तमेषु गते ।
क्रूरैर्निरीक्ष्यमाणे बन्धोस्तीत्यादिशोत्क्षिप्रम् ॥११२॥

Stanza 112.—If Saturn occupies the 5th, 9th, 4th, 8th or 7th identical with a malefic owned Rasi and is aspected by malefics, one suffers prison life.

NOTES

Malefic-owned Rasis are Aries, Leo, Scorpio, Capricorn and Aquarius. If Saturn occupies any of these signs and is aspected by malefics, incarceration is indicated. But here one should be careful to see in which place the afflictions occur as from Lagna and the Moon.

अचिरेण चरे मोक्षः स्थिरभे मोक्षस्तु दीर्घकालेन ।
द्विशरीरगते सौरे मध्यमकालेन मोक्षः स्यात् ॥११३॥

Stanza 113.—If Saturn occupies a movable sign, the person will be liberated from prison soon; if a fixed sign, he suffers a long-term of imprisonment; and if in a common sign, the period will be neither very long nor very short.

असतामशुभफलानां भेदः प्रोक्तस्तथैव सौम्यानाम् ।
भेदोभीष्टफलानामपि कृष्णीये विलिख्यते सोपि॥११४॥

Stanza 114.— The general effects of the planets whether good or bad, have been detailed before. But the particular effects of the planets have not been given. They are noted in *Krishneeya* which are reproduced herewith for the benefit of the readers.

भौमो रोगं कुरुते भोगं शुक्रस्त्वरोगतां सौम्यः ।
सौरो मरणं दिनकृन्नाशं चिरजीवनं जीवः ॥११५॥

Stanza 115.—Mars is capable of causing sickness ; Mercury, good health ; Venus, enjoyment ; Saturn, death ; the Sun, loss or destruction ; and Jupiter long life.

NOTES

Here the ascribed results happen provided the evil planets are unfavourably situated and benefics favourably disposed.

द्यूनस्थौ कुजभानुजौ खलु रुजे स्यातां तयोः कस्यचि-
द्योगोन्यस्य मदस्थितिश्च मृतये रिप्फोर्थसंस्थौ च तौ ।
पापः स्युश्चतुरश्रगाश्च मृतिदाः प्रोक्तं त्विदं चिन्तनं
भावानां तदधीशकारकविहङ्गानां त्रयाणामपि ॥११६॥

Stanza 116.—Mars and Saturn in the 7th cause sickness. If one is in Lagna and the other in the 7th, or if they are in the 2nd and 12th or if malefics occupy the 4th and 8th, there will be death. These principles should be applied to the Bhava, the lord and the Karaka.

NOTES

These stanzas are capable of any number of interpretations. Mars and Saturn in the 7th cause sickness. It may be 7th from Lagna, or from Lagna lord or from Lagna Karaka. Extending the same principles : If Mars is in the 7th (Kalatrabhava) and Saturn is in the 7th from 7th (Lagna) or *vice versa* or if Mars is in the 8th (2nd from 7th) or 6th (12th from 7th) or if these malefic dispositions obtain from the 7th lord or from Venus, death of the wife may be predicted. In actual practice, all malefics may be considered and not merely Mars and Saturn.

QUARRELS AND MISUNDERSTANDINGS

चन्द्रे पापयुतेथवा भृगुसुते कामेथवा वेश्मनि
स्त्रीभिः स्यात्कलहोऽथ बन्धुकलहः पापे भवेद्बन्धुगे ।
मातृक्लेशकरो शुभोस्तसुखगः सौम्येस्तगे बन्धुगः
पापश्चेदबलावशात्स्वजननीं प्रष्टाधिकं पीडयेत् ॥११७॥

Stanza 117.—If the Moon or Venus in association with malefics is in the 7th or 4th house, there will be quarrels with women. If a malefic occupies the 4th house, the native quarrels with relatives. If malefics occupy the 4th and 7th, mother will suffer from troubles. If a benefic is in the 7th and a malefic in the 4th house, the person ill-treats the mother.

VISIBLE AND INVISIBLE HEMISPHERES

विद्यादृश्यार्धमास्थानमदृश्यं विजनस्थलम् ।
लग्नाधिपः स्थितो यत्र तद्वासी पृच्छको भवेत् ॥११८॥

Stanza 118.—Visible hemisphere indicates a crowded place; invisible hemisphere denotes a lonely retreat. According as the lord of Lagna is in the visible hemisphere, the person lives in a crowded spot or in a lonely place.

NOTES

The visible half of the zodiac are the six houses counted from Lagna *via* the 10th. The remaining six belong to the invisible half.

एवं धनादिभावानां स्पष्टतां च निगूढताम् ।
विद्यादीशैः प्रकाशत्वमपि सूर्येन्दुयोगतः ॥११९॥

Stanza 119.—This principle can be applied to other Bhavas also, so that the open or hidden nature of their significations can be detected. Similarly the association of the Sun and the

Moon reveals the true, *i e.*, the internal or external nature of the Bhavas.

अदृश्यार्धस्थितेस्तैशे प्रष्टः स्याद्गूढकामता ।
स्पष्टकामो भवेत्प्रष्टा द्यूनेशे दृश्यभागगे ॥१२०॥

Stanza 120.—For example, if the 7th lord is in the invisible half, the querist's sensual desires will be hidden. If the lord is in the visible hemisphere, his desires will be quite open and known to all.

शुभोशुभर्क्षे जीर्णं संस्कृतादिभ्यां यदीरितम् ।
तत्सर्वं सर्वभावेषु योजनीयं हि युक्तितः ॥१२१॥

Stanza 121.—Benefic planets, benefic Rasis confer a cultured and fair bride. With regard to all Bhavas, all these factors have to be carefully considered.

॥ इति प्रश्नमार्गे चतुर्दशाध्यायः ॥

पञ्चदशाध्यायः

देवैर्वा धर्मदेवैः फणिपितृगुरुभिर्ब्राह्मणैः प्रेतभूतैः
पीडा या स्यात्कृता सा तदनु भवति या दृग्भवा
वाग्भवा वा ।
या स्याद्भूयो विषोत्था पुनरिह रिपुभिर्या कृता सा च तासां
हेतुश्चापि क्रमेण प्रतिविधिरपि च प्रोच्यते पृच्छकानाम्
॥ १ ॥

Stanza 1.—The miseries of men are due to the wrath of Devas, Dharma-devas, serpents, parents, preceptors, Brahmins, Pretas, and Bhutas. They are eleven in number. They are also due to evil eye, curses, the evil acts directed by enemies and other afflictions. Causes and remedies for such miseries are given for the benefit of the querist.

NOTES

The commentator gives the following causes as the reason why men suffer. (*a*) The anger of the gods, (*b*) the wrath of Dharma devas, (*c*) the fury of the serpent-god, (*d*) the dissatisfaction of the manes, (*e*) curses of seniors and preceptors, (*f*) curses of Brahmins, and (*g*) troubles caused by ghosts and those resulting as a reaction of wounding words and expression, poison and abichara.

Favourable and Unfavourable Karma

दैवानुकूल्यं प्रतिकूलतां वा विचार्य सत्यां
प्रतिकूलतायाम् ।
तदानुकूल्याय विधिर्विधेयो यतस्ततः सम्प्रति कथ्यते
तत् ॥२॥

Stanza 2.—Whether one's past Karma is favourable or unfavourable and in what manner it expresses itself, should be carefully divined by the astrologer.

NOTES

Here the term *deva* means the Karma or destiny factor. What we cannot explain by known causes, falls under Daiva or the Karmic factor.

e.f., पूर्वजन्मकृतं कर्म तद्दैवमिति कथ्यते ।

The causes of Karma—whether caused by wrath of deities, or the curses of parents, etc., have already been given elsewhere.

सर्वेश्वराणां धिषणेस्ति नित्यं सान्निध्यमस्माद्धिषणोनुकूले ।
प्रायोनुकूलास्सकलाश्च देवास्तत्प्रातिकूल्ये सति नानुकूलाः
॥ ३ ॥

Stanza 3.—Jupiter represents the one supreme divinity. If he is favourable, all deities will favour the native. If he is not favourable, all the deities will be unfavourable.

अर्कः शंभुरुदाहृतोखिलगृहेष्वर्को यदि द्वन्द्वभे
द्रेक्काणे प्रथमे गृहोत्र कथितो विघ्नेश्वरो मध्यमे ।
दुर्गा शीतकरो बली स विबलः काळी स एवाबल-
श्चामुण्डीप्रमुखास्तमोगुणजुषो भौमालयस्थो यदि ॥ ४ ॥

Stanza 4.—The Sun irrespective of the sign he is in, represents Siva. He also stands for Subrahmanya or Ganapati according as he occupies the 1st or 2nd Drekkana of a common sign. The Moon if strong stands for Durga; if weak, represents Bhadrakali; and if in addition to being weak he occupies a martian sign, denotes Chamundi with dark attributes.

NOTES

Here the different deities (causing good or evil Karma) rule the fortunes and misfortunes of men :

Planet	*Condition*	*Deity*
The Sun	In all signs	God Siva
The Sun	1st drekkana of a common sign	God Subrahmanya

Planets	*Condition*	*Deity*
The Sun	2nd Drekkana of a common sign	God Ganesha
The Moon	Strong	Durga
The Moon	Weak	Bhadrakali
The Moon	Weak and in martian signs	The darker aspects of Chamundi

Raktheswari, Raktha Chamundi, etc., fall under the category of 'dark aspects'.

कुमारो भैरवादिर्वा स्वाश्रितर्क्षवशान्कुजः ।
चामुण्डीभद्रकाल्याद्याः स चेद्युग्मसमाश्रितः ॥ ५ ॥

Stanza 5.—Mars in odd signs denotes the deities Subrahmanya, Bhairava, etc. In even signs, the deities signified are Chamundi, Bhadrakali etc.

NOTES

Subrahmanya is implied only when the odd sign is a satwic one. Other odd signs signify Bhairava, Chandrakesha, etc. Similarly with reference to even signs, the aggressive or passive nature of the deity depends upon the *satwic*, *rajasik* or *thamasik* nature of the even sign in which Mars is placed.

Satwic signs: Leo, Sagittarius, Cancer and Pisces.

Rajasic signs: Gemini, Libra, Taurus and Virgo.

Thamasic signs: Aries, Aquarius, Scorpio and Capricorn.

AFFLICTIONS DUE TO DEITY

श्रीरामाद्यवतारविष्णुरितरक्षेत्रेषु चन्द्रात्मजो
प्यन्त्यत्र्यंशगतः स्थिरे तु भवने यद्येष गोपालकः :
त्र्यंशेन्त्येत्र स विष्णुरेव हि पुनर्जीवो महाविष्णुर-
प्युक्तोयंह्याखिलेश्वरोत्र तु भिदा ज्ञेया ग्रहर्क्षान्वयात् ॥६॥

Stanza 6.—Mercury in movable and common signs governs Avataras of Vishnu. If he occupies the first and the second Drekkanas of fixed signs, he indicates Sri Krishna. If he occupies the third Drekkana of the same, he stands for Vishnu in general. Jupiter represents Vishnu. As he governs divinity in general, his nature can be understood from the sign he occupies and from the planets he associates with.

NOTES

For example, if Mercury occupies Leo or joins with the Sun or has any Varga connections with the Sun, he governs Siva. If he has any connections with the Moon, he stands for Durga. If he is connected with Mars, he stands for Subrahmanya and so on.

अन्नपूर्णेश्वरी लक्ष्मीर्यक्षी वा भृगुनन्दनः ।
मन्दश्शास्त्रादिकं दैवं राहुः सर्पगणः स्मृतः ॥ ७ ॥

Stanza 7.—Venus signifies Annapoorneswari, Lakshmi and Yakshi. Saturn rules Sastha and Kiratha and Rahu symbolises the 'serpent god'.

NOTES

Venus in own house signifies Annapoorna; in the house of a benefic, Lakshmi and in an evil house Yakshi; or in Satwika signs Annapoorna, in Rajasa signs Lakshmi and in Tamasa signs Yakshi. In odd signs with male planets, Sukra signifies Ganapati.

बाधकाधीश्वरास्सन्तो यदि सूर्यादिखेचराः ।
देवतानां निजोक्तानां पीडां ब्रूयुरनिष्टगाः ॥ ८ ॥

Stanza 8.—When planets owning 'houses of harm' (*badha*) occupy unfavourable places, they cause affliction appropriate to the deity ruled by them.

NOTES

Houses of harm are given in stanzes 110 and 111. Unfavourable houses are 6, 8, 12; and 3 also according to some writers.

कोपस्य कारणं कोपशमनाय प्रतिक्रिया ।
देवतानां ग्रहारूढस्थानभेदादथोच्यते ॥ ९ ॥

Stanza 9.—The reasons for the 'wrath' of the deities and the remedies for alleviating them can be known by the positions of planets in various houses.

सूर्यादीनां ग्रहाणां व्ययभवनगतः पापखेटो यदि स्या-
त्वोक्तानां देवतानां वपुषि विकलता डुण्डुभस्पर्शनं
स्यात् ।
संयोगे मान्दिराह्वोरथ रविजयुतौ जीर्णता वाशुचिर्वा
योगे भौमस्य रक्षाविहतिरभिहिता रक्षकस्वान्तभेदात्
॥१०॥

Stanza 10.—A malefic in the 12th from the Sun and other planets, signifying the wrath of deities, suggests disfigurement of the idol of the said deity. Gulika or Rahu, conjoining the anger-signifying planets, denotes the idol is polluted by the contact of Dundubha. Saturn's association reveals that the idol or temple or both have become worn out and polluted. Martian association indicates that the deity is not well looked after by the temple-guardians owing to dissensions amongst themselves.

लग्नस्थे पापयुक्ते सति खलु विहगे बिम्बदोषोत्र वाच्यो
बिंबं भिन्नं हि तस्मिन् धरणितनुभुवा शुद्धिरेवान्य-
खेटैः ।
बिंबं तत्र प्रदेयं भवति खलु मुदे खेचरैंथालयस्थे
जीर्णं वेश्मालयं तन्नवमथ कुरुतां दीयतां वान्यवेश्म
॥११॥

Stanza 11.—If the above mentioned planet occupies Lagna and joins with an evil planet, the idol is not in proper order. If the evil planet is Mars, the idol is broken; if Saturn and other evil planets, it is dirty and polluted. If the angry planet in conjunction with an evil one occupies the 4th house, the temple is a very old one and requires repairs.

NOTES

Here Lagna and the 4th house should also be 'houses of harm'. 'Not in proper order' implies cracks or uncleanliness. If the idol is broken, it is to be changed. If it is unclean, purificatory ceremonies have to be performed.

PALLIATIVES FOR AFFLICTIONS

नृत्तं द्यूनगते कुजार्कगृहगे खेटे प्रदीपः स्मृतः
शुक्रेन्द्वालयगे तु पायसमपि क्षीरं घृतं वा पुनः ।

बौधे चन्दनमार्यमन्दिरगते माला प्रसूनानि वा
मन्दर्क्षे खलु भूषणानि वसनं तत्तन्मुदे दीयताम् ॥१२॥

Stanza 12.—When the angry–planet is in the 7th house, the palliative is divine dance. If he occupies the signs of Mars and the Sun, illumination must be arranged; in those of the Moon or Venus, offering of milk, ghee and *payasa*; Jupiter, anointment with sandal paste; and Saturn, offering of ornaments and dress.

NOTES

If the 'angry planet' is in the 7th house, one should engage the performance of 'divine dance'; in the houses of the Sun and Mars, arrange 'illumination'; in the signs of the Moon or Venus, offer milk, ghee and *payasa*(sweetened rice or other grain preparation) as oblations. If he is in the house of Mercury, anoint the idol with sandalwood paste. If he happens to be in the house of Jupiter, adorn the idol with garlands of flowers and worship with sacred flowers. If he is in the house of Saturn, offer ornaments and dress.

रन्ध्रगे कर्मसंस्थे च पूजा वा बलिकर्म वा ।
गीतं वाद्यं च रिप्फस्थे तत्तत्प्रीत्यै प्रदीयताम् ॥१३॥

Stanza 13.—If the Badhaka planet is in the 8th or 10th house, perform puja or bestow Bali

Karmas. If he is in the 12th, employ music and sounding of drums.

NOTES

Worship to the deity should be offered both in the morning and in the evening with due observance of spiritual disciplines.

लग्नादौ प्रतिबिंबदानजपपूजाधामसंतर्पणै
रुक्शान्तिः प्रतिकारनृत्तबलिदेवोपासनैश्च क्रमात् ।
दन्तिस्कन्धसमर्पितेन बलिनाम्भस्तर्पणेनान्यगे
बाधोक्तौ तु तदीश्वरे न च ततः प्रोक्तं न किञ्चिद्व्यये
॥१४॥

Stanza 14.—Remedies for the disposition of 'the angry planet' in Lagna and other houses are respectively the gifting away of one's own image (pratibimbadana), recitation of mantras (japa), worship of God (puja), construction of temples (dhama), feeding (santarpana), pratheekara bali, dancing before the deity (nrithya), Propitiatory oblation (bali), invocations (devopasana), dantiskandha, dedication (tarpana). As the 12th house is not a 'house of harm', its lord is also not harmful.

NOTES

The remedial measures given in this stanza are according to other treatises, which the author quotes for ready reference

अर्के वार्कगृहस्थे वा विहगेनिष्टसंस्थिते ।
देवाराधनमाधेयं पृच्छतां रोगशान्तये ॥१५॥
चन्द्रे वा तत्गृहस्थे वा यवागूप्रतिपादनम् ।
शंखाभिषेकधाराद्यमपि देवे विधीयताम् ॥१६॥
देवे दीपसमर्पणम् च हवनं भौमे च तत्क्षेत्रगे
चान्द्रौ तद्गृहगे च नृत्तकरणं जीवे तत्क्षेत्रगे ।
कर्तव्यं द्विजभोजनं च वितरेद्देवाय होमादिकं
शुक्रे तद्गृहगे च रोगशमनायान्नं प्रदेयं बहु ॥१७॥
मन्दे मन्दगृहस्थे वा विहगेनिष्टसंस्थिते ।
नीचानामन्नदानं स्याद्भूदानं चार्तिशान्तये ॥१८॥

Stanzas 15 to 18.—If the Sun, the Moon,etc., are 'angry' or if the 'angry' planet occupies the sign of the Sun, Moon,etc., the palliatives, in the order of planets are divine worship (Devaradhana), Sankabhisheka and free distribution of rice-water, illumination and havanas, dance before deity, homas and feeding Brahmins, liberal feeding, and feeding of all classes of people.

NOTES

Here the reference is to the Moon etc., being themselves afflicted, or 'afflicted planet' occupying the signs of the different planets. Thus if an 'angry' Sun or any planet occupying Leo joins an unfavourable house, 'Aaradhana' should be performed. An angry Moon or a planet in Cancer requires the free distribution of rice water to the poor. An angry Mars or a planet occupying his houses will be pacified by illumination and 'Homas'. 'Natya' (ceremonial dance) is recommended for Mercury or for a planet occupying the sign of Mercury. Jupiter and the planets occupying his signs will be satisfied by free feeding of Brahmins and offering of ornaments. Venus and the planets occupying his house will be easily satisfied by the free feeding of the people in general. And Saturn and the planets occupying his signs require the feeding of backward classes.

लग्नस्थेषु ससत्स्विनादिषु वदेत्तद्देवतानुग्रहं
प्रष्टृयामथ बाधकालयगते धर्माधिपे प्राक्चिरम् ।
यत्किञ्चित्समुपास्य दैवतममुष्योपेक्षया साम्प्रतं
तत्कोपोस्ति भजेत दैवतमदो भद्रार्थमित्यादिशेत् ॥१९॥

Stanza 19.—If any planet in association with a benefic occupies Lagna, then say that the deity governed by that planet will favour the native. If the lord of the 9th occupies 'the house of harm', then the deity, he used to worship before, has been neglected and hence the trouble.

MISAPPROPRIATION OF DEITY'S PROPERTY

बाधकाद्यहितस्थाननाथे लाभार्थगे ग्रहे ।
तत्तद्दैवतकोपः स्याद्देवस्वस्यापहारतः ॥२०॥

Stanza 20.—If the lords of the 'houses of harm' occupy the 2nd or the 11th, then it must be construed that the native has misappropriated the property of the deity signified by the planet concerned.

NOTES

If the lord of 6, 8 or 12 occupies either the 2nd or the 12th, then the native's suffering will be due to the curse or wrath of the deity ruled by the said lord, whose property the native will have misused.

NATURE OF MISAPPROPRIATED PROPERTY

हेतुर्धातुरुदाहृतश्चरगृहे धतुग्रहे वोदिते
मूलं मूलखगे स्थिरे द्वितनुभे जीवश्च जीवग्रहे ।
मूलं भूमिमहीरुहाद्यमुदितं हेमादयो धातवो
जीवा मर्त्यचतुष्पदप्रभृतयो राशेस्समानाश्च ते ॥२१॥

Stanza 21.—The misappropriated property will be Dhatu, Moola or Jeeva, according as the Lagna happens to be either chara, sthira or dwiswabhava ; or the planet occupying the Lagna happens to be a Dhatu, Moola or Jeeva one.

NOTES

If movable signs happen to be Lagna or if a Dhatu planet occupies Lagna, misappropriation of mineral wealth such as gold, silver,copper, etc., is the cause of the deity's displeasure ; if fixed signs happen to be Lagna or if the planet ruling 'Moola' is in it, misappropriation of 'Moola Dravyas' such as lands, trees, plants, etc., will be the cause. If common signs be the Lagna or Jeeva Grahas occupy it, then misappropriation of 'Jeeva Dravyas', *viz*., living beings (man, quardapad, etc.), is the causc of the anger. Here again the planet must be a Badhaka. The position of lord of Lagna should also be similarly considered. A Badhaka (*i.e*., the lord of the 3rd, 6th or 11th) should occupy the Lagna. The Dhatu, Moola or Jeeva signified by the planet would be the property misused by the afflicted person ; or the mere fact of the Lagna being chara (movable), sthira (fixed) aad dwiswabhava (common) would give the clue as to the source of affliction. Just as Lagna, the 2nd house can also be considered.

जीवे हेतौ त्वात्मना कल्पितानां पश्वादीनामीश्वरस्या-
प्रदानात् ।
कोपो देवस्याप हृत्याथवैषां जीवार्थं वागर्पितानर्पणाद्वा
॥२२॥

Stanza 22.—Whenever the cause is found to be 'Jeeva', it must be inferred that the native vowed to present cattle as free gifts to the Diety, but did not act up to it; or he misappropriated the cattle for himself; or having promised to give money, etc., for any person or animal connected with the Deity, he retracted his promise.

धातौ हेतौ देयहेमाद्यदानात्स्वीकाराद्वा देवसंबन्धिनोस्य ।
मूले हेतौ भूमिधान्यादिकानां कोपो देवस्यापहाराद्यवधैः ॥२३॥

Stanza 23.—When 'Dhatu' is the cause of the Deity, the native has not acted up to the vow to give money as free gift or misappropriated the Deity's wealth. Similarly for 'Moola' he should be considered as having misused lands, trees, grain, etc., endowed to the Deity.

चन्द्राराह्यसिताः सूर्यशुक्रौ ज्ञार्यौ चरादयः ।
धतुर्मूलं च जीवश्च क्रमेण ग्रहराशयः ॥२४॥

Stanza 24.—The Moon, Mars, Rahu and Saturn, and all movable signs signify Dhatu. The Sun and Venus and all fixed signs represent Moola. Mercury and Jupiter and all common signs denote Jeeva.

चन्द्रारोरगसौरैर्धातुर्मूलं किलार्कशुक्राभ्याम् ।
जीवो जीवबुधाभ्यां मेषाश्विन्यादि धात्वादि ॥२५॥

Stnaza 25.—According to *Krishneeya*, the Moon, Mars, Saturn and Rahu are Dhatu. The Sun and Venus are Moola. Mercury and Jupiter are Jeeva. Similarly the signs Aries, etc., and the stars Aswini, etc., should be considered as Dhatu, Moola and Jeeva in regular order.

NOTES

They are to be considered in order of Dhatu, Moola and Jeeva in succession. With regard to Nakshatras, Aswini, Bharani, Krittika, Rohini, etc., represent Dhatu, Moola, Jeeva, Dhatu, etc., in cyclic order.

जीवो जीवेन वाच्यः क्षितिसुतफणिनौ धातुदौ सर्वपक्षे
धातुर्मूलं विकल्पाद्रविरवितनयौ द्वौ च धत्तो द्वयं च ।
जीवो मूलं च तद्वद्बुधभृगुतनयौ धातुजीवौ शशाङ्को
धातुर्मूलं च जीवः क्रमश इह मता राशयो वै चराद्याः
॥२६॥

Stanza 26.—According to all views, Jupiter represents 'Jeeva', and Mars and Rahu 'Dhatu'. The Sun stands for Dhatu only and Saturn for Moola only. According to some others, both these planets stand for both Dhatu and Moola.

In the same way, Mercury stands for Jeeva and Venus for Moola, while yet some say that both these planets stand for both Jeeva and Moola. The Moon stands for both Dhatu and Jeeva. Aries onwards indicate Dhatu, Moola, etc., in regular order.

NOTES

Stanza 26 is clear enough. But in view of the conflicting views, we can take the principles given in stanza 24.

धर्मदैवकृता बाधा तदनु पोच्यतेत्र तु ।

अर्कः शंम्वादिभिः पद्यैस्तद्भिदा च.वगम्यताम् ॥२७॥

Stanza 27.—The affliction caused by the deities—the Sun representing Siva, etc., should be considered as given in previous stanzas.

NOTES

Dharma Daivas or deities are to be understood as given in stanzas 4, 5. 6 and 7.

INTENSITY OF DEITY'S WRATH

वाधाधीशे गतवति सुखं वाधकस्थानसंस्थे

वेश्मेशे वा सुखपतिगृहाधिष्ठिते बाधकेशे ।

वेश्मेशे वाप्यमुकगृहगे धर्मदैवस्य बाधा

वाच्या प्रष्टुः पुनरधिकता लक्षणाधिक्यतोस्याः ॥२८॥

Stanza 28.—If the Lord of the 'house of harm' is in the 4th; or if the Lord of the 4th house occupies a 'house of harm'; or if the lord the 'house of harm' occupies the sign of the lord of the 4th; or if the lord of the 4th occupies the sign owned by the 'lord of harm'; then the native is subject to the wrath of deity.

NOTES

'Houses of harm' have already been enumerated in the earlier stanzas. Lord of the house of harm in the 4th sign or *vice versa*, Lord of the 4th in the sign of a *badhara* planent or a badhaka planet in the sign of 4th Lord indicates that the querist's sufferings is due to the anger of the deity appropriate to the badhaka planet. The *badha* or affliction will be due to the cessation of the appropriate ritas that were conducted for the deity.

चतुर्थनाथस्य तु दैवतं यत्तस्यानुरूपं खलु धर्मदैवम् ।
तत्प्रीतये यत्क्रियते स्वपूर्वैः पूजादिकं तन्तु विधेयमत्र
॥२९॥

Stanza 29.—Determine the 'family deity' as per the 4th lord and recommend the resumption of the old rites.

कोपे हेतुः प्रतिविदिरमुष्यापि यो देवतानां
पूर्वं प्रोक्तः स इह सुधिया योजनीयोपि योज्यः ।

बाधासंस्थे शशिनि च रवौ धर्मदैवस्य बाधा
वाच्या भक्त्या प्रतिसममिदं पूजनीयं समृध्यै ॥३०॥

Stanza 30.—The causes and remedies detailed before regarding the 'anger of Gods' may be repeated in this connection also. If the Sun and the Moon occupy the house of harm, the source of affliction will be the anger of 'family deities'. They must be worshipped with devotion for prosperity.

ANGER OF SERPENT GOD

जीवः सन्बाधकेशो व्ययमृतिरिपुगो यद्यहेः केन्द्रसंस्थः
सर्पाणामुत्तमानां यदि स सुरगुरुर्मान्दिकेन्द्रेधमानाम् ।
पीडा वाच्याथ बाधाभवनमुपगते चोरगे सर्पबाधा
तेषां हीनोत्तमत्वं शशिदिनकरयोर्योगवीक्षादिभिः
स्यात् ॥३१॥

Stanza 31.—If Jupiter as lord of a 'house of harm' occupies the 6th, 8th or 12th and these happen to be the kendras of Rahu, then it must be inferred that the person has earned the 'wrath' of 'superior serpents'. If Jupiter happens to be in the kendras of Gulika, inferior ones have turned against him. If Rahu occupies the 'house of harm', then the trouble is from serpents. In this yoga also, if Rahu has any connection with the Sun, then the trouble is from good serpents; if with the Moon, from bad ones.

राहौ बाधकषष्ठरन्ध्रखगते कार्यो बलिः प्रीतये
वेश्मस्थे खलु चित्रकूटकरणं गानक्रिया रिष्फगे ।
लग्नेस्ते च सुधापयोवितरणं नृत्तक्रिया वास्तगे
स्थानेष्वेष्वपि कीर्तनात्प्रतिविधेर्बाधोच्यतां भोगिनाम्
॥३२॥

Stanza 32.– If Rahu is in the 6th, 8th or 10th or in the house of harm, Sarpa Bali should be performed; if in the 4th, Chitra Kuta stone should be dedicated to the Serpent God; if in the 12th, 'singing' must be arranged; if in Lagna, milk and 'siddhapayasa' (milk and water) should be offered; and if in the 7th house, devotional music must be sung.

स्थानेष्वष्यखिलेषु सर्वबलिरेवोदीर्यतां वा पुन-
स्तृप्यन्त्युत्तमभोगिनस्तु बलिना नीचास्तु गानादिभिः ।
सर्वेषां बलिकर्म तुष्टिकरणं वक्तव्यमेवं हि वा
सर्पप्रतिरवश्यमेव करणीयारोग्यपुत्राक्षये ॥३३॥

Stanza 33.—Whatever be the house Rahu occupies, Sarpa Bali is to be performed. Some say that good serpents alone will be pacified by Sarpa Bali, while songs and dance are required to allay the fury of bad ones. If the serpents are not satisfied, sickness and other calamities may come in. If they are satisfied, children, good health and general prosperity will come in.

अण्डानां चरगे किशोरफणिनां नाशोसुरे द्वन्द्वगे
लग्नस्थे तदिदं द्वयं स्थिरगते बाधाकरो भूरुहाम् ।
कृत्वाण्डान्यहयश्च नीचफणिनां ताम्रेण हेम्ना मुदे
दोयान्युत्तमभोगिनां यदि नगा नष्टाश्च तान् स्थापयेत्
॥३४॥

Stanza 34.—If Rahu occupies a movable sign, the curse is due to the wanton destruction of the serpents' eggs. If he is in a common sign, it is due to killing of small ones. If he is in a fixed sign, it is the result of felling trees found near the serpent's abode. If such destruction is found, eggs and small serpents of gold and copper should be made and installed in the places of worship. For destruction of trees, fresh ones should be planted.

एकादश चरे लग्ने द्वन्द्वे सप्त स्थिरे नव ।
अण्डानि चाहयश्चेति सम्प्रदायविदां वचः ॥३५॥

Stanza 35.—According as Lagna is movable, fixed or common, the 11, 9 or 7 images (of eggs or small serpents) made in gold or copper, should be installed, according to tradition.

राहुर्मान्दियुतस्तदस्तनवमापत्यस्थितो वा यदि
प्रषुः स्यात्फणिबाधनं क्षितिसुतः केन्द्रे तु सहोर्यदि ।
बाधाहेतुरुदीर्यतां फणिगृहे क्षोणीरुहच्छेदनं
भूमेर्वा खननं विहिंसनमहेर्वल्मीकभेदोथवा ॥३६॥

Stanza 36.—The curse of serpents is to be inferred if Rahu conjoins Mandi, or if he is in the 5th, 7th or 9th from him. If Mars occupies a kendra of Rahu, the reasons for their trouble are destruction of trees or removing the earth or killing them or levelling their abodes or setting fire to the trees near or ignoring to replant fresh trees or breaking their favourite anthills.

यद्वोद्यानमहीरुहादिदहनं वा चित्रकूटच्छिदा
राहोः केन्द्रगतः पुनर्यदि शनिर्मान्दिश्च नागालये ।
मूत्रोच्छिष्टशकृद्विसर्गकरणं निष्ठीवनं वान्तिके
चण्डालोपगतिश्च सौरिभकरिप्रक्षोभणं वा पुनः ॥३७॥

Stanza 37.—If Saturn and Gulika occupy the kendras of Rahu, say that the abode of serpents has become unclean and polluted by heaping urine, stools, etc., all round, or by allowing sinners and other low-minded people to approach their quarters, or by allowing elephants to trample on them or by freely ploughing the places with bullocks.

मान्दिः केन्द्रगतो यदीह फणिनो निष्टीवनं मैथुनं
मूत्रोच्छिष्टशकृद्विसर्ग उत वा नागालये वान्तिके ।
वृक्षाद्यं यदि चेत्प्रणष्टमिह तत् कार्यं पुनः पूर्व-
वत्त्यक्तोच्छिष्टमलादिसंभव इदं पुण्याहमप्याचरेत् ॥३८॥

Stanza 38.—If Gulika alone stands in a kendra of Rahu, the abodes of the serpents have become unclean by spitting on them or by co-habitation or by excreting, etc., near them. If Saturn and Gulika occupy the kendras, the surroundings of their abode also should be well guarded and kept clean by fresh trees being planted and by regular rites of purification.

PARENTAL CURSES

भौमर्क्षांशकयोरशीतकिरणो बाधागतश्चेत् पितुः
शापेस्त्येत्रमुहृत्प्रभुर्यदि भवेच्छापं जनन्या वदेत् ।

पित्रोः शाप इनोडुनाथगृहयोश्चानिष्टगे स्यात् खरे
शुश्रूषार्थ समर्पणादिभिरिह प्रीतिं विधद्यात्तयोः ॥३९॥

Stanza 39.—According as the Sun or the Moon occupies the 'house of harm' which should happen to be the sign or Navamsa of Mars, the native is under the curse of the father or the mother. A malefic in Leo or Cancer which happens to be an unfavourable house from Lagna indicates the same result. To get rid of these curses, the parents should be better served if they are alive and their annual ceremonies must be performed with great devotion if they are dead.

पापश्चेद्बाधकस्थः सुरगुरुसहितस्तद्गृहे वा द्विजानां
देवानां वास्ति शापो यदि रविभवने तद्युतो वात्र पापः ।
पूर्वेषां वा गुरूणां यदि स धरणिजस्तर्हि शापो महान्
स्यात्
प्रीतिं देवद्विजानां स्वगुरुजनमनः प्रीणनं चात्र कुर्यात्
॥४०॥

Stanza 40.—If an evil planet is in the 'house of harm' in association with, or in the sign of Jupiter, there will be the curse of Brahmins and Devas. If the 'house of harm' is Leo or the Sun is there, the curse is again due to the dissatisfaction of father, grand-father or ancestors or seniors. This is known as Purva Sapa. If the evil planet happens to be Mars, the nature of the curse is very intense. Hence their dissatisfaction must be removed by suitable amends.

CURSES OF ELDERS

षष्ठेशो नवमे रिपौ नवमपः स्याच्चेत् पितुर्वा गुरोः
पूर्वेषामथवात्मनः स्वविषयं विज्ञेयमप्रीणनम् ।
सूर्ये षष्ठगते तदीशसहिते वा वाच्यमेतत् पितु-
श्चन्द्रेणापि चतुर्थषष्ठपतितश्चैवं जनन्या वदेत् ॥४१॥

Stanza 41.—If the lord of the 6th is in the 9th or if the lord of the 9th is in the 12th, then the father or preceptor or a family elder is not well disposed towards the native. The Sun occupying the 6th house or conjoining the 6th lord; and the Moon, similarly disposed, denotes respectively father's and mother's displeasure.

TROUBLES FROM GHOSTS

अब्ददीक्षादिलोपेन प्रेता याताः पिशाचताम् ।
स्वजनान् बाधमानास्ते चरन्तीति खलु स्मृतिः ॥४२॥

Stanza 42.—It is said if the obsequies of a person have not been properly performed, his soul without getting the necessary liberation will be wandring as a ghost molesting his kith and kin.

बाधा प्रेतोद्भवा स्यात् स्थितवति गुळिके बाधकेनिष्टभे वा
तत्रारर्क्षांशसंस्थो यदि कुजसहितो मान्दिरारेक्षितो वा ।
प्रेतः स्यादग्निशस्त्रप्रभृतिकृतमृतिर्मन्दसंबन्ध एवं
मान्देश्चेत् प्रेत एष स्वविरहिततया दुःखितः सन् परेतः
॥४३॥

Stanza 43.—If Gulika occupies the 'house of harm' or an unfavourable place, the person suffers troubles from ghosts. If he however occupies the sign or Navamsa of Mars or is associated with or aspected by Mars, then the man had an unnatural death, such as from burns, deadly weapons, or diseases like small pox, etc. If Gulika is in any way connected with Saturn, then the man will have died of misery and penury in a lonely and foreign place.

प्राप्तो मृत्युमसौ भुजङ्गदशनाद्युक्तेक्षिते राहुणा
नद्यादौ पतनेन तोयभवने मान्दौ सपापान्वये ।

संबन्धे गुळिकस्य चैवमासतां प्रेतास्तु दुर्मृत्यवो
विज्ञेया गुळिकांशराशिवशतो वाच्या च पुंस्त्रीभिदा
॥४४॥

Stanza 44.—If Gulika just mentioned has any connection with Rahu, then the person had died of serpent-bite. If Gulika is connected with evil planets and occupies a watery sign, then death will have been due to drowning. In this manner, by noting the connection of Gulika with evil planets, the unnatural causes of death resulting in the person becoming a Preta should be ascertained. The sex of the dead person depends upon the odd or even nature of the sign and Navamsa occupied by Gulika.

मन्देभ्र्रात्रादिभावस्थितितदधिपतत्कारकेक्षान्वयद्यैः
प्रेताः स्युः सोदराद्या स्थिरभवनगते मन्दजे प्रेत एषः ।
मृत्युं प्राप्तस्त्विदानीं स यदि चरगतः प्राक्तनः सोथ
मान्दौ
वेश्मस्थे तत्पतीक्षान्वयवति गृहसंबन्धवान् नान्यथा
चेत् ॥४५॥

Stanza 45.—If Gulika occupies Bhavas indicating brothers, etc., or is in any way connected with the lords or karakas of the respective Bhavas, then the dead person would be the brother, etc. If Gulika is in a fixed sign, the person died recently; if in a movable sign, long ago; if in the 4th, or connected with the lord of the 4th, the Preta or ghost is some way connected with the family. Otherwise the ghost is foreign to the house.

प्रेतस्य बालता वाच्या मान्दौ राश्यादिसंस्थिते ।
राश्यन्तस्थे जरन्नेव मध्यस्थे वय उह्यताम् ॥४६॥

Stanza 46.—If Mandi occupies the first part of a Rasi, then the Preta or ghost is that of an infant; if he occupies the last part, the ghost is that of an aged person. If in the middle, then it will be middle aged.

चन्द्राद्यालयतद्युक्ते मान्दावेकादिकं वयः ।
प्रेतस्यैके स्वबाल्यादिवशादुडुपतेर्वयः ॥४७॥

Stanza 47.—The age of the 'ghost' will also correspond to the age of the lord of the house in which Gulika is placed. In determining the Moon's age, however, his *avasthas* should be considered.

NOTES

The age of the dead person can be determined in another way. Note the position of Gulika in the various houses and calculate the years allotted to the lord of each house, or note the planet who associates with Gulika and calculate his years. Moon gives 1 year, Mars 2, Mercury 9, Venus 20, Jupiter 18, the Sun 20 and Saturn 50 years. In fixing the age of the Moon, there is another view. The avastha of the Moon determines the age. That is, if the Moon is in *balya avastha,* the Preta will be that of a child.

प्रेतस्य जातिजिज्ञासा जायते यदि कुत्रचित् ।
मान्द्याधिष्ठितराश्यंशजातिं तत्र विनिर्दिशेत् ॥४८॥

Stanza 48.—The caste and age to which the dead man belonged and the object are to be ascertained by noting the nature of the Rasi and Navamsa occupied by Gulika.

NOTES

The caste of the Preta in its worldly life should be ascertained on the basis of the Rasi and Amsa occupied by Gulika. Whether Rasi or Amsa should be taken, is again a problem to be determined by the astrologer's ability. Pisces is Brahmin, Aries is Kshatriya, Taurus is Vaisya and Gemini is Sudra. The triangular signs have similar 'castes'. According to some commentators, the caste of the Preta should be known from the caste of the lord of the sign occupied by Gulika. The castes of the planets are thus disposed : Brahmin—Jupiter and Venus; Kshatriya—Mars and the Sun; Vaisya—the Moon; Sudra—Mercury; and other so called low castes—Saturn. Of course other tendencies and objects of the Preta in afflicting the person should be guessed by noting the planetary strengths, exaltations, evil associations, dispositions, etc., of these lords.

REMEDIAL MEASURES

प्रेतबाधामिति ज्ञात्वा कार्यावश्यं प्रतिक्रिया ।
आपन्नो यदि तत्प्रीतौ सम्पच्चात्राभियुक्तवाक् ॥४९॥

Stanza 49.—Having ascertained that the affliction is due to troubles from ghosts, remedial measures should be adopted. Though the effects of trouble may be slow, the results of their favour will be easily seen.

कोपः प्रेतस्याकुर्यात्तनयविहननं च मयादीननर्थां
स्तत्प्रीत्यै पार्वणाद्यं पितृगणमनसः प्रीणनं श्राद्धकर्म ।
कुर्याच्च क्षेत्रपिण्डं तिलहवनमथो ब्राह्मणानां च भुक्तिं
प्रीताः प्रेतास्त्वमीभिर्विदधति सकलाः सम्पदः सन्ततिं च
॥५०॥

Stanza 50.—It is the 'anger' of *pretas* that brings about the death of children, sickness and poverty. To counteract such afflictions, *shraddhas*, *kshetra pindas*, *tilavahana*, etc.,should be carefully performed followed by the feeding of Brahmins. These remedies pacify the *pretas* and contribute to general well-being and prosperity of the person concerned.

EVIL EYE

अथ दृष्टिभवा बाधाः कथ्यन्ते तत्र ये नराः ।
नार्योऽथवाग्रहैर्बाध्याः शास्त्रोक्तान् कीर्तयामि तान् ॥५१॥

Stanza 51.—Drishti badha, the trouble that is brought about by seeing some unusual, uncommon 'grahas' capable of mischief will now be enumerated.

लुब्धं क्रूरं भयार्तं हृषितमतिशठं पूर्ववैरानुबद्धं
नष्टद्रव्यं वियुक्तं प्रीतहतमशुचिं प्राप्तकालं सरोगम् ।
हासान्धं कान्तदेहं निधिविलयकरं कातरं भूषिताङ्गं
रात्रावेकाकिनं च स्मरमथनगणास्तं पुमांसं ग्रसन्ति
॥५२॥

Stanza 52.—Persons who are miserly, or cruel in nature, or overpowered by extreme fear, thirst, or fatigued by extreme sexual indulgence, or stubborn, or spiteful, or ruined in wealth, or deserted by all, or disappointed, or unclean, or sickly, or maddened with joy, or very handsome, or squandering spend-thrifts, or deprived of mental strength, or having many ornaments on their bodies, and wandering alone in the nights, and persons to whom misfortunes are near, are attacked by five Bhutas.

तैलाभ्यक्तां प्रसूतामभिनवसुरतां मद्यपानानुरक्तां
नग्नामुत्पन्नसत्वां स्मरशरविवशां मुह्यमानां विहारैः ।
रथ्याशृङ्गाटकस्थामृतुसमययुतां पुंश्चलीकां रुदन्ति-
मेकान्तां कान्तदेहां स्त्रियमपि विषमा गुह्यकाः
संस्पृशन्ती ॥५३॥

Stanza 53.—Women anointed with oil, or in confinement, or engaged in sexual intercourse for the first time after puberty, or deeply drunk, or naked, or in pregnancy, or intensely passionate or fatigued by sensual and sexual pleasures; or standing often in streets, parks and junctions of highways; or having menstrual period, or steeped in immorality, or always complaining and crying or moving; or bewitchingly beautiful, are affected by *guhyakas*.

NOTES

The above three stanzas are from *Sarasangraha*.

Cause of Evil Eye

ग्रहाणां पीडने यानि कारणानिह तानि च ।
तेषां स्थानानि चोच्यन्ते परिहाराय दूरतः ॥५४॥

Stanza 54.—With a view to devising antidotes, the reasons for the attacks of these spirits and the spots from which they attack will be now taken up.

अवमानमृणं वैरं विघ्नो भाग्यविपर्ययः ।
ईश्वराज्ञा च कल्प्यन्ते कारणं ग्रहपीडने ॥५५॥

Stanza 55.—As a result of disrespect, debts, enmity and failure, man's good luck wanes and troubles from *grahas* arise as decreed by the Supreme Being.

NOTES

This stanza is variously interpreted. Disrespect implies irreverence to any divinity or deity. If one deprives the deity of what is due to it by way of gifts, pujas, etc., it constitutes a debt. The third is the old inherited enmity. Failure in one's debt towards the deity constitutes the fourth source of trouble. As a result of these four causes, the fortunes of the man are said to decline and he is said to suffer untold miseries. Divine Law orders punishment and then the troubles from grahas come in full force.

PLACES OF ATTACK

गृहाश्मकूटशैलाग्नवनोपवनसानुषु ।
सरिद्वापीसर कूपतटाकोदन्वतां तटे ॥५६॥
सङ्गमे सरिदावर्ते गोकुले शून्यमन्दिरे ।
एकवृक्षे चितास्थाने प्रभ्रष्टे देवतागृहे ॥५७॥
निधिदेशे रसक्षेत्रे विलद्वारे चतुष्पथे ।
ग्रामसीमान्तरे मातृस्थाने च क्षेत्रतीर्थयोः ॥५८॥
आरामोद्यानयोः सौधे प्रासादाट्टालकेषु च ।
क्रीडापरा वसन्त्येते स्थानेष्वेतेषु हि ग्रहाः ॥५९॥

Stanzas 56 to 59.—The various grahas frequent the following spots for amusement: caves, rocky places, tops of hills, forests, gardens, summits of mountains, banks of rivers, brinks of tanks and ponds, sides of wells; river confluences, whirls, cow-sheds, vacant houses, isolated trees, cremation grounds, ruined temples; places where treasure troves are found, chemical laboratories, mole-hills, centres of highways, outskirts of villages, places, where female deities are worshipped, places of pilgrimage; palatial mansions and places of sport.

NOTES

Causes for being afflicted by spirits have already been given. The spirits are generally said to frequent the places mentioned in stanzas 56 to 59 and they should be avoided.

संख्याः संज्ञाः स्वभावाश्च सन्ति शास्त्रान्तरोदिताः ।
बाधन्ते ये नरास्तेषां कथयन्ते तेप्यनन्तरम् ॥६०॥

Stanza 60.—The spirits that trouble man are many. Their number, their names and their general nature are explained below as based on other treatises.

NAMES OF SPIRITS CAUSING EVIL EYE

पीडका ये मनुष्याणां ग्रहास्ते सप्तविंशतिः ।
अष्टादश महान्तस्तेषूच्यन्तेत्राखिलाश्च ते ॥६१॥

Stanza 61.—The spirits that trouble man are 26 in number. Of these 18 are powerful spirits and 9 are secondary ones.

अमरा असुरा नागा यक्षा गन्धर्वराक्षसाः ।
हेद्रकश्चलनिस्तेजभस्मकाः पितरः कृशाः ॥६२॥

विनायकः प्रलापाश्च पिशाचान्त्यजयोनिजाः ।
भूताश्चेति समाख्याता अष्टादश महाग्रहाः ॥६३॥

Stanzas 62 and 63.—Amara, Asura, Naga, Yaksha, Gandharva, Rakshasa, Heydra, Kasmala, Nistheja, Bhasmaka, Pitris, Krisa, Vinayaka, Pralapa, Pisacha, Anthyaja, Yonija and Bhuta are the 18 Mahagrahas or great spirits.

अपस्मारो द्विजो ब्रह्मराक्षसोवनिभुग्विशौ ।
वृषलो नीचचण्डालौ व्यन्तराश्च नव ग्रहाः ॥६४॥

Stanza 64.—Apasmara, Brahmana, Brahma Rakshasa, Kshatriya, Vaisya, Sudra, Neecha, Chandala and Vyanthara are the 9 light or secondary spirits.

CATEGORIES OF SPIRITS

रुद्रक्रोदोद्भवा एते ह्यन्ये च बहवो ग्रहाः ।
बलिकामा रन्तुकामा हन्तुकामा इति त्रिधा ॥६५॥

Stanza 65.—These and many others had their origin from the anger of Rudra. These spirits can be divided into three categories based on their motives of attack; *viz.*, Bali Kama, Rati Kama, and Hanthu Kama.

NOTES

The origin of all these 18 great spirits (*mahagrahas*) and the secondary or light spirits (*laghu grahas*) is traced to the wrath of Rudra, and they are brought under three distinct categories, the basis being, their motive. Actuated by Bali Kama (wishing to eat the oblations given) some attack the man ; some are actuated by the wish to indulge in enjoyment with the victim (Rati Kama), while a few have their motive as the destruction of their victims (Hanthu Kama).

How to Distinguish Spirits

एते ग्रहाः पुनर्ज्ञेयाः सौम्यताग्नेयतावशात् ।
द्विधा च तद्विदा ज्ञेया ग्रहतत्तिथि भेदतः ॥६६॥

Stanza 66.—These spirits also can be divided into two, *viz*., passive and active and these can be distinguished from the natures and dispositions of the planets

बाधन्ते हन्तुकामाः कतिचन कतिचिद्देवता भोक्तुकामाः
पुंनारी रन्तुकामाः पुनरपि कतिचित्तासु या
हन्तुकामाः ।
घ्नन्त्येवैता गृहीत्वा बलिमिह विभृजन्त्यत्र या भोक्तुकामा
रन्तुं या बाधमाना अपि च बलिशतैर्नैव ता संत्यजन्ति
॥६७॥

Stanza 67.—Some 'devatas' attack persons to murder them; some do it for getting oblations, and some do it for enjoying with their victims.

The first do not leave their victims without killing them; the second leave the victims after getting their dues; and the third also do not leave their victims but they can be pacified.

NOTES

The terms 'devatas', 'grahas' and 'bhutas' are synonymous in the context in which they are now used.

देवग्रहादिभिः प्रोक्तं पीडितानां पृथक्पृथक् ।
लक्षणं तेन च ज्ञेया ग्रहभेदा हि तद्यथा ॥६८॥

Stanza 68.—The signs or symptoms by which the people affected by these Devatas can be distinguished, are detailed in other treatises. By examining them, the names of the Devatas also can be known.

स्नातः सुगन्धस्तेजस्वी हृष्टो देवालये रतः ।
अल्पवागल्पविण्मूत्रः स्वल्पभुक्तिरकोपनः ॥६९॥
गन्धमाल्यप्रियो धीरः सौम्यदृष्टिः सुरग्रही ।
देवान्निन्दन् स्तुवन् दैत्यान् ब्रह्मद्विड्जिह्मलोचनः ॥७०॥
दुष्टात्मा निर्भयो दक्षो गर्वहासी सविस्मयः ।
मुद्रां बध्नन् प्रभूताशी सकम्पाङ्गोऽसुरग्रही ॥७१॥

Stanzas 69 to 71.—A person affected by Deva Graha bathes early, anoints his body with scented perfumes, is calm, spends his time mostly in places of worship; talks, eats and estimates little; is not easily angered, likes flowers and perfumes and is strong in mind and gentle in looks. A person affected by Asura Graha decries Devas, praises Asuras, hates Brahmins, is cruel hearted, looks slantingly, is fearless and haughty, laughs patronisingly, exhibits signs of wonder at everything, displays dummy shows, eats much and shakes his body.

पानीयगुळदुग्धादिपिपासुः सृक्कणी लिहन् ।
भ्रुविप्रसर्पिरक्ताक्षः क्रोधालुरचले वसन् ॥७२॥
सकम्पाङ्गो दशन् दन्तान् पुष्पेच्छुर्नागपीडितः ।
धीरस्त्यागी मनोगामी रक्तकल्पानलेक्षणः ॥७३॥
भोगान्धो गन्धवाहाशी ज्ञेयो यक्षग्रही क्षमी ।
अल्पवाग्गन्धमाल्यादिप्रियः सङ्गीतनर्तनः ॥७४॥
पुळिनादौ वसन् जानन् परोक्षं मुखवाद्यकृत् ।
पिबन् क्षीरं हसन् क्रीडन् हृष्टो गन्धर्वपीडितः ॥७५॥

Stanzas 72 to 75.—One affected by Naga Graha is an addict of sweet drinks and curds (dugdha), bites his lips often, looks around with his red shot eyes, is very irritable and frequents hilly places, his body shivers and he quashes (or bites) his teeth and is fond of flowers. Yaksha Graha makes one brave, charitable, gives power of quick comprehension and seek pleasure always. Gandharva Graha makes one talk little, fond of perfumes and flowers, skilled in music and dance, sitting on mounds of sand, and produces melodious sounds with his facial movements, is fond of drinking milk, laughs and plays much.

प्रधावन्नात्ममांसानि खादन्मद्यासृजी पिबन् ।
शून्यग्रामोषितस्ताम्रो निर्लज्जो निष्ठुरः सरुट् ॥७६॥
शौचद्वेषी निशाचारी बलवान्ताक्षसग्रही ।
स्मेरास्योधोमुखः किञ्चिदपश्यञ्छन्नमुष्टिकः ॥७७॥
जानुन्यस्तशिराः क्रूरदृष्टिर्हृद्ग्रही नरः ।
विट्पङ्कलेपि निश्शौचो भस्मशायी रुदन् हसन् ॥७८॥
स्त्रीद्रोही त्रासयन् जन्तून् सदाश्नयन् कलहप्रियः ।
रागी परार्थहृत् क्रुद्धः स्वल्पवाक्कश्मलग्रही ॥७९॥

Stanzas 76 to 79.—One affected by a Rakshasa Graha is running to and fro, eats his own flesh, drinks blood and liquor, lives in a lonely place, his body is of copper colour, has no sense of shame, is quickly angered, is unclean, wanders in the nights and is hefty. One affected by Heydra Graha is smiling, has downward gaze, keeps his fingers folded, rests his head on his knee cap when sitting, and is fierce-looking. One affected by Kasmala Graha smears his body with dirt, is unclean, sleeps on ashes, laughs and weeps alternately for no reason, proves ungrateful to women, terrifies animals, always eats, is quarrelsome, sensual, misappropriates other's wealth, irritable, and talks very little.

निस्तेजा विडलः पश्यन्निर्निमेषणमब्रुवन् ।
परिहासितवैद्यश्च निस्तेजो ग्रहपीडितः ॥८०॥

Stanza 80.—If one is affected by Nistheja Graha, his body is lustreless, he is always tired and worn out, looks askance at all people,reserved and mocks at physicians.

असङ्गतार्थवाग्द्वेषी शीताङ्गस्तिर्यगीक्षणः ।
भुक्तावतृप्तः कृष्णाङ्गो निर्मलो भस्मकग्रही ॥८१॥

Stanza 81.—The person attacked by Bhasmaka Graha talks irrelevantly, hates others, has a cold and dark body, he will have angular looks, is not satisfied with any amount of food and is clean.

दर्भेषु निर्वपन् पिण्डान् प्रेतानाम् सोदकक्रियः ।
तिलमांसगुळादीनि कांक्षन् शान्तः पितृग्रही ॥८२॥

Stanza 82.—When a person is attacked by Pitru Graha, he performs *pinda kriyas*, is fond of flesh, sugar and gingelly seeds and is calm and unruffled.

एकान्तवासी शुष्काङ्गः प्रधावन् दारुणध्वनिः ।
पृष्टो न व्याहरन् भुक्तौ न तृप्यति कृशग्रही ॥८३॥

Stanza 83.—A person affected by Krisa Graha prefers solitude, is lean, runs to and fro, produces wailing sounds, does not reply even when questioned, and is not satisfied with any amount of food.

मार्जन् पादरजो मुञ्चन् शूत्कारान् छर्दयन् सदा ।
दन्तान् कटकटायन्यः स ग्रहः स्याद्विनायकः ॥८४॥

Stanza 84.—If a person is affected by Vinayaka Graha, he often removes the dust off his legs, produces sounds now and then, vomits always, bites his teeth making katakata sounds, (half-guttral and half-dental).

भञ्जन् गात्राणि शुष्काङ्गो नृत्यन् स्वस्थः सकृद्धसन ।
बहुभुग्बहुभाषी च प्रलापग्रहपीडितः ॥८५॥

Stanza 85.—A person influenced by Pralapa Graha, injures his own body, is lean, dances round, has no thoughts about anything, sometimes laughs and talks much without any purpose.

खररूक्षस्वरः शून्यभिन्नसेवी प्रलापकः ।
दुर्गन्धश्चाशुचिर्लोलः पिशाचग्रहपीडितः ॥८६॥

Stanza 86.—One possessed of Pisacha Graha exhibits harsh and hard voice, talks senselessly, likes dirty and worn-out things and his body is foul smelling.

तर्जयन् लोलरक्ताक्षो लुब्धो विदपङ्कलेपकः ।
बहुभुक्साङ्घ्रिकम्पश्च दीनवागन्त्यजग्रही ॥८७॥

Stanza 87.—If one is possessed by an Anthyaja Graha, he talks ill of others, his eyes are red and moving, he is niggardly, smears his body with dirt and refuse, eats much, shakes his legs for no reason and has plaintive speech.

बहुभुक्चिन्तितं जानन् पिशिताशि चलेक्षणः ।
निर्मर्यादो मेषगन्धः स्थिराङ्गो योनिजग्रही ॥८८॥

Stanza 88.—A person affected by Yonija Graha eats much, is able to read others' minds, likes flesh, eyes are swimming round, behaves shamelessly, smells like that of a goat, and he cannot move most of the limbs in his body.

प्रहरन् जनमारोहन् वृक्षानुच्चापशब्दवाक् ।
सर्वानुकारी विकृतो भवेद्भूतग्रही नरः ॥८९॥

Stanza 89.—Bhutha Graha can be recognised in a person who beats all who approach him, who climbs trees, talks incoherently and apes all, his nature is ever changing.

फेनोद्गारी विवृत्ताक्षो निस्संज्ञः पतितो भुवि ।
सङ्कोचयन् कराङ्घ्र्यादि पीताङ्गो दशनान् दशन् ॥९०॥
लब्धसंज्ञः पुनः स्वस्थः स्यादपस्मारवान्नरः ।
शुक्लमाल्यांबरादीच्छुः पठन् वेदं कुशादिधृक् ॥९१॥
विप्रानुष्ठानकृच्छुद्धो भजन् देवान् द्विजग्रही ।
प्रायस्तुल्यक्रियो विप्रग्रहेण ब्रह्मराक्षसः ॥९२॥

Stanzas 90 to 92.—A person possessed by an Apasmara Graha falls unconscious with shooting eye-balls after spitting large quantities of phlegm and is motionless, his body is yellow in colour, bites his teeth and after some time recovers consciousness. One affected by Brahmana Graha shows desire to get garlands of white flowers and dress, chants Vedas, spreading Kusa grass and observes all the religious ceremonies of a Brahmin and worships God. Similar conduct is exhibited by one who is affected by Brahma Rakshasa Graha.

रक्तपुष्पादिधृङ्‌ नित्यं धावन्वल्गन् हसन् लिखन् ।
सहिष्णुः क्षत्रचेष्टाकृद्धायन् गर्जन् नृप ही ॥९३॥

Stanza 93.—A person affected by a Kshatriya Graha likes red flowers and red dress, runs to and fro, dances round and round and laughs aloud, writes on palm leaves and paper, is able to stand excess of cold and heat and acts and roars like a Kshatriya.

जृम्भमाणो हसन् क्रन्दन्नाक्रोशन् कर्षको वणिक् ।
नृत्यन्नवाच्यवाक्कुप्यन्दुर्विनीतो विशातुरः ॥९४॥

Stanza 94—One affected by Vaisya Graha yawns, laughs and cries aloud, complains always, imitates a merchant, initiates selling and buying, dances round and round, talks rubbish, is quickly angered and is immodest in his actions.

विण्मूत्रादिभुगव्यक्तवाङ्नेढ्रस्पृग्रुदन् हसन् ।
विप्रद्विटस्त्रीप्रियः साङ्गकल्पः स्याद्वृषलग्नहि ॥९५॥

Stanza 95.—One affected by a Sudra Graha consumes his own urine and stools, talks indistinctly, rubs his private parts, cries and laughs for no reason, laughs at Brahmins, pretends love for women and his limbs shiver and shake.

मिश्रचिह्ना स्मृता नीचचण्डालव्यन्तरा ग्रहाः ।
मुञ्चामि किञ्चिद्देहीति ब्रुवन् गायन् हसन् मृदु ॥९६॥

Stanza 96.—One suffering from Neecha Graha, Chandala Graha or Vyanthara Graha has several signs mentioned before in a mixed form. One affected by Soumya Graha utters the words 'give me something, I shall go', he sings slowly and laughs gently.

न मुञ्चामीति वागात्मप्रहतो परुषं वदन् ।
सौम्याग्नेयग्रहावेतौ हन्तुकामं विवर्जयेत् ॥९७॥

Stanza 97.—One affected by Aagneya Graha says 'I will not go'. He beats his own body and utters harsh words. Hanthukama Grahas will not leave the body and hence no treatment is necessary.

निपतन् वप्रवृक्षादेर्वह्न्यगाधांभसो विशन् ।
विधून्वन्मूर्धजान् हृष्टो वैद्यं पश्यन् प्रभाषितः ॥९८॥
रुदन्नृत्यति रक्ताक्षो हन्तुकामग्रही नरः ।
पश्यन् समन्तादुद्विग्नः शूलदाहज्वरार्दितः ॥९९॥
क्षुत्तृष्णार्तः शिरोरोगी देहि देहीति यो ब्रुवन् ।
उद्विग्नः स्त्रीतन्नों क्रीडन् प्रियवाद्यनुपद्रवी ॥१००॥
स्नातो माल्याद्यलङ्कारी रतिं यो याचतेऽशुचिः ।
बलिकामौ रन्तुकामश्चैतौ साध्यौ मन्त्रिणा ॥१०१॥

Stanzas 98 to 101.—One exhibiting signs of 'Hanthu Kama' will try to jump down from trees, hillocks, plunge into deep waters or fall in the blazing fire. He will wring his hair, smile, dance round the physician talking and crying. If the Graha happens to be Bali Kama, he looks around and pretends fear; has stomach pains, excessive feeling of heat, high fever, hunger, thirst and severe headache,and says often 'give me what you owe me'. If the Graha is Rati Kama, he is always afraid of something; he plays on the bodies of women; talks of winning words, troubles none. he courts love after bathing and putting on flowers and ornaments; if his request is ignored, he lies down as if polluted. Bali Kama retires if he is given the Bali. Rati Kama does leave the man though his troubles can be minimised by periodical Balis and Pujas. Hanthu Kama is murderous.

चेष्टाभिरेवं पृथगीरिताभिर्विज्ञाय भूतान्यखिलानि
मन्त्री ।
तेषां चिकित्सां विदधातु तत्तद्योग्याभिरव्यग्रमनाः
क्रियाभिः ॥१०२॥

Stanza 102.—After examining these signs in detail,the Grahas or spirits must be identified and the necessary remedial measures prescribed.

PLANETS FAVOURING SPIRITS

ग्रहाणां पुनरेतेषां खेटसंबन्ध ईर्यते ।
तथैव बाधकस्थानमपि शास्त्रान्तरोदितम् ॥१०३॥

Stanza 103.—How these Grahas (or spirits) are connected with planets, what the houses of harm are, etc., have been explained in other treatises and they will be narrated here.

भानो रुद्रगणोग्रदेवभुजगाधीशा विधोः किन्नरा
यक्षाद्या ग्रहपन्नगाः क्षितिसुतस्योग्रा हि रक्षोग्रहाः ।
भूता भैरवदेवताश्च शशिजस्याट्टालगाः किन्नरा
वागीशस्य शुभग्रहाः शुभतरा नागास्त्रिमूर्त्यादयः
॥१०४॥

Stanza 104.—The Sun governs Rudraganas, Ugradevas and Nagas; the Moon rules over Kinnaras, Yakshas and Graha Pisachas; Mars denotes Rakshasa Grahas and Bhutas, Bhairava Devatas, etc., Mercury rules Attala Grahas and Kinnaras; Jupiter governs Deva Grahas, Naga Grahas and Thrimurthees.

यक्षीमातृभुजङ्गमा भृगुसुतस्यार्कात्मजस्याशुभा
भस्मारुक्षपिशाचकश्मलमुखा निस्तेजसंज्ञा ग्रहाः ।
राहोस्सर्पपिशाचपन्नगभृतः प्रेतग्रहाद्युद्भवाः
केतोस्तेऽखिलदेहिनां विदधते रोगाननिष्टर्क्षगाः ॥१०५॥

Stanza 105.—Venus governs Yakshee, Matrus and Nagas; Saturn—evil ones as Nisthejas, Bhasmakas, Pisachas and Kasmalas; Rahu denotes Nagas, Pisachas and Serpents; and Ketu—Pretagrahas and Pitris. Diseases are caused by these

Devatas indicated by planets occupying unfavourable positions.

बाधकस्थानगे सूर्ये शैवभूतादिपीडनम् ।
चन्द्रे दुर्गाकृतं रोगं धर्मदैवकृतं गदम् ॥१०६॥
भौमे स्कन्दकृतं व्याधिं भैरवादिनिपीडनम् ।
सौम्ये गन्धर्वयक्षादिविमानस्थानवासिनाम् ॥१०७॥
जीवे ब्राह्मणशापं च देवानामपि कोपनम् ।
शुक्रे यक्षीकृतं रोगं ब्रह्मराक्षसपीडनम् ॥१०८॥
मन्दे तु भूतनाथानां शैवानां पीडनम् तथा ।
राहौ सर्पकृतं रोगं केतौ चाण्डालदैवतम् ॥१०९॥
मान्दौ प्रेतकृतं रोगं प्रवदेन्मतिमान् नरः ॥११०॥

Stanzas 106 to 110.—According to *Santhana Deepika*, the different planets in the houses of harm cause troubles due to the wrath of different *devatas* thus: the Sun—Saiva Bhutas; the Moon—Durga and Dharma Daiva ; Mars—Subrahmanya and Bhairava; Mercury—Gandharva, Yaksha and other celestial denizens ; Jupiter—Brahmins and gods; Venus—Yaksha and Brahma Rakshasa; Saturn—Sasta, Kirata and five Bhuthas; Rahu—Serpents; Ketu—Chandala Devatas; and Gulika-Pretas.

HOUSES OF HARM

आरूढराशौ चर आयराशौ स्थिरे तु बाधा नवमे विचिन्त्या ।
तथोभये कामगृहे त्रयाणां केन्द्रेषु चैषामिति केचिदाहुः ॥१११॥

Stanza 111.—According as Arudha falls in movable, fixed or common signs, the houses of harm happen to be the 11th, 9th or the 7th from the concerned Arudha Rasi. Some are of the opinion that the quadrants from these places are also houses of harm.

NOTES

If Arudha falls in Aries, the house of harm is Aquarius. If Arudha is Taurus, the house of harm is Capricorn. If Gemini is Arudha, then the house of harm is Sagittarius. According to some, the cardinal signs from the places mentioned in this stanza can also be considered house of harm.

कुंभश्चराणामळिचापसिंहस्त्रीणामळिर्गोवृषभस्य नक्रः ।
कुंभस्य कर्की मिथुनस्य धन्वी मीनस्य चापं खलु बधकं स्यात् ॥११२॥

Stanza 112.—Aquarius is the 'house of harm' for all movable signs; Leo, Virgo, Scorpio and Sagittarius have Scorpio as house of harm. For

Taurus, it is Capricorn; for Aquarius it is Cancer; for Gemini and Pisces, Sagittarius is the source of harm.

बाधानिरूपणे पक्षास्त्रय इत्येषु गृह्यताम् ।
आदिमोन्त्यश्च सर्वत्र ग्राह्यो वा मध्यमः क्वचित् ॥ इति ॥११३॥

Stanza 113.—Thus, we see there are three distinct views regarding the fixing of houses of harm. Of these, the 1st and 3rd assignments are accepted by all. The 2nd is recognised by a few.

पित्तोष्णेत्यादयः श्लोकाः प्रश्नानुष्ठानपद्धतौ ।
ये प्रागुग्विषये प्रोक्ताश्चिन्तयेदिह तानपि ॥११४॥

Stanza 114.—Certain stanzas from *Anushtana Paddhathi*, have already been given. They may also be utilised in this context.

ASCERTAINING THE "DRISHTI BADHA"

बाधकाधिपतिर्लग्नं लग्नेशं वा यदीक्षते ।
त्रिदशादीक्षणेनापि बाधा स्याद्दृष्टिसम्भवा ॥११५॥

Stanza 115.—If the lord of harm aspects Lagna or the lord of Lagna, there is Drishti Badha. By aspect is meant the special aspects also.

NOTES

According to some, all aspects, including the special ones of Saturn and Mars, should be taken into consideration. If the aspects are partial, the *badha* will also be partial. For example, Lagna is Aries and the Sun, as badhaka graha is in Aquarius. The Sun's aspect on Lagna is only 1/3rd. The extent of badha or affliction is accordingly limited.

बाधकस्थानगेस्तेशे तद्द्वयाधिपयोर्मिथः ।

योगे दृष्टौ च वक्तव्या बाधा दृष्टिसमुद्भवा ॥११६॥

Stanza 116.—If the lord of the 7th is in the house of harm or both the lords join or mutually aspect, it must be inferred that there is Drishti Badha.

NOTES

If the lord of the 7th and the lord of house of harm join or in mutual aspect, the affliction obtains.

Some aver that here, 8th house aspect alone is to be considered.

चरराशियुते लग्ने धरासुतयुते मदे ।

लग्ने सहितपापे च देवतादर्शनाद्रुजा ॥११७॥

Stanza 117.—If Lagna being a movable sign is joined by an evil planet and Mars occupies the 7th house, then the affliction is due to the malefic aspect of Devatas.

NOTES

Some commentators imply a malefic's association with lord of Lagna instead of a malefic occupying Lagna.

शुभेतरयुते लग्ने सप्तमस्थे शनैश्वरे ।
चन्द्रे पापग्रहैर्दृष्टे पिशाचालोकनाद्रुजा ॥ इति ॥११८॥

Stanza 118.—If Lagna is occupied by planets other than benefics, Saturn joins the 7th house and the Moon is aspected by malefics, then the disease or affliction is due to Pisachas.

NOTES

Here the Moon's affliction in general either by aspect or association should be considered. The above 2 slokas are from *Santana Deepika*.

लग्नेशबन्धुर्यदि बाधकेशो रन्तु निहन्तं यदि तस्य शत्रुः ।
भोक्तुं समश्चेद्ग्रहपिडनं स्या देवं त्रिधा दैवविदो वदन्ति ॥११९॥

Stanza 119.—If the lords of harm and Lagna are friendly, the object of the Devatas in afflicting the person is *to enjoy* ; if inimical, the object is *to kill*; and if natural, the object is *to eat and drink*. The sources of the trouble should be minutely examined.

अन्ये तु लग्नेश्वरदृष्टयुक्ते रन्तु निहन्तुं मृतिषष्ठपाभ्याम् ।
बाधाधिपेन्यैरिह भोक्तुमेवं ग्राह्यौ विरोधे सति पूर्वपक्षः ॥१२०॥

Stanza 120.—According as the lord of harm is associated with or aspected by the lord of Lagna, or lords of 6 or 8 or lord of any other house, the intention of the Devata is to enjoy, kill or eat and drink. This is the opinion of some others. The effect of "any other lord" should be considered in the context of the previous stanza.

NOTES

As per stanza 120, if the lord of harm is joined by the lord of Lagna, enjoyment is the motive of the Devata. If lord of harm is with the lord of 6 or 8, destruction is the motive. If the lord of *badhaka* is connected with any other lord, the motive is eating and drinking. If lord of house of harm is with the lord of the 5th and suppose the lord of the 5th is an enemy, under such a circumstance, even though according to this sloka, the motive is eating and drinking, the motive should be considered as destruction. Here, one should fall back on stanza 119, and consider the friendly, inimical or neutral nature of the lord of other signs (than Lagna, 6th or 8th) towards lord of harm.

शुक्रर्क्षगोथ तद्दृष्टो बाधकस्थानगो ग्रहः ।

यदि भार्योद्भवं विद्याद्भार्याभर्तृसमागमे ॥१२१॥

Stanza 121.—If a planet in the house of harm is aspected by Venus or happens to be in a sign of Venus, then it must be inferred that the Devatas attacked the person while he was in intimacy with his wife.

Place of Attack

वाधासम्भवदेशस्तु बाधकस्थानराशिना ।
वाच्यो मेषादिराशीनां प्रदेशान् कथयाम्यतः ॥१२२॥

Stanza 122.—The place from which the attack comes is signified by the sign which happens to be the 'house of harm'.

मेषस्य धात्वाकररत्नभूमिः कुल्याप्रदेशो भुजगालयश्च ।
पूर्वप्रदेशो वृषभस्य पश्चात्कृषीवलक्षत्रसुरम्यभूमिः
॥१२३॥

Stanza 123.—The places signified by the different signs are: Aries—gold and silver mines, diamond mines, canals and serpent's abode. Taurus—all places mentioned for Aries and farm houses, fields of cultivation and beautiful spots.

उद्यानदेवालयरत्नभूमिर्यमस्य रम्यं प्रवदन्ति तज्ज्ञाः ।
देवाङ्गनावासतटाकरम्यं जलान्तिकं कर्कटकस्य राशेः
॥१२४॥

Stanza 124—Gemini—parks, places of worship, areas where precious stones abound and pleasure haunts. Cancer—neighbourhood of tanks and watery tracts and places where celestial nymphs frequent.

स्थानं मृगेन्द्रस्य तु तुङ्गदेशो गोक्षेत्रदेवद्विजवास भूमिः

देवालयाश्वद्विपमन्दिराब्धिक्षेत्रेषु वासो वनितागृहस्य ॥१२५॥

Stanza 125.—Leo—places frequented by lions and other wild animals, elevated places, cow-sheds, places frequented by Brahmins and Devas. Virgo—temples, horse and elephant stables, sea-coast and ladies' apartments.

जूकस्य वीथ्यापणकाननेषु कीटस्य वल्मीकतडाकयोश्च ।

आरामसेनागृहयुद्धभूमिसालेषु वासो नवमस्य राशेः ॥१२६॥

Stanza 126.—Libra—streets, bazaars and forests. Scorpio—anthills and ponds. Sagittarius-rest houses, military barracks, battlefields and walls and embarkments.

नदीमुखारण्यनिषादवासे ध्वेणस्य राशेर्घटभस्य तद्वत् ।

श्वभ्राम्बुपूर्णामरमन्दिरेषु झषस्य वासः कथितो मुनीन्द्रैः ॥१२७॥

Stanza 127.—Capricorn—river deltas, forests, areas inhabited by wild tribes; Aquarius—same places as Capricorn; and Pisces—deep caves, watery places and temples.

वनं क्षेत्रं पुरं कुल्या शैलग्रामापणाः क्रमात् ।

कूपकान्तारजलधितटाकसरितस्त्वजात् इति ॥१२८॥

Stanza 128.—The twelve signs from Aries onwards govern in regular order forests, fields, cities, canals, hills, towns, market places, wells, forests, oceans, lakes and rivers.

EVIL ARISING FROM WORDS

बाधकेश्वरदृष्टो वा युक्तो वा यदि वाक्पतिः ।

तर्हि रोगं वदेन्नृणां जिह्वादोषसमुद्भवम् ॥१२९॥

Stanza 129.—If the lord of the 2nd is associated with or aspected by the 'lord of harm', the person suffers disease due to Jihwa Dosha.

NOTES

Till now Drishtibadha was discussed. Now the discussion will be centred on Jihwa Dosha or evil arising from words.

बालग्रहाभिधा बाधन्तेऽर्भकानेव केवलम् ।

प्रसिद्धाः पूतनाद्या ये तत्पीडाथ निगद्यते ॥१३०॥

Stanza 130.—There are some Bala grahas which trouble only children. Now the important of them such as Puthana, etc., will be elaborated.

"BALA GRAHA" AFFLICTION

मन्दचन्द्रजयोरेको यद्वा मिथुननक्रयोः ।
बाधकस्थान संस्थश्चेद्बालपीडां विनिर्दिशेत् ॥१३१॥

Stanza 131.—If either Mercury or Saturn occupies the house of harm or if Gemini or Capricorn happens to be the house of harm, then the child suffers from the affliction of Bala Grahas.

NOTES

This verse is applicable only in queries bearing on children.

FOOD POISONING

मित्रे पुत्रे सप्तमे वाष्टमे वा मान्दौ वाहौ तिष्टति
क्ष्वेळभुक्तिः ।
तत्रस्थे चारीश्वरेरिप्रयुक्ता विज्ञातव्या सा न चेद्दैवयोगात्
॥१३२॥

Stanza 132.—If Gulika or Rahu occupies 4th, 5th, 7th or 8th, the disease is due to poisonous matter in the food. If the lord of the 6th joins this combination, then the poisoning will be due to enemies.

आरूढे सिंहराशौ कटुकरसयुते नागवल्लीदलाद्ये
भौमक्षेत्रे तथाज्ये मधुनि बुधगृहे तक्रदध्नोः सितर्क्षे ।
क्ष्वेळे वा कादळे वा विषममरगुरोर्धाम्नि निक्षिप्य दत्तं
पूपादौ मन्दगेहे लवणरसवति द्रव्य इन्दोर्द्रवे वा ॥१३३

Stanza 133.—The poison will have been administered mixed up with a hot substance, ghee, honey, curds, milk and fruits, cooked food or saltish juice according as Arudha Lagna happens to fall respectively in the signs of the Sun, Mars, Mercury, Venus, Jupiter, Saturn or the Moon.

NOTES

If Arudha Lagna is Leo, the poison has been given in some hot substances; if it is Aries or Scorpio, in ghee; Gemini and Virgo stand for honey; Taurus and Libra govern curd or buttermilk; Sagittarius and Pisces stand for milk and fruits; Capricorn and Aquarius stand for bread and other cooked food such as sweetmeats; and Cancer stands for saltish foods or liquid substances.

लग्नेशारीरासम्बन्धे हिंसार्थौ गरळार्पणम् ।
लग्नेशास्तेशसम्बन्धे स्याद्वशीकरणाय तत् ॥१३४॥

Stanza 134.—If the lord of Lagna is connected with the lord of 6th, then the object of giving poison is to harm the person. If the lord of Lagna is connected with the lord of 7th, then it is intended to win over the person.

TROUBLES FROM ENEMIES

दोषत्रितयसम्भूताः केवलं बधाया कृताः ।
द्वैविध्यमिति रोगाणां तद्भेदः प्राङ्निगद्यते ॥१३५॥

Stanza 135.—As already detailed, there are two types of disease *viz.*, those caused by the disorder of *thridoshas* and those brought about by mantric machinations of enemies which in their turn provoke the thridoshas.

NOTES

Now the discussion will relate to *satrubadha* or troubles from enemies.

आरूढे प्रबले वदन्ति सुधियो रोगोद्भवं बाधया
प्राग्लग्ने प्रबले तथामयगणा वाच्यास्त्रिदोषोद्भवाः ।
तद्वत्षष्ठपतौ बलिन्यपि गदान् बाधोद्भवान्निर्दिशे-
द्रन्ध्रेशेऽतिबले त्रिदोषजनिता रोगास्स्युरेवं द्विधा
॥१३६॥

Stanza 136.—If Mercury is stronger, the disease is due to Aabhichara. If Lagna is stronger, the disease is due to the disorder of thridoshas. If the lord of the 6th is stronger, the disease is due to enemies. If the lord of the 8th is stronger, then the disease is due to disturbance in the thridoshas.

व्याधीनामीश्वरो ज्ञेयः षष्ठपो रन्ध्रपस्तथा ।
बाधया सबलेरीशे रन्ध्रेशे रुक्त्रिदोषतः ॥१३७॥

Stanza 137.—The lords of disease are the rulers of the 6th and 8th. If the former is stronger, the disease is due to enemies. If the latter is strong, it is due to thridoshas.

NATURE OF TROUBLE

बाधेशस्यारिभे वा रिपुभवनपतेर्बाधकर्क्षे यदि स्याद्योगो
वा दर्शनं वा पुनरथ यदि वा तौ मिथः क्षेत्रसंस्थौ ।
बाधाधीशारिनाथावपि यदि सहितौ पश्यतोन्योन्यतो वा
शत्रोस्तत्राभिचारं वदतु बहुतया लक्षणानां स भूयान्
॥१३८॥

Stanza 138.—If the lord of the house of harm occupies or aspects the 6th; or when the lord of the 6th joins or aspects the house of lord of harm; or when these interchange houses; or occupy the same house; or when these aspect each other, it should be inferred that the afflictions come from the enemies.

NOTES

The disease or affliction will be due to enemies under the following conditions: (1) Lord of house of harm ocupies the 6th; (2) lord of house of harm aspects the 6th; (3) lord of 6th joins the house of lord of harm; (4) lord of 6th aspects the house of lord of harm; (5) lords of 6th and house of harm interchange; (6) lords of the 6th and house of harm are together; and (7) when the lord of the 6th aspects the lord of the house of harm.

महाभिचारो वक्तव्यः शुभश्चेद्बाधकाधिपः ।
पापश्चेत् क्षुद्र एष स्यादभिचार इति द्विधा ॥१३९॥

Stanza 139.—The affliction is of two kinds: If the lord of house of harm is a benefic, it is *mahabhichara*. If the lord is a malefic, it is *kshudrabhichara*.

महाभिचार एष स्याद्वैरिभिर्मारणादिकम् ।
यत् कर्म क्रियते क्षुद्रो यत् कीलादि निखन्यते ॥१४०॥

Stanza 140.—Mahabhichara consists of incantations calculated to cause death, etc. Kshudrabhichara consists of burying enchanted substances underground to bring about ruin.

WHO IS THE ENEMY?

रिपोश्च तन्नियोगाद्यो मारणादिकृदस्य च ।
जातिर्द्वयोश्च वक्तव्या तत्प्रकारोथ कथ्यते ॥१४१॥

Stanza 141.—When it is discovered that there is Aabhichara, we have to find who the enemy is and who did the work for him. The caste to which such persons belong is explained in the next verse.

वर्णो यः षष्ठराशेः स भवति हि रीपोः षष्ठराशीशितुर्वा
वाच्यो बाधाख्यराशेरथ तदधिपतेर्वापि वर्णः प्रयोक्तुः ।
विप्रः स्यान्मीनरशिर्द्धरणिपतिरजो वैश्य उक्षा नृयुग्मं
शूद्रः, स्यात्सन्निकोणं पुनरिह विहगा एव विप्रादिनोक्ताः
॥१४२॥

Stanza 142.—The caste and occupation governed by the 6th house or by its lord indicate the caste of the enemy. Similarly, the caste governed by the 'house of harm' or its lord is the caste of his accomplice. Pisces, Aries, Taurus and Gemini and their trines signify respectively Brahmins, Kshatriyas, Vaisyas and Sudras.

बाधकाधिपसम्बन्धो दृष्ट्या योगेन वा यदि ।
षष्ठभस्य रिपोर्वर्णं षष्ठराश्युदितं वदेत् ॥१४३॥

Stanza 143.—If the lord of the house of harm is in any way connected with the 6th house, then the enemy's caste is that of the sixth house.

बाधकस्थानतन्नाथयोगदृष्ट्यादयो यदि ।
षष्ठेशस्य रिपोर्वर्णस्तर्हि षष्ठाधिपोदितः ॥१४४॥

Stanza 144.—If the lord of the house of harm is in any way connected with the lord of 6th, the enemy's caste is that of the lord of the 6th.

षष्ठाधिपतिसम्बन्धो बाधकस्य गृहस्य चेत् ।
योगादिना प्रयोक्तुः स्याद्वर्णो बाधकभोदितः ॥१४५॥

Stanza 145.—If the lord of the 6th is bound up with the house of harm, then the accomplice in the deed belongs to the caste governed by the house of harm.

बाधकेशस्य चेत्षष्ठषष्ठेशेक्षान्वयादयः ।
वाधकाधिपतेर्वर्णं प्रयोक्तुस्तर्हि निर्दिशेत् ॥१४६॥

Stanza 146.—If the lord of the 6th is bound up with the lord of the house of harm, then the accomplice belongs to the caste of the lord of the house of harm.

विप्रावसुरसुरेड्यौ भौमार्कौ क्षत्रियौ शशी वैश्यः ।
शू द्रस्तु बुधो मन्दश्चान्तरवर्णो वराहमिहिरमते ॥१४७॥

Stanza 147.– According to Varahamihira, Jupiter and Venus are Brahmins, the Sun and Mars—Kshatriyas, the Moon—Vysya, Mercury—Sudra and Saturn—mixed caste.

ANOTHER VIEW

विप्रोत्तमः स्याद्गुरुरत्र शुक्रो विप्राथमोन्यग्रहरा-
शियोगात् ।
भेदोनयोः स्ययादथ सार्वभौमो भानुः कुजो माण्डलि-
कश्च वेद्यः ॥१४८॥

Stanza 148.—According to others, Jupitor is an exalted Brahmin while Venus is an ordinary Brahmin. When these join other planets, their qualities change. The Sun is the emperor, while Mars governs kingship.

भूमिजोनुपवीती स्वभ्द्राजतुल्योथ बोधनः ।
विद्वाननुपवीति सदेवदास इतीर्यताम् ।।१४९।।

Shanza 149.—Mars also signifies distinguished persons with no sacred thead, Mercury governs learned men and temple servents with no saered thread.

अन्चावीनी च पर्यन्तस्थान भेदाच्छनेरपि ।
देवदासादि चण्डालपर्यन्त जातयः स्मृताः ।।इति।।१५०।।

Stanza 150.—Saturn in exaltation rules over temples employees while in debilitation he rules over low-caste people.

विप्राह्वयौ गुरुसितौ नृपत्ती कुजार्को ।
वेश्यः शशि शशि सुतो वृषलोर्क जोन्त्यः ।।इति ।।१५१।।

Stanza 151.—Mahvacharya says that Jupitor and Venus represent Brahmins; the Sun and Mars, Kshatriyas; the Moon, Vaisyas; Mercury, Sudras; and Saturn, low cast people.

कृष्णीयश्च । विप्रौ भृगुदेवगुरु क्षत्रियभावो
दिवाकरोर्वीजो ।
वैश्यौ बुधचन्द्रमसौ शनैश्चरः शू द्रसङ्करकृत् ।इति।।१५२।।

Stanza 152.—According to *Krishneeya*, Jupitor and Venus govern Brahmins, the Sun and Mars Kshatriyas, the Moon and Mercury Vaisyas; and Saturn Sudras and the mixed caste.

अर्कस्य शुक्रो राजो वा शूद्रो वा मण्डलाधिपः ।
इन्द्रोर्विप्रोथवा वैश्यो भौमस्य द्विजशूद्रकौ ॥१५३॥

Stanza 153.—In *Sarasamuchaya*, it is said that the Sun and Venus govern kings of all castes, the Moon governs Brahmins or Vaisyas, Mars governs Brahmins and Sudras.

सौम्यस्य शूद्रो वैश्यो वा शनेः शूद्रोन्त्यजोपि वा ।
जीवस्य विप्रः शुक्रस्य शूद्रो विप्रोथवा स्त्रियः
नीचारिमूढगैरेतैर्नीचजातिं विनिर्दिशेत् ॥इति॥१५४॥

Stanza 154.—Mercury governs Vaisyas and Sudras, Saturn governs Sudras and low caste people. Jupiter governs Brahmins and Venus Brahmins, Sudras and women. When these planets are in inimical places debilitation or combustion, they govern only very low types

शत्रुप्रयोकात्वर्णोक्तावस्तिग्रन्थन्तरं च तद् ।
लिख्यते शत्रुताहेतुस्तत्रापि च मतान्तर म् ॥१५५॥

Stanza 155.—With regard to the enemy's caste, there are other views by which it can be determined.

षष्ठेशजातिं द्विषतोभिदध्यात् कर्मेशजातिं खलु कर्मकर्तुः ।
हेतुं च षष्ठेशसमाश्रितर्क्षनाथानुरूपं तमिहाभिधास्ये

॥१५६॥

Stanza 156.—The caste of the enemy is signified by the lord of the 6th, and the lord of the 10th signifies the caste of the accomplice. The motive for Abhichara Karma corresponds with the nature of the lord of the sign occupied by the lord of the 6th.

षष्ठशो यदि भौमवेश्मनि बुधैर्हेतुर्महीत्युच्यते
बैधे काञ्चनमार्यभे पणफलान्यच्छस्य रूप्यं तथा ।
वासो धान्यचतुष्पदाश्च शनिभे चण्डालदासायुधं
चन्द्रे भाजनमम्बु वार्कभवने ताम्रं च मूलं फलम् ॥

॥१५७॥

ENEMY'S MOTIVE

Stanza 157.—According as the lord of the 6th occupies the sign of Mars, Mercury, Jupiter, Venus, Saturn, the Moon or the Sun, the motive behind the deed happens to be lands, gold, fruits, silver, clothes, cattle or grain, servants, low caste people and weapons, vessels or water, or roots and fruits.

लग्नादिकेषु भावेषु यत्रास्ते बाधकेश्वरः ।
भावमेनं निमित्तीकृत्याभिचारं विनिर्दिशेत् ॥१५८॥

Stanza 158.—The motive of the enemy in resorting to Abhichara can also be gleaned according to the nature of the house occupied by the lord of house of harm.

NOTES

The view adumbrated in this Stanza is from 'other works'. The house containing the lord of house of harm reveals the motive behind the Abhichara. Thus if the lord of harm is in the 2nd, the motive is money: if in the 4th, property is the motive. In this way, the motive should be ascertained.

धात्वाधिभखेटानामुदयेनारातिबाधकेशाभ्याम् ।
आश्रितभाभ्यामथवा धात्वाद्या हेतवश्चिन्त्याः ॥१५९॥

Stanza 159.—Whether the motive behind the enemy's deeds springs up from Dhatu, Moola or Jeeva, can be ascertained by examining the rising sign, planets in the rising sign, lord of the sixth, lord of the house of harm, the house occupied by the lord of sixth, the sign occupied by lord of Lagna. Whether the enemy belongs to the same family as the querist or to outside family or whether the enemy is a near or a distant relative, should be carefully ascertained by noting the Lagna.

शत्रुः स्यात्स्वजनश्चरे स्थिरगृहे लग्ने सुहृच्छात्रवो
द्वन्द्वे स्यादितरोथवा गृहपतौ षष्ठस्थिते बान्धवः ।
पित्रेशे तनयादिकोथ मदपे भार्याथ धर्माधिपे
पित्राद्या गुरवो भवन्ति रिपवः शापोथवैषामिह ॥१६०॥

Stanza 160.—If the Lagna is a movable sign, the enemy is of the same kith and kin; if a fixed sign he is related; if common, the enemy is an outsider. According as the 6th house is occupied by the lord of the 4th, 5th, 7th, 9th, the enemy who is the cause of trouble will be a relative, son, wife or father or preceptor.

सहवासी स्थिरे लग्ने द्वन्द्वगेन्तिकदेशगः ।
चरे दूरगतः शत्रुर्ज्ञेयः स्निग्धजनोथवा ॥१६१॥

Stanza 161.—If the Lagna is a fixed sign, the enemy is a *sahavasi* (lives with the native); if it is a common sign, he is a neighbour; and if movable, the enemy belongs to a distant place, or is an old friend.

IDENTIFYING THE ENEMY

शत्रोर्दिग्रिपुनाथवैरिगृहयोरेकस्य वर्णोक्तवद्बाधाराशित-
दीश योरितरदिग्वाच्या प्रयोक्तुस्तथा ।
प्रागाद्येत्यमुनोदिता विहगादिकूप्रागादितो राशि-
दित्कासां दूरसमीपमध्यगतताजाद्यास्रभांशैस्तयोः ॥१६२॥

Stanza 162.—The direction and caste of the enemy and how far or near he is, should be ascertained from the 6th house or its lord. Similarly, the direction and caste of the mantric and how far or near he is, should be read from the Badhaka house or its lord.

NOTES

Whether it is the 6th lord or 6th house and whether it is the badhaka house or its lord, should be ascertained on the basis of Stanza 140 to 143. The directions and castes allotted to different Rasis are:

Rasi	*Direction*	*Caste*
Aries	East	Kshatriya
Taurus	South	Vaisya
Gemini	West	Sudra
Cancer	North	Brahmin
Leo	East	Kshatriya
Virgo	South	Vaisya
Libra	West	Sudra
Scorpio	North	Brahmin
Sagittarius	East	Kshatriya
Capricorn	South	Vaisya
Aquarius	West	Sudra
Pisces	North	Brahmin

If the Rasi and Navamsa in which the 6th house falls or the 6th lord occupies are movable, the enemy or *mantric* will be far off; if fixed, near; if common, not too far and not too near. If the said Rasi and Navamsa are different, then, the stronger of the two should be taken.

चरे विलग्ने रिपुनायदृष्टे कुजे ज लाभे स्थिरभे च धर्मे ।
द्वन्द्वेस्तराशौ प्रवदेन्नराणां रोगं रिपूणां कृतमभिचारैः
॥१६३॥

Stanza 163.—If the Ascendant happens to be a movable sign with Mars in the 11th, or a fixed sign with Mars in the 9th, or a common sign with Mars in the 7th and is aspected by the lord of the 6th, the native has sickness through Abhichara resorted to by an enemy.

होरानाथयुते भौमे लग्नकेन्द्रगतेथवा ।
रिपुनाथे विलग्नस्थे चाभिचार उदीर्यताम् ॥१६४॥
शत्रुस्थानाधिपे लग्ने कर्मण्यस्तं गतेथवा ।
लग्ने भौमयुते दृष्टे वाभिचार उदीयताम् ॥१६५॥
सुखभावगते केतौ कर्मलग्नगतेथवा ।
लग्ने भौमयुते दृष्टे वाभिचार उदीर्यताम् ॥१६६॥
सुखभावगते केतौ कर्मलग्नगतेथवा ।
केन्द्रे मान्दिसमायुक्ते रोगः क्षुदाभिचारजः ॥१६७॥

Stanzas 164 to 167.—The cause of sickness will be Abhichara under the following combinations. Mars in the Ascendant or in a quadrangular house and the lord of the 6th is in the rising sign; lord of the 6th in the Ascendant, 7th or 10th and Mars in or aspecting the Lagna; Ketu in the 4th, 10th or Ascendant and Mars in or aspecting Lagna; and Ketu in the 4th, 10th or Ascendant and Mandi occupying a kendra.

NOTES

Stanzas 163 to 167 are from *Santhana Deepika*. These stanzas give combinations to predict on the basis of the Prasna Chart, the source of sickness. The stanzas are easy to understand and do not need detailed elucidation. However, I should like to make a few observations. In all the combinations listed, importance is given to the 6th lord. According to Stanza 163, the 6th lord should aspect the Ascendant which should have Mars placed in the 11th, 9th or 7th, according as the ascending sign is movable, fixed or common. Stanzas 164 to 167 also require a certain disposition of Mars, Ketu or Gulika and the 6th lord involving only the Ascendant and the other quadrangular houses.

Means Adopted by Enemies

मारणोच्चाटनाद्यर्थं रिपुभिर्यन्निधीयते ।
चूर्णादिक तदुद्धारप्रकारोथ निगद्यते ॥१६८॥

Stanza 168.—To bring about death, exile, dissensions, madness, or ruin, marana and uchhatana—enemies prepare powders and other enchanted things and conceal them under the earth or in some hidden places.

NOTES

The astrologer will have to inform the client where these can be found, so that they can be removed.

WHERE THE KSHUDRA IS KEPT

उदयारूढचन्द्राणां गुळिके केन्द्रसंस्थिते ।
मन्दयुक्तेथ दृष्टे वा क्षुद्रं रिपुकृतं वदेत् ॥१६९॥

Stanza 169.—If Gulika occupies a quadrant from Lagna or Arudha Lagna or the Moon and is joined or aspected by Saturn, then the incanted articles (Kshudras) will be kept buried under the earth.

मान्दिश्चतुर्थराशौ वा चतुर्थांशेथवा स्थितः ।
यदि क्षुद्रं गृहे वाच्यं जलराश्यंशयोर्जले ॥१७०॥

Stanza 170.—If Mandi is in the 4th house or Navamsa, then the Kshudra will have been deposited inside the house. If the 4th house or Navamsa is watery, it will be kept immersed under water.

NOTES

Here the situation of Mandi in the 4th is with reference to Lagna, Arudha or the Moon. According to some, Mandi—whatever Bhava he may occupy—if it is a watery Rasi or Navamsa, the place of deposit shall be under water.

वर्गोत्तमांशगे तस्मिन्नभयत्र वदेदिदम् ।
मन्देन मान्दिना वापि युक्तेहौ सर्पसन्निधौ ॥१७१॥

Stanza 171.—If Mandi is in Vargottama, the Kshudra will be in two places—within the house and under water. If Rahu joins Mandi or Saturn, the substance is hidden near an ant hill.

तत्केन्द्रे चेद्रविभूक्षे केदारे भूमिजो यदि ।
जीवश्चाद्गृह एव स्याच्छुक्रश्चेच्छयनालये ॥१७२॥

Stanza 172.—According as a kendra (from Mandi or Saturn) is occupied by the Sun, Mars, Jupiter or Venus, the Kshudra is kept respectively in the branches of trees, in open fields, in the house itself or in the bedroom.

CONTAINERS USED

मन्दश्चेन्मलमूत्रादि परिहारोचितावनौ ।
मान्दिर्मेषत्रिकोणस्थस्तदंशस्योथवा यदि ॥१७३॥

शिरःकपाले निहितं व्यघ्रस्माखुभुजोथवा ।
गोत्रिकोणे घटे वाच्यं वंशादौ मिथुनस्य चेत् ॥१७४॥

कर्किंत्रिकोणसस्यश्चेत्कपालं निहितं च तत् ।
मान्दौसंहारनक्षत्रस्थिते वाच्या हि पुत्रिका ॥१७५॥

कीटराशिस्येते यन्त्रं चतुरंघ्रयंशकोस्थि च ।
एषां संख्या तु विज्ञेया मान्दिभुक्तांशकैस्समा ॥१७६॥

Stanzas 173 to 176.—If Saturn is in a kendra from Mandi, the Kshudra will be kept in latrines and urinals. According as Mandi is in Aries, Taurus, Gemini or Cancer (or their trines), the Kshndra will be kept in the skins of tigers and cats, water pots, bamboo vessels or cocoanut shells respectively. If Mandi is in Samhara Nakshatras (destructive asterisms), the Kshudra will be in the form of an image of a human. If Mandi is in Scorpio, it is in the form of an amulet. If it occupies the Navamsas of quadrupeds, it is in the form of bones. The number so kept or buried can be known from the expired number of Navamsa in the Rasi occupied by Gulika.

NOTES

Sambara Nakshatras are Krittika and Aridra.

From the description of the methods for finding the nature and source of sickness given in these stanzas, it is clear that at the time the author lived, the practice of causing harm through incantations, spells and other forms of base practices was widespread in Kerala. Even now not only in Kerala but also in other parts of India, resort is being had to such methods to cause harm to one's enemies. Some of the Kerala astrologers whom I had discussions with, say that these astrological principles pertaining to discovery of *abhichara* given in this work are almost always foolproof and that even now people consult astrologers on these lines.

The number of articles (Kshudras) on which the spell in cast corresponds to the number of Navamsas gained by Mandi in the Rasi he occupies. According to some, the total number of Navamsas from the beginning of Aries Navamsa should be considered. If for example, Mandi is in Libra Navamsa (Cancer sign) according to the first view, the number will be the 4, 3 Navamsas having completed. According to the others, the number will be 7, counting from Aries. Here again the figure has to be doubled if the amsa lord is exalted, etc.

ANOTHER VIEW

ऊर्ध्वास्ये बाधकाधीशे निहितं भूरुहोपरि ।
निखातं कावधो वक्त्रे तिर्यग्वदनगः स चेत् ॥१७७॥

पाषाणद्रुममध्यदिन्यस्तं चूर्णादिकं वदेत् ।
बाधेशतत्स्थराशिभ्यां द्रुमतत्स्थप्रदेशयोः ॥१७८॥

शुभोशुभर्क्षां इत्येतेनोह्या चोत्तमनीचता ।
बाधकाधिपतिः स्वांशान्नवांशे यावति स्थितः ।१७९॥

तत्संख्याः स्युर्द्रुमास्तत्र मध्यागांशकपोदिताः ।
तेषु बाधेशवृक्षो वा समीपे वास्य तत्स्थितम् ॥॥१८०॥

Stanzas 177 to 180.—If the lord of harm occupies Urdhwamukha Rasi, then the 'charm' has been placed on the tops of trees; if it is Adhomukha Rasi, it is under the earth; if it is Thiryangmukha, it is kept inside stones or logs of woods etc. By examining the Rasi held by the Badhaka, the family to which the trees wherein the Kshudra is deposited belongs should be known. If the Rasi is that of a benefic, the tree also belongs to a good family; if not the reverse. Count from the Navamsa owned by lord of Badhaka to the Navamsa occupied by him. This number gives the trees that grow there. Similarly is to be ascertained whether the Kshudra is in a particular tree or near a tree, etc.

NOTES

The nature of the tree can also be learnt from the Navamsa, as for example, Aries indicates a tree with thorns, Taurus a tree with flowers and Gemini a tree without fruits and so on.

बाधेशे जलराशिस्थे सिन्धुनद्यादिकूलगम् ।
जले क्षिप्तं निखातं वा वाच्यमूर्ध्वाननादिभिः ॥१८१॥

Stanza 181.—If the sign occupied by the lord of the house of harm is watery and it also happens to be Urdhwamukha, then the charm is kept on the bank of ariver or alake; if Adhomukha, buried under the waters; and if Thiryangmukha, has been allowed to float in the waters.

अर्के वार्केण युक्ते वा बाधेशे देवसन्निधौ ।
चन्द्रे चन्द्रान्विते तोयप्रदेशे वाथ सोषरे ॥१८२॥

कुजे वा कुजयुक्ते वा श्मशाने वाग्निसन्निधौ ।
युद्धोर्व्यां वैवमाद्येषु शशिजेवाथ तद्युते ॥१८३॥

विद्याभ्यासविहारोर्व्यामिय जीवे च तद्युते ।
देशान्ते कोशगेहे वा ततः शुक्रे च तद्युते ॥१८४॥

शय्यागृहे वा ग्रामान्ते ततो मन्दे च तद्युते ।
उच्छिष्टादिपरित्यागस्थाने चूर्णादिकं स्थितम् ॥१८५॥

Stanzas 182 to 185.—The Kshudra will be found to have been buried respectively near temples; watery tracts or places where springs sprout; burial grounds, battle fields or fiery places; places of learning or amusement; treasure-houses or state boundaries; village boundaries or bed-rooms; and dirty or deserted places, according as the Sun, the Moon, Mars, Jupiter, Venus or Saturn happens to be either lord of house of harm or occupies the house of harm.

युक्ते तस्मिन् राहुकेतुगुलिकैः सर्पसन्निधौ ।
दिगत्र रिपुनाथस्य वाच्या वा बाधकेशितुः ॥१८६॥

बाधकाधिपसंयुक्तराशेरण्यंशकस्य वा ।
अथत्रोद्धार्यमेव स्याद्बाधेशे चरराशिगे ॥
उभयस्थे प्रयत्नेन नोद्धार्यं तास्थिरस्थिते ॥१८७॥

Stanza 186 & 187.—If the lord of harm is conjoined with Rahu, Ketu or Gulika, then it has been kept in the serpent's abode or its vicinity. The direction where the Kshudra is kept should be ascertained from the lord of 6, lord of house of harm or lord of the Rasi and Navamsa occupied by the Badhaka lord. If the lord of harm is in a movable sign, the Kshudra can be easily removed; if he is in a common sign, it can be taken out with effort; and if he is in a fixed sign, it cannot be removed at all.

क्षुद्रं तत्स्थितिदेशं चैवं ज्ञात्वा, तदुक्तविधिना तत् ।
त्यक्त्वा रक्ष्यं स्थलमथ महाभिचारप्रतिक्रियां वक्ष्ये
॥१८८॥

Stanza 188.—Having ascertained the Kshudra, its location and whether it can be removed, the effects should be destroyed according to sastraic injunctions. I shall now describe the remedies for Mahabhichara.

REMOVING THE MAHABHICHARA

युक्त्वा षष्टपतिं विलग्नपतिना यो राशिरत्रागतः
सादित्यान्वितवीक्षितो यदि बलिं कुर्यादघोराहयम् ।
कार्यं चन्द्रमसा कपालहवनं स्याच्चक्रहोमं विदा
कर्तव्यं प्रतिकारकर्म गुरुणा प्रोक्तं तदेवार्किणा ॥१८९॥

भूमिजेक्षितयुतथ योगभे भूतमारणबलिर्विधीयताम् ।
खड्गरावणबलिं करोतु वा कृत्तिकाबलिमथातनोतु वा
॥१९०॥

शुक्रान्वितेक्षिते योगे प्रतिकारबलिक्रियाम् ।
करोतु शान्तये व्याघ्रेर्बलिं वा भूतमारणम् ॥१९१॥

Stanza 189 to 191.—According as the Rasi arrived at by adding the longitudes of the lords of the Ascendant and the 6th, is conjoined with or aspected by the Sun. the Moon, Mercury, Jupiter or Saturn, Mars or Venus, the remedial measures to be resorted to are respectively Aghorabali, Kapala Homa, Chakra Homa, Prathikarabali, Bhuthamaranabali or Khanga Ravanabali or Krittikabali, or Prathikara or Bhuthamaranabali.

NOTES

I do not propose to explain in detail' these remedial measures. There are even now experts in this subject and they may be consulted.

According to stanzas 189 to 191, add the longitudes of the lord of Lagna and the lord of the 6th and find out which planet occupies or aspects the resulting sign and prescribe the remedies as follows :—

The Sun	—	Aghorabali
The Moon	—	Kapala Homa
Mars	—	BhutaMaranabali, or Khangaravna bali or Krittika bali
Mercury	—	Chakra Homa
Jupiter	—	Prathikarabali
Venus	—	Parthikarabali or Bhuthamaranaabli
Saturn	—	Prathikarabali

अथवा दशमेनैव राशिना। तद्गतेन वा

तद्दृष्ट्रा वा विहङ्गेन विधीयन्तामिमाः क्रियाः ॥१९२॥

Stanza 192.—Or the remedies must be prescribed by taking into consideration the planet occupying or aspecting the 10th from Arudha Lagna.

NOTES.

If you find no association or aspect in the Rasi arrived at as per stanzas 189 to 191, then examine the 10th house from Arudha and see whether any planet joins or aspects it. Then recommend the above noted Balis.

दूतोक्ताद्यक्षरे दीर्घे रोगशान्तिस्तु गानतः ।
ह्रस्वे भोजनपूजाद्यैः संयुक्ते नृत्तकर्मणा ॥१९३॥

Stanza 193.—If the Prasna Akshara (length of the question) of the messenger is long, remedy to be prescribed is music; if it is short, puja and feeding; and if it is neither long nore short, temple dancing.

प्रोक्तः प्रतिक्रियाकर्तृभेदो दृष्ट्यापि पृच्छताम् ।
प्रश्नानुष्ठानपद्धत्यां तत्प्रकारोथ कथ्यते ॥१९४ ॥

Stanza 194.—In *Prasnanushtana Paddhati,* certain remedial measures have been suggested, based on the looks of the questioner.

व्याधेः शान्तिर्भवति मुखजैर्दक्षिणोर्ध्वावलोके ।
प्रष्टुर्दृष्टाविह पुनरधो देवतागायकैश्च ।

वामोर्द्धाधः सुदृढनिहितप्रेषणे तु प्रशस्तै-
श्चण्डालानामपि तदधमैः सा निरुक्ता क्रमेण ॥१९५॥

Stanza 195.—If the questioner looks towards the right side in an upward direction, the remedies should be performed by Brahmins: if he looks down, by temple musicians; if he turns his eyes up on the left side, the high class amongst the low-born; if he looks down on the left, then the inferior amongst the low-born ones.

बाधाभेदोत्र विज्ञेयः स्पर्शनेनापि पृच्छताम् ।
प्रायेण दृष्टिबाधायां खत्वेनदुपयुज्यते ॥१९६॥

Stanza 196.—By closely observing the parts of the body the questioner is touching (sparsa) when he puts the query, the nature of the badha (affllction) can also be ascertained.

DIFFERENT KINDS OF DEVATAS

वक्षो ललाटतलगुह्यतलानि नाभिं
प्रष्टा स्पृशेद्यदि वदन्ति हि देवतार्तिम् ।
पार्श्वे करांगुलिगळे च भुजङ्गपीडां
भ्रूकर्णकक्षयुगळेषु पिशाचपीडाम् ॥ इति १९७॥

Stanza 197.—According to *Anushtana Paddhati* if the questioner feels with his hand his chest, forehead, private parts, and navel, then the man has troubles from devatas; if he touches his sides, back fingers and neck, then he is troubled by serpents; and if he touches his eye-brows, ears and arm-pits, he has trouble from pisachas.

बाधकगततन्नाथग्रहतो ज्ञेया हि देवताभेदाः ।
तदधिष्ठितराश्यंशैरविभेदः स्यात्स कथ्यते तदनु ॥१९८॥

Stanza 198.—The different devatas causing afflication can be known by considering the planets owning or occupying the house of harm, as also on the basis of the Navamsas involving these lords.

सौम्यर्क्षांशकयोः स्थितो यदि भवेद्बाधाधिपः स्वालये
संस्थाप्यान्वहमर्चितोत्तमजनैर्बाधाकरी देवता ।
जीवर्क्षांशगयोः सुरालयगता मान्दे तु नीचार्चिता
भीमोद्यानानिवासिनी स यदि चेत्स्वांशेथवा स्वालये
॥१९९॥

Stanza 199.—If the lord of the house of harm occupies the sign of Mercury or his Navamsa, the trouble is from deities worshipped by high-class people in their homes; if the house or

Navamsa of Jupiter, the trouble will be from deities worshipped in temples; if the house or Navamsa of Saturn, the trouble is from deities worshipped by low-class people; if his own house or Navamsa, the trouble is from deities having their abode in solitary gardens.

दिवाकीर्त्यर्चिता वाच्या चामुण्डी सहकेतुना ।
पञ्चमी बुधयुक्तेन तत्क्षेत्रस्थेन चासृजा ॥२००॥

Stanza 200.—If Mars owning the house of harm joins Ketu, then the deity is Chamundi; if he joins with or occupies the signs of Mercury, the deity will be Panchami.

भौमेन भैरवो घण्टाकर्ण इत्यादयः स्मृताः ।
वाच्या रक्तेश्वरी रक्तचामुण्डयति भयङ्करी ॥२०१॥

Stanza 201.— If Mars occupies odd signs or odd Navamsas, then the deities are Bhairava· Kanta Karna, etc,; if he is in even signs or Navamsas, the deities are Rakteswari, Rakta Chamundi Atibhayakali, etc.

काळी चेत्यादयस्त्वोजयुग्मराश्यंश भेदतः ।
ओजयुग्मत्वभेदे तु भांशयोर्द्विविधा अपि ॥ इति
॥२०२॥

Stanza 202.—Effects suggested in stanza 201 should be stated if the lord of harm occupies an odd sign and an even Navamsa or an even sign and an odd Navamsa.

मेषाद्याश्रयभेदान्मूर्तिविशेषा दिवाकरादीनाम् ।
कथ्यन्ते संक्षेपणादिह खल्वन्यत्र विस्तरेणोक्ताः ॥२०३॥

Stanza 203.—When different planets occupy different signs, they signify different murthis or subsidiary deities. These are dealt with here briefly.

भौमक्षेत्रगतो रविस्त्रिणयनः कीटे स्वयंभूरजे
मर्त्यैरुच्चत ऊर्ध्वमत्र तदधो देवः प्रतिष्ठापितः ।
यक्षी गोगत एष जूकगृहगः काळी पुनः स्त्रीगतः
श्रीरामाद्यवतारविष्णुरथ विष्णुस्त्वेष वीणागतः ॥२०४॥

धर्मदैवं च नागाश्च भास्करः कर्कटस्थितः ।
सिंहस्थो देवता सा या पूज्यते नित्यमात्मना ॥२०५॥

गन्धर्वयक्षौ धनुषि स्थितोर्कस्तयोस्त्रियौ मनिगतस्तु-
भानुः ।
शास्ता पिशाचो मृगयाप्रधानः किरातमूर्तिश्च शनेर्गृहस्थः
॥२०६॥

Stanzas 204 to 206.—The Sun disposed in Aries to Pisces indicates respectiviely the following murthis or deities: Siva, Yakshi, Vishnu, snakes and Dharma Devas, one's own family deity, avataras of Vishnu, Bhadrakali, Swayambhu, Gandharva and yaksha, Ayyappa, Pisacha and hunter's deities, same as in Capricorn and Gandharva and Yakshi damsels. If within the exaltation parts of Aries, the deity of Siva will be one founded by a high personage, while in the rest of Aries, it will be deities installed by ordinary human beings.

NOTES

The commentator adds that when the Sun is in his exalted portion, the Deity may be that of Parasurama. Swayambhu means one grown nuturally. This also refers to Siva so that when the Sun is in Aries or Scorpio. the Deity will be the same. Likewise if the Sun is in Gemini the Deity is Vishnu, while in Virgo, it is Sri Rama and other Avataras of Vishnu. In Taurus it is Yakshi. In Libra it is Bhadrakali. In Sagittarius it is Gandharva and Yaksha. In Pisces the same deities in the female form. For Capricorn and Pisces the deities are the same.

चामुण्डी सुरसद्मगाजगशशी नीचार्च्चिता कीटाग-
श्चामुण्डी यदि मेषगः स विबलो वाच्ये उभे ते अपि ।
यक्षी शुक्रगृहस्थितः शिशिरगुर्वा धर्मदैवं बुध-
क्षेत्रस्थस्तु विमानसुन्दर उत स्त्री वास्य पुंस्त्रीवशात्

॥२०७॥

स्वगृहस्थः शशी नागो धर्मदैवं बली स चेत् ।

सिंहराशिस्थितश्चन्द्रो भगवत्यन्यपूजिता ॥२०८॥

चापस्थो व्योमगन्धर्वस्तत्स्त्री मीनगतः शशी ।

प्रेतशूलपिशाचाद्याः शशी मन्दगृहस्थितः ॥२०९॥

Stanzas 207 to 209.—The Moon in Aries indicates the temple God Chamundi; in Scorpio, the same goddess worshipped by low class people; if weak in these signs, both types of deities; in Taurus, Yakshi; in Libra, Dharma Daiva; in Gemini and Virgo, Vimana Sundara and Sundari; in Cancer, snakes if weak, and Dharma Daiva if strong; in Leo, Bhagavathi worshipped by others; in Sagittarius, Akasa Gandharva (male); in Pisces• Akasa Gandharva (female); and in Capricorn and Aquarius, Preta Soola Pisachas etc.,

स्याद्भूतराक्षसो ब्रह्मराक्षसो नरभोजिनी ।

बालप्रभक्षिणीत्याद्याः स्वर्क्षस्थः क्षितिनन्दनः ॥२१०॥

भौमो भैरवयक्ष एतदबला शौक्रध बौधे स्थितो

गन्धर्वो रतिकाम इत्ययमथो यक्षी च रुष्टो हरिः ।

कर्किस्थः परदेवता भगवती वा कृष्णचामुण्डच–

सृक्सिंहस्थो वनदेवताश्च शिवभूताश्च रुष्टः शिवः ॥२११॥

धनुर्झषस्थः खलु कुक्षिशास्ता स धीरभद्रोथ मृगे च कुम्भे ।
निजोत्सवध्वंसनरुष्टदेवः पराभिचारोद्भवदेवता च
॥२१२॥

Stanzas 210 to 212.—Mars in Aries, Bhuta Rakshasa, Brahma Rakshasa (male), etc.; in Scorpio—Narabhojini, Balaprabhakshani, etc. ; in Taurus—Bhairava, Yakshi (female); in Libra—Bhairava Yaksha (male); Gemini—Narasimha (terrible Vishnu Avatar) and Gandharva; Virgo—terrible Narasimha and Yakshi; Cancer—Bhagavathi, Krishna, Chamundi; Leo—terrible Siva Bhutas as Aghora Vana Devatas; in Sagittarius—Kushi Sasta; Pisces—Veerabhadra; Capricorn—a Deva angered by Abhichara.

भौमक्षेत्रबुधो ज्वरो भृगुगृहे गन्धर्व एष स्वभे
गन्धर्वोपि च किन्नरोथ हिमगोरम्भः पिशाचो गृहे ।
सिंहे पन्नगकन्यका गुरुगृहे रुष्टद्विजप्रेरिता
चामुण्डी कवची पिशाचयुगमाद्यताश्रितं मन्दभे ॥२१३॥

Stanza 213.—Mercury in Aries and Scorpio—Jwara Devata; Taurus and Libra—Gandharva; Gemini and Virgo—Gandharva and Kinnara; Cancer—Jala Pisacha; Leo—Naga Kanya; Sagittarius and Pisces—Chamundi charged with mischief by an angered Brahmin; in Capricorn and Aquarius—Kavachi, Sula Pisachi, Kala Pisachi.

भौमर्क्षे कुपितेशभूतनिवहो दुर्देवता चाभिचारोत्था
भूमिसुरस्य मार्गवगृहे यक्षी च यक्षोप्युभौ ।
तीव्रापस्मृतिदौ गुरुबुधगृहे क्लीबात्मिका देवता
विप्राणामपि चाभिचारजनिता वा देवकोपोद्भवा ॥२१४॥

Stanza 214.—Jupiter in Aries and Scropio—Siva Bhutas, Durdevata formed by the Abhichara of Brahmins; Taurus and Libra—Apasmara Yakshi and Yaksha; Gemini and Virgo –a neuter Devata formed by the wrath of Gods or by the Abhichara or Brahmins.

तुङ्गस्थः खलु देवताग्निगृहगा गन्धर्वमुख्यस्तथा
सिंहस्थो नृपसेवकैरिह नृणामुद्दिश्य कान्तं स्त्रिया ।
नारिणां च कृताभिचारजनिता दुर्देवता वाक्पति-
र्भस्माप्सङ्गिपिशाचकावधमगन्धर्वः शनेर्न स्वभे ॥२१५॥

Stanza 215.—Jupiter in Cancer indicates Davata in a Brahmin's house caused by his Agnihotra, Gandharva Chief; in Leo Davata caused by Abhichara of king's servants or caused by Abhichara of a woman performed against her husband; in Capricorn and Aquarius—Bhasma

Pisacha, Jala Pisacha, Adhama Gandharva; and in Sagittarius and Pisces—do not signify any Devatas.

भौमक्षेत्रभृगुस्तु जीववदजे यक्षस्तथा राक्षसः
स्वर्क्षो कर्कटके च यक्षसहिता यक्षी बुधर्क्षे पुनः ।
विद्याभ्यासभवाभिचार इनभे यक्षी सुरक्षेत्रगा
चापे ब्राह्मणशाप एव झषभे दुर्गा भवेद्भार्गवः ॥२१६॥

मन्दक्षेत्रगतः शुक्रः स्यादपस्मारदेवता ।
वात्याप्रभृतयः कालपिशाचश्चात्र बाधकः ॥२१७॥

Stanzas 216 and 217.—Venus in Aries and Scorpio—similar to Jupiter as in stanza 215, but in addition Yaksha and Rakshasa also : in Taurus, Cancer and Libra—Yaksha, Yakshi ; in Gemini and Virgo—Abhichara Devata of rival inimical co-scholars ; in Leo—temple Yakshi ; Sagittarius —a Murthi caused by curse of a Brahmin ; and Pisces—Durga Bhagavathi : in Carpicorn—Apasmara : and in Aquarius—Kala Pisacha.

असाध्यापस्मृतिर्मेषे कीटे प्राग्जन्मपीडितः ।
शिवालयस्थस्तद्भूतो वक्तव्यो भानुनन्दनः ॥२१८॥

गव्यपस्मारयक्षस्तद्यक्षीशापो द्विजस्य च ।
जूके शास्त्रादिभूतेशाः क्रुद्धा महविघाततः ॥२१९॥

चौथे काननदेवता शनिरपि प्रेतः सुहृत्प्रेषितो
दैवं नीचसमर्पितं सुरगृहे सिंहे सुरावासगः ।
शास्ताऽखेटपिशाचकश्च गुरुभे गन्धर्वभेदो मणी–
संघातार्तवविशृतोथ निजभे प्रेतः पिशाचाद्यपि ।।इति

।।२२०।।

Stanzas 218, to 220.—Saturn in Aries—effects of Apasmara Devatas not curable; Scorpio—a Siva Bhuta whom the native troubled in his last birth; Taurus—Apasmara Yaksha, Yakshi, curse of a Brahmin; Libra—Bhuthanathas as Kirata, Ayyappa, etc., originated by obstructing a festival: Gemini—Vana Devata: and Virgo—Pretas of relatives; Cancer—Devatas worshipped by low caste people: Leo—temple Sasta, Kirata, hunter's Gods, Pisachas: Sagittarius and Pisces—Mani (Gandharva); and Capricorn and Aquarius—Preta and Pisacha.

NOTES

So far the author has been reviewing the troubles caused by foes. He will now study how diseases can be cured.

एतच्छत्रुबाधानिरुपण विषयम् । अयव्याधेः शमन–
निरूपण प्रकारो लिख्यते ।।

बाधारूढाल्लग्नतो व्याधिशान्तिश्चिन्यारूढेपापयोगेक्षणार्धैः।
दोषैयुक्ते व्याधिवृद्धिर्गताधः प्राग्लग्ने सा भाविनी
पृच्छकानाम् ॥२२१॥

Stanza 221.—The nature of affliction is to be read from Arudha and the remedies to be employed are to be ascertained from the rising sign. If Arudha Lagna is afflicted, the progress of disease will be stopped. If the rising sign is afflicted, the illness will further increase.

भाग्यस्थानगते शुभे तदधिपे प्राणिन्यभीष्टस्थिते
लग्नेशे तपनेन वाथ धिषणेनालोकिते वान्विते ।
स्यादेवेश्वरसेवयोगदशमस्वद्वन्मनूनां जपै
र्लग्नेशे नवमे च दोषसहिते व्याधेः शमो दुर्लभः
॥२२२॥

Stanza 222.—If benefics occupy the 9th house, or the lord of the 9th is favourably disposed, or if the lord of Lagna is associated with or aspected by the Sun or Jupiter, the object of the remedial measures, *viz.*, the recovery of the patient, will be realised. If however the lords of the Lagna and the 9th are afflicted, then recovery is unlikely.

पृष्ठोदयजलह्रासचराधोमुखराशिभिः ।
लग्नस्थैर्व्याधिशान्तिः स्यात्तत्प्रश्नेन तदन्यथा ॥२२३॥

Stanza 223.—In a query pertaining to illness, *recovery* should be predicted if the rising sign be Prishtodya, movable, *adhomukha*, *jala hrasa rasi*. Othrewise there will be no relief

षष्ठाष्टमव्ययसुखे पापविमुक्ते शुभान्विते केन्द्रे ।
व्याधेः शान्तिप्रश्ने शान्तिर्भवतीति निर्दिशेन्मातिमान्
॥इति ॥२२४॥

Stanza 224.—Recovery should be predicted if the Ascendant, 4th, 6th, 8th and 11th houses are free from malefics and benefics occupy the 4th, 7th and 10th.

NOTES

Relief is to be predicted only after the due performance of remedial measures.

WHO SHOULD PERFORM REMEDIES?

बाधकविहगाधिश्रितभवनांशकयोर्न्निरीक्ष्यसत्वादिगुणान् ।
सात्विकराजसतामसकर्मास्त्वेतत्प्रतिक्रियाकर्त्ता ॥२२५॥

Stanza 225.—Remedies have to be suggested to be performed by persons of Sathvic, Rajasic and Thamasic nature according as the Badhaka planet occupies a Sathwic, Rajasic or Thamasic Rasi or Navamsa.

सूर्याचन्द्रमसोर्ग्रहांशकगतश्चेत् खेचरो बाधको
विप्रः कर्म करोतु निर्जनगुरोश्चेद्देवतागायकः ।
ज्ञस्य स्याद्यदि कुम्भकृत्प्रभृतयः शुक्रारयोर्वा शने-
श्चण्डालोत्तममध्यमौ तदधमस्तद्देवताप्रीतये ॥२२६॥

Stanza 226.—Remedies should be performed by different persons according to the situation of the badhaka planet thus: Badhaka planet in the sign or Navamsa of the Sun or the Moon—holy Brahmins; sign or Navamsa of Jupiter—temple songsters; sign or Navamsa of Mercury—potters; in the sign or Rasi or Amsa of Venus—high class amongst the Chandalas; sign or Amsa of Mars—ordinary Chandalas; and sign and Amsa of Saturn—very low amongst them.

मान्दित्रिकोणयोगेक्षाद्येतस्य यदि पुल्कसः ।
दिवाकीतिस्तथा केतुबाधक ग्रहयोगतः ॥ इति ॥ २२७॥

Stanza 227.—If the troubling or harming planet is combined with or aspected by Gulika or stands in the 5th or 9th house from him, Pulayas are to be employed. If the planet joins with Ketu, Parayas should perform the rites.

सौम्ये सौम्यगृहस्थे बाधेशे तत्प्रतिक्रिया विप्रैः ।
पापे तद्गृहगे वा चण्डालाद्यैरितीरितं कश्चित् ॥२२८॥

Stanza 228.—If the troubling planet is a benfic or occupies a benefic sign, the remedies should be done by Brahmins; if he is a malefic or occupie a maefic sign—low caste people should be employed for the purpose.

चिकित्सा तु कृता केन रोगशान्त्यै भवेदिति ।
प्रश्नोपि शमनप्रश्नवत्स्यात् कर्मात्र शक्तिमत् ॥२२९॥

Stanza 229.—To the query who should be the physician to whom the work of medical treatment should be entrusted, the anwser is similar to the one given in verse 32. In addition to what is given there, the 10th house also must have benficial influences.

मृत्युञ्जयगणपतिहोमादानां कर्तृचिन्तने धिषणः ।
अनुकूलो जलवृद्धिर्दशमगुणश्चास्तु लग्नमूर्ध्वमुखम्
॥२३०॥

Stanza 230.—With regard to the question to whom the remedial measures should be entrusted, the answer is to be read from the favourable disposition of Jupiter such as in 4, 9 or 11. The Ascendant should be *jala hrasa rasi,* 10th house must be benefic in character and the Lagna should also be *Urdhwamukha*.

इति प्रश्नमार्गे पञ्चदशाध्यायः

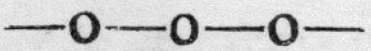

षोडशाध्यायः

अध्यायैः पञ्चदशाभिर्गतैरेतैः समीरितः ।

आयुः प्रश्नः सरोगारम्भान्तबाधाप्रतिक्रियः ॥१॥

Stanza 1.—In the last fifteen chapters, the question of longevity has been examined in detail, noting also when disease is likely to begin, how it originates and how it could be cured by suitable remedial measures.

पूर्वमायुः परीक्षेत पश्चाल्लक्षणमादिशेत् ।

इत्युक्त्यायुः परीक्ष्याथ लक्षणं किञ्चिदुच्यते ॥२॥

Stanza 2.—The longevity of the person is to be examind first and then the trends in the horoscope prognosticated. This is what great Rishis say.

WHEREABOUTS OF THE QUERIST

लग्ने चरे चरमुखांशकतः क्रमेण

दूरे नृणां चरणसंस्थिततद्द्वयानि ।

अभ्यर्णे एव तदिदं त्रितयं स्थिरर्क्षे

तद्वद्वदेत्तदुभयात्मनि मध्यदेशे ॥३॥

Stanza 3.—Considering the movable, fixed or dual nature of the Ascendant and the Navamsa Lagna, one has to infer the whereabouts of the questioner — whether he is at home or in a far away place, etc.

NOTES

If Lagna and Navamsa Lagna are movable, then the questioner is in a distant place travelling about on some work; if the Lagna is movable and Navamsa is fixed, he is in a distant place but staying without undertaking any long journeys; if the Lagna is movable and the Navamsa is common, he is in a distant place, and there he is sometimes staying at one place and sometimes journeying; if Lagna is fixed and Amsa is movable, he is in the neighbouring places and journeying from place to place; if Lagna is fixed and Amsa is also fixed; he is in a neighbouring place and stays without any long journeys; if Lagna is fixed and Amsa is common, he is in a neighbouring place and while there, he is sometimes journeying and sometimes staying in one and the same place; if Lagna is common and Amsa is movable, he can be found neither very far from his native place nor very near it, leading a nomad's life, if Lagna is common and Amsa is fixed, he can be found in the above-mentioned place leading a sedentary life; if Lagna and Navamsa are both common, he lives in the above-mentioned place leading both sedentary and travelling life. Here Lagna means Arudha Lagna. Lagna Rasi indicates distance, and Amsa signifies the nature of life.

आरूढाधीश्वरारूढराश्यंशाभ्यां च चिन्तयेत् ।
एतद्द्वयोश्च संवादे सति स्याल्लक्षणं दृढम् ॥४॥

Stanza 4.—The above can also be read from the Rasi and Amsa occupied by the lord of Arudha. If any contradiction is discovered between the two, the stronger of the two should be considered.

SUCCES OVER ENEMIES

जन्मलग्नाधिनाथस्य प्रश्नलग्नाधिपस्य च ।
दिशि सिध्येदयत्नेन कार्यं वैरिजयादिकम् ॥५॥

Stanza 5.—Success in life and victory over the enemy attends a person in the direction denoted by the lord of Lagna.

NOTES

Here, Lagna refers to the Ascendant at the time of birth, or Lagna rising at the time of question according as the chart under consideration is a radical or a Horary one.

अरूढे सप्तमे वास्य ग्रहश्चेदुच्चसंस्थितः ।
तस्योक्तं द्रव्यसर्वस्वं प्रभुरस्तीति निर्दिशेत् ॥६॥

Stanza 6—.If an exalted planet occupies Arudha or the 7th house from it, then the querist acquires wealth through sources signified by the planet concerned.

NOTES

This stanza is highly suggestive. There will be influx of money through sources signified by the planets exalted in Arudha or the 7th therefrom. Suppose the Sun is the planet involved in this combination. Then the income will be due to dealings in precious metals, medicines, etc., as per the stanza *arkamsethrinakanaka*, etc. If Saturn is the planet, the source will be dealings in products pertaining to bones, hides and skins, etc.

आरूढभतदीशाभ्यां लक्षणं यद्यदीरितम् ।
आरूढविषये पूर्वं तत्तदत्रापि योजयेत् ॥७॥

Stanza 7.—All those *lakshanas* (significations) mentioned earlier regarding Arudha and the lord of Arudha should also be made use of and suitably applied in this connection.

NOTES

Here the reference to ' earlier ' passages means to the 8th chapter.

Bright and Dark Future

सुखान्त्यार्द्धादि षड्भावस्थिता यदि शुभग्रहाः ।
सम्पत्स्यादुपरि प्रष्टुः पापश्चेदापदं वदेत् ॥८॥

Stanza 8.—The future of the person will be bright or otherwise according as the six houses from the latter part of the 4th are occupied by benefics or malefics.

कर्मान्त्यार्द्धादिषड्भावस्थितैर्भूतं शुभाशुभम् ।
तुलादिषट्के लग्नस्थे दैवविन्निर्दिशेदिति ॥९॥

Stanza 9.—If however the six houses from the latter portion of the 10th house are occupied, then the past life of the person would have been fortunate or otherwise according to the benefic or malefic nature of the planets. This applies to personsborn in the six Rasis beginning with Libra.

NOTES

The future or past being fortunate or otherwise, as per stanzas 8 and 9, applies only to persons born in Libra to Pisces.

मेषादिषट्के लग्नस्थे सुखान्त्यार्द्धादिषट्कगैः ।
गता स्यात्सम्पदापच्च भविषत्यन्यषट्कगैः ॥१०॥

Stanza 10.—For persons born in the six Rasis beginning with Aries, the past is indicated by the Bhavas 4 to 10 and the future by Bhavas 10 to 4.

NOTES

Here the unexpired portion of 4th house till the expired portion of the 10th house — and the expired portion of the 10th till the unexpired part of the 4th is implied. Benefics indicate good. Malefics signify misfortunes. Thus the past and the future are to be read from the eastern and western hemispheres.

MEANS TO ADOPT

सामादिषु प्रयोक्तव्य उपायः समयेत्र कः ।

इति जिज्ञासवे वाच्यं लक्षणं किमपीर्यते ॥११॥

Stanza 11.—If a question like "by what means or art can I win in this object" is put, then the method to be adopted to answer this question is given below :—

साम्नी जीवः स भृगुतनयो दण्डनाथौ कुजार्कौ

दानस्येन्दुः शिखियमबुधाः सासुरा भेदनाथाः

वीर्योपेतैरुपचयगतैर्लग्नगैः केन्द्रगैर्वा

तत्तत्सिद्धिं व्रजति तदहस्स्वंशके वापि तेषाम् ॥१२॥

Stanza 12.—The means indicated by the strongest of the planets occupying the Ascendant, Upachayas or Kendras should be adopted as follows :—Jupiter and Venus—gentle (same); the Moon—bribery (dana); Saturn, Rahu and Mercury —intimidation (bheda); and the Sun and the Mars—force (danda); The week-day or hour of the concerned planet is preferable.

NOTES

Jupiter and Venus govern arts of gentle persuasion. The Moon stands for offer of gifts and money. Mercury governs intimidation. Saturn, Rahu and Ketu also govern intimidation in different forms. Mars and the Sun govern open rupture and war. The first two come under diplomacy and arbitration. The last two come under war. The methods indicated by the strongest of the planets occupying Upachaya Rasis, or Lagna or Kendras should be used on the respective week days or at the time of their Kala Hora. Then the object can be accomplished.

Though Lagna is included in the Kendras it is repeated to show its importance. So is the 10th house repeated though it is included in the Upachaya Rasi. The week-days and Kala Hora for Rahu and Ketu are similar to those of Saturn and Mars.

Locating a Treasure Trove

एतस्मिन् भवने किं वा धनमस्ति न वेति यः ।
जिज्ञासुर्वाच्यमेतस्मै लक्षणं सम्प्रतीर्यते ॥१३॥

Stanza 13.—To a query "whether a treasure trove can be found in this house", the answer is to be given thus :

यदि कण्टकवर्तिनः शुभाः स्युर्यदि वैकादशवेश्मगाः विलग्नात् ।
धनवद्‌ग्रहमादिशेत्तदानीं द्वारं च स्वदिशि परं वदेद्धिधिज्ञः ॥१४॥

Stanza 14.—If all the benefics occupy Kendras or 11th and 4th houses, then there is wealth in the house mentioned by the questioner. In the dik or direction indicated by the benefics, there will be openings as windows or doors, etc.

प्राच्यादीत्युदितिने यत्र विधिना गेहस्य भागे भवे–
त्सौम्यः कण्टकलाभगोत्र निहितं तस्योदितं तद्धनम् ।
स्वोच्चस्थो यदि भूरिवैरिगृहनीचस्थः स चेत्तल्लघु
क्रूराधिष्टितगेहभागानिहितं वाच्यं च शल्यादिकम् ॥ इति
॥१५॥

Stanza 15.—The treasure-trove will be located in the direction signified by the benefics adverted to in the previous stanza. According as the planet is exalted or occupies own house, or is debilitated or in inimical house, the fund will be much or little. It can also be located in the direction indicated by malefics.

NOTES

Say there is wealth in the quarter of that house or building indicated by benefics in Lagna or 4 or 11 (the Sun is East, etc.). If that benefic is exalted or in Moolatrikona, the quantity is appreciable. If he is debilitated or in an inimical Sign, it is very little in the diks indicated by malefics.

DRESS WORN BY VISITORS

भानुः कौसुम्भवासाः सितवसनधरो ग्लौरसृग्रक्तवासाः
पालाशाच्छादनो ज्ञो वसनमथ गुरोः पीतमच्छस्य चित्रम्।
कोणः कृष्णांबरः स्यादय कथयतु तैर्लक्षणं केन्द्रसंस्थै
रायस्थैर्वा स्ववासोधरयुवतिनृणामागमं प्रश्नकाले ॥१६॥

Stanza 16.—Strong planets disposed in quadrants or the eleventh house indicate that at the time of the query there will be visitors—male or female—according to the sex signified by the concerned planet—wearing the dress of different colours thus: the Sun—red, the Moon—white, Mars—red, Mercury—green, Jupiter—yellow, Venus—variegated, and Saturn—black.

NOTES

The strongest planet indicates the sex as well as the colour of the dress worn by the visitor.

NATURE OF PERSONS MET WITH ON THE WAY

प्रस्थानलग्नास्तगतैर्बलिष्ठैः केन्द्रस्थितैर्वा विहगोदितानाम् ।
विप्रादिनारीनरवस्त्रभाजामभ्यगमो वर्त्मनि कीर्तनीयः
॥१७॥

Stanza 17.—In a query bearing on journeys, the powerful planets in the 7th or in quadrants indicate the caste and sex of the person one will meet on his way and the colour of the dress he or she wears.

मार्तण्डो व्रणवान् व्रणी धरणिजो वाचस्पतिः काचदृ-
ङमन्दो वामपदे व्रणाङ्कसहीतः पार्श्वे तिलाङ्को भृगुः ।
चन्द्रो माषतिलादिलञ्छनयुतः सौम्यः सिरासन्ततो
योऽयं प्राक्तनलक्ष्मणोर्वरकळत्रादेश्च लक्ष्मण्यदः ॥१८॥

Stanza 18.—The Sun and Mars govern wounds and sores; Jupiter—copper coloured eyes; Saturn—wounds in the left leg; Venus—moles on the sides; the Moon—moles and scars; and Mercury—swollen nerves in the body. These details can be used in questions bearing on journeys and marriage.

CHARACTERISTICS OF BRIDE AND BRIDEGROOM

आरूढनाथेन तु लक्ष्म वध्वास्तदस्तनाथेन वरस्य वाच्यम् ।
प्रश्ने विवाहस्य परत्र लग्नपुत्रादिकैः प्रष्टृसुतादिकानाम्
॥१९॥

Stanza 19.—In a query bearing on marriage, the characteristics of the wife should be read from the lord of Arudha, and those of the husband from the lord of the 7th from Arudha. In all queries—marriage or otherwise—particulars about

the native should be gathered from the Lagna lord, those of the children from the 5th lord and so on.

NOTES

According to the commentator, if for example, the lord of Lagna is the Sun, the wife will be having some wound or sore; if the lord of the 7th from Arudha happens to be Jupiter, the husband or bridegroom will have copper coloured eyes (**मार्जारेक्षण:**); In this way in queries bearing on marriage or on other aspects, the *lakshanas* should be applied.

लक्षणकथनेमुष्मिन् खचरवपुर्द्रव्यजातमपि यद्यत् ।
संज्ञास्वस्वदशाफलकथितं तद्योजनीयमखिलमपि ॥२०॥

Stanza 20.—The characteristics, significations etc., attributed to different planets in the chapter on preliminaries should be approximately adapted in answering the various questions.

NOTES

Lakshana means attributes or properties or characteristics assigned to various planets while dealing with preliminaries. Here reference is made to 'vapu', 'dravya' etc., signified by different planets. According to Varaha Mihira for instance, the Sun has fair appearance (**मधुपिङ्गलदृक्**). He rules copper (**ताम्रस्या**). He signifies nails, teeth, **नखदन्तपचर्मः** etc. According to stanza 6 (given above) (**भानुः कौसुलभः**) the Sun represents red colour wounds, etc.

All these characteristics should be carefully. considered. Suppose in a query, the Sun is strongly placed in a *kendra*. This means that a person wearing red coloured clothes, having wounds in the body, with a squarish face will make an appearance at the time of the query; or article made of gold, copper, nails, teeth, etc,. would be broughts in. In Prasana bearing on marriage, if the lord of arudha Lagna is the Sun, then the bride will have a square face. I the lord of the 7th from Arudha happens to be the Sun, then the characteristics are applicable to the bridegroom. Similarly details can be used in other queries also, bearing on husband, children, etc.

यद्यद्वस्त्विह लोके तत्सर्वं धातुमूलजीवमयम् ।
कृष्णीयप्रभृतिभ्यः शास्त्रेभ्यस्तद्भिदा ज्ञेया ॥इति ॥२१॥

Stanza 21.—All matters in this world can be classified into Dhatu, Moola and Jeeva. The details regarding them given in *Krishneeya* and other treatises, should be carefully ascertained.

NOTES

The various minerals, vegetables, etc. assinged to different planets should be ascertained from standard books on the snbject. According as the indicators of the various Dhatus, etc., are in the house of gains or destruction access to or deprivation of them should be predicted.

Stanzas 22 to 24 have been omitted as they deal with *lakshanas* covered in Chapter II.

RULERS OF DIFFERENT PARTS OF DAY

आदित्यदिदिनेष्विनादिफणिपर्यन्ताः क्रमेणोदयं
स्वस्वाद्याः स्वदिनेषु यान्ति दिवसाष्टांशेषुखल्वष्टसु ।
जीवज्ञास्फुजितां क्रिया हि सकलाः सिध्येयुरिन्दोः शनै–
नोन्येषामुदये वदेदिति सुधीः सञ्चिन्त्य पृच्छाविधौ ॥२५॥

Stanza 25.—The eight parts of the day beginning from sunrise, are ruled respectively by the week-day lord and other planets in the order of the Sun to Rahu. If the ruling period at the time of a query is that of Jupiter, Mercury or Venus, the objects of the question will be fully realised. If the ruler of the period is the Moon, the object will be fulfilled in due course. If the periods belong to the Sun, Mars, Saturn or Rahu, the result is failure.

प्रश्ने दिनगतविघटीर्विन्यस्य विभज्य शेखरैः शेषात् ।
विज्ञेयो विहगानामुदयो वक्तव्यमसुनेदम् ॥२६॥

Stanza 26.—Convert the ghatis at the time of the query into vighatis. Divide the product by 225. The quotient represents the number of the period.

NOTES

Stanzas 25 and 26 give a simple method for finding out the results of a query—irrespective of the nature of the query. According to stanza 26, the duration of day (in terms of vighatis) should be divided by 225. The quotient represents the number of the rising period, which should be reckoned from sunrise.

The day (diurnal duration) is divided into 8 parts. The lord of the first part is the lord of the week-day. The lords succeed in the order of the Sun, the Moon, etc. Thus on a Sunday, the ruler of the first part is the Sun; of the 2nd the the Moon; the 3rd Mars; the 4th Mercury; the 5th Jupiter: the 6th Venus: the 7th Saturn and of the 8th Rahu. The division of the day into 8 parts has nothing to do with the planetary hours, described in other books, where the lord of the week-day rules the 1st hour, the subsequent hours being ruled by the planets in the order of Saturn, Jupiter, Mars, Sun, Venus and the Sun.

To take an example : Suppose a query is put at 4-5 p.m. at Bangalore on 21–5–1960. The number of ghatis from sunrise will be 25 and therefore the number of vighatis is 1500. This divided by 225 gives the quotient as 6 and the remainder as 150. Therefore the 7th part is rising. The week-day being Saturday, lord of the 1st part is Saturn, that of the 2nd Rahu, of the 3rd the Sun, of the 4th the Moon, of the 5th Mars, of the 6th Mercury and of the 7th Jupiter. As the concerned planet is Jupiter, the object of the query will be fulfilled.

I must caution readers that this particular method of answering queries has its own limitations. Each part rules for nearly 1½ hours and queries put by different people in a particular division of the day would elicit the same answer. This method cannot be used after sunset and before sunrise. But the commentator adds that under the dictum वांराधिपात्तं चमाटया (the ruler of the 1st part after sunset will be the fifth planet from the week-day lord, in the order of the Sun to Rahu), the method can be utilised for answering questions put during nights also. Thus on a Sunday, the lords of the eight divisions, (from sunset to sunrise) will be respectively Jupiter (5th from the Sun lord of the week-day), Venus (2nd), Saturn (3rd), Rahu (4th), the Sun (5th), the Moon (6th), Mars (7th), and Mercury (8th).

गतनाडिकामुदधि संगुणां हरेदवनीधरैस्तु परिशेषितैः
क्रमात् ।
मृतिविभ्रमौ कलहसौख्यनिर्गमाः सकळत्रबन्धनमितीरयेद्-
बुधः ॥ इति ॥ २७ ॥

Stanza 27.—Multiply the query ghatis by 4 and divide the product by 7. If the remainder is 1, the result is death; 2 travel; 3 quarrels; 4 happiness; 5 departure; 6 happiness with wife; and 7 incarceration.

NOTES

This stanza is from *Anushtanapaddhati*. I do not propose to comment on the method which is generally used even now by village astrologers to give snapshot answers to questions. Sometimes the method works. Sometimes it does not.

CHARACTERISTICS DUE TO FIVE ELEMENTS

आत्मश्वासोद्भवो दूतवाक्यप्रथमवर्णजः ।

दिनयातघटीभूतो भूतानामुदयास्त्रिधा ॥२८॥

Stanza 28.—The orgin of Pancha Bhutas can be known in three ways; (1) from an examination of the astrologer's breath; (2) from the first letter of the word uttered by the messenger or queren; and (3) from the time of query.

अभयोः पुटयोस्तु दण्डसंस्था पृथिवीतोयमधः
कृशानुरूत्वम् ।
पवनस्तु तिर्यङ्नसोथ मध्ये गगनं भूतगतस्तन्दूद्भवेयम्
॥२९॥

Stanza 29.—While breathing out it the air comes out of both the nostrils and is of the shape of the of a straight stick, it is Prithvibhuta; when it passes straight down and not in the shape of a stick it is Jalabhuta; when it passes upwards, it is Agnibhuta. When it passes in angular shape, it is Vayubhuta; and it when passing out of both the nostrils, the breath joins together and continues as one, it is Akasabhuta.

भूमेरकारं पयसस्त्विकारं वह्नेरुकारं मुनयो वदन्ति ।
एकारमोकारमपि क्रमेण वायोश्च वर्णं नभसश्च वर्णम् ॥३०॥

Stanza 30.—The letters a (अ), e (इ), u (उ), ye (ए) and o (ओ) respectively signify Prithvi. Jala, Agni, Vayu and Akasa Bhutas.

यामः स्याद्दिवसष्टभाग इह तेष्वोजे महिपूर्वको
युग्मे स्याद्गगनादिगश्च दिवसे रात्रौ च भूतक्रमः ।
भूमे, पादयुता घटी तु पयसो नाडयाङ्घ्रहीना शुचे–
र्नाडयर्द्धं पवनस्य खस्य घटिकापादो द्वयोर्यामयोः ॥३१॥

Stanza 31.—Of the eight Yamas into which the day-time is divided, the odd ones begin in Prithvi Bhuta or Tatwa and end in Akasa Bhuta. The even ones rise in Akasa Bhuta and end in Prithvi Bhuta—the duration of the Tatwas in a Yama in terms of vighatis being; Prithvi 75, Apa 60, Agni 45, Vayu 30 and Akasa 15. Similar is the case with regard to the night.

NOTES

In Chapter II, reference has already been made to the method of answering questions by considering the exhaled and inhaled air current. Here again reference is made in stanzas 29 to 31, to the Panchabhutas governing (*a*) the expired air current of the astrologer, (*b*) the first letter of the question or the message, and (*c*) the time of the day. It is not poseible for the average astrologer to study the nature of his breath and the Bhuta under which the expired air current at a particular moment falls. According to Gheranda the standard length of the body of Vayu is 72 inches or six feet. The ordinary length of the air current when expired is 9 inches. The length varies when man performs different kinds of work. Thus in singing, it is said to become 12 inches; in eating 15 inches and so on. The astrologer must be able to say whether at the time of the query, the breath one exhales is from one nostril or both the nostrils; and whether it is cloudy and resembles a a straight stick; whether it goes upwards or downwards and so on and then decide the Bhuta under which it falls.

The first letter of the query or message should also enable the astrologer to discover the predominant Bhuta at the time. The first letters अ,इ,उ,ए,ओ respectively represent the Bhutas Prithvi, Apa, Agni, Vayu and Akasa. All letters of the alphabet can be brought under the above 5 letters. Thus if the first letter is (ki) it is like इ and represents Apa-bhuta. Here no distinction is made between a consonant and a vowel.

Stanza 31 gives the periods in a day or night when the different *tatwas* will be predominant. The duration of day and night are each divided into 8 parts. In odd parts—Ist, 3rd, etc., the first 75 vighats (30 minutes) represent the Prithvitatwa, the next 60 vighatis (24 minutes) Jalatatwa, the next 45 vighatis (18 minutes) Agnitatwa, the next 30 vighatis (12 minutes) Vayutatwa and the last

15 vighatis (6 minutes) Akasatatwa. In even *Yamas*, the reverse holds good, *i.e.*, the first 15 vighatis (6 minutes) represent Vayutatwa, the next 30 (12 minutes) Agnitatwa and the last 75 vighatis (30 minutes) Prithvitatwa. The length of each interval (Yama) is taken as $3\frac{3}{4}$ ghatis ($1\frac{1}{2}$ hours) assuming the duration of the day as 30 ghatis (12 hours). When the duration of day is more or less than 30 vighatis, the duration of each Yama and the tatwa change proportionately.

Thus in a day of equal diurnal and nocturnal duration, the following periods represent the total period of each tatwa:

Prithvi	—	20	ghatis	(8 hours)
Jala	—	16	"	(6h. 24m.)
Vayu	—	8	"	(3h. 12m.)
Agni	—	12	"	(4h. 48m.)
Akasa	—	4	"	(1h. 36m.)

भूतानामुतयेन च विचिन्तयेत् प्रष्टकार्यमखिलमपि ।
न मृतिर्न रोगशान्तिर्द्धरणेरुदये जलोदये तु पुनः
॥३२॥

इप्सितमचिरात्सिध्यति वह्नेरुदये मृतिर्विरोधश्च ।
वायोरुदये सर्वं सिध्यति गमनागमादि चलकार्यम्
॥३३॥

व्याध्यारंभो नाशः स्थिरकार्यं चाहवश्च तथा ।
आकाशोदयकाले सिध्यत्यशुभं विशेषेण ॥३४॥

Stanzas 32 to 34.—By noting the Bhuta in these three ways at the time of Prasna, predictions can be made. If the Bhuta is Prithvi, the sick man will neither die or recover. If it is Jala Bhuta, the desired things will soon be accomplished. If it is Agni, enmity and death will take place. If it is Vayu, all activities such as going and coming will be successful. If it is Akasa, new diseases will crop up, business will fail and prosperity will decline. But some permanent activities will be successful.

LAKSHANAS GIVEN IN OTHER WORKS

प्रागात्मश्वासविषये विस्ताराद्यदिहेरितम् ।
पञ्चानामपि भूतानां फलं तदपि चिन्तयेत् ।।इति ।।३५।।

Stanza 35.—What has been already described regarding these Bhutas, etc., in earlier chapters may also be utilised with advantage.

NOTES

Here, the reference is to Chapter II where the astrological significance of these five bhutas have been enumerated.

लग्नेशोशुभसंयुतो यदि नृभे प्रष्टविपत्तिर्नृभिः
पश्वाद्यैश्चतुरङ्ि.घ्रमेषु यदि चेत्तद्भेदतो निर्दिशेत् ।
सर्पाख्यैस्तु सरीसृपाख्य भवने यद्यंबुराशौ नदी-
कूपादौ पतनं झषाधिजलजन्तूपद्रवो वा यदि ।।३६।।

Stanza 36.—If the lord of Lagna joins with an evil planet, there will be danger and it will come from men or beasts according to the nature of the rising sign. If it is Taurus, it is from horned animals; if it is *sarisripa Rasi*, the danger will be from serpents. If it is a watery sign, he will fall in a well or tank or some aquatic animals will bite him.

NOTES

Here the sign refers to the sign occupied by the lord of Lagna. If it is a biped sign, the danger will be from men. If it is a quadruped sign, the danger will be from quadrupeds. Thus if it is Taurus, horned animals are meant; if it is Leo, animals having short teeth, etc., are meant. Cancer and Scoripo are *sarisripa* signs.

DANGER TO THE HOUSE

संहारोडुगतोर्कजः क्षितिभुवा युक्तोथवा वीक्षितः
प्रष्टुर्मन्दिरदाहकृत्स शिखिना युक्तेक्षितो वा तथा ।
संहारोडुगतोसदीक्षितयुतो लग्नाधिपः कुष्टका-
येवं राहुयुतोक्षिते तु तनुपे प्रष्टाहिदष्टो भवेत् ॥३७॥

Stanza 37.—If Saturn occupies a *samhara-nakshatra* in association with or aspected by Mars or Ketu, then the house of the native will be in danger of fire. If the lord of Lagna occupies a *samhara nakshatra* and joins with or is aspected by evil planets, the native will be affected by leprosy. If such an evil planet is Rahu, then the danger will be from serpents.

LOSS OF METALS

मार्तण्डे तनुगे भृगौ धनगते हेमागमः पृच्छतां
लग्नस्थे भृगुजे व्ययस्थित इने हेम्नो विनाशो भवेत् ।
मन्दे लग्नगतेऽर्थगे च शशिजे लाभोऽयसः कथ्यतां
मन्दे रिष्फगते बुधेऽथ तनुगे नाशश्च वाच्योयसः
॥३८॥

Stanza 38.—If the Sun occupies Lagna and Venus is in the 2nd, the native will get plenty of gold; if *vice versa*, there will be loss of gold. If Saturn is in Lagna and Mercury is in the 2nd, he will get a large quantity of iron. If Saturn is in the 12th and Mercury is in the Ascendant, there will be loss of iron.

लाभस्ताम्रस्य वाच्यो वपुषि यदि भृगुर्भूमिपुत्रो धनस्थो
भूपुत्रे लग्नसंस्थे पुनरपि भृगुजे रिष्फगे ताम्रनाशः ।
वक्तव्योत्रार्थलाभः क्षितिभुवि तनुगे सूर्यपुत्रे धनस्थे
रिष्फस्थे भूमिपुत्रे वपुषि यदि शनिः कथ्यतामर्थनाशः
॥३९॥

Stanza 39.—If Venus is in Lagna and Mars is in the 2nd, he will earn much copper. If Mars is in Lagna and Venus is in the 12th, there will be loss of the metal. If Mars is in Lagna and Saturn is in the 2nd, he will gain much wealth. If Saturn is in Lagna and Mars is in the 12th, there will be loss of wealth.

भानोर्लग्ने पशुगजतुरङ्गादिकानां विनाशः
कीटोत्थापत्तपनबुधयोर्मृत्युभीतिः कुजस्य ।
इन्दोः सूनोर्विपदिह सुहृत्पुत्रयोः कीर्तनीया
नीचारिस्था रविहतकरा ये फलं प्रोक्तमेषाम् ॥४०॥

Stanza 40.—If the Sun occupies Lagna which happens to be the sign of his debility or enemy, there will be destruction of cattle, horses and elephants. According as Mercury or Mars is similarly placed there will respectively be trouble from vermin and danger to relatives and children; or fear of death.

स्वोच्चस्थितो देवगुरुर्भृगुर्वा चन्द्रेण युक्तो यदि लग्नसंस्थः।
प्रीतिर्भवेदेव जनात्समस्तात् पक्षेण लाभश्च चतुष्पदानाम्
॥इति ॥४१॥

Stanza 41.—If Jupiter or Venus in exaltation or own house is in conjunction with the Moon in

Lagna, then the gods and all the people will look on the native with favour and he will acquire quadrupeds within 15 days.

INTERPRETING FIRST LETTER OF QUERY

पञ्चघ्नेऽष्टविभाजितेक्षरगणे दूतोदिते शिष्यते
तत्रैकं यदि देवराट्शिखिमुखा दिक्पा यदि व्यादिकम् ।
दूतोक्तोर्णगणे त्रिभिः खलु हृते शिष्टैकता चेद्गदः
साध्यो नूनमसाध्य एव युगळे शिष्टे त्रिके दुश्शमः ॥४२॥

Stanza 42.—Multiply the number implied by the first letter in the word spoken by the messenger by 5 and divide the product by 8. If the remainder is 1, the disease will have been caused by Devendra; 2 by Agni; 3 by Yama; 4 by Nirithi; 5 by Varuna; 6 by Vayu; 7 by Vaishravana; and 8 by Siva. Divide the number above mentioned by 3. If the remainder is 1, say that the sick man will recover; if it is 2, he will not recover; if it is 3, he will recover with remedial measures and good treatment.

NOTES

The Deities mentioned in stanza 42 are the lords of the eight cardinal points of the compass. It is one of these Deities that is supposed to afflict the questioner.

व्याधीनां शमनं करोति वलभिद्देवस्य पूजादिकै-
रग्निर्होमविधानतोऽथ पितृपूजाभिः पितृणां पतिः ।
रक्षः सूचयति व्यथार्दितनृणां रुग्ब्रह्मरक्षोमुखा-
वेशेनेति विधानमस्य शमनायाधीयतां धीमता ॥४३॥

तैलभिषेकाच्च घृताभिषेकाद्दैवे सधारादपि तर्पणाद्वा ।
पाशी विधत्ते गदशान्तिमेषां वक्त्यन्यभावादिक-
मार्तिहेतुम् ॥४४॥

मालापटीरागरुगुल्गुलूत्थधूपप्रधानाभरणार्पणाद्यैः ।
देवप्रसादेन गदोपशान्ति करोति नृणां खलु मातरिश्व
॥४५॥

देवद्विजार्चनविधिं जनिभे जनानां रुक्शान्तये विहित-
वानलकाधिनाथः ।
गीतेन नृत्तकरणेन च भारतेन त्रय्या च देवपरितोषण-
मप्युमेशः ॥४६॥

Stanzas 43 to 46.—The sick man can recover by adopting the following remedial measures. If the afflicting or disease-causing Deity is Indra, worship Ishta-devata or family god ; if it is Agni-perform Mrityunjaya Homa; if it is Yama, propitiate the manes; if it is Niriti, satisfy the Brahmarakshasa; if it is Varuna, perform *abhisheka* to God Siva with holy water, oil and ghee; if it is Vayu, decorate God with holy ornaments and flowers, anoint Him with perfumes and sandal paste and fill the atmosphere with scented fumes; if it is Vaishravana, worship the Gods and Brahmins on a birthday; and if it is Siva, arrange Bhajanas, sacred dances, reading of scriptures and recitation of the Vedas.

NOTES

Stanza 42 enables us to find out the Deity causing the sickness or affliction and whether or not recovery either naturally or by treatment is possible. In the latter circumstance, remedial measures are to be performed as per stanzas 43 to 46. According to some the total number of letters of the query and not the number of the first letter should be taken.

Providing the Deity with ornaments or charging the temple atmosphere with scented fumes or the performance of holy dance, recitation of Vedas, Puranas, etc., are generally done either on one's birthday or on a day ruled by one's birth star.

PREDICTING BY BETEL LEAVES

प्रष्ट्रा वितीर्णताम्बूलैः शुभाशुभमशेषतः ।
वाच्यं द्वादशभावोत्थं तत्प्रकारोथ लिख्यते ॥४७॥

Stanza 47.—By examining the betel leaves presented by the querist, the good and bad results pertaining to the 12 houses can be predicted.

ताम्बूलैः प्रष्टुदत्तैरपि फलमखिलं तस्य वक्तव्यमेवं
प्रारभ्योपर्यधस्ताद्गणनमिह वपुः पूर्वमह्नोर्द्धयोः स्यात् ।
म्लनिक्षत्याद्युपेतं तदयुतमपि यद्भावसम्बन्धि पत्रं
तस्य व्याध्याद्यनिष्टं भवति शुभमपि प्राप्तिसंवर्द्धनाद्यम्
॥४८॥

Stanza 48.—According as the time of query happens to fall (*a*) after midnight and before noon, or (*b*) after midday and before midnight, the leaves should be counted from top to bottom or from bottom to top. The first and subsequent leaves represent the first and subsequent Bhavas. Faded, squeezed, torn or damaged leaves denote affliction to the Bhavas they signify while broad and soft leaves in proper form indicate prosperity to the Bhavas concerned.

NOTES

If we believe in the theory that nothing in this universe can happen by chance or accident, then there is bound to be some sort of correlation between the nature of articles we may come across unexpectedly and the events likely to happen in the future. The querist presents some betel leaves and nuts (thamboola) to the astrologer. The leaves are chosen at random by the querist. Some are damaged and some are in excellent condition. After the leaves are counted either from top to bottom (if the time is after midnight and before midday) or from bottom to top (if the time is between midday and midnight), they must be arranged as 1, 2 ,3 etc. The first leaf represents the first Bhava, the 2nd the 2nd Bhava, and so on. If the leaves are fresh and undamaged, only good can be expected from the Bhava concerned. If on the contrary, the leaf is dry, and eaten by pests, the events signified by the Bhava are in danger. According to this theory, gains and losses can be noted by comparing the sizes of the 11th and 12th leaves. Longevity can be studied by comparing the 1st and 8th leaves.

I have not personally tested this method. Therefore I can say nothing either for or against the theory. But some of the Kerala astrologers with whom I discussed the matter are of the opinion that in Prasna or Horary astrology, predictions based upon this 'betel leaf theory' generally come correct.

The leaves have to be held in the left hand and the counting has to be done by the right hand.

ताम्बूलसंख्यां द्विगुणां शरघ्नां सैकां हरेत्सप्तभिरत्र शिष्टैः ।
सूर्योदिकानामुदयोत्र कल्प्यो ग्रहोदयो यत्र स लग्नराशिः
॥४९॥

Stanza 49.—Double the number of leaves. Multiply this by 5. Add 1 to it. Divide the total by

The remainder represents the planet in the order of the week-days. The sign occupied by the planet in the Horary chart is the Thamboola Lagna.

दुःखाय भानुरुदितः सुखकृच्छशाङ्कः
प्रष्टुः कुजः कलहकृद्धनदौ ज्ञजीवौ ।
शुक्रोखिलाभिमतकृन्मरणाय मन्दो
लग्नादिभावविहगैश्च वदेत् फलानि ॥ ५० ॥

Stanza 50.—According as the Sun to Saturn (in the order of week-days) rises in Thamboola Lagna, there will respectively be sorrows, general happiness, quarrels, acquisition of money, gratification of desires, death and destruction.

NOTES

Stanzas 49 and 50 link up the* betel leaf indications with the chart cast for the time of query. The formula suggested is

$$\frac{2. \text{ (No. of betel leaves)} \times 5 + 1}{7} = \text{quotient} + \text{remainder.}$$

(*) One of the Panikkars tells me that stanza 49 is a bit confusing. According to him, Thamboola Lagna sign will be at the horizon when the concerned planet rises. This means one has to find the time at which the planet rises on the day in question and then calculate the ascendant for this time. But the concensus of astrologers say that the sign occupied in the Prasna chart by the planet revealed by the leaves is Thamboola Lagna.

The remainder represents the planet whose position in the Prasna chart gives the Thamboola Lagna. Suppose the number of betel leaves is 14. Then,

$2\ (14) \times 5 + 1 = 141/7 = 20\ 1/7$
Remainder = 1 = Sun

Since the Sun is in Thamboola Lagna, the result is "quarrels".

Acquisition of Elephants

गजलाभो ममेदानीं किमु स्यादिति कश्चन ।
प्रभुः पृच्छति चेत्तस्मै वाच्यं लक्षणमुच्यते ॥५१॥

Stanza 51.—Queries made by rulers regarding the capture of elephants can be answered according to the principles given below :—

लग्नद्युनतपस्सुतेषु धिषणः पाथोनराश्यंशगः
प्रश्ने कुञ्जरलाभकृन्नरपतेस्तत्रायनाथो यदि ।
नाथः संश्चतुरङ्घ्रिभस्य नियतं केन्द्रत्रिकोणाश्रितः
शीघ्रं तत् खलु केन्द्रगौ यदि तदा कर्मेशभाग्याधिपौ
॥५२॥

Stanza 52.—If at the time of query Jupiter occupies the 1st, 7th, 9th, or 5th house which should have reference to Virgo Rasi or Navamsa, elephants will be secured by the querying kings. Here the lord of the 11th should own a quadrupedal Rasi, and occupy a quadrant or a trine. Again if the lords of 9 and 10 should occupy kendras, the capture will be easy and without any effort.

NOTES

In these days of democracy when kings have disappeared, this yoga can be applied for all gains. Instead of quadrupedal signs, signs corresponding to the gains intended could be substituted.

पृच्छायां गुळिकं पूर्वं सम्यग्विस्पष्टमानयेत् ।
तत्कालजान् ग्रहांश्चान्यान् पुनर्लक्षणमादिशेत् ॥५३॥

Stanza 53.—The correct longitudes of Gulika and other planets at the time of the query should be determined to ascertain the *lakshanas* or indications.

INDICATIONS FOR SICKNESS

भानौ मान्दियुतेक्षिते निजगृहे कस्यापि पुंसो रुजा
कोपो वा नृपतेस्तदीयपुरुषस्यान्यायतो वागमः ।
शीतांशौ कलहो भवेदबलयोः स्त्रीहेतुकः सोथवा
यः कश्चित्कलहोथवा पुनरिह श्रूयेत दूरादपि ॥५४॥

Stanza 54.—If Gulika is conjoined with or aspected by the Sun, someone will be sick in the house of the querist; or the king wili be angry with him; or some messenger from the ruler unexpectedly arrives in the house. If Gulika is associated with or aspected by the Moon, two women in the querist's house will be quarrelling; or men will be quarrelling because of a woman; or the story of a quarrel that happened in a distant place will be reported in the family.

भूपुत्रे कलहो भवेत्परिसरे श्वद्वीपिनोर्नायकै-
रन्योन्ये यदि वा शवोपनयनं यद्वाथ मांसागमः ।
शीतांशोस्तनये तु नूतनघटानीतिः प्रधानागमो
यद्वा नूतनलोहजाद्युपगमो वा विग्रहः पुंस्त्रियोः ॥५५॥

Stanza 55.—If Mars is the planet joining Gulika, there will be quarrel amongst the owners of dogs or keepers of tigers or between dog-owners and tiger-keepers in the neighbourhood of the querist's residence, or a corpse or flesh will have been brought; if Mercury, new mud or earthenware vessels will be brought to the querist's house, or a distinguished personage will turn up, or vessels made of metals will be brought or there will be quarrel between men and women (in his house).

जीवे भूमिरुहः पतेद्यदि चरे भग्नः समूलं स्थिरे
मध्ये यद्युभये तदीयविटपस्तत्स्याज्झषे वा हये ।
आयानां विमनोद्विजस्य यदि वा यद्वात्र पक्वागमो
यद्वापन्निजपूर्वहेतुरथवा तेषां नु शेषक्रिया ॥५६॥

Stanza 56.—If it is Jupiter, a tree will fall down, broken, or uprooted or branches torn off, according as the sign involved is movable, fixed or common; the falling of the tree will be in the direction indicated by Pisces (ईशान्य) or Sagittarius (वायव्य) or a Brahmin will turn up with a worried mind, or in affliction; or someone will bring plantain fruits; or some unhappy incident will happen, brought about by the patriarch of the family; or the senior member of the family will die.

शुक्रे छेदनमाखुनाथ भविता वस्त्रस्य पात्रक्षति-
र्दघ्नो वा पयसोथवोपनयनं विप्रागमोन्यायतः ।
गृहणीयात्पुनराखुरोतुमथवा पादायुधं वाग्रतो
मन्दे कश्चन दीक्षितो गृहमुपेत्याथो रुषा यास्यति
॥५७॥

चण्डालस्य मृतिः स्थले तु निजके तद्विग्रहो वाऽऽयस-
द्रव्याणामथवा हतिः पुनरहौ श्वव्याघ्रयोर्विग्रहः ।
यद्वा पन्नगदंशनं फणियुगानीतिश्च तत्राथवा
दुग्धस्योपनयो वदेदिति सुधीः केतोः फलं राहुवत्
॥५८॥

Stanzas 57 and 58.—If Venus joins or aspects Gulika, there will be trouble from rats, or vessels will be broken, or somebody will bring milk or curd, or a Brahmin will come in without any reason uninvited, or a cat will pounce upon a rat or a hen in front of the querist. If it is Saturn, a holy Brahmin (Deekshita) will come to the house and depart in anger, or low caste people in the neighbourhood will die or quarrel, or some vessels made of iron will be brought to the house. If Rahu is so conjoined, a dog and a tiger will fight or a serpent will bite either him or his relative or two serpents will be brought to the house of the native or milk will be brought to his house by an outsider. The effects of Ketu will be similar to those of Rahu.

NOTES

After giving the methods of predicting with the aid of betel leaves, the author switches on to the regular subject-matter of astrology. The translation of stanzas 54 to 58 is clear enough and they do not need further remarks. How far the results ascribed to Gulika's association with the different planets, can be used in interpreting horary charts in the light of society as it is constituted today, is left to the discretion of the intelligent reader.

PERFORMING OBSEQUIES

एष शेषक्रियां कुर्यात् किमु पित्रोर्नवेति यः ।
प्रश्नोथास्योत्तरं वक्तुं लक्षणं किमपीर्यते ॥५९॥

Stanza 59.—If the query "will I be able to perform the obsequies of my father and mother" is made, the answer should be given thus:

स्वांशे राशौ चरे वा स्थितिरिननवमाधीशयोरेनयोश्च
दृष्टी रिप्फे स्थितिर्वा यदि तदुपगतांशर्क्षयोः केन्द्रगत्वम् ।
सम्यग्दीक्षा पितुः स्याद्यदि कथितगुणेष्वेषु नैकोपि दीक्षा
नैव स्यात्सम्भवेच्चेदपि बहुविपदः सम्भवेयुर्गदाद्याः
॥६०॥

Stanza 60.—The person will be able to perform the obsequies if the Sun and the lord of the 9th (*a*) occupy their own or movable signs, or their own or movable Navamsas; (*b*) or are posited in or aspect the 12th; (*c*) or are in kendras or Navamsas of kendra houses. In the absence of any one of these combinations, the ceremonies cannot be performed because of obstacles, such as sickness and other calamities.

NOTES

Stanza 60 requires the presence of either the lord or the karaka in the prescribed places. According to combination (c), the Sun or the lord of the 9th should be in a quadrangular place.

धर्मेऽस्ति पापान्वयवीक्षणं चेद्दीक्षा विहन्येत शुभासतोश्चेत् ।
अग्रे शुभश्चेद्विहतिस्तु मध्ये पृष्टे स चेत्तां परतोलभेत
॥६१॥

Stanza 61.—If the 9th house is afflicted by malefic planets, the ceremonies will not be performed. If however both benefics and malefics occupy the 9th and if the former have a higher longitude in the Rasi, the ceremonies will be begun properly but towards the end, they will have to be stopped; if on the other hand malefics happen to be in front, then the ceremonies will be started by a third party but towards the end, the native will complete the functions.

NOTES

'In front' means a greater longitude. Suppose two planets are in a sign, one in the 15th degree and the other in the 18th, the latter will be 'in front' of the former.

मातृदीक्षाविचारे तु धर्मधर्मेशभास्वताम् ।
प्रोक्तस्थानेष्विह ग्राह्याश्चतुर्थेतत्पतीन्दवः ॥६२॥

Stanza 62.—By substituting the 4th house, the 4th lord and the Moon respectively for the 9th, 9th lord and the Sun, prediction about the mother's funeral ceremonies should be made.

जातो यः पितृजन्मरन्ध्रभवने यल्लग्नगस्तत्पतिः
कुर्यातां पितृकर्म तौ पितृमृतीशोडुतये यः पुनः ।
जातः सात्मजपौत्रयुक्च विधिना कुर्याच्च दीक्षां पितु-
र्ज्जातो व्योम्नि पितुस्समस्तदधिपे लग्नस्थिते चाधिकः
॥६३॥

Stanza 63.—The son will be fortunate enough to perform the funeral ceremonies of the father if the 8th from the Moon in the father's horoscope happens to be the rising sign in the son's horoscope; or if the lord of the 8th from the Moon in the father's chart happens to occupy the ascendant in the son's chart. One born in one of the asterisms owned by the lord of the 8th from the Moon in the father's horoscope will not only be blessed with children, prosperity and long life, but will also be able to do the ceremonies properly. If the 10th house from the Moon in the father's horoscope happens to be the rising sign of the son, he will resemble his father in everything ; if, in addition to this the lord of the 10th occupies the rising sign of the son, the son will surpass his father in good qualities and wealth.

NOTES

Janma means Chandra Lagna. But according to some commentators, it may mean the rising sign also. The Lagna of the son may also mean the son's Chandra Lagna. Similarly, some commentators think that the 10th means 10th from Lagna and not from Chandra Lagna. We need not bother about these apparent differences in interpretations. Both Lagna and Chandra Lagna are equally important.

यस्य स्यात् पितृजन्मतोऽत्र नवमो लाभो द्वतीयोथवा
चन्द्राधिष्ठितराशिरेष सततं तातानुवर्ती भवेत् ।
यस्य स्यात् पितृजन्मभं स्वजनिभाल्लाभे त्रिकोणेथवा
लग्नेशाश्रितभाल्लभेत सकलं वित्तं स पित्रार्ज्जितम्
॥६४॥

Stanza 64 .—If the rising sign of the son happens to be the 9th or 11th (or 2nd) house from the Moon in the father's horoscope, the son will be guided by the father in all principles of life. If the rising sign of the father happens to be the 11th house from the Moon in the son's horoscope, or if the rising sign of the father happens to be the 5th, 9th or 11th from the sign occupied by the lord of Chandra Lagna in the son's horoscope, then the son will be able to inherit and enjoy all his father's property.

लग्नेन्दुभ्यां पितृगृहपतिः स्वस्वलग्नायगश्चेत्
प्रीतिं कुर्यात् पितुरिह तु शुश्रूषया दीक्षया च ।
लग्नाधीशो नवमपतिना भानुना वा समेतो
भाग्यस्थो वा यदि जनकवद्वृत्तिविद्यादयुपेतः

॥६५॥

Stanza 65.—If the lord of the 9th occupies the 11th, and the lord of the 9th from Chandra Lagna occupies the 11th from the Moon, the son will serve the father lovingly. If the lord of Lagna joins the Sun or lord of 9, or occupies the 9th house, the son will be similar to the father in occupation, education, character and all good qualities.

NOTES

Stanzas 64 and 65 can be used for predicting the mutual relations between a son and his father. The son becomes worthy of the affection of his father, if (*a*) the son's ascendant falls in a sign which should be the 2nd, 9th or 11th from the Janma Rasi of the father; (*b*) the father's ascendant falls in a sign which should be in the 11th from the Janma Rasi of the son; (*c*) if the father's ascendant is in a sign which in the son's horoscope happens to be the 5th, 9th or 11th from the sign occupied by the lord of Chandra Lagna in the son's horoscope ; (*d*) lords of the 9th from Lagna and Chandra Lagna are in the 11th respectively from Lagna and Chandra Lagna; (*e*) if the lord of Lagna joins the Sun or lord of the 9th or occupies the 9th.

HAPPINESS AND SORROW TO PARENTS

जातो यः पितृजन्मरिष्फपतिनक्षत्रेषु कुर्यात् पितु-
र्दुःखं दूरगमादिभिः स सततः, वैरी भवेद्वैरिभे ।
यद्रिष्फाधिपसंयुतः खलु पितुर्जन्माधिपो यस्य वा
रिष्फस्थः स च तावुभौ पुनरृणं नूनं लभेतां पितुः
॥६६॥

Stanza 66.—A son whose asterism happens to be owned by the lord of the 12th from Chandra Lagna in the father's horoscope will cause sorrow to the father by his travels and other actions; if the son's ascendant happens to be the 6th from the Janma Rasi of the father, or if the son's asterism happens to be ruled by the lord of 6th from father's Janma Rasi, he will be an enemy to his father. If the lord of Janma Rasi in the father's horoscope joins the 12th house or the lord of the 12th in the son's horoscope then the son will be required to redeem the debts of his father.

NOTES

Suppose the Janma Rasi (the sign occupied by the Moon or Chandra Lagna) in the father's horoscope is Aries. The lord of the 12th is Jupiter. The asterisms of Jupiter are Punarvasu, Visakha and Poorvabhadra. If the son is born in any one of these stars, he will cause sorrow to the father by his undesirable activities.

The 6th from the Janma Rasi of the father is Virgo ; Mercury who owns this sign has lordship of Aslesha, Jyeshta and Revati. If the son's ascendant is Virgo or if his Janma Nakshatra (birth-star) is Aslesha, Jyeshta or Ravati, he will be his father's enemy.

Lord of father's Janma Rasi is Mars. Suppose the son's ascendant is Virgo. If Mars (in the son's horoscope) occupies Leo (12th from Lagna in the son's chart) or is in conjunction with the Sun (lord of the 12th in the son's horoscope), the son will have to redeem the debts of his father.

भावश्चेन्नवमश्चरे तदधिपो वायं व्यये चाष्टमे
भानुर्वैवमिह स्थितिर्न सविधे तातस्य मृत्यौ भवेत् ।
मार्गे स्यान्मरण श्रुतिर्द्वितनुभे स्थानं स्थिरे सन्निधौ
सत्स्वमीक्षितसंयुते नवमभे नाथेस्य चार्के तथा ॥६७॥

Stanza 67.— If the 9th house happens to be a movable sign or if the lord of the 9th occupies a movable sign and if the lord of the 9th or the Sun occupy the 8th or 12th, then the son will not be near his father when he dies. If the above combination happens in a common sign, the son will hear the news of his father's death when he is away. If the yoga occurs in a fixed sign and if benefics aspect or join the 9th house or its lord, the son will be near his father, serve him on his death-bed and perform all death ceremonies carefully.

AFFLICTIONS TO RESIDENCE

कालोस्मिन् वासभूमेम गृहदोषोस्ति वा न वा ।

इति प्रश्ने कृते वक्तुं लक्षणं किमपीर्यते ॥६८॥

Stanza 68.—To a query as to whether or not there are any planetary evils afflicting the house in which the native lives, the answer is to be made as follows :—

AVAKAHADA SYSTEM

अकला यदि नामादौ भूमेर्लग्नं तु मेषभम् ।

आङवा इच क्ष): पश्चादीन्गळाः कर्कटोदयः ॥६९॥

उ ट ०० ऊणनाः पश्चादेहळा एनबा अळी ।

ए प ५०; ओमळाः पश्चादोय १० और ना झषः ॥७०॥

Stanzas 69 and 70.—Take the first letter in the name of the house, and fix the Lagna. The signs Aries to Pisces signify the letters: आक, अङ, इच, ईञ, उट, ऊण, एत, एन, ऐप, ओम, ओय and और. ल व ञ ह ळ are ruled by Aries to Leo. If any name begins with intervening letters it must be treated as belonging to the first letter in the varga.

NOTES

The explanation given below for these two stanzas is based on the clarification provided by an astrological savant in Kerala whom I met at the Astrological Conference held at Trichur in 1958.

In the assignment of letters to the zodiacal signs, especially in regard to consonants, the peculiarity is if ka (क) is ruled by Aries, nga (ङ – the last in the series ka, kha, ga, gha ङ) is ruled by Taurus. If the name commences from say kha (ख) or ga (ग) or gha (घ), then it must be treated as belonging to the first letter in the varga or series, viz., ka (क). Similarly the letter ta (ट) is ruled by Leo and nna (ण) the last letter in the varga is ruled by Virgo which means the intervening three letters, *viz.*, tta (ठ), da (ड) and dha (ढ) should be considered as belonging to the first later t which means the Rasi is Leo. The savant also suggsted that the theory that la (ल), va (व), ra (र) etc., are ruled by two Rasis, could be ignored and la (ल), va (व) (श ष स ह ळ) taken to be ruled by Aries, Taurus, Gemini Cancer and Leo respectively.

I must confess that I have neither used nor tested the principles given in these two stanzas. It is for the enterprising student to experiment with the methods suggested.

According to the method given in stanzas 69 and 70, the Lagna of the land in which the house of the querist is situated is determined. Evidently this method is based on symbology and not on astrology proper.

लग्नत्रिकोणे गुरुरत्र लग्ने चरे गुरुस्तूभयराशि संस्थः।
द्वन्द्वे विलग्ने चरगः सुरेडचस्थिरे तु लग्ने स तु लग्न एव ॥७१॥

Stanza 71.—According as the ascendant (as per above two stanzas) happens to fall in a movable, fixed or common sign, Jupiter's situation in the horoscope of residence or land will be in the 9th, 1st or 5th sign respectively from the ascendant.

NOTES

If the Lagna so determined is in a movable sign, then Jupiter is supposed to occupy the 9th from it. If the Lagna is a fixed sign, then Jupiter will be in the ascendant itself. If the Lagna is a common sign then Jupiter will be in the 5th from it.

अ व क ह डादिकविधिना विज्ञातव्यं हि जन्मनक्षत्रम्।
नक्षत्रे विज्ञाते विज्ञेया स्थितिरनेन चन्द्रमसः ॥७२॥

Stanza 72.—The Nakshatra at the Bhumi Jataka should be ascertained on the basis of Avakahada and then the position of the Moon determined.

NOTES

The Nakshatra and Padas of the land or house should be ascertained according to what is called Avakahada principle. This principle has been discussed in may *Muhurtha* or *Electional Astrology* to which the reader may refer for further details.

चन्द्राश्रिते वेश्मनि लग्नभे वा तयोर्द्वयोर्वाष्टमयोश्च पापाः ।
स्थिता यदास्मिन् समये मृतिः स्यात्तद्वासिनां गोनर पूर्वकाणाम् ॥७३॥

Stanza 73.—When malefic planets transit the Lagna or 8th from it or Chandra Lagna or the 8th from it, evil will befall the persons tenanting the land or the house in question. Livestock found there will also suffer from diseases or even death.

NOTES

Here the reference to the Lagna and Chandra Lagna is in terms of stanzas 69, 70 and 71.

लग्नात् पञ्चमथभेवा नवमभे यद्वा शशाङ्कात्सुते
धेर्मे वा धिषणप्रवेशसमये तद्वासिगर्भोद्भवः ।

धर्मापत्यगराशिभेदवशात् स्त्रीणां गवां वा महिष्यादी-
नामथवा सदा स्थितिजुषां गर्भग्रहस्तत् क्षितौ ॥७४॥

Stanza 74.—When Jupiter passes (in tiansit) through Bhumi Lagna or Bhumi Chandra Lagna or 5th or 9th from them, the women or cows or buffaloes will conceive.

NOTES

If the sign transited happens to be Aries, goats will conceive; if it is Taurus, cows and buffaloes will conceive. If the sign is Gemini, women will become pregnant. Similarly other signs should be dealt with.

अरिभवने सहजे वा बृहतां पत्यौ स्थिते कलहः ।
नृपपीडा निधनगते लग्नेन्दुभ्यां वधो व्ययगे ॥७५॥

Stanza 75.—According as Jupiter is in the 3rd or 6th or 8th or 12h from the Lagna or the Moon. there will respectively be quarrels on the land, the land will suffer due to the wrath of the ruler or murder will take place there.

NOTES

Some authors say the situation of Jupiter should be considered from Arudha Lagna and from the Moon.

If Jupiter (in the land horoscope) occupies the 3rd or 6th from Lagna or the Moon some quarrel will take place soon. If Jupiter is in the 8th the land will suffer due to the wrath of the ruler. If Jupiter is in the 12th house, a murder may take place in the land.

BECOMING THE HEAD

आधिपत्यं भवेत् किं मे न वेति यदि पृच्छति ।
प्रभूणां कुलजः कश्चित्तं वक्तुं लक्ष्म कथ्यते ॥७६॥

Stanza 76.—If a person born in a royal family asks when he would become the head or chief, the answer is to be given thus :

तत्र प्राग्जन्मकालीनविहगाः खलु सुस्फुटाः ।
गणनीया विशेषेणज्ञेयास्तारा स्तदाश्रिताः ॥७७॥

Stanza 77.—The asterisms occupied by the different planets at the time of birth of the querist should be carefully determined.

सूर्येन्द्वारविलग्नकर्मपतयस्ते येषु भेषु स्थिता
स्तेष्वाद्यांशकपास्तदंशभवगा लग्नत्रिकोणेथवा ।
वीर्यान्वाः खलु यस्य स स्वककुलज्यैष्ठ्यं लभेताचिरा-
त्तैस्तेशा इतरत्र चेद्व्यमृताद्विड्भ्यः शनैर्ज्यैष्ठ्यदाः ॥७८॥

Stanza 78—Find out the asterisms occupied by the Sun, the Moon, Mars, the lord of Lagna and the lord of the 10th house from Lagna.

If the lords of the first quarters of these asterisms occupy 1st, 5th, 9th or 11th from the rising sign, the person will become the head very shortly. If these lords occupy 6th, 8th or the 12th, there is no chance of getting such overlordship. If they occupy positions other than those mentioned above, the person has to wait for a long time to get it.

NOTES

Suppose the asterisms occupied by the Moon, Mars, lord of Lagna and the lord of 10th are respectively Aswini, Pubba, Krittika, Swati and Purvashadha. The lords of the 1st quarters of these stars are respectively Mars, the Sun, Jupiter, Jupiter and the Sun. It is the disposition of these planets that is to be considered as per stanza 78.

सूर्यादिकेतुचरमद्युचरेषु केचित्तारासु चेन्निगृतिश
क्रपदास्थितासु ।
मित्रादिकेषु पुनरष्टसु वात्र शीघ्रं ज्यैष्ठ्यं पदे सुरपतेः
पयसां च पत्युः ॥७९॥

Stanza 79.—If three or four planets are situated in the asterisms belonging to Indra or Nirithi groups or one of the eight asterisms beginning from Anuradha, the person gets overlordship very soon.

कृत्तिकादिभरण्यंताः प्रदक्षिणतया स्थिताः ।
सर्वास्वपिदिशास्वीशकोणादारम्य सर्वतः ॥८०॥

Stanza 80.—Beginning from Krittika and ending with Bharani, the 28 asterisms are allotted in a clockwise order to the eight cardinal points, in groups of three and half stars each.

NOTES

Including the Abhijit, there are twenty-eight asterisms. They have been allotted to the 8 cardinal points in the following order :—

Nakshatras	*Direction*
Krittika Rohini Mrigasira Aridra	North-East
Aridra 2 Punarvasu Pushyami Aslesha	East
Makha Pubba Uttara Hasta 2	South-East
Hasta 2 Chitta Swati Visakha	South

Nakshatras	*Direction*
Anuradha Jyeshta Moola Poorvashadha 2	South-West
Poorvashadha 2 Uttarashadha Abhijit Sravana	West
Dhanishta Satabhisha Poorvabhadra Uttarabhadra 2	North-West
Uttarabhadra 2 Revati Aswini Bharani	North

If three or four planets in the Prasna chart occupy constellations belonging to the groups of Indra (Aridra, 3rd and 4th quarters, Punarvasu, Pushyami and Aslesha), Varuna (Poorvashadha, Uttarashadha, Abhijit and Sravana), Niruthi (Anuradha, Jyeshta, Moola and Poorvashadha 2 quarters), he will become head of the estate at a very early date.

Kalachakra or Time Cycle

नक्षत्रैः कालचक्रस्यैर्योगिन्य मृत्युना तथा ।
सम्प्रदायान्तरोक्तानि कथ्यन्ते लक्षणान्यथ ॥८१॥

Stanza 81.—By examining Kalachakra, Nakshatra, etc., we can work out 'Yogini and Mrityu'. From these processes also some effects can be predicted.

STAR POSITIONS IN KALACHAKRA

चतुरश्रत्रिकं कुर्यादन्तर्मध्ये बहिः क्रमात् ।
दण्डांश्च चतुरस्ताद्दिक्क्रेणगांश्चक्रसिद्धये ॥८२॥

दण्डानां प्रत्येकं चतुरश्रसमागमेषु मध्ये च ।
अभिजिद्युक्तास्ताराः स्थाप्याः स्युः सप्त सप्त गणनाय
॥८३॥

दण्डाग्रादामध्मं निर्गत्यततोन्तिकस्थदण्डेन ।
एवं पुनः प्रवेशो निर्गमनं प्रोक्तवच्च गणनमिह ॥८४॥

Stanzas 82 to 84.—Draw three squares, one inside the other and prepare a Chakra as given in the following diagram. Beginning from the centre of the top horizontal line establish the 28 stars (including Abhijit) in the 28 parts in the order shown in the diagram. Starting from No. 1, the count should be done in the order in which the figures are shown in the Chakra.

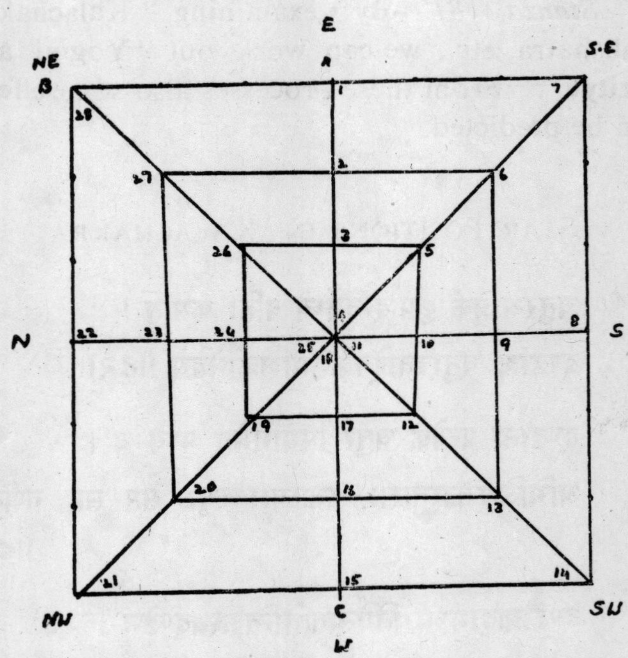

प्राग्दण्डाग्रादधस्ताद्दिनकरगतभाद्गण्यमाप्रश्नतारम्
प्राणोत्र प्रष्टृतारात् पुनरिति गणिते दक्षिणेनात्र देहः ।
वामं शर्वुस्य कोणाद्धुतभुज उडुनो गण्यतां प्राग्वदत्र
स्थानं मृत्योस्त्रयेस्मिन् स्थितवति मरणं प्रष्टुरेकत्र दण्डे
॥८५॥

Stanza 85.—Assign the star occupied by the Sun at the time of query to No. 1. Count from this to the star held by the Moon at the time of query and the point arrived at is Prana. Assign birth star to No. 1 and count from it to the Prana star. The point arrived at is Deha. Always assign Krittika to 28. Count from here to horary star in the anti-clockwise order. The point arrived at is Mrityu. If all these three points fall in the same line, it indicates death.

दण्डैक्यं यदि तत्र मृत्युवपुषो रुग्वृद्धिर्दैर्घ्याधिकं
मूर्च्छालस्यकृदेकदण्डवसतिर्मृत्योश्च जीवस्य च ।
प्राणाद्यग्निभपूर्वके च गणने पूर्वापरादन्यतो
दण्डैक्यं गुळिकोर्कभार्तजननोडूनां विदध्यामृतिम् ॥८६॥

Stanza 86.—If Deha and Mrityu points fall on one and the same pole, then the sickness will be prolonged. If Mrityu and Prana fall on one and the same, the person will be dull and will have fits every now and then. Assign Krittika to 1. Count from it serially to the stars held by Gulika, by the Sun and by the birth Moon. If the three points fall in the same line or pole (except AC), then death is likely.

NOTES

In the diagram given on page 644 A is the point from which the start of the count should be made. Suppose at the time of query, the Sun is in Aslesha, and the Moon in

Chitta while the birth star is Mrigasira. The points of Prana, Deha and Mrityu have to be ascertained thus :

Prana : 1 represents Aslesha, the star held by the Sun. Counting from this to Chitta, the star held by the Moon, in the order given in the diagram (the point of Prana) falls in 6.

Deha : 1 represents Mrigasira the birth star. Counting from Mrigasira to Chitta in the same order, D (point of Deha) falls in 10.

Mrityu : 28 always represents Krittika, the starting point. Counting from this to Chitta (in the reverse order) M (point of Mrityu) falls in 17.

It will be seen that the three points have fallen in different lines or poles.

Just as in the case of Prana, Deha and Mrityu, stanza 86 requires the consideration of the points arrived at by counting from Krittika (putting at No. 1) to the stars held by Gulika, the Sun and the birth Moon. Here also the points should not fall in the same pole. The centre pole (AC) is excepted which means that the three points, as per stanza 86, falling in AC, is not harmful.

It is also implied if the three points, either as per stanza 85 or 86, fall in three different poles, the affliction does not arise.

POSITION OF YOGINI

योगिन्यर्कगतोडु पुच्छदुडु यद्योकतगं ततुतं
प्रष्टुर्मृत्युरिहैकदण्डगमिदं सम्बन्धिमृत्युप्रदम् ।

प्राग्दण्डाग्रकृशानुबाधिकमधः संगण्यतां दक्षिणं
चक्रेऽस्मिन् खलु योगिनी च चति प्रोक्तक्रमात्
प्रत्यहम् ॥८७॥

Stanza 87.—Assign A to Krittika: Count from it clockwise to the star held by the Sun. If this happens to coincide with the point signified by the birth star and Yogini, the native may die. If all the three points fall in the same line or pole, some of the relatives may die. The movement of Yogini is given below :

NOTES

Suppose the birth star is Mrigasira and the star held by the Sun at question time is Dhanishta and Yogini falls at 12 (in the Kalachakra diagram). Counting from Krittika (A) to birth star the point arrived at is 3. Counting again from A to Dhanishta (the star held by the Sun) the point arrived at is 21. Then the three factors do not fall in the same point. Nor do they fall in the same line. Hence the results ascribed in stanza 87 do not apply in this case.

CALCULATING THE YOGINI

अर्कारार्यबुधाच्छमन्दशशिषु प्राच्यादिदिक्षूदिता
गत्वाष्टासु दिशासु सायमुदयस्थानं पुनश्च व्रजेत् ।
मध्यं स्वोद्गमदण्डतः पुनरतो दण्डद्वयं वामत-
स्त्यक्त्वान्येन बहिर्व्रजेत्प्रथमयामे तद्गति स्त्रीदृशी ॥८८॥

तस्मान्मध्यमतोथ दण्डयुगळं वामेन हित्वेतरे-
णोर्ध्वं यातिगति पुनरितिस्यादन्ययामेष्वपि ।

यामत्त्र्यंशविनाडिका नगसुगीज्ञैयः स कालो गते-
र्व्याप्तान्तर्वृतिमध्यमाङ्कणदलेष्वायाननिर्याणयोः ॥८९॥

Stanzas 88 and 89.—Yogini rises on Sunday to Saturday in the east (1), north (22), south-east (7), south-west (14), south (8), west (15) and north-east (21) respectively. After rising it travels in the course of the day, through all the 8 directions and returns to the starting point by sunset. In the night it starts from the same point and moves once more through the various directions.

NOTES

The rising and course of Yogini on different week-days and during different Yamas are as follows :—

Sunday: Yogini rises in the east at point 1 (in the Kalachakra diagram) and in the first Yama travels through 2, 3, 4, 19 and 10 reaching north-west (21). In the 2nd Yama, it starts from north-west (21) and passes through 20, 19, 18, 10 and 9 reaching south (8).

3ad Yama : 8, (south) 9, 10, 11, 26, 27 (north-east)
4th Yama : 29 (north-east) 27, 26, 25, 17, 16 (west)
5th Yama : 15 (west), 16, 17, 18 5, 6 (south-east)
6th Yama : 7 (south-east) 6, 5, 4, 24, 23 (north)
7th Yama : 22 (north), 23, 24, 25, 12, 13 (south-west)
8th Yama: 14 (south-west) 13, 12, 11, 3. 2 (east).

Suppose the birth or the query time is at Gh. 25–30 after sunrise on a Sunday. Assume the su nrise to be a 6 a.m. This means that the birth has occurred when 3t ghatis have passed in the 7th Yama, the 6th having ended at Gh. 22–30 the duration of each Yama being Gh. $3\frac{3}{4}$ ($1\frac{1}{2}$ hours). In each Yama, Yogini traverses 6 points so that it takes 37.5 vighatis to traverse each point. In the 7th Yama. 4 points (4 × Vi. 37.5 Gh. $2\frac{1}{3}$) have heen completed and the 5th point is being traversed.

According to the table, (see p. 648) the 7th Yama starts at point 22 (north) and the 5th in the series happens to be 12 (south-west). Therefore the Yogini's place is at 12.

The eight directions are signified by the following numbers thus :—

East = 1, North-East = 28, North = 22, North-West = 21 West = 15, South–West = 14, South = 8, and South-East = 7.

The rising and movement of the Yogini on other weekdays can be tabulated as follows:

Yogini Rising Table (both for day and night)

Yama	Monday	Tuesday	Wednesday	Thursday	Friday	Saturday
	1	2	3	4	5	6
1st	North 22	South-East 7	South-West 14	South 8	West 15	North-West 21
2nd	South-West 14	North 22	East 1	North-East 28	South-East 7	South 8
3rd	East 1	South-West 14	North-West 21	West 15	North 22	North-East 28

	1	2	3	4	5	6
4th	North-West 21	East 1	South 8	South-East 7	South-West 14	West 15
5th	South 8	North-West 21	North-East 28	North 22	East 1	South-East 7
6th	North-East 28	South 8	West 15	South-West 14	North-West 21	North 22
7th	West 15	North-East 28	South-East 7	East 1	South 8	South-West 14
8th	South-East 7	West 15	North 22	North-West 21	North-East 28	East 1

After Yogini rises according to above table on different week-days, it traverses 6 points (commencing with the point assigned to the direction of rising) in each Yama in the order given for Sunday (*vide* notes above). To make it more clear: On Monday, in the 1st Yama, Yogini rises in the North, *i.e.*, at point 22 and therefore follows the order 22, 23, 24, 25, 12 and 13 (*e.g.* order in 7th Yama on Sunday). In the 2nd Yama on Monday, it rises in the south-west, *i.e.*, at point 14 and traverses 13, 12, 11, 3 and 2 (*e.g.*, order in 8th Yama on Sunday). Take again Saturday. The Yogini rises in the 1st Yama in north-west (point 21) and moves through 20, 19, 18, 10 and 19 (*e.g.*, order in the 2nd Yama on Sunday).

For applying stanza 87, the exact point of Yogini (in Kalachakra chart) has to be decided.

Example :—Required the position of Yogini at 2h. 16m. p.m. (I.S.T.) on Wednesday 16-10-1918.

Duration of day Gh. 29–21 = 29 35
Time of birth in Ghatis Gh. 20–33 = 20.55

Duration of each Yama will be $\frac{3\ 75}{30} \times 29.35$

$= \text{Gh. } 3.67$

For the required time 5 Yamas have elapsed = 3 67 × 5= 18.35, Gh. 2–12 (Gh. 2, Vi. 12) having passed in the 6th Yama This means the Yogini is $\frac{2.18}{3.67} \times 6$ in the 4th point.

On Wednesday Yogini rises in the West (15) in the 6th Yama and moves in the order of 15, 16, 17, 18, 5, 6. The fourth point held by Yogini happens to be 18. In Kala-chakra diagram 18 falls on S.E. in the centre. In the same case, the Sun is in Chitta and the Janma Nakshatra is Satabhisha. Counting from Krittika (A) Chitta falls at 12 and Satabhisha falls at 22. The Yogini has fallen in central line or pole. The Sun has fallen in the 1st pole towards the south and the Moon on the last pole towards the north. Thus there is no affliction.

अहो यातविनाडिका मुखरयामत्वंशकाभ्यां हरेद्यामाः
प्रष्टृगृहे बहिर्वृत्तिमुखस्थानं च यातं फलम् ।
योगिन्युक्तवदेव मृत्युचरणं चक्रेस्ति वारक्रमा-
न्नित्यं वायुदिगादि चास्य गमनं प्रोक्तं मरुत्प्रद्यतः
॥९०॥

Stanza 90.—Convert the time (of question or birth) into Vighatikas after sunrise. Divide this by 225. The quotient is the number of Yamas expired from sunrise. Divide the remainder by 37½. The quotient represents the point of Yogini in the diagram. The path of Mrityu is similar to that of Yogini. But there is difference with regard to its rising. On all days it rises in the north-west and passes through the various diks or cardinal points.

मरुद्यमेज्ञम्बुपवह्निसोमरक्षःसुराधीश्वरदिक्षु नित्यम् ।
उद्धृत्य वामं दिवसेष्टवारं भचक्रगोर्कोदयतः क्रमेण ॥९१॥

Stanza 91.—According to some, eachday in the first Yama Mrityu rises in the north-west (21); in the 2nd Yama south (8); in the 3rd Yama, north-east (28); in the 4th —west (15); 5th—south-east(3); 6th—north (22); 7th—south-west (14) and 8th—east (1). At the end of the 8th Yama it comes to east where it rises in the first Yama of the night repeating the same cycle.

NOTES

Yogini rises at different points (diks) on different week-days; but Mrityu rises on all week-days at point 21 (corresponding to north-west). Its movement during the

8 Yamas is as follows: It takes, as in the case of Yogini, 37.5 Vighatis to pass through each point of a Yama.

1st Yama	...	21, 20, 19, 18, 10, 9
2nd Yama	...	8, 9, 10, 11, 26, 27
3rd Yama	...	28, 27, 26, 25, 17, 16.
4th Yama	...	15, 16, 17, 18, 5, 6
5th Yama	...	7, 6, 5, 4, 20, 23
6th Yama	...	22, 23, 24, 25, 12, 13
7th Yama	...	14, 13, 12, 11, 3, 2
8th Yama	...	1, 2, 3, 4, 18, 20, 21

The position of Mrityu can be located on the same basis as that of Yogini.

मेषादिकचरभानां दिश्युदयोऽन्तेषु मृत्युयोगिन्योः ।
मिथुनादिद्वन्द्वानां मध्येष्वग्न्यादिकोणेषु ॥९२॥

Stanza 92.—If Yogini and Mrityu rise in the posion of diks, take it as the end of the movable signs. When these rise in the corners, take it as middle of common signs.

NOTES

In this stanza, we are enabled to locate the positions of Yogini and Mrityu in terms of zodiacal signs. If either Yogini or Mrityu occupies points denoting east, west, north or south, then the Rasis are Aries, Cancer, Libra, Capricorn, etc. If the Yogini or Mrityu is in an angle (north-east, north-west, south-west or south-east), then it is said to be in a common sign (Gemini, Virgo, Cancer, etc.). No fixed signs have come into the picture.

FEATURES OF YOGINI

दंष्ट्रायुग्मभयं कराञ्जननिभा संरक्तवृत्तेक्षणा
नादापूरितदिङ्मुखा वधरुचिः संध्याभ्रस्क्तांबरा ।
मेदोमांसवपाविभूषिततनुर्भोगीशभोगाङ्गदा
जन्तून् खड्गधारा निहन्ति निखिलान्
मत्ता भृशं योगिनी ॥९३॥

Stanza 93.—Yogini has two frontal teeth, She is fearful to look at. She is yellow in colour. Her eyes are red. Her terrible voice can be heard in all quarters. Her special taste is for killing. Her dress is of red hue as twilight. She adorns herself with the spoils of killing. Her bangles are serpents. She has a sword in hand which she uses for killing all. She is always deep drunk.

स्वाधिष्ठितराशेः सा पादेनाक्रम्य तुर्यभं सुदृढम् ।
प्रहरत्यपि खड्गेन द्यूनं हन्येत तत्रगस्तु तया ॥९४॥

Stanza 94.—Yogini tramples on the 4th house from the sign she stands in ; and cuts the 7th house with her sword.

NOTES

The fearful appearance of *Yogini* is described to impress the unfortunate effects flowing from its position in the chart.

If the Aroodha Rasi of the questioner falls in the 4th or 7th from the sign held by Yogini, the querist will die. Of the two signs, the 7th is the worst.

सूर्याद्यहस्सु योगिन्याः पक्षभेदो न चोद्गमे ।
तच्चारे पुनरस्त्येप श्लोकपादैरथोच्यते ॥९५॥

Stanza 95.—With regard to the rise of Yogini in different directions according to week-days, there is no difference of opinion. But with regard to its path, some authors hold different views and they are explained below.

MOVEMENTS OF YOGINI ON WEEKDAYS

केसरीभोगशेषो हि सङ्गहारी कलावती ।
राजा गुणवता सेव्यो वारणासितदापगा ॥९६॥

लोकभीषणसंहारी मार्गतोहसिकेरवः ।
तत्र सम्पदसेगेण सूर्यवारादिपु क्रमात् ॥९७॥

एकादिसंख्यावचनैरिहार्णै-
रीन्द्राग्निपूर्वाः यथिता हि काष्टाः ।
अद्यासु दिक्षुदयनं क्रमेण
चान्यासु चारः प्रतियाममाख्याः ॥९८॥

Stanzas 96, 97 and 98.—On Sundays, Yogini rises in the east (1) and moves through 7, 2, 6, 3,

5, 6 and 8 diks respectively in the eight Yamas. Monday—7, 5, 8, 2, 1, 3, 4 and 6; Tuesday—2, 8, 3, 5, 4, 6, 7 and 1; Wednesday – 4, 2, 5, 7, 6, 8, 4, 3; Thursday—3, 1, 4, 6, 5, 7, 8, 2; Friday—5, 3, 6, 8, 7, 1, 2 and 4; and Saturday—6, 4, 7, 1, 8, 23 and 15.

The numbers 1 to 8 respectively denote east, south-east, south, south-west, west, north-west, north and north-east, and also signify the 8 Yamas.

NOTES

The author explains *matha bheda* or difference of opinion and gives another method (we shall call it B) in vogue amongst a certain section of ancient astrologers in the matter of the movement of Yogini. (The earlier method described we shall term as A.) In the matter of the initial rising of Yogini in the 1st Yama, there is agreement. But in regard to its movement there is difference. And indeed the difference is formidable

Take for instance Sunday. According to method B, in the first Yama it rises in the east; (1) in the 2nd Yama it is in the north (7); in the third Yama south-east (2); in the fourth Yama, south-west (6); in the 5th Yama, west; in the 6th Yama west (5); in the 7th Yama north-west (6); and in the 8th Yama north-east (8). For the convenience of the readers, the rising of Yogini (on Sunday) according to methods A and B is tabulated as follows :

Ywama	*Method A*	*Method B*
1st	East (1)	East (1)
2nd	north-west (21)	north (7)
3rd	south (8)	south-east (2)
4th	north-east (28)	south-west (4)
5th	west (15)	south (3)
7th	north (22)	north-west (6)
8th	south-west (14)	north-east (8)

According to method A, numbers given in brackets represent direction as shown in the Kalachakra diagram. According to method B, numbers indicate the directions in the regular order of east (1), south-east (2), etc.

According to method A Yogini having risen say in the east on Sunday touches points 2 3, 4, 19 and 20, in the 1st Yama, whereas according to B, no such movement within the Yama is indicated.

सूर्याद्यिहस्सु यस्यां दिश्युदयोतः परा दिशः ।
यामक्रमेण गत्वान्त्ये यामे यात्यष्टमीं दिशम् ॥९९॥

Stanza 99.—Thus Yogini after rising in a particular Dik traverses through the various Diks in different Yamas and reaches the 8th Dik after 8 Yamas.

NOTES

Suppose on a particular week-day it rises at a particular Dik, or direction, *e g* , Sunday, in the east in the 1st Yama. In the 2nd Yama it reaches the 7th cardinal point (Dik) therefrom ; in the 3rd Yama, the 4th therefrom ; in the 4th Yama the 3rd therefrom; in the 5th, the 8th from it; in the 6th, 3rd from it; in the 7th, the 2nd from it; and in the 8th Yama the 3rd from it. This is the order in which the Yogini moves on all days. In other words, Yogini returns to the 8th Dik from the starting Dik at the end of the 8th Yama.

For example, take Monday. Yogini rises in the north in the 1st Yama; in the 2nd Yama the 7th Dik (from the north) *viz.*, west. In the 3rd Yama it moves into the 4th therefrom (west), *i.e.*, north-east; in the 4th Yama it moves into the 3rd from north-east, *viz*, south-east; in the 5th Yama it moves into the 8th from south-east, *viz*, east. In the 6th Yama it gets into the 3rd from east, *viz.*, south. In the 7th Yama it traverses the 2nd from south, *viz.*. south west; and in the 8th Yama Yogini gets into the 3rd from west, *viz.*, north-west which Dik happens to be the 8th from the rising Dik north.

Longitudes of Yogini and Mrityu

चोळेनेष्टघटीर्निहत्य विभजेदह्नः प्रमित्या फलं
राशिः शिष्टत आनयेल्लवकलाः संशोध्य भान्मण्डलम् ।
शिष्टं शोधित चक्रसंख्यमतिहायोर्ध्वात्त्यजेत्स्थानतः
केसर्यादिमरुध्यमादिषु तदा तत्तत्स्फुटं संभवेत् ॥१००॥

Stanza 100.—Multiply the Ishta Ghatis by 96. Divide the product by 30. The quotient is the

Rasi. Reduce the remainder to degrees, minutes, etc. Expunge multiples of 12. (*a*) Note the Rasi Yogini is in at the required time. (*b*) Then deduct (*a*) from (*b*). The exact *sphuta* of Yogini is obtained. By a similar process the position of Mrityu can also be known.

NOTES

Let us again take the example given under stanzas 88–89, *viz.*, birth on Wednesday 16–10–1918 at about 2h. 15m. or Gh. 20.33 (*i e.*, 20 55) after sunrise.

Duration of day = 29.35

On the day and at the time of birth Yogini is in the 4th point in the 6th Yama, which means the point held by Yogini happens to be 18 in the Kalachakra diagram and this falls on S.E. in the centre. This means Yogini is in the middle of Virgo (15°) or Kanya.

Now applying this stanza

$$\frac{\text{Ishta Ghatis} \times 96}{30} = \frac{20.33 \times 96}{30}$$

$$= 65.056$$

$$= 65 \text{ signs and } 1^\circ\ 40'\ 45''$$

Expunging multiples of 12 we get 5s 1° 40′ 48″ (*a*)

Yogini's Rasi position is 3s 15° (*b*)

Deducting 5s 1° 40′ 48″ (*i.e.*, *a*) from 5s 15° (*b*) we get

5s 15° 0′

5s 1° 40′ 48″

0 14° 40′ 48″

= The longitude of Yogini is Aries 14° 40° 48″.

Regarding the position of Mrityu in the above example (*a*) is common to both Yogini and Mrityu. As regards (*b*), *i.e.*, the Rasi position of Mrityu. It rises each day in the N.W. (corresponding point 21) unlike Yogini which rises in different directions on different days.

In the 6th Yama the 4th point happens to be 25 (*vide* stanza 91) which means north. The Rasi position of Mrityu is Capricorn 30°. Therefore *b* – *a*, *i.e.*, 300° – 151° 40′ 48″ = 148° 19′ 12″, *i.e.*, the position of Mrityu = Leo 28° 19′ 12″.

मृत्योरन्तः प्रवेशो वितरति मरणं निर्गमे नैव मृत्यु-
स्तन्निर्याणं पुरस्ताद्यदि तरुपतनं गोमृतिर्वह्निकोणे ।
कार्तान्त्यां मर्त्यमृत्युर्निरृतिदिशि मृगस्यांशुपे कासराणां
चण्डालैतन्निकृष्टद्विजमृतिरनिलेन्द्वीशदिक्षु क्रमेण
॥१०१॥

Stanza 101.—If the query is made at the time when Mrityu is passing into the *interior* predict that the questioner will die.

If Mrityu happens to go *out*, then the native will not die. If he goes out through the *east* at the time, a tree will fall down. If he issues out through south-east, cows will die. If he goes out through south, some of his near relatives will die. If he goes through south-west, animals such as deer will die near. If he goes out through west, female buffaloes will die. If he goes out through north-west, high amongst Chandalas will die. If he goes out through north, low amongst Chandalas will die. If he goes out through north-east, Brahmins near will die.

Carefully study the diagram and see when he goes in and when he *goes out* by noting points.

MOVEMENT OF MRITYU

नरृैत्यां भृत्यनाशो वावारुण्यां वा चतुष्पदाम् ।
जीवन्ति रोगिणो नूनमेतेषां सति संभवे ॥१०२॥

Stanza 102.—According as at the time query is put Mrityu issues out through south-west or west then servants or quadrupeds of the questioner will die If these events happen, then it can be predicted that the questioner will not die.

प्राच्यामन्तःप्रवेशे प्रभुजनमरणं वह्निकोणेऽग्निभीति-
र्मूर्च्छा कस्यापि पुगाशनत इनजदिश्यात्मनोतश्च दौस्थ्यम् ।
नैरृत्यां पाशभृद्दिश्यतिसरणमपि छर्दिरित्यब्जरोगा-
श्चापे चौर्योत्थरावः शशिनि स मृगभूः प्रष्टमूर्च्छेशकोणे
॥१०३॥

मृत्योरन्तर्गमने यल्लक्षणमिति समीरितं तस्य ।
संभव इह यदि मरणं प्रष्टुनिस्संशयं प्रवदेत् ॥१०४॥

Stanzas 103 and 104.—In the Poorvardha of a yama if Mrityu gets in through the east Dik at the time of the query, death of a person belonging to the ruling class may happen in a near place. If Mrityu gets in through south-east Dik, incendiarism is to be feared. If through south, some person falls unconscious due to excessive eating of nuts; if south-west, the questioner himself may get sick by eating nuts; if west, he will have watery diseases as dysentery, vomitting, etc.; if north-west, trouble from thieves and consequent uproar; if through north-east, sudden fits. If these ominous signs take place, you can predict the death of the questioner is certain.

अर्कारजीवबुधशुक्रशनैश्चरेन्दु–
वारोदयेष्वनुदिनं क्रमशोथ दिग्भ्यः ।
उद्वृत्य गच्छति हि मृत्युरिह क्रमेण कालोन्यथाह्नि
निशि राशिषु च त्रिवारम् ॥१०५॥

Stanza 105.—According to *Sara Samgraha* Mrityu rises thus at the the time of sunrise. Sunday in the east, Tuesday south-east, Thursday south, Wednesday south-west, Friday west, Saturday north-west and Monday north. It traverses through the 8 points of the compass thrice in the day-time and thrice in the night-time in a clock-wise direction. 'Kala' also rises in the same Diks as Mrityu but traverses through the cardinal points in an anticlockwise direction thrice in day-time and thrice in night time.

NOTES

How Mrityu and Kala are to be calculated have been given in Chapter V, Verse 23.

योगिन्यत्रसहोदिता मृतियमस्थाने दिनाष्टांशकं
नीत्वा गच्छति वारदिश्यनुदिनं त्वीशानदिश्यष्टमे ।
प्राच्यांचेत्स्थितिरेव मेषवृषयोर्दृष्टिस्तुलाकीटयो-
र्याम्यादौ च तथैव यामदळयोः कोणेषु यामावधि
॥१०६॥

इन्द्रेन्द्वग्न्यसुरान्तकांबुपमरुद्दिक्ष्वर्कचन्द्रारवि-
द्वागीशस्फुजिदर्कपुत्रदिवसेषूद्याति सा योगिनी ।
यामैस्सप्तभिरेव सप्तसु दिशास्त्वेकैकयामक्रमा-
दास्थायन्तिमयामथोर्दिननिशोरीशानदिकस्था भवेत्
॥१०७॥

Stanzas 106 and 107.—Yogini stays along with Kala and Mrityu in the Dik (cardinal point) where these rise, during the first Yama on all days. In the 2nd Yama Yogini stays in the rising direction of the next day; in the 3rd, in the rising direction of the 3rd day; in the 4th Yama the fourth day and so on. In the 8th it will stay in the north-east on all days. East signifies Aries and Taurus The first and the second parts of the Yama denote Aries and Taurus respectively. Similarly, south signifies Cancer and Leo, the west Libra and Scorpio and north Capricorn and Aquarius. South-east, south-west, north-west and north-east respectively represent Virgo, Sagittarius, Pisces and Gemini. Yogini aspects the 7th sign from the sign occupied by it. If the Arudha Lagna of the querist happens to be the 4th or 7th from Yogini, death may take place.

NOTES

In the matter of calculation of Yogini, etc., there appears to be much repetition. Therefore one will do well to stick to the methods suggested in the earlier stanzas of this chapter.

According to stanzas 106 and 107 the movement of the Yogini will take place thus:

SUNDAY

1st Yama—east, 2nd north (same as 1st on Monday), 3rd south east, 4th south-west, 5th south, 6th west, 7th north-west, 8th north-east.

MONDAY

1st north, 2nd south-east (same as 1st on Tuesday), 3rd south-west, 4th south, 5th west, 6th north-west, 7th east and 8th north-east.

The 1st on Tuesday will be south-east (the 2nd on Monday).

This way the Yogini cycle can be calculated for all week-days.

Stanza 107 merely clarifies what is given in stanza 106.

YOGINI MOVEMENT

अष्टानां च तिथीनां दळद्वये तद्वदष्टयामेषु ।
योगिन्याश्चारदिशो वक्ष्यन्ते श्लोकपादेन ॥१०८॥

Stanza 108.—The movement of Yogini through the various tithis or lunar days are described in the form in which Yogini's movement during the week-days has been given.

कंसारिभोगमतिदा सोमदाराः कलावती ।
रजोंणुणवती सेयं भाद्रमासि तदापगा ॥१०९॥

लोकवर्तिशिसंहरि शार्ङ्गी तद्दासपुत्रवान् ।
स्तंमे सकृदरोगेण हतः कालोत्र भौमसः ॥११०॥

दळद्वये प्रतिपदः कंसारीत्युदिता दिशः ।
यामेष्वष्टसु विज्ञेया द्वितीया दळयोर्द्वयोः ॥१११॥

सोमदारादिकासद्वत्तृतीयादळयोः पुनः ।
रजोगृणवतीत्यादी चतुर्थिदळयोरथ ॥११२॥

भाद्रमासीति गादिताः पञ्चम्या दळयोस्ततः ।
लोकवर्त्यादिकाः षष्ठ्याः शार्ङ्गीत्याद्या दिशःस्मृताः ॥११३॥

स्तंभेस्ताद्यास्तु सप्तम्या अष्टम्याश्च हृतादिकाः ।
नवम्यादिषु तद्वत्स्याद्यथा प्रतिपदादिषु ॥११४॥
दळद्वये योगिनी स्यादित्युक्ता तिथियोगिनि ॥११५॥

Stanzas 109 to 115.—Yogini rises and moves during the eight Yamas in the eight directions on different lunar days as follows :—

Prathama and Navami (1st and 9th) : east, north, south-east, south-west, south, west, north-west and north-east ; *Dwiteeya and Dasami* (2nd and 10th) : north-west, north-east, south-east, east, south-west and north-west ; *Triteeya and Ekadasi* (3rd and 11th) : south-east, north-east, south, west, south-west, north-west, north and east ; *Chathurthi and Dwadasi* (4th and 12th) : south-west, south-east, west, north, north-west, north-east, east and south ; *Panchami and Trayodasi* (5th and 13th): south, east, south-east, north-west, west, north, north-east and south-east ; *Shashti and Chaturdasi* (6th and 14th) : west, south, north-west, north-east, north, east, south-east and south—west ; *Saptami and Pournamasya or Amavasya* (7th and 15th or 30th) : north-west, south-west, north-east, south-east, south and west ; and *Ashtami* (8th) : north-east, north-west, east, south, south-east, south-west, west and north. The same arrangement holds good both for bright and dark halves.

NOTES

These stanzas deal with the rise and movement of Yogini on different lunar days Except *ashtami* (8th day), two lunar days are clubbed together implying that on both these days the same arrangement holds good. For instance let us take *shashti* (6th) and *chaturdasi* (14th). The Yogini rises in the west in the first Yama, goes to south in the 2nd Yama, to north-west in the 3rd Yama, north-east in the 4th, north in the 5th, east in the 6th, south-east in the 7th and south-west in the 8th Yama.

The Diks or points of compass are indicated in letters. Their conversion into numbers is given in the appendix.

योगिन्या यदि दृष्टौ लग्नारूढौ च जन्मलग्ने वा ।
मृतिदौ भवतो जीवौ योगिन्या मुखगतश्चापि ॥११६॥

Stanza 116.—If Yogini aspects the birth Lagna or Arudha Lagna, the querist will meet with his death.

NOTES

The birth Moon is also included in this combination. Yogini should not aspect the birth-Moon.

HELL AND HEAVEN

पातः किं नरके मे किं वासः स्वर्गे घनागमः ।
काथंवेति कृते प्रश्ने वक्तव्यमथ कथ्यते ॥११७॥

Stanza 117.—For questions like "shall I fall in hell", "will I go to heaven", "can I get wealth" answers should be given as follows:

स्थूणत्रयत्रिषघटिका विष्टिर्गण्डान्तर्वैधृतो लाटः ।
परिवेषव्यतिपातक धूमार्गळमन्दपूर्वचतुरुदयाः ॥११८॥

एते दोषा नरकपतनं सूचयन्तीह नृणां
प्राग्लग्ने वा तुहिनरुचि वा संभवन्तोथवार्के ।

दुःखं मानक्षयमघनतां नारकानेव विद्या-
दस्मिन् लोके पुनरतितरां चन्द्रदोषैः स्युरेतैः ॥११९॥

Stanzas 118 and 119.—The three sthunas, vishaghatika, vishtikarana, gandantha, vaidhriti lata parivesha, vyathipatha, dhuma, ekargala, rising of Saturn, rising of Rahu, rising of Ketu and rising of Gulika are the *doshas*. If these doshas afflict the ascendant, the Moon or the Sun, the native suffers hell in this world itself, which consists of sorrow, dishonour and poverty.

NOTES

The three *sthunas* are (1) Kantakasthuna, (2) Rakta-sthuna and (3) Sthuna.

अर्कक्षोणीसुतारव्यां भवति गणनया नैरृतं यावदस्मा-
त्तावत्यौ तारके द्वे क्रमश इह मते कण्टकस्थूणसंज्ञे ।
नाभ्यामामूलसंख्याद्वययुति गणितः कण्टकस्थूणनामा-
रक्तस्थूणोवसिष्टं क्षितिसुतरहिते सिंहधृत्यंशके स्यात्
॥१२०॥

विषादिदोषैरुदितैः समेते प्रश्नातिलग्ने निरयः परत्र ।
आरूढभे प्रश्न उडुप्रभौ वा दोषान्वितेत्रोष्णकरे परत्र
॥१२१॥

Stanzas 120 and 121.—The asterism arrived at by counting from Moola, the same number as intervenes between the nakshatra held by the Sun at the time of query to Moola, is called *kantaka* nakshatra. The same reckoning with reference to Mars gives *sthuna*. The asterism arrived at by counting from Moola that number which is the sum of the kantaka and sthuna asterisms gives *kantakasthuna*. By subtracting the longitude of Mars from 138°, *raktasthuna* is obtained. If these doshas afflict Arudha Lagna or the Moon at the time of query, the native's life in this world will be equivalent to hell. If the Sun either in the birth chart or in the query chart is afflicted by these doshas, the native goes to hell after death.

NOTES

How to calculate the *sthunatraya* (three sthunas) have been explained in the above two stanzas.

(1) Count from the star or constellation held by the Sun to Moola. Note the number. Count the same number from Moola, the star held by *kantaka* is obtained.

Example.—The Sun is in Aslesha. Counting from this star to Moola we get 11. Counting 11 from Moola we get Bharani. Therefore *kantaka* is in Bharani.

(2) Mars is in Pubba. Counting from Pubba to Moola we get 9. Counting 9 from Moola we get Revati. Therefore the position of *sthuna* is Revati.

(3) Adding the number of the kantaka star (Bharani– 2) to the number of the sthuna star (Revati—27) we get 29, *i.e.*, 2, after expunging 27. The 2nd from Moola is Poorvashadha. Therefore *kantakasthuna* is in Poorvashadha.

(4) Longitude of Mars is 125°. Subtracting this from 138° the result is 13°. This falls in Aswini. Therefore, *aktasthuna* is Aswini.

SIGNS OF KRITA YUGA ETC

नृणामायुः सहस्रं कृतयुगसमये तद्दलं तस्य चार्द्धं-

त्रेतायां द्वापरे वा कलियुग उदितः स्यात् सहस्राष्टभागः ।

पूर्णार्धाङ्घ्र्यष्टभागान् निजनिजशरदां तत्तदाख्यालयांशा
रूढाः खेटाः प्रदद्युस्त्वजमुखभवतुष्कत्रिकोणः कृताद्याः
॥१२२॥

Stanza 122.—The longevity of man in Krita, Treta, Dwapara and Kali Yugas respectively are 1000, 500, 250 and 125 years. Planets occupying the signs and Navamsas of Krita, Treta, Dwapara and Kali Yugas contribute their Dasa years, in full. half, quarter or one-eighth respecttvely as the longevity of the person.

NOTES

The *Kritayuga* signs are Aries Leo and Sagittarius; *Thretayuga* signs are Taurus, Virgo and Capricorn; *Dwapara yuga* signs are Gemini, Libra and Aquarius ; and *Kaliyuga* signs are Cancer, Scorpio and Pisces.

यज्जननं कृतयुगभे दैवनियोगादुपेत्य सकलजनाः ।
धनपस्मै दद्युरथ त्रेतायामर्थलब्धिरटनेन ॥१२३॥

द्वापरभे स्वीयधनव्यापारात् कलियुगे न केनापि ।
एवं फलदा विहगाः कृतपूर्वयुगाभिधानराशिगताः
॥१२४॥

स्वदशापहृतिप्रभृतिषु समयेष्विह चिन्त्यतां तदंशोपि
॥१२५॥

Stanza 123 to 125.—Persons born in Krita yuga signs or Navamsas get everything unasked. Those born in Tretayuga signs will get wealth, etc., if they aspire for them. Those born in Dwaparayuga signs will be able to make money by trade, etc. Those born in Kaliyuga signs cannot get wealth by any of these ways.

This theory can be skilfully used for interpreting Dasa and Bhukti results.

NOTES

In interpreting effects of planets occupying signs of different categories listed above, one has to take due note of their own inherent strengths and weaknesses. A literal application is not called for. It is also suggested that in regard to questions bearing on financial matters, the principles given in the above three stanzas could be applied. Thus if at the time of query, the lord of the 2nd is disposed in the 11th which happens to be a Krityuga sign, then the forecast can be made that without much effort his financial problems will be straitened.

CONCLUSION

The sixteen Chapters of the first part have been completed. The work *Prasna Marga* has been written in deference to the wishes of my desciples.

Prasna Marga has been divided into two parts—Purvardha and Uttarardha.—The first part ends with 16 Chapters.

॥ इति प्रश्नमार्गे षोडशोध्यायः ॥

APPENDIX I

Rise of Gulika Kala etc., during day and night in Ghatikas

Week day	Gulika		Kala		Ardha Prahara		Yama		Rahu
	D.	N.	D.	N.	D.	N.	D.	N.	D. N.
Sunday	26	10	30	6	14	30	22	6	$26\frac{1}{4}$
Monday	22	6	2	14	26	10	18	2	$3\frac{3}{4}$
Tuesday	18	2	22	6	6	22	14	26	$22\frac{1}{2}$
Wednesday	14	26	2	30	18	14	10	22	15
Thursday	10	22	6	2	30	26	6	18	$18\frac{1}{2}$
Friday	6	18	14	22	10	6	2	14	$11\frac{1}{2}$
Saturday	2	14	6	2	22	18	26	10	$7\frac{1}{2}$

D = Day ; N = Night

For example on Sunday Gulika's position coincides with the Lagna rising at Gh. 26 after sunrise ; at Gh. 10 after sunset. Similarly with regard to other tertiary planets.

APPENDIX II

	Siddha Yoga	Amrita Yoga	Mrityu Yoga	*Dagda Yoga	Asubha Yoga	Vara Soola Yoga
Sunday	Hastha	Moola	Makha	Dwadasi	Bharani	West–12
Monday	Sravana	Sravana	Visakha	Ekadasi	Chitra	East–8
Tuesday	Aswini	Uttara	Aridra	Panchami	Uttarashadha	North–16
Wednesday	Anuradha	Krittika	Moola	Dwiteeya	Dhanista	North–16
Thursday	Pushyami	Punarvasu	Satabhisha	Shashti	Jyeshta	South–20
Friday	Revati	Uttarabhadra	Rohini	Ashtami	Purvashadha	West–12
Saturday	Rohini	Swathi	Uttarashadha	Navami	Revati	East–8

Explanation : **Sunday coinciding with Hasta gives Siddha Yoga.**
Monday coinciding with Ekadasi (11th lunar day) gives Dagdha Yoga

APPENDIX III
Mrityu Bhagas of Planets and Rasis

		♈ Mesha	♉ Vrishabha	♊ Mithuna	♋ Kataka	♌ Simha	♍ Kanya	♎ Thula	♏ Vrischika	♐ Dhanus	♑ Makara	♒ Kumbha	♓ Meena
Ravi	☉	20	9	12	6	8	21	16	17	22	2	3	22
Chandra	☽	26	12	13	25	24	11	26	14	13	25	5	12
Kuja	♂	19	18	25	23	29	28	14	21	2	15	11	6
Budha	☿	15	14	13	12	8	18	20	10	21	22	7	5
Guru	♃	19	29	12	27	6	4	13	10	17	11	15	28
Sukra	♀	28	15	11	17	10	13	4	6	27	12	29	19
Sani	♄	10	4	7	9	12	16	3	18	28	14	13	15
Rasi		1	9	21	22	25	2	4	23	18	20	10	24
Rahu	☋	14	13	12	11	24	23	22	21	10	20	18	8
Ketu	☋	8	18	20	10	21	22	23	24	11	12	13	14
Gulika	P	23	24	11	12	13	14	8	18	20	10	21	2

APPENDIX IV

Chandra Kriya

1. Displaced from position, 2. Do penance, 3. Enjoy with other women, 4. Steal, 5. Ride on an elephant, 6. Sit on a throne, 7. To be a king, 8. Kill the enemies, 9. To be a Commander, 10. To do good to others, 11. To be lifeless in everything, 12. To be wounded in the head, 13. To have hands and legs wounded, 14. To be imprisoned, 15. To be ruined, 16. To be a king, 17. To study Vedas, 18. To sleep, 19. To think about good stories, 20. To do good actions, 21. To be born of a noble family. 22. To get treasures, 23. To keep a balance in one's hand, 24. To annotate, 25. To kill enemies, 26, To be sick, 27. To be defeated by enemies, 28. To leave one's native place, 29. To be a servant, 30. To be without money, 31. To be in a wrong place, 32. To be with a good minister, 33. To govern another's country or property 34. To be with a wife, 35. To be afraid of elephants, 36. To be timid in warfare, 37. To be timid in everything, 38. To remain hidden from view, 39. To give food freely, 40. To occupy a fiery spot (to sit on fire) 41. To be hungry, 42. To eat food, 43. To travel, 44. To eat flesh, 45. To be wounded in war by arrows, 46. To marry, 47. To play balls, 48. To gamble, 49 To be a king, 50. To be miserable, 51. To set on a bed, 52. To be served by enemies, 53. To be with relations, 54. To be engaged in meditation, 55. To be with wife, 56. To eat plentifully, 57. To drink milk. 58. To do good actions, 59. To have mental peace, 60. To enjoy.

APPENDIX V

Chandra Vela

1. Headache, 2. Delight, 3. Worship of Devas, 4. Desire in happiness, 5. Disease in the eyes, 6. Enjoyment, 7. Slay with women, 8. High fever, 9. To put on ornaments, 10. To shed tears, 11. To drink pioson, 12. To cohabit with women, 13. To have stomach complaints, 14. To play in water, 15. To laugh, 16. To paint, 17. Anger, 18. Play, 19. To drink ghee, 20. To sleep, 21. To sing, 22. Disease in the teeth, 23. To quarrel, 24. Journey, 25. To get mad, 26. To jump in water, 27. Opposition, 28. To do as he pleases, 29. Fear from hunger, 30. Education, 31. To amuse oneself, 32. To fight, 33. To do good action, 34. To do bad actions, 35. To do cruel actions, 36. Delight.

APPENDIX VI

Chandra Avasthas

1. To go to a foreign place leaving one's profession, 2. To occupy a throne, 3. Loss of life, 4. Kingship, 5. To do actions befitting one's family, 6. Sickness, 7. To occupy a wrong place, 8 Fear, 9. Hunger, 10. To marry a woman, 11. To lie on a good bed, 12. To take good food

APPENDIX—VII
Nature of Drekkanas

Rasi	First Drekkana	2nd Drekkana	3rd Drekkana
Mesha	Nara, Purusha, Ayudha Krura Drekkana	Sthira, Mriga, Soumya	Purusha, Ayudha and Misra
Vrishabha	Sthree, Agni, Misra	Purusha, Mriga, Soumya	Purusha, Jalachara
Mithuna	Sthree, Soumya	Purusha, Pakshi, Misra	Purusha, Ayudha, Jalachara
Kataka	Purusha, Chatushpada, Jalachara	Sthree, Sarpa, Krura	Purusha, Sarpa, Jalachara, Misra
Simha	Pakshi, Chathushpada, Nara, Krura	Nara, Ayudha, Mishra, Raja	Purusha, Chathushpada, Ayudha, Krura
Kanya	Stree, Agni, Soumya	Purusha, Nara, Jalachara	Sthree, Soumya
Thula	Purusha, Soumya	Pakshi, Purusha, Misra	Purusha, Chathushpada, Vana
Vrischika	Sthree, Sarpa, Krura	Sthree, Sarpa, Krura	Chathushpada, Vana, Nara, or Kurma Mukha Jhala—Krura
Dhanus	Narmukha, Ayudha, Chatushpada, Misra	Sthree, Soumya	Nara, Ayudha, Soumya
Makara	Nara, Nigala, Krura, Chathushpada	Sthree, Soumya	Purusha, Aswamukha, Ayudha, Misra
Kumbha	Pakshi, Nara, Krura	Sthree, Vana, Soumya	Nara, Oushadha, Vana, Soumya
Meena	Nara, Jala	Sthree, Jhala	Purusha, Sarpa, Agni, Vana, Krura

APPENDIX VIII

Finding Time with the help of the Sun's Shadow

Ghatikas	Leo and Aries		Virgo and Pisces		Libra and Aquarius		Scorpio and Capricorn		Sagittarius		Taurus and Cancer		Gemini	
	′	″	′	″	′	″	′	″	′	″	′	″	′	″
1	64	0	63	0	64	0	68	0	70	0	67	0	69	0
2	32	0	31	0	32	0	34	0	35	0	33	0	34	0
3	21	0	20	0	23	0	22	0	23	0	22	0	22	0
4	15	0	15	0	15	0	16	0	17	0	16	0	16	0
5	12	0	12	0	12	0	12	0	13	0	12	0	13	0
6	9	3	9	1	9	5	10	0	11	0	9	5	10	0
7	7	4	7	3	7	7	8	6	9	1	8	0	8	2
8	6	1	6	1	6	5	7	3	7	6	6	5	6	7
9	5	0	5	0	5	4	6	3	6	7	5	3	5	5
10	4	0	4	0	4	5	5	4	5	6	4	3	4	5
11	3	1	3	1	3	7	4	7	5	3	3	4	3	7
12	2	3	2	3	3	3	4	2	5	0	2	6	3	1
13	1	5	1	6	2	7	4	1	4	5	2	1	2	4
14	0	6	1	3	2	6	4	0	4	4	1	5	2	0
15	0	3	1	1	2	5	3	7	4	3	1	2	1	5
16	0	0	0	0	0	0	0	0	0	0	1	1	1	6

8 Angulams = 1 foot. ′ = Foot, ″ = Angulam.

N.B.—These ghatikas are to be calculated both after sunrise and before sunset. Eg., if the shadow is 64 ft. it is either 1 ghatika after sunrise or before sunset in the months of Simha and Mesha (1st). For other dates find out by proportion.

APPENDIX IX
"Yogini" Diks

Dik	*Bright Half (Sukla Paksha)*		*Dark Half (Krishna Paksha)*	
East	1. Prathama	11. Ekadasi	6. Shasthti	...
North	2. Dwiteeya	12. Dwadasi	7. Saptami	...
South-East	3. Thritheeya	13. Trayodasi	8. Ashtami	...
South-West	4. Chaturthi	14. Chaturdasi	9. Navami	...
South	5. Panchami	15. Pournami	10 Dasami	...
West	6. Shasti		1. Prathama	11. Ekadasi
North-West	7. Saptami		2. Dwiteeya	12. Dwadasi
North-East	8. Ashtami		3. Thritheeya	13. Thrayodasi
Akasam	9. Navami		4. Chathurthi	14. Chaturdasi
Bhoomi	10. Dasami		5. Panchami	15. Amavasya

AN INDEX OF TECHNICAL TERMS

A

Abhichara	...	Incantations meant to harm others
Adhomukha	...	The sign occupied by the Sun
Adhrishta	...	Invisible or supernatural cause of events
Adrishta nimittaja	...	Events arising from unknown causes.
Aghorabali	...	Sacrificial offering to a form of Siva or the Sun
Agnitattva	....	Fiery signs Aries, Leo and Sagittarius
Amaya	...	*Costus speciosus*
Amita	...	Longevity beyond hundered years
Anasana	...	Fasting
Angara	...	North-west ; charcoal
Angula	...	One eighth of an inch
Anishta	...	Houses 6, 8, 12 from the Ascendant
Antara Bhavas	...	Part of the house indicating the internal
Anujanma	...	The tenth and the nineteenth stars from the birth star
Apasmara	...	Epilepsy
Ara	...	Mars
Ari	...	Enemy ; sixth house

Arishta ... Death within 12 years; harmful

Artha ... Fortnight

Arudha ... The sign rising at the time of the query

Ashtamangala ... An elaborate method of horary astrology described in Chapter 7

Ashtama Rasi ... Eighth house

Ashtottari ... A system of the periods of the planets covering 108 years

Aspada ... Tenth house

Asthi ... Bone, ruled by the Sun

Astodaya ... Heliacal setting and rising of a planet

Asu ... Sixth part of a Vighati; four seconds

Asura graha ... demonaic spirit

Avastha ... State or condition attributed to a planet on the basis of the sign occupied. See p. 235

Aya ... Eleventh house

Ayana ... Six months

Ayushkaraka ... Saturn

Ayyappa ... The deity Sasta

B

Badhaka ... A planet that obstructs or is harmful. It is the lord of the eleventh sign for

		movable ascendants, the lord of the ninth for fixed ones, and the lord of the seventh for common signs. Also see Chap. 15 : 111–113
Baghyabhava	...	Part of the house dealing with external affairs
Balagraha	...	Spirits of children who had a premature or unnatural death
Balaprabhakshini	...	An evil spirit preying on children
Bali	...	Sacrifice
Balikarma	...	Act of offering a sacrifice
Balya	...	A planet in a friend's house
Bandhu	...	Relatives ; fourth house
Bhadrakali	...	A form of protecting Goddess
Bhairava	...	A deity who follows Sivag
Bhaktavirodha	...	Loss of appetite
Bharadwaja	...	Skylark, a Sage
Bhasa	...	Vulture
Bhasma	...	Ashes ; North
Bhasmaka graha	...	A spirit that causes unappeas-ing appetite
Bhasma pisacha	...	A spirit of evil
Bhava	...	House. The sign is called Rasi. Eleventh house.
Bhuja	...	Arc. Also called Koti
Bhumi	...	East ; North-east

Bhuta ... Elements called earth, water, fire, wind and ether. Sometime it means a spirit

Bhutamarana bali ... Sacrifice to Mars and Venus in order to destroy evil spirits

Bhutanatha ... Siva

Bhuta Rakshasa ... A demon

Bhutattava ... Earthy signs—Taurus, Virgo and Capricorn

Brahma Rakshasa ... A fierce demon

Budha ... Mercury, rules wind, bile, phlegm and skin

C

Chamundi — A form of the Goddess Durga

Chandra ... Moon. Rules blood, wind and phlegm

Chandrakriya ... Arc traversed by the Moon in a star converted into minutes and multiplied by 60, and then divide it by 800 and add one to the quotient (see Appendix)

Chakora ... A song-bird like the partridge

Chakra ... Zodiacal diagram. The fixed one is posited on the earth around the astrologer. The movable one is in the sky. The former refers to the directions. The latter is

		the basis for fixing the Ascendant
Chakra homa	...	A sacrificial offering to Mercury
Chara	...	Movable or cardinal signs
Charaphala	...	Position of a planet as per its mean motion converted into an arc
Chatushpada Rasi	...	Leo, Aries, Taurus, the second half of Sagittarius and the first part of Capricorn
Chaya	...	Shadow ; measuring time on the basis of the shadow caused by the Sun ; South
Chatra Rasi	...	The sign obtained from the Vidhi Rasi. Count the number of signs from Arudha to the ascendant and then count this number from the Vidhi Rasi to get Chatra Rasi
Chitra Kuta	...	A stone
Chittottha	...	Seventh house ; mental diseases

D

Dagdha Yoga	...	An evil moment. See note on page 44
Dakshinayana	...	From the time the Sun enters Cancer and leaves Sagittarius

Dantiskandha	...	Offering an elephant's tooth
Darbha	...	Sacred grass called Kusa
Darvi	..	Medicine ; powder of conch
Dasa	...	Number of years ruled by a planet. Its sub-periods are called Antardasa or Bhukti.
Deha	...	Multiply the Moon's longitude by eight and then add the longitude of Mandi
Devagraha	...	Divine or benefic spirit
Dhanus	...	Sagittarius
Dharmadeva	...	These are given in Chapter 15.4-7
Dhatri	...	Emblic myrobalan
Dhatu	...	Mineral. In odd Navamsas the Dhatu Navamsas are 1, 4, 7. In even signs, 3, 6, 9
Dhuma	...	From three hours to six after suntise. It also means smoke. There are five temporory planets. These are Dhuma (sun's longitude plus 133°) ; Vyatipata (360° minus Dhuma) ; Parivesha (180° plus Vyatipata) ; Indrachapa (360° minus Parivesha) ; and Ketu (Indrachapa plus 17 degree)
Dhumni	...	Future
Dhvaja	...	Flag ; a point in Ashtamangala
Digdaha	...	Reddish colour at sunset

Digit	...	**The central digits are serpant, mouse, elephant, hare. Their corresponding unit digits are Garuda, cat, lion, and dog respect lvely**
Dinagata	...	**Time of birth after query**
Dipta	...	**Three hours from sunrise**
Dirgha	...	**Longevity of a hundred years**
Dravya	...	**Substance. Jeeva dravya refers to organisms. Muladravya refers to immovable property. Dhatudravya signifies minerals**
Drekkana	...	**Ten degrees of a sign. The three parts are ruled by the lord of the sign, and by the lords of 5 and 9 from that sign (see Appendix VII)**
Dridha	...	**Karma acquired in the past**
Drigganita	...	**Astronomical calculation that agrees with observations**
Drishta	...	**Perceived cause of a result**
Drishtibadha	...	**Suffering caused by the evil eye of a person.**
Dundubha	...	**A large drum**
Durdevata	...	**An evil spirit**
Durga	...	**Supreme Goddess**
Durmuhurta	...	**It has a duration of 48 minutes and varies from day to day. It is inauspicious. See notes on pages 46 to 48**

Dustha	...	Planets in a malefic sign
Dutalakshana	...	Omens
Dvadasamsa	...	A twelfth part of sign
Dvisvabhava	...	Common signs—Gemini, Virgo, Sagittarius and Pisces

E

Ekargala	...	An unfavourable time
Ela	...	Cardamom

G

Gaja	...	Elephant
Gana	...	Metrical foot
Ganapati	...	Deity who destroys obstacles
Gandanta	...	The conjunction of Pisces–Aries, Cancer–Leo and Scorpio–Sagittarius
Gandharva	...	A semi-divine being ; musician
Ganita	...	Astronomical calculations
Ghantakarna	...	Divine being
Ghatika	...	24 minutes. It is also called Nadi or Nadika. Its sub-division is Vighati or Vinadika coveing 24 seconds
Gochara	...	Transit influences of planets
Godha	...	Alligator
Gola	...	Spherical astronomy
Gridhramukha	...	Last decanate of Leo and Aquarius and the second of Libra (see Appendix VII)
Griha	...	House ; fourth house

Grishma ... Summer
Guhyaka ... A class of demigods following Kubera
Gulika ... A sensitive point; on pages 160 to 162 the calculation is given
Gulma ... Abdominal ulcer
Guru ... Jupiter. Rules flesh and the 10th house

H

Hantukama ... An evil spirit eager to kill
Havana ... Fire sacrifice
Hinga ... Asafoetida
Homa ... Sacrificial offering
Hora ... Half of a sign; science of astronomy and astrology

J

Jala ... Water; West
Jala graha ... The Moon and Venus
Janma Nakshatra ... The constellation through which the Moon was passing at the time of birth
Janma Rasi ... The sign occupied by the Moon at the time of birth
Jala Pisacha ... A water demon
Japa ... Chanting of the sacred mantra
Jataka ... Horoscope
Jihva dosha ... evil arising from words
Jiva ... In odd signs its navamsas are 3, 6, 9 and in even signs 1, 4, 7

Jrimbhika	...	Yawning
Jwala	...	Flame ; East

K

Kala	...	Refers to the sign and the condition ; First house
Kala Chakra	...	A system of periods of the planets and signs
Kala Hora	...	The order in which the lords of the horas follow is Saturn Jupiter, Mars, the Sun, Venus, Mercury and the Moon The first hora is that of the lord of the week-day
Kala Paisachi	...	An evil spirit
Kala Sphuta	...	The calculation is given on pages 167–8
Kali	...	Fierce Goddess
Kali Yuga	...	Began in 3102 B.C.
Kana	...	A kind of corn called *premna spinosa* or *longifolia*
Kapha	...	Phlegm
Kanya	...	Virgo
Kapalahoma	...	Sacrifice to propitiate the Moon
Karka, Karkataka	...	Cancer
Karaka	...	Significator
Karana	...	One of the five elements in the Panchanga or Hindu calendar

Karma ... The result of actions done in the past. See notes on 1.34, 38 and pages 280, 413–4, 480–6
Kasmala graha ... Polluted planet, a base spirit
Kaumara ... Planet in its own house
Kavacha ... Amulet
Kemadruma ... When there is no planet on either side of the Moon
Kendra ... Houses 1, 4, 7, 10
Ketu ... South node of the Moon
Khadga Ravana Bali ... Sacrificial offering to Mars
Khara ... Donkey
Kinnara ... A demigod
Kirata ... Huntsman
Kolamukha ... The first decanate of Cancer and Capricorn and the last one of Scorpio (see Appendix)
Kona ... Houses 1, 5, 9
Krodhagni ... The mantra beginning with 'Jatavedase'
Krodhani ... Angry
Krittikabali ... Sacrifice to Mars
Kshaya ... Consumption
Kshana ... 48 minutes
Kshata ... Sixth house
Kshema ... Fourth star from the birth star
Kshudram ... Incantated article
Kshurdamantra ... Incantation for an evil spirit

Kshetra Pinda	...	Offering
Kukshi Sasta	...	A Deity
Kuja	...	Mars. Rules bile and muscle
Kumbha	...	Aquarius
Kushmandabali	...	Sacrificial offering of a pumpkin to Durga
Kushtha Kana	...	A plant
Kunda	...	Number 81
Kutumba	...	Second house

L

Lagna	...	Ascendant
Lakshana	...	Signification

M

Madhuka	...	Liquorice root
Madhya	...	Longevity of seventy years
Magadhi	...	Long pepper
Mahagraha	...	Eighteen great spirits described in Chap 16, Verse 63
Majja	...	Muscle
Makara	...	Capricorn
Malina	...	Soiling of body
Mana	...	Tenth house
Mandi	...	A sensitive point. See pages 160-161
Manduka Gamana	...	In Kalachakra system there is a leap from Virgo to Cancer
Manjishtha	...	Madder.
Mani	...	A Gandharva
Manu	...	Mantra
Maraka	...	A planet that inflicts death

Marana	...	Eighth house
Masa	...	Month
Matri	...	Seven divine mothers
Mesha	...	Aries
Meena	...	Pisces
Mithuna	...	Gemini
Mitra	...	Eighth star from the birth star, friend
Mohini	...	Beguiling
Mriduvarga	...	Benefic vargas of Mercury
Mrita	...	Planet in debilitation
Mrittika	...	South west
Mrityu	...	A sensitive point obtained by multiplying Mandi's longitude by seven and adding the Sun's.
Mrityu bhaga	...	Fatal degrees. These are 1, 9, 22, 23, 25, 2. 4, 23, 18, 20, 24 and 10 from Aries onwards. The Moon's are 26, 12, 13, 25, 24, 11, 26, 14, 13, 25, 5, 12.
Mrityu Chakra	...	Horary time in Vighatis to be divided by 15 to get Mrityu Rasi. This plus the longitude of the Sun or the Moon in Navamsa gives the position of the Sun or the Moon in Mrityu Chakra See pages 172–174 (5.28).

Mrityu Nakshatra	...	**This is calculated from the Trisphuta Nakshatra. See page 195.**
Mrityu Prada	...	**Death-inflicting planet.**
Mrityu sphuta	...	**Multiply the longitude of Mandi by 9 and divide it by 30. Likewise calculate Deha and Prana Sphutas as given on page 249.**
Mrityu Yoga	...	**It arises from Sunday to Saturday coinciding with certain stars. See page 44**
Muhurta	...	**Auspicious moment**
Mula	...	**Animals. In odd and even signs the Navamsas are 2 5 and 8**
Mulatrikona	...	**A special area of a sign in which the planet has great strength**
Murcha	...	**Swooning**

N

Nadika	...	**Same as Ghati or 24 minutes. It has 60 Vinadikaṣ or Vighatikas. In northren India it is called Pala.**
Nadi	...	**These are three Nadis employed in Pranayama or breath control. These are Ida, Pingala and Sushumna.**
Naga	...	**Snake**

Naga Kanya ... Snake woman

Naidhana ... Seventh star from the birth star

Nakshatra ... Constellation. These are 27 and sometimes with Abhijit these are 28. These are important in calculating the periods of planets. Each Nakshatra covers 13° 20′

Nakshatrapada ... One-fourth of a constellation. It co ers 3° 20′

Narasimha ... The fierce form of Vishnu

Navamsa ... Ninth part of a sign

Neecha ... Debilitation

Needra ... Sleepiness

Nigala ... Second decanate of Scorpio (See Appendix)

Nija Roga ... Natural ailment. The acquired one is agantuka

Nimitta ... Cause, condition

Niryana Rasi .... Multiply the longitude of a planet by the number of the expired Navamsa. The result is the sign of death given by the planet

Nisheja graha ... A weak spirit

Nocturnal signs ... These are the first four from Aries, and 9, 10 and 12. The others are diurnal signs

P

Pakshi Drekkana	...	Second decanate of Libra and the first of Leo and Aquarius (See Appendix)
Panchakshari	...	A five-lettered mantra of Siva
Panchami Devata	...	Deity of death
Papakartari	...	A sign or a planet having malefics on either side
Parahita	...	A method of astronomical calculations
Parivesha	...	See under Dhuma
Parva	...	Lunar days 1, 8, 14, 15, 16, 23, 29, 30
Pasa drekkana	...	Second decanate of Cancer, the first of Scorpio and the last of Pisces (See Appendix)
Paramamitra	...	Ninth star from the birth one
Pati	...	Husband, seventh house
Patni	...	Wife, seventh house
Phala	...	Result. It is based on the causal law
Phaladata	...	Planet that gives results
Pindakriya	...	Offerings made to the dead ancestors
Pisacha	...	Demon
Pitta	...	Bile
Pradosha	...	Twilight
Pramana	...	That which demonstrates the truth of a given statement

Pramana Gulika ... For a day birth add 180° to the longitude of Gulika of the previous night. For a day birth the position of Gulika on that day is the longitude

Pranakalantara ... A principle considered in Driggsnita

Prana Sphuta ... Multiply the longitude of the ascendant by 5 and add that of Mandi

Prasna ... Query

Prasnakriya ... Horary astrology. The act of putting questions and getting replies

Prasnakshara ... The letters in the query

Pratikarabali ... Sacrifice to avenge or to pacify a curse. It is offered to Jupiter and Venus

Pratyak — The fifth star from the birth one

Prayascitta — Expiatory rite

Preta — The spirit of the recently dead one

Prishthodaya — The signs Aries, Taurus, Cancer, Sagittarius and Capricorn

Prishthatogamana ... In Kalachakra system the movement is sometimes backwards from Leo to Gemini

Punya	...	**Vedic rite of purification**
Purvasapa	...	**Curse given earlier**
Putana	...	**The demon who wanted to kill Sri Krishna by suckling him**
Putra	...	**Fifth house**

R

Rahu	...	**North node of the Moon**
Rahu–Sun–Moon chart		**This is explained on pages 169 and 170 with example**
Raja	....	**A planet in exaltation**
Raja Prasna	...	**Enquiry about the ruler**
Rakshasagraha	...	**Demonaic spirit**
Rakta	...	**Blood ruled by the Moon**
Rakta Chamundi	...	**The blood red Deity**
Randhra	...	**Eighth house**
Ranimusta	...	**A plant**
Rantukama	...	**A spirit desiring sex**
Rasa	...	**Flavour. There are six called sweet, acid, salt, sour, bitter and hot**
Rasi	...	**Sign of the zodiac. The Sattvik signs are Cancer, Leo, Sagittarius and Pisces. The Rajasik are Taurus, Gemini, Virgo and Libra. The Tamasik are the rest**
Ravi	...	**The Sun. Rules bile**
Riksha sandhi	...	**Junction of two signs or two constellations**

Ripha	...	Twelfth house
Ritu	...	Season There are six seasons
Rodani	...	Wailing
Rudragraha	...	A spirit following Rudra

S

Sadhana	...	Practice
Sadydrishta	...	Death within one year
Sahottha	...	Third house
Sama	...	One year
Samayajala Samriddhi	...	Three signs from the Moon are of rising ebb. The next three fall or flow. Then three ebb or rise The last three fall or flow
Sampal	...	The second star from the birth star
Sandhi	...	Junctional points. These are (*a*) the first and the last 24 minutes of a lunar day and star. (*b*) the first and the last 2 minutes of a sign; and (*c*) the first and the last 24 seconds of a Navamsa
Sani	...	Saturn. Rules tendons and wind
Sanjna	...	Technical terms

Sankalpa	...	The desire with which one undertakes to perform a rite
Sankhabhisheka	...	Sprinkling ritual water on the Deity through a conch
Sankhapushpa	...	A plant
Sankranti	...	Solar ingress into a sign
Sannipata	...	Combined disorder of the three humours of the body causing dangerous fever
Saptavarga	...	Rasi, Hora, Drekkana, Saptamsa, Navamsa, Dvadasamsa and Trimsamsa
Sarasvati	...	Goddess of learning
Sarat	...	Autumn
Sariba	...	Kusa or sacred grass
Sarirottha	...	Bodily ailment
Sarpabali	...	Sacrificial offering to propitiate the serpent Deity
Sarpa Drekkana	...	The first decanate of Scorpio and the last ones of Cancer and Pisces
Sarpa Siras	...	The second half of Vyatipata Yoga
Sarvashtakavarga	...	A method whereby the strength or weakness of a planet or a house can be found out
Sasta	—	Ayyappa who is both Siva and Vishnu

Sayana	—	Tropical Zodiac. Deduct Ayanamsa to get the sidereal zodiac
Saumyagraha	—	Mild or benefic spirit
Shadvarga	—	The same as Saptavarga minus Saptavarga
Siddhartha	—	White mustard
Siddhi	—	Obtaining mastery of a mantra
Sighra Varga	—	Asvini, Hasta, Pushyami
Simha	—	Leo ; Lion
Simhavalokana	—	A leap in Kalachakra system from Pisces to Scorpio
Sindhuttha	—	A plant
Sirshodaya	—	The signs are Gemini, Leo, Virgo, Libra, Scorpio, Sagittarius and Aquarius
Sisira	—	Winter
Sivabhuta	—	Spirit attending on Siva
Skandha	—	A branch of astronomy
Sopha	—	Swelling, tumour
Sosbani	—	Drying up
Sphuta	—	Correct longitude. Add the longitudes of the Ascendant, the Moon and Mandi to get Trisphuta. Add this to the Sun's to get Chatusphuta. Add this to Rahu to have Panchasphuta
Sraddha	—	Offering to the dead ancestors on the day of their death

Sprishtanga — The sign corresponding to the organ touched by the querist

Srishti — Asvini is creative (srishti) constellation. Bharani is the sustaining one (sthiti). Krittika is the destructive one (sambara). The series are in this order

Sthira — Fixed signs

Stunga — The numeral 74

Subha — Ninth house

Subhakartari — Planet or house having benefics on both sides

Subrahmanya — A Deity, son of Siva

Sudarsana — The mantra for Vishnu

Sudhapayas — Milk in the form of nectar

Sukla — Seminal fluid

Sukra ... Venus. Rules seminal fluid, wind and phlegm

Sukshma Trisphuta ... This is obtained by adding Prana, Deha and Mrityu sphutas

Sulacakra ... Allocation of constellations with reference to the constellation through which the Sun is passing at birth or query

Sulapaitachi ... A demon that causes suffering and pain

Sutra	...	Thread ; aphorism. Ordinary (anya) Sutra is determined by the ascendant. The ownership (Adhipati) Sutra is to be noted by the lords of the ascendant at birth and at the time of query Amsaka Sutra is arrived at from the Navamsa Lagna. Nakshatra Sutra is calculated by the birth' star of the questioner and the asterism at the time of query. Mahasutra is worked out by Arudha and the tenth from it. These are respectively earthy, watery, fiery, aerial and ethereal
Sva	—	Second house
Svasana	—	Gasping
Svastha	...	Doing well. A question about health.
Svayambhu	...	Brahma the creator.
Svayathu	...	Dropsy
Tantra	...	Texts dealing with the operation of the mantras.
Tanu	...	Body ; first house.
Tapani	...	Making weak due to tenperarture.
Tiktaka	...	Khadira tree.

Tilahoma	...	Sacrificial offering of sesamum,
Triyanmukha	...	The sign to which the Sun will be moving.
Tithi	...	A lunar day. Rikta Tithis are 4, 8, 9, 14 of lunar month. These are Chidra tithis.
Trijanma nakshatra	...	Birth star and the tenth and nineteenth from it
Triphal	...	Three myrobalans called Hirda, Behada, and amlakathi.
Trivrid	...	Plant possessing valuable purgative properties.
Tula	...	Libra.
Tumba	...	Gourd.
Tundgamsa	...	Exaltation degree in sign or in navamsa.
Tvak	...	Skin.

U

Ubhayodaya	...	The sign Pisces.
Uccatara	...	Invocation.
Udayalagna	...	The sign rising at sunrise.
Ulkapata	...	Fall of meters.
Upachaya	...	House 3, 6, 11.
Urdhvamukha	...	The sign left by the Sun.
Urdhvodaya	...	These are Gemini, Leo, Virgo, Scorpio and Aquarius.

Ushna ... Some period in each constelation. See under 14 2.

Uttarayana ... The Suns's ingress into Capricorn till he leaves Gemini.

V

Vacha ... Aromatic root

Vakya ... Traditional method of calculation

Vanadevata ... Sylph

Vakra ... Grain

Vargottama ... Planet occupies the same signs in Rasi and Navamsa

Varsha ... Year ; Rainy season

Vara ... Marrow of flesh ruled by Jupiter

Vasanta ... Spring

Vasara ... Week

Vashasa ... Tendon, nerve ; ruled by Saturn

Vata ... Wind

Vayutattva ... Signs Gemini, Libra, and Aquarius

Vedana ... Pain

Vepathu ... Shivering

Vidhi Rasi ... If the Sun is in Taurus, Cancer Gemini or Leo, the sign is Aries. If he is in Scorpio, Capricorn or Aquarius, it is Gemini. If he is in the other signs, it is Taurus.

Vidyadhara	...	A demigod
Vikrama	...	Third house
Vilanga	...	A plant
Vimsottari	...	120 year system
Vimana Sundara	...	A deity
Vipat	...	Third star from the birth star
Vira	...	Number 24
Visha drekkana	...	First decanates of Aries, Cancer, Leo, Virgo, Sagittarius, Capricorn and so on
Visha Nadi	....	Starting from Asvini, the ghatis are 50, 24, 30, 4, 14, 11, 30, 20, 32, 30, 20, 18, 22, 20, 14, 14, 10, 14, 20, 24, 20, 10, 10, 18, 16, 24, 30
Vishama Vyadhi	...	Incurable disease
Virabhadra	....	Follower of Shiva
Vismriti	...	Forgetfulness
Visvavyaghata	...	Pepper (Santh)
Vriddha	...	Planet in enemy's house
Vrischka	...	Scorpio
Vrischikali	...	A plant
Vrishabba	...	Taurus
Vyatipata	...	See notes on page 43
Vyaya	...	Twelfth house

Y

Yaksha	...	A demigod
Yama	...	3.75 ghatis
Yamakantaka	...	A sensitive harmful point
Yashti	...	Liquorice

Yauvana	...	Planet in its Moolatrikona
Yoga	...	See Chapter 2 and Verse 18
Yogarishta	...	Harmful period for longevity
Yogasphuta	...	The sign for Sun and Moon and Saturn
Yogayus	...	Longevity given by the planets
Yogini	...	A spiritual being
Yoni	...	In Ashtamangala this refers to flag, smoke, lion, dog, ox, donkey, elephant and crow

—o—

ERRATA

Page	*Verse*	*Read*
9	13 last line	धर्मं, अर्ग्यं
10		जन्मना, कर्मणा
12	17 omit व in	मव
16	21	स्युः
17	Footnote	सन्नस्तु, स्पष्ट···
21	Last verse	भृतो
23	34	क्षन्य
28	45	यदुक्तं
30	1	कर्माखिलं
31	2	किं जन
39	15	श्रुती···
49	26	निम्नो···
50	28	कार्यं
52	31	Last 6 Syallables do not fit into the metre
56	38	भू···हुत···
57	39	तोतः
62	49	संशयः
67	65	वक्ष्नो···
70	71	संप्राम्नोति
84	104	नद्न्यर्ण···तद्गण
85	107	वर्गेशाक्षर

Page	*Verse*	*Read*
87	Last lines	The verse is in Sardula Vritta and the first is in मगण
88	110	कारोऽथ
	127	दृढतर···ऊर्ध्वेक्षण रहितो
99	134	सङ्गहे···योगस्तु
101	143	पश्यति
102	146	पुष्पं
105	155	क्षते
108	3	पत्रेच···प्रछाद्यं
112	12	तत्पञ्चम
114	13	दूतः
116	17	यद्यदृज्ञान
	18	तृणा न्योतानि
122	31	द्वरान्निरेति···द्वारा
126	5	प्रश्नेषु
130	9	मृत्युञ्जयी
137	24	रोम
141	32	साद्रीश
146	51	जेत्ररु
147	54	ष्टश स्त्य क्रा ?
160	16	आने
168	24	नुलोम
182	18	श्रायुर्वीर्यं
191	31	त्स्र पृयक्षा
193	37	कृद्दवि रतिसारं
		वाज्ञन
198	46	प्रहुरिन्दुं

Page	*Verse*	*Read*
205	62	वाङ्मनसोः
206	65	विस्फुटो···also in V. 66
	66	तद्दीशा
210	3	भूतानि
	4	चन्द्राहयः
	6	धूमो
211	8	क्शिरो
242	27	त्यज्योतपि
249	38	दृष्ट्यादि
250	39	क्षीणे
255	50	Add तथा after the eighth syllable of the first half
256	53	सूर्यस्य
258	61	क्षीण
265	12	धिषणा
266	13	सत्स्वपि
267	14	रायु
268	19	दशौ
270	24	विचिन्त्याः
277	36	सौख्य···विषयेषु गुण दोष विमिश्रितेषु
277	37	देहो
	38	लग्नाधि
278	39	केन्द्र गतेषु
	40	रोग
279	42	भ्यधत्त
	43	युक्षिन्त्यते

Page	*Verse*	*Read*
280	46	मास्ति
281	49	समायोगा
282	53	Read at the end दशायुश्च दशाक्रमात्
282	54	वदाम्यथ
283	55	मध्य दीर्घामितायुष
286	62	विलग्नेन्द्वो:
	64	लग्नपते:
288	68	सन्धि
	70	केन्द्रायुर्मृत्यु
291	75	निर्णीते, निर्णीतं
293	4	तद्बी, मृत्युदा
305	21	राह्वा
317	34	मान्द्यादय:
320	41	मृतिर्मान्द्यश
324	48	समाह
333	3	वस्मसा
335	10	गुरुणा वेपयु: पादे दक्षि···
339	14	गुल्माङ्गो···
343	17	भास्कर:
345	18	युत:
	19	कथितानीति
349	30	प्र चतुष्पादां
355	39	निर्णीते
369	25	यच्छुतं
	27	ष्ण
371	31	मूर्तौ
378	50	रन्ध्र

Page	*Verse*	*Read*
380	55	व्यस्ता
381	56	कूष्माण्ड
391	78	पापदृष्ट
397	1	श्चन्द्रो
400	5	समुद्गमः or समुद्भवः
401	7	ल्पता
402	9	प्राप्त
405	13	व्याधि, रुजा
409	20	शिष्टेषु
411	21	पञ्चताम्
	22	इदं
413	25	शमनाय
415	30	तांना···मुदितं···पाप्मा
417	34	श्चित्तं
417	35	प्रतिश्रयम्
418	38	सोन्मादके
422	4	हर्येत
423	7	पुण्यम्
424	10	सर्वप्रणा
427	18	भोजयितृ
431	23	ह्रस्व
432	25	जन्मतो
433	27	द्विर्द्वादश
	28	तद्वदाप्त
434	29	तदधिप
438	31	द्युमणिरथ
440	36	सुतं च दत्ते

Page	Verse	Read
446	46	मूल्या
454	50	त्यूह
	59	रोगवि–हो one syllable is missing
464	80	कांक्षायां
468	86	पापान्वया
474	92	सेनानी
	93	बुद्धिवृद्धेः
475	94	श्चार्य
487	108	समीरितम्
		स्याथ
490	112	शेत्क्षिप्रम्
491	116	पापाः
495	1	गुरुभिर्ब्रा
498	5	वशात्कुजः
499	6	त्यंशेन्यत्
		ह्यखि
500	7	मन्दद्दशास्तादिकं
		सर्पगणः
501	10	2nd line begins द्रुत्कनां
507	21	धातुर्ग्रहे
508	22	स्यापि
509	23	वधैः
	24	धातु
510	26	धत्ते
511	27	प्राच्यतेत्र तु
512	29	तत्तु
	30	विधि

Page	*Verse*	*Read*
514	33	सर्प प्रीति
515	34	कृत्वा···देयान्यु
516	36	तु राहो र्यदि
517	39	शापो स्त्ये महः प्रभु
518	39	इनोहनाथ
519	42	बाध यन्त्येते चरन्तीति
521	44	मसतां
	45	मान्देर्भ्रांत्राादि
		न्वयाद्यैः
524	49	विहननं चामया···
526	53	विवशां
527	54	कारणानीह
528	56	शैलाग्र
529	60	कश्यन्ते
	62	हेद्र
532	70	द्विह जिह्मा ?
537	87	विपङ्क
538	92	द्विज
540	95	वाङ्मेद्र
		द्विट्
		ग्रही
541	100	क्षुत्तृ···तवोः
	101	सु मन्त्रिणा
542	104	द्दालकाः
545	112	बाधक
546	113	ग्राह्यो
	114	Second line first six letters are not correct

Page	*Verse*	*Read*
	115	दृष्टि
548	119	समश्चेद् ग्रह पीडनं
549	121	तद् दृष्टो
553	132	राहौ
554	135	बाधया
556	138	न्योन्यतो वा
	139	वक्तव्य:
557	142	रिपो:
558	143	वर्णै
	145	स्याद्वर्णौ
559	148	स्यादथ
560	149	द्वाननुपवीती
	150	उच्चावनीच
	151	ह्व, नृपति
561	155	प्रयोक्तृ, ग्रन्थान्तरं
562	157	षष्टेशो, ताम्र
564	161	शत्रुर्ज्ञेय:
565	162	विहग दिक्, राशि दिक् तासां, गतता बाधारप
566	163	नाथ, कृतमाभिचारै:
	167	क्षुद्राभि···
569	172	चेद्रविर्वृक्षे, जीव श्चेद्
570	174	व्याघ्र
	176	चतुरं घ्र्यंश
571	178	मध्यादि, तस्य
572	179	तेनोच्च्या
	180	मध्यगांश
573	183	चैवमा···

Page	*Verse*	*Read*
	187	अथात्रो
575	189	रत्रागतः, राह्वयम्
	190	युतेथ
	191	व्याधेर्बलिं
576	192	मिमाः
578	196	स्वत्वेन तदुप···
579	199	मर्दितो
581	203	संक्षेपेण
	206	गृहस्थः
583	211	शोक्रो थ
585	215	नरीणां
586	217	पिशाचाश्चात्र
587	Last but one line	अथ व्याध्रेः
588	221	शान्तिश्चिन्त्या
		दोषैर्युक्ते
589	224	न्मतिमान्
590	227	कीर्तिस्तथा
591	229	शान्त्यैः
	230	होमादीनां
593	2	दुच्यते
595	6	आरूढे
600	15	भागनिहितं
601	16	स्यादथ
	17	मभ्यागमो
602	18	सहितः, लाञ्छन
608	29	रूपम्
		स्तदिन्दूद्भवेयम्